ENCYCLOPEDIA OF ARCHITECTURE

ENCYCLOPEDIA OF ARCHITECTURE

Doreen Yarwood

Facts On File Publications
New York, New York • Oxford, England

Library of Congress Cataloging-in-Publication Data

Yarwood, Doreen.
Encyclopedia of architecture.

Bibliography: p.
Includes index.
1. Architecture—Dictionaries. I. Title.
NA31.Y37 1986 720′.3′21 86–735
ISBN 0–8160–1423–X

10 9 8 7 6 5 4 3 2 1

Printed in Great Britain

FRONTISPIECE
The Royal Hospital for Seamen, Greenwich, the Chapel, 1696 onwards

Preface

The intention in this book is to present a copiously illustrated and easy-to-use reference work upon architects, materials, building methods and architectural terms.

There are several excellent dictionaries and glossaries available which give biographical articles upon individual architects and craftsmen and/or definitions of architectural and building terms. Few are heavily illustrated or contain broadly based articles upon the history of architectural subjects.

In this one-volume work the subject matter is handled in an encyclopaedic manner so that, for instance, the development of Baroque, classical or modern architecture, church structure and design, or town planning is generally and chronologically discussed. Specific terms and the contribution of individual architects are handled in shorter articles. Limitation of space has precluded the inclusion of biographies on individual craftsmen. The stress in this book is upon British architects and architecture but a number of major articles are written from an international viewpoint, for example, Modern Architecture, Temple, Town Planning, Renaissance Architecture, Palladian Architecture. Furthermore, as may be judged from the index, a considerable proportion of the illustrations represent buildings outside Britain.

So that the reader may quickly and easily find the required information a comprehensive index is provided. It is not possible to present an equal comprehensiveness in the list of books recommended for further reading but an attempt has been made to provide in classified form at least one reference for each subject and period from books easily available in libraries or for purchase.

This book is the result of over 30 years' research and on-the-spot study of architectural history. The drawings are my own, made from photographs taken on extensive personal travels. The great majority of photographs in the book were taken by my husband, John Yarwood. Apart from these, the author and publishers wish to express their thanks to the following for permission to reproduce photographs:

A. F. Kersting for 31, 231, the British Museum for 134, 429, the Science Museum for 188, 191, Edwin Smith for 196, James Stirling for 344, Fibreglass Ltd. for 191, Pilkingtons for 188, the Department of the Environment for 96 and Wates Ltd. for 149.

In a book of this coverage, however painstaking the compilation; mistakes will occur, particularly in the light of recent research. I should be deeply grateful to receive any corrections from colleagues with specialist knowledge.

DOREEN YARWOOD
East Grinstead, 1984

Contents

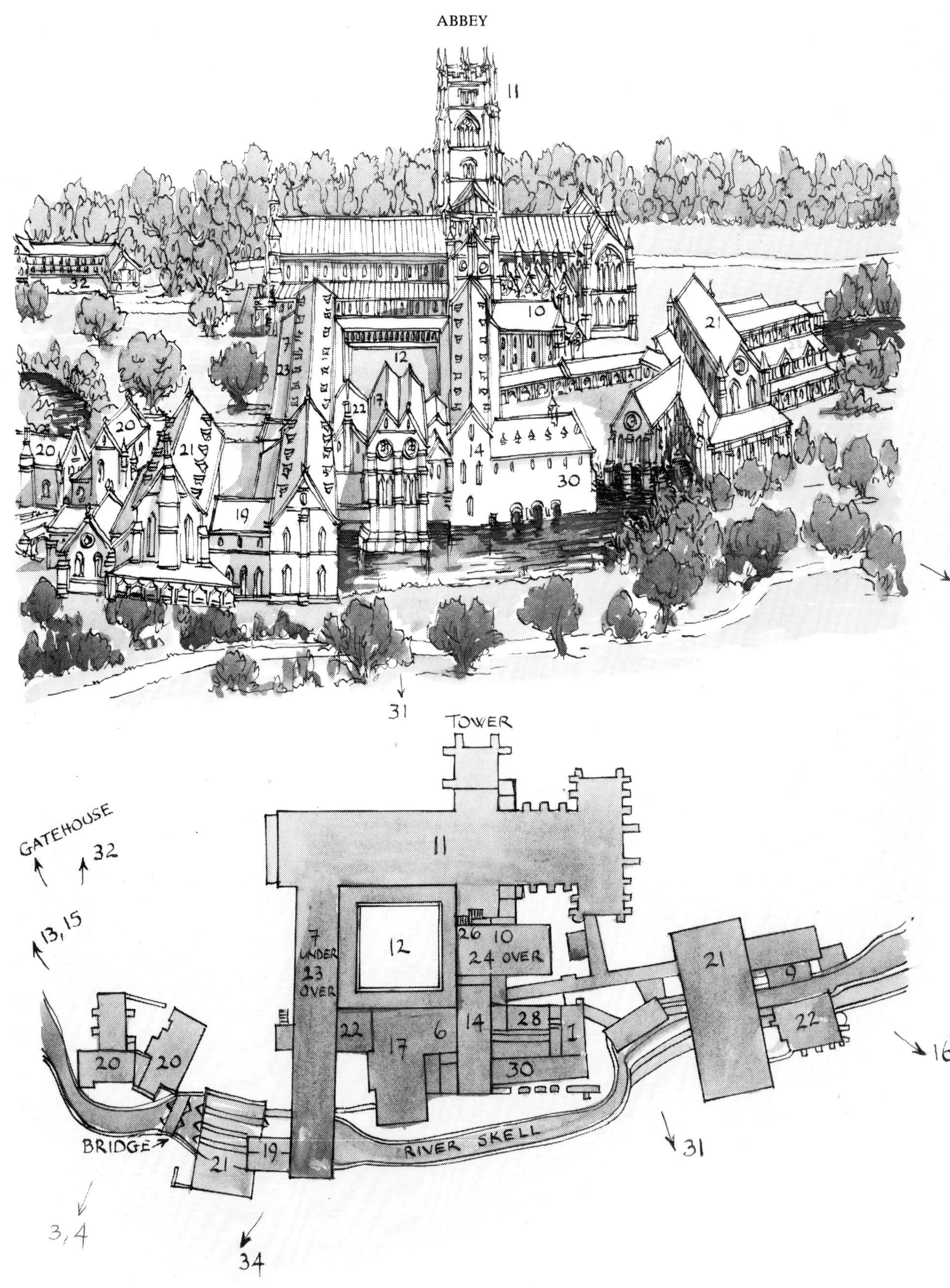
11
32
10
21
7
23
12
22
17
20
20
21
14
30
19
31
TOWER
GATEHOUSE
32
13, 15
11
26 10
24 OVER
7
UNDER
23
OVER
12
21
9
22
22
17
6
14
28
1
20
20
30
16
BRIDGE
21
19
RIVER SKELL
31
3, 4
34

ABACISCUS

1. A square compartment which encloses a design in a mosaic pavement.
2. An obsolete synonym for 'abacus', derived from the Greek diminutive of this term (see 'abacus' in CLASSICAL ORDER).

ABBEY, MONASTERY, PRIORY The monastic way of living originated in Egypt in the early centuries AD, where some men adopted a solitary, wandering life as recluses or hermits. The word monastery derives from the Greek *μοναδτλριον* which, in turn, comes from *μονάζειν* (='to live alone'). In the fourth century some of these monks (this word has a similar derivation) began to group together, still living alone but sharing a chapel and refectory. They are described as 'coenobites', in distinction from those who continued to live in a totally isolated manner who are referred to as 'anchorets'. This monastic movement spread westwards and soon monks began to establish communities, still living in their own huts, but grouping these to form larger units. In fifth-century Ireland, St Patrick, himself a British Christian, son of a Roman provincial official, came from Gaul to convert the Irish.

From Ireland these monks went forth to spread the gospel to Scotland, Wales and Cornwall, whence Christian arts and learning were slowly disseminated to the rest of Britain. St Ninian founded the Celtic monastery at Whithorn (Scotland) in, it is thought, about 400 AD and, in 563, St Columba left Ireland to found the Celtic monastery on the island of Iona. From here, later, the Celtic Church spread to Northumbria, where St Aidan established the monastery at Lindisfarne.

Isolated and, often, island sites were favoured by these Celtic monks who wished to lead the contemplative life. They built small structures in stone and wood, comprising one room or cell (see BEEHIVE CONSTRUCTION). These cells

Fountains Abbey, Yorkshire: reconstruction and plan, *c.* 1500
Key to both drawings

1. Abbot's or Prior's accommodation
2. Almonry: a room where food and alms were distributed to those in poverty and distress. Dispensing was carried out by the Almoner.
3. Bakehouse
4. Brew house
5. Buttery: a place for storing wine and ale. From Old French *boterie* and Latin *botaria* (='cask, bottle'). The term was extended, during the Middle Ages, to a place for storing all kinds of provisions, possibly due to its similarity to 'butter' (see MANOR HOUSE).
6. Calefactory: warming room, heating centre of monastery. From Medieval Latin *calefactorium*.
7. Cellarium: storeroom partly or wholly below ground. Generally constructed under the dormitory on the west side of the cloisters.
8. Cemetery
9. Chapels
10. Chapter house (see CHAPTER HOUSE)
11. Church
12. Cloister
13. Corn mill
14. Dormitory (dorter): sleeping apartments
15. Farm
16. Fish ponds
17. Fraterhouse (*fratery*): refectory, dining-room
18. Garden
19. Garderobes (see GARDEROBE)
20. Guest houses
21. Infirmary (Medieval Latin *infirmaria*): a building to house the sick and infirm, generally with chapel and kitchens
22. Kitchen: in the Middle Ages, a separate building because of the danger of fire
23. Lay brothers' accommodation: a lay brother was a man who had taken the vows of the religious order but was occupied mainly on manual work and exempt from the scholastic studies of the monk
24. Library
25. Locutory: an apartment where conversation was permitted. Also, a grille through which the monks might talk to someone from the world outside
26. Night stairs
27. Piggery
28. Prison and punishment cells
29. Quarry
30. Reredorter: a small room at the back of the dorter or dormitory which contained wooden-seated, compartmented closets and a drain of running water
31. Smithy, forge: generally set some distance from other buildings because of the danger of fire
32. Stables
33. Workshops

Tintern Abbey, Gwent, viewed from the south-west, thirteenth century

Fountains Abbey, Yorkshire: undercroft (*cellarium*), twelfth century

The night stairs in the south transept, Hexham Abbey Church, Northumberland, thirteenth century

Buildwas Abbey, Shropshire: nave and crossing, 1135

Cloister garth lavatory cistern, Much Wenlock Priory, Shropshire, *c.* 1160

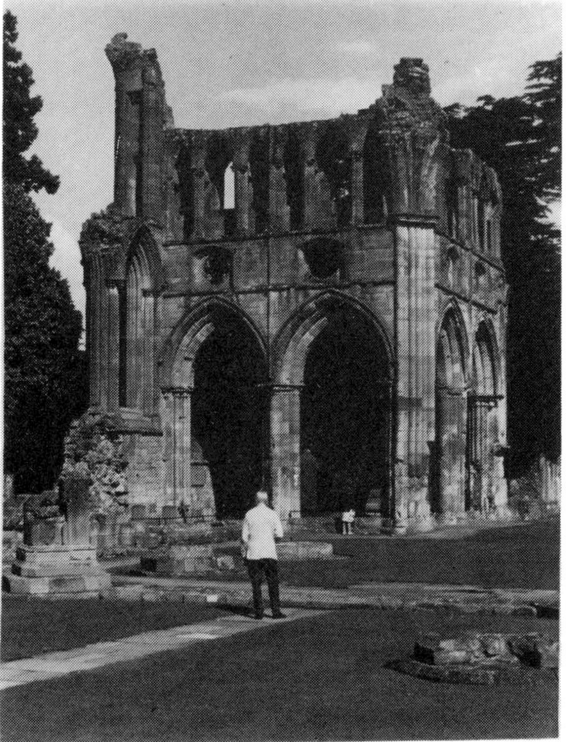

Dryburgh Abbey, Berwickshire: north transept, thirteenth century

were separate small buildings but often intercommunicated. Remains of these in Britain are fragmentary, but in Ireland there are a number of sites where ruins exist indicating a church or chapel with monks' cells clustered round it. One such instance is on the island of Skellig Michael where there are nine buildings comprising two oratories, six huts and the church.

The monastic way of life which was developed in medieval Britain and western Europe stemmed from that initiated at Montecassino in Italy by St Benedict, who laid down his 'Rule' in about 529 AD. This idea of a monastic establishment where a community of persons lived together in seclusion and under solemn vows to work in study, physical labour and prayer to the glory of God and for the benefit of mankind was introduced to Britain by St Augustine, who landed in Kent in 597 with his 40 Benedictine monks.

During the Middle Ages monastic communities provided education, shelter and guidance and the monks themselves were among the learned and educated members of society. They lived a retired, communal life, working hard on the farm, in the fields—for each monastery was self-sufficient—and in the library, study or workshop, carving in wood and stone and copying and illustrating manuscripts. They spent many hours in prayer by day and by night for the living and for the dead. In Britain the religious houses were at their most numerous and expansive in the early fourteenth century. Between 1000 and 1300 AD, 500 abbeys and priories had been founded or re-established under the jurisdiction of different Orders; the chief of these were the Benedictine, the Cistercian, the Cluniac, the Augustinian, the Premonstratensian and the Carthusian as well as Orders of the Friars and the Knights of St John.

The terrible visitation of the plague, the Black Death of 1348–9, seriously reduced the numbers of monks in religious houses and these never fully recovered. At the Dissolution the monasteries were allowed to fall into decay and their lands were forfeit and sold or given away to create new estates. Some of the finest abbey churches survived for use as cathedrals and parish churches. These, which included such superb examples as the *cathedrals* of *Canterbury, Durham, Gloucester* and *Norwich* as well as the *abbeys* of *Westminster* and *Sherborne*, were situated in towns where an adequate population could support them but the more remote monasteries such as those of the Cistercian Order, which by the nature of their Order had been built in lonely situations, could not be used in this way and fell into ruin. This circumstance has had the advantage, however, that the churches and conventual buildings, though in ruin, have not been partly rebuilt in later architectural styles as have their Continental counterparts, the Gothic structures of which have been often re-clothed in a Baroque skin. During the sixteenth, seventeenth and eighteenth centuries British monasteries fell into ruin, the stone being taken for local building and time and weather completing the decay. Since the mid-nineteenth century this process has been halted and repair work has prevented the total loss of such fine structures as *Glastonbury Abbey*, Somerset, *Tintern Abbey*,

Gwent, *Fountains* and *Rievaulx Abbeys* in Yorkshire and *Dundrennan* and *Melrose Abbeys* in Scotland.

An abbey is a monastery where monks live under the jurisdiction of an abbot, or nuns an abbess. The word 'abbey' refers to the jurisdiction and function of the community as well as to the monastic buildings. Typical of the great Cistercian abbeys is *Fountains* which, until the Dissolution, was one of the finest in Britain. Though now in a ruined condition, the whole monastery is still in a fair state of preservation and sufficient remains of the conventual buildings to give a clear impression of how it appeared in the fifteenth century. The tower still dominates the Skell valley, the river flowing along the southern side of the site and the wooded escarpment rising above. The remains of the great church are considerable and the high quality of the Early English workmanship which went into such abbeys is visible in the ruins of the thirteenth-century transept known as the 'Chapel of the Nine Altars' (see ground plan of the layout and conjectural restoration of the abbey remains).

In architectural design monastic buildings reflected the characteristics of ecclesiastical structure through the Romanesque and then the different phases of Gothic architecture. The buildings were laid out and built in a practical manner so as to enable the monks to live and work together as efficiently and harmoniously as possible. The building pattern of the different Orders varied in architectural design and detail, for the Mother Houses of most of these were on the Continent, primarily France; but in general the layout was similar, so that a monk from one Order could easily find his way about the monastery of another. This was the result of years of developing the best and most convenient way of laying out a large, complex group of functional buildings.

The important structures of a monastery were first of all built in wood in a temporary manner then, over the years, rebuilt in stone. Often, large sections of the monastery were left in timber, with thatch roofing, for many years, rendering them vulnerable to periodic, devastating fires; these parts were then rebuilt in the architectural style of the day. Thus, although the eleventh and twelfth centuries were the energetic years of building, most monasteries today are the remains of later, Gothic styles of workmanship, replacing the Norman building destroyed by fire.

The monastic church (see CHURCH DESIGN AND STRUCTURE) was generally cruciform in plan, aisled and having a central tower with a stumpy spire over the crossing. Cistercian abbey churches were, in accordance with the dictates of their Order, plain and simple. Early Romanesque ones were aisleless and had no tower over the crossing. Later twelfth-century examples, such as *Buildwas Abbey* and *Fountains Abbey*, were built with a low central tower, though Fountains received the addition of the existing tall, Perpendicular, transeptal tower in the fifteenth century. It is interesting to note that, whereas the traditional Norman abbey nave was designed with circular Romanesque columns supporting semicircular arches and, above, triforium and clerestory, as at *Dunfermline Abbey* (Benedictine Order), the design favoured by Cistercian Romanesque builders was for pointed arches to the nave arcade and, above, plain walling without a triforium stage. Again, Cistercian churches almost invariably terminate the eastern arm in a square, not apsidal, manner. The large number of churches built in this way by the Order in Britain was undoubtedly an influential factor in developing this characteristic here for other ecclesiastical building in contrast to the apsidal termination more usual on the Continent.

The domestic buildings of the monastery were generally arranged round a quadrangle one side of which was formed by the nave of the church, while its transept provided one right-angle corner of the court. In the centre of this was usually a lawn—the *cloister garth*. On all four sides was a stone-flagged walk with an open, stone screen and lean-to roof covering it. This was called the *cloister* and has survived intact in many cathedrals and abbey churches. The cloister was commonly built on the south side of the church nave, facing the sun and protected from the north-east wind. Parallel to the nave, on the opposite side of the cloister, were the refectory and kitchens, while on the west and east sides were usually built the dormitories one of which was connected to the transept of the church. Through this the monks could enter the church under cover during the night for services, by way of the night stairs. Under the dormitory were often extensive cellars for storage of food and wine. Other courts and layouts were designed to accommodate guest houses, library, chapter house, infirmary and abbot's house. For details of the layout of a typical large monastery see annotated plan and perspective conjectural reconstruction drawing.

ABERCROMBIE, SIR LESLIE PATRICK (1879–1957) A well-known pioneer in the field of British town-planning, Abercrombie established his reputation in 1913 with his scheme for the replanning of Dublin. He later devised plans for many British cities, including Bath, Bristol, Stratford-on-Avon and Sheffield. During the years 1915–35 he held the Chair of Civic Design at Liverpool University; he then moved to London where he occupied the Chair of Town Planning at University College.

Abercrombie was particularly known for his extensive work in replanning Britain's cities bombed during the Second World War, for example Plymouth and London. In 1944 he presented his Greater London Plan, emphasizing the need for decentralization and anticipating an overspill from the Metropolitan area. From this scheme developed the New Towns policy and, later, many of his proposals for green and agricultural belts and regional planning were put into operation. Much of his scheme for

London's redevelopment of road systems was shelved as being too costly.

Abercrombie established the profession of town planning in Britain and trained the next generation to continue his work (see HOLFORD, LORD WILLIAM GRAHAM). His fame spread beyond the confines of Britain and his advice was sought in countries as far apart as the USSR and Abyssinia, Palestine and Ceylon.

ABUTMENT The solid mass of masonry or brickwork from which an arch springs or against which it abuts; the abutment thus resists the lateral thrust of the arch or vault. The abutment may be a pier or wall or, in the case of a bridge, for instance, solid rock (see also BUTTRESS).

ABUTMENT
Pier: church of St Bartholomew-the-Great, London, *c.* 1123

ADAM, ROBERT (1728–92) Originator of the elegant form of neo-classicism prevalent in Britain in the later eighteenth century and innovatory genius presiding over the firm of Adam Brothers, Robert Adam was born at Kirkcaldy in Fifeshire. He spent his early childhood in the coastal town on the Firth of Forth then, when he was 11, the family moved to Edinburgh where his father, William, had established his practice.

William Adam (1689–1748) was the son of a stonemason who, after initial training from his father, worked for the Scottish architect Sir William Bruce (see BRUCE, SIR WILLIAM). Adam was an energetic businessman who made himself proficient as an architect, becoming in his middle years the man best known in his profession in Scotland. Most of the nobility and gentry went to him for new houses and alterations for existing ones. He was appointed Master Mason in North Britain to the Board of Ordnance and carried out a great deal of work in the building of forts in the Highlands.

Most of William Adam's civic work has been destroyed or altered; it is in his country houses that his style of building can still be seen. This is based chiefly upon the English work by Vanbrugh and Gibbs (see VANBRUGH, SIR JOHN and GIBBS, JAMES). Adam was attracted by powerful designs, Baroque in their monumentality and curves. He used Palladian ornament and façade treatment but, in general, English Palladianism was too formal and prescribed for him (see PALLADIAN ARCHITECTURE). His best and most typical work can be seen at *Hopetoun House*, near Edinburgh (*c.* 1723), the *Drum* and *Duff House*, Banff (1730).

William and Mary Adam had ten children, four sons and six daughters. William Adam sent his sons to the local high school in Edinburgh and Robert and James, the second and third sons, to university there. Robert attended from 1743 when he was 15 but his studies were inter-

Medieval bridge of S. Martin, Toledo

ROBERT ADAM, Duff House, Banff, Scotland. Architect: William Adam, 1730–9

South front, Kedleston Hall, Derbyshire. Architect: Robert Adam, 1760–80

rupted by the '45 rebellion, after which he was ill and never returned to the university to graduate.

John Adam (1721–92), the eldest son, remained all his life in Edinburgh working, first for his father, then taking over the architectural practice on the latter's death. John's work was rather like his father's, bearing in mind the changes in fashion in the succeeding years, to which he had responded. He designed a number of schemes in Edinburgh which include the *Exchange* (1753–60) and work on the original *North Bridge* (1772). The Exchange façade (High Street) is still there but, since the building has been swallowed up in the larger City Chambers, it is now the existing main elevation inside the courtyard.

After William Adam's death, Robert Adam joined his brother John in the family firm in Edinburgh and between 1750 and 1754 carried out architectural commissions in Scotland; the third son James soon joined them also. It is interesting to see the work which the brothers

The library, Kenwood, London, 1761

Cast-iron stove, saloon, Kedleston Hall

20 St James's Square, London, 1772

Wall and ceiling detail, library, Mellerstain House, Berwickshire, from 1768

Saloon lighting decoration, Kedleston Hall, Deıbyshire, from 1760

Charlotte Square (north side), Edinburgh New Town. Built to Adam's design of 1791

James Adam (1732–94) joined his brother in London on his return from his Grand Tour in 1763. He was a more light-hearted personality, pleasant, well-informed and cheerful. He had many ideas, but lacked the application and determination which drove Robert. He became a neat, capable draughtsman and an ideal second-in-command of the family firm. Under Robert's guidance he was reliable and hard-working. When this was removed he found it hard to concentrate or get things done on his own. He was a genuine lover of the arts and of beautiful things, and had a wide and scholarly knowledge of their history and evolution. Little is heard of William, the youngest

achieved in completing the interiors at *Hopetoun House*, which William had been working upon, and at *Dumfries House* in Ayrshire (1754). The work shows nothing of the brilliance of Robert's later style but the interior décor at Hopetoun in the red and yellow drawing rooms, despite the inexperience of the young architects, displays the beginning of Robert's break away from Palladianism to a lighter, rococo touch.

In 1754 Robert Adam set off on his Grand Tour with Lord Hopetoun's younger brother, the Hon. Charles Hope. Adam was away for over three years in France and Italy, carrying out an energetic programme of work, never wasting time and always conscious that this was his one great opportunity to amass the knowledge in notes and drawings to carry out his architectural ambitions. During this time Adam met a number of artists and craftsmen in Italy who influenced his ideas, and, later, worked with and for him. Of particular importance was his relationship with *Charles-Louis Clérisseau* (1721–1820), the brilliant French draughtsman. Adam arranged for Clérisseau to live in the same house and to teach him drawing and painting as well as a knowledge of the antique. Later, Clérisseau accompanied James Adam on his Grand Tour and Robert continued as the Frenchman's patron as did other architects, notably Sir William Chambers. Adam also met and later employed Joseph Wilton and Giovanni Battista Cipriani and was particularly interested by his discussions with Piranesi, famous for his dramatic interpretations of the ruins of ancient Roman architecture (see PIRANESI, GIOVANNI BATTISTA). They went on sketching expeditions together in Rome and in the Campagna, together with Clérisseau and the painter *Laurent Pêcheux*.

Robert Adam returned to Britain in 1758, set up in practice in London and, within a very short time, became the most fashionable architect of the day. By 1762–3 his services were in great demand. He was offering a new version of the neo-classical style, lighter, more elegant and infinitely more varied, both in architectural massing and in interior decoration, than had the Palladians. By his imaginative planning of suites of rooms, the introduction of varied room shapes and a clever use of columnar screens, apses and ceiling designs he succeeded in producing exciting interiors as well as altering the appearance of existing rooms in an earlier style, a commission which he was often called upon to carry out.

Adam was convinced by his research in Italy, as was Piranesi, that the ancient Romans had never abided by rigid rules such as those which the Palladians had followed (see PALLADIAN ARCHITECTURE), but had adapted their classical orders to need and scale (see CLASSICAL ORDER). Adam did this too. He would take an order, re-create its proportions and decoration and alter the accepted rulings; the result would have more of the essence of the source material than anything seen in Britain in the first half of the century.

It is widely known that Adam designed everything in a building down to the smallest detail in order to achieve homogeneity, so much so that we tend to remember the details rather than the whole. His interiors varied from delicate stucco arabesque-covered walls and ceilings to the Roman grandeur of the columned hall at Kedleston or the palatial richness of the ante-room at Syon. He included colour in a number of his designs; many of these can be studied in the Soane Museum and they show a grading of light ground colours with, often, white stucco ornamentation. Gilt is used sparingly.

What Adam admired greatly in a building was 'movement' (his concept of the Baroque qualities of Borromini's and Bernini's architecture). He achieved his interpretation of this by a delicacy and lightness in his interiors. There exist fewer exteriors by Robert Adam because he was so often asked to alter, enlarge or redecorate an existing building. At Bowood, the Admiralty screen, Fitzroy Square and Edinburgh he showed himself equally an exterior architect.

Adam's first commissions were to design the stone *screen* to front the *Admiralty Building* in *Whitehall* in London and to redecorate the apartments in *Hatchlands*, Admiral Boscawen's house in Surrey. Adam did not play safe. He took the opportunity of trying out his new ideas. The work is immature compared to the great houses of the 1760s but it illustrates the lively, imaginative Adam approach.

Adam's work can be neatly categorized into three decades, each showing a change of mood. The 1760s were the years of his greatest success and of his best-quality work. This was the decade of the great country houses of which *Syon House*, Middlesex (from 1762) and *Kedleston Hall*, Derbyshire (1758–68) are the masterpieces. Only slightly less superb are *Harewood House*, Yorkshire (1761–71), *Osterley House*, Middlesex (1761 onwards) and *Kenwood*, London (1767–8), while there is a great deal of fine work surviving at *Bowood*, Wiltshire (1761–71), *Croome Court*, Worcestershire (from 1769), *Mersham-le-Hatch*, Kent (1762–72), *Newby Hall*, Yorkshire (1765–83) and *Nostell Priory*, Yorkshire (from 1765).

Adam drew on many sources for the designs in these houses, believing that the mode should be suited to the commission. For his palatial style he drew on the grandeur of ancient Rome found in thermal baths and triumphal arches and the late Roman work which he had studied in Diocletian's Palace in Split. For more intimate apartments he adapted the delicate stucco and painted wall decoration he had seen at Herculaneum and which his brother James later recorded at Pompeii. He also used the purity of Greek ornament and orders, Byzantine richness of colouring and, in his exteriors, Italian Baroque concave and convex curves. A favourite Adam theme was to repeat or create a design in floor covering similar to that of the ceiling above. At Syon, in the ante-room this is in scagliola; at Saltram and Harewood, for example, it is in the form of a carpet woven to Adam's design.

Doorcase, drawing-room, Syon House, Middlesex, from 1762

brother (1738–1822). He also joined the family firm in London; he designed some buildings but there exists little data about them. His main function seems to have been to act as business adviser and accountant. Many of the business dealings and patents are in his name.

The decade of the 1770s was a less harmonious one for Robert Adam. Pressure of work caused him to lower his superbly high standard of craftsmanship; his work became thinner, the decoration in relief so low as to be almost spidery; the plastic quality of 'movement' waned. He carried out a great many commissions of which the chief were his town houses, the Adelphi and the country houses of *Saltram*, Devon (from 1779) and *Mellerstain*, Berwickshire (from 1768).

His *London houses*, of which only a few remain, were planned to give accommodation for lavish entertainment and maximum privacy for the owner behind a narrow façade. Behind this front was a carefully planned suite of rooms of different shapes and sizes integrated with an originally designed staircase and landings. The two outstanding examples are 20 St James's Square and 20 Portman Square (see STAIRCASE; TOWN HOUSE).

In 1768 all four of the Adam brothers participated in the ambitious speculative enterprise of the *Adelphi* project on London's waterfront. The site was behind the present-day Victoria Embankment Gardens where the Thames was not then embanked and the project was to construct terraces of luxury town houses above warehouses which, it was hoped, the government would take over. This part of the project failed but the terraces were built and only destroyed by demolition order in 1937. Only a few of the houses behind the river terrace survive in streets named after the Adam brothers. The word Adelphi derives from the Greek ἀδελφοι (= 'brothers').

In the 1780s Robert Adam's enthusiasm and originality returned. He rediscovered his zeal for architectural plasticity and his exteriors were once more characterized by the vitality of their monumental designs. The interiors showed more colour and form and less of the spider's-web tracery of the previous decade. These were the years of the great projects many of which foundered on bureaucratic and other obstacles. *Cambridge University* was one example, *Edinburgh University* and *New Town* another (see TOWN PLANNING). But Adam built the *Register House* in the city, a number of projects in Glasgow and several castellar-romantic country houses. These had neo-medieval exteriors and elegant classical interiors; *Culzean Castle* in Ayrshire (1776–92) is a superb example.

Adam produced two widely known publications in his lifetime, the first the result of his Grand Tour studies in Split in 1758 entitled *Ruins of the Palace of the Emperor Diocletian at Spalatro in Dalmatia* (1764), and the other, *Works in Architecture of R. and J. Adam*, in three volumes.

Robert Adam had a host of imitators and architects who based their ideas upon his. In his heyday, he was irritated by James Wyatt's adoption of his style (see WYATT, JAMES). Later, architects in a number of countries, France, Sweden, Ireland, for instance, modelled their work closely upon that of Adam. In particular, Charles Cameron (*c.* 1740–1812), a fellow Scot, was one of these. Like Adam, he studied in Italy but then went to Russia in the employ of the Tsaritsa Catherine and spent most of his life there. At the royal summer palace of *Tsarskoe Selo* (now Pushkino) one felt, before the severe damage caused in the Second World War, that one had entered one of Robert Adam's most sumptuous apartments. Here, on the Gulf of Finland, richer materials were at the architect's disposal and, where Adam had used stucco, marble and ormolu, Cameron used as well porphyry, porcelain and agate.

Clérisseau, who also influenced Cameron, spent many of the later years of his immensely long life in Catherine's service. As a result, many of his drawings, including some of those done with Robert in Italy, are in the Hermitage Museum in Leningrad. Among other architects who adopted the Adam style abroad was *Charles Bulfinch* in the USA.

(See also articles AFFRONTED; ALABASTER; CARYATID; CEILING; CHIMNEYPIECE; CLASSICAL ARCHITECTURE; CLASSICAL ORDER; CLASSICAL ORNAMENT; CLASSICISM; DOOR; DOORWAY, DOOR FURNITURE; GRAND TOUR; PALLADIAN ARCHITECTURE; PANELLING; PEDESTAL; PLASTERWORK; TERRACE ARCHITECTURE; TOWN PLANNING; WINDOW.)

ADDORSED A term used to describe two similar or identical figures set back to back. A decorative motif used especially in Romanesque capitals and neo-classical friezes, when the figures were generally animals, fishes, monsters or mythical beings.

ADDORSED
Choir capital, Church of S.-Pierre, Chauvigny, France, twelfth century

ADIT An approach or entrance to a building.

AEDICULE Originally, in classical architecture, a small room or sacred shrine. The term came to be used for a niche or shrine containing a statue and enclosed by flanking columns carrying an entablature and pediment. In Renaissance building an aedicule is such an enclosure of any opening: window, door, niche.

AFFRONTED A form of ornamentation similar to addorsed but with the animals or figures facing one another (see ADDORSED).

AEDICULE
Aediculated window, Somerset House, London, *c.* 1780

AFFRONTED
Admiralty screen, Whitehall, London, Robert Adam, 1760

AGGER A Latin word denoting the materials for filling a hollow or forming a mound. The term was applied in Roman construction to an earthwork, an embankment mound, a platform for artillery or movable towers, a raised causeway, dam or dyke. The material could be excavated earth, logs, brushwood, sand or stone.

AISLE From Latin *ala* (='wing'), a contraction of *axilla*. In Medieval Latin *axilla* became *ascella* and referred to the wing of a building or a corridor. In ecclesiastical architecture the term was applied to a lateral division of a church where, often, aisles flanked the nave and choir on both sides, divided from these by an arcade or colonnade.

AISLE
Early Christian basilica in Rome, in which Ionic colonnade separates nave and aisles: S. Lorenzo 'fuori le mura', built AD 434 and 578

Sometimes there was only one aisle, generally on the north side, or a church might be double-aisled, giving five parallel chambers. The aisles were generally roofed at a lower level than the central nave and choir (see CHURCH DESIGN AND STRUCTURE).

ALABASTER A fine, translucent variety of gypsum in white, yellow or reddish-brown and sometimes shaded with delicate markings. An easily carved material used for decorative sculpture, especially in church interiors. It is also employed to dramatic effect in several great houses, notably in the hall at *Holkham* where the columns are of Derbyshire alabaster (white with red markings) and at *Kedleston* where the hall columns are in creamy-white veined in red and grey (see ADAM, ROBERT; COUNTRY HOUSE AND MANSION; KENT, WILLIAM).

ALCOVE From the Arabic *al-qobbah* (='the vault') via Spanish *alcoba* (='bedroom or recessed chamber within a bedroom'). In English the term refers to a vaulted recess which might be part of a chamber and separated from it by an entrance partition or balustrade, or may simply describe a large niche or garden recess, perhaps containing a seat.

ALDRICH, DR HENRY (1647–1710) While Dean of Christ Church, Oxford, and later Vice-Chancellor of the university, this man of versatile talents made extensive contributions to the city and university architecture. His chief work was the *Peckwater Quad* at *Christ Church* (1705–11) in which he planned three almost identical sides, pilastered in the Ionic Order and each with a pedimented columned centrepiece. The design of the fourth

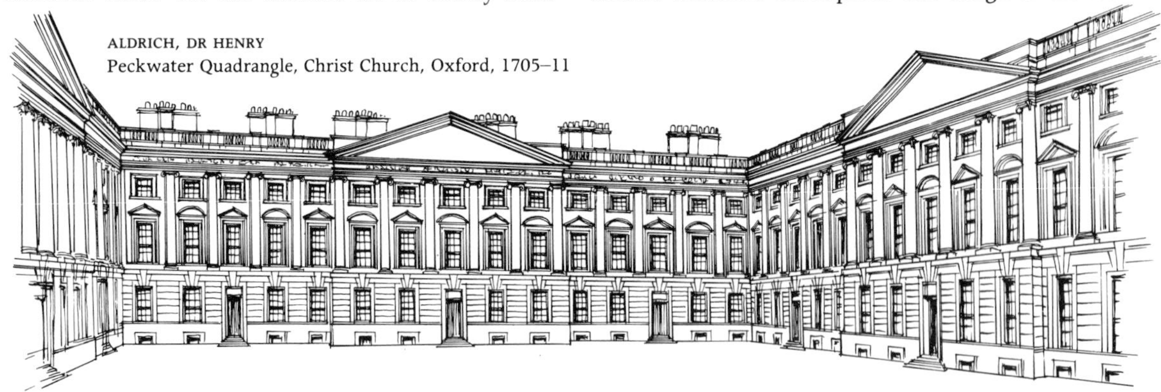

ALDRICH, DR HENRY
Peckwater Quadrangle, Christ Church, Oxford, 1705–11

side was several times altered. It is different from the others and was not built until 1717–29.

He is believed to have been the architect of *All Saints' Church* (1707–10) where he was involved in the building construction and is thought to have been connected with the design of *Trinity College Chapel* (1691–4) and, possibly, the Fellows' Building at *Corpus Christi College* (1706–12).

ALMSHOUSE A house endowed (generally by private charity) for the shelter of the aged poor.

ALTAR From the Latin *altare*, the high or raised place, upon which offerings to a deity were placed or sacrificed. Classical altars took a variety of forms in stone or marble. In the Early Christian Church the altar was often constructed over the place where a saint's relics were interred. From the early Middle Ages the Christian altar was usually of stone or marble in the form of a table or rectangular slab, which traditionally contained the saint's relics and was decoratively carved in front and at the sides. After the Reformation, wooden communion tables generally replaced such stone altars in Britain. In the

Carved stone reredos, Winchester Cathedral, late fifteenth century (figures modern)

ALTAR
(*left*) Baroque altar, by the Asam brothers. Osterhofen Abbey Church, Germany, 1726–40

Renaissance carved retablo, by Alonso Berruguete. Subject: Visitation of the Virgin. Toledo, sixteenth century

Greek Church the chamber or receptacle under the altar where relics are placed is known as a *catabasion*.

During the Middle Ages the principal altar in larger churches—the *high altar*—was usually placed at the east end of the chancel (see CHURCH DESIGN AND STRUCTURE). It stood upon a raised step, the *predella* (this term was also sometimes used to refer to the shelf at the back of the altar which supported the reredos) and the front of it was covered by a decorative cloth or a painted or carved panel known as the *antependium* or *altar frontal*. Many altars were fitted with a *retable* which was a shelf or ledge raised above the altar back on which ornaments could be placed or was a panelled, decorative back attached to the altar.

The *reredos* was a decorative screen behind and above the altar, separate from it and usually covering the wall itself. Some examples in the later Middle Ages were extremely richly decorated with stone and wood carving of pinnacles with niches containing sculptured figures and/or painted panels. Even more flamboyantly ornamented were the late Gothic and Baroque reredos screens in Spain, Germany and Austria.

ALTAR-TOMB A tomb resembling an altar but not used as such. Often there was a recumbent effigy on top of the slab.

ALURE A walk or passageway, in particular that behind the parapet of fortified walling, a castle or a church. *Aluring* refers to alure-work, that is, the construction of an alure.

AMBULATORY A place for walking; a covered way, as in a cloister. In a church the term refers more specifically to the roofed passageway passing behind the high altar and between it and the chapels of the chancel at the east end of the building. On the Continent the ambulatory, which links the two chancel aisles, generally follows an apsidal plan (see APSE); in Britain it is more often square with right-angled corners (see CHURCH DESIGN AND STRUCTURE).

ALTAR-TOMB
Late Tudor altar-tomb, Stoke d'Abernon Church, Surrey

ALURE
Medieval city walls, York

AMPHITHEATRE A circular or elliptical walled structure with an open space—the *arena*—in the centre and tiers of seats rising all round. Derived from the ancient classical theatre, the amphitheatre is in the form of a double theatre, two structures being joined together to provide an oval or circular space for contests, exhibitions and spectacle with ideal viewing facilities for many thousands of people.

The Romans developed the theme of the amphitheatre first in wood but later, due to fire risk, using stone and concrete. All important towns possessed their own amphitheatre, one of the earliest at *Pompeii*, the largest the Flavian Amphitheatre, later popularly known as the *Colosseum* in *Rome*. Even in ruin this great construction illustrates clearly the Roman method of dealing with the problems of erecting such a structure on a level site to accommodate some 45–50 thousand spectators. The solid foundations are largely of volcanic materials, the supporting walls of brick, tufa and travertine and the vaults of more porous volcanic substance to reduce weight. The decoration, seating and classical orders are in marble. The

AMBULATORY
Choir and ambulatory of the Grote Kerk, Brouwershaven, Holland, early fourteenth century

AMPHITHEATRE
The Flavian amphitheatre (Colosseum) AD 70–82

supporting construction consists of wedge-shaped piers which are set to radiate inwards. These support concrete vaults which slope downwards towards the arena. Access to seats is adequately planned with the provision of staircases built between the walls and by passages between the seat ranges. The arena—287ft × 180ft—was originally encircled by a 15ft high wall, its floor carried on joists. Under the floor was space for scenery, storage and animals.

As with the majority of larger Roman amphitheatres, the Colosseum combines an arcuated structure with the decorative use of classical orders. The intact parts of the exterior walling show four tiers with the Doric Order used on the ground storey, above Ionic then Corinthian and, at the top, the Corinthian in pilaster form (see CLASSICAL ORDER and PILASTER). Between the three-quarter columns of the first three tiers are arched openings, 80 on each stage and each of which originally contained a statue. On the fourth stage, between the pilasters, are still visible the corbels which supported the masts of the *velarium*—the covering curtain which could be drawn across the open auditorium when needed.

The Colosseum exterior wall is built of travertine blocks; there is no mortar, the blocks being held by metal cramps. The walling is 157ft high and the dimensions from one side to the other measure 620ft × 513ft.

A number of other Roman amphitheatres survive in a fair state of preservation and several of them are still in use for modern spectacular performances, particularly of opera and bullfights. Interesting examples include the structures at *Verona, Capua* and *Pozzuoli* in Italy, *Nîmes* and *Arles* in France, *Pula* in Yugoslavia and *El Djem* near Carthage.

ANTECHURCH, FORECHURCH An extension to the west end of a church consisting of several bays in depth and of a width comprising nave with aisles (see CHURCH DESIGN AND STRUCTURE and NARTHEX).

ANTECOURT An outer court, an approach to the principal court of a mansion.

ANTE-ROOM A room preceding, or acting as an entrance to, a principal chamber.

APEX STONE, SADDLE STONE The summit stone in a gable.

APOPHYGE The concave curve where the shaft of a column joins, at the upper end, the capital and, at the lower, the base. The apophyge at the top of the shaft curves outward to the astragal (see ASTRAGAL); at the bottom of the shaft the apophyge curves outward to the fillet above the base (see MOULDINGS).

APOPHYGE
The Pantheon, Rome, AD 120

APOPHYGE
The Erechtheion, Athens, 421–405 BC

APRON A decorative, raised panel immediately below a window sill. Particularly to be seen in Renaissance architecture.

APSE A polygonal or semicircular recess or termination, usually vaulted or domed. The basilica of ancient Rome had an apse at one or both ends and this type of termination became traditional to Early Christian church design

APRON
Sudbrooke Lodge, *c.* 1718

APSE
Mosaic-decorated apse in the church of S. Apollinare in Classe, Ravenna, Italy, AD 534–49

which was based upon the basilican plan. Throughout the Middle Ages the chancel or eastern arm of the church continued to be finished by one or more apses and in some countries, notably Germany and Italy, Romanesque churches in particular had transepts finished with apses. In Britain, from the early Gothic period onwards, the square termination was more usual. The term apsidal is used to describe a building or part of a building which has the form of an apse (see also AMBULATORY, CHEVET and CHURCH DESIGN AND STRUCTURE).

ARCADE A row of arches carried on columns, piers or pilasters. These can be free-standing or used decoratively against a wall; this type of decoration is often seen in Romanesque architecture and is referred to as a 'blind arcade'. The term 'arcade' is also used for the principal arched division marking a church nave from the aisles. In the nineteenth century, undercover shopping arcades were built in cities, generally constructed with iron and glass and having vaulted roofs.

Nineteenth-century shopping arcade: the Galleria Vittorio Emmanuele II, Milan

Triforium arcade, St Alban's Cathedral, Norman

Interlacing-arch blind arcade, Canterbury Cathedral, twelfth century

Triforium arcade, Exeter Cathedral, fourteenth century

ARCH A structure of wedge-shaped blocks of material over an opening which support one another by mutual pressure and are thus capable of carrying considerable weight.

Building by the structural use of arches (*arcuated* construction) is of ancient origin. The triangular relieving slab was known to the Mycenaeans (for example, the *Lion Gate* entrance to the citadel of *Mycenae*); this was a form of construction thought to have come from Egypt. The Etruscans built true arches with radiating voussoirs, a number of examples of which survive in town gateways in Italy, those at *Volterra* and *Ferentino* for instance, but it was the Romans who adapted this method of construction most extensively to suit their more complex needs. They used it in many of their building structures from baths to basilicas and nowhere more characteristically than in the monumental or *triumphal arch* where they based a complete structure on the arch form (see TRIUMPHAL ARCH).

The *classical arch* seen in ancient Rome and in its revived form in Europe in Renaissance and Baroque architecture is round or semicircular, as is also the *Romanesque arch* of the early Middle Ages. Much of the building style of Romanesque work, at least in southern France, in Italy and Spain, was strongly derivative of classical work because of the wealth of Roman architecture then surviving in these areas. The round Romanesque arch in Britain and the rest of Europe could be *semicircular* with its centre on the springing line, or might be *segmental* where the centre is below the springing line, or *stilted* where it is above. The *horseshoe arch*, especially common

Roman triumphal arch: Arch of Constantine, Rome, AD 312

Horseshoe arch: Church of St John the Baptist, Baños de Cerrato, Spain, AD 661

Sculptured, triangular relieving slab: the Lion Gate, citadel of Mycenae, from 1350 BC

in Italy and Spain, is of Islamic origin. Here, the curve is carried below the semicircle; it is a form rarely used in England.

The medieval arch which appeared in a great variety of forms was mainly based on the *pointed arch*, aptly termed by the French the *arc brisé* (='broken arch'). It was the development of this pointed arch which opened up the

Trefoil recessed arch: principal doorway in the façade of Salamanca New Cathedral, Spain, 1515–31

Etruscan arch: town gateway, Volterra, Italy, third century BC

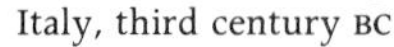

Triangular-headed window opening: Deerhurst Church, Saxon, tenth century

Recessed Norman doorway: Lincoln Cathedral, *c.* 1150

Interlacing arches: Bolton Priory Church, Norman, twelfth century

Lancet window opening: Fountains Abbey Church, *c.* 1204–47

(*left*) Equilateral arch: choir of Ely Cathedral, Early English, thirteenth century

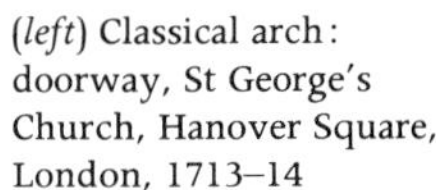

(*left*) Classical arch: doorway, St George's Church, Hanover Square, London, 1713–14

Ogee-shaped head to church doorway, fourteenth century

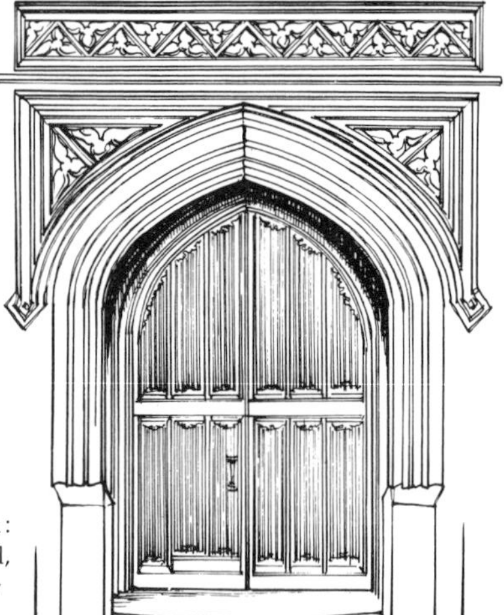

(*right*) Four-centred arch: gatehouse, Gifford's Hall, Stoke-by-Nayland, early sixteenth century

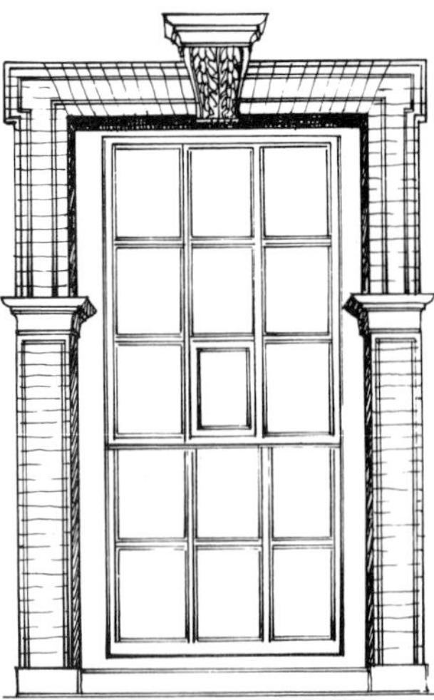

Straight arch: brick voussoirs at Balls Park, Hertfordshire, *c.* 1640

way to Gothic architecture with its complex vaulting systems and arcades. The chief forms of the Gothic arch, from the early *lancet* through *equilateral* and *ogee* to *four-centred*, are listed below and illustrated (see GOTHIC ARCHITECTURE; VAULTING).

Arches are constructed with radiating wedge-shaped blocks of stone (or bricks) called *voussoirs*. The central one at the top is the *keystone* and the horizontal ones at the sides, the *springers*. The *springing line* is the point or level at which the arch springs from its support; this is often marked by a projecting, bracket form of moulding, the *impost*. The solid walling or support on or against which the arch rests is the abutment (see ABUTMENT). The outer curve of the line of voussoirs is called the *extrados* and the inner the *intrados*; the under-surface is also known as the *soffit*. The *span* of an arch is the distance between the supports or abutments and the *rise* (or height) that measured from the springing line to the intrados (see illustration of arch construction).

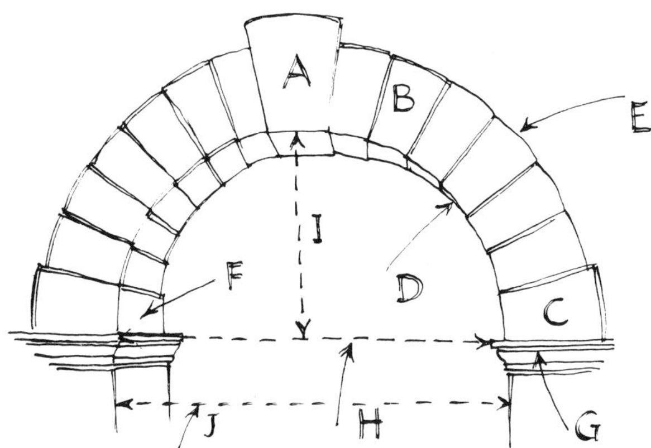

ARCH CONSTRUCTION
A Keystone B Voussoir C Springer D Intrados E Extrados F Soffit G Impost H Springing line I Rise J Span

Types of arch

Basket, basket-handle, three-centred: an arch constructed with arcs from three centres resembling the handle of a basket (see drawing).
Compound, recessed: as in a doorway where a number of concentric arches are set within and behind each other (see drawing).
Diminished: a round arch of segmental type.
Discharging, relieving: where a round or triangular arch, often of segmental design, is built into a wall above a lintel or arched opening in order to relieve it of much of the weight pressing from above (see drawings).
Drop, obtuse: a low, pointed arch with a span greater than the radius (see drawing).
Elliptical: an arch shaped like a half-ellipse rising above the springing line.
Equilateral: a pointed arch with its radii equal to the span. The proportions of all pointed arches are governed by the position of the two centres from which the curves are struck. In the equilateral arch each radius is equal to the span (see drawings). When the radii are larger than the span the height of the arch is increased and, similarly, when they are less than the span the arch height is lower.
Foil: in varied groupings, trefoil, cinquefoil, multifoil, found especially in Moorish architecture but also in western Europe and Britain in Romanesque and Gothic work (see drawings).
Four-centred: a depressed arch used especially in Britain in the late Middle Ages. Constructed with four arcs, the inner and upper two from centres well below the springing line and the two outer from centres on the line (see drawings).
Horseshoe: an Islamic form found especially in Spain where the centre is above the springing line and the curve is prolonged to narrow the arch at impost level giving a horseshoe shape. This can be seen in round and pointed form (see drawings).

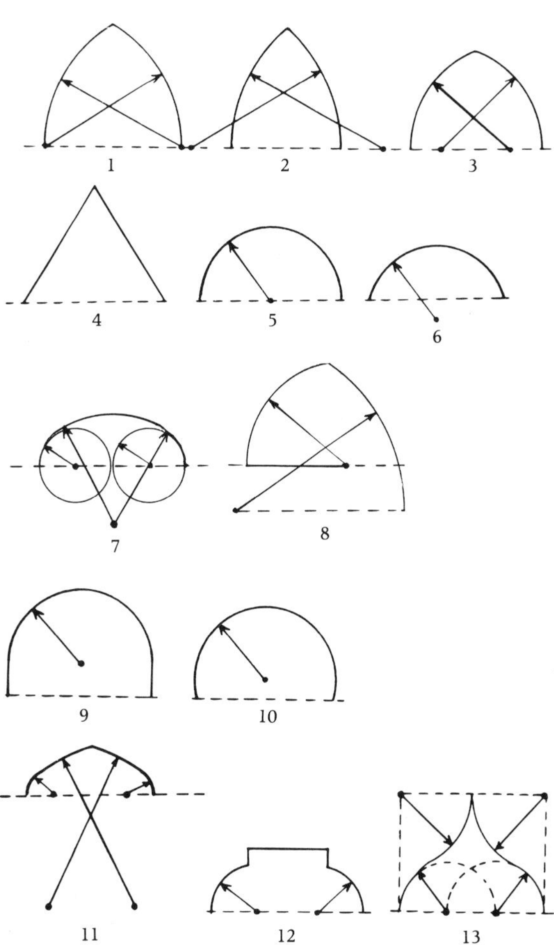

TYPES OF ARCH
1. Equilateral 2. Lancet 3. Obtuse 4. Triangular 5. Semicircular 6. Segmental 7. Basket 8. Rampant 9. Stilted 10. Horseshoe 11. Four-centred 12. Shouldered 13. Ogee

Interlacing: semicircular arches which cross and overlap, found especially in Norman (Romanesque) architecture (see drawing).
Inverted: an arch built upside-down in foundation work.
Lancet: a pointed arch of a tall, narrow shape, its radii larger than the span. This is the classic design of the early medieval period, in England called Early English but also lancet style after the characteristic, narrow lancet-headed windows (see drawings).
Ogee: a four-centred arch widely employed in the later Middle Ages; it was introduced about 1300 and was used in England mainly in the fourteenth century. Two of the centres of the arcs are outside the arch and two within so producing a compound curve, one part concave and the other convex (see drawings).
Rampant: an arch where the springing is at a different level on one side from that on the other (see drawing).
Rear: an arched opening on the inner face of a wall.
Segmental: a round arch forming a segment of a circle, its centre below the springing line (see drawing).
Shouldered: a false arch with a horizontal lintel joined to the doorway jambs by corbels which give concave or convex forms (see drawing).
Stilted: a tall, round arch with the springing line raised above impost level (see drawing).
Straight: a rectangular opening as in classical architecture, with a lintel made up from radiating voussoirs using the arch principle (see drawing).
Strainer: an arch inserted, usually, across an aisle or nave to prevent the walls from leaning.
Triangular, mitre: a triangular-headed arch formed by two slabs joined in a mitre at the top. Used, for example, in Saxon architecture (see drawings).
Tudor: a more extreme form of the late-fifteenth-century four-centred arch where the upper curves are almost flat (see drawing).

ARCHER, THOMAS (1668–1743) One of the three leading architects of the English Baroque school. Archer's architectural training, unlike that of his colleagues Vanbrugh and Hawksmoor (see VANBRUGH, SIR JOHN and HAWKSMOOR, NICHOLAS), was in the classic tradition followed by most eighteenth-century architects. He went to Oxford then studied on the Continent for four years, seeing at first-hand in Italy the ancient classical buildings as well as the work of the Italian Baroque architects Bernini and Borromini. This preparation gave him advantages in breadth of vision as well as knowledge of the wide spectrum of classical design.

Much of Archer's work has been lost or altered, particularly in the secular field but the pilastered bow front of Chatsworth's north elevation survives. His reputation rests chiefly on three churches where he displays a variety and sensitivity in design as well as a certain individuality. In 1709–15 he built the Church of St Philip in *Birmingham*, now the *Cathedral*. This is a large structure, finely sited in the centre of the city. The Baroque tower is of special interest. Its four faces are concave with belfry openings flanked by coupled Corinthian pilasters; above is a graceful cupola.

The other two churches are in marked contrast to one another. *St Paul's Church, Deptford* (1730) is a graceful building of considerable beauty standing in pleasant garden surroundings in a drab district of London (see PORTICO). The body of the church is solid and powerful, fronted by a Baroque Doric portico, but above rises a slender, delicate steeple in the style of Wren. The *Church of St John*, in Smith Square, *Westminster* was gutted in 1941 and stood, controversially, a stark, burnt-out shell for many years before it was rescued and restored to its original condition in 1964–9 to be used as a concert hall. The controversy existed between its admirers who wanted to restore it as soon as possible and its equally passionate detractors who wished to demolish it. There is

Cathedral of St Philip, Birmingham. West front, 1709–25

St John's Church, Smith Square, Westminster, 1714–28

The pilastered bow north front (shown here to the left of the photograph) of Chatsworth House, Derbyshire, 1704–5

nothing delicate or reminiscent of Wren about St John's. It is a massive, uncompromising, Baroque church, standing four-square with its corner towers and matching elevations filling completely the London square which it occupies. Like Vanbrugh's Blenheim and Hawksmoor's Christ Church, Spitalfields, St John's is an individual, powerful building, handled with vitality. Inside, several times rebuilt, the church is more traditionally designed and decorated in the Roman Baroque manner, with barrel-vaulted ceiling carried on giant Corinthian columns. The wood side galleries are supported on Ionic columns.

ARCHITECTS' CO-PARTNERSHIP A group of English architects, the practice founded by Capon, Cocke, Cooke-Yarborough, De Syllas, Grice and Powers. Their first commission to bring recognition and arouse considerable interest was the rubber factory at *Brynmawr* in South Wales (1949) (see ARUP, SIR OVE). The sculptural quality of this structure and its simple, yet powerful forms, became characteristic of the group's buildings and this commission was followed by a number of projects in architecture for education which included students' accommodation at *St John's College, Oxford* and *King's College, Cambridge* as well as a number of schools. These were followed by the Biochemistry Building at *Imperial College*, London (1961–4).

ARCHIVOLT The concentric mouldings which form the face of a classical arch.

ARMATURE A metal structure used for reinforcement in sculptural decoration, tracery, canopies and slender columns.

ARRIS The sharp edge produced at the meeting of two flat or curved surfaces. In architecture this occurs, for example, in the raised edges which separate the flutes of a Doric column (see CLASSICAL ORDER) or in a V-shaped gutter.

ART NOUVEAU An aesthetic, romantic, ephemeral movement which showed itself in most of the countries of Europe between the late 1880s and 1910 but which had burnt itself out by 1914. It was a movement engendered by those who were searching for a new mode of artistic expression which would take them away from the revamping of styles which had been the chief pattern of the nineteenth century and, and at the same time, would lead to a resurgence of the quality of craftwork and away from the pressures of a technological age.

Art Nouveau was a decorative rather than an architectural movement and, in architecture, was concerned more with surface decoration than with plastic structure. Though short-lived and limited in scope, it is important historically in architecture as an early attempt to break away from eclecticism. It was not entirely successful in this but manifested a deeply felt striving to do so. It was an escape for architects who sought new forms of design yet shied away from the current trend towards industrialization. They preferred the world of the individual, the craftsman, the cottage industry. Art Nouveau was an extension of the ideas of Morris and Ruskin (see MORRIS, WILLIAM and RUSKIN, JOHN). Despite the search for new ideas in design the movement was based upon backward-glancing, and upon a return to craftsmanship and the smaller population of pre-industrial times: it could not last. The First World War finally broke down the illusions and post-1918 architects were either eclectics or moderns.

The term Art Nouveau stems from the name of a shop

ART NOUVEAU
Casa Milà, Barcelona. Architect: Antonio Gaudì, 1905

which opened in Paris in 1895 to sell merchandise of modern, that is non-derivative, style. Different countries adopted different names for the movement, calling it after individual architects or journals, or using descriptive terms. In England it was first called the 'modern style', in Belgium the *coup de fouet* (='whiplash'), after the characteristic flowing lines of the designs. Germany called it the *Jugendstil* after the Munich journal *Jugend*, France the *style Guimard* after the architect *Henri Guimard* who designed the ornamental *Paris Métro* entrances in 1899, though the French also used the descriptive term *style nouille* ('noodle style'). The Austrians called it the *Sezessionstil* after the Sezession group of artists in Vienna, the Spaniards *Modernismo* and the Italians the descriptive *lo stile floreale* or *lo stile Liberty* after the Regent Street store which was famous at that time for selling textiles with Art Nouveau designs.

Art Nouveau had begun as a decorative movement in book illustration, textiles, glassware and furniture. Predominant motifs were undulating plant forms, flames, moving waves or flowing hair. Abstract and geometric

Casa Castiglione, Milan. Architect: Giuseppe Sommaruga, 1903

Kingsgate Bridge (footbridge) over River Wear, Durham, 1963

St John's College, Oxford. Residential accommodation, 1975, by Arup Associates

forms were also used but had the same quality of line and movement. Decoration then extended to the use of faïence, stained glass, terracotta and veneers. In architecture, iron and glass were favourite materials as well as coloured glass and stucco. Typical works were *Victor Horta's Hôtel Tassel* in Brussels (1892–3) and *August Endell's Studio Elvira* in Munich (1897). *Otto Wagner* in *Vienna* was introducing the ornamental style into his *Stadtbahn* stations, as Guimard was doing in Paris, and his block of flats, the *Majolika Haus*, was decorated across the façade in floral designs, as was the ironwork of the balconies and grilles.

The Latin approach in Italy and Spain was more extrovert. Characteristic is *Sommaruga*'s apartment block in the Corso Venezia in *Milan* (1903), where the doorway and lower windows appear to be hewn from the living rock, the decorative window panels swirl and curve and, on the second floor, *putti* in pairs cling precariously to their window frames. Art Nouveau in Spain is embodied in the work of *Antonio Gaudì*, but in a manner which is personal to the architect and which went much further towards individual and original design than the Art Nouveau movement generally achieved, as in his masterpiece the *Church of the Holy Family* in *Barcelona*. Typical of his Art Nouveau work are the plastic façades of the Barcelona apartment blocks, the *Casa Battlò* and the *Casa Milà*, both built 1905–7. In the larger of the two, the Casa Milà, the façades undulate like waves. There are no horizontal or vertical straight lines or planes; all is movement. The chief motif is the sea, not only in waves but in fronds of plant life, seaweed and rocks. This maritime element is seen mainly in the iron balconies on each floor. It is a controversial building and totally non-eclectic.

Early architectural examples in Britain were on the fringe of the movement, as evidenced by *C. Harrison Townsend's Whitechapel Art Gallery* of 1900 (see TOWNSEND, CHARLES HARRISON). In the later phases of the movement Art Nouveau in structural rather than ornamental form was shown in the work of *Charles R. Mackintosh* where he interpreted anti-eclecticism in a clean-cut rectangularity of line and mass, an astringent quality to be seen in his *Glasgow School of Art* of 1898–1909 (see MACKINTOSH, CHARLES RENNIE).

ARUP, SIR OVE (*b.* 1895) One of Britain's leading consultant engineers, Arup was born in Newcastle-upon-Tyne of Scandinavian parents. He went to school in Hamburg in Germany and Soro in Denmark, then took a degree in mathematics and philosophy at the University of Copenhagen (1914). After this he graduated from the Royal Technical College in Copenhagen as a civil engineer, specializing in the theory of structures.

Arup retained close ties with the Continent for some time and worked as a designer in Hamburg for the Danish civil engineering firm of Christiani and Nielsen. In the early 1930s, in England, he became consultant to the firm of *Tecton* (under the direction of Berthold Lubetkin) and was closely associated with the leading projects of the time—the *Highpoint flats* at Highgate, the *Penguin Pool* at the London Zoo, and the *Finsbury Health Centre*—where he helped to pioneer new techniques in the use of concrete as a structural material. In 1938 Arup set up his own firm of Arup and Arup Ltd (see TECTON).

In 1945 he left the firm and formed a new one, Ove Arup and Partners, to devote himself entirely to consultancy work, giving advice to architects on structural planning and development. Later, in 1963, he established a parallel partnership of architects and engineers (Arup Associates) led by Philip Dowson and others.

In the years since the Second World War, Arup has been associated with many important projects as consultant to a number of well-known architects in Britain and abroad. In the early years he was associated with the *Architects' Co-partnership* in the factory at *Brynmawr* (see ARCHITECTS' CO-PARTNERSHIP) and later for the footbridge over the River Wear at Durham, with *Sir Basil Spence* at *Coventry Cathedral* and the *University of Sussex* (see SPENCE, SIR BASIL), with *Arne Jacobsen* at *St Catherine's College, Oxford* and with *Joern Utzon* at the *Sydney Opera House* (see MODERN ARCHITECTURE).

ASHBEE, CHARLES ROBERT (1863–1942) An idealist, social reformer and man of wide interests and activities, he was one of the leaders of the progressive group of architects and designers whose centre was the Art Workers' Guild. Ashbee read history at university then entered the office of the architect G. F. Bodley (see BODLEY, GEORGE FREDERICK), but soon became deeply interested in the ideas and achievements of Ruskin and Morris. With these in mind in 1888 Ashbee founded a Guild of Handicraft in Mile End Road in London's East End where young men could study arts and crafts in its workshops. In 1902 he moved out of London with 150 of his craftsmen to create a new art and craft colony in Chipping Camden in the Cotswolds. The project did not transplant satisfactorily in such different surroundings and slowly died though many of the craftsmen stayed in the area for the rest of their lives.

Ashbee remained in Chipping Camden until 1917 when he undertook town planning work in Cairo and later became Civic Adviser to the City of Jerusalem, specializing in Arab arts and crafts. He returned to England in 1924 where he wrote many books, mainly on arts and crafts, established the Essex House Press, designed a quantity of jewellery and metalwork and carried out church restoration. Ashbee's few architectural works included some houses in Cheyne Walk in Chelsea, one of which was his own office.

ASTRAGAL A small moulding, semicircular in section, sometimes enriched with bead and reel decoration (see CLASSICAL ORNAMENT), which marked the division

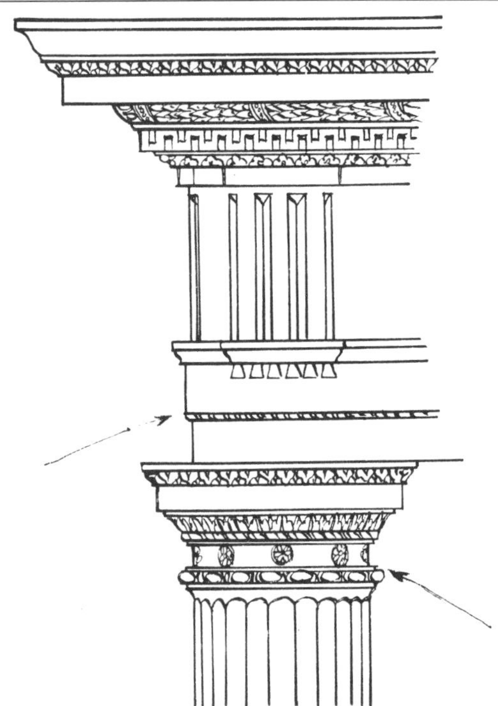

ASTRAGAL
The Doric order at the Baths of Diocletian, Rome, AD 290–300

between the shaft of a column and its capital. The term is also applied to a similar moulding dividing the faces of the architrave (see ENTABLATURE).

ASTYLAR Describes a classical façade without columns or pilasters.

ASTYLAR
The Reform Club, London, 1828–30. Architect: Sir Charles Barry

ATRIUM In domestic architecture of ancient classical times an open courtyard surrounded by rooms which were covered by roofs sloping towards the centre (see ROMAN DOMESTIC ARCHITECTURE).

ATRIUM
Church of S. Ambrogio, Milan, *c.* 1140

In Early Christian and Romanesque churches an atrium was an entrance colonnaded court.

In modern architecture atria have sometimes been incorporated into designs for ecclesiastical or domestic building.

ATTIC In classical architecture the *attic storey* is the one above the main entablature of the building and is treated in a similar architectural manner, with columns or pilasters. The rooms inside such an attic storey do not have sloping ceilings but the term *attic* is more imprecisely applied to such rooms, generally having dormer windows, built into the gables at the top of Victorian-style houses.

ATTIC
No. 68, The Close, Salisbury, *c.* 1735–40

AXONOMETRIC PROJECTION Axonometry, from the Greek ἀξονμετρια (='measurement of axes'). A drawing depicting a building in three dimensions. It is shown at a chosen angle so that the verticals and horizontals are to scale but diagonals and curves are distorted (see also ISOMETRIC PROJECTION).

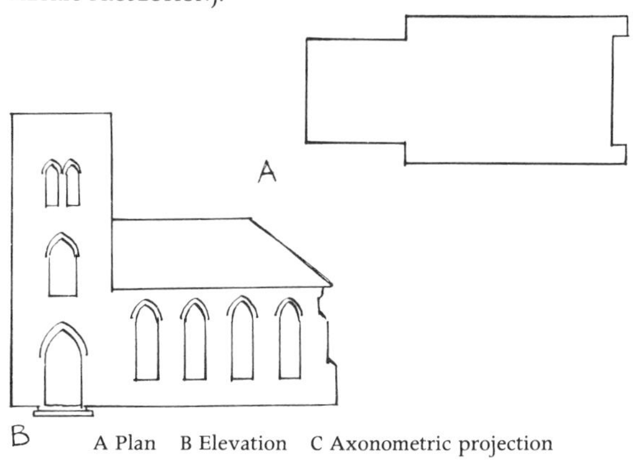

A Plan B Elevation C Axonometric projection

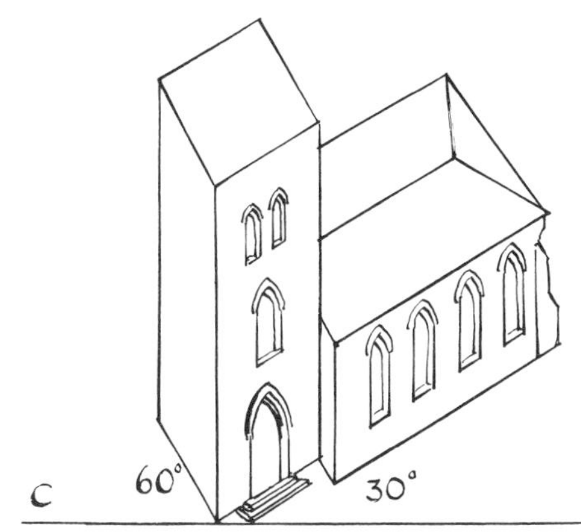

BADIGEON

1. A mixture of plaster and freestone used for repairing sculpture.
2. A preparation of glue and sawdust used for repairing woodwork.

BAKER, SIR HERBERT (1862–1946) Much of Sir Herbert Baker's work was carried on outside Britain, notably in South Africa and India. He designed a number of buildings in Johannesburg and Pretoria, mainly in 1902–13, then joined Lutyens in his extensive civic work at New Delhi (see LUTYENS, SIR EDWIN LANDSEER). Baker's work is of large-scale, classical type but much less original and interesting than that of Lutyens. An unfortunate instance of his vacuous classicism of the inter-war years is his immense superstructure added to Soane's Bank of England headquarters in the City of London. More satisfying are his India House in Aldwych (1925–9) and *South Africa House* (1930), both in *London. India House* is a large building with a curved façade to Aldwych. It is plain, with restrained decoration, the focal centre being the entrance doorway. On either side of this are Indian

India House doorway and detail, Aldwych, London, 1925–9

columns with elephant bases and, perched on top of the columns, seated tigers. Among his less ambitious projects carried out between the wars are *Rhodes House* at Oxford and the War Memorial Cloister at *Winchester College*.

BALCONY A platform projecting from the interior or exterior wall of a building; this may be carried on brackets, consoles or columns or it may be cantilevered. The platform, which might have a straight or curved front, is generally guarded by an ornamental railing.

Balcony supported on brackets. New Steyne, Brighton, early nineteenth century

Theatre and cinema balconies or balconied boxes are usually carried on columns or are cantilevered.

BALDACHIN, BALDAQUIN, BALDACCHINO In contemporary usage a canopied structure, supported on decorative columns, suspended from the ceiling or projecting from a wall, cantilevered or carried on brackets, which is placed above an altar or throne. A famous example is Bernini's bronze baldacchino enclosing the throne of *St Peter's Basilica* in *Rome* (1624–33). The word comes from the same source as 'baudekin', a rich, embroidered fabric traditionally woven with a warp of gold thread and a weft of silk and this was the original meaning of the word. Both terms stem from the Italian word for Bagdad (*baldacco*) and the old French *baudekin*. Bagdad was the city where the fabric was first made.

A domed canopy over the altar, usually carried on columns, is also known as a *ciborium*. This term has a different derivation and stems from the Latin word *ciborium* (='drinking cup') and so refers to its shape rather than the fabric from which it was originally made.

BALDWIN, THOMAS (1750–1820) One of the architects working in *Bath* in the second half of the eighteenth century, creating civic and terrace building in classical style. Baldwin designed the *Guildhall* in 1776. The interior layout included a banqueting hall some 80ft by 40ft, and 30ft in height, with an elaborately decorated stucco ceiling; the Corinthian Order in fluted columns standing on pedestals was used all round the hall (see CIVIC ARCHITECTURE). Baldwin rebuilt the *Great Pump Room* of the city's thermal baths between 1791 and 1792. The façade giving on to the street in the centre of the city possesses a fine colonnade. The Ionic Order is used and

High Altar baldacchino suspended from above in the centre of the Cathedral of Christ the King, Liverpool, 1967. Architect: Sir Frederick Gibberd

BALDWIN, THOMAS
Bath Street, *c.* 1791

the colonnade is in two sections joining three building blocks. Each colonnade has a central pedimented feature in which the tympanum is decorated by sculptured sphinxes—flanking an oval wreath which surrounds a relief head. The centre block dividing the two colonnades is the Pump Room itself. Here the Corinthian Order is used in the form of engaged columns with entablature and parapet above and rusticated storey below. The interior of the Pump Room was completed later, in 1796, by John Palmer. The *Bath Street* scheme, laid out by Baldwin in 1791, survives, with its attractive Ionic colonnaded promenades (see TERRACE ARCHITECTURE).

BALISTRARIA A cruciform aperture in the walls of medieval fortified structures through which the crossbow-men discharged their weapons. The word stems from the Latin *ballistrarius* (='arbalestrier' or 'crossbowman'). The word 'balistraria' was also used to describe the room in which the arbalests (crossbows) were kept.

BALISTRARIA
Great gatehouse, Herstmonceux Castle, Sussex, *c.* 1445

BALUSTRADE Short pillars or posts in series supporting a handrail and standing upon a base or string. The posts are known as *balusters*. Balustrades made up from turned stone balusters are constructed as parapets on classical buildings and bridges. Wood or stone balustrades made from a series of balusters are used in staircase construction but staircase balustrades may also be designed with iron or carved wood scrolling and panelling (see STAIRCASE).

BALUSTRADE
St Catharine's College Chapel, Cambridge, late seventeenth century

BAPTISTERY The part of a church devoted to the rite of baptism and containing the font (see FONT). In the Early Christian churches of the fourth to the sixth centuries, the baptistery was nearly always a separate building constructed near the church, most usually in the atrium (see ATRIUM). Such baptisteries were generally round or octagonal and provided for baptism by immersion. Following this tradition of the Early Christian churches in Italy, most Italian baptisteries during the Middle Ages continued to be built adjacent to the church. Internationally famous examples include those of the cathedrals at Pisa, Cremona, Ferrara, Parma, Grado and Florence. It was more usual in medieval churches in Britain for the baptistery to be part of the church and this was most often near the west end in the nave arm. In some instances, a screen or grille marked off the baptistery section of the church. This idea of setting the baptistery apart and of creating a focal centre in it with the font has been revived in a number of modern churches. At Frederick Gibberd's *Metropolitan Cathedral of Christ the King* in *Liverpool* (1962–7), for instance, the baptistery takes the form of a circular chapel with a centrally placed font and the chapel is separated from the nave by bronze gates (see GIBBERD, SIR FREDERICK). In Basil Spence's *Coventry Cathedral* (1954–62), the font is set to one side of the nave and stands against the backcloth of John Piper's superb baptistery window, its 195 lights scintillating with the spectrum colours (see SPENCE, SIR BASIL).

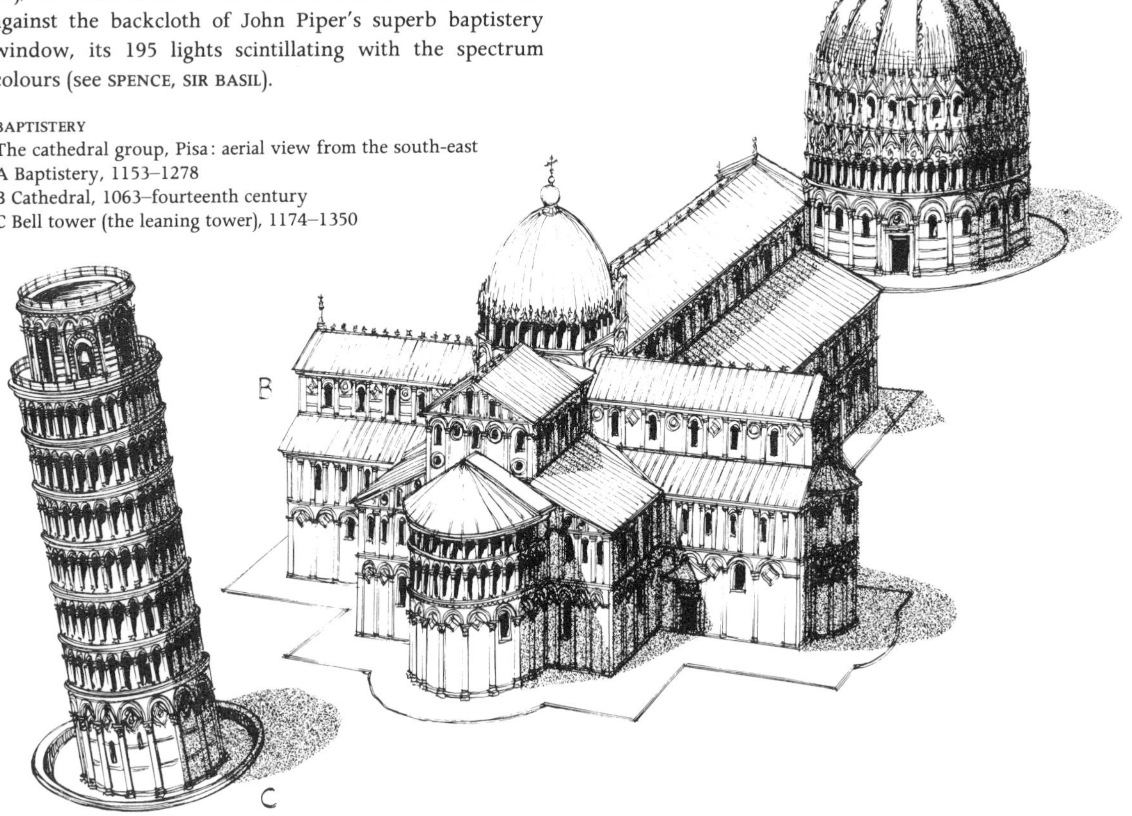

BAPTISTERY
The cathedral group, Pisa: aerial view from the south-east
A Baptistery, 1153–1278
B Cathedral, 1063–fourteenth century
C Bell tower (the leaning tower), 1174–1350

BARBICAN A fortified outer defence to a town or castle. Often a massive, double-towered strongpoint built over a gate or bridge which acts as a first line of defence before the gatehouse is reached; also serves as a watch tower. Because the barbican was the outer defence of the castle it has, in most instances, survived less well than the gatehouse further in (see GATEHOUSE). At *Harlech* in North Wales, for example, and at *Chepstow*, Monmouthshire, little but the site remains and at *Bodiam* in Sussex, where the barbican was built on the causeway spanning the moat, only part of a wall survives. Of the interesting extant examples that at *Goodrich Castle*, Herefordshire, built in the fourteenth century, is particularly well preserved and illustrates the defensive strategy of the time. An attacker would have to cross the moat under fire, capture the barbican, then cross an open bridge and negotiate a drawbridge to reach the gatehouse. The barbican illustrated, at *Lewes* in Sussex, is, unusually, one of the best preserved parts of the castle. It is a three-storey, machicolated structure straddling the road bridge into the castle, which was originally protected by two portcullises (see PORTCULLIS).

BARGE BOARD Carved timber projecting board fronting the gable of a building to prevent rain driving under the barge course (see below) and to conceal the structure of the horizontal roof timbers behind. Barge boards were particularly decoratively carved in the fifteenth and sixteenth centuries.

BARGE COUPLE Roof beams, mortised and tenoned together, to strengthen the roof structure.

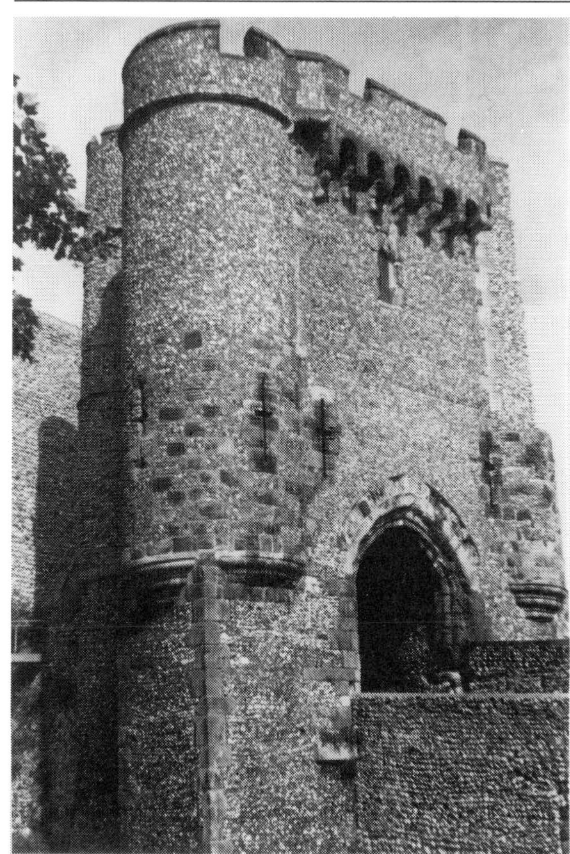

BARBICAN
Lewes Castle, Sussex, fourteenth century

BARGE COURSE Roof tiles carried forward to project at the gable end and made good with mortar to keep out the rain and snow.

BARN A covered storage structure for keeping grain, hay, straw etc. A number of fine examples of medieval barns survive. These were the important ones, built in stone and usually *abbey barns*, where the produce of the wealthy monastery was stored, or *tithe barns* which were built to contain the tithes collected from the population. This form of tax or tribute, originally set at one-tenth of a

BARGE BOARD
Carved barge board, Ford's Hospital, Coventry, 1529

man's property or produce was, in Britain in the Middle Ages, a payment which might be due to king, lord of the manor or clergy. Medieval barns were mostly built of wood; the important stone examples had open timber-framed roofs and small windows for ventilation. The larger ones were divided inside into nave and aisles as in a church and were strongly buttressed. Of surviving examples, a number are in the West Country such as the fourteenth-century *tithe barn* at *Bradford-on-Avon*, Wiltshire and the *abbey barn* at *Glastonbury*, Somerset. From the fifteenth century are the barns at *West Pennard*, Somerset, *Abbotsbury*, Dorset and *Ashleworth*, Gloucestershire.

BAROQUE ARCHITECTURE A classical form of architecture prevalent in the seventeenth and part of the eighteenth century characterized by curved forms, chiaroscuro and a bold massing of large-scale shapes. Although several theories have been put forward for the origin of the term Baroque, it is thought that the most likely is that it derives from the Portuguese word *barocco*, meaning an imperfect or grotesque pearl. It was first applied in a derogatory sense rather in the same way that the word Gothic had been coined earlier (see GOTHIC ARCHITECTURE), and was a contemptuous reference to the curving, bizarre and sometimes bulbous shapes to be seen

Tithe barn, Bradford-on-Avon, Wiltshire, mid-fourteenth century

West front, St Paul's Cathedral, London, 1675–1710. Architect: Sir Christopher Wren

Church of S. Carlo alle Quattro Fontane, 1638–40. Architect: Francesco Borromini

Façade, Murcia Cathedral, 1740–54 Architect: Jaimé Bort y Meliá

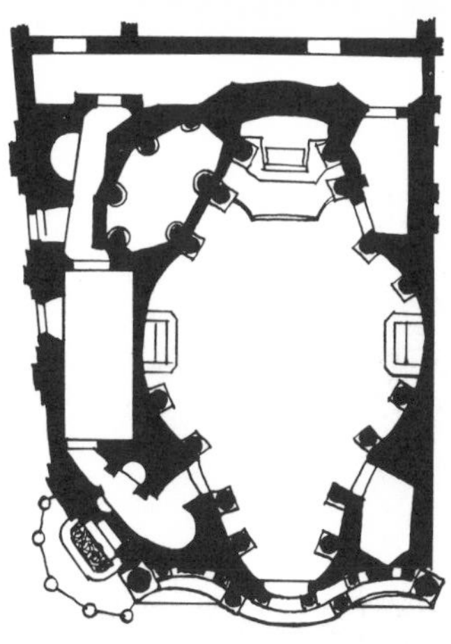

Ground plan of the Church of S. Carlo alle Quattro Fontane, 1638–40. Architect: Francesco Borromini

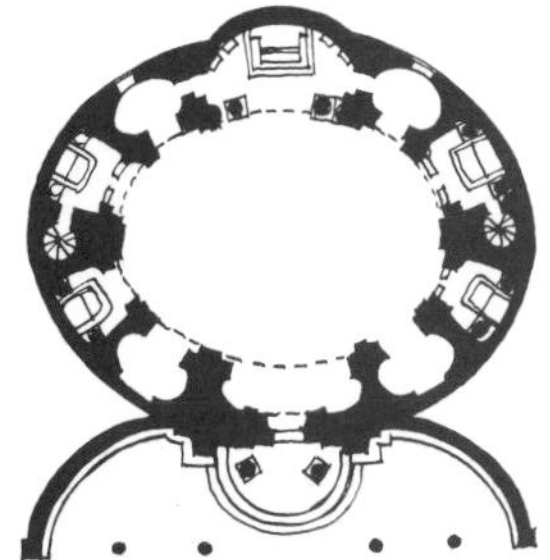

Ground plan of the Church of S. Andrea al Quirinale, Rome, 1658–78. Architect: Gianlorenzo Bernini

South porch, St Mary's Church, Oxford, 1637

Pilgrimage Church of Vierzehnheiligen, Germany, begun 1743. Architect: Balthasar Neumann

BAROQUE ARCHITECTURE
Piazza Colonnade of St Peter's Basilica, Rome, 1656–67. Architect: Gianlorenzo Bernini

Kaisersaal, the Residenz, Würzburg, Germany, 1733–52. Architect: Balthasar Neumann. Ceiling painter: Gianbattista Tiepolo

Garden front of Castle Howard, Yorkshire, begun 1700. Architect: Sir John Vanbrugh

in this type of architecture.

Italy was the source of Baroque architecture, as it had been for the Renaissance. The underlying force of the Baroque movement was spiritual, turning away from Renaissance humanism back towards the Roman Catholic church. A deep feeling had arisen, a desire for a re-introduction of spiritual values; evidence of man's need for belief in something greater than himself. This movement had begun in Italy in the mid-sixteenth century. By the seventeenth it had become organized and its leaders appreciated that, to provide for the spiritual needs of the people, it must appeal to everyone.

The new art form used all media–architecture, sculpture, painting, music, literature–to make the Church real and vital to all. Its greatest artistic exponents were *Francesco Borromini*, the master of handling the oval shape and using walls whose form alternated between the concave and the convex and *Gianlorenzo Bernini*, whose superb, dramatic handling of form and lighting in the media of stone and wood appealed so vividly to the Latin peoples. Baroque architecture is, like that of the Renaissance, classical in concept, using the orders constructionally and decoratively. Its interpretation of these and of classical ornament is much freer, with the use of curves, not only in ceiling design but in whole walls which move sinuously from concave to convex. The whole appearance is of vitality and movement and to this is added dramatic lighting effects by only one or two sources as in a Rembrandt painting. The dynamic quality of Baroque is accentuated by broken pediments, entablatures and columns separate and broken forward and the incorporation of vital, naturalistic sculpture and painting integrated into the architectural design. The favourite ground plan is oval, demonstrating the maximum quality of movement, and this is echoed in the ceiling above, which pulses with warmth and richness of colour (see TOWN PLANNING).

From Italy the Baroque architectural forms spread throughout Europe but the style was suited chiefly to the southern, Latin peoples of the Catholic faith. This was partly for its religious significance and partly because it is an extrovert, rich and colourful form. There is no parallel to Italian Baroque in Britain and northern Europe, where it gained only a foothold and where, for much of the eighteenth century, classical architecture remained cool and aloof, in straight lines and pure tones. Apart from Italy, Baroque architecture is found in its more vigorous and characteristic manner in southern Germany, Austria, Switzerland, Czechoslovakia, Hungary, Spain and Portugal.

Baroque architecture in England takes a diverse form. There is no sinuous curving, no theatrical presentation but the movement, violent and discordant, is present, evidenced in the strong massing of shapes, and three-dimensional, large-scale grandeur. It was a short-lived movement, beginning about 1690; and by 1730 it was

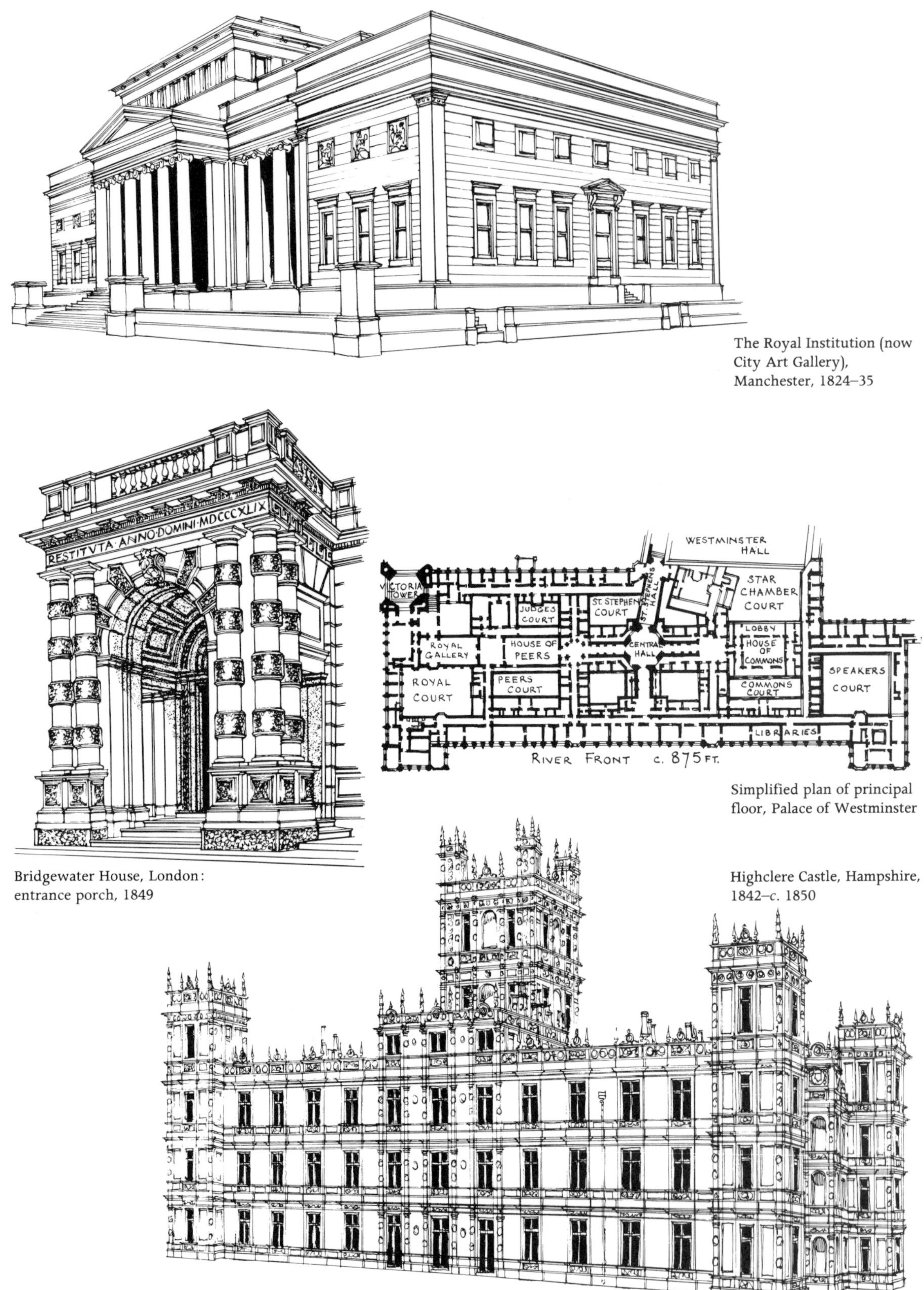

The Royal Institution (now City Art Gallery), Manchester, 1824–35

Bridgewater House, London: entrance porch, 1849

Simplified plan of principal floor, Palace of Westminster

Highclere Castle, Hampshire, 1842–*c.* 1850

over. Britain turned to Palladianism, its order and discipline more suited to the temperament of the people than the violence and voluptuousness of Baroque.

Different in interpretation though it may be, the later work of Wren, that of Talman and, especially, the designs of Vanbrugh, Hawksmoor and Archer cannot be termed anything other than Baroque for the buildings display the chief characteristics of the concept. Wren's designs showed a tendency towards Baroque in his late-seventeenth-century work. The west towers of *St Paul's Cathedral*, for instance, and, even more, the domes and colonnades at *Greenwich*, are plastic and vigorous. But Wren's Baroque was always restrained and controlled; classicism was paramount. In this, as always, Wren was essentially English (see CHURCH DESIGN AND STRUCTURE; DOME; WREN, SIR CHRISTOPHER).

Of the next generation of architects Vanbrugh was the most colourful. In *Castle Howard* and *Blenheim* he set the pattern for his style, grouped buildings of forceful, powerful masses, often discordantly contrasting with one another. Vanbrugh was a master of handling three-dimensional form in stone, creating strong patterns of sun and shade in settings of grandeur (see COUNTRY HOUSE AND MANSION; VANBRUGH, SIR JOHN).

Hawksmoor's Baroque is personal, strongly stated and large scale. His churches, *Christ Church, Spitalfields*, for example, are highly individualistic and uncompromising in their bold massing. His university work also showed a personal Baroque theme, in classical form at *Queen's College*, Oxford, but a kind of Baroque-Gothic interpretation in *All Souls' quadrangle* (see GOTHIC REVIVAL; HAWKSMOOR, NICHOLAS). The work of the third member of Britain's group of Baroque architects, Thomas Archer, was less self-consciously personal except, perhaps, for his *Church of St John* in Westminster (see ARCHER, THOMAS).

BARRY, SIR CHARLES (1795–1860) The leading architect in England in the years 1830–60, establishing Early Victorian architecture, Barry's approach was characteristic of architects of his time: he showed considerable versatility in suiting the style to the commission. Though he lived until 1860, Barry was not a Gothic Revival architect and, despite the great reputation which he acquired for the Perpendicular Gothic Palace of Westminster, he carried out also a wide variety of commissions in styles based upon Greek Revival, the Italian Renaissance palace and the Elizabethan country house.

Barry had no family architectural background but was articled at the age of 15 to a London surveyor. With a legacy left to him by his father he travelled extensively abroad between 1817 and 1820, studying buildings and making drawings in France, Italy, Greece, Turkey, Egypt and Syria. On his return to England he began his architectural career by designing a number of churches for the Church Commissioners. He found that the Commissioners preferred Gothic or Grecian churches so he designed two in Manchester then won the competition for *St Peter's, Brighton*, built 1824–8. This church shows his inexperience in handling Gothic but it is a good, stone church sited as a terminal stop to the Steyne and it has a well-

Halifax Town Hall, tower, 1859–62

The Palace of Westminster: the river front, 1836–65

proportioned, tall, slender tower. Barry then designed *St Andrew's Church, Hove* (1827–8) in Italian Renaissance style and then three churches in Islington (1826–8).

In 1824 Barry won the competition for the *Royal Institution* (now the City Art Gallery), *Manchester*, where he designed a simple, strong, Greek building, using the Ionic Order. He then moved on to his London clubs, the *Travellers'* (1830–2) and the *Reform* (1838–41), which he based upon the Italian Renaissance palace pattern. The principal rooms are placed at the front and rear of the site while the centre is lit from a court covered with iron and glass roofing—in Italy this would have been open. This palace style was widely adopted for large town buildings thereafter, in particular based on the Reform Club with its astylar façades (see ASTYLAR).

Barry then went on to develop the Italian Renaissance palace theme in the design of town mansions such as *Bridgewater House* in London (1846–51) and to adapt it to country house design when he rebuilt the south front at *Cliveden*, Buckinghamshire (1849–51) after a fire, and remodelled part of *Shrublands* in Suffolk and *Harewood* in Yorkshire. At *Highclere Castle* in Hampshire, he carried out the remodelling in an indigenous Elizabethan/Jacobean style (1842–*c.* 1850).

Like most Victorian architects who designed in both classical and Gothic form, Barry used the classical format for civic architecture. An impressive instance of this is his *Treasury Building* in Whitehall (1846). Also in London he continued Nash's layout in *Trafalgar Square*. *Halifax Town Hall* (1859–62) was one of his last works; he died before it was finished and his son, E.M. Barry, completed it. This is a large, asymmetrical building, dominated by the imposing tower set at one corner which, though classical, has a flavour of Gothic in its upper stages.

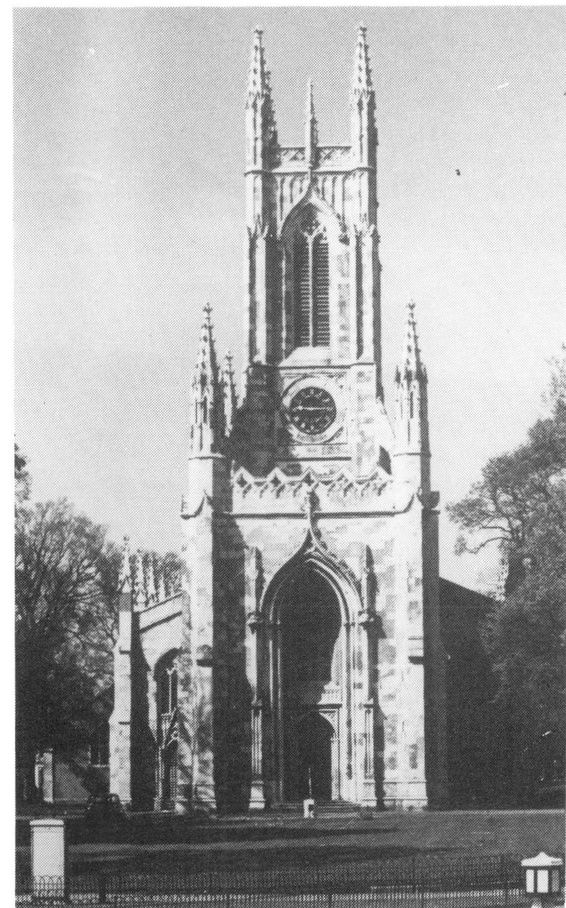

St Peter's Church, Brighton, 1824–8

Barry's greatest architectural contribution is the *Palace of Westminster*, a building classical in the symmetry of its river façade but clothed in panelled Gothic dress and with its two towers and flèche between, creating a romantic, asymmetric skyline. It is fortunate that the building was designed in the 1830s before the Gothic Revival had gathered momentum and acquired such rigidity. In 1834 the old Palace was destroyed by fire. It was decided by the Parliamentary Committee which was set up that a competition should be held for the work of rebuilding and 96 architects submitted designs. The committee also decided that the new Palace should be Gothic in style to harmonize with the nearby Westminster Abbey, and the design must incorporate the medieval Westminster Hall and St Stephen's Chapel which had survived from the old Palace. Barry won the competition and the first stone was laid in 1840. The chaste, rectilinear simplicity of the Perpendicular form of Gothic appealed to the architect and he also felt it to be most in sympathy with the Henry VII Chapel of Westminster Abbey opposite. His handling of the design problems was masterly. He retained Westminster Hall and, in the centre of his new building, made an octagonal chamber with lantern above—a chamber which gives direct access through St Stephen's to Westminster Hall. At the south-west corner of the Palace he set the great Victoria Tower and at the other end the more delicate Clock Tower (containing Big Ben). The House of Commons was first occupied in 1852. Owing to members' complaints of its acoustic qualities, Barry was compelled to lower the ceiling, spoiling the proportion of the chamber. He pointed out that the fire hazard was now greater—this was confirmed in 1941. The House of Lords is lavishly decorated with a richly ornamented ceiling incorporating the royal emblems and medieval motifs in gold. The walls are ornately carved and panelled. Most of the Gothic detail, both on the exterior and inside, was the meticulous work of Pugin, whom Barry commissioned for the task (see GOTHIC REVIVAL and PUGIN, A. W. N.).

Two of Barry's sons were architects, *Charles Barry* (1823–1900), who is best known for his rebuilding of *Burlington House*, in Piccadilly, where he used his father's club style of Italian Renaissance palace design, though this is heavier in detail—a reflection of its period, the late 1860s—and *Edward Middleton Barry* (1830–80) who, apart from building a new *Covent Garden Opera House* and a number of houses, completed his father's town hall at Halifax and the Palace of Westminster. A third son, *Sir John Wolfe Barry* (1836–1918), was a civil engineer known especially for his work on *Tower Bridge* in London. A fourth son, later Bishop of Sydney, wrote Sir Charles's biography.

BARTIZAN A battlemented turret projecting from the top of a tower. A term coined in the nineteenth century for a medieval feature.

BASE In architecture, the part of a column between the shaft and the pedestal or pavement. (For classical bases see CLASSICAL ORDER.)

Eleventh-century Norman bases were insignificant in comparison with the capitals, consisting only of a quarter-round moulding standing on a square plinth. Later examples were more weighty and elaborate but all had round mouldings on a square plinth. In later work, the angles between the square and round sections were filled by carved decorative foliage or animals: these were called spurs. Some examples resembled the Attic base (see CLASSICAL ORDER), having two round mouldings, or one round and a quarter-round, separated by a hollow or chamfer.

In Gothic architecture, Early English bases were commonly on the Attic principle but, in later work, a multiplicity of mouldings was used on a deeper pedestal. In the early fourteenth century bases were composed of triple rolls but these were replaced later by ogee mouldings. Bases tended to become taller and were set upon an octagonal plinth. In the last, fifteenth-century, phase of Gothic architecture, bases were tall and slender and finely proportioned. It was usual to have a roll moulding at the top then a double ogee and further rolls. Bell-shaped bases were common. Below this came the octagonal plinth in one or more members (see also MOULDINGS).

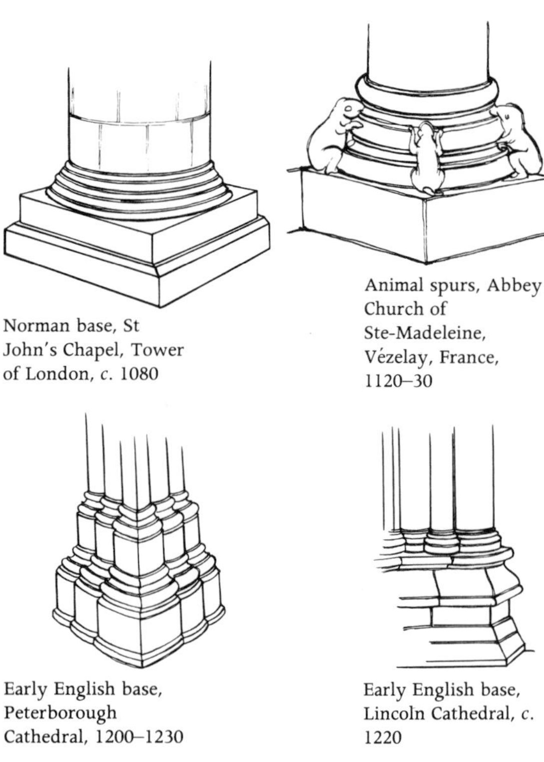

Norman base, St John's Chapel, Tower of London, *c.* 1080

Animal spurs, Abbey Church of Ste-Madeleine, Vézelay, France, 1120–30

Early English base, Peterborough Cathedral, 1200–1230

Early English base, Lincoln Cathedral, *c.* 1220

Fourteenth-century base, Exeter Cathedral

Perpendicular pier base

BASEMENT The lowest storey of a building, often partly or wholly below ground level.

BASEVI, GEORGE (1794–1845) A classical architect of the first half of the nineteenth century, Basevi died comparatively young but, despite this, a considerable quantity of his work survives. He was a pupil of Soane for three years (see SOANE, SIR JOHN) and, following a further three years' study in Europe, began private practice in 1819. He made an important contribution to the speculative terrace housing development in the *Belgravia* area of London, work on which he was largely engaged between 1825 and 1840 (see PORCH; CUBITT, THOMAS). These façades are characteristic of the high quality of urban development then being carried out in many cities especially in the south of England, in Cheltenham and Brighton and Hove, for instance. In *South Kensington* Basevi's astylar façade of *Pelham Crescent* is simpler and less palatial. In addition to a number of country houses he collaborated with Sydney Smirke (see SMIRKE, SIR ROBERT) in building the *Conservative Club* in London (1843–4).

Basevi's best known single building is the *Fitzwilliam Museum* in Cambridge (1836–45), for which he won the competition in 1835. He worked on the building until his death; it was continued by Cockerell, who was responsible for the impressive entrance hall though the staircase is High Victorian (1870–5) (see COCKERELL, CHARLES ROBERT). Basevi's early work had been influenced by Grecian lines and proportion but gradually his buildings had become more Roman in style. The Fitzwilliam Museum is in a heavier, almost Baroque Roman style, with an imposing Corinthian, pedimented portico and weighty attic.

BASILICA The basilica was one of the most important buildings of ancient Rome and wherever the Romans built

Belgrave Square, London, from 1825

BASEVI, GEORGE
Pelham Crescent, South Kensington, London, 1820–30

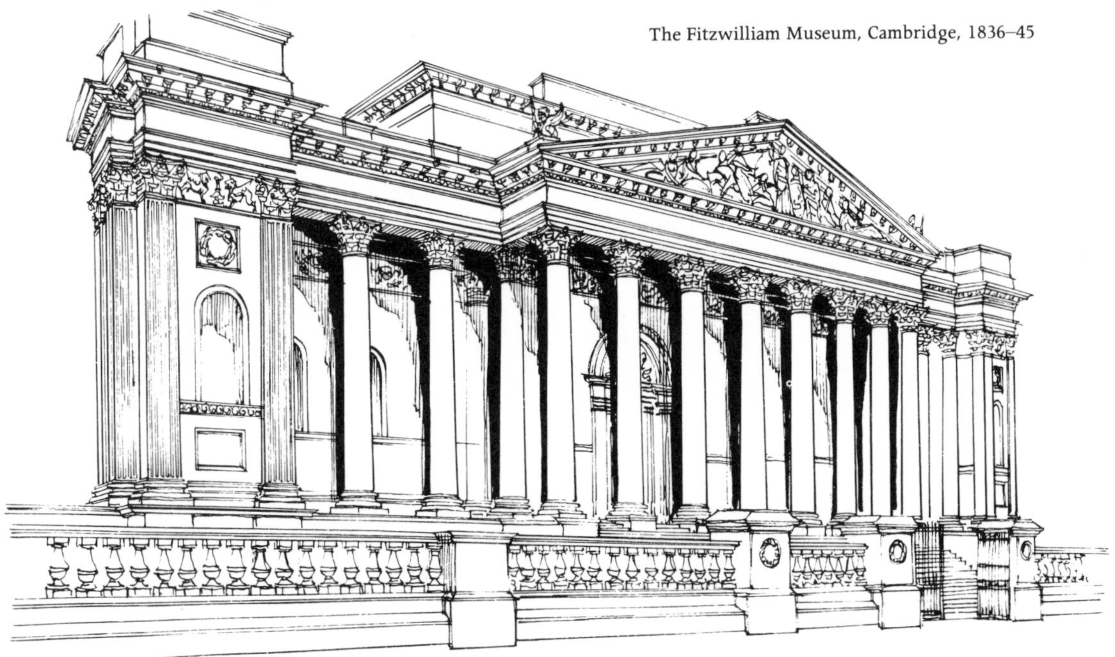

The Fitzwilliam Museum, Cambridge, 1836–45

a city the basilica would occupy a central position in or near the forum. The basilica was a hall of justice and a centre for commercial exchange. The word 'basilica' referred to this function, not its design as a building; but, in general, the basilican form was of rectangular plan with an apse at one or both ends of the shorter sides or, alternatively, the entrance in the centre of one of the longer sides might face an apse on the longer side opposite. The rectangular space was divided longitudinally by columned arcades into a wider central area and two narrower areas flanking it at each side. These colonnades supported walls which were pierced above with windows to light the building and an open timber roof which might be enclosed by a flat, decorative ceiling. Later and larger basilicas were roofed with concrete vaults which were carried on a few, very large piers. The most famous basilica in Rome of this type was the *Basilica of Maxentius (Constantine)*, begun in AD 308. Four massive piers, each 14ft in diameter, supported a vaulted roof. In front of these stood eight gigantic marble columns, one of which was removed by Pope Paul V and now stands in front of the Church of Sta Maria Maggiore in the city. Despite an earthquake in the ninth century and being used as a quarry for building during the Middle Ages, the remains of the Basilica in the Forum Romanum are considerable.

Probably due to its simple plan and the many examples surviving in Rome and other large Italian cities when the Emperor Constantine, by his Edict of Milan in AD 313, gave recognition to Christianity as the official religion of the Empire, the basilica was adopted by the early Christian Church for its building prototype. Later, in the eastern part of the Empire, this plan gave place to the Byzantine Greek cross layout but, in western Europe, basilicas have continued to be built until today, though this is a design more characteristic of Italy and France than Britain, where the cruciform plan has been predominant.

The term 'basilican' applied to churches and cathedrals is often loosely used and given to buildings of a variety of plans and constructions. A basilican church, like the early Christian ones, is characterized by:

1. A rectangular, not a cruciform plan, therefore no transepts.
2. A division into a broader and higher nave and narrower, lower aisles by columns.
3. Commonly an apse at one end (usually the east) or at both ends.
4. Walls (in a true basilica) which are not reinforced and therefore cannot bear a stone vault. It has an open timber roof or a flat wood ceiling.

In the early Christian church the apse contained the altar from the beginning but this was not necessarily orientated to the east (for example, S. Maria Maggiore in Rome). The plan included the addition of a narthex at the west end (or that opposite the one occupied by the high

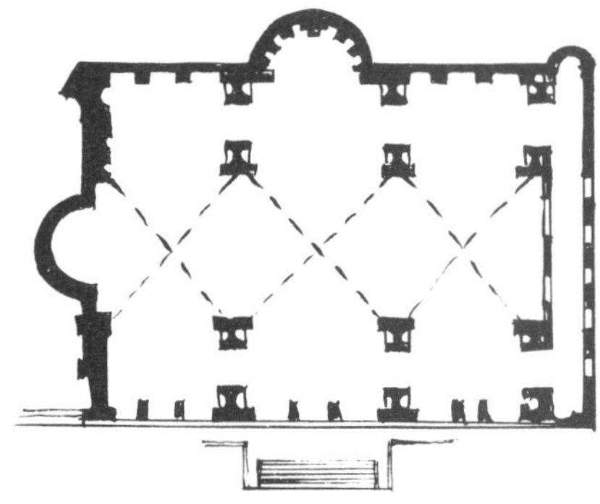

Ground plan of Basilica of Maxentius, Forum Romanum, Rome, begun AD 308

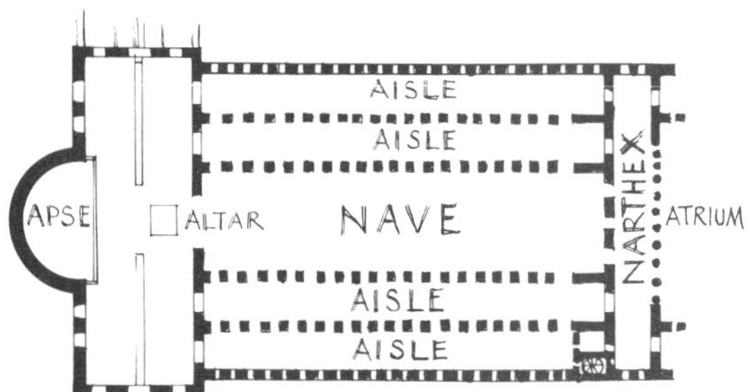

Ground plan of S. Paolo-fuori le Mura (St Paul-without-the-Walls) Rome

Basilica of S. Paolo-fuori-le-Mura, Rome, built 380 AD, rebuilt to original design after destruction in 1823

altar). This narthex was a portico extending across the whole width of the façade and was built to accommodate those, such as penitents, who were not permitted to enter the church, and enable them to hear the service. The atrium was in front of the narthex and this generally contained the separate baptistery (see ATRIUM; BAPTISTERY; CHURCH DESIGN AND STRUCTURE; NARTHEX; TRIBUNE).

BASTARD, JOHN (*c.* 1688–1770) The reputation of John Bastard and that of his brother William was, as with a number of other provincial architects in the eighteenth century, associated specifically with one town or part of the country. Instances of this include the Hiorns in Daventry, John Carr of York and Thomas White in

BASTARD, JOHN
Blandford Church, Dorset, 1735–9

Worcester (see CARR, JOHN). In the case of John and William Bastard it was *Blandford* in Dorset. The fire of 1731 had caused great damage to the town, the centre of which was rebuilt in a sustained operation in less than 30 years. The brothers took an important part in this rebuilding which achieved a remarkably homogeneous layout of good-quality, simple early Georgian architecture. Of particular interest are the church, the town hall and the Red Lion public house.

BASTION A projecting part of the angle of a fortification which enables the defenders to have a view of the ground before the ramparts.

BATTEN A long piece of timber of small, rectangular section, a scantling, used as a fixing or support for laths in plasterwork or roofing slates.

BATTER An inclined face or receding slope. A term used to describe a wall, tower or façade which is thicker at the base and thinner at the top.

BATTLEMENT An indented parapet at the top of a wall, used in the early Middle Ages especially for fortified structures but in the fifteenth and sixteenth centuries and later, as architectural decoration to church towers, houses and other buildings. The indentations are called *embrasures* or *crenelles*, the raised portions between are *merlons* or *cops*: both are finished with a coping. A crenellated parapet is one which has battlements.

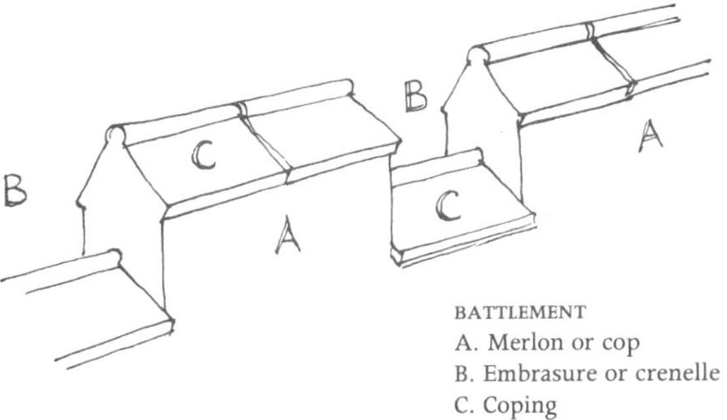

BATTLEMENT
A. Merlon or cop
B. Embrasure or crenelle
C. Coping

BAUHAUS A school of arts and crafts had been founded at Weimar in Germany in 1906 by the Grand Duke of Saxe-Weimar, who appointed *Henri Van de Velde* (1863–1957) as Director. Van de Velde was an Art Nouveau architect and designer. He had spent many years studying painting and industrial design then turned to architecture about 1895. He was born in Antwerp but spent much of his working life in Germany helping in the foundation and establishment of the Weimar School of Applied Arts, where he enunciated progressive ideas, training the students in the basis of workshop technique as well as in art studios. He left Germany for Switzerland in 1917 and recommended Gropius as his successor.

Walter Gropius (1883–1969) (see MODERN ARCHITECTURE) was appointed in 1919 to head the art college. Two institutions had been amalgamated, the Grand Ducal School of Applied Arts and the Grand Ducal Academy of Arts. Under Gropius the new institution became the *Staatliches Bauhaus* and was reorganized. Gropius put into practice his strongly held ideas. He was so successful that this small college, which trained only a few hundred students in the limited years of its existence, became world famous, attracting architects, artists and students from all over Europe, who saw here something new which would free them from the strait jacket of the academic approach to design in medieval or classical idiom. This applied to all the visual arts. Artists of the stature of Paul Klee from Switzerland and Vassili Kandinsky from Russia were two who joined his orbit and worked harmoniously with the whole group.

Gropius' idea was to set up an institution where students in all the arts and crafts could work together and learn from one another. He abhorred the artificial barriers which existed between artists and craftsmen and between artists in different media; he believed that all artists should be craftsmen and saw them all as interdependent. He felt that manual dexterity was as essential and vital as creative design. The phrase so often heard to denote lack of academic ability but compensating dexterity, 'he is good with his hands', would have found no favour with Gropius. Every Bauhaus student, whatever his field of work or talent, took the same workshop training. He studied and observed what was required to create the complete design. When qualified he was able to understand and supervise all the aesthetic and constructional processes which made up his field of work.

The basis of this idea was not new. It had been practised by architects of the Renaissance and the Baroque and by eighteenth-century designers such as Kent and Adam who not only worked out every detail of a building but fully comprehended the arts and crafts, as well as the building science, which went into it. During the nineteenth century this realistic approach had been lost and Gropius and his staff re-established it, trying for collaborative design in a building.

The early, enthusiastic ideals of craftsmanship, inspired by such men as Morris (see MORRIS, WILLIAM), underwent a metamorphosis in the 1920s and the momentum was lost. The aims of the Bauhaus changed direction towards an industrialized design dominated by stark simplicity and functionalism. In an effort to break the shackles which had constricted architects for hundreds of years, tying them to the medieval/classical design pattern, designers over-reacted. Bauhaus building became mechanical, excessive in its studied plainness. It lacked humanity, warmth and colour. This was far from the aims of the builders but they were held in the grip of an intensity of desire to build something new, something functional, clean and stripped of tawdry decoration.

In 1924 the Bauhaus in Weimar had to be closed because of political changes. Gropius was invited to leave Weimar and go to Dessau to re-establish the Bauhaus in new premises. He designed the new purpose-built school which, itself, became a prototype for the new architecture (1925–6). Gropius left the Bauhaus in 1928. He was succeeded by *Hannes Meyer* who was dismissed for political reasons in 1930. *Mies van der Rohe* took over (see MODERN ARCHITECTURE) but, due to the growth of National Socialism, he too was dismissed and the school was closed in 1932.

The Bauhaus was the most important school of art of the twentieth century. A measure of its influence is the intensity of the reaction to it—for and against. Its opposers included architectural reactionaries in the 1920s all over Europe; the Nazis in the 1930s, who described the work as Art-Bolshevism; and, at the same time, the Russians, who thought it bourgeois.

BAY A vertical division of the exterior or interior of a building. The division can be marked by buttresses, by an order or by fenestration, for example, the Regency bay window extending the full height of a house. In the early cruck form of building the structure was constructed in bays, each of which was about 16 feet wide, the divisions being marked by pairs of crucks (see CRUCK BUILDING). The Normans introduced into their cathedrals and churches articulation into bays and marked the divisions by the tall vertical shafts which extended from floor to wooden ceiling. Later, where a church was stone vaulted, this shaft, or group of shafts, terminated in a capital which supported the vault and springing. The vaults were themselves divided into bays by ribs and timber roofs by principal rafters (see also CHURCH DESIGN AND STRUCTURE, CLASSICAL ARCHITECTURE, ROOF and VAULTING).

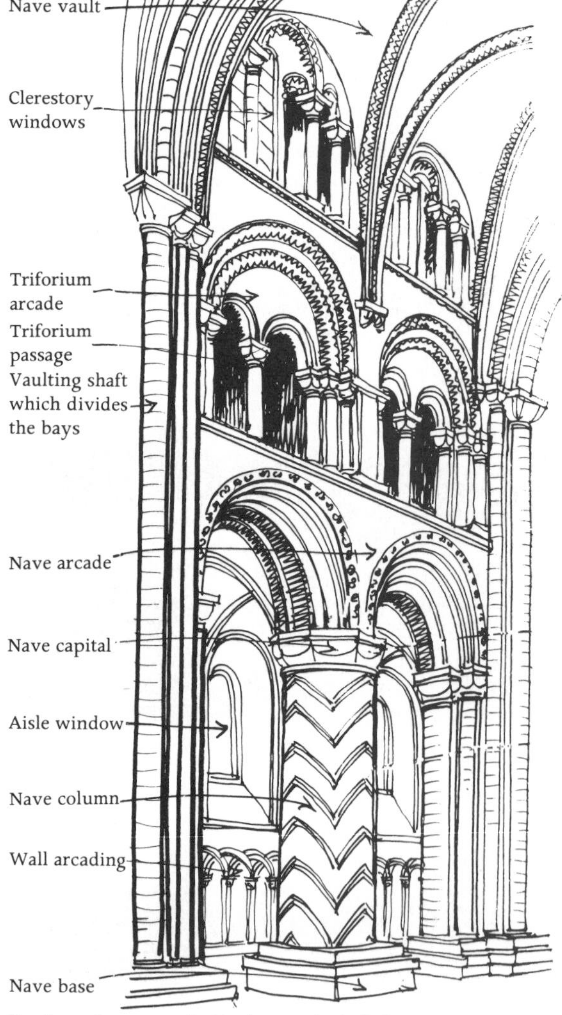

One bay of nave arcade, Durham Cathedral, from 1093

Bays marked by fenestration: sea-front terrace, Hastings, *c.* 1820–30

BEARER A member or material used as a support or stay.

BED

1. The under-surface of a stone, brick or slate.
2. Mortar joint spread to receive a course of stone or bricks.
3. In stone, marble and slate, the direction of the natural stratification of the material.

BEEHIVE CONSTRUCTION Simple, one-roomed structures of beehive shape were made in various materials by many primitive societies. Prehistoric examples of a circular conical form have been found in Sardinia: these are called *nuraghi* (singular *nuraghe*). In remote areas of Ireland and Scotland stone beehive cells were built by Celtic monks in the early centuries AD. These are usually of dry masonry, each course corbelled inwards to converge at the top to make a domed vault (see ABBEY, MONASTERY, PRIORY).

The circular beehive shape was also used by ancient cultures for tombs. A notable instance of this is the *tholos tombs* at *Mycenae* in the Peloponnese in Greece. These are

BEEHIVE CONSTRUCTION
Etruscan tumulus, Cerveteri, Italy, seventh to fifth century BC

Street of *trulli*, Alberobello, Italy

underground, circular chambers covered with a mound of earth and approached by means of a *dromos* (a stone-faced passage). Inside the tomb is faced with squared blocks of masonry set in horizontal courses which are corbelled to meet at a domed centre overhead. Such tombs are constructed by first cutting the open passage (dromos) into the hillside until the ground is rising high enough above it. After the last burial the dromos is filled in. Only the mound of earth is then visible and the tomb would last as long as the vault withheld the water from the earth above. Good examples have buttress walls encircling the vault to protect it and to take the thrust.

The best and most famous tholos tomb at Mycenae is that known as the *Treasury of Atreus*, built *c.* 1330 BC. This is finely contructed with dressed, curved conglomerate blocks. Inside the dome each block overlaps and counterweighs the one below on a cantilever system. The blocks are wedge-shaped and the interstices are filled with clay and stone. The chamber is 47½ft in diameter and 43ft high. The dromos approach is 120ft long and 20ft wide, its side walls regularly laid with blocks of dressed conglomerate. The 18ft-high doorway inclines inwards. The lintel blocks, inner and outer, above the doorway are gigantic, each weighing 100 tons.

The Etruscans also built a type of tumulus in this way. This was a beehive-shaped burial mound, made of earth, circular in plan and surrounded at the base by a stone wall. It was entered by a rectangular doorway and the elaborate chamber inside was lined with stone blocks.

Houses with conical beehive roofing are still in use in Apulia in southern Italy. These are made of stone blocks in a similar manner to the Celtic monks' cells but are larger in order to accommodate more than one room. In Alberobello, near Bari, there is a whole street of these houses, which are called *trulli*.

BEHRENS, PETER (1868–1940) An important innovator in the modern architectural movement in Germany, Behrens became first a painter then a designer in Art Nouveau forms. By the first years of the twentieth century he had become interested in architecture, his designs mainly on the lines of the contemporary neo-classicism. A turning point in his career was his appointment in 1907 as architect and consultant to AEG, the Berlin electrical company. His *Turbine Factory* in Berlin (1909), which survives, was a breakthrough in design. Built in concrete, steel and glass, this is a severely functional building. Two more factories followed in Berlin in 1910, then in 1913 he built the large AEG plant at Riga. He became in demand for industrial work, completing an office building for the *Mannesmann Steel Works* in *Düsseldorf* (1911–12, destroyed) in a more traditional but emasculated classicism and an extensive scheme for *I. G. Farben* at *Frankfurt* (1920–4), reflecting the current Expressionism. In England, Behrens is known for the house *'New Ways'* which he designed at *Northampton* in

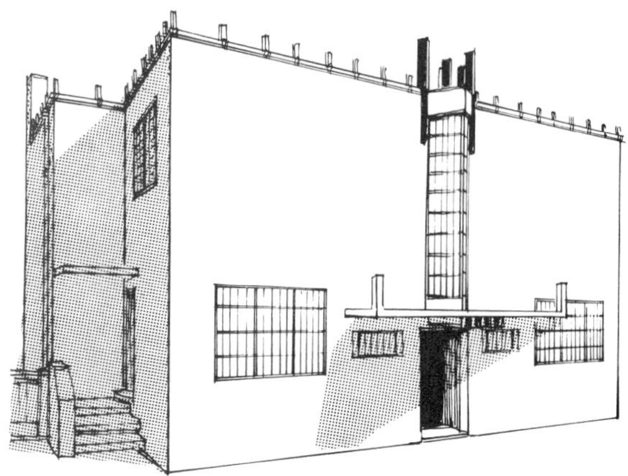

BEHRENS, PETER
'New Ways', Northampton, 1925

1925–6. This is in the characteristic modern style of the Continent in the 1920s but an innovation for England at that date. Behrens numbered among his pupils in the years before the First World War some of the most famous of modern architects—Gropius, Mies van der Rohe and Le Corbusier (see MODERN ARCHITECTURE).

BELFRY Derived from the Middle English *berfrey, berfray* and Old French *berfrei*. The meaning of the word has changed over the centuries; applied to a pent-house or a movable tower used by besiegers of a town or castle in the early Middle Ages, it referred to a watch tower, alarm-bell tower and bell tower in the later medieval period. Since that time a belfry has been either an upper storey in a church tower where the bells are hung or the bell tower itself (see BELL TOWER).

BELL, HENRY (1647–1711) One of a number of seventeenth- and eighteenth-century architects whose life and work was spent mainly in one locality. It is for his achievements in *King's Lynn*, where he was twice mayor, that Bell is known. The *Exchange* for merchants (1683) is his chief building; it became the Custom House in 1718 and is still used as such. It is a well-proportioned, two-storeyed, stone structure, articulated with Doric pilasters on the ground floor and Ionic above, surmounted by a steeply pitched roof with dormers and, above, a balustrade and lantern. Bell's other works include a house in King's Lynn and the church at *North Runcton*.

BELLCOTE, BELL GABLE A turret, gable or other framework on a roof from which bells are hung.

BELL TOWER A tower attached to or separate from a church built for the ringing of bells (see also BELFRY). The Italian term *campanile* is sometimes used especially when referring to a separate structure.

BELVEDERE From the Italian *bel vedere*, a sight or view

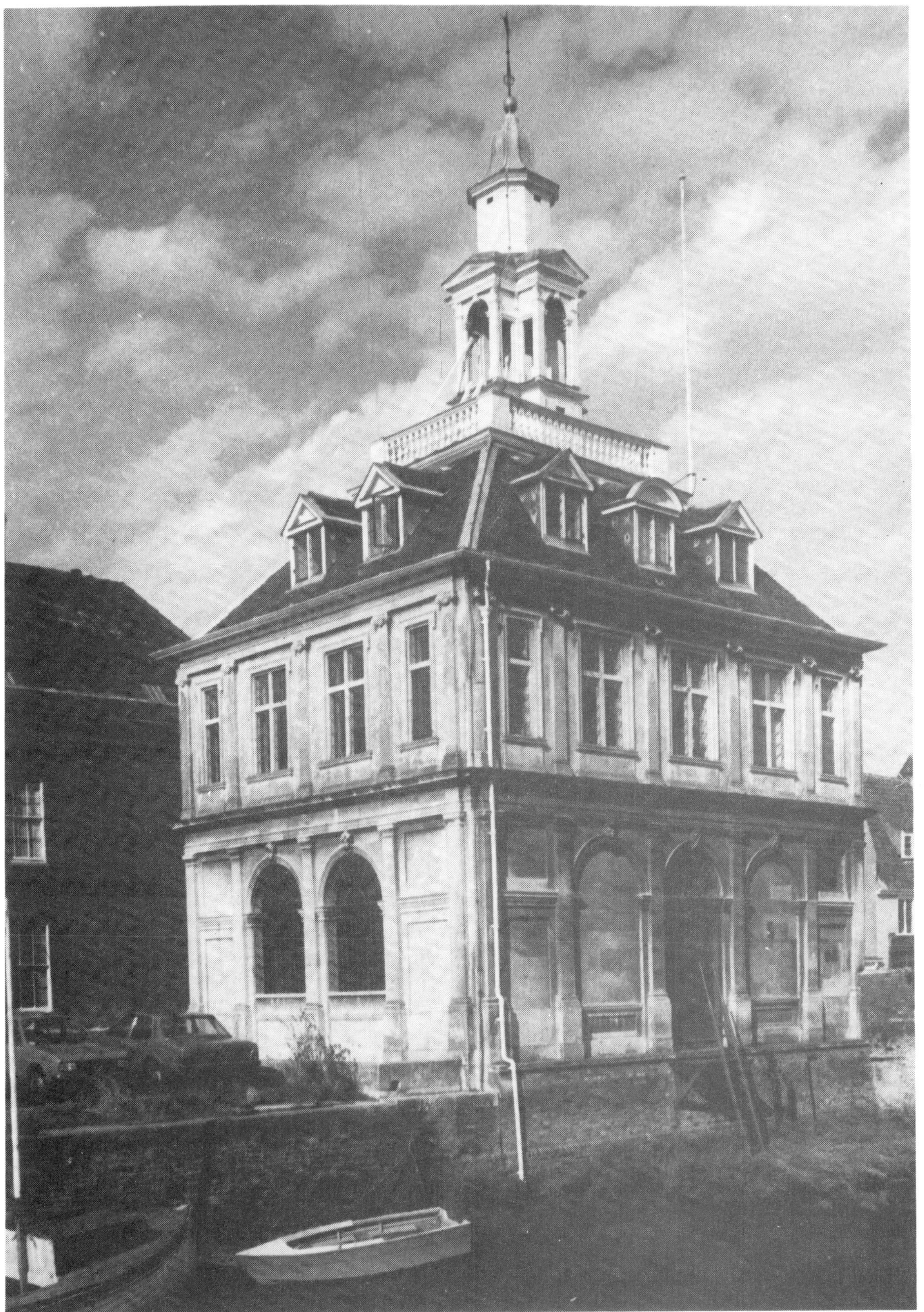

The Custom House, King's Lynn, Norfolk, 1683

of beauty. A raised turret or lantern on the top of a house from which a view can be obtained (see also GAZEBO).

BEMA From the Greek word *βημα*, meaning 'step'. In ancient Greece this was a platform from which an orator addressed his audiences. In the Early Christian church it was a raised stage or platform from which the clergy addressed the congregation and was stituated in the apse or chancel. In the Byzantine church the bema is a raised area behind the iconostasis which contains the altar (see ICONOSTASIS). In the present day, 'bema' can also refer to the chancel of a church.

BENTLEY, JOHN FRANCIS (1839–1902) Most of Bentley's work was in church design and the majority of these churches were Roman Catholic ones—Bentley himself became a Roman Catholic. He was a pupil of Henry Clutton then set up in practice for himself in 1862. For some time he designed church furniture and carried out additions and alterations to churches. In 1868 he built the *Convent of the Sacred Heart* at *Hammersmith*—a restrained, impressive structure—then went on to the *Church of the Holy Rood* at *Watford* (from 1887) and the *Church of St Francis* at Barking in Essex in 1893. The Holy Rood is in great contrast to the Hammersmith church,

BELL TOWER
Adjacent bell tower in the style of an Italian *campanile*: Church of St Mary and St Nicholas, Wilton, Wiltshire, by Wyatt and Brandon, 1840–6

BENTLEY, JOHN FRANCIS
Cathedral Church of the Most Precious Blood, Westminster (Roman Catholic), begun 1895

being a richly decorated, superbly handled Gothic Revival design.

Bentley's *chef d'oeuvre* is the *Roman Catholic Cathedral of Westminster* which he designed in 1894. Work began in 1895 and the shell was complete by 1903. He based the banded pattern of the exterior on the Italian cathedrals of Siena and Orvieto but, whereas these are striped in black and white marble, Westminster is in red brick banded with white stone. The immense interior is Byzantine in conception, superbly handled with shallow, concrete domes over the nave, crossing and sanctuary. Architectural decoration is sparing for Bentley intended the interior to be completely covered in marbles and mosaics which, slowly and with splendid effect, is taking place. The tall, slender, elegant campanile is one of London's finest landmarks. For many years this and the domes were the only part of the cathedral easily visible but since 1976, with the rebuilding in Victoria Street, there has been a clear view of the main body of the building.

Bentley's largest domestic commission was his decoration of E. W. Pugin's *Carlton Towers* in Yorkshire which he carried out after the architect's death in 1875. This is a particularly rich and splendid scheme (see PUGIN, A.W.N.).

BLANK DOOR OR WINDOW An imitation or fake door or window.

BLOCKING COURSE A plain course of brick or stone above a classical cornice. The term can also be used for a plain projecting course at the base of a building.

BLOMFIELD, SIR ARTHUR
Chapel, Selwyn College, Cambridge, *c.* 1895

BLOMFIELD, SIR ARTHUR (1829–99) An influential architect of his day with a large practice devoted to ecclesiastical and collegiate work. Blomfield began practice in 1856, became President of the Architectural Association in 1861, was knighted in 1889 and won the RIBA Gold Medal in 1891. He designed many churches, particularly in the 1880s. Many of these were in brick, some were plain and inexpensive, others more elaborate: nearly all were Gothic. Examples include *St Mary's, Portsea, St Matthias', Croydon,* and *St John's, St Leonard's-on-Sea* (see GOTHIC REVIVAL). His collegiate work included *Whitgift School* at *Croydon,* the *King's School* at *Chester* and *Queen's School, Eton.*

Selwyn College, Cambridge dates from 1882. Much of the huge quadrangle surrounded by brick buildings in Tudor Gothic style was designed by Sir Arthur from 1895 onwards. The chapel elevation is built with a large Perpendicular Gothic window flanked by cupola-topped towers while the gatehouse has one turret tower and a central oriel window over the carved Tudor Gothic doorway.

BLOMFIELD, SIR REGINALD (1856–1942) Born of an ecclesiastical family, Blomfield entered his uncle's (Sir Arthur Blomfield) office as a pupil after successful studies at Exeter College, Oxford. Like his uncle, Reginald Blomfield built up a large architectural practice and his work ranged over a wide field which included houses, bridges, monuments, civic architecture and collegiate building. He was principal architect to the Imperial War Graves Commission and, in this capacity, designed many memorials on the Continent of which his *Menin Gate* at *Ypres* (1923–6) is the most outstanding. This is a massive memorial, movingly suited to its conception.

At the turn of the century it was decided to rebuild *Regent Street* and much of *Piccadilly Circus* but to retain the curve of Nash's Quadrant. Norman Shaw was asked to design the layout which he did in 1905 at the age of 75. He died in 1912 with much of the scheme incomplete (see SHAW, NORMAN). It was after the First World War that Blomfield was asked to present a new design. It comprises the Quadrant, County Fire Office and Swan and Edgar façades. It is a professional, suitable scheme but lacks the warmth of Shaw and the panache of Nash. Blomfield's other work includes *Lambeth Bridge* (1929–37), the *Public Library* at *Lincoln* (1913), the *Cottage Hospital, Rye* (1929), the new façade to the *Middlesex Hospital, London* (1929) and much of the work on the new building at *Lady Margaret Hall, Oxford* (up to 1930).

Sir Reginald Blomfield was also known as a critic and writer on art and architecture. Among his standard works are the two-volume *History of Renaissance Architecture in England* (published 1897), his *History of French Architecture* (published 1911) and his *Life of Norman Shaw* (published 1940). He became President of the RIBA in 1912, an RA in 1914; and was knighted in 1919.

BLORE, EDWARD (1787–1879) An antiquarian and medievalist, Blore spent much of his life making drawings of English medieval architecture and most of his own work was in the Gothic style. He developed a large architectural practice, building houses and churches, and restoring a number of medieval buildings. He was Surveyor to *Westminster Abbey* between 1827 and 1849 and became architect to King William IV; in this capacity he completed *Nash's Buckingham Palace* in the 1830s (see NASH, JOHN) and carried out various commissions at *Windsor Castle* and *Hampton Court Palace*.

BOASTED WORK Masonry or woodwork hewn into the broad shape required in readiness for being carved.

BODLEY, GEORGE FREDERICK (1827–1907) A pupil of Scott (see SCOTT, GEORGE GILBERT), Bodley worked in the Gothic style, chiefly in church architecture. His churches, mainly of late Gothic derivation, display a professional quality and refinement of taste especially in decorative detail. Among his earlier commissions were *St Michael's, Brighton* (1859–62) and *St Martin's-on-the-Cliff, Scarborough* (1861–3). Bodley was a close friend of a number of the Pre-Raphaelites—Rossetti, Burne-Jones and Morris—and, as in these two churches, he was an early patron of the Morris firm (see MORRIS, WILLIAM).

In 1869 Bodley went into partnership with *Thomas Garner* and the firm designed and decorated a number of churches. Among these, in the 1870s, were two examples showing a varied approach in their work; the *Church of the Holy Angels* at *Hoar Cross*, Staffordshire had a richly ornate interior, while *St Augustine, Pendlebury* in Lancashire was an instance of monumental simplicity, strongly influenced by the Catalan and south-east French type of Gothic design as at Albi and Barcelona cathedrals, where the building is aisleless and has passages constructed through internal buttresses.

Apart from Pendlebury, two of Bodley's best church designs were those at *Clumber*, Nottinghamshire (1886–9) and *Holy Trinity, London* (1901). He was also designer, with Vaughan, of Washington Cathedral in the USA. In Britain Bodley was architectural adviser for many years to the cathedral chapters of Exeter, Manchester, York and Peterborough.

BODY

1. In a church, the nave or central aisle.
2. In a pillar, the shaft; in a compound pier, the central shaft.

BONOMI, JOSEPH (1739–1808) Born in Rome, Bonomi came to England in 1767 to work for Robert Adam (see ADAM, ROBERT) and, later, Leverton (see LEVERTON, THOMAS), chiefly on interior decorative work. In the 1780s he branched out for himself and designed a number of country houses but they lacked the quality of Leverton's work. Among these houses were *Longford Hall*, Shropshire (1789–92) and *Eastwell Park*, Kent (1793–9).

BOSS A carved, ornamental, projecting knob placed at the intersection of ribs in a stone vault or the beams in a timber roof or ceiling (see VAULTING).

BOSSAGE Stones laid in a wall, projecting, and to be carved at a later date.

BOX FRAME OR CROSS WALL CONSTRUCTION A concrete structure designed in a formation of boxes where the loads are carried on the cross walls. It is a type of construction suited to compartmented accommodation such as flats or offices which can then be repeated throughout the building.

BRACKET A member projecting from a wall, generally made of stone, wood or metal, plain or ornamentally shaped and carved, which acts as a support for a statue, shelf, cornice, arch, beam etc. (see also CONSOLE and CORBEL).

BRATTISHING A carved decorative cresting to a screen, parapet or cornice to be seen chiefly in the late Middle Ages, consisting usually of formalized leaves and flowers, sometimes within a battlemented form.

BRESSUMER, BREASTSUMMER The principal horizontal beam, often decoratively carved, in a timber-framed building, which carries the superstructure (this is sometimes projecting) and the first floor joists are tenoned into it. The term is also used for a heavy beam spanning a wide opening such as a fireplace (see SUMMER).

BRICKWORK A block of regular form, moulded and cut from a soft material such as clay, then hardened, its particles consolidated by fusion, under heat from the sun or by being burnt in a kiln. The colour and texture varies according to the clay in use, the method of burning and the process of manufacture.

Brick has been widely used by Man as a building material for over 6000 years. It has many useful qualities. It is inexpensive to produce and the raw material is readily to hand. It can be made in different sizes, colours, qualities and textures. It is durable, withstands the weather and is a good insulating material. It can be used in conjunction with other materials as, for example, in Roman walling, where the bricks provided bonding courses at intervals between others of flint or rubble masonry, and in a decorative form as infilling to timber framing or with stone dressings—a treatment often employed by Sir Christopher Wren (Hampton Court Palace, 1689–1701).

Early brick-making in areas of the world where the climate was hot, such as Egypt and Mesopotamia, used

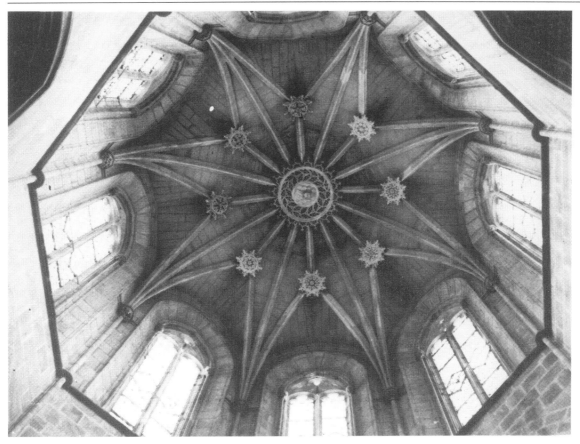

BOSS
Bosses at intersection of star vault of cupola. Founder's Chapel, Batahla Abbey, Portugal, fifteenth century

BRATTISHING
Carved stone brattishing, fifteenth century

BRESSUMER
Early medieval Norwegian construction: Sør-fron, *c.* 1300

the sun to dry and heat the material. The Spanish word *adobe*, meaning a sun-dried brick, reflects a method employed until modern times and such brickwork can be seen in many parts of the world including Spain, south-east Europe and South America. Burnt bricks were being made in the Near East by 3000 BC and, in Britain, some examples have been found which pre-date the Roman occupation. These bricks are not very hard and certainly much softer than Roman ones.

The Romans widely employed bricks for building, especially in provincial work. This was so in Britain, where brickwork was practised extensively. The bricks were used as bonding courses in walling, as can be seen in remains of town walls such as those at Colchester in

Essex, and also as facing to a concrete core. Roman building bricks were large and thin, resembling large tiles and the mortar courses between were of a thickness generally about the same as the bricks themselves. The bricks, which were hard and well-burnt, varied in size from one inch to one-and-a-half inches in thickness and could be square or rectangular, the latter ranging from 18in × 12in to 12in × 6in. Floor bricks were rectangular but smaller and thicker and those made to build up into *pilae* (underfloor piers for the heating system) were square. Hollow box bricks were made for insertion into walls for cavity heating methods. Many examples of Roman bricks can be seen in Britain but these have chiefly been re-used in Saxon and Norman times and in the Middle Ages. These hard bricks were durable and existed in quantity so were incorporated into churches, cathedrals and fortifications where strong materials were needed. St Alban's Cathedral and the Castle and St Botolph's Priory in Colchester are typical examples.

After the Romans left, brick-building died out in Britain and, unlike northern Europe in the Hanseatic Towns along the Baltic coast, and unlike France and Italy, where brick was widely used from the twelfth century onwards, the craft was slow to re-appear. There are very few instances from about 1200 of the use of brick dressings in Britain but the first example where a considerable number of bricks was used, in conjunction with other materials, was *Little Wenham Hall* in Suffolk (*c.* 1275). It is likely, though this is not documented, that these bricks of varied hues were made on the site. Brick continued only in limited use as a building material in Britain until the seventeenth century. *Holy Trinity Church* in *Hull* is one of the few fourteenth-century examples and, even in the fifteenth century, when the material was more widely used, this was chiefly for cottages and small houses. Brick was, however, beginning to be found useful in areas where stone was not available, for the great forest covering of the country was at last showing signs of depredation. These areas are in the east of the country from Kent and East Sussex to East Anglia and north to Lincolnshire and East Yorkshire. This need for brick as a building material, added to the fact that the Continental influence from the Hanseatic League and Flemish building traditions was strongest in this area, led to some fine examples of brick building in larger structures. These include *Tattershall Castle*, Lincolnshire, *Oxburgh Hall*, Norfolk, *Eton College*, Buckinghamshire, the entrance gateway at *Queens' College*, Cambridge and *Hurstmonceux Castle*, Sussex (which has stone dressings and machicolations).

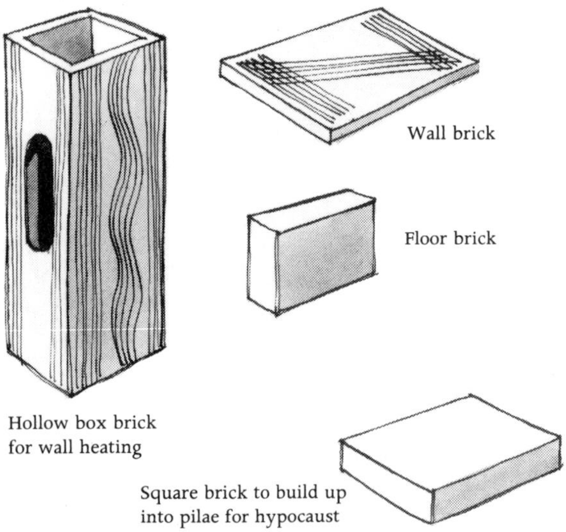

The word 'brick' seems to have come into use in Britain only in the mid-fifteenth century; before this the general term was *waltyle* (wall tile), or the Latin *tegula* (the Roman roof tile) was used. The word 'brick' appears to derive from the meaning of a broken piece of a baked material as in the Teutonic *brekan* (='to break') and the Old French *briche* or *brique*.

In the Tudor period, brick building developed more quickly. During the time of Henry VIII the work was more skilfully handled, both in the making of bricks and in the laying of them. Decoration was attempted on an ambitious scale and in a manner which had been traditional in the Hanseatic towns of Holland, Germany or Poland since the thirteenth century. Diaper patterns were produced by using headers with darker, more heavily burnt ends (see *Brickwork terms*). The picturesque skylines of the time with their numerous chimney-stacks provided the opportunity for the greatest variety of ornamentation in brick (see CHIMNEY). Notable examples include *Hampton Court Palace*, *Horham Hall*, Essex, *Compton Wynyates*, Warwickshire and *Hengrave Hall*, Suffolk. Terracotta was also used to decorate brick buildings. In this period such work was usually carried out by Italian craftsmen as in the superb craftsmanship at *Sutton Place*, Surrey. After 1560, in the Elizabethan and Jacobean periods, a number of large buildings, especially houses, were constructed chiefly or wholly of brick, though the material was still too costly to encourage the small house-builder. Famous Jacobean examples are *Hatfield House*, Hertfordshire, *Bramshill House*, Hampshire, *Charlton House*, Greenwich and *Aston Hall*, Birmingham.

A further advance in the handling of brick was apparent in the 1630s and 1640s. Classical architecture was beginning to be accepted and, particularly in houses, the varied forms of decorative gable were fashionable. Both these architectural factors provided a challenge to the brick builders since the material is more difficult to handle in the precise form required than stone which can more easily be carved. In Mannerist brickwork designs, *Kew Palace* (1631), *Broome Park*, Kent (1635–8) and *Balls Park*, Hertfordshire (*c.* 1640) show how skilfully brick was shaped to form classical columns, pilasters and moulded openings. Some stone was used for dressings and

Roman bricks

Wall brick

Floor brick

Hollow box brick
for wall heating

Square brick to build up
into pilae for hypocaust

Church of St Peter-on-the-Wall, Bradwell, Essex: re-used Roman bricks, tenth century, Saxon

Gatehouse, Oxburgh Hall, Norfolk, from 1482

Decorative brick gable in Hanseatic style, Pernaja Church, Finland, late fourteenth century

Herringbone brickwork and lacing courses, Guildford Castle: re-use of Roman bricks, Norman, twelfth century

Aisle vault of stone with brick infilling, Cathedral of S. Bavon, Ghent, Belgium, medieval

Herstmonceux Castle gatehouse, *c.* 1440

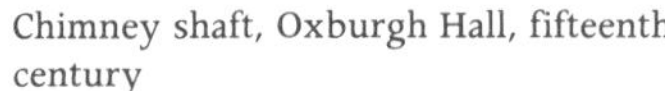

Doorway, Church of St Nicholas, Burnage. Architects: Welch, Cachemaille-Day and Lander, 1931

Chimney shaft, Oxburgh Hall, fifteenth century

at *Raynham Hall* in Norfolk (*c.* 1635–6) the classical orders and dressings are in stone. In these and other buildings of this time another new phase had been entered upon in the gradual replacement of *English bond*, as the most usual bonding method, by *Flemish bond* (see BONDING). At the same time, especially at Kew Palace, *gauged brickwork* was introduced and this made possible the elegant, semicircular window openings with radiating voussoirs (see BRICKWORK TERMS).

The century which commenced in 1660 was the great age of English brick building. High-quality bricks were made from a variety of fine clays, and were beautifully laid and used to decorate all kinds of buildings from Wren's Hampton Court Palace to whole streets of houses in towns large and small. All features of classical architecture were produced in good brickwork—even, in some instances, Corinthian capitals; and classical mouldings were enriched with the traditional acanthus, anthemion and egg-and-tongue; arch voussoirs were cut to precise shape. Eighteenth-century work showed a taste for polychromy in soft reds, greys and yellows. Brick building became much less costly as bricks were manufactured on a larger scale so, gradually, towns (especially London) replaced half-timber buildings with fire-proof brick ones. Even in counties with adequate stone supplies brick was fashionable and was soon also cheaper for building. The brick tax, imposed in 1784 and twice increased, had an effect on the use of brick for smaller buildings. The cost became prohibitive and there was a return to timber in rural areas. There was also a successful attempt to beat the tax by making larger bricks since the tax was levied on the number of bricks used, not their size. Brick continued in use for larger buildings though, due to architectural fashion, it was commonly faced with stucco and painted, partly to imitate stone—considered to be a more dignified, quality material—and partly because the smooth surface of stucco lent itself to the architectural style of the day. This was especially fashionable in the years 1780–1830.

The brick tax was repealed in 1850. At the same time the rapidly increasing population was requiring a tremendous increase in the tempo of building for all purposes—industrial, civic, ecclesiastical and domestic. The architectural mood of the day demanded the abolition of all sham and imitation; bare bricks were thought better than stucco-covered ones. The combination of these circumstances led to a boom in brick building and brick was far and away the most usual Victorian building material. Technical advances and improvements in brick-making rendered the material the cheapest and most readily to hand. In different qualities and by different processes bricks were made for all purposes from the extra hard 'engineering bricks', manufactured for industrial use in factories, railways, viaducts, etc., to the attractively textured ones for facing and cheaper, softer ones for everyday use. Brick played an important part in the 'railway

Monk bond, Guildford Cathedral, Surrey, 1936–61. Architect: Sir Edward Maufe

Bryanston House, Dorset, 1890. Architect: Norman Shaw

Brick nogging, seventeenth century, Aarhus, Denmark

age' in the second half of the century (see RAILWAY ARCHITECTURE). It was widely employed as a structural material in railway stations, tunnels, cuttings and viaducts. Some of these structures were immensely high and long and, despite closures, a number of fine viaducts survive. Among these is *Digswell Viaduct*, near Welwyn in Hertfordshire (*c.* 1850). Nearly 13 million bricks went into its construction, only slightly more than the $12\frac{1}{2}$ million in Westminster Cathedral (see BENTLEY, JOHN FRANCIS).

The wider range of colours available, especially the stronger hues, appealed to many later Victorian architects and polychromy was ultra-fashionable in the years 1865–85. *Keble College*, Oxford, is a typical example (see BUTTERFIELD, WILLIAM). Brilliant red brick was also favoured by many architects as in, for example, the *Prudential Assurance Building* in London (see WATERHOUSE, ALFRED). Another Waterhouse scheme which finely illustrates the Victorian use of terracotta as a decorative medium on brick buildings is the *Natural History Museum* in London (1873–9). Since it has been cleaned recently this high-quality work may be seen to advantage. A further reason for the popularity of brick for building was its durability. It stood up to the polluted atmosphere of Victorian cities far better than stone which began to crumble as its surface was attacked.

In reaction from High Victorian polychromy and strong red hand-edged machine-made bricks, came a number of architects of the years 1890–1940, for example Lutyens, Champneys and Shaw (see individual entries), who built extensively in brick but encouraged the use of the high-quality hand-made product, which they utilized for facing in a variety of soft colours. Despite the increasing use of the modern materials of concrete and steel, brick is still a major building material in Britain and about two per cent of the product is hand-made.

Brick-making

The making of bricks from clay by a heating or burning process, as distinct from the more primitive system of leaving them to dry in the hot sun, requires three principal stages of production. This has been so since Roman times, though the methods for carrying out these processes have become more complex and mechanized as time has passed. The raw material has to be dug out of the ground, it must be prepared and moulded into shape, then it is burnt.

After the clay had been excavated from the ground it had to be *puddled*. This process was one of preparing the clay for burning and included removing pebbles and other extraneous material, then mixing and squeezing the residue with water and sand to acquire an even consistency. Often, more than one clay was used in the mixture in order that the qualities of one substance should counteract those of the other, so giving an even-firing result. Before the seventeenth century, puddling was done by men treading the material barefoot. Gradually, this system was replaced by the *pug-mill* which was cylindrical and contained a central, vertical shaft with blades attached which extended horizontally, churning the mixture into a smooth consistency. The mill was powered by a horse or donkey walking round in circles. Later, the pug-mill would contain rotating wheels and be powered by water, steam or electricity.

The next stage was to shape the brick into the required form. The primitive method was to beat the material by hand into the shape required. By the later Middle Ages each brick was pressed into a wooden mould then left to dry for some time. Later the mould was made with a detachable base, called a *stock board*. The brick was removed by reversing the mould on to a pallet board and was further left to dry as it was necessary to remove as much surplus water as possible before burning in order to avoid uneven shrinkage.

The final stage of burning was, in early times, carried out in clamps. These clamps were stacks of bricks in which the fuel (faggots of brushwood) was intermingled. This was lit from outside and allowed to burn out. Bricks burnt in clamps were unevenly fired, those on the exterior being less burnt than those inside. This caused unevenness in size and colour, the bricks which were burnt most being darker in colour and smaller than the others. This is one of the chief reasons for the interesting

Brick-making

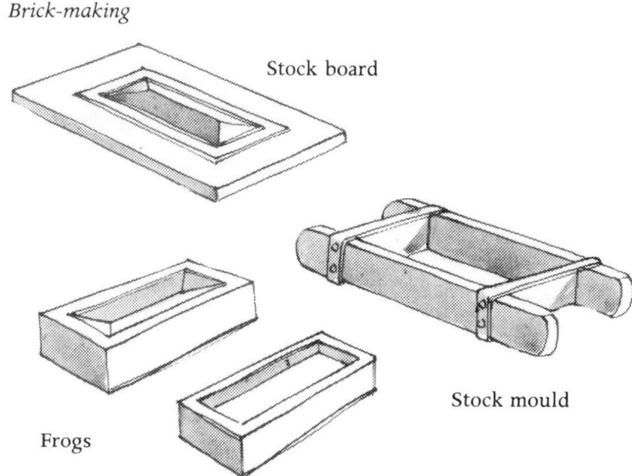

varied quality of medieval and Tudor brick building. The spaces in the uneven sizes of bricks were made up with mortar. The clamp system was followed by burning in kilns, which were permanent structures in which the raw bricks were loosely stacked with spaces between through which the heat could pass. Bricks were generally fired in these for about 48 hours. Fuel was wood until about 1700 when, due to shortages, it became necessary to use coal more often.

Improvements and technical advances had been made in brick-making processes over the centuries but it was not until the second half of the nineteenth century that such advances led to a mass-produced article which was needed to supply the quickly expanding building programme. Many of the old hand processes were replaced by machinery, and this mechanization saved time and labour. It was no longer necessary to spend time waiting for the bricks to dry before firing—machines could dry them. The development of the Fletton process in the 1890s was particularly relevant in this part of manufacture. Fletton is the area near Peterborough where a specific shale-clay is found in quantity. The material possesses a low degree of pliability because of its reduced water content so can be pressed into a brick ready for firing without previous drying. The composition of this shale-clay also includes about 10 per cent of carbonaceous material so less coal is needed to fire it. The time spent in the intermittent kiln system, where it had been necessary to fire and cool each setting of bricks over a period of a fortnight before another could be undertaken, was now eliminated with the *Hoffmann* continuous kiln invention of 1858. In this there were a number of chambers and the firing process could operate continuously with the brick stacks at different stages of firing or cooling. Large numbers of bricks were handled at controlled temperatures. These mechanical processes resulted in uniform bricks, perfect in size and colour and the brick-making costs were greatly lowered. Further advances followed, all processes being streamlined and accelerated leading to greater variety in colour and texture.

Bricks have always been made in a variety of shades. This is due to the chemical constituency of the raw material and to the process of and material used in burning. At one time the colouring was a haphazard business but in more recent times chemicals are added to produce a certain colour. The red in bricks is caused by the firing of material with an iron content. Other colouring agents include manganese, sand, lime and cobalt. The most common brick colours are red, yellow, brown and bluish-grey.

Bonding

A uniform arrangement of bricks in all walls to ensure strength and for decoration. Certain rules are generally followed to provide good bonding, the main one of which is to avoid continuous vertical joints on the outer or inner face of the wall. In walls of nine-inch thickness headers are introduced to bond the stretchers across the wall.

In early brickwork the design was so irregular and so intermingled with flint and stone that it followed no bonding pattern. By the late thirteenth century a bonding system began to be followed and this was most commonly *English bond* (alternate courses of headers and stretchers). This type of work, which seems to have been imported from France, was in general use throughout Tudor building but was slowly replaced in popularity from the mid-seventeenth century onwards by *Flemish bond*, which is characterized by alternate headers and stretchers on the same course. An early example of Flemish bond (which was rarely to be seen in Flanders) is *Kew Palace* (1631). Many types of bonding have been in use over the centuries, a number of which are variations on English and Flemish but with *breaking joints*, that is, on every alternate course the joint would be moved to the left or right. More than one type of bond may be used in a building or on a wall. The most common types of bonding include—

American bond: American term for English garden-wall bond.

Brick-on-edge bond: bricks laid on edge, usually headers, and suitable for a sill, flat arch or wall coping.

Brick-on-end bond: a similar function for stretchers laid on end rather than on bed.

Broken bond: where the length of the wall or pier between windows or doorways does not allow for the continuity of the bonding sequence. The broken bond is then placed in the centre of the space available in order to preserve symmetry.

Dearne's bond: alternate courses of headers and stretchers but with the headers laid on bed and the stretchers laid on edge (see also *Silver-lock's bond*).

Dutch bond: a variation of English bond in which the stretcher courses are moved half a brick to right or left to stagger the pattern.

English bond: a very strong but expensive bonding consisting of alternate courses of all headers and all stretchers.

English cross bond: a staggered English bond, similar to

Dutch bond but, due to the insertion of closers, the pattern is further staggered.

English garden-wall bond: a widely used bonding which is less costly than English bond because an odd number of stretcher courses, generally three, are used to one course of headers (see *American bond*).

Flemish bond: each course consists of alternate headers and stretchers. Single Flemish bond is where the bonding on a nine-inch wall is only followed on the face. In double Flemish bond it is followed on exterior and interior faces.

Flemish garden-wall bond: a Flemish bond but where an odd number of stretchers, generally three, are used between each header. Also known locally as 'Scotch' or 'Sussex bond'.

Flemish stretcher bond: the courses of alternate headers and stretchers are separated by several courses, of stretchers only, generally three.

Header bond: where the face of the wall shows all headers. A method of bonding used for footings or curving walls because of its great strength.

Irregular bond: where no uniform bonding pattern is used but the vertical joints are broken to avoid weakness.

Monk bond: a variation of Flemish bond where two stretchers are set between each header. Also known as 'flying Flemish bond'.

Raking bond: used in very thick walls or footing courses. Normal bonding, generally English or Flemish, used on outer and inner faces of wall but with infilling of diagonal or herringbone brick courses.

Rat-trap bond: a variation of Flemish bond where all the bricks are laid on edge so forming a cavity between the stretchers on a nine-inch wall.

Silver-lock's bond: similar but where only the stretchers are laid on edge.

Stack bond: courses of bricks laid on end with continuous vertical joints. May not be built for load-bearing walls.

Stretcher bond: a cavity wall bonding composed entirely of stretchers.

A glossary of general brickwork terms

Air brick: a perforated brick made of brick earth, terracotta or cast iron inserted in a wall for ventilation purposes.

Bat: a portion of a brick cut or broken across its length, used in bonding to make up a space.

Bed: bottom horizontal surface of a brick when laid. Also mortar spread to receive a course of bricks. *Bed-joint* is the horizontal joint between two courses of brickwork.

Black mortar: contains ashes to darken the material.

Brick earth or clay: a clay from which bricks are made.

Brick nogging: brick infilling to timber-framed walls.

Brick-tile: a tile with one end moulded as the end or face of a brick. Bedded into plaster or mortar or nailed to battens to cover pebble rendering. Also known as a mathematical tile or wall-tile (see TILES).

Bonding

Brick-on-edge bond

English bond

Flemish bond

Header or heading bond

English garden-wall bond

Monk bond

Flemish garden-wall or Sussex bond

Stretcher or stretching bond

Rat-trap bond

Stack bond

Brickwork terms

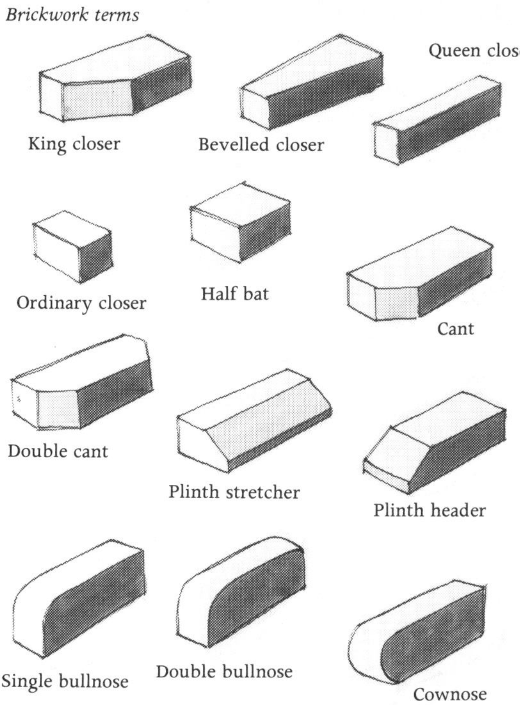

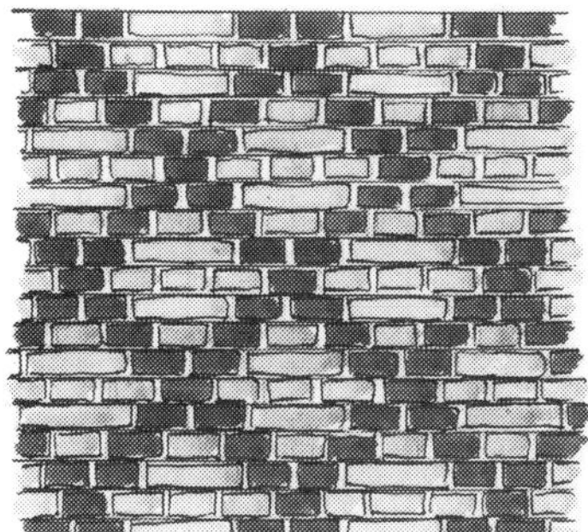

Diaper pattern using flared headers

Bullnose brick: one with a quadrant corner, that is, where the edges on one side are rounded. If one end of the brick is so treated, it is a single bullnose, if both ends, it is a double bullnose. A brick where the edges on top and bottom are so treated is a cownose brick.

Canted brick: one with a bevelled corner or corners.

Cavity wall: a form of construction in which two walls, generally $4\frac{1}{2}$in thick, are built with an air space (generally 2in) between them. The purpose of such construction is to improve thermal insulation and prevent penetration of dampness. In recent times it has become common practice to fill the cavity with a porous material to improve still further the thermal insulation while still maintaining a moisture barrier.

Chequered brickwork: the use of squares of brickwork alternating with ones of other materials (see CHEQUER WORK).

Closer: a piece of brick, narrower than the others, inserted near the end or corner of a wall to close the row and maintain the bond. Different-shaped pieces carry specific names, for example 'king', 'queen', 'bevelled', 'ordinary closers' (see illustrations).

Diaper brickwork: a diamond pattern produced in the wall by means of the use of coloured bricks (headers).

Dog-leg brick: one made to span the corner where two walls intersect at a wide angle.

Dutch clinker: a small, well-burnt paving brick.

Efflorescence: white powdery deposit on new brickwork which is drying out caused by the presence of salts in the bricks and/or mortar.

Engineering brick: one which is dense, durable and of uniform size, used for heavy-duty walling in industrial and large structures, for example, railway viaducts.

Facing brick: one whose colour, texture and general appearance are suitable for the exposed face of a wall. Such a brick may be glazed, rough-textured or sand-faced.

Flared brick: one which is darker at one end due to its position close to the heat in a kiln or clamp. Traditionally such bricks were laid as headers to form patterns in a wall, especially diaper patterns.

Fletton: a light pink brick, machine-pressed and burnt in a continuous kiln. Used particularly for interior and backing work.

Frog: indentation on one or both sides of a brick formed for several reasons: it makes a key for the mortar, the brick is easier to handle, strength is given to the wall against lateral pressure and the brick is denser because of the pressure exerted to form the frog.

Galleting: insertion of small pieces of tile, stone or pebbles into the mortar for decoration and for added strength.

Gauged brickwork: bricks which are cut with a wire bow-saw to a precise measurement and shape and rubbed smooth, generally with York stone, to give a fine surface finish. They are then laid with fine joints. Arch voussoirs are a specific example of such bricks. Gauged work was introduced in Britain in 1630. Before this thicker mortar and wedge-shaped pieces of brick were inserted to make up any inaccuracies in the size and shape of bricks.

Glazed brick: applied to one face and/or end of a brick before firing. Salt-glazing, providing a brown shiny surface, is done by throwing salt into the kiln during burning.

Header: a brick laid so that only its end appears on the face of the wall. A *bull header* is one which is specially made for circular work in which one end is thicker than the other. A *snapped header* is one used in a $4\frac{1}{2}$in wall and so must be cut or 'snapped' in two in order not to project forwards or backwards.

Herringbone brickwork: a bond where the bricks are laid in a herringbone pattern, that is, diagonally at right angles to each other.

Hoffmann kiln: a kiln with a number of chambers in

which a continuous operation of firing and cooling can be carried out.

Honeycomb brickwork: walling in which the bond provides for the omission of certain bricks to allow ventilation or give a decorative effect.

Jointing: spacing between bricks filled by mortar. This can be treated or finished in various ways; for example, left flush with the brickwork or scored by a trowel to mark the horizontal bonds. If the mortar is pressed at an angle to the bottom or the top of this horizontal joint, this

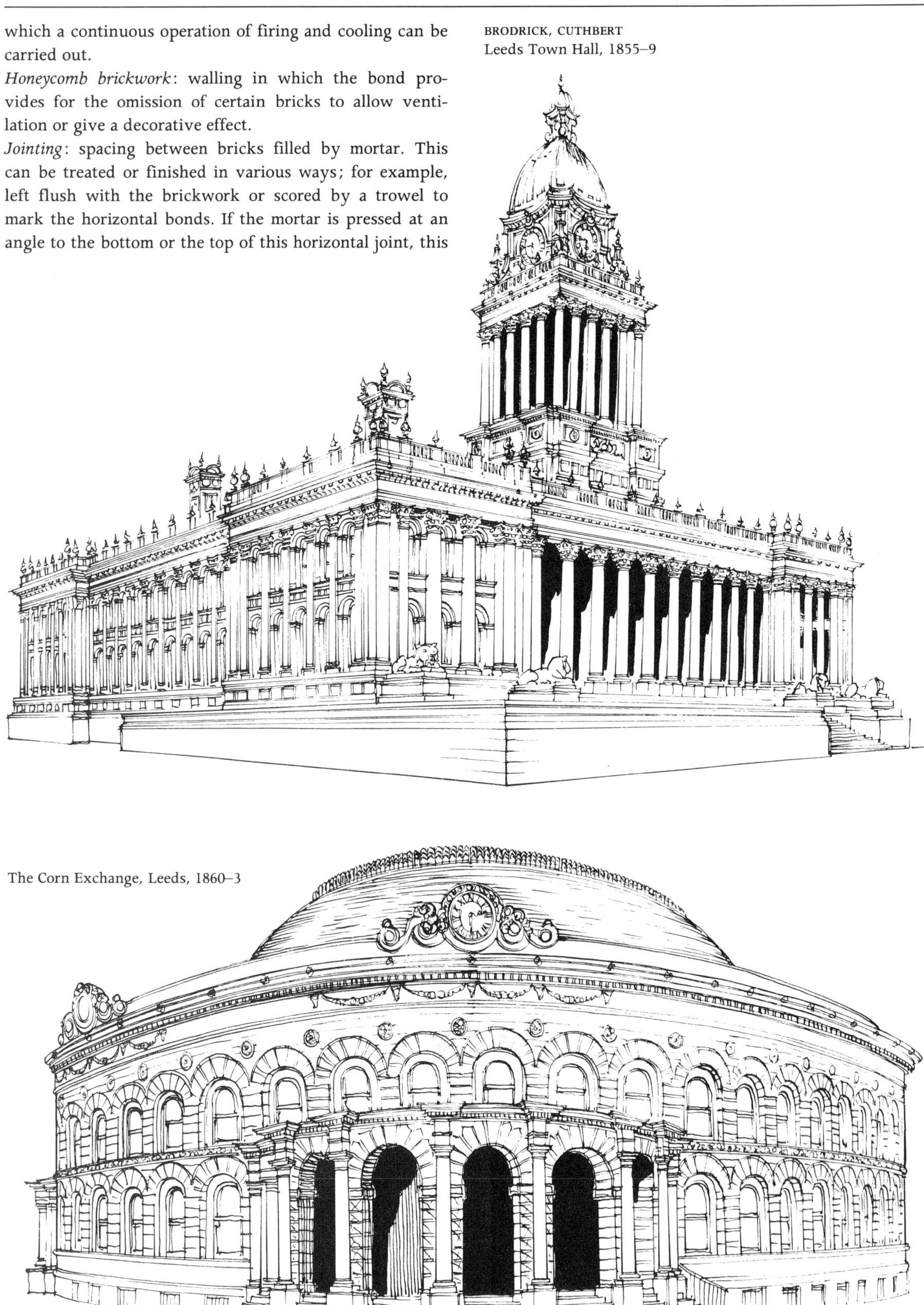

BRODRICK, CUTHBERT
Leeds Town Hall, 1855–9

The Corn Exchange, Leeds, 1860–3

gives a different finish; the former is called a *struck joint*, the latter a *weathered joint*.

Lacing course: an interlacing course of bricks to bond a rubble and flint wall.

Lap bonding: where one brick projects over the one on the course below.

Perpend: vertical joint in a brick wall.

Plinth brick: one chamfered, generally about $2\frac{1}{4}$in, to adjust to the different planes of the wall face and its plinth.

Pointing: the filling with a richer mortar of the raked-out joints of a brick wall to prevent penetration of moisture and to give a pleasant appearance. Coloured mortars are sometimes used.

Pressed brick: one which is machine-pressed before firing.

Putlog holes: holes in the brickwork into which the putlogs—the horizontal short tubes on which a builder's scaffold boards are supported—are inserted.

Stock brick: one hand-made by the use of a stock mould and board. (Also, later applied to the ordinary brick of certain localities, for example, London stock bricks.)

Straight joints: where two vertical joints in bonding are aligned immediately and precisely above one another.

Stretcher: a brick laid with its long side to the face of the wall.

Wire-cut brick: one formed from a continuous, rectangular slab of plastic clay extruded from a machine which is then cut crosswise at the correct intervals by a series of wires. Such bricks do not have frogs and are less dense than pressed bricks.

BRIDGE-STONES Paving stones laid over an area in front of a doorway; the pavement is generally supported by an arch.

BRISE-SOLEIL An adjustable screen made of vertical or horizontal fins fixed to reduce the sun's glare upon window glass.

BRODRICK, CUTHBERT (1822–1905) A Yorkshire architect born in Hull who designed several large-scale, secular buildings in the High Victorian period in the north of England. Brodrick worked for some time for Lockwood and Mawson, the Yorkshire firm of architects, then set up practice for himself in 1845 after some time studying on the Continent. His most unusual building was the elliptical *Corn Exchange* in *Leeds* (1860–3), its boldly severe rusticated exterior derived from Florentine Renaissance palace design. His immense and powerful rectangular *town hall* in Leeds (1853–8) dominates the centre of the city; its Baroque Corinthian colonnades are repeated in pilaster form all round the building. The clock tower is a city landmark; it rises on a square plinth which supports a Corinthian colonnade and cupola above. Equally vital and imposing is the *Grand Hotel* at Scarborough (1863–7), magnificently sited on the cliff tops overlooking the sea. Strongly influenced by French Renaissance designs, the hotel has four corner domed pavilions joined by a deep, projecting cornice and mansard, dormered roofs.

BROOKS, JAMES (1825–1901) A Gothic Revival architect who built many churches, the chief of which are in London. He preferred to design in Lancet (see GOTHIC ARCHITECTURE) style using brick as a building material. Typical of these churches are the *Transfiguration, Lewisham* (1880), *St Michael's, Shoreditch* (1863), the *Ascension, Battersea* (1876) and the *Annunciation, Chislehurst* (1868–70).

BROWN, LANCELOT ('CAPABILITY') (1716–83) Designed a number of Palladian country houses which included *Croome Court*, Worcestershire (1751) and *Claremont*, Surrey (1771–4). Lancelot Brown's reputation, however, rests upon his contribution as a landscape gardener. He worked with William Kent on laying out the grounds at *Stowe* in 1740 and by 1749 established himself as a consultant in this field.

Brown's major contribution was to provide a suitable setting for the Palladian country house (see PALLADIAN ARCHITECTURE). He laid out a particularly English kind of garden and parkland with sweeping lawns and great spreading trees. He engineered serpentine lakes out of streams and rivers, moved whole hillsides and strategically planted great clumps of cedars and oaks to set off the formality of the rectangular house. Amidst the trees and hills he incorporated, in eighteenth-century fashion, sham classical ruins. Brown's reputation grew apace and he was much in demand by the great country-house owners of the day. What he created was essentially indigenous to England and very different from the formality of French and Italian gardens derived from the style of Versailles. It was a natural-seeming landscape but one carefully engineered, not Nature run wild. Some other European nations emulated these parklands. One particular admirer was Catherine the Great of Russia, who had some parks created in this style near St Petersburg.

Brown's nickname 'Capability' arose because of his habit of stating the capabilities of the development of an estate, when called in by a new client to express his opinion. Among the many fine estates and parks which he laid out and/or improved are *Croome Court*, Worcestershire (from 1751), *Audley End*, Essex (1763), *Blenheim Palace*, Oxfordshire (1765), *Bowood*, Wiltshire (1761 on) and *Dodington Park*, Gloucestershire (1764).

BRUCE, SIR WILLIAM (*c.* 1630–1710) After the Restoration Bruce brought to Scotland the purer, Italian Renaissance form of classical architecture which had been introduced into England by Inigo Jones and which he combined with the Scottish vernacular. He also began to establish the profession of architecture (see JONES, INIGO).

Though not of the stature of the outstanding English architects of that time, Bruce's work was competent and interesting. In 1671 he was appointed King's Surveyor and Master of the Works in Scotland. His most important work in this office was the reconstruction of the *Palace of Holyroodhouse* in *Edinburgh* (1671–8). This was not an easy task as he had to incorporate medieval structures which included the remains of the beautiful old church and parts of the later palace. Set against the background of Arthur's Seat and the Holyrood Park, the palace stands bold and four-square, evincing still its Scottish/French heritage in the dormers and chimney-stacks and in the great corner towers capped by conical turrets though the entrance is classical, articulated by flanking, coupled columns. Inside is the open, arcaded court patterned on the Renaissance palaces of Rome.

Bruce designed another classical building, his own house at Kinross, in 1681. A more important work was the commission he received from the Earl of Hopetoun to build the great new mansion of *Hopetoun House* near Edinburgh, where Bruce worked from 1699, though much of his design has been obscured by the later work by the Adam family. The central part of the façade on the garden elevation survives from Bruce's house as does also the interior wood staircase with its finely carved and panelled walls. After Bruce's death Lord Hopetoun asked William Adam to extend the building and bring it up to date in the current architectural idiom. This Adam did, though the work was accomplished so slowly that both architect and patron died before it was completed. Hopetoun House is on the grand scale with an entrance elevation extending over 500ft and fronted by lawns and drives. There is a great centre block and quadrant colonnades leading to terminal pavilions. A giant Corinthian Order spans the *piano nobile* and the second storey, taken up in Doric form in the pavilions. This is in the Palladian manner but the skyline and the sweeping contrasting curves of bays and quadrants are Vanbrugh-inspired Baroque as is the weightiness of the whole composition (see ADAM, ROBERT).

BUILDING MATERIALS The principal materials which have been used in Britain for building structures of particular architectural interest are discussed in individual entries: see BRICKWORK; CLAPBOARD; CONCRETE; CRUCK BUILDING; FACING; GLASS; MASONRY; PLASTERWORK; ROOF; SLATE; STONE; TILES; TIMBER-FRAMING; WALLING. Other materials, which have been widely used, were employed in primitive times, or for smaller, everyday dwellings, or were traditional for building in certain parts of the country where other materials, such as stone or wood, were not readily available in quantity. Most important among these are the earths, wood, thatch, flint and pebbles, which are discussed here.

Unburnt clay *earth*, necessarily mixed with some other substances, has been a traditional building material in Britain since very early times. By the sixteenth and seventeenth centuries its use was mainly confined to rural structures—cottages and small farmhouses—but in Norman times many town houses had mud walls. There are several ways of using earth for building and these methods have been developed in different parts of the country (and under various names) because of the local content of the material to be found there. Construction using earths can be of the plastic type where a clay earth is mixed with water to a stiff mud consistency or it can be of dry earth rammed to give cohesion. Clay earth mixed with water to give a stiff mud must contain lime to make it set, also straw, gravel and sand. The gravel may be small pebbles or fragments of slate or similar aggregate. Common names for such 'mixes' are *cob* (mainly used in the south-west of the country), *clob* (in Cornwall) or mud. *Wichert* was made from a hard earth containing a quantity of chalk. Buildings made of plastic earths need to be based on a plinth of brick, stone, flint or rubble up to about $1\frac{1}{2}$–2ft in height in order to keep the base dry and prevent invasion by vermin. Cob walls are usually 3–4ft thick at

BRUCE, SIR WILLIAM
Palace of Holyroodhouse, Edinburgh, 1671–8

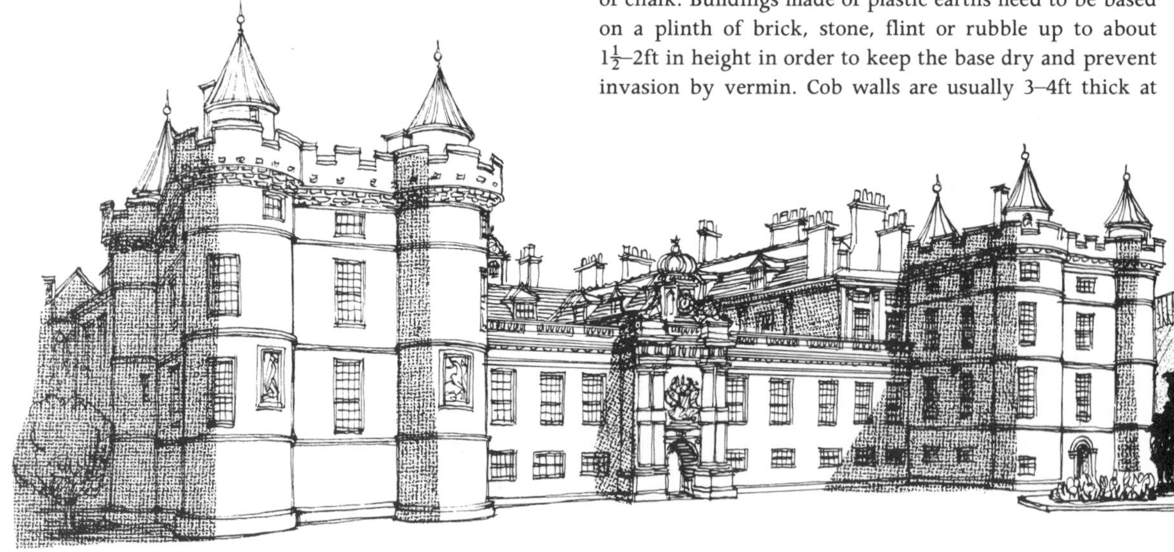

base, and need to be faced with plaster and colour-washed annually; thus treated they are weatherproof and provide good insulation; they may then last for centuries. The colour of the wash varies from area to area but is most often white.

The rammed earth method, known as *pisé*, was traditional to many parts of the world—Europe, Africa, Asia and America. In Europe it was used by the Romans and was widely employed in France though, in Britain, its use has been limited. This is possibly due to the climate, since dry weather is vital for satisfactory building in this material. The clay earth (contained between shutterboards) was beaten or rammed against a hard surface by a hardwood rammer till it cohered into a hard block or mass which could be used for building. A more modern substitute is *stabilized earth* which is mixed with cement so rendering it stronger and easier to handle.

A version of the Spanish *adobe* (see BRICKWORK) was used for building in parts of East Anglia. This was a clay which was mixed with water and straw, then pressed into wooden moulds to make blocks which were then left to dry thoroughly, in the open air. These unburnt 'bricks' were large, about 18in × 18in × 6in, and were used for walling, with a clay mortar. They were then faced with plaster or brick or might be tar-washed for protection. This type of block building was known as *clay lump*.

The most usual roofing material traditionally used for buildings made from these various types of clay earth, as well as those of half-timber construction (see TIMBER-FRAMING), was some form of thatch. This was because it was the most lightweight of roofing means and therefore suitable for walls which would not bear a great load. Throughout northern Europe buildings had been roofed since earliest times with turves, moss, heather or reeds and, often, a mixture of more than one of these. From Norman times the most usual thatching materials had been reed, straw or heather, the last being especially used in moorland areas where the material was plentiful, such as Scotland, northern England and the West Country. The

Timber-framed structure with hazel wattle infill and thatched roof, seventeenth century, Weald and Downland Museum, Sussex

chief problem with such roofing materials was fire danger and, because of this, restrictions on thatching in towns came into force as early as the thirteenth century, and a plaster covering was often added to such roofs to attempt to counter this hazard. In rural areas thatch as a roofing material has survived to the present day. The thatcher's art has been developed over the centuries and many roofs are decoratively cut and trimmed especially along the ridge where reinforcement is needed.

While earth and clay made into mud were the earliest materials for building in Britain, in general use before the coming of the Romans, *wood* was also utilized before the first century BC, but for the more important structures. Almost nothing survives of buildings made of wood before the Middle Ages, when timber-framed structure was developed (see TIMBER-FRAMING). One interesting example is the *Church of St Andrew* at *Greensted* in Essex. In the tenth century a small wooden chapel was built here with walls composed of trunks of oak trees, split in half lengthways. These were set upright, closely together, with the curved side of the trunks falling outwards and were let into a sill at the base and a plate at the top; they were fastened with wood pins. These timbers still form the basis of the nave walls of the present church though they had to be removed in the nineteenth century, shortened and set into a brick plinth because of decay at the foot. This type of construction, profligate in its use of oak trunks, was typical for centuries in areas of Europe where wood was plentiful, as in Norway and the forest areas of Rumania. For a doubtless similar reason, it was not uncommon in Saxon England, but it is quite different from the later English construction of timber-framing.

A more primitive type of walling, and one of the earliest means of construction, was *wattle and daub*. In this a row of vertical stakes or branches (wattles) were interwoven horizontally by smaller branches or reeds. Clay mud (daub) was plastered on to one or both sides and dried out in the sun; it was reinforced by turves and moss. A majority of Saxon houses was constructed in this way and capped by a thatch roof. This structural method was used throughout the Middle Ages. Laths replaced branches and hair and straw were incorporated into the mud to give greater strength and durability. Such a technique was used as infilling in timber-framed structures when surfaces were usually plaster-covered and painted.

Flint is an extremely durable material which has been used for building in England from the Iron Age onwards. It is a pure form of silica, extremely hard but easy to

Flint and brick house with thatched roof, sixteenth and seventeenth centuries, Weald and Downland Museum, Sussex

split. Flints occur in chalk deposits and are irregularly shaped nodules, white on the exterior from their long sojourn in the chalk, but with shades of dark grey or black inside. The use of flint has been traditional in chalk areas in south-east and southern England as far west as Wiltshire and Dorset. The finest-quality work, architecturally and decoratively, is in East Anglia where, in the Middle Ages, flint was a predominant building material for churches.

Prior to the fourteenth century flints were used whole, embedded in mortar. For strong walling it was necessary to incorporate stone rubble and lacing courses of stone or brick. The Romans widely used flint for their walling; in conjunction with their extremely durable mortar and lacing courses of their hard, tile-like bricks, it produced in many areas town and fortified walling which still survives. Building with flint continued during Saxon and Norman times through the Middle Ages and after.

Although flint is a durable material, the strength of walling depends upon the cohesion of this substance with its mortar so, during the Middle Ages, it was used more and more in conjunction with other building materials. Also, uncut or complete flints are not materials of beauty and lend monotony to a wall surface. From about 1300 onwards it became customary, at least in important buildings, to split the flints. This process, known as *knapping*, became a specialized technique. It is not difficult to fracture a flint but the art lies in trimming it to the desired shape and thickness. The knapped flints were set in mortar close together, the split face outwards, to form definite shapes and patterns. They were used in conjunction with stone or brick most often in a chequer pattern, and a high standard of craftsmanship evolved. The flint faces were set flush with the stone or brick outer face.

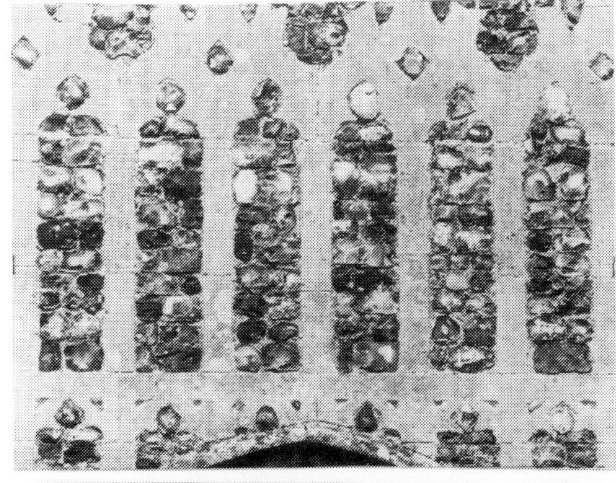

BUILDING MATERIALS
Flushwork: Long Melford Church, Suffolk

From the early fourteenth century onwards a specialized form of decoration using knapped flints was developed. This was known as *flushwork*. By the fifteenth and sixteenth centuries a high degree of skill and experience was producing elaborately ornamented surfaces of church towers and porches, gatehouses and civic façades. This technique, especially characteristic of East Anglia, used flints in conjunction with stone. Slabs of cut stone used as facing were mortared to a flint rubble wall. Panels were cut or left open in specific designs and these were filled with knapped flints, their shiny black surfaces contrasting with the light stonework. Medieval patterns were varied and intricate; trefoils, quatrefoils, cinquefoils, cusped panels and heraldic insignia were interspersed with floral motifs. Characteristic examples of flushwork are the *churches* at *Eye* and *Long Melford* in Suffolk and the gatehouse of *St Osyth's Priory* in Essex. The *Guildhall* at *King's Lynn* is a classic example of flint and stone chequer work.

Similary used are *cobbles* and *pebbles*. Cobbles are pieces of rock which have been broken away by the action of glaciers or water and have been collected and used for rubble wall building or facing since early times. Cobbles vary greatly in size from three or four inches in diameter to a foot or more. Pebbles, which are smaller, are particularly in use in sea-coast areas.

BUNGALOW From the Hindustani word *banglā*, meaning 'of, or belonging to, Bengal'. A one-storeyed house or temporary dwelling originally with a thatched roof. The term was at first applied to the light, veranda-style houses built in India for British officials in the nineteenth century.

BURGES, WILLIAM (1827–81) The son of a marine engineer, Burges was first trained in engineering; then he turned to architecture and worked in the offices of first Blore, then Wyatt (see BLORE, EDWARD and WYATT, SIR MATTHEW DIGBY). Burges travelled widely, particularly in France, Germany, Italy and Belgium. He became interested in monumental structures richly decorated in medieval forms, in French as well as English design. In his own work he was a Gothic Revivalist and an Ecclesiologist but his interest was architectural rather than moralist (see GOTHIC REVIVAL). While still a young man he won, in conjunction with *Henry Clutton*, the competition for the Cathedral of Lille but this design was not carried out.

Burges's chief works were his extensive additions and remodelling to *Cardiff Castle* (1868–81) and *Castell Coch*, near Llandaff (1876–81), both for Lord Bute. These interiors are richly 'revivalist medieval', displaying a fertile imagination and variety of design in high quality carving, gilding and painting. Another important commission was the *Church of Ireland Cathedral* in *Cork* (1862–76), beautifully sited and a fine complex building with three towers on French Gothic pattern. He carried out a good deal of

BURGES, WILLIAM
Cardiff Castle with nineteenth-century remodelling

Knightshayes, Devon. Garden front, 1869–75

ecclesiastical work, adding the east end to *Waltham Abbey*, Essex in 1859 and building *St Mary's Church* at *Studley Royal*, and *Skelton Church*, both in 1871. In the secular field his own house in *Melbury Road, Kensington* (1875–80) and *Knightshayes* in Devon (1869–75), built for John Heathcote-Amory, were typical both of the Gothic Revival work of the time and of that of the architect.

BURLINGTON, RICHARD BOYLE 3rd EARL OF (1694–1753) The best-known and most influential of the aristocratic patron/architects of the eighteenth century, doyen and inspiration of Palladianism in England, Lord Burlington dominated the architectural scene for three decades after he returned from his second trip to Italy in 1719. He first visited Italy in 1714–15; there he acquired a general interest in classical architecture. On his return he was able to study two new publications: Colen Campbell's *Vitruvius Britannicus* and an English edition of Palladio's *I Quattro Libri dell'Architettura*. The latter work had first been published by the architect in Italy in the sixteenth century but in 1715–16 a translation by Dubois appeared in two volumes, largely illustrated by Leoni, who had come to England to supervise the publication (see LEONI, GIACOMO). Lord Burlington became extremely interested in Palladio and also liked what he saw in Campbell's publication. He commissioned Campbell to undertake the remodelling of his London home, *Burlington House* in *Piccadilly* (see CAMPBELL, COLEN).

In 1719 Lord Burlington returned to Italy and spent some months in Vicenza, studying Palladio's work there and in the surrounding region, and making a collection of the architect's drawings. When he returned to England he had acquired a first-hand knowledge and understanding of Palladio's work which, added to his knowledge of the buildings of ancient Rome and his growing appreciation of the seventeenth-century contribution of Inigo Jones in England, provided a three-fold basis for his energetic sponsorship of the Palladian school of architecture in Britain. He was not the originator of the style but he was responsible for its countrywide acceptance as the logical pattern of building for the next 30 years. His patronage of the leading architects of the style—Kent, Campbell and Leoni—and his enthusiasm and encouragement led to the publication of learned works and numerous pattern books over the years so that local builders and craftsmen had a sound basis to follow, thus ensuring an excellent quality of general building standard. It was due largely to Lord Burlington that in Britain Palladian architecture became so firmly established and found favour for so long.

Lord Burlington had met William Kent in Rome. He brought him back to England and employed him to work at Burlington House to carry out decorative painting (see KENT, WILLIAM). This was the beginning of a close collaboration which lasted for the remainder of both their lives, not only in the field of architecture but in landscape gardening, furniture and interior decorative design where the personalities and talents of the two men complemented each other. Lord Burlington himself became an architect but he did not personally design a large number of buildings—his predominant influence was as a patron of other architects, not only financially but with architectural and intellectual advice also as at Holkham. His own work is meticulous in quality and in its close adherence to pure classical standards, not only those set by Palladio, but returning to the first principles of Rome. Because of this deep concern with unfailing obedience to the classical rule book, Lord Burlington's own work became more pedantic and ascetic though its taste is faultless. Among his designs were the *Dormitory* at *Westminster School* in London (1722–30), and *Northwick Park*, Worcestershire (1730).

Lord Burlington's two chief surviving works are Chiswick House in London and the Assembly Rooms in York.

Chiswick House, London, 1725–9

Chiswick House was begun *c.* 1723. It is closely based upon Palladio's Villa Capra (the Rotonda) near Vicenza which is the domestic equivalent of Bramante's Church of S. Pietro (see RENAISSANCE ARCHITECTURE), a centrally planned villa completely symmetrical with a central domed hall. The whole *piano nobile* of the Villa Capra is raised on a square podium with four identical porticoes with entrance steps, one to each side. The Chiswick villa has only two porticoes and the chief of these is approached by a double staircase. The dome, which covers the hall, is shallow, carried on a hexagonal drum. Lord Burlington has returned, more than Palladio at Vicenza, to the theme of the Roman thermal baths in a sequence of rooms of differing shapes, a theme which Robert Adam was to develop later in the century (from the same source of inspiration) at Syon and other houses (see ADAM ROBERT; PALLADIAN ARCHITECTURE).

In the *Assembly Rooms* at York (1731–2) (re-fronted in 1828) Lord Burlington again reverted to ancient Rome and combined this with Palladio's interpretation of the layout of the Roman baths. There is a central ballroom, its design derived from the Vitruvian theme of an Egyptian hall as interpreted by Palladio. The room measures 112ft × 40ft; its ceiling is supported by 48 Corinthian columns. Leading from the ballroom is a suite of rooms of various sizes and forms. The Assembly Rooms were built by public subscription and became one of the fashionable centres for assemblies and entertainment in eighteenth-century England.

BURNET, SIR JOHN (1857–1938) and **TAIT, THOMAS** (1882–1954) Two Scottish architects who worked in partnership first in Glasgow then, from 1905, in London. Burnet was the son of an architect. He studied in Paris, at the Ecole des Beaux Arts, but his early work was tradi tional and unremarkable. Typical were the *Glasgow Institute of Fine Arts* (1879–80) and, in *London*, the Edwardian wing of the *British Museum* built from 1905 onwards.

Much more original were two large steel-framed structures in London, the *Kodak Building* in *Kingsway* (1911) and *Adelaide House* on *London Bridge* (1921–4). These are two of the earliest examples in London of modern building methods and, unlike the earlier Ritz Hotel where the steel-framing is concealed by stone classical dress, the two Burnet and Tait buildings clearly show in the vertical emphasis of their design the structural methods in use.

In 1934 Sir John Burnet retired. Tait, now head of the firm, was joined by a new partner, *Francis Lorne*. In the 1930s the firm designed and built a number of plain brick structures on the lines of some of the Swedish and Dutch architecture of more than a decade earlier. One of the best examples is the *Royal Masonic Hospital* at *Ravenscourt Park* (1932–3), which was awarded the RIBA Medal for its year. It combines a pleasant exterior with a highly functional interior. The floors and roof are of concrete and the flat roof is available for open air accommodation. There are also large semicircular balconies.

BURTON, JAMES (1761–1837) and **BURTON, DECIMUS** (1800–81) James Burton, a Scotsman, was one of the most enterprising and successful builders of his time. In *London* he developed much of Bloomsbury, taking over sites and letting out some of the work to other builders, although supervising the whole himself. By this means he kept up a high standard of building. His son Decimus designed much of the work for his father who built a great deal for Nash, including many of the Regent's Park terraces, and parts of Regent Street and Waterloo Place.

BURNET, SIR JOHN AND TAIT, THOMAS
Adelaide House, London Bridge, 1921–4

Nash, in turn, sponsored Decimus early in his architectural career. James Burton was largely responsible for laying out *Russell Square* (1800–14) and surrounding area, *Tavistock Square*, Burton Street and *Bloomsbury Square*.

Tunbridge Wells had developed as a resort in the seventeenth century but much of the architecture is Regency. James Burton built the *Calverly Estate* here which was designed by his son Decimus. Calverly Park is laid out with detached and grouped houses on a curve which fronts the park itself. Local sandstone has been used for building. The scheme is not severe or stately classicism but more romantic and informal, with delicate balconies and verandas. The houses have curved bay fronts. Calverly Crescent behind is more formal. It is elegant with a slender iron colonnade. James Burton also built extensively at *Hastings* and *St Leonards-on-Sea* and here too Decimus was the architect. Not a great deal survives of their work but typical is *Pelham Crescent* (*c.* 1823), a seafront terrace with bow windows and canopied iron balconies (see TERRACE ARCHITECTURE).

Decimus Burton, so-called as the tenth child of his father James Burton, lived late into the Victorian age but is usually considered as a Regency and Early Victorian architect because all his major work was done before 1850; furthermore he continued to design in the classical idiom, having little inclination towards Gothic Revival architecture. His architectural career began early, as he helped his father with the building of some of the Regent's Park terraces and, at the age of 21, he designed *Cornwall Terrace* under Nash's direction (see NASH, JOHN). In 1825 he undertook the *Hyde Park* improvements which included his *arch* and *screen* at Hyde Park Corner which he envisaged as a triumphal entrance and connecting link from Hyde Park to Green Park. The screen, consisting of three arches and an Ionic colonnade, still acts as an entrance to Hyde Park. The arch, which he based on the Arch of Titus in Rome, was later moved to the top of Constitution Hill and its angle to the screen changed. Burton had intended that a sculptured quadriga should be set on top but, instead, an equestrian statue of Wellington was placed there in 1846; this was replaced in 1912 by Adrian Jones' much larger quadriga.

Decimus Burton designed the *Athenaeum* in *Pall Mall* in 1827. It is interesting to note here, as well as on the Hyde Park screen and the United Service Club on the opposite side of Waterloo Place, the Greek style of sculptured frieze extending round the buildings. These were all inspired by the arrival of sections of the Parthenon frieze (the Elgin Marbles) which had been acquired for the nation in 1816. The architect also designed a number of country houses and villas as well as working for his father on terrace building at Tunbridge Wells, Hastings and St Leonards-on-Sea. In *Hove* he was responsible for the impressive *Adelaide Crescent* (1830–4).

Decimus Burton was also interested for much of his life in projects which combined architecture and engineering and he collaborated with engineers on such structures. Early in his career he designed a *conservatory* in *Regent's Park* (dem. 1875) which was covered by a very large dome. Later, in the 1840s, he collaborated with *Richard Turner* to build the Winter Gardens in Regent's Park (demolished) and the extant *Palm Stove* in *Kew Gardens* (see IRON AND GLASS).

BURTON DECIMUS
The Athenaeum Club, London, 1827–30 (the later upper storey has been omitted)

BUTTERFIELD, WILLIAM (1814–1900) Reserved, aloof and deeply religious, Butterfield was a man of austere principles; faith was one with his architecture. He was a staunch adherent to the Ecclesiologist philosophy and

BURTON, DECIMUS
Hyde Park Screen, London, 1825

BUTTERFIELD, WILLIAM
Keble College Chapel, Oxford, 1873–6

most of his work was ecclesiastical (see GOTHIC REVIVAL). After an early apprenticeship in the building industry Butterfield carefully studied medieval church architecture in England and on the Continent. He set up practice in the 1840s when he carried out early designs at Coalpit Heath and at *St Augustine's College* at *Canterbury*. His first major commission was the *Church of All Saints* in *Margaret Street* in London's West End. This church illustrates his fully developed, highly individualistic style, one which is characterized by a strong massing of shapes, lofty steeples and an addiction to polychromy. He used strong, harsh colours and left few surfaces undecorated. He did not believe in painted or stained colour, but preferred durable materials used with high-quality craftsmanship, and so achieved his colour ornamentation by use of mosaic, tile, brick, marble, stone and alabaster. All Saints' (1849–59) is an original church and its interior makes a forcible, dramatic first impression. The site is poor; narrow and cramped, in a side street behind Oxford Street. The only possible direction for expansion was upwards and upwards All Saints' went with an asymmetrically placed lofty steeple. The church is built of red brick decorated with black brick and bands of stone. The exterior today is hemmed in by other buildings but the interior can still be seen. Here, Butterfield created a vividly rich effect by patterning almost every surface with marble and tile, marquetry, gilt, coloured glass, carving, semi-precious stones and alabaster. Among his other London churches were *St Augustine's, Queen's Gate* (1870–7) and *St Alban's, Holborn* (1858–63) damaged in the Second World War. He built the church at *Baldersby St James* in Yorkshire (1856) and *All Saints'* at *Babbacombe* in Devon.

In addition to his churches, Butterfield carried out much ecclesiastical work in collegiate commissions. This included chapels at *Rugby School* and at *Balliol College, Oxford*. At *Keble College, Oxford*, which was opened in 1870, he was college architect over the years 1868–82 and so had a free hand to design a large new quadrangle including a chapel, library and hall. Keble College is a striking monument to High Victorian Gothic and for many years aroused fierce controversy. Typical of Butterfield's work, it is an exercise in polychromy. He used red brick decorated in stripes and checks with stone and black and white brick. In the nineteenth century this must have presented a startling appearance but time has mellowed the surfaces harmoniously. The *chapel* (1873–6) is the finest building of the college; it is well proportioned and

BUTTERFIELD, WILLIAM
Detail: Keble College Chapel

richly decorated, especially the interior. A small memorial chapel contains Holman Hunt's well-known picture 'The Light of the World'.

Butterfield continued designing churches and schools for many years but after 1875 such violent polychromy became less fashionable and his later work aroused less interest. He maintained close ties with the Ecclesiological Society and was particularly interested in designing for church furniture and interior decorative schemes in quality, durable materials.

BUTTRESS A reinforcement to and projection from a wall. Its use makes unnecessary the building of a thicker wall to provide stability, so economizing in building materials and often increasing the aesthetic appeal of the structure. As window openings weaken a wall, buttresses are provided between them. Buttresses are needed most because of the thrust from the roof. With a timber roof this outward thrust is partly counteracted by the tie and collar beam construction but with a stone vault stronger buttresses are necessary. Saxon and Norman buttresses are often wide but of low projection as, with the thick walling, no greater reinforcement was needed.

With the development of Gothic architecture thinner walls were constructed, windows became larger and the ribbed stone vault evolved (see VAULTING). Thus stronger buttresses were required; so were of greater projection, deeper at the base and diminishing in stages towards the roof level. These stages were marked by set-offs with the top finished by a slope or a triangular head or pinnacle. By the fourteenth century, in the Decorated period of Gothic architecture, buttresses were nearly all built in diminishing stages and usually finished with a crocketed pinnacle. Richer designs have carved niches and canopies. The surfaces of fifteenth-century buttresses are, like those of the rest of the building, often panelled and their set-offs have bold, plain slopes.

Types of buttresses

Angle buttress: two buttresses meeting at an angle of 90° at the corner of a building. Widely used from the thirteenth century onwards.

Clasping buttress: a less common design where a large square buttress encases (or clasps) the corner, usually of a tower or porch.

Diagonal buttress: more common from the fourteenth century, a buttress set diagonally at the right angle corner of a building or of a tower.

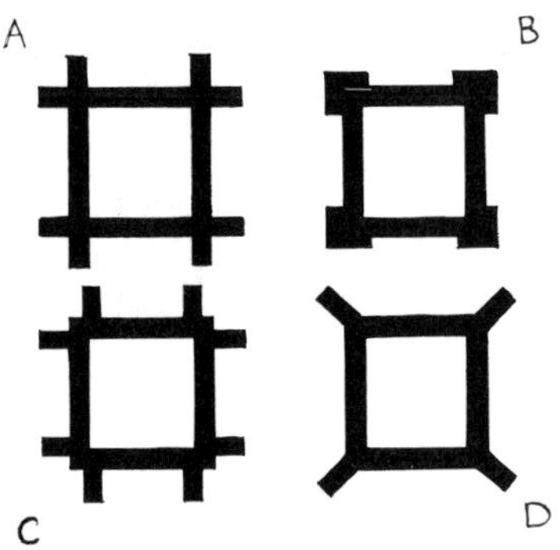

BUTTRESS
Tower sketch plan showing types of buttress
A Angle
B Clasping
C Setback
D Diagonal

Diagonal buttresses at corners of building: Willington Stables, Bedfordshire *c.* 1520

Angle buttress, thirteenth century

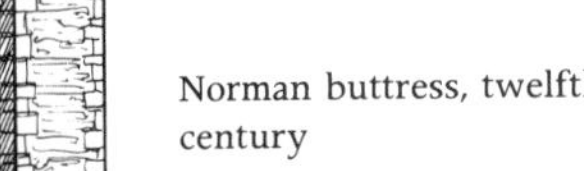

Norman buttress, twelfth century

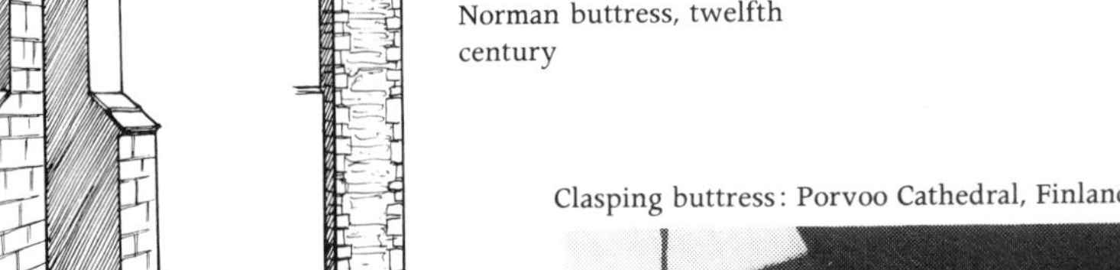

Flying buttresses: Apse, Reims Cathedral, France, 1210

Clasping buttress: Porvoo Cathedral, Finland, 1414–18

Setback buttress: St Mary's Church, Taunton, fifteenth century

Flying buttress: Henry VII Chapel, Westminster Abbey, *c.* 1505

Flying buttresses: St Mary's Church, Beverley, fifteenth century, also angle buttress

Flying buttress (arch buttress): a buttress in which the thrust of a vault is transmitted from the top of the wall to the outer buttress by means of an arch. The flying buttress was developed during the long period of medieval building because of the evolution of the stone vault in large churches. The covering of larger and larger spans created a strong outward and downward thrust at the same time as larger window areas were weakening the wall structures. By the later fourteenth and the fifteenth century, walls were pierced by numerous large windows while vaults were being constructed higher and wider than ever before. The thrust was counteracted by a development of the abutment system which provided a strengthening of the wall from the exterior face at the point where the greatest thrust was to be expected. Trial and error established this to be just below the springing line of the vault on the interior wall face (see VAULTING). The flying buttress system serves a dual purpose: the counter-thrust at a given place on the exterior wall surface conveys the vault pressure away from the building and down to the ground and also, by means of a

heavy pinnacle above, helps to offset the vault thrust. By the fifteenth century large buildings displayed a forest of flying buttress arches and pinnacles. This was most marked in French Gothic architecture at the east end of a cathedral with its complex chevet (see CHEVET) as at, for example, the cathedrals of Le Mans and Reims. In England the nave of *Canterbury Cathedral*, the *Henry VII Chapel* at *Westminster Abbey* and *St George's Chapel, Windsor* show some of the outstanding examples.
Setback buttress: a design similar to the angle buttress but where two buttresses are set back slightly, leaving the corner of the building exposed between them.

BYZANTINE ARCHITECTURE In AD 330 the Roman Emperor Constantine transferred the Imperial seat of government to Byzantium, a small city founded in 666 BC by the Dorian Greeks and occupying the strategic site on a hill overlooking the Golden Horn on the Bosporus, commanding the Mediterranean and the Black Sea. Constantine planned a new city and when, later in the century, the Roman Empire was divided into eastern and western parts, Byzantium, later Constantinople and now Istanbul, became the capital of the eastern empire. After the collapse of the western half Constantinople, as the remaining capital, became the centre of the empire, having dominance over lands from the Euphrates to the Danube. By mid-sixth century, under Justinian, the Byzantine Empire reached its zenith of influence and greatness; it covered an area of about a million square miles.

Byzantine architecture was based on the classical pattern traced from Greece through Rome. Because of Byzantium's geographical position straddling the worlds of west and east, an eastern influence from Persia, Syria and Armenia soon showed itself in the architecture. The classical orders and ornament appeared less and less, brick was a prime building material, carved decoration was replaced by mosaic and marble cladding and the domed covering was developed. All this was combined with the massive brick and concrete structural forms initiated by the Romans and the designs of the Early Christian churches. A distinctive Byzantine style of architecture and decoration evolved during the sixth century, a style which provided a basis for buildings as far apart as Russia and Italy. The chief remains are of churches and monasteries and less is known of Byzantine secular architecture though there is no reason to doubt its importance and magnificence. The spread of Byzantine culture was greatest in two chief periods of expansion, the first stemming from the Empire of Justinian in the sixth century and the second in the eleventh to thirteenth centuries. From the first period came the great *Church of S. Sophia* in *Istanbul*, and in the same city *S. Irene*, the churches in *Ravenna* and the cathedrals of the *Ravennate* in Italy and *Istria* in

Aquileia Cathedral, Italy. Interior ninth to eleventh century; mosaic pavement Roman AD *c*. 320

S. Sophia, Istanbul, 532–6, interior looking south-east

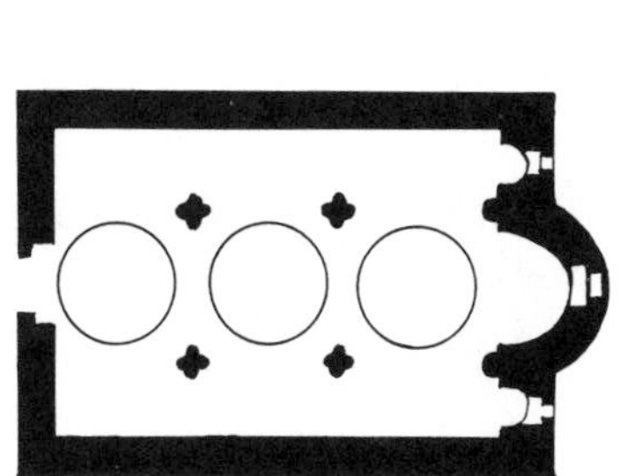

Ground plan, S. Cataldo, Palermo, Sicily, 1161

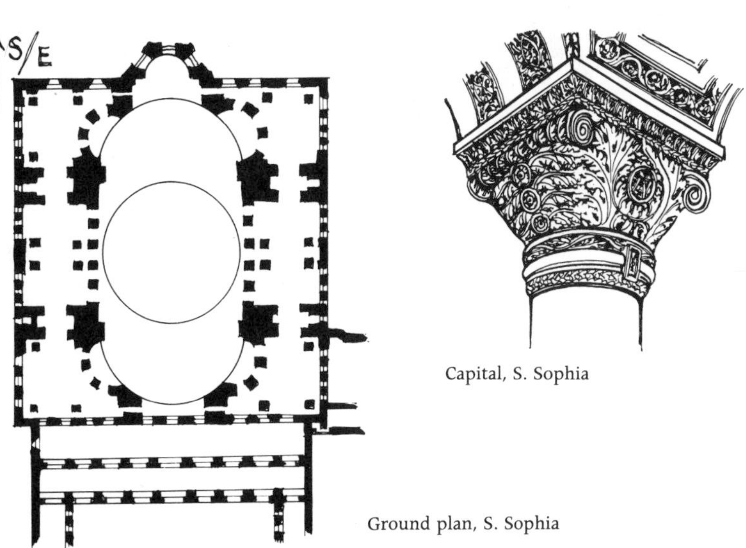

Capital, S. Sophia

Ground plan, S. Sophia

Cathedral of St Mark, Venice, viewed from the south-west and from above in campanile. Thirteenth-century domes delineate Greek cross plan; fifteenth-century additions to façade

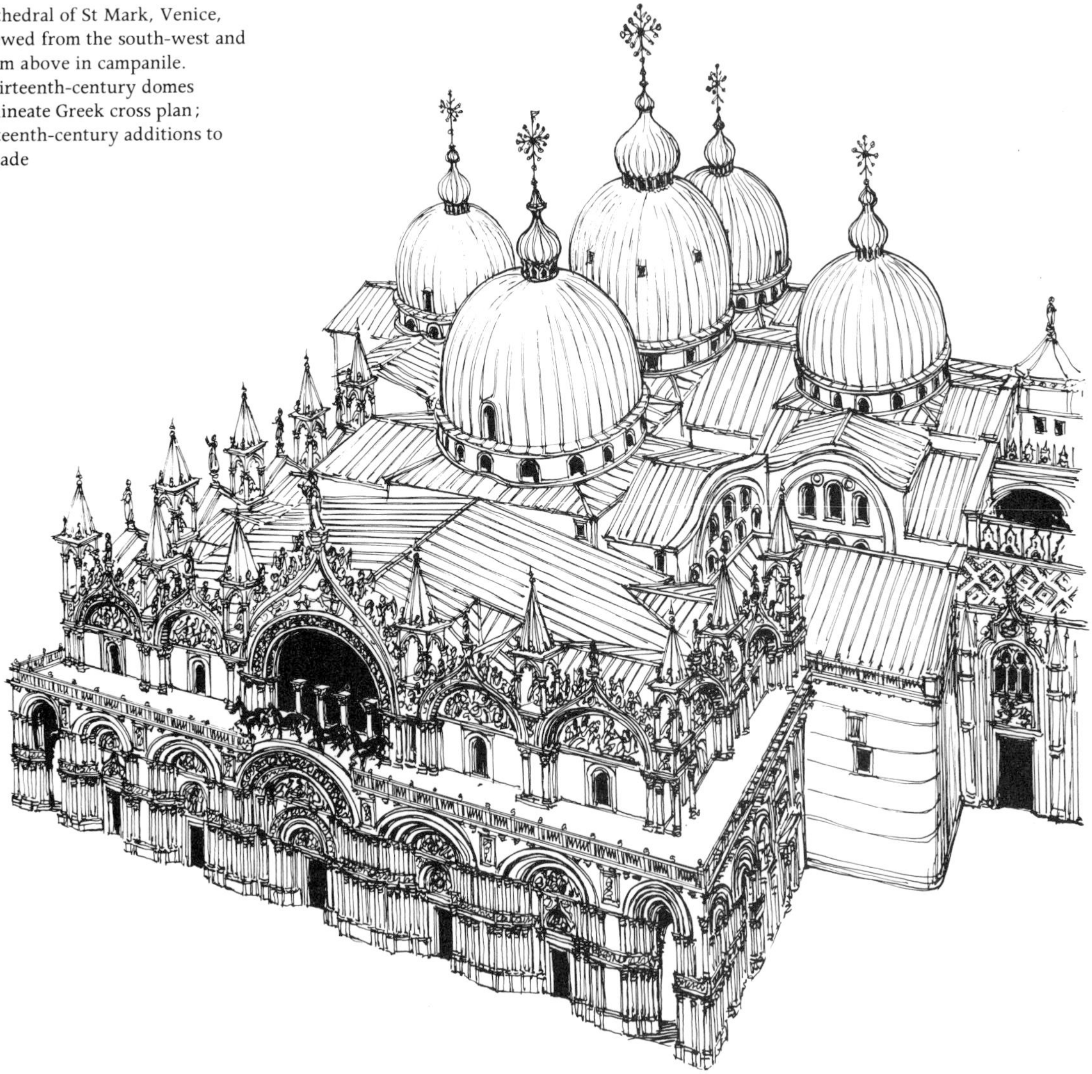

Ground plan, St Mark's Cathedral

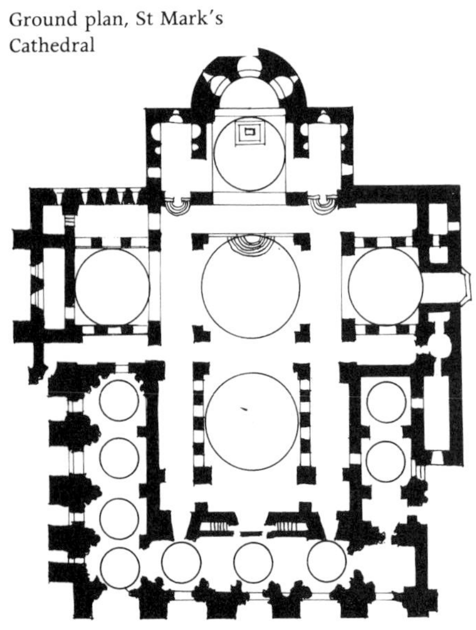

Church of St John of the Hermits, Palermo, Sicily, 1132

Church of St Alphege, Bath: modern version of a Byzantine church. Architect: Sir Giles Gilbert Scott

Capital, Church of St Alphege, Bath

Yugoslavia, while from the second period date such superb and varied examples as *St Mark's Cathedral* in *Venice* and nearby *S. Fosca* on the *Island of Torcello*, the *Palermo* churches in Sicily, the Yugoslav churches at *Gračanica* and *Studenica*, the church of *S. Saviour in Khora*

Capital, Poreć Cathedral, Yugoslavia, 535–43

in *Istanbul*, many of the *Greek* churches and monasteries as well as in *Rumania*, *Bulgaria* and *Russia*.

Despite the considerable differences in form in these countries of such differing cultures and climate, wherever it is to be found the Byzantine church displays certain characteristics which differentiate it from Early Christian, Romanesque or Gothic buildings. The exterior is plain, almost undecorated and very simple (the Cathedral of St Mark in Venice is an exception, a fact which marks the strong western influence in its design and later alterations). It is usually of brick with terracotta decoration or marble facing. There is no tower—the existing minarets and bell towers are later additions. The essential spirit of a Byzantine church is to be found inside. Here is mystery, semi-darkness pierced by shafts of light from tiny windows creating a shimmering effect as they fall on the mosaic surfaces which originally covered the whole area of the church. To give maximum effect the internal architectural forms are simplified into plain shapes providing wide, curving surfaces best suited to displaying the pictorial decoration. The scenes were depicted in gold and brilliant colours over walls, vaults, domes and apses and told the story of Christianity to an illiterate population in a similar manner to the sculptured portals of Gothic cathedrals. The mosaic pictures have a three-fold purpose: as decorative adjuncts to the architectural scheme, to give information in the Christian world and to depict the symbolism of the Byzantine church as a microcosm of the world and setting of Christ's life on earth. Thus, by tradition, certain subjects occupy specific places in the scheme. For instance, the central dome simulated the vault of heaven and showed a representation of Christ Pantocrator (Ruler of All) surrounded by angels and apostles. In the drum were prophets, on the pendentives, evangelists. Each part of the walls and vaults received its own quota of the Bible story.

The Byzantine church evolved from two types of plan, the basilica and the domed centrally planned structure. The basilican plan was taken from the Roman civic building (the basilica) and the Early Christian church and examples are chiefly to be seen in western Europe as in the *Cathedrals* of *Grado* and *Aquileia* in the Ravennate in Italy, *Poreć* in Istria and the two Ravenna churches of *S. Apollinare*. The structure was similar to the Early Christian examples but was plainer and mosaic covered the wall surfaces instead of classical entablatures and arcades. The centrally planned design came from the east. This was most often of Greek cross plan with a dome over the crossing. In Sicily, Greece, Turkey and, further east, in Rumania and Russia, for example, the multi-domed church evolved with a domed covering to each arm of the cross and possibly the narthex also. Sometimes the domes were shallow saucer types, in other instances they were raised on tall drums. In the sixth century the two basic plans were blended so that many Byzantine churches display characteristics of both basilican and centrally planned structures.

The Byzantine building form survived until about 1200 and the Byzantine artistic decoration almost until the fall of Constantinople in 1453. It was revived in western Europe in the nineteenth-century age of eclecticism but less extensively than the western medieval forms of Romanesque and Gothic architecture, as the Byzantine was so clearly better suited to the colourful eastern cultures. In Britain a number of churches were designed in Byzantine form, especially in the later nineteenth century and the first three decades of the twentieth. One outstanding example is *Westminster Cathedral* (see BENTLEY, JOHN FRANCIS). A twentieth-century architect who used Byzantine themes in some of his collegiate and ecclesiastical work was Scott as for instance, in his *Church of St Alphege* in Oldfield Park, Bath, and his chapel at *Lady Margaret Hall*, Oxford (see SCOTT, SIR GILES GILBERT). For other articles describing Byzantine architecture see ATRIUM; BASILICA; CAPITAL; CHURCH DESIGN AND STRUCTURE; DOME; ICONOSTASIS; NARTHEX.

CAISSON From the French word meaning 'large box' or 'locker'.

1. A water-tight air chest or chamber used for construction under water, for example, in bridge building.
2. The sunken panels in a vault or ceiling (see also COFFER).

CALIDUCT A pipe or channel for conveying hot air, water or steam for heating purposes.

CAMBER A shallow convex curve given to a horizontal member such as a tie beam in a timber roof.

CAMPBELL, COLEN (1676–1729) A Scottish architect and the first of the Palladian school. Little is known of Campbell's early life until he was commissioned to remodel Burlington House in 1717 (see BURLINGTON, EARL OF). In 1715 he had published the first volume of his *Vitruvius Britannicus* in which he included a series of plates of works by English architects as well as a number of his own designs. It was this publication which attracted Lord Burlington's attention to him. He subsequently published two more editions in 1717 and 1725. The main idea was to advertise his own work but he also performed a considerable service to architecture by the publication of so many plates of important buildings. Campbell stated that his work was based on the three-fold sources—classical antiquity, Vitruvius and Palladio—and so was established the concept of the Palladian movement (see also VITRUVIUS and PALLADIAN ARCHITECTURE). His first design, *Wanstead House*, Essex (1715–20), now demolished, was evidence of this and became a pattern for large country houses. Its 260ft frontage displayed a marked symmetry and gave predominance to the *piano nobile* and the great portico.

Campbell's other great mansion was *Houghton Hall*, Norfolk which he designed for Sir Robert Walpole in 1721 and illustrated in 1728 in *Vitruvius Britannicus*. The design was revised by Thomas Ripley who added cupolas

CAMPBELL, COLEN
Stourhead, Wiltshire, 1718–24, east front; wings added *c*. 1800

CAMPBELL, COLEN
Mereworth Castle, Kent, 1723

to Campbell's corner towers. This is an imposing house, its façade extending over 450 feet and comprising a central block connected to pavilions by colonnades. *William Kent* was commissioned to design the interior (see COUNTRY HOUSE AND MANSION; KENT, WILLIAM) and, assisted by the Italian stuccoist *Artari* and the sculptor *Rysbrack*, they jointly decorated the great stone hall. This is in the Roman tradition of splendour with its first floor gallery, classical doorways and chimneypiece and coved ceiling ornamented with gambolling *putti*.

These two great houses were influenced chiefly by Rome and Inigo Jones and only indirectly by Palladio. Two smaller designs, of villa rather than mansion proportions, are *Stourhead*, Wiltshire and *Mereworth*, Kent, both much more closely connected to Palladio's own work. Stourhead, which was completed in 1724, is a square, symmetrical central block with portico, to which wings were added later in the century. (The central block was gutted by fire in 1902 but was rebuilt to the original plan by Sir Aston Webb.) Campbell's version of *Palladio's Villa Capra*, Mereworth Castle, is the rendering in England closest to the prototype, being a square block with four identical porticoed elevations and a central drum and dome covering a central hall. The design built by Palladio was suited to the Italian climate where the idea was to avoid the sun by moving around the hall to the rooms leading off it according to the time of day and the shade required. In England, under a 60ft high dome with a 38ft diameter, the result is magnificent but chilly.

CANCELLI Bars of lattice work as in lattice windows or the lattice grille or screen separating the choir from the body of a church. The actual screen is usually termed *cancello* as in the Italian word for gate or railing.

CANOPY A suspended or projecting covering or hood over a statue, pulpit, altar, tomb, door, window etc.

CANOPY
Perpendicular Gothic canopy: choir screen, Canterbury Cathedral, *c.* 1400

CANTILEVER A specially shaped beam or girder supported securely at one end by a downward force behind a fulcrum and carrying a load at the other free end or with the load distributed uniformly along the beam. A cantilever bracket is used to support a cornice or balcony of considerable projection (see BALCONY; CORNICE). The cantilever principle is widely used in designs of large bridges as in the Forth Railway Bridge. Stairs are often constructed on the cantilever principle. In this case the steps are built at one end into a side wall and are unsupported at the opposite end though the steps partially support each other (see STAIRCASE).

CAPITAL The crowning feature of a column or pilaster. The function of a capital is to give an area from which an arch may spring or on which an entablature may rest larger than the supporting column or pier. A capital also ornaments the junction between arch or entablature and column and is a helpful feature in identifying a period or style of architecture. The top member of the capital is a flat slab called the *abacus*. This varies in form according to the style of architecture and type of capital; in the Doric Order it is a deep, square slab, in the Corinthian its sides are concavely curved (see CLASSICAL ORDER), while in medieval building it might be square, round or octagonal and variously moulded. The lower part of the capital is more slender. This is the *necking*; the division between it and the shaft is usually marked by a narrow moulding. The capital in the shape of a bell turned upside down is a traditional design used especially in classical architecture but also in many Gothic designs. Classical capitals are discussed under CLASSICAL ORDER.

Byzantine capitals show great variety of form and detail. Some closely followed classical design—the windswept acanthus type, for example, is a version of the Corinthian capital—while some were of Ionic pattern but with much smaller volutes (see CLASSICAL ORDER and CLASSICAL ORNAMENT). The most typical Byzantine form is the *basket* or *cubical* capital which is decorated by plaitwork, leaves, circles and scrolls. Such capitals are characterized by deeply incised lines and drilled holes which give a strongly defined light-and-shade effect. Many Byzantine capitals are surmounted by a larger block set between the arch and the abacus of the capital. This is called a *dosseret* or *pulvino* (see BYZANTINE ARCHITECTURE; DOSSERET).

In Romanesque architecture ('Norman' in England) capitals were massive to match the piers and support the arch. The abacus was a solid square or round block and, in the early work, constituted the whole capital. Soon mouldings were added below and capitals were circular with simple, broad mouldings which could be plain or richly carved. The most typical Norman design is the *cushion* capital (also known as a *block* capital). This is a cube of masonry (or wood) with its lower parts rounded off to conform to the circular shaft of the column, leaving a flat face (the lunette) on each of the four sides. From the

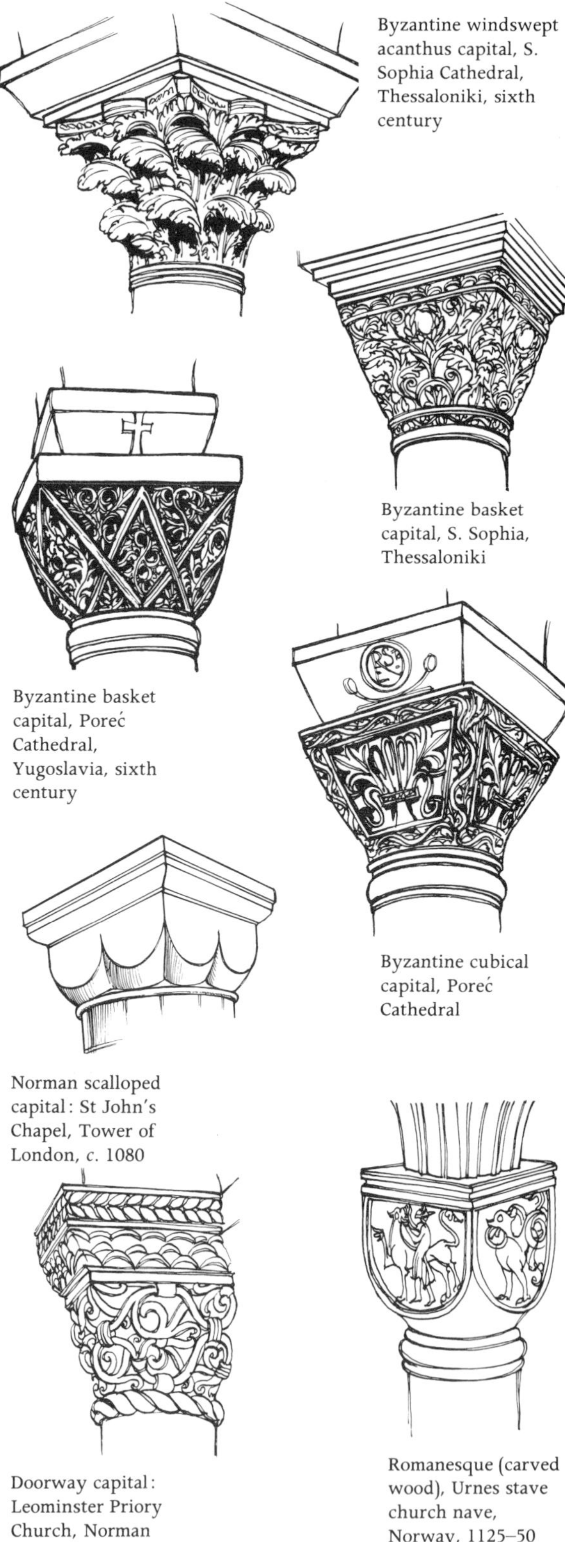

Byzantine windswept acanthus capital, S. Sophia Cathedral, Thessaloniki, sixth century

Byzantine basket capital, S. Sophia, Thessaloniki

Byzantine basket capital, Poreč Cathedral, Yugoslavia, sixth century

Byzantine cubical capital, Poreč Cathedral

Norman scalloped capital: St John's Chapel, Tower of London, *c.* 1080

Doorway capital: Leominster Priory Church, Norman Cushion capital,

Romanesque (carved wood), Urnes stave church nave, Norway, 1125–50

Choir capital, church of S. Pierre, Chauvigny, France, twelfth-century Romanesque

Choir capital, Lincoln Cathedral, thirteenth century

Moulded capital, West Walton Church, Norfolk, thirteenth century

Choir capital, Lincoln Cathedral, thirteenth century

Transept capital, Southwell Minster, thirteenth century

Chapter house, Southwell Minster, thirteenth century

cushion design evolved the *scalloped* capital where the lunettes are sub-divided into cone shapes. Later Romanesque capitals are carved in foliated designs or animal, bird and figure forms, though the latter are comparatively rare in England apart from the work of the Herefordshire school of sculptural ornament. In France, in particular, Romanesque animal and figure capitals are rich in variety and imaginative design (see ROMANESQUE ARCHITECTURE; ROMANESQUE ORNAMENT).

In Gothic architecture, Early English capitals were generally of moulded or foliated type. The abacus was usually round and moulded. In compound piers the abacus mouldings extended round the whole pier. Foliated capitals were carved stiffly, the stalks standing out from the capital bell and, later, falling in heavy clusters. Some fine examples can be seen in Lincoln Cathedral and the vine-leaf capitals in Southwell Minster are famous. Specific types of foliated capital of the period include the *crocket* capital, which has stylized leaves formed into tiny classical volutes, the *stiff-leaf* capital, which developed from it and the *water-leaf* capital shaped into plain broad leaves curving towards and turned over at the angles of the abacus.

By the fourteenth century foliated capitals were carved more naturalistically with shorter stalks and a profusion of flowers and fruit. The abacus was generally carved in the same block of stone as the capital, whereas earlier it had often been separate and, as in the thirteenth century, sometimes of a different material and colour.

In fifteenth-century Perpendicular Gothic designs the plain moulded capital was generally in use, often in octagonal shape set on circular columns. Capitals were sometimes designed separately for each shaft but more often continued in mouldings round a compound group of shafts. Carved and foliated capitals were used in larger buildings but these were more stylized than before, lower in relief, and included foliage and figures in the form of angels (see GOTHIC ARCHITECTURE; GOTHIC ORNAMENT).

Doorway sculptured capital, Kilpeck Church, Herefordshire, Norman

CARPENTER, RICHARD CROMWELL (1812–55) A disciple of the doctrine of the Cambridge Camden Society (see GOTHIC REVIVAL) and a friend of Pugin (see PUGIN, A. W. N). Carpenter crowded a considerable quantity of work in the Gothic style into his short working life. His feeling for Gothic was instinctive, sincere and highly competent. He was no fanatic but he appreciated the ecclesiological approach.

One of his early essays into the style was in a London square where he used what was considered suitable at the time, Tudor Gothic, for a homogeneous layout of terraced houses. This was *Lonsdale Square* in *Islington*, begun in 1838. He was then later taken up by the Ecclesiologists and built a number of churches, the best known of which are *St Paul's, Brighton* (1846–8), *St. Peter's, Chichester* (1848) and, most notable, the *London* church of *St Mary Magdalene* in Munster Square (1849–52).

In the 1850s, in the short time before his premature death Carpenter was chiefly engaged in school and collegiate work. He designed *St. John's College* at *Hurstpierpoint* in Sussex (1851–3), but the most outstanding example of his work in this field is at *Lancing College* in Sussex. The college was founded in 1848 by the curate of New Shoreham, Nathaniel Woodward. Carpenter designed the residential and teaching accommodation round two quadrangles, using stone and flint in traditionally local

CARPENTER, RICHARD CROMWELL
Lonsdale Square, Islington, 1838–42

manner. Building began in 1854 and, after Carpenter's death a year later, the work was continued by his partner William Slater and later still by his son *Richard Herbert Carpenter* (1841–93) who was responsible for the design of the great chapel, only recently completed.

CARR, JOHN (1723–1807) Although considered a provincial architect, for most of his extensive practice was carried on in the north of England, Carr's work was little inferior to that of many London architects of the time. He began his career as a mason, helping his father in Wakefield then, in his twenties, built *Kirby Hall*, Yorkshire, to the designs of Lord Burlington and Roger Morris. He entered architectural practice soon after 1750. He became a Palladian architect in the manner of Taylor and Paine and built a number of large country houses in this style (see TAYLOR, SIR ROBERT and PAINE, JAMES). He designed *Harewood House* in Yorkshire (1759) and built the north front before Adam took over (see ADAM, ROBERT); he built the east front of *Wentworth Woodhouse*, Yorkshire (1770) and designed *Lytham Hall*, Lancashire (1757–64) and *Basildon Park*, Berkshire (1776). Among his smaller houses are

CARR, JOHN
The Assize Courts, York, 1777

The Crescent, Buxton, Derbyshire, *c.* 1780–90

Denton Hall, Yorkshire (1770–80) and, in *York*, where he was twice mayor, *Fairfax House* (c. 1765) (see TOWN HOUSE). Also in York in his *Assize Courts* (1777) and, opposite, the Female Debtors' Prison, now the *Castle Museum* (1780). In *Horbury* in Yorkshire, where he was born, Carr built the church at his own expense (1791), which has a tall classical steeple and lateral, Ionic porch; he is buried here. His chief large-scale work was the *Crescent* in *Buxton*, Derbyshire (c. 1780–90), which he designed in the current terrace form of architecture using the giant order in a manner evolved by Wood in his *Royal Crescent* in *Bath* (see WOOD, JOHN, II).

CARTOUCHE Ornament in the form of a shield or tablet, often inscribed or bearing a heraldic device, enclosed in scrolls representing rolled up paper.

Cartouche

CARYATID In classical architecture, a female figure used as a column support of an entablature. The term traditionally derived from the destruction of the city of Carya by the Greeks who carried the females into captivity and retained them, as then attired, in a state of servitude. Different names are usually given to human figures employed architecturally as supports. Male supporting figures are termed *Atlantes* (plural of 'Atlas') or *Telamones*; female figures carrying baskets on their heads are *Canophorae*; and figures merging into pedestals, used especially in chimneypiece design in the eighteenth century, are *Herms* or *Terms* (the former are generally human in form; the latter may be human, animal or mythical beings).

CASEMATE A vaulted chamber, with embrasures, constructed in the thickness of the walls of a fortress. Used as a battery or barracks.

CARYATID
From the south porch of the Erechtheion, Acropolis, Athens, 421 BC

CASEMENT

1. A hollow moulding (see MOULDINGS).
2. A type of window frame opening on hinges affixed to the vertical side of the outer frame (see WINDOW).

CASINO Originally a small house (from the diminutive of the Latin and Italian *casa*), a summer house, lodge or pavilion. In the eighteenth and nineteenth centuries the term was used to describe a large public room, a dancing or music saloon. In more modern times it generally refers to a building used primarily for gambling.

Herm on the fireplace at Hopetoun House, Scotland, 1753–4

CASSON, SIR HUGH (*b.* 1910) A man of wide interests and abilities, the senior partner of the architectural firm of Casson, Conder and Partners has held a variety of posts and represented his profession in a number of important organizations: RIBA representative for the National Trust, Trustee of the British Museum, President of the Architectural Association, architectural consultant to the towns of Brighton, Bath and Salisbury and President of the Royal Academy.

Casson returned to architectural practice after the Second World War, years which he had spent partly as a camouflage officer at the Air Ministry and partly as technical officer in the research group of the Ministry of Town and Country Planning. In 1948 he was appointed Director of Architecture for the 1951 *Festival of Britain*, when some 40 architects co-operated under his direction to reclaim the South Bank. In particular, he was responsible for the 1851 Centenary Pavilion. After this he became Professor of Interior Design (later Environmental Design) at the Royal College of Art. His architectural achievements cover a wide field, notably *university* projects of libraries, laboratories, lecture rooms and faculty buildings at Cambridge, Birmingham and Belfast, *civic design projects* in a number of cities and specialized designs such as the oast house form of the *Elephant House* at London's Zoological Gardens.

CASTELLATED Constructed in the style of a castle, having battlements (see BATTLEMENT and CASTLE).

CASTLE A strongpoint, habitation or town centre, fortified for defence.

It was the Normans who developed the art of castle building in Britain. After the Conquest life was turbulent and insecure. Protection was equally important to the baron, lord of the manor and the meanest of servants. Security was provided by the grouping together of the community in a fortified centre which varied in size and defensive structure according to the wealth and extent of lands owned by the nobleman.

Before 1100 most castles were built of wood with thatch roofing on the *motte-and-bailey* principle. The *motte* was a large natural or artificially made mound or hill. A deep ditch was dug around its base. Round this was the *bailey*, an area of land enclosed by a wooden palisade which, in turn, was encircled by an earth *rampart* (see RAMPART) and a further, outer ditch. If possible, a stream or lake was diverted to fill this ditch or *fosse* with water. On top of the motte was built the castle in which lived the lord, his family and servants; it too was enclosed by a wooden fence. Inside the bailey were constructed wooden buildings of all kinds, their number and extent determined by the needs of the people of the community. In a large castle bailey there would be storehouses, granaries, barns, a smithy, bakehouse, kitchens, quarters for soldiers, cottages for villagers and stables for horses. When under attack everyone retreated inside the bailey and the castle could withstand quite a long siege as well as the means of attack of the time. The only access route, via fortified bridges spanning the ditches, was easily defended.

In the twelfth century the wooden structures in the more important centres were replaced by stone ones. The hill castles were rebuilt in the form of *donjon* strongpoints or keeps. These were of two types, the shell keeps and the rectangular ones. Both types were built in large numbers during the second half of the century but few of the shell keeps, being less strong, have survived. Like the eleventh-century motte-and-bailey castle, the stone shell keep was set on a mound, natural or artificial. Stone walls 8–10ft thick were then built on a circular or polygonal plan round the top of the mound enclosing an area some 40–100ft in diameter. The walls were generally of rubble with ashlar plinth and quoins and were 20–25ft high. Within these walls were then built residential quarters in stone and/or timber. Remains of such shell keeps, in some places partly rebuilt, can be seen at *Cardiff Castle*, *Carisbrooke Castle* (Isle of Wight), *Berkeley* and *Windsor*. In *York* William the Conqueror built two artificial mounds, one on each side of the river, and erected a wooden keep upon them. These have now disappeared but the thirteenth-century stone keep erected upon the eastern motte, which replaced William's wooden keep, gives an impression of the shell keep design; this one, called *Clifford's Tower*, is quatrefoil in plan.

The great, square Norman keeps, rebuilt in stone in the

Norman shell keep on its motte: Carisbrooke Castle, Isle of Wight, twelfth century

(*left*) Norman keep: The White Tower, Tower of London, 1078–90 (windows enlarged later)

Norman keep: Goodrich Castle, Herefordshire, *c.* 1160

St John's Chapel, Tower of London, *c.* 1080

twelfth century, and mainly in the second half, were massive constructions. The design came from the French *donjon* and was immensely strong, virtually impregnable in its period against the weapons employed. The keep had to be built on solid ground, being too heavy for an artificial mound, and the highest natural eminence within the outer bailey walls was chosen. The walls of the keep, over 100ft high, were immensely thick, up to 20ft at base and with flat buttresses at the corners and in the centre of the four faces. These buttresses died away into the splayed base. Passages, bedrooms and garderobes were built into the thickness of these massive walls. Turrets were constructed at the corners of the keep which contained spiral, stone staircases with a central newel which extended through all the four or five floors, each of which could be defended by one man at the top (see STAIRCASE).

The basement or undercroft was used for storage; it had a stone vaulted roof and unpierced, blank walls. Often the dungeons were on this floor or lower still. Above, the ground floor was used by the garrison and servants and had only slit windows. The principal living accommodation of the castle was on the first floor. This was the great hall which occupied the whole floor. In larger keeps this would measure about 45ft square and be about 30ft high: a span too great for timber baulks so a stone dividing wall was built across the centre, pierced with arches, so that the room could still be used as one chamber. Ceiling timbers then spanned each half with great baulks slotted into the stonework and smaller rafters crossed them at right angles. This gave a flat roof to one storey and a floor to the one above. Fireplaces were set into the outer walls with flues extending upwards and outwards to the outer face. Sanitation was provided by the garderobes built into the wall thicknesses. These had stone seats and a vent gave exit to the wall outside or a cesspool below. The chapel was an important chamber in larger keeps (see CHAPEL). The best surviving example is

Rochester Castle, plan of second floor of Norman keep, *c*. 1130

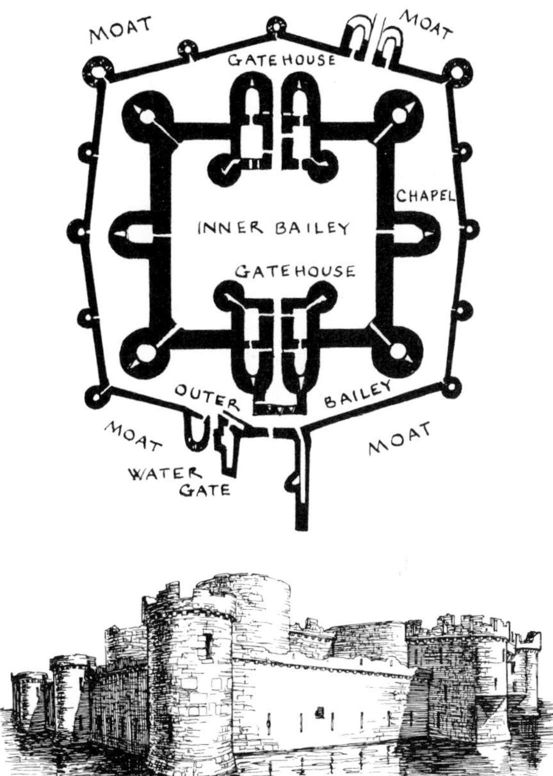

Beaumaris Castle, Anglesey, plan and view, 1295–1325

St John's Chapel in the *Tower of London*. The Norman keep here was one of the first to be built (*c*. 1077–80). Chapels were usually built into the thickness of the walls of a keep on the second floor, the same one on which the lord and his family had their apartments. Above this was the battlemented roof where there were kitchens and ovens. Used for preparing food in peaceful times, these could quickly be adapted when under siege for heating up defensive weapons and missiles.

The Norman keep was strongly defended from without. The main entrance, on the first floor, was covered by another building or tower which was connected, usually by an inside stair, to a second tower. The main doorway had heavy oak doors with iron fittings held in place by massive bars across them which slid into wall sockets on each side. An oak and iron portcullis often protected the doorway (see PORTCULLIS) and a *drawbridge* (which could be raised and lowered) spanned the gap between the two outer towers (see BARBICAN and GATEHOUSE). Keeps were also sited according to their defensive needs. Those belonging to the lord of the manor and probably situated in open country were sited, where possible, on cliffs or hills and surrounded by a natural or man-made ditch. Castles which were built by the King or by barons to command major towns were often built inside and near to the city walls as in, for example, *London*, *Colchester*,

Caernarvon Castle, North Wales, 1283–*c.* 1330

Herstmonceux Castle, Sussex, *c.* 1445

Chepstow Castle, Gwent, 1067–1300
A Norman keep
B Great gatehouse, 1225–45
C Great Tower, 1290–1300
D Barbican

Worcester and *Winchester*. Impressive remains of great square Norman keeps survive at the *Tower of London* (White Tower), *Dover, Rochester, Castle Hedingham, Colchester, Guildford, Portchester* and *Goodrich Castles*.

By the mid-thirteenth century the castle with a central strongpoint, the keep, was found to be inadequate. It was immensely strong and continued to be almost impregnable (apart from mining at the corners) but its virtues were entirely defensive and the needs of the time began to require a fortified strongpoint which could be used also as a base for offensive operations, so the *concentric castle* gradually replaced the donjon. In Britian such castles are often called 'Edwardian' after Edward I who was responsible for the creation of a number of them in order to consolidate his domination of Wales and Scotland. The concentric system was being used in England before Edward became king but it was developed under Edward and his name is associated primarily with such Welsh castles as *Caernarvon, Beaumaris, Conway* and *Harlech*.

In a concentric castle there is no reliance upon a central strongpoint but the castle consists of rings of walls, built one inside the other, defended along their whole length by fortified towers. These mural towers are designed to give covering fire from every point of the compass. No part of the structure was then weaker than another. There are generally three defensive rings of walls, each thinner than those of a Norman keep.

New structures based on this design needed no keep and used the central space as an open courtyard where, round it within the inner ring of walls, was constructed domestic accommodation in separate buildings for the great hall, chapel and living space. Between the inner and the second ring of walls were built other necessary structures and in the outer bailey was room for garrison buildings, stables, smithy, cattle and villagers. Beyond the outer wall was a moat defended by a gatehouse and/or barbican. Typical is *Beaumaris Castle* on the Island of Anglesey where the moat is still water-filled and the mural towers are in good condition. *Caerphilly*, in South Wales, remains one of the finest concentric castles in Britain, though partially ruined. It has a rectangular inner ward of 70 by 53 yards with a drum tower at each corner and a gatehouse in the centre of each end wall. The hall (72 × 33ft) is flanked by a chapel and private apartments. The second ward is 106 × 90 yards; its walls descend some 20ft into the water. The water for the lake here at Caerphilly, as at *Leeds Castle* in Kent, was provided by damming a stream. A third ward is defended by gatehouses, towers and portcullis and was connected to the second by a bridge.

In a number of instances Norman castles were converted into concentric ones. The central keep was retained for accommodation and as a final strongpoint whilst the curtain walls with their mural towers, gatehouses and moat were constructed round the keep. The *Tower of London* is one such example, where the *White Tower*, the original keep, is now surrounded by many other towers and walls. On the borders of England and Wales are two more: *Goodrich Castle*, Herefordshire and *Chepstow Castle, Gwent*. These castles had the best of both worlds, a spaciousness of living accommodation unknown to the Normans yet, if the concentric system failed, the donjon remained as a last line of retreat.

Kidwelly Castle, Carmarthenshire. An Edwardian castle, *c.* 1275–1325

A number of fourteenth-century castles were built as part of a town's defences and were designed in a rather different form. In North Wales there are two famous examples: *Caernarvon* and *Conway*. These are roughly rectangular in plan and have strong mural towers set round one chief ring of walls. Such castles have to be built on commanding and, if possible, impregnable sites. Caernarvon Castle, with polygonal towers, is almost encircled by the river estuary. Conway, with its circular towers, rises steeply above the harbour's edge.

By 1375–80 the quadrangular plan began to supersede the Edwardian form of concentric design. *Bodiam Castle* in Sussex is an excellent example of such castle building. It is approached over an oak bridge, which spans the moat, to the octagon. During the approach the invader would be under fire from the towers and would have to pass the barbican, cross a 10ft moat, over which the drawbridge could be raised if required, and storm the main gatehouse. This was fitted with three portcullises. Bodiam still presents the shell of a great castle. Its outer walls, lapped by the moat, are in good condition. The barbican is in ruins but the main gatehouse is preserved. On entering one steps into a quadrangular court surrounded by buildings and towers and containing the great hall, chapel, private chambers and kitchen.

Castles and fortified residences continued to be built during the whole of the fifteenth century but, as the military importance of such buildings decreased, domestic comfort and spaciousness increased and larger castles became palaces and smaller ones slightly fortified manor houses (see COUNTRY HOUSE AND MANSION; MANOR HOUSE). Interesting examples include *Hever Castle*, Kent, *Warwick Castle* and *Hurstmonceux Castle*, Sussex. (See also BALISTRARIA; BARBICAN; BARTIZAN; BASTION; BATTLEMENT; BRICKWORK; CASEMATE; CASTELLATED; MACHICOLATION; PORTCULLIS.)

CATHEDRA The chair or throne of a bishop in his cathedral church, originally placed in the apse behind the high altar.

CEILING Related to the verb 'ceil', a medieval term describing the action of lining the roof or walls of an apartment with plaster, wood boarding or a canopied hanging (see also CELURE).

Before the sixteenth century in Britain much of the interior roofing for larger buildings was by stone vaults or open timber structures (see TIMBER TRUSSED ROOF; VAULTING). From about 1470 onwards the flat wood or wood and plaster covering began to replace the open design and the term ceiling was used to describe it. The flat ceilings of the first half of the sixteenth century were supported by massive wooden beams, plain, moulded or decoratively carved, augmented by smaller cross rafters. The panels between were boarded or plastered.

By the 1540s ceilings covered entirely by decorative plaster were being introduced. Skilled craftsmen from Italy illustrated the possibilities of the medium which, as the English acquired the necessary skills, became popular because it was decorative and inexpensive. Elizabethan craftsmen experimented with the material, introducing sand, quicklime, horsehair and fibre to their plaster and some followed the Italian custom of adding finely-ground marble to the final coat to give a polished lustre finish to the work. The ceiling designs were simple at first, based on Gothic ribbed vaulting, and consisted of narrow, moulded ribs on a plain ground. The ribs were applied in geometrical patterns, predominantly octagons, and shields, heraldic bosses and floral motifs decorated the panels and intersections. Many ceilings were of pendant design, where the ribs descended to bosses and finials. As the sixteenth century advanced designs became more

Wooden-beam and plaster-panel ceiling: Tudor Parlour, *c.* 1530. Based upon Abbot's Room, Thame Park, Oxfordshire

Pendant plaster ceiling of the Hall, Trerice Manor House, Cornwall, 1572

Coffered octagon ceiling of the Gallery, Croome Court, Worcestershire. Architect: Robert Adam

Gilded plaster. Rococo decoration in ceiling cove. Hopetoun House, West Lothian, 1750–4

Plaster strapwork ceiling at Athelhampton Manor House, Dorset, early seventeenth century

ornate. Ribs became wider, flatter and bolder and the ornament spread all over the ceiling surface. Strapwork evolved and all kind of motifs were introduced: flowers, animals, birds, fruit, scrolls, heraldic insignia and *putti* (see STRAPWORK). By the end of the century designs were in high relief and free in treatment. Colour was widely used.

In the seventeenth century Jacobean ceilings continued to be decorated with richly ornamented strapwork patterns but the purer classical influence of Inigo Jones began to be reflected in the ceiling designs of the 1640s and 1650s. The all-over design was replaced by one with a raised centrepiece, which might be circular, oval or rectangular and which was ornamented by naturalistic, classical motifs. These included leaves, fruit, swags and *putti*, all in high relief. A classical cornice (see CLASSICAL ORDER and CORNICE) marked the junction of ceiling and walls and the area between this and the centrepiece was often deeply coved, especially in large apartments. A *cove* is a wide, concave form extending from the horizontal surface of the ceiling to the vertical one of the walls. In large, important rooms the central and other ceiling panels were generally painted with allegorical or historical scenes. In the second half of the century the classical influence became stronger and classical ornament was used on the mouldings. The bold, high-relief panelled ceilings were reserved more for larger buildings and smaller rooms had simple, ribbed designs. The centrepiece type of ceiling pattern was retained until the end of the century.

Eighteenth-century ceilings were mainly of classical design. Palladian interiors had white ceilings with bold classical cornices, often deep, wide coving and a high-relief ceiling pattern, the moulded ribs enriched with classical ornament and often containing paintings in the panels. Gilt was used on the enrichment. Many ceilings in larger apartments were coffered in Roman fashion (see CAISSON; COFFER). The ceilings of the second half of the century continued in classical form but the designs were in lower relief and more delicate in colouring and treatment. The Adam mode of stucco handling dominated the work of the years 1760–90 and was widely imitated (see ADAM, ROBERT). The coloured ceiling with delicate stucco work picked out in white rather than gilt replaced the heavier Palladian designs. Ornament became more restrained and sparing in use as the century neared its end.

In larger buildings the Gothic Revival influenced ceiling patterns during the nineteenth century. Cusped and traceried panelled and ribbed ceilings were designed and these could be white or coloured with gilt on the enrichment and mouldings. In the home the plain, white ceiling with cornice and central rose, from which the light fitting depended, was more common.

For further reference to and illustration of ceiling design see also ADAM, ROBERT; BAROQUE ARCHITECTURE; CAMPBELL, COLEN; JONES, INIGO; KENT, WILLIAM; PALLADIAN ARCHITECTURE; PLASTERWORK; VANBRUGH, SIR JOHN; and WREN, SIR CHRISTOPHER.

CELURE A canopy, the word probably derives from a source such as 'ceil' (see CEILING). In architecture, it is the painted, panelled section of a 'wagon' roof above the church altar.

CENOTAPH An empty tomb. A monument to a person or persons buried in another place. The well-known example in Britain in Lutyens' Cenotaph in Whitehall to the memory of the dead of the First World War. A wood and plaster model was erected in 1919 for the peace procession of that year. The design so appealed to both the public and critics that it was perpetuated in Portland stone (see LUTYENS, SIR EDWIN LANDSEER).

CENOTAPH
The Cenotaph, Whitehall, 1919. Architect: Sir Edwin Lutyens

CENTERING A temporary framework, generally made of timber, set up to support a vault, arch, bridge or dome while under construction. The centering is removed (struck) when the mortar of the permanent structure has set.

CHAIR RAIL A moulding applied to the walls of a room at suitable height, to prevent the backs of chairs from damaging the wall if pushed back against it. Also known as *dado rail* (see DADO).

CHAMBERS, SIR WILLIAM (1723–96) Son of a Scottish merchant, Chambers was born at Göteborg in Sweden. He spent much of his boyhood in Yorkshire then returned to Sweden where at the age of 16 he joined the Swedish East India Company. During the following nine years in this employment he made voyages to China and Bengal. He left the Company when he was 25 and went to Paris to study architecture where he worked under Jean-François Blondel and became acquainted with a number of French architects, notably Jacques-Germain Soufflot. After a year he went to Italy where he studied for five years, returning to England in 1755. He set up practice where success came quickly to him. He progressed steadily from honour to honour. He became architectural tutor to the Prince of Wales who, later as George III, showed his appreciation of Chambers's work and appointed him Architect to the King. He became Comptroller in 1769, was knighted in 1770 and became Surveyor-General in 1782. He played a leading part in the foundation of the Royal Academy and was its first treasurer in 1768.

One of Chambers's early commissions was, in his capacity as architect to the Princess Dowager, to lay out the *Gardens* at *Kew* and ornament them in classical and oriental manner. Between 1757 and 1763 he did this, designing the Pagoda, the classical Orangery, some temples and alcoves. He published in 1757 his *Designs of Chinese Buildings*, in which he used first-hand drawings he had made while in China. In 1759 he published his first edition of *A Treatise on Civil Architecture*, which became a standard work. He compiled it from many of his own first-hand studies in addition to works by Italian architects including Bernini, Peruzzi, Palladio, Vignola and Scamozzi. This comprehensive study of Italian architecture includes whole designs and a wealth of detail on classical forms in doorways, window openings, ceilings and chimneypieces.

Chambers was a proud, reserved, sensitive, humourless man. He was ambitious and convinced that his views on classical architecture were the correct interpretation for English architects. He resisted all incursion into the Greek forms of classicism and based his own work on Palladianism mellowed fractionally by Parisian neo-classicism (see CLASSICISM; PALLADIAN ARCHITECTURE). In the current 'battle of the styles' he was wholeheartedly 'Roman'. His detail, ornament and proportions were meticulously correct; his work was sincere, intellectual, and of superb quality.

Chambers designed a number of houses which are characteristic of his work. In the country-house field his *Peper Harow* in Surrey (1765–75) is a simple, three-storeyed building with slightly projecting central block. It is set in beautiful grounds and is now a school. Like his mansion *Duddingston* in Midlothian (1762–8), the house retains one of the fine staircases for which Chambers is noted. Of his town houses, the façade of *Melbourne House, Piccadilly*, (1770–4), survives, though the building was enlarged and altered in 1804 to become the Albany Chambers. His *Dundas House* in St Andrew's Square, *Edinburgh* (1771–2) became the Royal Bank of Scotland and *Wick House* on *Richmond Hill* in Surrey, which he designed for Sir Joshua Reynolds, has been considerably altered. A small-scale work, the *Casino*, a little pavilion at *Marino*, near Dublin (1757–69), is one of Chambers's most attractive works. Perfectly proportioned and handled, built on Greek-cross plan, this building contains some beautiful interiors clearly influenced by his Parisian studies.

Chambers was the leading official architect of his day and so was commissioned to design *Somerset House* in London (1778–86), his most important work. For a number of years a scheme had been discussed to house several government departments together in one building

The River front, Somerset House, London, 1778–86

The Strand front, Somerset House, London, 1778–86

Peper Harow, Surrey, 1765–75

Entrance doorway, Melbourne House, Piccadilly, 1770–4

The Royal Bank of Scotland, St Andrew's Square, Edinburgh, 1772

in the centre of the capital. This building was to be designed to accommodate these as well as the Royal Society and the Royal Academy of Arts. The site chosen was that of the old riverside palace which, when demolished, gave a new site with a south front facing the Thames 800ft long, and a much narrower north elevation to the Strand of about 135ft, roughly in the centre of the long façade. Chambers designed the Strand front in a manner reminiscent of Inigo Jones's previous work on the old palace. It is two-storeyed with rusticated arches on the lower stage and the Corinthian Order in column form above. The centrally placed entrance has three round-arched openings which lead to a central court, each façade of which has a Corinthian pavilion in its centre. In the elevation which faces the Strand front entrance is a principal feature which also forms a focal centre for the river front; it is surmounted by a pediment and a dome.

Somerset House is one of London's most impressive waterfront monuments. It presented Chambers with a number of problems which he solved intelligently. One major difficulty was the unusual shape of the site, with one immensely long façade and one short one. Another was that, since the river was not then embanked, the water would lap the building. Chambers built a masonry platform above tide level and constructed on it a basement storey for warehouses and offices. He then fronted this by a rusticated masonry arcade. The façade was divided into three blocks by a central archway and two side watergates so that the tide was controlled by the water's entry into these archways. At the time, as contemporary drawings show, the building had a more impressive appearance, for now much of the effect has been diminished by the building of the modern roadway and embankment.

CHAMBERS, SIR WILLIAM
The Pagoda, Kew Gardens, 1761

The river façade has a certain monotony of design, especially since the addition of wings in the nineteenth century. Also, the dome in the central court, while satisfactory when viewed from the court or from the Strand, is insignificant when seen from the waterfront. The building is finely constructed in Portland stone; it is beautifully finished and ornamented and many of the interiors are elegantly and superbly designed and decorated (see AEDICULE).

CHAMBRANLE A decorative border on the top and sides of doors, windows and chimneypieces.

CHAMFER To cut away the square sharp edge or arris of a stone block or wood beam. The cut surface is generally at an angle of 45° to the horizontal and vertical surfaces of the block. When the cut surface is concave, it is termed a *hollow chamfer*. When it is cut in parallel mouldings, it is a *moulded chamfer*; when it is a flat but sunk surface, it is called a *sunk chamfer*. A *stop* or *stopped chamfer* is one where the chamfer is only carried part way along the block or beam and is stopped by a carved splay.

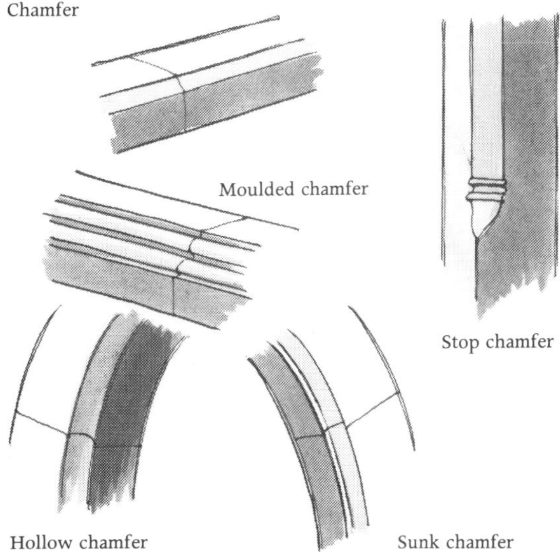

CHAMP In architecture, a field or ground which bears an area of raised relief carving.

CHAMPNEYS, BASIL (1842–1935) In a long career Champneys was practising, for the majority of his time, at the height of nineteenth-century eclecticism though, from the 1880s onwards, this was leavened by the revival of indigenous architectural forms. He designed in Renaissance and medieval manner with equal competence. Among his most pleasing works are those in brick in the English, gabled style of the second half of the seventeenth century as at, for example, *Newnham College, Cambridge*. Much of Champneys's work was in the collegiate field. Other examples include the large quadrangle surrounded by buildings in the Gothic style at *Mansfield College, Oxford* (founded 1886), and *Bedford College* in Regent's Park in *London* (1900–2). He also designed the Butler Museum at *Harrow School* (1886) and the *Indian Institute* in Oxford (1882). His most important work, for which he was awarded the RIBA Gold Medal in 1912 was *Rylands Library* in Manchester (1885), a stone building in ecclesiastical, Perpendicular Gothic dress. The central hall of the library is 125ft long and 44ft high. It terminates in an apse and has a vaulted roof. Champneys also designed a number of churches.

CHAPEL A room or a small building reserved for Christian worship. In the Middle Ages manor houses, palaces, castles and monasteries possessed chapels for private worship and it became the custom for chapels to be built for universities, schools, colleges, prisons, garrisons and other institutions. Such chapels were consecrated and had altars (see St John's Chapel, Tower of London, under CASTLES).

The word chapel derives from the Late Latin and the Italian *cappella*, diminutive of *cappa*, meaning 'little cloak'. This was in reference to the cloak of St Martin which, preserved as a sacred relic by the Frankish Kings, was traditionally regarded as a saintly relic upon which oaths may be sworn. In time the term came to be applied to a sanctuary in which holy relics were preserved and where prayers were said. Early chapels were also known as oratories.

Churches and cathedrals, especially those built in the Middle Ages, contain one or more chapels dedicated to certain saints or to specific purposes or activities. These are built into the aisles, most often in the eastern arm of the building. The largest chapel, traditionally situated on the end of the eastern termination, is the *Lady Chapel*, dedicated to the Virgin.

The word chapel is also often applied to a building erected for Christian worship of a denomination which differs from that of the established Church of a country. In Britain this might apply for instance to buildings for worship by Methodists, Baptists or Roman Catholics.

There are a number of types of chapels which have been built for specific functions. A *chantry chapel* is one where prayers were said for the dead, in particular for the founder of the building. The mass was originally sung or chanted and the word derives from the Old French *chanterie* and the Medieval Latin *cantaria*. In great monasteries and cathedral churches in the Middle Ages the chantry chapels were enriched by beautifully carved stone screens and canopied niches and tombs. The donors or founders of such chapels vied with one another in their lifetime to decorate an apartment with superb craftsmanship in which masses would be celebrated for the well-being of their souls. A *chapel of ease* was one built by the roadside, in a hamlet or on a bridge for the convenience of travellers. There are several *royal chapels* which are burial chapels dedicated to the interment of one or more royal

CHAMPNEYS, BASIL
Newnham College, Cambridge, 1880 onwards

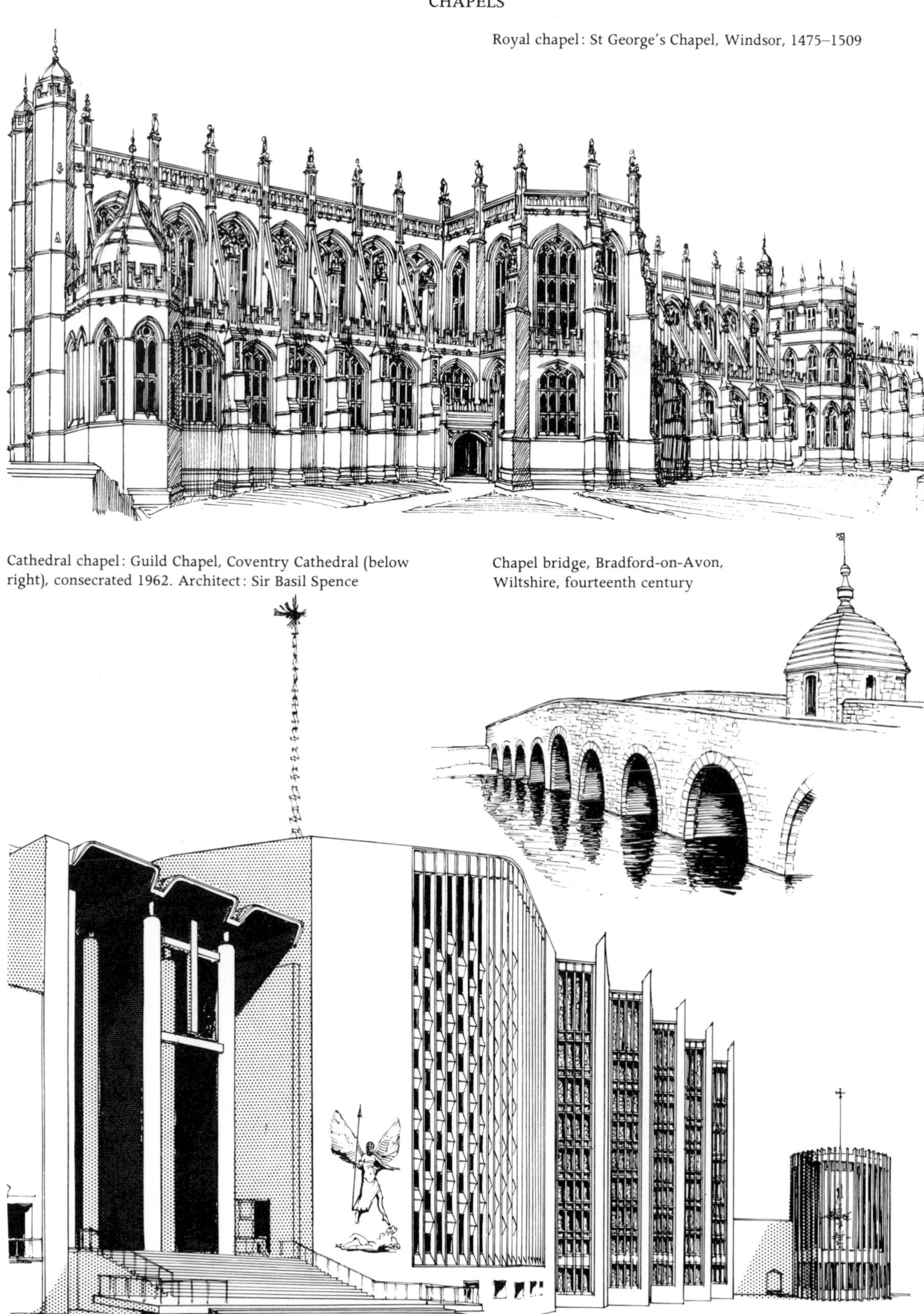

Royal chapel: St George's Chapel, Windsor, 1475–1509

Cathedral chapel: Guild Chapel, Coventry Cathedral (below right), consecrated 1962. Architect: Sir Basil Spence

Chapel bridge, Bradford-on-Avon, Wiltshire, fourteenth century

personages. Of particular architectural beauty are the *Henry VII Chapel* in Westminster Abbey, and *St George's Chapel* at Windsor.

CHAPTER-HOUSE The chapter of a monastery or a cathedral church is its governing, administrative body. The chapter-house, where the chapter holds its assembly for discussion of business, is a building adjacent or attached to the cathedral or abbey church. In Britain the chapter-house is most often polygonal in plan and has a pointed exterior roof. Inside, in a number of instances, a single column supports the interior stone vault. Round the walls are canopied stalls for seating. Fine medieval examples can be seen at *Wells, Lincoln* and *Salisbury Cathedrals, York* and *Southwell Minsters* and *Westminster Abbey*.

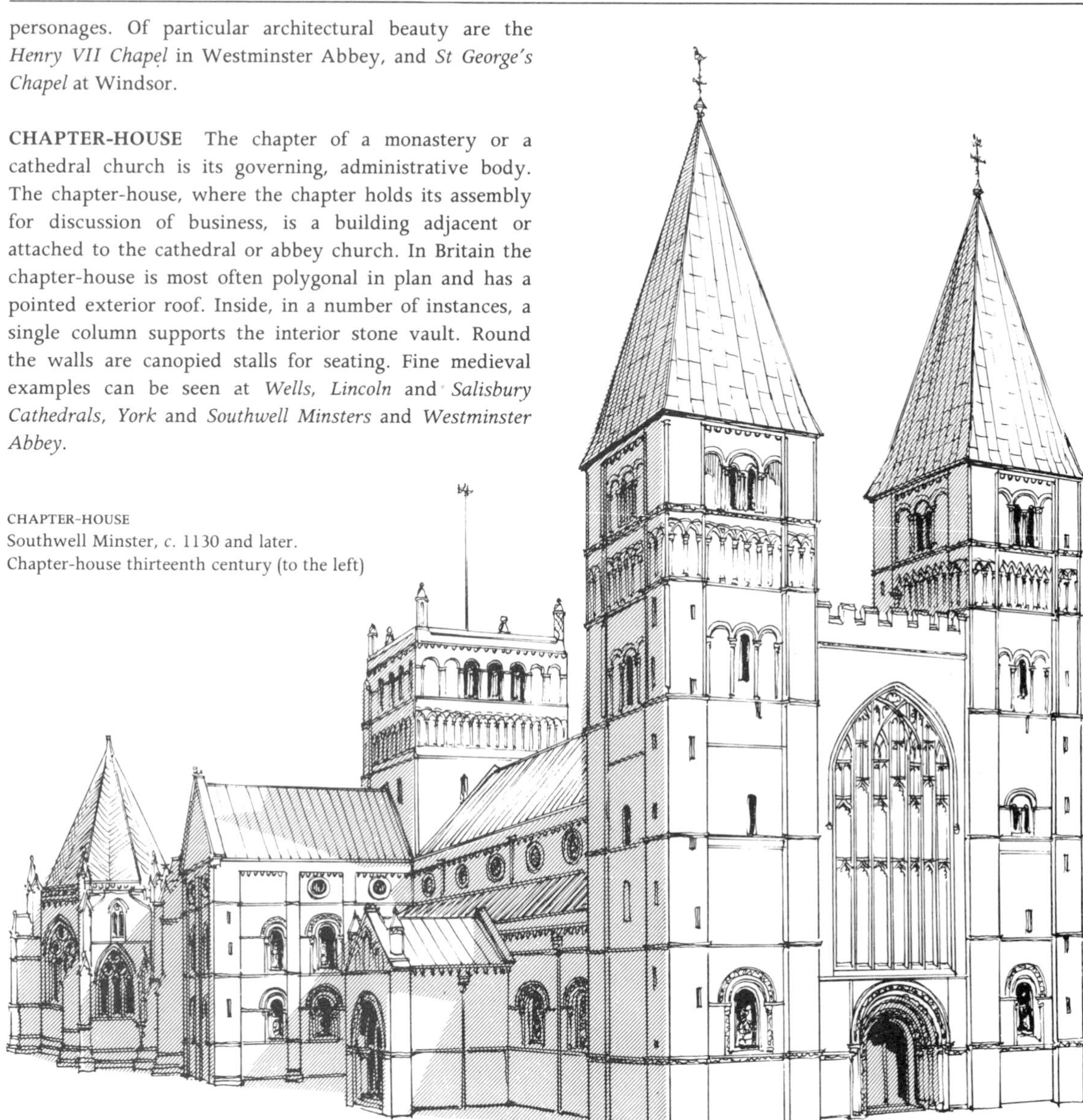

CHAPTER-HOUSE
Southwell Minster, *c.* 1130 and later.
Chapter-house thirteenth century (to the left)

CHARGE From the late Latin *carrica*, 'load which is borne'. In heraldry this refers to the device borne by the shield; in architecture it refers to the ornamentation borne by a member such as a frieze.

CHARNEL HOUSE From the late Latin *carnale* and the Old French *charnel*, referring to a burial place. In the Middle Ages charnel houses were used extensively to store bodies and, generally, a chantry chapel was part of the building (see 'chantry chapel' under CHAPEL).

CHEQUER WORK A method of wall and pavement decoration in which a 'chessboard' pattern of alternating squares of contrasting material is used. Typical, especially in the fifteenth to seventeenth centuries, was the alternating of squares of knapped flint and stone.

CHIMNEY, CHIMNEYPIECE, GRATE Derived, via the Middle English *chimenee* and the old and modern French *cheminée*, from the Latin *caminus*, which meant a furnace, a forge and a fireplace or hearth used for warming the room and/or for cooking. By the sixteenth century the term also came to include the flue and the exit stacks on the roof. Inside the building the structure which contains the flue is called the *chimney-breast* while the lintel bar which supports the fireplace opening is the *chimney-bar*. The decorative framework surrounding the fireplace, which could be made of marble, stone, brick or iron, is

CHEQUER WORK
Flint and stone chequer work, Hall of the Trinity Guild, King's Lynn, fifteenth and sixteenth century

Enlarged detail of above

the *chimneypiece* or *mantelpiece*. Often this incorporates a shelf—the *mantelshelf*—and might extend above to the ceiling in an ornamental framework including mirrors, a painting and/or niches and shelves for ornaments. A chimney built into the corner of a room is called an *angle-chimney*. Chimney flues could be constructed within the very thick walls or, later when walls were thinner, were made so that they projected on the exterior walls of a building. The structures, which were built above roof level to dissipate the smoke away from the building, are called *chimney-stacks* if they are large and contain a number of flues and *chimney shafts* if they contain only one. On top of the stack or shaft are *chimney pots* which cap the flues.

Until the fourteenth century chimneys were rare. It was more usual to heat the chamber with a central hearth of stone or brick with iron fire-dogs against which great logs were stacked. The smoke then escaped through a louvre in the open timber roof above. In larger buildings the louvre could be an ornamental Gothic lantern structure as at Westminster Hall. From the late thirteenth century onwards fireplaces began to be installed in other rooms and were built on outside walls. A stone hood was constructed over the top of these fireplaces to direct the smoke up the flue which, at this time, usually had its outlet to the outside air in the outer wall only a few feet above the fireplace. In the fourteenth century flues were constructed to ascend vertically through the massive walls and the smoke escaped through a chimney shaft set on the roof ridge or gable peak. Such shafts were generally round or octagonal and had apertures on all sides for the escape of smoke.

In the fifteenth century fireplaces were made of brick or stone and had larger hearths. The four-centred arch prevailed by the end of the century and some chimneypieces were decoratively carved. By this time also chimney-stacks became a decorative feature of the exterior of a house being designed in single shafts or clustered into groups. Most of these were in stone. It was in the first half of the sixteenth century that such shafts and stacks became a notable ornamental part of the skyline. Many at this time were made in decorative brickwork and terracotta, at Hampton Court Palace for example, and designs were very varied. Shafts were cylindrical or octagonal and were ornamented by zig-zags, scrolls, crossed beading, circular holes, honeycomb patterns and fluting. The bases could be octagonal, square or diamond-shaped on plan and were also moulded and fluted. Inside, the large fireplace was still enclosed in a four-centre-arched opening with a stone or brick chimneypiece.

Elizabethan and Jacobean chimneypieces were the dominant ornamental features in a room, a tradition which continued in varied decorative form throughout the seventeenth and eighteenth centuries. The Flemish influence on Elizabethan design was particularly apparent in the chimneypiece which was intricately carved in wood, marble or stone. The fire-opening was flanked by carved pilasters, columns or caryatid figures which sup-

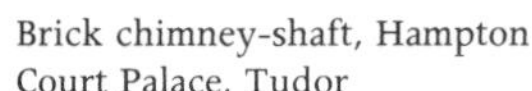

Brick chimney-shaft, Hampton Court Palace, Tudor

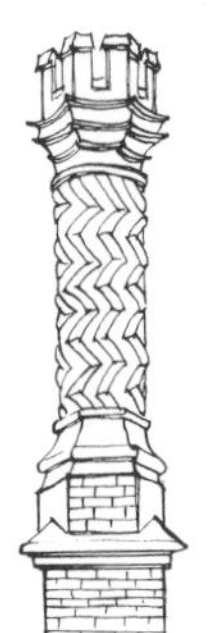

Chimney-stack, Lacock Abbey, Wiltshire, stone, *c.* 1530

Carved stone chimneypiece, iron fire-dogs, *c.* 1510

Stone hooded fireplace, 1180–1200

Domestic chimney stack by Sir Edwin Lutyens, 1899

Carved and inlaid oak chimneypiece, *c.* 1570–5

Brick chimney-stacks, Holkham Hall, Norfolk, 1734, Palladian

Chimneypiece of glass with clock and gas fire, 1935–40

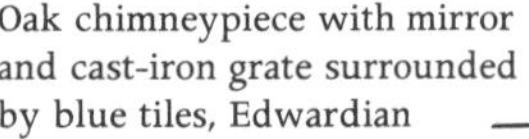

Oak chimneypiece with mirror and cast-iron grate surrounded by blue tiles, Edwardian

ported an ornate mantelshelf, while above was an overmantel or second tier also vigorously carved and perhaps incorporating mirrors or paintings. Motifs were varied. They included masks, grotesques, animals, human figures, flowers, fruit, strapwork and scrolls. Inlay with coloured woods was employed as well as carved decoration. Chimney-stacks were still decorative but plainer than early Tudor designs.

With the second half of the seventeenth century came purer classical chimney designs both outside and inside a building. Chimney-stacks were tall, rectangular forms with classically moulded tops. The chimneypiece was less riotously carved and its decoration was in classical form with orders, supporting columns and enriched mouldings. Above the mantelshelf was often a rectangular frame containing a mirror or a painting and this would be surmounted by a classical cornice and carved decoration. The Grinling Gibbons style of wood-carving in free profusion of fruit, flowers and birds was characteristic of the 1670s and 1680s in overmantel design. Cast-iron fire-backs and *basket* or *dog grates* began to supersede the iron fire-dogs as coal was burnt more often.

In the eighteenth century the chimneypiece was part of the general design of the room. A classical scheme of moulded panels, cornice and wainscot incorporated all the features of the room: doorcase, window openings and chimneypiece. In the early Georgian period the latter was richly and boldly carved in marble or wood or could be decorated in gilded or painted stucco; the overmantel extended to the cornice of the room. Mirrors formed an integral part of eighteenth-century room décor and most chimneypieces incorporated one or more mirrors set among the carved framework which also included candleholders. In mid-century rococo carved designs were paramount; carved and gilded pinewood frames were often designed in one with the chimneypiece below and, amid the leafy scrolls, were intertwined carved birds, shells and fruit.

During the years 1765–75 the rococo scrolls were largely replaced by more architectural chimneypieces, often single-storeyed and with a framed painting or mirror above the mantelshelf. The Adam mode was predominant until the 1790s in which a mantelshelf and entablature were generally supported on flanking classical columns or caryatid figures. Marble, scagliola or wood

Part of chimneypiece of the double-cube room, Wilton House, Wiltshire, 1653

Carved and painted pinewood chimneypiece in rococo style: marble fireplace, steel firegrate, 1756

were employed with the classical decoration inlaid or carved. Low sculptural relief, especially of draped classical figures and compositions, was a favourite design feature. A variety of materials was used for the ornamentation. Particularly favoured were carved and inlaid marbles, ormolu, bronze or brass, Wedgwood plaques and painted decoration. The ornament was concentrated on the frieze and side panels of the chimneypiece. During the later eighteenth century fire openings became smaller and almost all grates had cast-iron fire-backs attached to a fire-basket grate for coal burning; this had replaced the earlier open fireplace with fire-dogs and fire-back. The *basket grates* were designed in a number of forms. The Adam designs were characteristic. These were generally of steel and iron and were elegant, enriched by classical ornamentation and with urn finials. Later in the century *hob grates* were more usual. These fitted into each side of

White marble chimneypiece inlaid with coloured marble; cast-iron hob grate, 1795–1800

Hall chimneypiece of white marble with plaster figure decoration above, steel and brass firegrate and fender. Kedleston Hall, Derbyshire. Architect: Robert Adam, 1758–68

the fireplace instead of being free-standing in the centre of the fire opening as before. They were made of cast iron, with wrought iron bars, and the side panels were enriched with classical relief decoration.

Regency chimneypieces were similar but smaller and plainer. Grates were of hob design or could be sarcophagus grates which stood on paw feet and were decorated with Egyptian motifs. After about 1845 chimneypieces became ornate. They were made of brass, iron, marble or stone or could be of painted iron or wood. Velvet draperies with fringe and tassel edging were added to the chimneypiece design and a similarly decorated overmantel contained niches and shelves to accommodate a profusion of ornaments. Grates were most commonly of cast iron, fitted into the fire-opening. Fire-irons and fenders were of brass or steel.

Until the advent of central heating during the twentieth century the chimneypiece continued to be the dominant decorative feature of the room, its style determined by that of the period. Ornate designs, mainly in black-leaded or painted cast iron, marble or polished wood remained fashionable until the 1890s when simpler classical eclectic chimneypieces were preferred. The Gothic Revival influenced many designs; this was seen in cusped panelling and arched openings. At the turn of the century plainer, rectangular chimneypieces were usual, the fire-opening surround usually faced with glazed tiles. In smaller houses often an iron cooking range was combined in one design with a drawing-room grate. From about 1910 the fireplace was a plain feature, sometimes with a superstructure and a mirror, but more often not. Brick and marble were widely used for the chimneypiece which could be designed for a coal grate or for a gas or electric fire.

Cast-iron chimneypiece and grate, brass fender and fire-irons; mahogany overmantel with mirror and tasselled velvet hangings, 1870–5

Simple stone or brick classical chimney-stacks were constructed throughout the eighteenth and part of the nineteenth century. Victorian chimney-stacks, particularly on smaller and middle-class housing, were utilitarian, of brick, grouped to accommodate a multiplicity of chimney-pots. With the advent of central heating the roof chimney has slowly disappeared.

CHINOISERIE A term used to describe European interpretations of Chinese art which appeared in the seventeenth century and became very fashionable in the second half of the eighteenth century. Chinese design themes and motifs were incorporated especially into interior ornamentation in stucco and wood carving, wallpaper, furniture and porcelain. The pagoda in Kew Gardens is one manifestation. Some of the interiors in the Royal Pavilion at Brighton are fine examples of Regency interpretations.

CHURCH DESIGN AND STRUCTURE More than one suggestion has been put forward for the origin of the word 'church'—meaning a building for public Christian worship—and its allied forms in many other European languages which derive from the same source. It is now generally accepted that it came originally from the Greek κυριακόν, meaning 'of the Lord', this, in turn, deriving from κυριοζ (='Lord'). The earliest cited instances of this Greek word being used to refer to a 'House of the Lord' date from about 300 AD, after which time the word was often used in this sense and the Emperor Constantine named several of his churches κυριακά. The Western Germanic and the Old Saxon word *kirika*, in general use from the fifth century, is believed to have been taken from the Greek source as were the Old English *circe* or *cirice* and the Middle English *chirche*, *cherche*.

Until the early fourth century AD Christianity had been celebrated in houses and community structures. In 313 the Edict of Milan gave to the Christians under Roman rule the right to practise their religion openly on an equal basis with other faiths and, from 325, Christianity became the official religion of the Roman Empire. It was from this time onwards that Christian churches were built for the purpose of worship and a form of Christian architecture

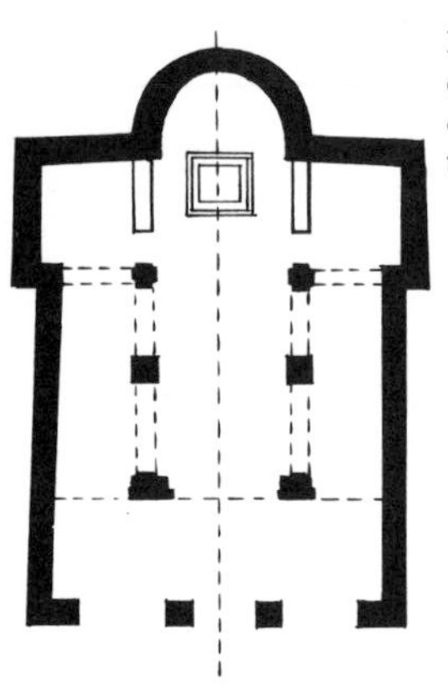

Plan of basilican Christian church at Roman city of Silchester, fourth and fifth centuries AD

Nave and chancel of Saxon church, Escomb, Durham, seventh century.

The chancel arch, Escomb church

Ground plan of Saxon church, Boarhunt, Hampshire, eleventh century.

Nave and chancel

Centrally planned Early Christian circular church: S. Costanza, Rome, *c.* 340 AD

Circular Church of the Holy Sepulchre, Cambridge, *c.* 1130

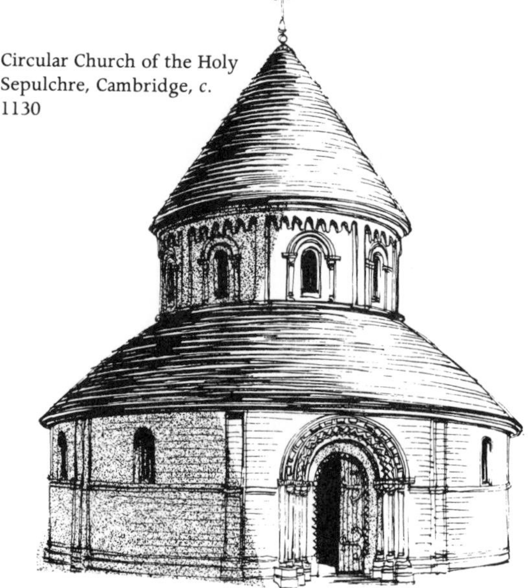

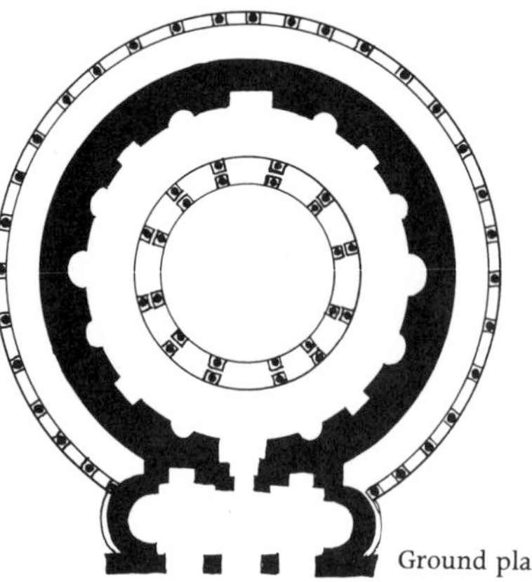

Ground plan, S. Costanza

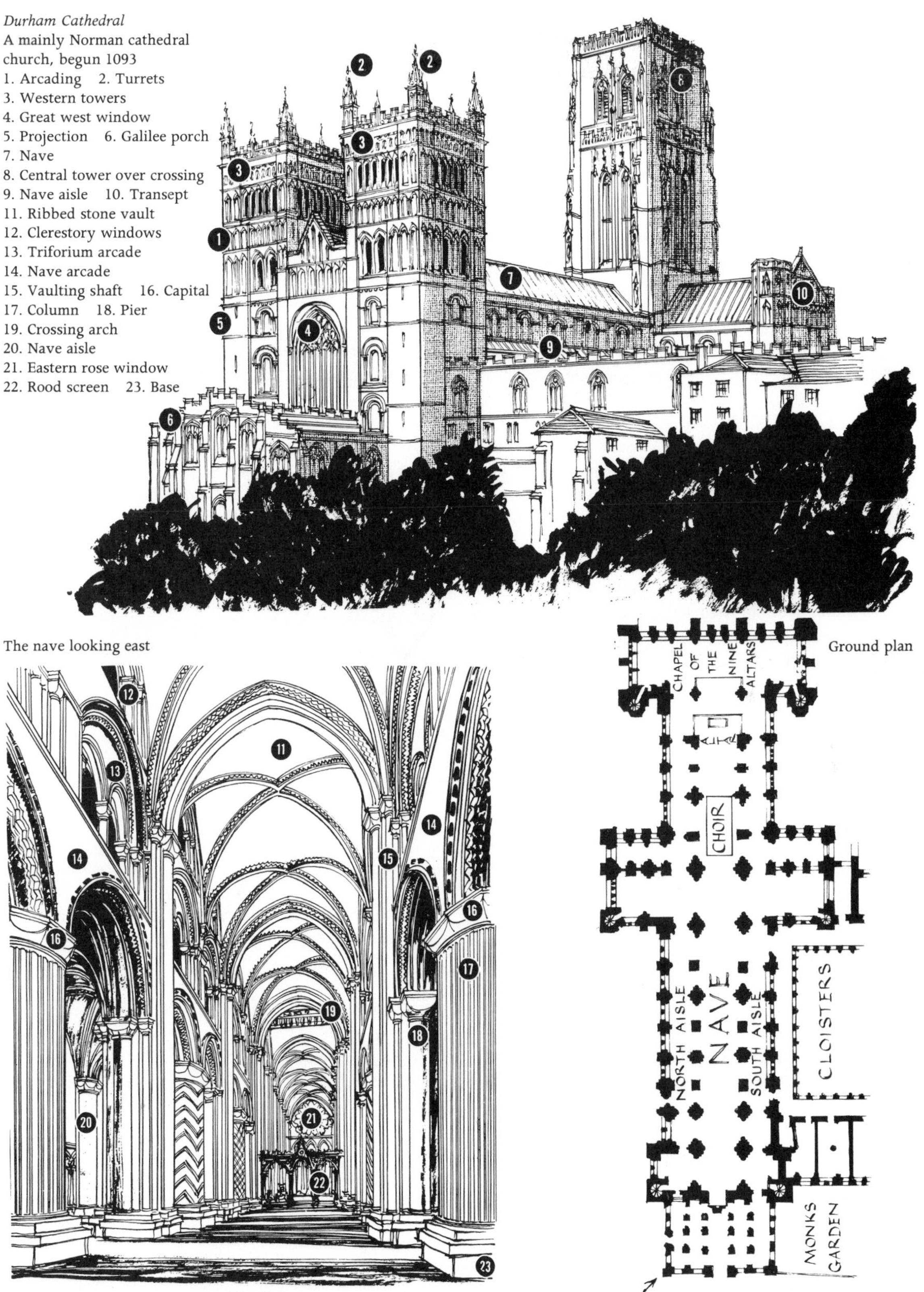

Durham Cathedral
A mainly Norman cathedral church, begun 1093
1. Arcading 2. Turrets
3. Western towers
4. Great west window
5. Projection 6. Galilee porch
7. Nave
8. Central tower over crossing
9. Nave aisle 10. Transept
11. Ribbed stone vault
12. Clerestory windows
13. Triforium arcade
14. Nave arcade
15. Vaulting shaft 16. Capital
17. Column 18. Pier
19. Crossing arch
20. Nave aisle
21. Eastern rose window
22. Rood screen 23. Base

The nave looking east

Ground plan

evolved. These Early Christian churches were based upon the plan and construction of the basilica, the Roman hall of justice and commerce (see BASILICA).

During the succeeding centuries the plan and structure of Christian church building could take one of several forms and this continued to be so during the Middle Ages. From the time of Constantine until the end of the fifteenth century the *basilican plan* was widely adopted. This was rectangular with no transepts but with the space divided longitudinally into nave and aisles, the former being roofed with wood at a higher level than the aisles and divided from them by a colonnade. One or both of the ends of the building was apsidal (see APSE). This basilican plan was one which continued to be followed in Italy, the country where the tradition had originated, and in France. In Britain Saxon churches in the south of England, built by the Canterbury Augustinian school, also followed the basilican pattern, as in Rome and, throughout the Middle Ages, some churches continued to be built in this way, but they were comparatively few. The medieval *hall churches* of Germany were also rectangular in plan and aisled but, unlike the basilica, the chief characteristic of a hall church is that the vaults or roof of aisles and nave are of equal height, so that the nave can have no triforium or clerestory, but is lit by exceptionally large aisle windows to compensate.

Saxon churches in the north of Britain, in Northumberland and County Durham, for example, were of simpler plan, consisting only of tall, aisleless naves and small rectangular chancels. These were based on the Celtic pattern and it was a style followed in small, country churches for many years.

A few churches were built in England on *centrally planned* lines, these circular buildings following the ancient traditions of many earlier cultures from the circles of standing stones, classical temples and the Roman mausoleum. A number of the Early Christian churches were circular, generally adaptations of mausolea or martyria: examples in Rome include *S. Costanza* and *S. Stefano* of the fourth and fifth centuries. In Britain these churches were built mainly in the Norman period in Anglo-Romanesque architectural style instead of classical, as in the Rome examples, but they have the same circular plan with an inner ring of arcaded columns supporting triforium walling and arcade. There is usually a conical roof over the central part above the clerestory windows and a lower roof, at triforium level, over the circular aisle. The Knights Templars and the Knights Hospitallers built most of their churches on this pattern, traditionally supposedly based upon the Rotunda of Constantine's Church of the Holy Sepulchre in Jerusalem; the *Temple Church* in *London* (1185, rebuilt after World War II) and the *Holy Sepulchre Church* at *Cambridge* (c. 1130, restored 1840s) are examples of these.

In Britain, from the eleventh century onwards and throughout the Middle Ages, the most usual plan was based on a cross, that is, it was *cruciform*. This plan, resembling Christ's cross at His Crucifixion, had one arm longer than the others and this type of design is known as a *Latin cross*. This is in distinction from the *Greek-cross plan* which has four equal arms and is more common in eastern Europe and in later Renaissance work. In a church it is the nave which occupies the longer and western arm and the chancel the eastern, shorter one. The cross-bar, the transepts, is aligned north and south and the square area where this intersects the nave-chancel axis is known as the *crossing* above which is generally constructed a tower, steeple or dome.

The *orientation* of a Christian church is with the altar at the east end of the building (though in some of the first Early Christian churches in *Rome* it was at the west as in, for example, the Church of *S. Maria Maggiore*, (432–40). The eastern arm of the church is the *chancel*, which contains the choir and the altar and was originally reserved for the clergy, though after the Reformation the chancel was opened for the receiving of Holy Communion by the congregation. The chancel was separated from the western arm, the nave, by a decorative screen known—according to the type of church—as a *chancel* or *choir screen*, *rood screen* or *pulpitum*. The word 'chancel' derives from the Latin *cancellus*, referring to the bars of lattice-work in the screen which enclosed the area. In many older churches a large stone arch marked the division between chancel and nave; this is the *chancel arch*. The eastern part of the chancel, where the altar is placed, is reserved for the clergy. This is the *sanctuary* or *presbytery* (from the Late Latin *presbyterium*, 'council of elders').

The western arm of the cruciform church is occupied by the *nave* where the congregation assembles. The word derives from the Latin *navis* (='ship') and is symbolic in that it represents the place of safe passage of souls over the stormy waters. In German the word *Schiff* is still used to designate the nave of a church, with *Hauptschiff* or *Mittelschiff* to denote the central nave as opposed to its side aisles. At the west end of the nave are generally to be found the *font* and the *stoup*. The west doorway is normally the principal entrance to the church from the exterior.

The transverse section of the cruciform church comprises the north and south transepts. In a more complex, large church there may be more than one set of transepts as at *Beverley Minster* in Yorkshire, but this is more common in Continental churches than in Britain. The *pulpit* is generally to be found on the eastern side of the north transept and the lectern in a similar position in the south transept. Transepts may be terminated apsidally though, again, this is more usual in Europe than in Britain and is most often to be found in Germany. Some churches are built with transeptal towers, of which *Exeter Cathedral* is an example.

A *cathedral* is the principal church of the diocese and is so called because it contains the bishop's throne. This

Typical medieval parish churches

Interior of nave looking east
1. Nave timber roof 2. Corbel supporting beam 3. Clerestory window 4. Aisle roof 5. Nave arcade 6. Capitals 7. Chancel arch 8. East window 9. Altar 10. Chancel screen 11. Nave piers 12. Aisle windows 13. Bases 14. Pulpit 15. Lectern

Exterior
1. Western tower 2. West end of church 3. Nave 4. Nave aisle 5. South porch 6. East end of church 7. Parapet and pinnacles 8. Porch entrance 9. Chancel 10. South transept

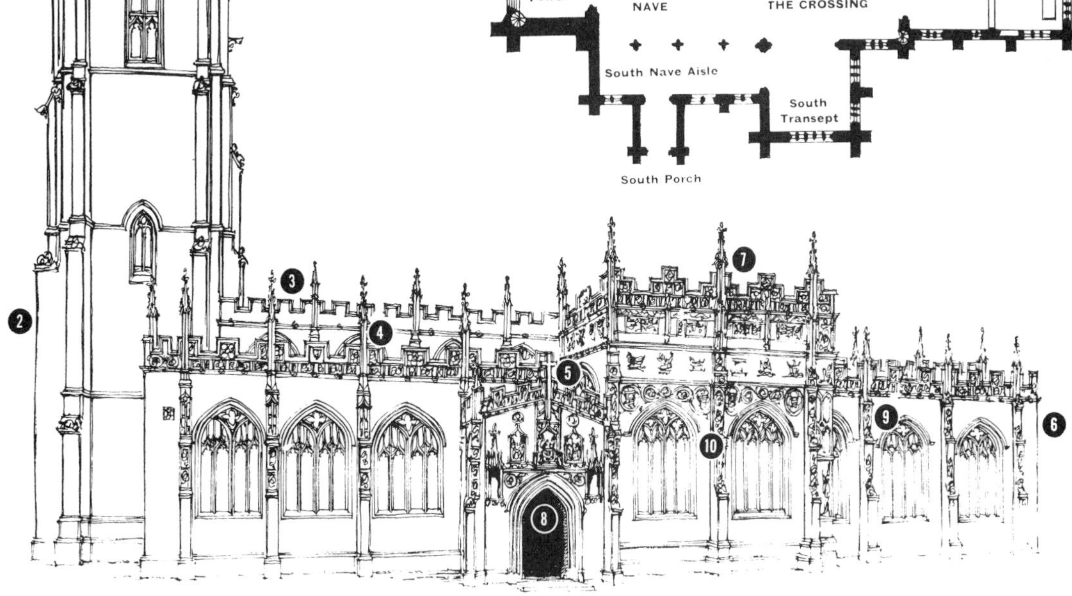

Ground plan

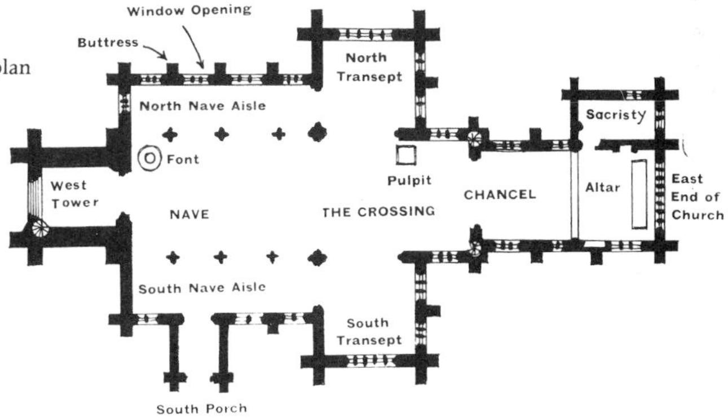

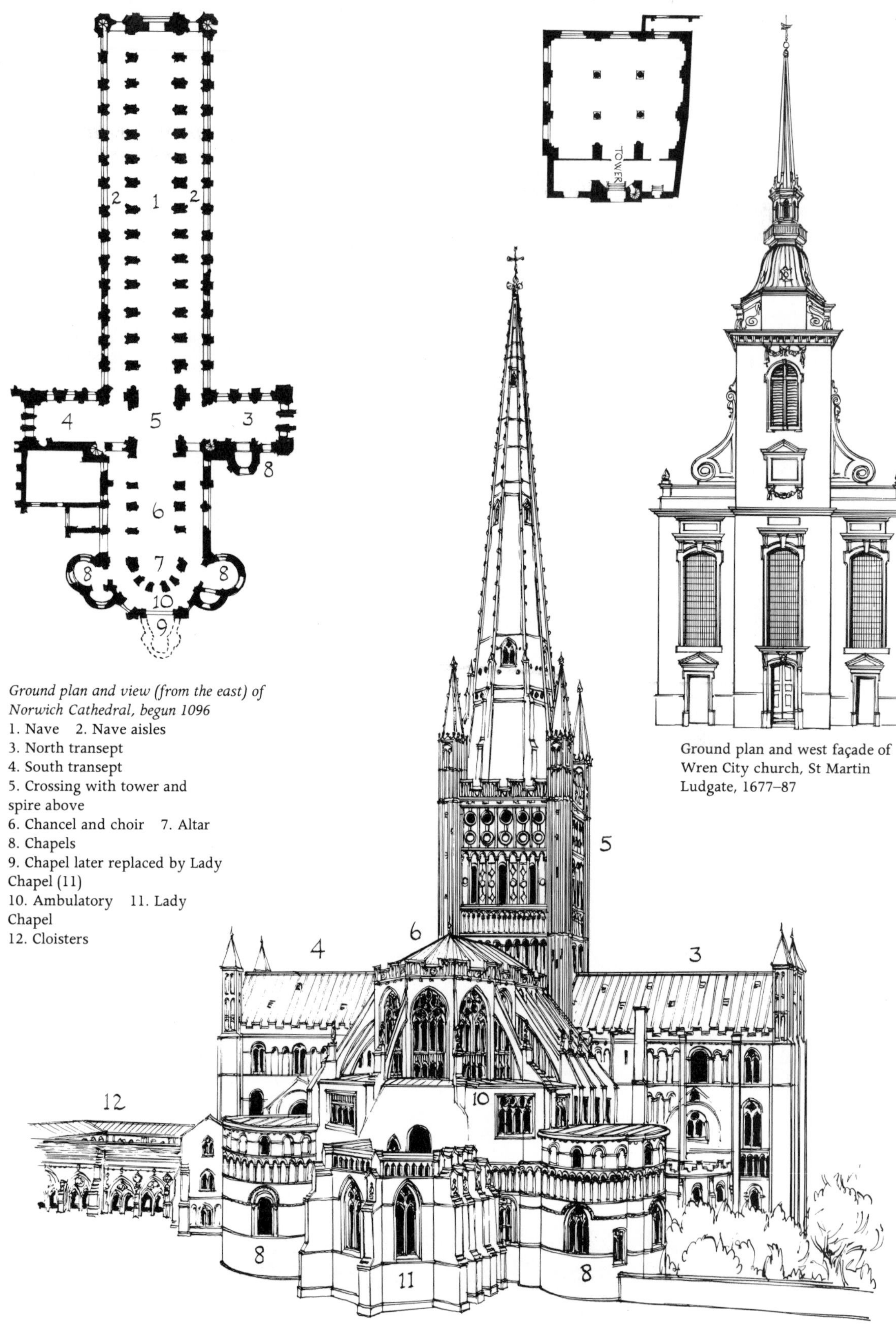

Ground plan and view (from the east) of Norwich Cathedral, begun 1096
1. Nave 2. Nave aisles
3. North transept
4. South transept
5. Crossing with tower and spire above
6. Chancel and choir 7. Altar
8. Chapels
9. Chapel later replaced by Lady Chapel (11)
10. Ambulatory 11. Lady Chapel
12. Cloisters

Ground plan and west façade of Wren City church, St Martin Ludgate, 1677–87

throne, the *cathedra*, was originally placed in the apse behind the high altar. Later in the Middle Ages it became the most imposing of the stalls of the choir. A *collegiate church* in England is similarly a large important building, one endowed for a body corporate or a chapter but with no bishop's see. A *minster* is the church of a monastery or one which has been a monastic church. The name can now also be applied to a collegiate or cathedral church of note. In Britain parish boundaries were established in Norman times and each parish had its own church ministered to by its own parish priest to whom ecclesiastical dues were paid. In later times, with increases of population, parishes were sub-divided, each new area having its own *parish church*.

In Britain many of these parish churches mirror the changes in architectural style from the time of the Normans onwards as well as illustrating the economic trends and social and ecclesiastical needs in the passing centuries. Because of their importance in medieval community life, and the consequent care and materials with which they were erected, it is ecclesiastical buildings which have survived from these early times more than secular ones. Built in the Norman age in Romanesque architectural style, of massive structure and durable materials, the great cathedral, abbey and parish churches exist all over the country. Many have Saxon foundations and fragmentary remains (more considerable in a number of instances, see SAXON ARCHITECTURE) and a quantity of building surviving from the eleventh and twelfth centuries of Norman workmanship. During the thirteenth to fifteenth centuries churches were enlarged to supply the needs of a larger population and to conform to the architectural style of the day so the majority of Norman churches show work characteristic of different centuries.

The typical English cathedral church of the eleventh and twelfth centuries developed from the Normandy pattern introduced by the Normans after the Conquest. This is cruciform, has twin western towers, a long nave and short choir (both aisled), transepts and apsidal termination to the choir and, often, to the transepts also. At this time the worship of saints was a growing custom and more chapels were needed for this in the eastern part of the cathedral. These were built out from the transepts and in the aisles of the chancel. The French solution in the rebuilding of the Abbey of Cluny in 981 was to extend the aisles eastwards past the transepts and complete these with apses to contain chapels. Alternatively, in other instances, these chancel aisles were prolonged as an ambulatory round the eastern apse (see AMBULATORY and APSE). The French developed the *chevet* from this construction in which chapels radiated from the eastern apse. *Le Mans Cathedral* in France is a classic example of this, the eastern arm being built in the thirteenth century. In England, *Norwich Cathedral* was constructed with chancel ambulatory and three radiating chapels in the twelfth century, two of which remain but the centre one was later replaced by a Lady Chapel (see CHAPEL). After 1100 the English plan began to diverge from the Continental pattern by playing down the importance of the eastern apse or apses. Sometimes the transepts were built forward with chapels also flush with the central apse and, later, the east ends of the majority of English cathedrals were altered to square terminations, Ely, Durham, Winchester, for example. Generally this was achieved by building on to the eastern arm a *Lady Chapel* or *retro-choir*. This provided greater space here but at the same time it was no longer possible to walk round the ambulatory in the chancel behind the high altar.

Inside, the cathedral church was usually designed in three horizontal stages. On the ground floor was the arcade of nave, chancel and transepts, above this was the *triforium* arcade and the third storey comprised a row of windows. These are termed *clerestory* (clearstory) windows, in distinction from the triforium arcade, which is also known as the 'blind-storey'. The clerestory windows light the building while behind the triforium arcade is a passage often extending all round the church. This backs on to the sloping roof which covers the aisles and extends from the lower part of the clerestory to the upper aisle arcade (see also BAY).

Similar styles of building and plan were attempted in parish churches but on a less ambitious scale. Some churches were very simple, consisting only of aisleless nave and chancel, others were aisled, sometimes with only one. A central tower with short spire was often built over the crossing; alternatively, some churches had western square or round towers. Many chancels were apsidal (see ROMANESQUE ARCHITECTURE).

Between 1150 and 1550 many new churches were built but also the Norman churches were enlarged and adapted to current needs. The Norman crossing tower was often replaced by a single or twin western towers and tall spires were added in a number of instances. The eastern apse was generally re-designed to give a square termination and the chancel lengthened to provide more space for chapels. Aisles were added to nave, chancel and transepts and, when these were roofed, it was often necessary to increase the height of the original walls and insert clerestory windows to light the interior. Windows were constantly being altered and enlarged in order to improve the illumination and buttress systems were adapted to provide the necessary stability (see BUTTRESS). In larger churches and cathedrals stone vaults more and more replaced timber roofs; this also required a reappraisal of the buttress system (see VAULTING).

Britain possesses a superb heritage of medieval churches (see GOTHIC ARCHITECTURE) and this is especially so of those built or enlarged in the years 1375–1550 in Perpendicular Gothic style. Many of these are very large, reflecting the prosperousness of the country and are crowned by tall, elegant towers and steeples. The structures are panelled inside and out in stone and glass and contain

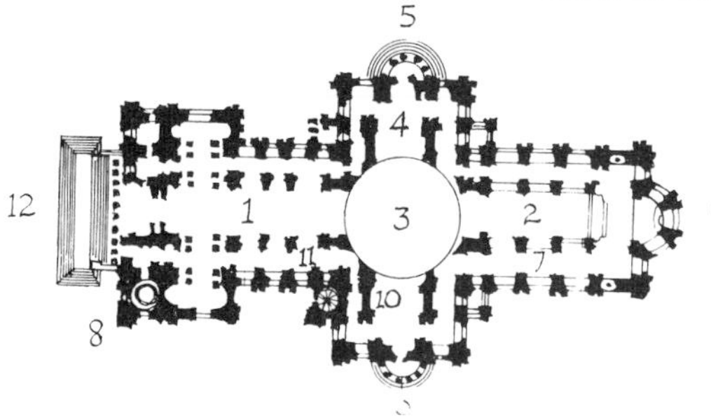

St Paul's Cathedral, London, 1675–1710, from the south-east. Architect: Sir Christopher Wren
1. Gilt cross, 365ft above ground level 2. Lantern 3. Dome 4. Drum 5. Drum parapet 6. Apsidal east end 7, 8. Western towers 9. South porch 10. South transept 11. Chancel

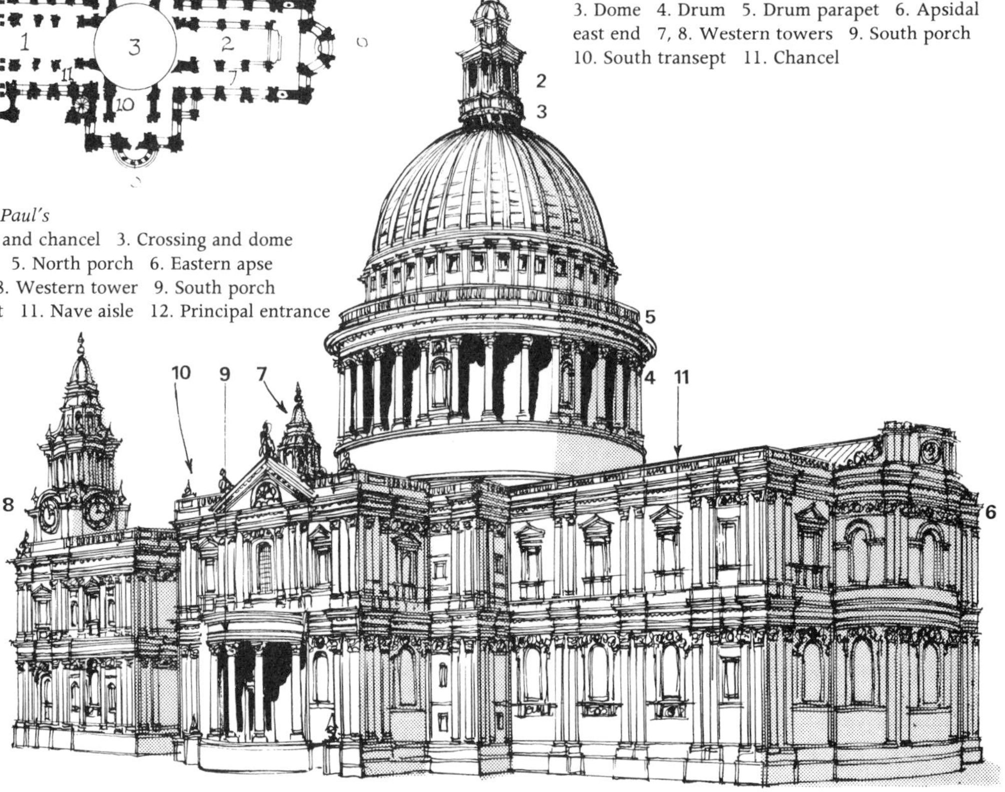

Ground plan of St Paul's
1. Nave 2. Choir and chancel 3. Crossing and dome 4. North transept 5. North porch 6. Eastern apse 7. Chancel aisle 8. Western tower 9. South porch 10. South transept 11. Nave aisle 12. Principal entrance

Interior of St Paul's Cathedral, looking east
1. Crossing and drum of dome
2. Nave
3. Piers supporting dome
4. Choir
5. Whispering gallery
6. Chancel
7. Nave ceiling
8. Nave arcade
9. Eastern apse windows
10. Pulpit
11. Nave aisle

Coventry Cathedral, 1954–62. Architect: Sir Basil Spence
1. Vaulting canopy (reinforced concrete) 2. Organ 3. Nave pier 4. The Sutherland tapestry 5. Nave aisle 6. Pulpit 7. Polished marble floor 8. Crown of thorns as canopy over choir stalls 9. High Altar

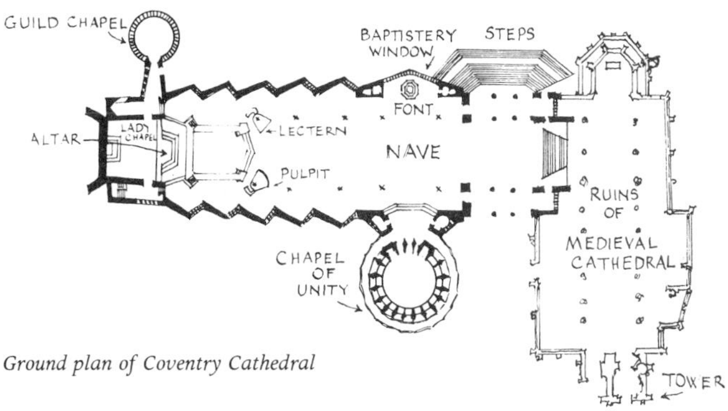

Ground plan of Coventry Cathedral

Guildford Cathedral from the south-west. Begun 1936, consecrated 1961. Architect: Sir Edward Maufe
1. West doors 2. Narthex 3. Nave 4. Nave aisle 5. South transept 6. Central tower 7. Chancel 8. South door

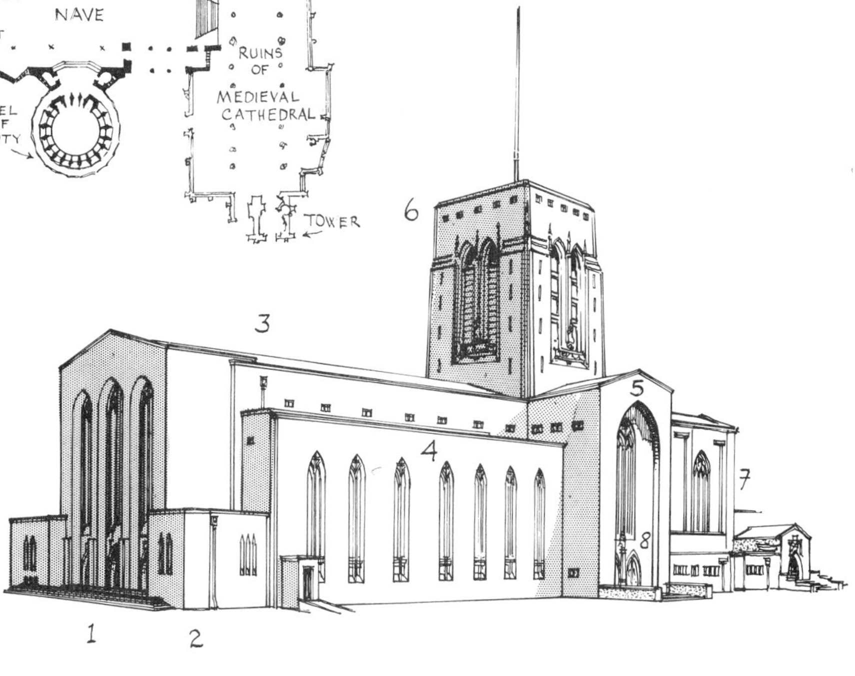

some fine carved woodwork and stonework in choir stalls, pews, monuments and fonts (see FONT; PEW; STALLS).

Few churches were built in Britain in the sixteenth and early seventeenth centuries and it was the Fire of London in 1666 which provided the opportunity for extensive church building when *Sir Christopher Wren* replaced the lost city churches. His designs were quite different from the medieval church. They were varied but were mostly in the classical style of architecture (see CLASSICAL ARCHITECTURE and RENAISSANCE ARCHITECTURE), not Gothic, and for these he returned mainly to the plan of the Roman basilica—triforium and clerestory were replaced by a simple colonnade or a gallery supported on classical columns or piers; in a number of instances the church was a simple rectangle with walls articulated by a pilastered order. Wren bore in mind that these were Protestant churches, though being re-erected on Catholic sites. He planned them simply, making the pulpit visible to everyone and placing it so that the preacher should be audible and so able to establish a rapport between himself and his congregation. These are light interiors, the large, round-headed, classical windows filled with plain glass in contrast to the earlier decorative coloured glass. While the plan and layout are simple the interior decoration is often rich, with fine carving in wood and stone and craftsmanship in glass and iron. The towers are plain but the steeples varied and picturesque. The dome was introduced in classical churches, though it was never used in England to the extent that it was on the Continent. *St Paul's Cathedral* is the chief example, the dome, supported on pendentives (see DOME), rises over the crossing of this Latin cross structure (see WREN, SIR CHRISTOPHER).

In following centuries churches were built on both classical and Gothic lines, following traditional patterns. Modern churches are simpler, using new materials and methods of construction and many show original ideas in design. The *Metropolitan Cathedral of Christ the King* in *Liverpool*, designed by *Sir Frederick Gibberd* and built 1962–7, is a successful example on cathedral scale (see GIBBERD, SIR FREDERICK).

Glossary of Terms

Those marked * are the subject of a separate article.

*Altar**

*Ambulatory**

*Antechurch**

*Apse**

*Baldacchino**

*Baptistery**

*Basilica**

*Bay**

*Bell tower**

*Bema**

Chancel: the eastern arm of a church

Chancel arch: the arch which divides the chancel from the nave or crossing.

Chancel screen: a screen erected to divide the chancel from the nave and crossing.

Chapel (including *Lady chapel* and *chantry chapel*)*

*Chapter house**

Chevet: construction of the eastern arm of a church with ambulatory and radiating chapels.

Choir (quire): the part of a church where services are sung. The term is also used more generally to refer to the eastern arm of the building.

Clerestory (clearstory): the upper storey of the church, higher than the aisle roofs, pierced by a row of windows.

Cloisters: see ABBEY*

Confessio: a recess or chamber near the altar for containing relics.

Crossing: the area where nave and choir are intersected by the transepts.

Crypt: a vaulted chamber partly or wholly underground, generally constructed beneath the chancel, to contain graves and relics. Many crypts are large chambers containing one or more altars and were made to accommodate a considerable number of pilgrims who had come to pay homage at the shrine.

*Font**

*Galilee**

*Gallery**

Greek-cross plan: that of a church with four equal arms.

*Iconostasis**

Latin-cross plan: that of a church with one arm longer than the other three.

Lectern: the reading desk or support on which the Holy Bible rests and from where passages are read aloud. Could be made of wood or stone but often of brass with the rest in the form of an eagle.

Misericord: see STALLS*

*Narthex**

Nave: the western part of the church where the congregation assembles.

Orientation: the placing of a church in relation to the points of the compass. The altar and, therefore, the chancel, are generally at the east end.

*Pew**

Presbytery: the area in the eastern part of a church where the altar is placed and reserved for clergy.

*Pulpit**

*Pulpitum**

Reredos: see ALTAR*

Retable: see ALTAR*

Retro-choir: the area behind (east of) the high altar.

Rood: a large crucifix erected at the entrance to the chancel and often flanked by a figure of the Virgin Mary at one side and St John on the other.

Rood loft: the gallery on which the rood was placed.

Rood screen: screen built below the rood loft. With the Reformation the roods and lofts were, in many cases, destroyed. The screen often remained as a chancel screen.

Sacristy: a room attached to a church where sacred vessels are kept.

Sanctuary: the holiest part of the church where the high altar is placed.
*Sedilia**
*Stalls**
Stoup: a vessel to contain holy water placed near the west door of a church. It may be free-standing or set in the wall.
Transept: the transverse arms of a cruciform church aligned north and south.
Triforium: the galleried arcade in a medieval church extending round the building at second floor level. Also termed blind-storey, as it has no windows to the exterior, being level with the aisle sloping roof.
Vestry: a room in or attached to a church where the vestments are kept and where the clergy and choir robe.

Kensington Cinema, London. Architects: Leathart and Granger, 1926

CINEMA ARCHITECTURE In the years between the two World Wars the rapid growth of the cinema industry created a new form of architecture based on need and function. Picture houses were being built in large numbers in the USA from 1910 onwards but in Britain it was not until after 1920 that purpose-built cinemas were being constructed; before this cinemas were converted music halls or theatres. For the first few years after this even new cinemas were based on the layout of the music hall or theatre and were eclectic in architectural design, using varied source material from classical to Chinese or Assyrian and, especially, Egyptian. Historical origins were adapted and mixed to provide an often garish and extravagant result, especially in interior decoration. One of the first of the new cinemas was the *Regent* at *Brighton* (1921, by *Robert Atkinson*). This was followed by *Frank Verity's Shepherd's Bush Pavilion* in London (1923), which had a more modern exterior and set the pattern for the beginning of an architectural form especially suited to the needs of the cinema.

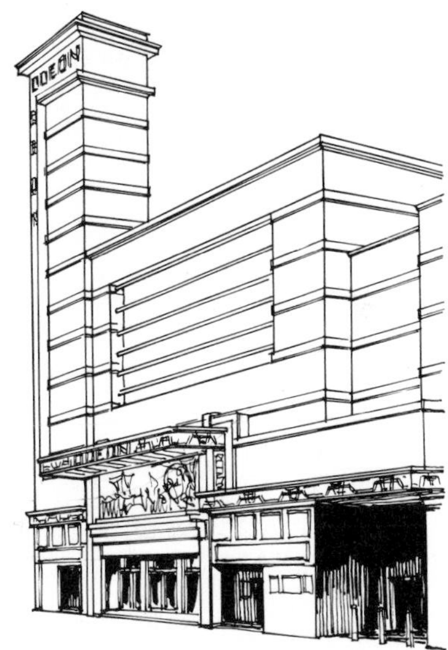

The Odeon Cinema, Leicester Square, London. Architect: Harry Weedon, 1937

The architectural firm of *J. R. Leathart* and *W. F. Granger* designed a number of cinemas in the 1920s. Their work was modern but not ultra so. The interior concept remained traditional but the exterior was more streamlined. Their *Kensington Cinema* of 1926 is characteristic of the time, basically classical but with a minimum of decoration. Their *Twickenham Cinema* and *Sheen Cinema* (demolished) of the years 1929 and 1930 were plainer still on the exterior. Their *Richmond Cinema* followed the American pattern inside in creating an ambitious illusion, in this case of a Moorish courtyard open to the sky, the illusion fostered by cleverly arranged changes of coloured lighting from concealed sources.

Regent Cinema, Bournemouth (later Gaumont), 1927

In Britain the tempo of cinema building increased until 1930, when the depression curtailed construction for a year or so, but after 1934 building accelerated. The years 1928–38 were the age of the super-cinema. These were built larger and larger, veritable cathedrals, to accommodate greater audiences in comfort, with ever more lavish interior décor, often in questionable taste. The quantity of cinema construction in Britain was second only to that in America; every town and village had its cinema.

In London, impressive, large-scale structures were erected, *Frank Verity's Carlton, Haymarket* (1927) and *Lamb* and *Matcham's Empire, Leicester Square* (1928, but now demolished), for example. Further afield came the *Regent, Bournemouth* and the *Playhouse, Glasgow,* the latter seating over 4000 and a record size for its date. The big circuits began to build their own cinemas. The *Astorias* in London, designed by *Edward Stone,* were closely modelled on the American pattern. They were designed to suit the London suburbs and were large and impressive, contrasting blatantly with their drab surroundings. Typical were those at *Brixton, Streatham* and the *Old Kent Road,* all 1929–30. Their architectural inspiration was not original—it was Egyptian, Italian Renaissance or Moorish Spain, larger than life and lacking sophistication. *Granada* followed. Also eclectic, this series of buildings was even larger-scale, with elaborate plaster decoration inside in high relief, taken from sources as far afield as Cordova palaces and the Gothic Revival. Characteristic were those at *Tooting* and *Woolwich* of the late 1930s. On an immense scale were *George Cole's Trocadero* at the *Elephant and Castle* (1930, now demolished) and *Robert Cromie's Gaumont Palace* at *Hammersmith Broadway* (1932, now Odeon). Both of these were monumental but the former was chiefly Italianate, the latter remains cleanly modern.

British cinema design remained closely allied to the American prototype. It was on the Continent and, especially, in Germany that a more original line was followed. These were smaller cinemas than the American and British ones but were of better architectural design and a higher standard of interior decoration. Aesthetically the buildings were more original and interesting. Typical of such work in the 1920s were *Hans Poelzig's Capitol Cinema* and *Erich Mendelsohn's Universum Cinema,* both in *Berlin.* From the mid-1930s, National Socialism discouraged such 'decadent' modern themes.

It was the *Odeon* circuit in Britain which produced a range of cinema designs which were characteristic and unusual, so that an Odeon cinema was recognizable by its single tower and plain, tiled façade. Most notable is the *Odeon, Leicester Square,* its black granite structure erected on the site of the old Alhambra Theatre (1937). This is a classic instance of a building designed for illuminated advertising which, at night, becomes the whole feature as the black façade fades into the darkness. Other interesting Odeon designs include those at *York* and *Colwyn Bay* (1936) and *Morecambe* (1937) all built under the aegis of the Harry Weedon design office at Birmingham. By the 1930s, following the Odeon example, modern architecture became accepted for cinema design and structures such as the *New Victoria Cinema* (1930) and the *Curzon Cinema, Mayfair* (1934, now demolished) by Burnet, Tait and Lorne were less vigorously criticized. Less severe, but of characteristic design of the period, was *Margate's Dreamland* (1934) by *Iles, Leathart and Granger.* Made in a variety of materials, this was designed satisfactorily to withstand the atmospheric conditions of its exposed seafront site.

British cinema-building before the Second World War predominantly utilized steel construction, especially for the balcony, stage and proscenium. The widespread use of reinforced concrete was rare. A number of materials were used for building but facing included a variety of coloured materials such as faience tiles, glazed terracotta, concrete slabs, black vitrolite and glass mosaic. Inside, the super cinema was generally designed with a single, wide balcony. Smaller examples had rising tiers of seats. Lighting was generally concealed or indirect. Interior decoration tended to be over-elaborate, even 'marzipan', but the exteriors, by the 1930s, were often very plain and vehicles for large-scale advertising—a trend which has increased in post-war years.

The cinema has had to adapt, since 1955, to television competition. Few new cinemas of note have been built; the general trend has been towards the sub-division of existing cinema buildings. Of interest among the few new large-scale ventures has been the use of reinforced concrete as in, for example, *T. P. Bennett's Marble Arch Odeon* as part of an extensive mixed development (1966) and a similar project at the *Elephant and Castle,* where *Ernö Goldfinger* has constructed his new *Odeon* on the site of the old Trocadero (1966). This is notably original in the spatial handling of the material.

CITADEL A fortress commanding a city. Alternatively, an inner fortified city, generally sited upon an eminence, round which the city later expands.

CIVIC ARCHITECTURE During the Middle Ages the guildhall and the market hall were centres of commercial and administrative activity in the towns of Britain. These were important buildings and so were made of durable materials and reflected the current architectural style. Because of this—it was customary to rebuild from time to time as the architectural mode changed—and because they were constructed on costly sites in the centre of towns, not many examples survive without considerable alteration. The *Guildhalls* of *London* and *York* were superb examples of their kind but both have been altered over the years and were largely rebuilt after devastation in the Second World War. More examples survive from small towns in rural areas, for instance the half-timber structure at *Lavenham,* Suffolk (*c.* 1529) and the Elizabethan market hall at *Rothwell,* Northamptonshire. The *tolbooth,* especially in Scotland, survives in a number of instances as a picturesque feature of the town's main street. This was the forerunner of the town hall. Here taxes and tolls were collected; it also contained a court room and cells below for debtors. *Edinburgh's Canongate Tolbooth* (1592) is an interesting example.

The Market House, Tetbury, Gloucestershire, 1700

The Guildhall, Lavenham, Suffolk. Half-timber, *c.* 1529

Lewisham Town Hall, 1931, Architects: Bradshaw, Gass and Hope

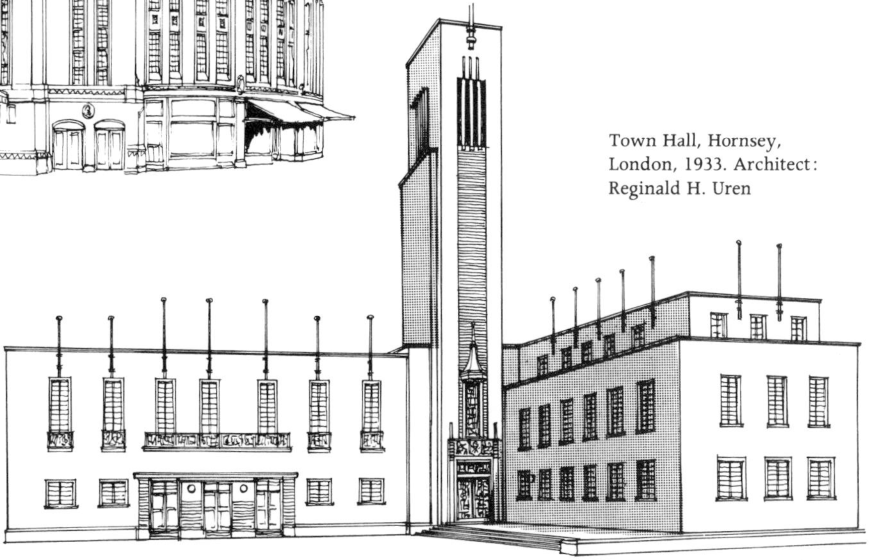

Town Hall, Hornsey, London, 1933. Architect: Reginald H. Uren

The City Centre, Cardiff, 1897–1920. Architects: Lanchester, Stewart and Rickards

By the later seventeenth century town and city halls were being erected to accommodate the administrative needs of the town as well as custom houses, exchanges, market halls and guildhalls. From this time onwards a monumental classical style of architecture chiefly prevailed for such important structures though, in rural areas, a less formal classicism was sometimes adopted. From the seventeenth and eighteenth centuries *Abingdon Town Hall* (1677–80), the *Custom House* at *King's Lynn* (1681, see BELL, HENRY), the *Mansion House, London* (1739–53, see DANCE, GEORGE) and the *Guildhall* in *Bath* (1775–6, see BALDWIN, THOMAS) are examples of the former and *Amersham Town Hall*, Buckinghamshire, *Tetbury Market House*, Gloucestershire (1700) and *High Wycombe Guildhall*, Buckinghamshire (*c.* 1757–60) of the latter. One of the most impressive civic structures of the eighteenth century is *Somerset House* in London (1778–86, see CHAMBERS, SIR WILLIAM). During the eighteenth century the town hall was, more and more, expected to accommodate a court-house and necessary offices in addition to commercial and administrative needs. Several notable examples in neo-classical and Greek Revival design survive, the latter based upon the temple form. Imposing and characteristic are *St George's Hall, Liverpool* (begun 1839, see ELMES, HARVEY LONSDALE) and *Birmingham Town Hall* (begun 1831, see HANSOM, JOSEPH ALOYSIUS).

It was in the second half of the nineteenth century that a great number of immense and imposing town and city halls were erected all over Britain. The tremendous and rapid increase of population and the acceleration of the movement of the work-force from country to town made such administrative centres necessary. Some of these town halls were ugly and tasteless, but some (and a number survive) were fine architectural schemes. Many were built in a classical style, notably *Leeds* (see BRODRICK, CUTHBERT), *Halifax* (see BARRY, SIR CHARLES) and *Sheffield* (1891–6, see MOUNTFORD, EDWARD WILLIAM). Some Gothic Revival architects countered the convention and built in

Northampton Town Hall, 1864. Architect: E. W. Godwin

Gothic. Many of the largest and most dramatic of such town halls are in the industrial cities of the north of England. The most famous of these is *Manchester's* magnificent town hall (1869, see WATERHOUSE, ALFRED). Others include those at *Rochdale* (1866–71 by *W. H. Crossland*), *Chester* (1865–9 by *W. H. Lynn*), *Middlesbrough* (1883–8, by *G. G. Hoskins*) and *Bradford* (1869–73) where the architects were *Lockwood* and *Mawson*, builders of Sir Titus Salt's mill and houses at nearby *Saltaire* (see TOWN PLANNING). *Northampton* and *Congleton* town halls represent the less imposing Gothic approach (1864, see GODWIN, EDWARD WILLIAM).

Civic centres and buildings in the twentieth century have faithfully mirrored the changing architectural fashions. In *Cardiff*, at the turn of the century, the city centre was laid out with buildings of grand Baroque style (after the Paris Grand and Petit Palais) by *Lanchester, Stewart and Rickards*, who were also responsible for the smaller *Deptford Town Hall* in London (1902). Equally successful but in marked contrast, reflecting the extreme plainness of the late 1920s and early 1930s, is the *City Hall* at *Swansea*, South Wales (see THOMAS, SIR PERCY). In classical mode is the *London County Hall*, fronting the Thames near Westminster Bridge and noted for its central convex colonnade (1912–22, *Ralph Knott*). In the emasculated classicism so typical of the early 1930s in Britain is *Vincent Harris's Civic Hall* at *Leeds*. Also typical, but displaying more originality and less dependence on past themes now exhausted, is *Lewisham Town Hall* (1931, *Bradshaw, Gass and Hope*) and *Reginald Uren's* design at *Hornsey* (1933–5). Post-war civic structures have followed the modern architectural trends but, in Britain, these have not excited significant interest (see also TOWN PLANNING).

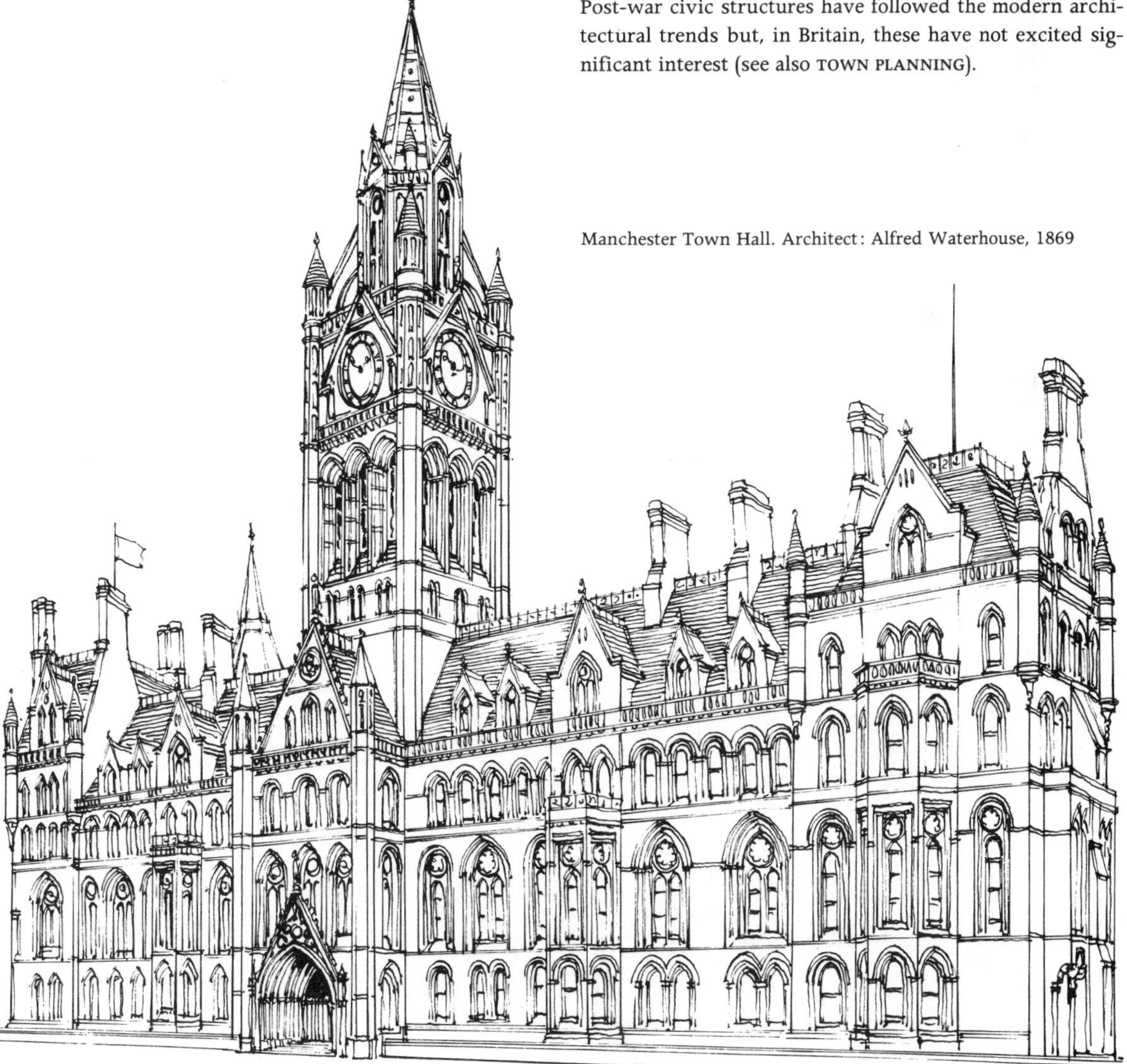

Manchester Town Hall. Architect: Alfred Waterhouse, 1869

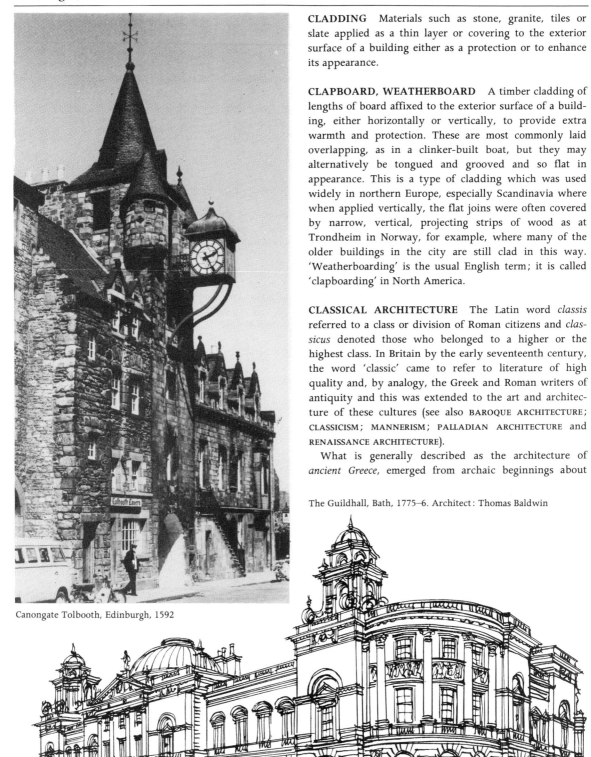

Canongate Tolbooth, Edinburgh, 1592

CLADDING Materials such as stone, granite, tiles or slate applied as a thin layer or covering to the exterior surface of a building either as a protection or to enhance its appearance.

CLAPBOARD, WEATHERBOARD A timber cladding of lengths of board affixed to the exterior surface of a building, either horizontally or vertically, to provide extra warmth and protection. These are most commonly laid overlapping, as in a clinker-built boat, but they may alternatively be tongued and grooved and so flat in appearance. This is a type of cladding which was used widely in northern Europe, especially Scandinavia where when applied vertically, the flat joins were often covered by narrow, vertical, projecting strips of wood as at Trondheim in Norway, for example, where many of the older buildings in the city are still clad in this way. 'Weatherboarding' is the usual English term; it is called 'clapboarding' in North America.

CLASSICAL ARCHITECTURE The Latin word *classis* referred to a class or division of Roman citizens and *classicus* denoted those who belonged to a higher or the highest class. In Britain by the early seventeenth century, the word 'classic' came to refer to literature of high quality and, by analogy, the Greek and Roman writers of antiquity and this was extended to the art and architecture of these cultures (see also BAROQUE ARCHITECTURE; CLASSICISM; MANNERISM; PALLADIAN ARCHITECTURE and RENAISSANCE ARCHITECTURE).

What is generally described as the architecture of *ancient Greece*, emerged from archaic beginnings about

The Guildhall, Bath, 1775–6. Architect: Thomas Baldwin

CLAPBOARD, WEATHERBOARD Weatherboarded houses in Sandvick, Bergen in Norway

700 BC and reached its highest point in beauty and quality in the mid-fifth century BC. Many fine buildings dated from the later Hellenistic period even after 146 BC when Greece became a subject state of Rome, but in quality the later fifth-century work was never surpassed. Remains of Greek structures include temples, theatres, stadia, town fortifications, stoas and other civic buildings. These show the preference of Greek builders for the *trabeated* form of architecture (from Latin *trabes*, ='beam'). This type of construction, often called post-and-lintel, consists of vertical supports (in this case, columns) and horizontal beams or blocks of stone or marble. From the early discovery that a lintel stone supported on two columns could form an opening, the colonnade evolved, in which a row of columns would carry a long, extended lintel and so form the exterior elevation of a building. Greek architecture was suited to the climate and mode of life, which was outdoor in character. Colonnades supported porticoes and roofs and these gave shelter from the hot sun and sudden rainstorms. Windows were unimportant but doorways were finely proportioned, simply designed rectangles. Vaults and arches were rarely constructed. Roofs were generally of timber, covered by terracotta or marble tiles and interior ceilings were of coffered marble. The roof pitch was low (the climate made a steeper pitch unnecessary) and the rake of the end pediments was determined by this, which gave the pleasing proportions characteristic of the low Greek pediments which differ from the steeper, later northern European, Renaissance examples.

The beauty of Greek architecture derives not from its diversity of form, for this is limited and very simple, but from its subtle and detailed attention to proportion and line. The Greeks developed a system of *orders* wherein the proportions of the individual parts were studied and crystallized (see CLASSICAL ORDER and CLASSICAL ORNAMENT). The prime feature of Greek architecture is its intellectual quality. The Greeks did not show a great desire for innovation. They developed to an intensely high degree a standard of architectural perfection.

Part of this striving for excellence was the development of a series of refinements of line, mass and curve the purpose of which was to give to a building vitality and plasticity and to make it appear to be correctly delineated. For the true horizontal and vertical line, particularly when silhouetted against a brilliantly blue sky, appears concave to the human eye. To offset this illusion the Greeks created a convex line and form so subtle and

The Acropolis, Athens. Left to right: Propylaeum, Temple of Athena Nike, Erechtheion, Parthenon

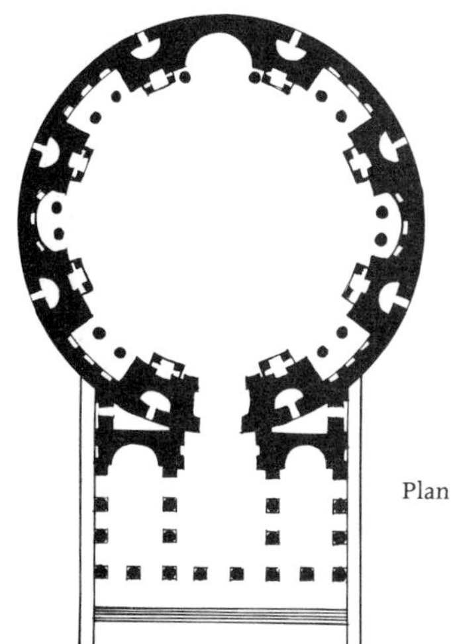

minutely calculated as to appear to be a straight vertical or horizontal. In the Parthenon in Athens, the finest illustration, all 'horizontal' and 'vertical' lines are curved to counteract this visual illusion—from columns, stylobate and entablature down to the abaci of the Doric capitals. The curves are not arcs of a circle but parabolas and the correctional refinement is very small; for instance, the stylobate rises four-and-a-quarter inches in a length of 228ft. Columns diminish in diameter from bottom to top but also have an *entasis* whose widest point is about one

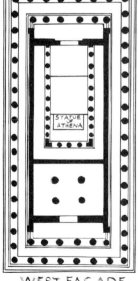

Plan and interior of the Pantheon, Rome, AD 120 onwards

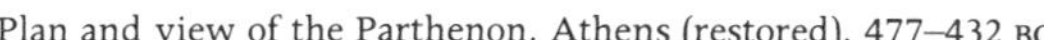

Plan and view of the Parthenon, Athens (restored), 477–432 BC

third of the way up from the base (the term derives from the Greek word for distension). Each flute curves in tune with the general entasis which is about three-quarters of an inch for a height of 34ft. The column spacing also varies (see COLUMN); the outside columns are closer together than the ones nearer the centre in a colonnade or portico and angle columns are generally wider than their neighbours. This is because a silhouetted column appears narrower than one with a similar-toned background. All the columns incline slightly inwards as do the faces of the entablature and pediments in order to lend a pyramidal form to the building. These refinements were costly to produce and are only to be found to this exactitude on such important buildings.

In early times the Greeks built with sun-dried bricks, terracotta, wood and stone. Later, stone and marble were the chief materials. In Greece itself most of the important buildings were made of marble, chiefly Pentelic and Hymettian from the mountains behind Athens, Parian from the island of Paros and the grey Eleusian from Eleusis. In areas where limestone and conglomerate had to be used, as at Paestum in southern Italy, the Greeks coated the material with a stucco made from powdered white marble. Colour was widely used on the exterior and interior of buildings for decorative purposes. The Greeks rarely used mortar but fitted the blocks of stone and marble with utmost care, using metal dowels and cramps to hold them together. The drums of the columns were so finely fitted that the joints were barely visible. Stone and marble walls were built in large blocks without mortar and the lowest course was generally twice as high as the others. Sometimes hollow wall construction was employed to reduce weight or economize in material.

The Roman civilization under the Republic continued building in the Greek tradition during the Hellenistic period (*c.* 300–27BC), though the architectural form was influenced from the Middle East and there was greater variety in style and function of building. The Romans also built in the trabeated manner and used the *orders,* adapting the Greek ones and adding further variations (see CLASSICAL ORDER and CLASSICAL ORNAMENT). The Romans adapted the trabeated construction to suit their more complex needs. Under the Roman Empire (27BC–476AD) they increasingly incorporated the arch and vault into their architectural style, using both structural forms in one building, which enabled them to construct four or five storeys to the Greek one or two. In Greek trabeated architecture, the length of the lintel determined the intercolumniation (distance between the columns). As the Romans turned more and more towards arcuated construction, using the orders in a decorative capacity, there was no such restriction and columns are sometimes separated by a distance as great as their height. In multi-storeyed buildings they frequently used a different order on each storey, lining the columns up one above the other, the entablatures acting as string courses. The Colosseum shows the fine architectural effect that such a system can provide (see AMPHITHEATRE).

Roman orders, mouldings and ornament are generally coarser and more heavily enriched than the Greek and their building proportions less subtle. The Romans lacked the superb artistic sense of the Greeks and never reached the standard of perfection to be seen in the Parthenon. Their outstanding abilities lay elsewhere—in their engineering achievements in vaulting such constructions as the *Basilica of Maxentius* and the *Baths of Diocletian,* in the building of amphitheatres such as the *Colosseum* and in schemes on a great scale as evidenced in the *Palace of Diocletian* in Split and *Hadrian's Villa* at *Tivoli.* It is in such works that the Roman genius for architectural effect and scale in planning can be appreciated (see AMPHITHEATRE; AQUEDUCT; ARCH; BASILICA; CIRCUS).

The Romans were fortunate in the wide availability of building materials in Italy. Much of their work was in brick (see BRICKWORK) and concrete faced, in republican times chiefly with stucco and, under the empire, with marble. A useful selection of stone was to hand: travertine from the Tivoli area and tufa and peperino, both of volcanic origin. These were all used in large blocks for strong walling and arch voussoirs (see STONE). The material which, more than any other, influenced the whole course and design of Roman architecture was *concrete* and this made the vaulting of huge spans possible (see CONCRETE and VAULTING). The exceptional strength and durability of Roman concrete was due to the substance *pozzolana,* a volcanic ash, found in quantity in the volcanic areas around Rome and Naples and named after Pozzuli near Naples where the best quality supplies were available. *Pozzolana,* when mixed with the excellent lime from the local limestones, formed an extremely hard concrete to which base was added brick and travertine fragments to provide a solid core for walling and vaulting. With brick reinforcement, the concrete was poured between boards to make walls and over centering for arches and vaults. The increasing use of concrete as structural material led to a more daring development of domed circular temples. Here, the Pantheon in Rome is the supreme example. In continuous use, first as a temple, later as a church, this remarkable building has survived, its interior a masterpiece of construction and lighting effect. The only source of daylight is the central unglazed oculus. The concrete coffered dome (142ft diameter), supported on brick-faced concrete walls reinforced by brick relieving arches, diminishes in thickness to a mere 4ft at crown.

Marble was not in general use in Rome until the early days of empire, hence Augustus' boast that he found Rome a city of bricks but left it a city of marble. Even so the marble was a veneer and the bricks were still present underneath. From about 25 BC Italian quarries were developed—especially Carrara, Cipollino and Pavonazzo—to provide marbles, while marbles were also imported

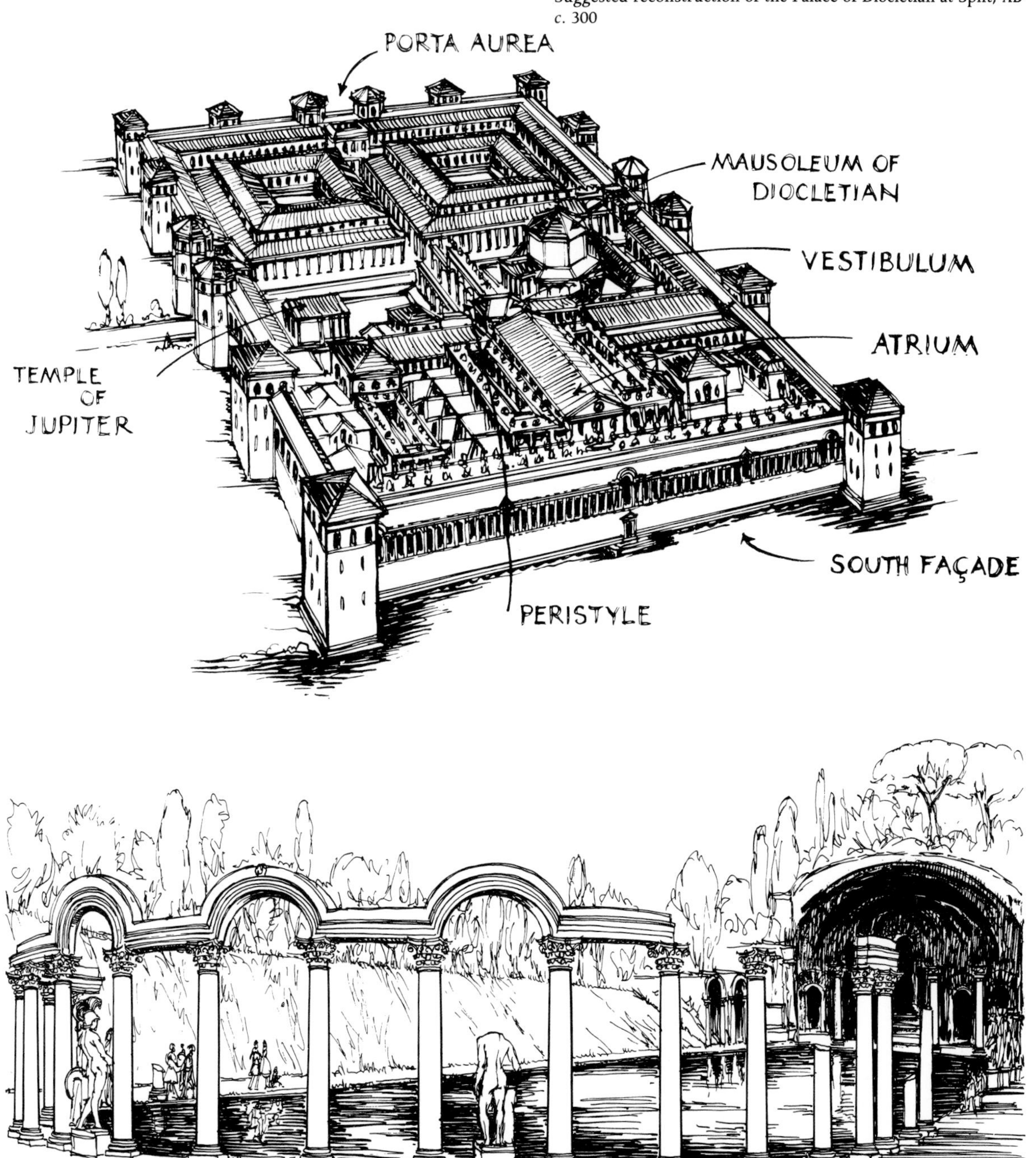

Suggested reconstruction of the Palace of Diocletian at Split, AD *c.* 300

Hadrian's Villa Tivoli. Canal of Canopus and Temple of Serapis AD 118–138

from all over the empire, notably from Greece, as well as granite, alabaster and porphyry. As in ancient Greece, a marble stucco was applied to brick and concrete structures.

For further information on classical architecture see also ASTYLAR; BLOCKING COURSE; CLASSICAL ORDER; CLASSICAL ORNAMENT; CLASSICISM; COLONNADE; COLUMN; PEDESTAL; PEDIMENT; PODIUM; PORTICO; PROPYLAEUM; ROMAN BATHS; ROMAN DOMESTIC ARCHITECTURE; STOA; STYLOBATE; TEMPLE; TOWN PLANNING; TRIUMPHAL ARCH; TYMPANUM; XYSTUS.

CLASSICAL ORDER
Greek Doric capital, Parthenon, Athens

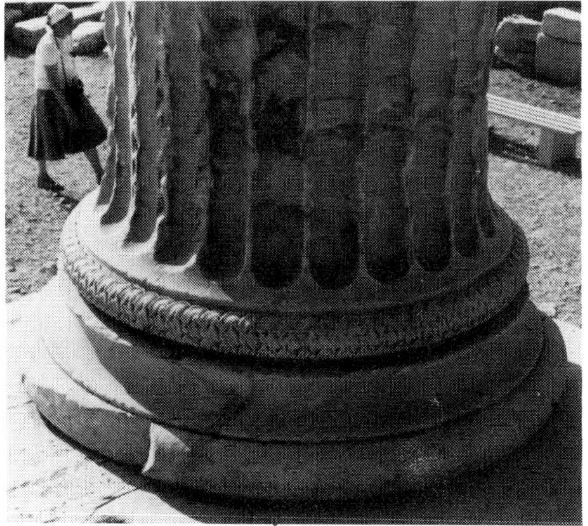

Attic base, Erechtheion west porch, Athens

Metope, Parthenon, Athens, 447–432 BC: Lapith and Centaur

CLASSICAL ORDER All the countries in Europe as well as those in the New World have, for long periods in their architectural history, used a system of 'orders' in classical architecture, a system first devised by the Greeks, adapted by the Romans and revived with the Renaissance. It is a formula which has survived, though later modified, for some 2500 years and was still in use in the early twentieth century. The term 'order' refers to a grouped number of parts which, in Greek architecture, were evolved in three designs: Doric, Ionic, Corinthian. Each order consists of an upright column or support (see CARYATID and COLUMN) which, in most instances, has a *base* at the foot. It has a *capital* at the head, upon which is supported a horizontal lintel. This last member, called the *entablature*, is divided into three parts; the lowest member is the *architrave*, the centre member the *frieze* and at the top is the *cornice*. Each order possesses specific relative proportions between its parts, and certain distinguishing features and mouldings peculiar to itself. The size of a building does not affect these proportions which remain constant and the differing scale does not impair the perfection of such proportions. The Greeks never used a part of one order with a part of another or, except in Hellenistic times, employed more than one order on a building façade, though they might use one for the exterior and another for the interior. The proportions of the orders were developed by trial and error over a long period of time. Earlier Greek examples of the seventh and sixth centuries BC have massive columns, capitals and entablatures and narrow intercolumniations. Later, fifth- and fourth-century buildings have slender columns, wider intercoluminations and mouldings and curved forms are more refined. Evidence of this can be seen by comparing the echinus in a Doric capital from the temples at *Paestum* or *Agrigento* with those of the *Parthenon*. The former are more bulbous, almost semicircular in section, the latter of a most subtle, flatter silhouette. The Greeks preferred the Doric Order and used it on the Greek mainland particularly for large buildings and exterior work. The Ionic Order is seen more frequently in eastern, colonial areas, especially in Asia Minor and the Aegean islands.

The Greek Doric order

This is the most massive of the Greek orders and the one upon which the Greeks lavished most care. The columns are placed close together and have no bases but stand directly on the stylobate (see TEMPLE). As in all Greek orders the shaft is fluted, in this case in shallow, subtle arcs divided by arrises. The number of flutes per column varies; in the ideal design such as the *Parthenon* there are 20 but a greater or smaller number is used according to material and proportion; for example, at *Paestum* in the *Temple of Hera* there are 24 while in the *Temple of Poseidon* at *Sounion* only 16. Including the capital the column has a height of four to six-and-a-half times the base diameter and, in general, the earlier the building the thicker the column. The *capital* consists of a square *abacus* at the top and below this a curved *echinus* and *annulets* or annular rings. Below this is the *necking*, then a groove called the *hypotrachelium*.

The *entablature*, usually about a quarter the height of the order, has a plain *architrave* and a *cornice* which projects strongly and under whose soffit are flat blocks called *mutules* set one over each triglyph and one between; they have each 18 *guttae* in three rows beneath. The *frieze* of the Doric Order is distinctive; it is divided into *triglyphs* and *metopes*. The triglyphs are most usually placed one over the centre of each column and one between (a *monotriglyph* design), except at the angles where, the columns being closer together, the external triglyph is placed at the extreme edge of the frieze and not over the centre of the angle column. The triglyph is carved with flutes or channels, called *glyphs*, and the spaces between are *shanks*. If there are only two glyphs it is termed a diglyph. An alternative variation includes a *ditriglyph* design where there are two triglyphs between columns. The metopes are the spaces between triglyphs; these were rectangular in early examples and square in later ones. These are often decorated with sculptural groups, as in the *Parthenon*, so many of whose metopes are on display in the British Museum and the Louvre. These metope sculptures, together with the pedimental groups, constitute the beauty of the Greek Doric Order which epitomizes the ideal union of simple, perfectly proportioned architectural masses relieved by sculptural decoration. The frieze is separated from the architrave by a narrow fillet moulding called the *tenia*, while below each triglyph is another moulding, the *regulus*, from each of which six guttae depend.

The Greek Ionic order

This order is generally a later development than the Doric but early prototypes have been found, particularly in Asia Minor, from where the *Aeolian capital* (from Aeolis in north-west Asia Minor) stems. This has two volutes with palmette between, flattened to accommodate the architrave. Below, the echinus is formed by a water lily shape. This design is related to both Egyptian and Syrian capitals. The true Ionic capital dates from the late sixth century and has two scroll volutes (see VOLUTE), based upon a shell formation or that of an animal's horns, which face the front elevation, though in an angle column the corner volute may face outwards at an angle. Below this is an *echinus* moulding with egg-and-dart enrichment. The necking is sometimes, as in the *Erechtheion*, decorated with anthemion ornament (see CLASSICAL ORNAMENT).

The order is proportioned differently from the Doric; it has a much slenderer column, in height about nine diameters, carved into 24 flutes of semicircular section separated by fillets not arrises, and it is completed by a moulded base which is often enriched by carving. Often, but not

COMPARATIVE ORDERS

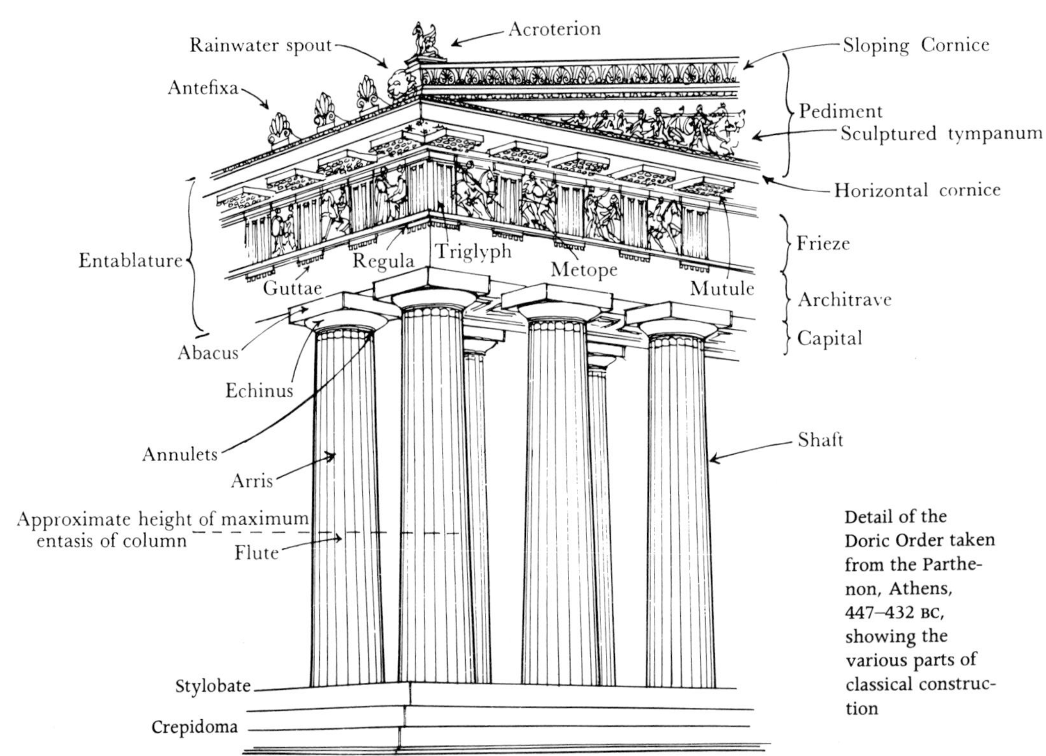

Detail of the Doric Order taken from the Parthenon, Athens, 447–432 BC, showing the various parts of classical construction

Roman Corinthian: The Pantheon, Rome, AD 120

Roman Composite: Arch of Titus, Rome, AD 81

Italian Baroque Doric/Tuscan: St Peter's Piazza, Rome. Architect: Bernini, 1656–67

Italian Renaissance, Doric: S. Pietro in Montorio, Rome. Architect: Bramante, 1500

Italian Renaissance, Corinthian: Il Gesù, Rome, Architect: Della Porta, 1573

Italian Baroque, Composite: S. Agnese, Rome. Architect: Borromini, 1645

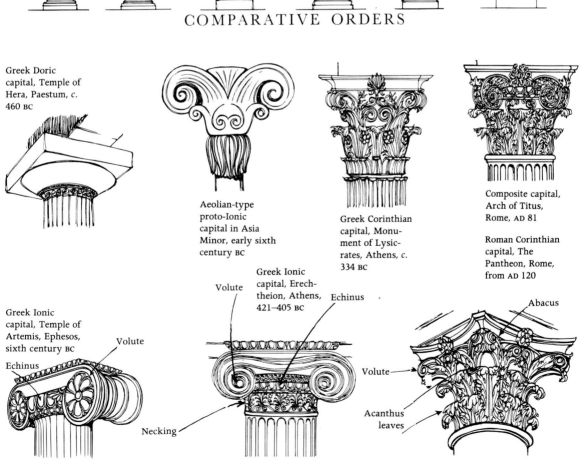

Greek Doric capital, Temple of Hera, Paestum, *c.* 460 BC

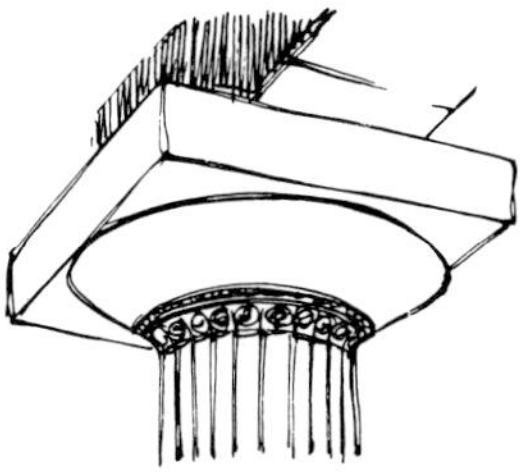

Aeolian-type proto-Ionic capital in Asia Minor, early sixth century BC

Greek Corinthian capital, Monument of Lysicrates, Athens, *c.* 334 BC

Composite capital, Arch of Titus, Rome, AD 81

Roman Corinthian capital, The Pantheon, Rome, from AD 120

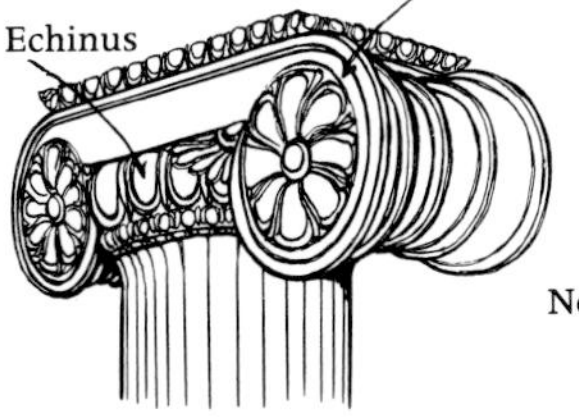

Greek Ionic capital, Erechtheion, Athens, 421–405 BC

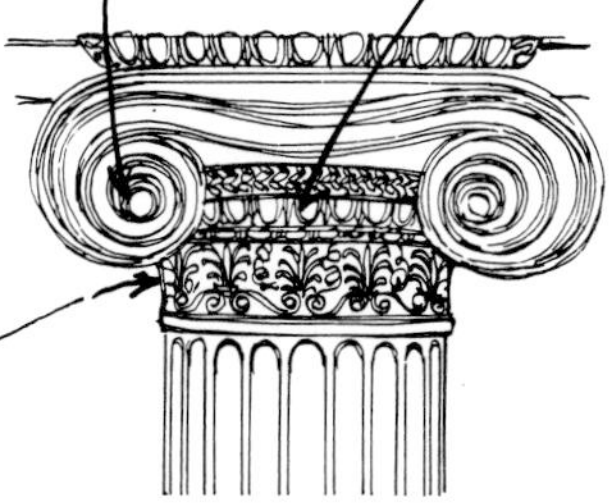

Greek Ionic capital, Temple of Artemis, Ephesos, sixth century BC

Volute

Echinus

Volute

Echinus

Necking

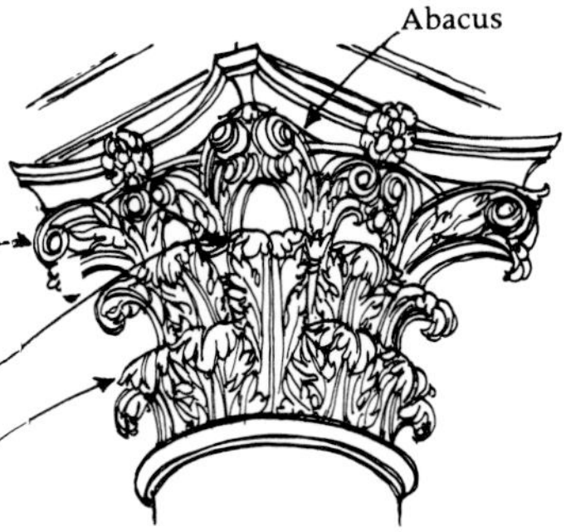

Abacus

Volute

Acanthus leaves

always, this is an *Attic base*, that is one with two convex rounded mouldings, the lower one larger than the upper, separated by a broad, concave moulding. The former are torus mouldings, the latter scotia (see MOULDINGS).

The *entablature* is less deep, generally one-fifth of the whole order, and has an *architrave* set forward in a three-plane fascia, a *frieze* without triglyphs or metopes but often decorated by a continuous band of sculpture as in, for example, the *Erechtheion*, and a *cornice* of smaller projection than the Doric, without mutules, but generally with dentil ornament, surmounted by a corona and cyma recta moulding (see CLASSICAL ORNAMENT and MOULDINGS). The order is graceful and well-proportioned and was used by the Greeks for smaller buildings, interiors and, often, in Asia Minor.

The Greek Corinthian order

This order was employed much less by the Greeks and not many examples survive. It was developed in fifth-century Athens and was later adopted with enthusiasm by the Romans. The most usual design, has a richly ornamented entablature with deep cornice, the upper member of which is supported by pairs of *modillions* (brackets). It is similar to the Ionic Order except for the *capital* which has a four-faced abacus. Below this it is shaped like a concave bell which is encircled by two rows of acanthus leaves above which are the *caulicoli*, each of which is surmounted by a calyx from which emerge the corner volutes and these support the angles of the abacus. There were a number of variations of the Greek Corinthian capital and these are simpler designs. Generally one of the rows of acanthus leaves has been replaced by a row of lotus or palm leaves. If this was the upper row, the volutes could also be omitted as in the *Tower of the Winds* in *Athens*.

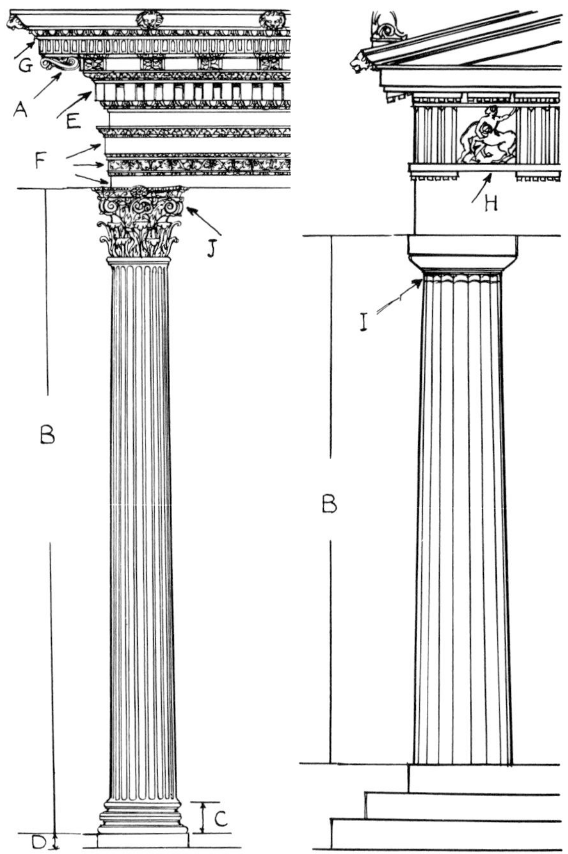

CLASSICAL ORDER
Roman Corinthian Order, Temple of Castor and Pollux, Rome
Greek Doric Order, Parthenon, Athens
A Modillion B Column C Base D Plinth E Dentil F Fascia G Corona H Tenia I Hypotrachelium J Volute

Roman orders

The Romans used the three Greek orders and developed two more of their own. The proportions differed from the Greek prototypes, the mouldings and carved enrichment were less subtle and, generally, more ornate. This is emphasized by the fact that the Greeks preferred the plainer Doric Order, and the richer Cornithian had a greater appeal for the Romans. Vitruvius gives us a clear account of the form of the Roman orders but, having lived in the days of Augustus, he was unable to describe the Composite Order (see VITRUVIUS).

Cornice, from the forum at Ostia.

The *Roman Doric Order* is less massive and less refined than the Greek and, being slenderer, is given a base. The metopes which beautify the Greek frieze are frequently replaced in Roman work by garlanded bulls' skulls. The capital is less subtle; the Greek echinus becomes a quarter-round moulding and fillets replace the Greek annulets. The Roman variation of their Doric Order is the *Tuscan*, derived from Etruscan prototypes. It is rarely fluted and its mouldings are generally plain. Roman examples have disappeared but Renaissance architects revived it from Vitruvius's *De Architectura*. Bernini used it in his colonnade in front of *St Peter's Basilica* in *Rome*.

The *Roman Ionic Order* bears a close resemblance to the Greek prototype though mouldings are more richly decorated in Roman examples. The capital angle volutes are often turned to present faces to both elevations.

One of the reasons for the popularity of the *Corinthian*

CLASSICAL ORDER
Greek Corinthian capital, the Olympeion, Athens, 174 BC–132 AD

Order with the Romans was that, since all four faces of the capital are alike, it presents an interesting view from all angles for the decoration of public buildings. The shaft is plain or fluted. The capital bell is strongly delineated, richly decorated and uses the softer acanthus leaf (see CLASSICAL ORNAMENT). In later examples all mouldings are enriched. The Romans evolved their *Composite Order* (as the name suggests) from a mixture of the Ionic and Corinthian. It is only the capital that differs materially. Here the volutes are large as in the Ionic capital and the caulicoli and scrolls are replaced by an echinus moulding enriched by egg-and-dart and a lower bead-and-reel (see CLASSICAL ORNAMENT). The Composite Order, being richly ornate, was especially employed on triumphal arches; its use on the *Arch of Titus* in AD 81 is the first recorded instance of its appearance.

The orders were employed as a basis for design with the revival of classical architecture in Renaissance Italy. Until the eighteenth century it was the Roman orders which served as a model, one which was more or less faithfully followed, apart from the Flemish and German Mannerism of the sixteenth century in northern Europe. With the Classic Revival of the later eighteenth century the Greek forms were reintroduced. During the nineteenth century all sources were studied and emulated though liberties were taken with proportion and design (see also BAROQUE ARCHITECTURE; CLASSICAL ARCHITECTURE; CLASSICAL ORNAMENT; CLASSICISM; COLUMN; ELIZABETHAN ARCHITECTURE; JACOBEAN ARCHITECTURE; PALLADIAN ARCHITECTURE; REGENCY ARCHITECTURE; RENAISSANCE ARCHITECTURE; TRIUMPHAL ARCH; VICTORIAN ARCHITECTURE and VOLUTE).

CLASSICAL ORNAMENT *Greek ornament* was of the highest quality and has never been surpassed in classical architecture. Designers used decoration sparingly in order to enhance the architectural form. The motifs came from many sources, Egyptian, Assyrian, Minoan and Mycenaean, and were mainly based upon natural plant and animal forms. The Greeks did not use these naturalistically but conventionalized them. Each moulding and part of the building was assigned its own ornament, all forms of which were characterized by simplicity of line, refinement and symmetry. Colour and gold were used to pick out the enrichments in carved marble.

Composite capital, Ostia Antica, Italy, *c.* third century AD

Among the natural motifs common to Greek ornament are the *acanthus leaf* (the spikier *spinosus* variety), the *anthemion* (honeysuckle), the *palm* (often referred to as *palmette*), the *sphinx*, the *griffin* and the *lion's head*. Mouldings were carved with ornament of which the most often used are the *egg and dart* (representing life and death), *leaf and dart* or tongue, *bead and reel*, the *dentil*, the *bay leaf garland*, where ribbons are crossed over bay leaves arranged horizontally, the *guilloche*, which resembles a complex plait, the *fret* or *key pattern* and many forms of scroll.

Greek anta capital, Erechtheion, Athens. Ornament top to bottom: leaf and dart, bead and reel, egg and dart, bead and reel, anthemion, bead and reel

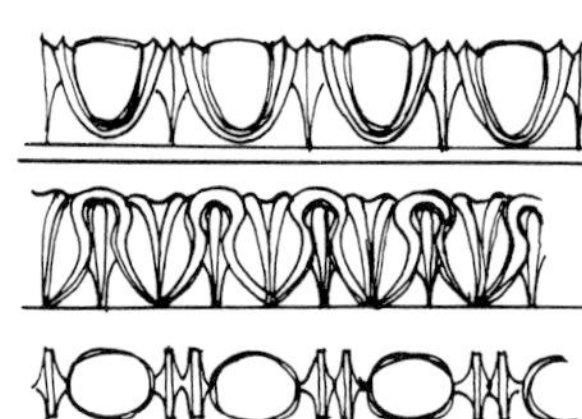

Roman patera

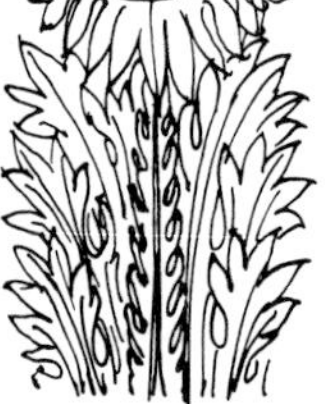

The Greek acanthus (spinosus) leaf

The Roman acanthus (mollis) leaf

Anthemion decoration

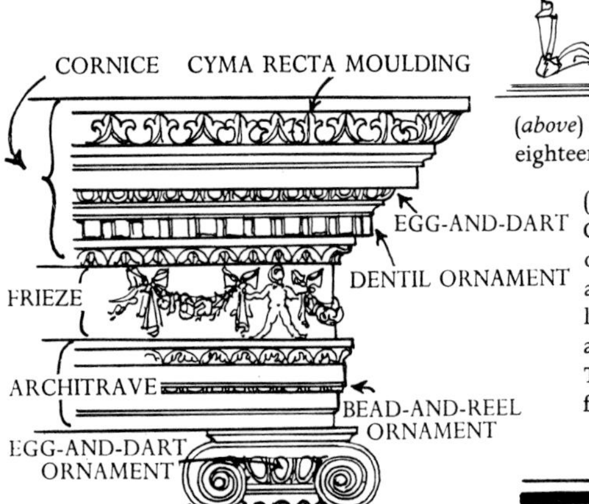

Roman Ionic order

(*above*) Bucrane, English, eighteenth century

(*right*) Greek entablature ornamented with anthemion, fret, lions' heads, paterae and triglyphs. Tholos, Epidauros, fourth century BC

Fret

Roman scroll ornament

Bay-leaf garland

Guilloche

Roman scroll panel, Trajan forum, Rome

Vitruvian scroll

Greek anthemion and bead-and-reel ornament, Delphi, sixth century BC.

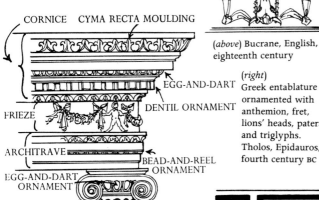

Fragment of Roman Corinthian capital showing caulicoli, Ostia, Italy

Roman Arch of Galerius, Thessaloniki. Carved mouldings—top to bottom: egg and dart, Vitruvian scroll, acanthus, scroll decoration, sculptured frieze, bay-leaf garland

Greek capital necking enriched with anthemion and bead-and-reel ornament

Roman ornament is a continuation of development from the Greek, using the same motifs but in a bolder, more vigorous manner, displaying less refinement. A greater surface area was decorated in Roman work than in Greek. The Roman version of the *acanthus leaf* is usually based on the more rounded *Acanthus mollis* plant rather than the spikier Greek *Acanthus spinosus*. The Romans frequently used acanthus foliage in scroll decoration where spiral lines were clothed by foliage and sheaths with terminal rosettes. They also designed panels and borders with arabesques having mythological forms such as the chimera and griffin as well as birds and animals. In capitals, panels and friezes other foliage was also employed: water leaves, ivy, the vine and the olive leaf. A circular relief ornament called a *patera* was a common wall and frieze decoration and, on friezes, especially the Doric, the ox skull and garland (*bucrane, bucranium*) was widely used.

CLASSICISM The various revivals of classical architecture which followed upon one another in the western world from the Renaissance until the early twentieth century (see CLASSICAL ARCHITECTURE). The building style during these revivals prior to the second half of the eighteenth century was based upon that of ancient Rome. Though study of the Greek literature and theatre had been made, it was a widely held view in the sixteenth and seventeenth centuries that ancient Rome was the fountain of classical art and, since the Italians had made the early discoveries and studies, this was a natural development. From the early Renaissance works of *Brunelleschi* in the fifteenth century a classical theory of architecture was evolved based principally upon the manuscripts of Vitruvius (see VITRUVIUS).

From this Roman classical basis the architectural style evolved into Mannerism and then Baroque, Italy always in the lead until the end of the seventeenth century. These different interpretations of the classical form present considerable contrasts to one another. Renaissance work was patterned closely upon ancient Roman temple and palace building and *Bramante's* circular *Tempietto* in S. Pietro in Montorio in *Rome* is regarded as a perfect interpretation of this. But, after 70 or 80 years, architects wanted something new. They toyed with Mannerism which broke many of the classical rules; it put decoration where it was not usually placed or set columns which bore no load. It was Roman Baroque which finally broke away from the precepts of what was believed to be the work of ancient Rome and the mainspring of this was a movement and plasticity often created by convex and concave forms. *Borromini* and *Bernini* were two of its principal exponents (see BAROQUE ARCHITECTURE).

In Britain it was *Inigo Jones* in the early seventeenth century, much later than Brunelleschi in Italy, who began to build in a Roman classical form based upon the Vitruvian pattern. In the previous century Elizabethan architecture had been patterned upon a variety of classical sources obtained at second, third and even fourth hand, which produced a robust, vital but impure style (see ELIZABETHAN ARCHITECTURE, JACOBEAN ARCHITECTURE and JONES, INIGO). After Inigo Jones more varied interpretations followed, less precisely correct but representing some of the finest of English classical work, a fusion of sources as varied as Dutch Palladianism and French and Italian Baroque, blended to create finally Wren's inimitably English classicism (see WREN, SIR CHRISTOPHER). There followed the short interludes of English Baroque under *Vanbrugh, Hawksmoor* and *Archer,* the personal style of *Gibbs* (see ARCHER, THOMAS; BAROQUE ARCHITECTURE; GIBBS, JAMES; HAWKSMOOR, NICHOLAS and VANBRUGH, SIR JOHN) and then English architecture was set back on the Vitruvian principle by *Lord Burlington's Palladian* school, which dominated English building for forty years (see BURLINGTON, EARL OF; CAMPBELL, COLEN; KENT, WILLIAM; LEONI, GIACOMO; PALLADIAN ARCHITECTURE).

A new spirit was abroad in the 1740s and 1750s which resulted in a reversal of thought on the origins of classical art and later overthrew Palladianism completely. A growing desire for travel to study 'on the spot' arose in all the countries of western Europe, especially among Englishmen, Frenchmen and Germans. People travelled distances according to their means from the nobility on their Grand Tour of two to three years to architects and artists who worked as they travelled (see GRAND TOUR). Interest was aroused in Greece, Dalmatia and even lands as far away as Syria. One factor which excited interest and controversy was the discovery of the nature of the Greek Doric Order. Ever since Brunelleschi in the fifteenth century, the Roman Doric or Tuscan had been the model, based on Vitruvius and the ruins of Roman buildings, then reiterated in succeeding publications through the sixteenth and seventeenth centuries (see comparative orders in CLASSICAL ARCHITECTURE). The drawings now seen in the books published by those who had studied *in situ* showed the Doric Order of the *Parthenon,* sturdy, fluted, without base and with its deeper, magnificent entablature, all this giving to the order quite different proportions of height and width. This Greek Doric version horrified the Palladians and they were even more shocked when they saw drawings of the older temples of *Paestum* and *Sicily,* with their shorter, stockier columns, enormous capitals and weighty entablatures. They are the most powerful-looking Doric buildings in western Europe. The English adherents to the Roman style in the second half of the eighteenth century, led by *Sir William Chambers,* thought this work primitive and barbaric (see CHAMBERS, SIR WILLIAM).

This second half of the century was the time of *Neoclassicism* or the *Classic Revival.* It developed into the *Greek Revival* when a fiercely pro-Greek school arose, its adherents as loyal to the Greek pattern as the Romans were to their ideal. The two schools of thought ran contemporaneously for some years but, in the last decades of the century, the Greek model was more often preferred and buildings were plainer, even severe, and the classical structure returned more to the trabeated form with the columns bearing their load and not merely acting as wall decoration. The years 1770–1820 witnessed the building of much great architecture as well as a great deal which was banal. A personal imprint was placed on the structures of a number of original architects (see ADAM, ROBERT; NASH, JOHN; SOANE, SIR JOHN; WYATT, JAMES), who drew on the variety of classical sources then available and interpreted them in many differing ways (see also GEORGIAN ARCHITECTURE and REGENCY ARCHITECTURE). The classical pattern was followed throughout the nineteenth century and into the early twentieth reproduced in a bewildering multiplicity of forms and gradually becoming less severe and more richly ornamented as time passed (see BARRY, SIR CHARLES; SMIRKE, SIR ROBERT; VICTORIAN ARCHITECTURE and WILKINS, WILLIAM).

COADE STONE An artificial stone, a stoneware ceramic material, which was fired in a kiln. The Coade formula, now established by modern methods of analysis, was based upon the combination of china clay, sand and various fluxes together with considerable quantities of grog, that is, crushed and finely ground already fired stoneware. Indeed, Mrs Coade referred to this custom of incorporating a proportion of pre-fired stoneware in the original name of the firm which was *Coade's Lithodipyra Terra-Cotta or Artificial Stone Manufactory*: 'lithodipyra' being a word of Greek origin which would translate as 'stone-twice-fire'. This mixture produced a material which was remarkably stable during firing with a very low rate of shrinkage and so made possible its use for extra-life-size statuary and large architectural features to be incorporated into buildings.

The Coade business was started in 1769 by Mr and Mrs George Coade (who were then elderly) and was run by their unmarried daughter Eleanor who, apart from her training and experience as a modeller, was a gifted businesswoman. Eleanor Coade (1733–81, usually called 'Mrs' as a courtesy business title) made a great success of this firm which was established in Lambeth in a private house with attached studio and a factory behind. It was situated in Narrow Walk (now Belvedere Road) and backed on to the river so that supplies of raw materials could be brought in by barge and there unloaded and stored. The factory was enlarged and altered over the years but was only finally demolished in 1950 to make way for the Festival of Britain.

Coade stone was widely used by many of the leading architects of the later eighteenth and early nineteenth centuries, notably Adam, Chambers, Nash, Soane and Wyatt. The material so resembled stone that it is often mistaken for it, but is so hard and resistant to weather that it retains sharpness of detail much better than the natural substance.

The many examples of the material still *in situ* include sculpture, ornament and architectural detail on *No. 20 Portman Square, Buckingham Palace,* the *Royal Naval College, Greenwich,* the *Royal Society of Arts,* the *Soane Museum,* all in *London,* and *Liverpool Town Hall, Culzean Castle, Scotland* and *St George's Chapel, Windsor.*

Apart from the qualities of the actual material, the firm's reputation was greatly and quickly enhanced by the high quality of its classical statuary. In the eighteenth century it was modelled by or under the direction of the sculptor *John Bacon* (1740–99). His classical figures were then mass-produced by pressing the material in moulds and firing. One example which was widely reproduced was the female caryatid figure from the south porch of the Erechtheion on the acropolis of Athens. A drawing of this had appeared in the second edition of Stuart and Revett's *Antiquities of Athens* in 1789 (see DILETTANTI SOCIETY and STUART, JAMES) and many copies were made from the original Coade model. Sir John Soane used them more than once on, for example, his own houses in Lincoln's Inn Fields (the Soane Museum) and Pitzhanger Manor (Ealing Public Library).

Eleanor Coade died in 1821. Her manager, a relation, William Croggon, bought the firm and ran it until 1833 after which his son continued for a while. In 1840 H.N. Blanchard, who had been a Coade employee, bought many of the moulds and models and his firm continued manufacture of the stone until mid-Victorian times, after which architectural fashion turned to polychromy and richer, stronger colouring in materials so the use of Coade stone died away.

COATES, WELLS WINTEMUTE (1895–1958) Born and brought up in Japan of Canadian missionary parents, Coates was tutored by Englishmen but also studied Japanese painting and drawing, silk rearing, weaving and dyeing, as well as how to build boats. At the age of 18 he went on a world cruise then settled in Canada where he studied arts and science at McGill University and engineering at the University of British Columbia. He became a fighter pilot in the First World War. After 1918 Coates, who later changed his name by deed poll to Wells-Coates, worked at a variety of occupations in Canada: journalism, lumbering, engineering. In the 1920s he moved to London and experimented with a number of fields of design: interiors, furniture, radio sets (ECKO). He designed shops and showrooms, displaying an original talent for handling of space, and developed the open-plan theme; his work evidenced a paring-down to essentials, a stripping-off of all superfluous decoration.

Wells-Coates strongly interested himself in designing architecture and interiors in tune with the modern world and its needs and saw a close link between architecture and engineering. His monolithic concrete block of flats in *Lawn Road, London,* built by a company called Isokon

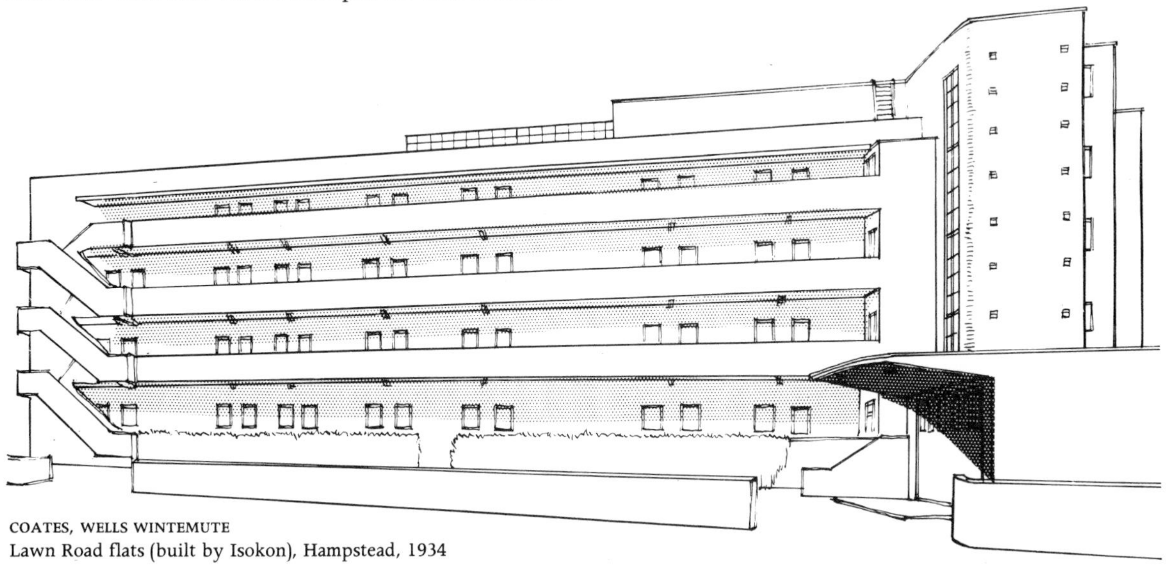

COATES, WELLS WINTEMUTE
Lawn Road flats (built by Isokon), Hampstead, 1934

(1934), was a pioneer expression of a theory, held by a number of modern architects of that time, of 'minimum dwelling', that is, homes designed for people who wished to live as 'lightly' as possible, with a minimum of possessions and fittings. His essay in space-economy here was followed by further flats in *Embassy Court, Brighton* (1934–6) and a venture in split-level planning in *Palace Gate, London* (1939).

Wells-Coates was one of the leaders of the modern movement in architecture in Britain in the 1930s; he was one of the founders in 1933 of the Modern Architectural Research Group (MARS) (see MODERN ARCHITECTURE). He did not have the opportunity to carry out a large number of commissions but retained his interest in a wide field of design from studio interiors for the BBC to experimental sailing craft. After service in the Second World War as an RAF staff officer, he contributed the *National Film Theatre* to the 1951 Festival of Britain, then returned to Canada to live and work. At the time of his death he was engaged in the early stages of a number of large-scale town planning projects which included the new town of Iroquois to be built on the banks of the St Lawrence seaway.

COCKERELL, CHARLES ROBERT (1788–1863) The son of S.P. Cockerell (see COCKERELL, SAMUEL PEPYS), he worked for five years in his father's office before studying in Italy, Sicily and Greece for seven years. In Greece he participated in the archaeological discoveries of the time, notably at the temple of Aphaia on Aegina. In 1817 he returned to England and entered architectural practice. Over the years Professor Cockerell—he held the chair of architecture at the Royal Academy—became the accepted authority on antique Greek architecture though, due to his in-depth studies of Italian Renaissance work and his deep admiration for the achievements of Wren (see WREN, SIR CHRISTOPHER), his own style was scholarly yet less pedantic than the narrower vision of the dedicated Greek Revivalist. Cockerell was awarded the first Gold Medal of the Royal Institute of British Architects and was a member of academies in Athens, Rome and other Italian cities as well as Copenhagen and Munich; he gained the reputation of being the 'grand old man' of the classical school.

In 1825 Cockerell built *Hanover Chapel* in Nash's Regent Street (see NASH, JOHN). Demolished in 1896, the chapel had a Greek Ionic portico with flanking towers and a dome-covered atrium. He succeeded his father as Surveyor to the fabric of St Paul's Cathedral and, in 1833, followed Soane as architect to the *Bank of England* (see SOANE, SIR JOHN). Taylor (see TAYLOR, SIR ROBERT) and Soane had worked on the London headquarters building; Cockerell made his contribution in building branch banks in the chief industrial cities, notably Bristol, Plymouth, Manchester and Liverpool. The Liverpool bank is typical of these dignified designs; the giant Doric Order is used on the main elevation and above the entablature is a central pediment. The decoration is restrained and broadly treated. He also designed a number of other banks and insurance offices which included the *London and Westminster Bank*, Lothbury (1837–8, demolished 1928), the *Sun, Fire and Life Assurances Offices*, Threadneedle Street (1840–2, demolished 1971) and, in Liverpool, the *Liverpool and London Insurance Offices* (1856–8).

Cockerell's chief works are the *Cambridge University* (now Law) *Library* (1837–40) of which only the north wing was executed) with its fine, coffered barrel vault and the *Ashmolean Museum* and *Taylorian Institute* in Oxford (1841–5). The Oxford building stands on a corner site and its main façade (Beaumont Street) has two projecting end wings and a central portico also set forward. The rest of

The Bank of England, Liverpool, 1845

The Taylorian Institute (Ashmolean), Oxford, 1841–5

the elevation is in low relief, contrasting with the bolder wings and portico. The St Giles Street front has typical Cockerell free-standing columns carrying their own entablatures with classical sculptured figures above, as on Soane's design at Pitzhanger Manor, Ealing (see SOANE, SIR JOHN). The Greek Ionic Order is used, taken from Cockerell's own drawings which he made of the temple of Apollo Epicurius at Bassae in Greece. The detail is finely handled and executed. The building comprises a library, art gallery and lecture rooms. Cockerell was also responsible for completing the classical interiors, after the architects' deaths, of Basevi's *Fitzwilliam Museum* in *Cambridge* and Elmes' *St George's Hall* in *Liverpool* (see BASEVI, GEORGE and ELMES, HARVEY LONSDALE).

COCKERELL, SAMUEL PEPYS (1753–1827) A pupil of Sir Robert Taylor, then entered architectural practice where he designed a number of churches, for example, Banbury (1792–7), and became Surveyor to St Paul's Cathedral, the Admiralty and the East India Company. Cockerell is known primarily for *Sezincote*, the country house in Gloucestershire which he designed for his brother Sir Charles Cockerell in 1803. This is traditionally English in plan but Indian in style, incorporating onion domes and oriental arches.

COFFER, COFFERING Sunken panels in a ceiling, vault or dome, also known as *caissons* or *lacunae*. In classical architecture these coffers may be square, diamond, hexagonal or octagonal and in Roman and Renaissance work they are enriched with decorative mouldings and central motif (see CAISSON; CEILING).

Roman coffered vault, Basilica of Maxentius, early fourth century AD

COLLCUTT, THOMAS EDWARD (1840–1924) Worked in Street's office for some time (see STREET, GEORGE EDMUND), where he received a sound training in Gothic Revival architecture. In his own work he was more variously eclectic, blending Renaissance and Romanesque forms from many sources in pleasant, large-scale secular buildings, erected for different purposes. Typical of his best-known work was the *Imperial Institute* in South Kensington (1887–91), of which only the elegant tower survives. A catholic mixture of styles—Romanesque, Byzantine, Renaissance—in red brick, stone and terracotta was fused into a harmonious and successful whole. Collcutt's other works included *Wakefield Town Hall* (1877–80) and the Strand section of the *Savoy Hotel* (1903).

COLLCUTT, THOMAS EDWARD
The Imperial Institute, South Kensington, 1887–91

COLONNADE A row of columns supporting an entablature or arches (see BASILICA; CLASSICAL ARCHITECTURE; COLUMN; PORTICO and TEMPLE).

COLONNETTE A small column as in a triforium, window recess or font.

COLUMN Columns have been used as supports and in decorative schemes in many styles of architecture (see BASE; CAPITAL; CARYATID; CLASSICAL ARCHITECTURE; CLASSICAL ORDER; GOTHIC ARCHITECTURE and ROMANESQUE ARCHITECTURE). A column may be used in various ways. It may be complete, used singly or in pairs as in a colonnade

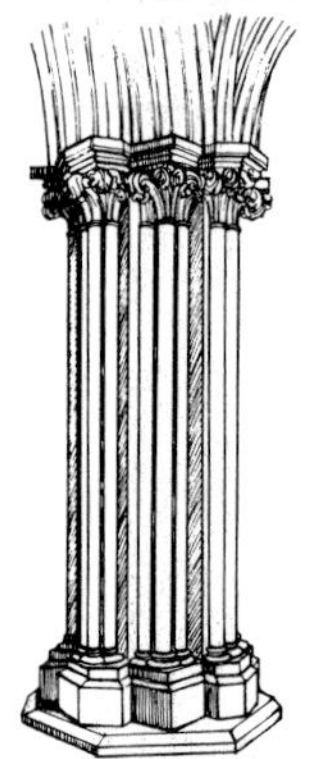
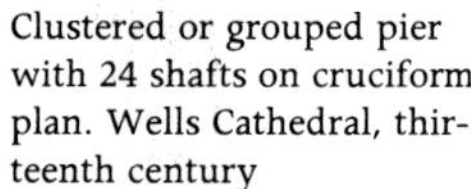

Clustered or grouped pier with 24 shafts on cruciform plan. Wells Cathedral, thirteenth century

Engaged columns with banding of rustication, York House Watergate, London, c. 1626

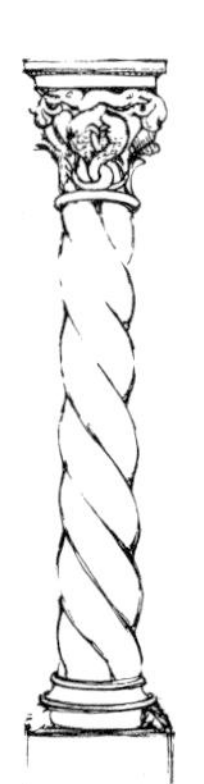

Twisted column, Church of S.S. Mary and Nicholas, Wilton, 1840–6. Architects: Wyatt and Brandon

Decorative banded columns in brick and terracotta in Gothic Revival style. Natural History Museum, London, 1873–9. Architect: Alfred Waterhouse

or it might be partly or wholly attached to a wall or another column. Pairs of columns are described as '*coupled*'. An *engaged, applied* or *attached* column is one where a part of its surface is in contact with the wall; in a *half* or *demi-column* only half the column projects from the wall. These forms are most often used in classical architecture; in Gothic architecture a number of columns may be grouped round a pier. In this design there is a central shaft or pier and round this are set several slenderer columns. This is referred to as a *grouped, clustered* or *compound pier*. In Renaissance and Baroque architecture rustication was introduced into column design. Such column shafts were banded by intermittent rustication (see MASONRY). In Baroque architecture the twisted column was favoured; this was graphically termed the 'barley-sugar' column or the 'Solomonic' column (from its supposed use in Solomon's temple). When entwined with vine or other leaves, it was termed a *wreathed column*. The rostral column, the *columna rostrata*, is one dating from Roman times. Decorated with projecting prows of ships, it is traditionally used for commemorating naval victories.

The term *columniation* refers to a building where columns are employed. *Intercolumniation* is the space between the columns which, in classical architecture, is measured at the lower part in multiples of the diameter of a column. Vitruvius (see VITRUVIUS) laid down five principal ratios: pycnostyle, where the columns are one-and-a-half diameters apart, systyle (two), eustyle (two-and-a-quarter), diastyle (three) and araeostyle (more than three). Eustyle is most generally adopted.

A column is divided into capital, shaft, base and plinth (see CLASSICAL ORDER). In classical architecture the shaft is often fluted, that is, cut in vertical channels each separated by an arris or fillet. The arris, as in the Greek Doric Order, is a sharp form (see ARRIS), the fillet is a flat moulding between the hollowed channels (see MOULDING). Some fluted columns are *cabled*, that is, a convex moulding is introduced into the flutes, almost filling up the hollow from the base of the column to about one third the way up the shaft. The column shaft connects the base at the bottom to the capital at the top; in each instance it is joined by a gentle curve (see APOPHYGE).

In Gothic architecture, clustered columns and piers are often banded part way up; these are described as 'annulated'. Such bands may encircle the shafts at top or bottom also. These may be referred to as annulets, shaft rings or cinctures.

CONCH The semi-domed covering of a semicircular apse or niche. The word derives from the Latin *concha* (= 'shell-fish') and smaller apses are often decorated with a shell design.

CONCRETE One of the oldest building materials made by Man, it is composed of four major ingredients: sand, stone, cement and water. The first two of these are comparatively inert, the latter two are the active participants. Thus when all four are mixed together, so producing a wet plastic substance which can be deposited and moulded at will, the cement and water cause a chemical reaction which gradually transforms this substance into a rock-hard conglomerate. The word concrete derives from the Latin *concretus* (= 'grown or run together').

The stone content may be in the form of pebbles or flints, crushed rock or broken up material of many kinds: clinker, cinder, slag, bricks or old concrete. Especially suitable are granite, hard sandstone and rounded pebbles found in natural gravel beds.

In early times the word 'cement' referred to a mixture of broken stone held together loosely by a binding material of lime, clay or burnt gypsum and sand. The word derives from the Latin *caementum* (= 'rough stones', 'rubble', 'building material'). This 'almost concrete' sub-

CONCH
Conch carved with shell ornament over niche. St Catharine's College Chapel, Cambridge, seventeenth century

stance preceded the use of true concrete. With its advent the source of the cement was primarily quicklime (calcium oxide). It was generally obtained by burning pulverized limestone, a process known as *calcining*.

It is not known when concrete was first made as the early development of cementing agents produced a mortar which was not strong enough to bind the whole mass durably together and, being friable, such materials have not survived. The oldest example of concrete found so far was made about 5600 BC. Concrete was certainly made and used in ancient Egypt; wall paintings exist which depict these processes and fragments have been found in a number of places where it acted as an infill mortar in stone walling. The Greeks also made a lime or burnt gypsum (calcium sulphate) mortar for walling with sun-dried bricks.

It was the Romans who developed the use of concrete in a structural manner, not merely as an agent for binding and covering as hitherto (see CLASSICAL ARCHITECTURE). It seems likely that their first use of the material was in emulation of Greek builders and examples of their work have been found which date from about 300 BC. It was towards the end of the second century BC that they experimented with a volcanic earth which they found in the region of Pozzuoli near Vesuvius. It resembled a reddish-coloured sand; the Romans took it for sand and mixed it with lime to make concrete. This concrete was of exceptional strength and hardness because the *pozzolana*, as it is called after its town of origin, is in reality a volcanic ash which contains alumina and silica and this combines chemically with the lime to produce a durable concrete. It seems likely that the Romans were not aware of the reason why their new concrete was so superior but there is no doubt that their engineers and architects quickly appreciated its importance. They experimented with the material and discovered that it would set equally well under water as in air. They mixed it with an aggregate of broken stone and brick and faced it with bricks, stone and marble.

By the first century AD the Romans had become adept at handling concrete and at taking full advantage of its possibilities as a structural medium. It enabled them to span and roof spaces of great magnitude, achievements which were not equalled until the introduction of steel construction in the nineteenth century. They built aqueducts, breakwaters, bridges and massive foundation rafts, and vaulted the civic structures and *terme* of the day. They experimented with reinforcement of the concrete with bronze strips and dowels in order to improve its tensile strength. Although the metal helped in this way the experiment was not successful because, having a higher rate of thermal expansion than the concrete, in hot weather it caused cracking.

The Romans then built walls and vaults of massive thickness which, in the hard, durable *pozzolana* concrete would resist any stress (see VAULTING). But walls of such thickness had problems of weight so the Romans developed a system of lightening the structure by the introduction of relieving arches and earthenware jars into the wall. They also mixed a quantity of volcanic rock, which is porous, into the aggregate. Such lightweight concrete was used in the construction of the *Colosseum* and *Pantheon* (see CLASSICAL ARCHITECTURE).

In Roman Britain *pozzolana* was not available but it was found that a quantity of powdered brick mixed with lime would give a satisfactory result for this also contained silica. The Romans used this concrete extensively in building farmhouses and villas. In the major examples mosaic was laid on the concrete floor as a decorative finish. In one of the largest building projects in Britain, *Hadrian's Wall*, concrete was an important material.

Pozzolana concrete was widely used for building in Europe for 800 years. The extent of this work in concrete was an important factor in the survival of many structures. The Romans had developed the use of the material as an immensely important structural medium. Yet, after the collapse of the western half of the Empire in the fifth century, the greater part of this knowledge and experience was lost for about 1300 years. The making of concrete did not die out but its use was largely confined to infilling in walling and as a foundation material. The Normans built concrete foundations to many castles and medieval masons did the same for churches and cathedrals. The thirteenth-century structure of *Salisbury Cathedral* is a noted example.

The development of cement

It was in the middle of the eighteenth century that builders began to search for a means to make a cement which would set quickly and be strong and durable. *Pozzolana* and lime mixtures had been imported from Italy by English builders since the sixteenth century but the secret of Roman concrete had not been appreciated or understood. The first major success in finding a way to make a satisfactory cement was achieved by *John Smeaton* (1724–92), an English engineer who was commissioned to build a new Eddystone lighthouse in 1756, the third on the site which is a rocky reef in the English Channel some 14 miles off Plymouth. Smeaton decided that the new lighthouse must be of stone (the earlier ones which had been destroyed had been of wood) and he spent a long time studying the properties of mortars obtained from different types of limestone in order to find which would be most suitable for cementing his stone blocks into a structure, built in such an exposed position, strong enough to withstand the sea. Smeaton need a hydraulic cement, that is, one which would set under water, as Roman *pozzolana cement* had done. He found that the best hydraulic cement was mixed with lime made from limestone which contained an appreciable quantity of clay. He used a Welsh limestone, included some Italian *pozzolana* and produced a cement which, used in the building of the lighthouse in 1759, lasted for over 100 years. It was not until 1876 that the lighthouse was finally dismantled and replaced. Smeaton's lighthouse was re-erected on Plymouth Hoe, where it still stands. He recounted his research experience in *A Narrative of the Eddystone Lighthouse*, published in 1791.

During the succeeding 60 years further experimentation was made in a number of European countries to improve upon Smeaton's cement. In 1796 an Englishman *James Parker* took out a patent for a substance which he called *Roman cement* because he believed it to be similar to that used by the Romans. It was made in Northfleet in Kent by calcining stones found on the beach on the Isle of Sheppey. These 'noddles of clay', as they were called, were of limestone with a high clay content; they were burnt at a high temperature and then powdered.

In 1812 the French engineer *Louis J. Vicat* (1786–1861) began a detailed investigation into various limestones found in France and later published his conclusions, which were that the best hydraulic lime was produced from limestone containing clay which provided silica and alumina. He experimented with the effects of adding different clays in varying proportions to slaked lime and burnt the mixture. Vicat's work encouraged other investigators to experiment with making artificial cements from clay and chalk (calcium carbonate). Among these was the Englishman *James Frost* who patented his *British cement* in 1822. This was made at Swanscombe in Kent.

The work done by Vicat and Frost marked the beginning of the development of artificially prepared cement. It was *Joseph Aspdin* (1779–1855), an English bricklayer who, in 1824, patented a better product: this he called *Portland cement*. Aspdin's cement was also made from a mixture of chalk and clay but calcined to a higher temperature before being ground to powder; it was an improved and more reliable product than that of Vicat or Frost. He used the name Portland because he thought it resembled in colour the famous limestone quarried on the Island of Portland. Aspdin's cement works were in Wakefield in Yorkshire but his son, *William Aspdin* (1816–64) set up another works at Rotherhithe on the Thames. It was earlier, in this area, that Portland cement is thought to have been used for the first time in an engineering structure when *Sir Marc Brunel* ordered it from the Wakefield Works in 1828 for use in building his Thames Tunnel.

Aspdin's Portland cement was quite different from the modern product which is the result of many different later improvements. It was *Isaac Charles Johnson* (1811–1911), manager of the White and Sons Cement Works at Swanscombe in Kent who produced a Portland cement in 1845 which was much nearer to the modern product. In his process the raw materials were burnt at a much higher temperature, until the mass was almost vitrified, and the resulting clinker was finely ground to produce a cement which was far in advance of Aspdin's earlier product.

In the second half of the nineteenth century concrete was beginning to be employed more widely but its adoption as an important building material was inhibited by the high cost of making Portland cement. Gradually new ideas were adopted in production in order to reduce this cost. One improvement was in apparatus for grinding the clinker. At first this was done between mill stones. In the 1880s iron mills were introduced and these were later replaced by tube mills filled with pebbles; later still, steel balls replaced the pebbles.

The major hindrance to a faster and, therefore, cheaper production, was in the design of kiln. Parker's Roman cement, for example, was made in a *bottle* or *dome kiln*, traditionally used for burning lime. Isaac Johnson introduced an improvement, a *horizontal chamber kiln* and this, in turn, was replaced by a *shaft kiln*. This was a vertical shaft which enabled the raw materials to be burnt continuously. The chief drawback to this design, however, was the difficulty of ensuring even burning of the clinker but improvements to the pattern gradually eliminated the problem. Finally the cost of manufacture was markedly reduced by the introduction of the *rotary kiln* which is the basis of modern design. One of the earliest of these, a continuous process rotary cement kiln, was erected in 1887 at Arlesey in Hertfordshire to the designs of *Frederick Ransome*. This measured 26ft in length and 5ft in diameter, small indeed compared to a modern kiln which would probably exceed 300ft in length.

Reinforced concrete

Concrete used by itself is very strong in compression, that is, it resists the weight of a load which tries to crush it. It is, however, extremely weak in tensile strength, that is, it cannot resist forces which threaten to pull it apart. If, therefore, plain concrete is used for beams or arches or domical coverings, the outward and downward bending forces will cause the material to fail. When the Romans used concrete to construct their barrel vaults and domes they built massively, with walls up to about eight metres in thickness. This was to withstand the roofing which was of solid concrete, resting vertically on the supporting walls and so exerting no outward thrust. The *Pantheon* dome in Rome is an example of this (see CLASSICAL ARCHITECTURE).

If concrete is reinforced by metal bars, wires or cables embedded within it, the elastic strength of the metal will absorb all tensile and shearing stresses and so complement the high compression resistance of the concrete to provide an immensely strong constructional material. The Romans experimented with using bronze for this purpose but found it to be unsatisfactory. Experiments with iron in the late eighteenth and early nineteenth centuries showed

Reinforced concrete: Palazzetto dello Sport, Rome, 1957.
Architects: Annibale Vitellozzi and Pier Luigi Nervi

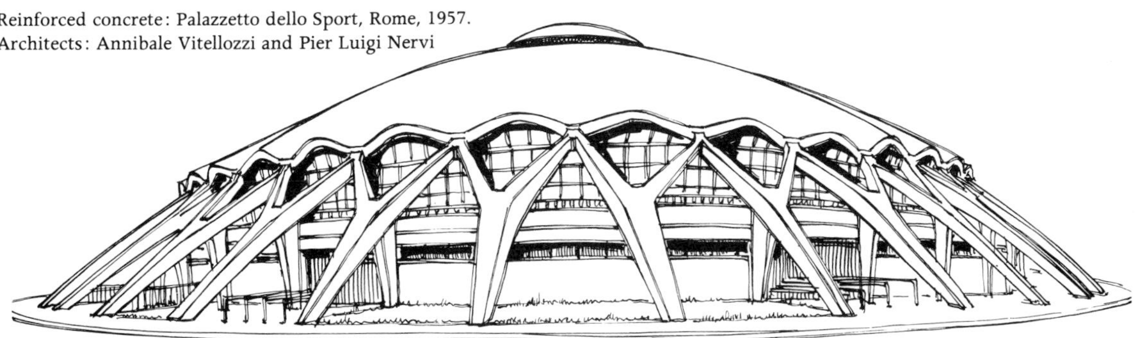

Concrete on-site pre-casting by Wates system at Highfield, Feltham. Floor slabs being lowered into position on low-rise block. Photograph by courtesy of Wates Ltd.

that here was a material highly suited to the purpose because it has about the same coefficients of thermal expansion and contraction as concrete over the normal range of temperatures. In modern construction, using steel in this way economizes in the use of the expensive material and the concrete, which shrinks around the reinforcement as it sets, grips the metal firmly, so protecting it from rusting and weathering. It also reduces the fire hazard, for the steel, which would warp and bend if it became sufficiently hot, is protected within the concrete casing.

The idea of reinforcing concrete with iron to increase its tensile strength was put forward by architects in France in the late eighteenth century. The theory was tested by *Rondelet*, Soufflot's collaborator, in building the Church of Sainte-Geneviève, now called the *Panthéon*, in *Paris*, where he used a metal-reinforced mortar and rubble aggregate. An early trial in England was the experimental arch constructed by *Sir Marc Brunel* in 1832 in building his Thames Tunnel. He incorporated strips of hoop iron and wood into a brick-and-cement arch.

During the nineteenth century experimentation with the idea of metal reinforcement of concrete was carried out in several countries; the concept was not the property of one individual but ripe for general development. Iron and, later, steel, became widely used as structural and decorative materials so it was natural that they should act as reinforcement to concrete. In England *William B. Wilkinson* took out a patent in 1854 for embedding wire ropes or hoop iron into concrete blocks for constructing fireproof warehouses and dwellings. It is not clear, though, to what extent Wilkinson applied this patent.

The French were pioneers on the Continent in developing reinforced concrete construction. *Joseph Monier* (1823–1906) first experimented with large garden tubs reinforced with wire mesh (patented in 1867) and ten years later had developed a system of reinforcing concrete beams. He took out patents for reinforcement of bridges and stairways. In the same period *François Coignet* (1814–88) exhibited a technique of reinforcement with iron bars at the Paris Exposition and *François Hennébique* (1842–1921) developed hooked connections for reinforcing bars patented in 1892, using steel and iron.

During the late nineteenth century reinforced concrete construction began to develop quickly in Germany and Austria and in America. As early as 1862 a patent was taken out for filling a cast iron column with concrete and in 1878 steel rods were inserted into concrete columns. In the early years of the twentieth century there was extensive experimentation into reinforcement of columns by spiral steel hoops which produced a stronger column than the vertical rods. Reinforced concrete was being widely used to construct bridges; an early example in *Copenhagen* was built in 1879. Longer spans were being handled in the USA, France and Germany in the 1890s, for example, the bridge at *Châtellerault* in France in 1898.

In Britain reinforced concrete construction advanced more slowly though, by the late nineteenth century, plain concrete was being more widely used. *Pre-cast concrete* had been available from about 1845 for paving and decorative features such as balustrades and finials. In 1875 *William Lascelles* patented a system for building houses from pre-cast concrete slabs; these were fixed to a wooden framework. Some of the panels for ceilings and walls were cast with all-over relief decoration. Plain concrete was also being widely employed for dock and factory buildings, warehouses and even bridges. The *Glenfinnan Viaduct* in the Scottish Highlands, which carries the railway from Fort William to Mallaig, is a survivor of this type of design. It was built in 1897 by *Robert McAlpine* and has 21 massive concrete arches. *J. F. Bentley* also used plain concrete in the massive Roman manner in the domes of his *Westminster Cathedral* (see BENTLEY, JOHN FRANCIS).

It was the Frenchmen *François Hennébique* and *François Coignet* who played a major part in establishing construction in reinforced concrete in Britain. Hennébique opened an office in London in 1897 and within a decade his constructional system was being taken up by a number of clients. His fellow-countryman Coignet followed by opening a London office in 1904. Early examples of this type of work were still largely industrial—water towers, bridges, wharves and reservoirs. In 1908, however, work was begun on Britain's first reinforced-concrete-frame skyscraper (see HIGH-RISE BUILDING). This was the 15-storey *Royal Liver Building* in *Liverpool* which was, though, clad in stone as was traditional practice at the time.

Pre-stressed concrete

The reinforcement of concrete by iron and steel had created a structural material with immense and varied possibilities and it was after the First World War that these began to be realized on a large scale. The next advance was in the field of *pre-stressed concrete*, a development which, in its turn, enormously increased the potential of the material. The purpose of pre-stressing is to make a more efficient and economic use of materials. It makes possible the creation of slender elegant forms which are at the same time immensely strong. The theory is that the metal reinforcement should be stretched before the concrete is poured into position and the pull maintained until the concrete is hard and strong. Such reinforcement is in the form of wire cables threaded through ducts and these are so placed to create preliminary compressive stresses in the concrete in order to avoid cracking under conditions of working load.

Pre-stressing, to be successful, requires high quality concrete and high-tensile steel. Early experiments with the theory in the late nineteenth century were not satisfactory because such materials were not then available. It was the French engineer *Eugène Freyssinet* (1879–1962)

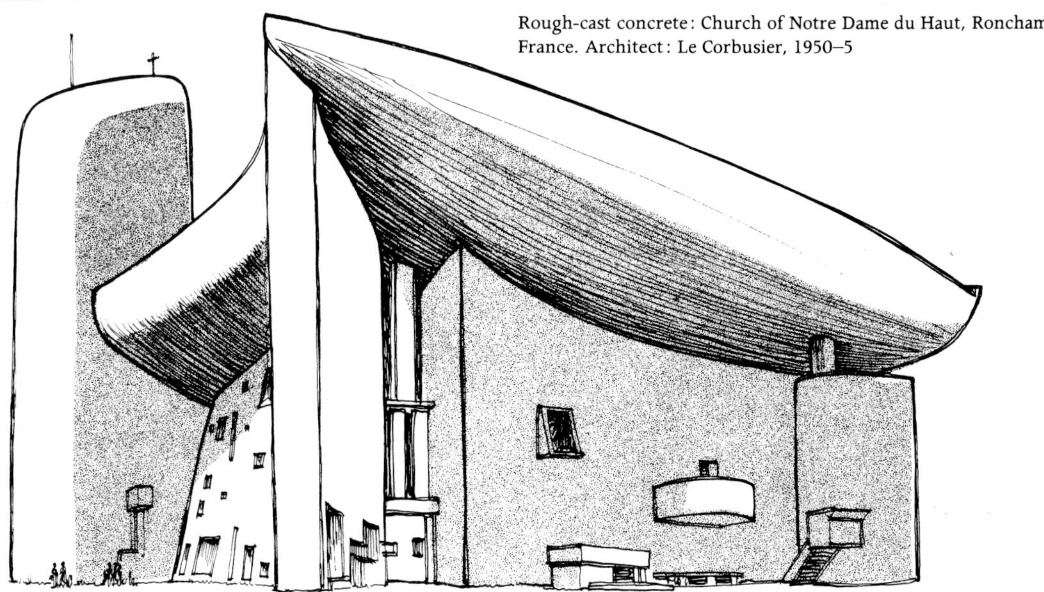

Rough-cast concrete: Church of Notre Dame du Haut, Ronchamp, France. Architect: Le Corbusier, 1950–5

who pioneered pre-stressed reinforced concrete. He experimented with building concrete bridges while an army engineer and later, after 1918, formed his own company to develop his ideas. These proved highly successful and brought him fame when, in 1934, he succeeded in saving the *Ocean Terminal* at *Le Havre* from sinking into the mud and being covered by the sea by building new foundations of pre-stressed concrete.

After the Second World War steel was in limited supply and architects turned more and more to reinforced pre-stressed concrete. With increased knowledge of these techniques it was realized that the structural possibilities of the concrete were virtually unlimited. It became a desirable material, partly because it was not expensive but also because the needs of an individual project could be exactly calculated in terms of reinforcement and strength of concrete. Further, it could be cast in any form and so gave a freedom of design to architects which they had not possessed previously and was particularly suited to modern architecture.

Outstanding among the great engineers of Europe who demonstrated some of the exciting possibilities which could be achieved with reinforced concrete was the Italian *Pier Luigi Nervi* (1891–1979). From his early work on the *Florence Stadium* (1927–30) and the later imaginative concrete hangars at *Orvieto* and *Orbetello*, where he developed the use of pre-cast concrete elements, he went on to create original and beautiful structures of infinite delicacy and variety of which the *Palazzetto dello Sport*, built for the 1960 *Rome* Olympics, was a typical example. This was a 'big top' but in concrete not canvas, a structure 194ft in diameter anchored by 36 concrete ties. In the 1940s Nervi felt constrained by the limitations imposed by the use of timber formwork to shape the concrete and went on to experiment with his own version of *ferro-concrete* in which he erected the metal-framed skeleton structures to support the cladding, a method with which much of his subsequent work was identified. The great roof of the 1949 *Turin Exhibition Hall* is a major instance of this. (Formwork, also called *shuttering*, is the timber or metal form into which the concrete is poured. The formwork is removed when the concrete has set, leaving the imprint of its surface marking upon the concrete.)

Nervi had been pressed to use his ingenuity in reinforced concrete by a shortage of steel in post-war Italy. Similarly, necessary economies in a number of countries led to the development of building methods which saved time and, therefore, cost. Pre-cast cladding in high-rise construction was one answer and *Le Corbusier*'s experiment in urban living, the *Unité d'Habitation* in *Marseilles* waa a pace-setter. From this structure and others inspired by it there was coined in England in 1954 the term *brutalism*. This referred to the use of concrete in its most overt, naked form, handled in strong masses. It was an English derivation from the French *béton brut*, meaning concrete left in its natural state, unfinished, after the formwork had been removed, and displaying the timber graining impressed upon it. Other means of producing a rough but even texture on the concrete included *bush-hammering*. In this a bush-hammer with a grooved head was employed to mark the surface of the concrete after it had set.

During the 1950s and 1060s a tremendous number of buildings of all kinds were erected all over the world in reinforced pre-stressed concrete. By the 1970s disillusion was setting in. Concrete was a cheap structural building material and it was malleable and manageable but it weathered badly and drearily. Much effort has been spent in trying to improve this surface problem and with some

BOARDED CONCRETE
Queen Elizabeth Hall, South Bank, London. GLC Architects' Department, 1967

success. Better-quality concrete structures are now being erected. When concrete is faced, as it so often is in Mediterranean countries, by mosaic, faience, marble and stone, its structural advantages are undeniable. In great engineering projects, such as the *Thames Barrier Scheme* (opened 1984) reinforced concrete has no rival (see MODERN ARCHITECTURE).

CONSOLE A decorative scrolled bracket used in classical architecture to support a cornice. Consoles are most often placed on either side of a door frame to hold up the cornice of the frame. A console is characterized by being taller than it is wide or deep, in contrast to the modillion, which takes a similar form but is set horizontally to support the projecting mouldings (see CLASSICAL ORDER). Consoles are also referred to as *ancones*, though this word is also used to denote the working projections left, while building is in progress, on column drums to facilitate construction (see also BRACKET and CORBEL).

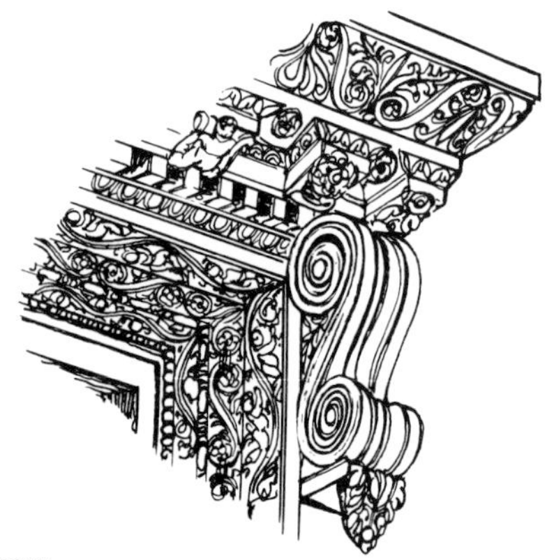

CONSOLE
Temple of Jupiter (now baptistery of cathedral), Split, Yugoslavia. Roman, *c.* 300 AD

CONURBATION A twentieth-century town-planning term for a group of adjacent towns or urban areas which are planned together or have developed into a large unit, often with a common industry or function.

CONVENT A building or group of buildings used by a company of men or women living together under the discipline of a religious order. The church in this group of buildings is known as a *conventual church* (see also ABBEY; CHURCH).

COPING A protective capping, covering the top of a wall and designed to throw off rain water. For this purpose the capping may be gently rounded, sloping or gable-shaped.

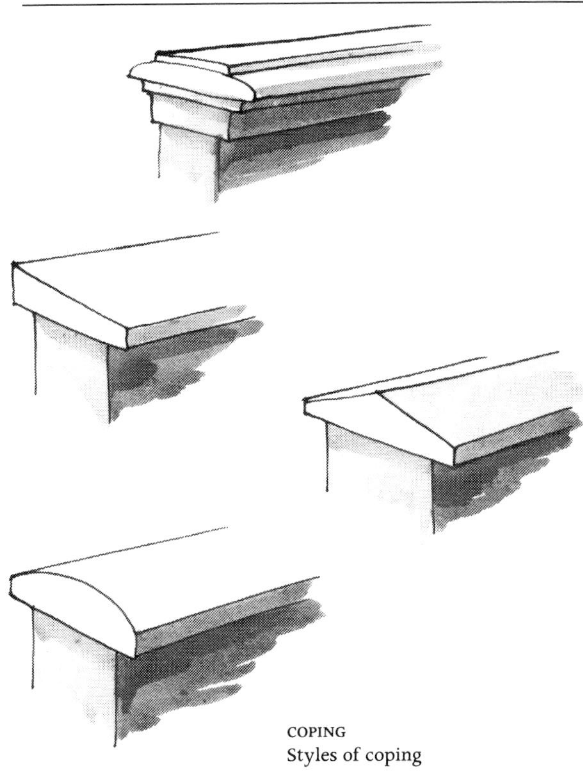

COPING
Styles of coping

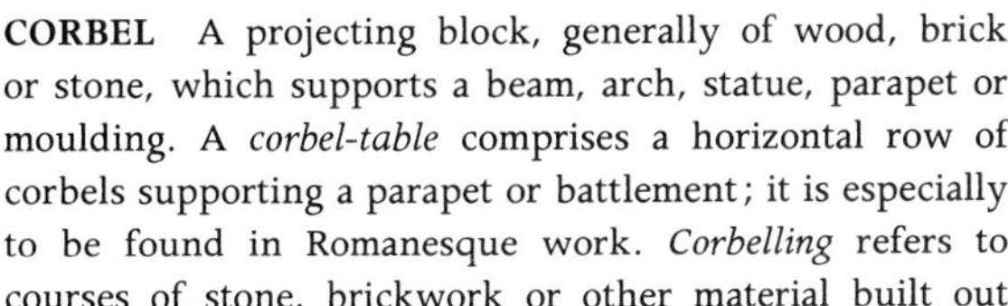

CORBEL A projecting block, generally of wood, brick or stone, which supports a beam, arch, statue, parapet or moulding. A *corbel-table* comprises a horizontal row of corbels supporting a parapet or battlement; it is especially to be found in Romanesque work. *Corbelling* refers to courses of stone, brickwork or other material built out each beyond the one below in order to support a projection as in a chimney-stack or oriel window (see also GOTHIC ORNAMENT).

Corbelling of oriel window in decorative terracotta and brick. Infanta's Palace, Guadalajara, Spain, 1461

Corbels supporting apse arcading, Benedictine Convent of Königslütter, Germany, *c.* 1140

Corbel, Lund Cathedral, Sweden, twelfth century

CORNICE A moulded projection which crowns a wall, building or arch. In classical architecture, the top member of the entablature (see CLASSICAL ARCHITECTURE and CLASSICAL ORDER).

CORPS DE LOGIS A French term applied to the main part of a building.

CORTILE An Italian word for a courtyard. In Renaissance architecture a cortile is an interior court generally surrounded by arcaded storeys.

COSMATI WORK A decorative technique employed especially in medieval Italy, in which marble panels were colourfully inlaid with mosaic, stones and gilding.

COTTAGE ORNE A small country house displaying an artificial, coy rusticity. It was fashionable to build such derivations from the Picturesque movement in the late eighteenth and the first half of the nineteenth century, as decorative cottages for workers and as country retreats for the gentry. These buildings were characterized by their asymmetry, thatched roofing and an over-fanciful carving and decoration of barge boards and weather-boarding.

COUNTRY HOUSE AND MANSION, GREAT HOUSE The tradition of the English country mansion dates from the time of the first Elizabeth. Since the mid-fifteenth century the need for defence fortifications had been declining and the manor house had gradually become more spacious, with an accent on greater privacy for the owner and his family. There was a tendency to increase the window area and towards less restricted living and sleeping areas. As England became more settled and wealthier the country house reflected these conditions.

Impetus was given to an acceleration of these trends in the 1560s by the introduction into the country of architectural treatises and pattern books from the Continent showing the new forms of Italian and French Renaissance designs. At the same time, in contrast to the Middle Ages and the earlier sixteenth century, few churches were being erected and there was little civic or university building so the greater part of the new wealth was funnelled into domestic construction. The aristocracy commissioned, and partly designed, great country houses on a palatial scale, vying with one another in the provision of a sufficiently lavish and impressive house to attract the monarch, accompanied by her court retinue, on a visit during her summer progress.

In plan there was a trend away from the medieval enclosed courtyard to a more open design often based on the 'E' or 'H' form. The house was a rectangular block with projecting end-wings and entrance porch. Following the classical tradition symmetry began to replace the earlier asymmetrical designs so that the apartments on one side of the entrance porch were balanced by others on the opposite side, each with an equivalent number and form of windows. In the later decades of the century a greater symmetry was achieved when bay window matched bay window, gable matched gable and chimney-stack matched chimney-stack. The window area was much increased and the skylines were lively and varied with the contrasting shapes of cresting, curving gables and decorative chimney-stacks. The entrance porch—the 'frontispiece'—was a focal feature of the house. It was often two- or even three-storeyed, adopting on each stage a different version (loosely interpreted and imperfectly understood) of one of the classical orders.

Inside the house, as the need for defence had declined and the desire for privacy had increased, the use of the hall as a living and sleeping room had been abandoned. The Elizabethan country mansion possessed a far greater range of rooms than its medieval predecessor. The hall was now smaller and the solar had been replaced by several reception rooms of which the main chamber (the great drawing room) was the largest. Generally on the first floor, this possessed an architectural and decorative scheme second in richness and quality only to the hall. It was not so lofty and there was no carved screen but the ornamentation and treatment of windows, ceiling and walls was similar. Bedchambers were now more numerous though they were still passage rooms. As there were few corridors in the house, the bedrooms were actually only a wide passage divided up and having a door at each end which led to adjoining rooms. Because such rooms were draughty, the large bedstead, with its ornately carved headboard, posts and canopy frame, enveloping curtains and frill, provided a cosy room within a room.

Characteristic of the Elizabethan mansion were two new developments: the long gallery and the staircase. The purpose of the gallery was to create a suitable place where the household and guests could amuse and disport themselves together, especially in the winter months; the children could play and the adults sit and talk, do needlework, make music, dance or stroll. The gallery, usually on the first or second floor of the house, extended along the whole of one long façade with windows on three sides and fireplaces on the fourth, inner, side. A number of such galleries survive and some are of great length, up to 170ft, though only about 20ft in width and 15ft in height (see GALLERY).

It was in the Elizabethan mansion that the impressive staircase evolved as a distinctive and decorative feature of the house. Staircases were built massively of oak, on generous proportions to accommodate the farthingale skirts of the time, and were of dog-legged design. In the early seventeenth century Jacobean staircases had further developed into open well designs, still massive and ornately carved but of more sophisticated form and execution (see STAIRCASE).

The Jacobean great house continued to develop on similar lines to the Elizabethan. Its size increased, with a greater number and variety of rooms, larger windows and richer interior decoration. A number of these mansions survive, many of them retaining original decorative schemes and some furniture. Fine examples include the Elizabethan *Longleat House*, Wiltshire (1550–80), *Hardwick Hall*, Derbyshire 1591–7), *Cobham Hall*, Kent (1594–9), *Montacute House*, Somerset (1588–1601), *Wollaton Hall*, Nottinghamshire (1580–8), *Burghley House*, Northamptonshire (*c.* 1585); and the Jacobean *Castle Ashby*, Northamptonshire (*c.* 1624), *Hatfield House*, Hertfordshire (1607–12), *Bramshill House*, Hampshire (1605–12) and *Knole House*, Kent (*c.* 1605). These mansions are built of stone and/or brick. There exist also a number of large half-timber houses of which *Speke Hall*, Lancashire (*c.*

Entrance front of Cobham Hall, Kent, 1594–9. Elizabethan

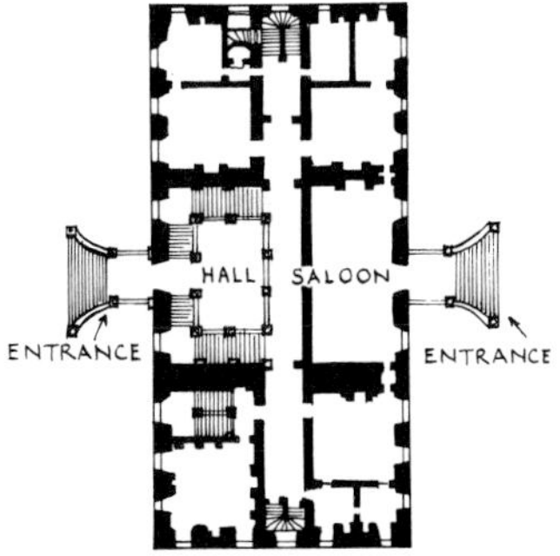

Ground plan of Coleshill House, Berkshire, 1650–2 (house destroyed by fire 1952). 'Dutch Palladian'; architect: Sir Roger Pratt

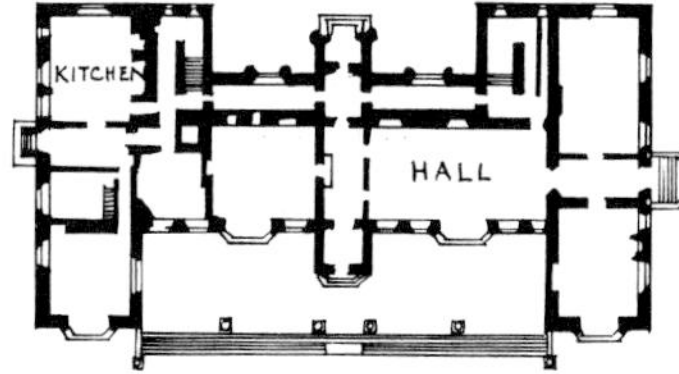

Ground plan of Montacute House, Somerset, 1588–1601

Long gallery: based upon Sudbury Hall, Derbyshire, *c.* 1676

Belton House, Lincolnshire, 1685–9. Architect: William Stanton

Entrance (north) front of Blenheim Palace, Oxfordshire, 1705–22. Baroque; architect: Sir John Vanbrugh

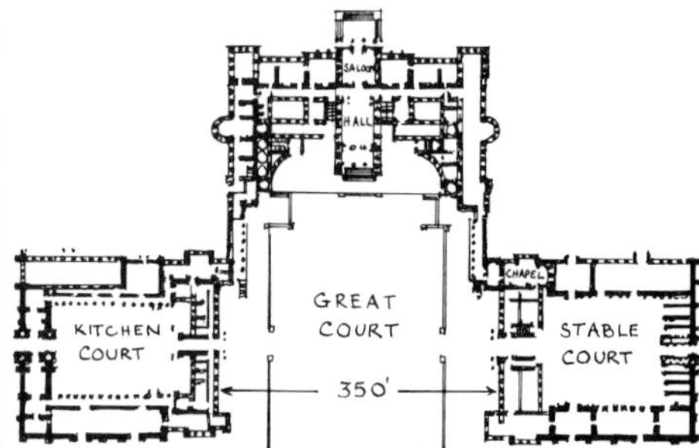

Ground plan of Blenheim. Total frontage 856ft

The stone hall, Houghton Hall, Norfolk, 1721–30. Palladian; architect: Colen Campbell

1598) is a good example (see also ELIZABETHAN ARCHITECTURE; JACOBEAN ARCHITECTURE; RENAISSANCE ARCHITECTURE; SMYTHSON, ROBERT).

By the second half of the seventeenth century the country house was much more closely modelled on the purer Renaissance classical lines. In the 1650s and 1660s the Dutch Palladian house was a symmetrical rectangular block displaying classical orders and ornament (see MAY, HUGH; PRATT, SIR ROGER and WEBB, JOHN). Towards the end of the century a number of large country houses were built of this type with projecting side wings added to the rectangular central block and often with a centrally placed entrance porch slightly advanced also. The skyline might be broken by a lantern or cupola. *Belton House* in Lincolnshire (1685–9) was one such example; of equal interest, but on a different plan is *Petworth House*, Sussex (1688–9).

The garden was now becoming an essential part of a country house scheme and the preference for an apparently casual, natural landscaping was beginning to be followed, in contrast to the formal French and Italian layouts. Gardens included a vegetable and orchard section also.

With the adoption of Italian and French palace design the principal apartments were set on the *piano nobile*, the lofty first floor. Here were to be found the hall and reception rooms while on the second floor above would be the gallery and bedrooms. The latter were now proper chambers, not just part of the passage; they were larger than before, more lavishly furnished and had a coal-burning fireplace. The kitchen was now part of the house and no longer outside in a separate building but it was still situated far from the dining room in whatever part of the house it could be fitted. The principal apartments had priority of position and their aesthetic appearance, on the exterior as well as the interior, was of prime consideration to the architect, who rated his clients' comfort, as well as that of their staff, as secondary.

The short period of Baroque house building in England (see BAROQUE ARCHITECTURE), which created such palatial residences as *Blenheim Palace*, Oxfordshire (1705–22) and *Castle Howard*, Yorkshire (1699–1712) (see VANBRUGH, SIR JOHN), exercised a certain influence on the construction of other, somewhat less immense, conceptions. From 1700 the rectangular block with slightly projecting wings gave place to a main rectangular block which was extended round a three-sided forecourt by curving or straight colonnades which, in turn, connected to side wings or grouped buildings. The *piano nobile* was given even more precedence than before and much of the plan of the rest of the house was sacrificed to height and nobility of the reception apartments on this floor. A fine example of a large country house of this time is *Chatsworth* in Derbyshire, built over the period 1686–1705 by several architects (see ARCHER, THOMAS and TALMAN, WILLIAM).

The eighteenth century was arguably the greatest age of country house building in Britain. The large estates were being farmed more efficiently and thousands of acres of land, previously covered by woodland and heath, were enclosed and put to the plough to become productive. All over the country, on medium-sized and great estates, owners were putting their profits into land and buildings and the ambition to own a beautiful house in fine parkland and grounds resulted in superb houses, some new, others altered and enlarged from an earlier age, and all beautifully decorated and furnished. The sons of the well-to-do and aristocratic families took the Grand Tour of Europe. They now spent two or three years instead of one in France, Italy, Greece and the Middle East. They brought back antique and Renaissance sculpture and paintings, books, coins and ceramics and, above all, ideas and knowledge which would assist them in planning and building their new homes, apartments and art galleries.

The paramount style in the years 1720–50 was Palladian (see PALLADIAN ARCHITECTURE). Here the exterior of the house was monumental, somewhat austere, symmetrical and correctly classical. A rectangular, central block was generally connected to side pavilions by low galleries and colonnades. Straight lines prevailed in reaction from Baroque curves. The ground floor was rusticated and, above this, was the *piano nobile*. The entrance front generally faced north or east and on the opposite long side was the garden façade. Both long elevations usually had a central classical portico with pediment. Apart from this, the plain façade was normally only broken by the rectangular sash windows and parapet above. Great Palladian houses appear to be four-square, solid and indisputably English. What makes them into masterpieces, on the exterior, is the siting and surroundings, for the gardens and parkland are in contrast and complementary to the architecture. The Palladian house was carefully set on rising ground or at the foot of a vista or by a stream or lake. The art of landscape gardening in the specifically English manner was brought to perfection in these years, creating an apparently natural, though carefully studied backcloth to the mansion (see BROWN, LANCELOT (CAPABILITY); PALLADIAN ARCHITECTURE).

The interior of the Palladian house was often a vivid contrast to its exterior. Here was Roman splendour in gilt and marble, large-scale decorative furniture and a host of mirrors reflecting the light of hundreds of candles. The principal rooms were still on the *piano nobile*. The living apartments led off a large, imposing central hall which was entered from the portico or main doorway, approached by a staircase. These apartments would include a dining room, a small and large drawing room or saloon (which generally faced south) and a library, and upstairs would be bedrooms and dressing rooms. Kitchens and servants' quarters were relegated to the basement or, in very large houses, to the terminal pavilions in the wings of the house. Stables and service rooms were also accommodated in these wings. The inconvenience of food being chilled by the time it was served in the dining room because of the considerable distances between here and the kitchen was not thought to be of importance; servants were in plentiful supply and the prestige and splendour of the house was the prime consideration. Characteristic of the great Palladian mansions are *Holkham Hall* (begun 1734) and *Houghton Hall* (designed 1721) in Norfolk (see CAMPBELL, COLEN and KENT, WILLIAM). Other fine examples include *Clandon Park*, Surrey (1731–5, see LEONI, GIACOMO), *Nostell Priory*, Yorkshire (1733–50, see PAINE, JAMES), *Prior Park*, Bath (1735, see *Ralph, Allen*) and *Wrotham Park*, Middlesex (1754, see WARE, ISAAC).

Architectural and decorative design became more diverse in the second half of the eighteenth century. Its expression (apart from a vogue for Chinoiserie, see CHINOISERIE) and the Romantic School continued to be primarily classical but eclecticism had a wider base than before. The extension of the Grand Tour to countries further afield, the archaeological discoveries in Greece and in the Middle East and a heightened interest on the part of scholars brought new sources of inspiration. Architects and artists used ideas from Greek architecture and ornament, studied the excavated remains from Pompeii and experimented with a variety of classical forms. Buildings and, particularly, decoration and interior schemes became finely drawn and sophisticated. The Georgian house of the Classical Revival was elegant and superbly decorated; a standard of excellence in craftsmanship was evidenced in the whole house from architectural construction to the smallest detail of ornamentation and furnishing. Rooms were finely proportioned and well lit by large sash windows in the day-time and the candlelight was augmented after dark by the quantity of mirror glass set in beautiful, carved frames. Graceful staircases led from one floor to another.

As Georgian merged into Regency the eclectic repertory was extended; Egyptian motifs vied with Greek and Roman; furniture was made in a wide variety of imported woods, inlaid, carved and painted. There was a feeling of lightness in Regency houses both in atmosphere and colour. The large windows were draped with light-coloured silk, linen or chintz curtains, often striped or delicately sprigged in line with the gowns of the day. The curtains were held back from the window to permit the light to enter the room. Wallpapers too were light and gay and often striped to blend with curtains and upholstery.

Many examples of beautiful eighteenth-century houses designed by famous architects survive in different parts of Britain and in a fair number of cases the interior deco-

Drawing room, 1810–20. Regency

Toddington Manor, Gloucestershire, 1819–40. Architect: Lord Sudeley. Victorian Gothic

'Wispers', Midhurst, Sussex. Half-timber, 1875. Architect: Norman Shaw

Tigbourne Court, Hambledon, Surrey, 1899. Architect: Sir Edwin Lutyens

'The Pastures', North Luffenham, Leicestershire, 1901. Architect: C. F. A. Voysey

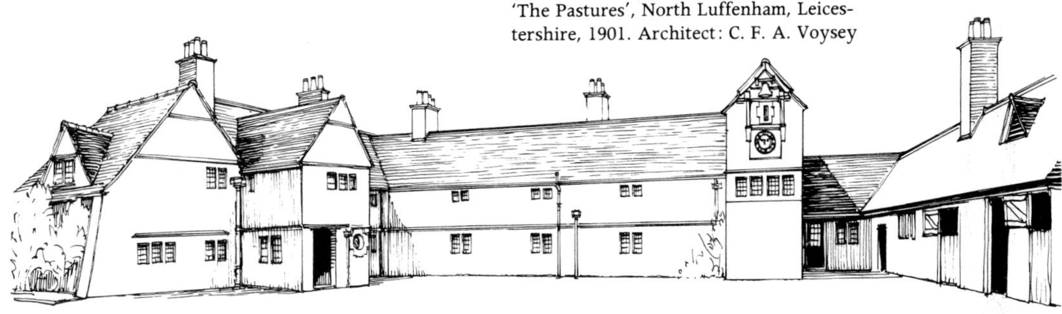

ration has been remarkably preserved or restored. Representative of the varied architectural styles and ornamentation are the Adam masterpieces of *Syon House* (1762–70) and *Osterley Park House* (from 1761) in Middlesex, *Kedleston Hall*, Derbyshire (1758–68) and *Harewood House*, Yorkshire (1759–71, see ADAM, ROBERT), *Attingham Park*, Shrewsbury (1784, see STEUART, GEORGE), *Peper Harow*, Surrey (1765–75, see CHAMBERS, SIR WILLIAM), Wyatt's *Heaton Hall*, Manchester (1772), *Ashridge Park*, Hertfordshire (1803–13) and *Dodington Park*, Gloucestershire (1797–82, see WYATT, JAMES), *Woodhall Park*, Hertfordshire (1778–82, *see* LEVERTON, THOMAS), *Southill*, Bedfordshire (1796–1803, see HOLLAND, HENRY) and Soane's *Moggerhanger*, Befordshire (1806–11) and *Tyringham Park*, Buckinghamshire (*c.* 1796, see SOANE, SIR JOHN) (see also CLASSICISM; GEORGIAN ARCHITECTURE and REGENCY ARCHITECTURE).

This great age of country house building in England ended with the Regency. Some new mansions (and alterations to existing ones) were designed and built throughout the nineteenth century, but the quality craftsmanship and originality of design were lacking. Many of the outstanding architects of the nineteenth century built one or more such houses, using a variety of styles based on earlier work, themes such as Elizabethan/Jacobean, ecclesiastical medieval, or Italian palace design. The houses were sometimes immensely large, with complex towers and turrets, coloured glass and vaulted ceilings. They must also have been inconvenient and, with their enormous halls and reception rooms, chilling to live in. Architecturally interesting examples include *Highclere Castle*, Hampshire (1842–4, see BARRY, SIR CHARLES), *Harlaxton Manor*, Lincolnshire (1831–55, see SALVIN, ANTHONY), *Scarisbrick Hall*, Lancashire (from 1837, see PUGIN, A. W. N.), *Kelham Hall*, Nottinghamshire (1858–61 see SCOTT, SIR GEORGE GILBERT), *Milton Ernest Hall*, Bedfordshire (1853–8 see BUTTERFIELD, WILLIAM), *Carlton Towers*, Yorkshire (1873–5, see PUGIN, A. W. N. and BENTLEY, JOHN FRANCIS).

In the last quarter of the nineteenth century a reaction had set in, especially in domestic architecture, against Victorian over-elaboration and the adoption of such a preponderance of external influences on design. A number of architects began to construct even large country houses in a much simpler manner, using traditional materials and returning to the vernacular for their design inspiration. Webb, friend of William Morris, was one of these and based his houses on the English farmhouse pattern; *Standen* in Sussex (1892–4) is a well-preserved example (see WEBB, PHILIP). The best known of these architects was Shaw, who designed many country houses, adopting differing styles to suit the client but all displaying tasteful simplicity and good craftsmanship. He was especially known for his half-timber 'Tudor' work, brick and terracotta houses and a classical design based on the English version of the Dutch Palladian pattern. Typical are '*Wispers*', *Midhurst* in Sussex (1875) and *Bryanston House*, Dorset (1890, see SHAW, NORMAN). Voysey's work, at the turn of the century, was much plainer and presaged the development of modern architecture. He designed on an informal plan asymmetrical houses using traditional materials. Roofs were long and steeply pitched, ceilings low and decoration at a restrained minimum. '*The Pastures*' at *North Luffenham*, Leicestershire (1901) is characteristic (see VOYSEY, C. F. A.).

The last phase in large country house building came in the twentieth century in the years before the First World War. Many of this period were based on a classical, Georgian plan, others followed Voysey's approach and were nearer to the vernacular. Architects well known for their pleasant country houses of this time include Newton and Dawber (see NEWTON, SIR ERNEST and DAWBER, SIR GUY). The outstanding contribution in this field was made by Lutyens. Like Shaw he designed in a number of different styles and materials, suiting these to the commission and area. He built chiefly in stone or brick of the best quality, of local manufacture if possible. Characteristic of these years are *Heathcote, Ilkley*, Yorkshire (1906) and *Tigbourne Court*, Hambledon, Surrey (1899). Few private houses of any great size were built after this; after 1914, country house building was never the same again for architects, who were no longer untrammelled by thoughts of cost and the availability of land. Lutyens, however, continued to design a few large houses until well into the 1930s. They were all traditional but varied, for example, the stone, classical mansion *Middleton Park*, Oxfordshire (1935, see LUTYENS, SIR EDWIN LANDSEER).

For descriptions and illustrations of specific parts of country house building and decoration over the centuries see also CEILING; CHIMNEYPIECE; CLASSICAL ARCHITECTURE; CLASSICAL ORDER; CLASSICAL ORNAMENT; DOOR; PANELLING; PORCH; PORTICO; STAIRCASE; STUCCO; WINDOW.

COURSE A single, continuous layer of building material—bricks, stones, timber—of the same height. *Coursed rubble* is walling of rough stones laid in courses (see WALLING). A *string course* is a continuous horizontal projecting band, usually moulded, set in the facing wall of a building.

COWL A covering for the head as in a monk's cowl. Architecturally, it is a covering placed as a shield over a chimney or ventilation shaft. It is often constructed to turn with the wind and so improve ventilation.

CREST, CRESTING A decorative finish to the top of a

CREST
Stone parapet cresting, Hardwick Hall, Derbyshire; Elizabethan

wall, roof ridge, screen or other part of a structure (see also BRATTISHING).

CROCKET Carved projecting design of foliage used as ornamentation in Gothic architecture on spires, pinnacles and gables (see also GOTHIC ORNAMENT).

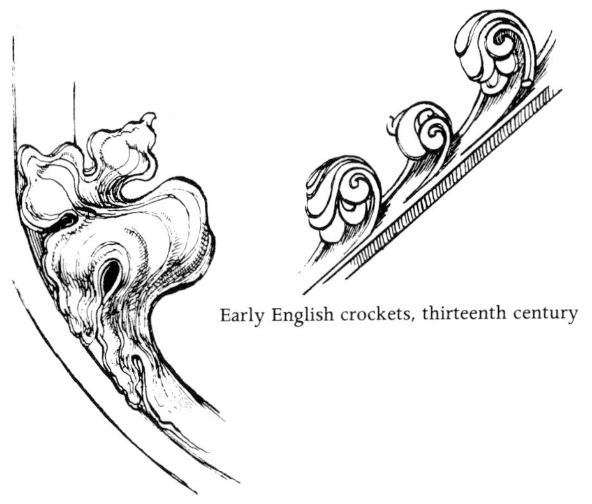

Early English crockets, thirteenth century

CROCKET
Crocket at Lavenham Church, Suffolk, *c.* 1485–1525

CRUCK BUILDING Crucks are pairs of massive curved timbers used in construction which meet at the apex of a building and act as the chief framing beams of wall and roof. The cruck form of house was constructed in Britain from Saxon times and for much of the Middle Ages, mainly in Scotland and the north, Midlands and west of England and, particularly, in Herefordshire.

The early structures were built in bays. Each bay was about 12–16ft wide and the number and spacing of these varied according to the wealth and position of the owner. The bay divisions were marked by the crucks which were bent tree trunks, meeting at the top in gable shape to support a ridge pole which ran horizontally to link the cruck pairs. Parallel to this were slenderer poles, called purlins, linked by crossing rafters. The interstices were filled with branches and the whole roofing, which extended to the ground, was covered on the exterior by brushwood, thatch, turf or heather. Such buildings lacked head-room as the walls and roof were in one curved piece.

Cruck construction evolved from these early buildings to a more sophisticated form. The crucks were cut from trees with a natural curve and were then further shaped

CRUCK BUILDING
Late- sixteenth-century long house: the old farmhouse at Castle Farm Folk Museum, Marshfield. Illustration shows the upper floor of the two-storeyed building. Crucks were tenoned into the tie beams (see right) which carried the upper floor joists

Cruck house, Weobley, Herefordshire

as desired in order to make a symmetrical arch from the pair. The crucks (called blades) were set at their bases into a low stone wall or timber sill instead of being rammed down into the ground as before. At first the buildings were of single storey construction but, as time passed, crucks were extended higher and an intermediate floor was put in. The upper storey seriously lacked head-room so the next stage was to extend the horizontal tie beams (which marked the upper floor level) beyond the crucks to support the wall plates (which were helping to support the roof). The ends of these tie beams were now lined up with the bases of the crucks and it became possible to construct vertical walls for the ground storey. By the fourteenth century crucks could be very long, 35ft or more, giving a good two-storey building, and barns and houses could consist of a number of bays. Roofs were still thatched but tiles were also used. Many cruck-framed buildings have survived though, in many cases, the fact is only visible internally as the exterior walls have been plastered over or additions have been made to the building.

The origins of cruck building are still obscure. Several theories have been advanced; one of these suggests that the construction derives from boat building (upside down) and Viking sources are proffered, another that it stems from an inverted Gothic pointed arch. It is now thought more likely that the form is closer to the early Irish stone oratories and churches (see also TIMBER FRAMING).

CRYPTOPORTICUS In ancient Rome a covered gallery or arcade enclosed and having, along one side, openings rather than columns.

CUBITT, THOMAS (1788–1855) The founder of the first building firm of the modern type. Until Cubitt's time work in different trades had been sub-contracted—bricklaying, masonry, carpentry, plumbing etc.—and, whereas the system had worked well enough until 1800, when large-scale development was involved as the nineteenth century required, it showed itself inefficient and slow. Cubitt bought land and workshops and set up a firm which included all craftsmen necessary to the building trade, on a permanent wage basis. To keep his firm financially solvent he had to provide continuous work for them. This he did by large-scale speculative building. His standards in art and architecture were high, far above those of the men who followed him.

Cubitt performed a major service to *London*. Many of his houses, squares and terraces survive, as sound and elegant as they were over 100 years ago. They expose as inferior much of the later phases of development which surround them. All his life Cubitt used his influence to combat the abuses of architecture, building and living standards to which speculative building is heir. He was especially interested in drainage, smoke control and London's sewage arrangements and constantly worked to improve these. His own houses were soundly built, pleasant to live in and created to last. He supplied first-class amenities in the way of land drainage, sewage disposal, lighting and roads.

Cubitt performed a major service to *London*. Many of Stoke Newington then moved on to St Pancras in Tavistock Square, Woburn Place and Euston Square. The façades of his houses were in stucco and Greek classical in style. His most extensive and best known enterprise was the creation of *Belgravia*. When Buckingham Palace was constructed from Buckingham House, he realized that the area was suitable for wealthy development. He leased an area of swampy ground from Lord Grosvenor and converted it into aristocratic squares. Belgrave Square is typical, designed by Basevi for Cubitt, who built it (see BASEVI, GEORGE). The square is lined with classical terraces with single large houses set at the corners. In the remainder of the Belgravia scheme, Cubitt and his brother Lewis made the designs. *Lewis Cubitt* was an architect and when Thomas laid out Lowndes Square he designed a five-storey block there on Italian palace lines. From Belgravia Thomas Cubitt went on to *Pimlico*, and Clapham Park.

Lewis Cubitt and his brother *Joseph* were also responsible for a good deal of work connected with railways and bridges. Their most outstanding contribution here was *King's Cross Station*, built 1850–2, of which the façade was designed by Lewis. This is an unusual design for its time, being simple and powerful. There are two tremendous, boldly projecting semicircular arches and a central clock tower. The lunettes are glazed and, below these on the lower storey, are six segmental-arched openings and a central porch. The façade is closely attuned to the fine train sheds behind. Lewis Cubitt was also responsible for *Dover Station* (1843–4), and Joseph for *Blackfriars Bridge* over the Thames in London (1863–9) (see RAILWAY ARCHITECTURE).

CULVERT Arched channel or tunnelled drain made of brick or stone for conveying water.

CUSP A point or apex in a decorative design and especially the point at which two curved shapes intersect. The term is applied, in Gothic architecture, specifically to the point of intersection of two foils (arcs) in tracery (see FOIL).

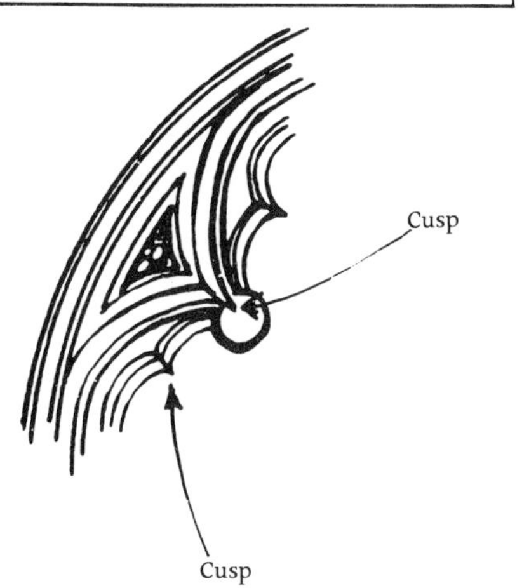

DADO, DIE In classical architecture, the solid block of the pedestal between the cornice above and the plinth or base below (see PEDESTAL). In the interior decorative scheme of a room, the dado is the lower part of the wall, to be found in the place corresponding to the one which it occupies on a pedestal. There is a plinth or skirting member below, reaching to the ground and, above, at a height of $2\frac{1}{2}$–3ft, a moulded rail which is known as a 'dado' or 'chair rail' (see CHAIR RAIL).

DAÏS A raised part of the floor of an apartment. In the Middle Ages the word daïs specifically referred to the platform at one end of a hall on which was placed the high table or seat of honour.

DANCE, GEORGE, the Elder (1698–1768) Holder of the post of Clerk of the City Works in London from 1733 until his death, and architect of the *Mansion House* (1739–53) there, which is a Palladian building using the Corinthian Order. Dance also built a number of London churches of which *St Leonard's, Shoreditch* (1736–40) is the most successful design: the steeple is reminiscent of that of Wren's St Mary-le-Bow.

GEORGE DANCE (THE ELDER)
The Mansion House, London, 1739–57

DANCE, GEORGE, the Younger (1741–1825) Son of the architect of the Mansion House, the younger Dance early displayed flair and imagination in his work. He went to Italy to study at the age of 17, remaining there several years and winning a gold medal at Parma in 1763 for a neo-classical design, ahead of its time and which showed considerable affinity with contemporary French themes. Soon after his return, as a young man of only 24, he designed the beautiful little church of *All Hallows* at

London Wall in the City of London (1765–7). The church interior is noted for its simplicity and clean, functional lines, the restraint of its decoration and the vault, supported on Ionic columns and pierced by large lunettes.

The quality of Dance's work was quickly recognized and he was elected as a founder member of the Royal Academy of Arts in 1768 and, in the same year, succeeded his father as Clerk of the City Works in London. His *Newgate Prison* there (1769–82) was one of the most original buildings of the eighteenth century. This impressive, unusual structure presented an appearance suited to its purpose; dynamic and austere, the mass of the building was enclosed by unbroken rusticated walling which lent an awesome atmosphere to the place. In the centre was the Governor's House, flanked by entrance lodges, the windows of which contrasted with the great areas of rusticated wall on either side. The prison was burnt by Gordon rioters in 1780, later rebuilt, but finally demolished in 1902 to make way for the Central Criminal Courts.

Dance's later work was equally original: for example, his *Council Chamber* in *Guildhall*, built 1777 but destroyed 1908. This had a remarkable dome, lit from a central opening which, as in the All Hallows vault, indicated the way later to be followed by his pupil Soane (see SOANE, SIR JOHN). By the turn of the century Dance turned to more austere Greek Revivalist design, evidenced by his house at *Stratton Park*, Hertfordshire (1803–6, largely demolished 1960).

DAWBER, SIR GUY (1861–1938) Born at King's Lynn and studied at the Royal Academy Schools in London, he became an articled pupil in King's Lynn, then assisted Sir Thomas Deane in Dublin and afterwards entered the office of Sir Ernest George (see GEORGE, SIR ERNEST). Dawber was primarily a domestic architect and, following in Newton's tradition (see NEWTON, SIR ERNEST), built many houses of vernacular type, mostly in the West Country. Characteristic was *Ashley Chase* in Dorset (1929), also *Stowell Hill*, Somerset and *Burdocks*, Gloucestershire. Deeply interested in the preservation of England's countryside, Dawber created the Council for the Preservation of Rural England. He won the Royal Gold Medal for Architecture in 1928 and was President of the Royal Society of British Architects 1925–7.

DEMILUNE A crescent-shaped outwork constructed, in military architecture, in the moat to protect a bastion.

DIAPER WORK A textile fabric, woven since the Middle Ages, diamond-patterned by the directions of the threads. In architecture the term is applied to an all-over surface decoration in diamond shapes or squares which are frequently enriched by carved or painted floral motifs; it is especially to be found in medieval Gothic architecture (see also GOTHIC ORNAMENT).

DIAPER WORK
Carved stone diaper decoration, fourteenth century

DIAPHRAGM ARCH Transverse arch which carries masonry partition walling, used particularly in timber roof structures in order to inhibit the spread of fire (see ARCH and VAULTING).

DILETTANTI SOCIETY Founded in England in the 1730s for artistic encouragement and patronage of excavation and research into the antique classical world, especially Greece. It published original papers, commissioned and financially supported expeditions by some of its members. *Robert Wood*'s journey to Palmyra (the results of his studies there published in 1753 as *The Ruins of Palmyra*) was one such expedition. *Stuart* and *Revett*'s journeys in Greece, which resulted in the publication in 1762 of *The Antiquities of Athens*, were also under the aegis of the society (see GRAND TOUR and STUART, JAMES).

DOBSON, JOHN (1787–1865) A Northumbrian architect and engineer whose work ranged from docks and railway structures to country houses and town planning. He is best known for his work in *Newcastle upon Tyne* where he was responsible for the *Central Station*, introducing an immense roof construction of iron and glass (1850). Dobson also designed many streets and squares in the city which were carried out in stone by Grainger, a speculative builder. These façades were designed in classical style but Dobson introduced neo-Gothic to the area in his churches and some of his country houses.

DOME (CUPOLA) A convex rounded roof, covering a part or whole of a building, with a base on the horizontal plane which is circular, elliptical or polygonal. In vertical section the dome may be hemispherical, partly elliptical, saucer-shaped or formed like a bulb. The English word dome derives from the Latin *domus* (='house') and the Italian *duomo* (= 'cathedral' or 'house of God'). It has been traditional in Italy to build domes over churches and cathedrals and consequently 'dome' has been adopted for this usage in England. The more usual Italian term is 'cupola', derived from the Latin *cupula*, diminutive of *cupa* (='flask', 'barrel'). 'Cupola' is also used in English but is more commonly applied to a small or lantern dome or the internal ceiling of a dome.

Unlike the arch and the vault, the dome had not been introduced to Renaissance Europe from the ancient classical world. The Romans had extensively developed the theme of the stone and concrete vault but had largely neglected the possibilities of domical coverings. The famous Pantheon dome in Rome (see CLASSICAL ARCHITECTURE) is supported upon walls of circular plan and so presents fewer structural problems. However, this system of construction limits the spatial capabilities of interior architectural design.

In Renaissance and, even more so, Baroque architecture, the dome became a fundamental characteristic of design and a variety of different forms of construction were attempted and built. To achieve, in particular the Baroque, spatial effects of lighting and of solid stone structures ornamented by painted and sculptured curved surfaces appearing to float upwards, it was necessary to support the dome upon free-standing piers instead of the more constricting walling. The basis for this type of construction was the Byzantine development of the dome, evolved in Constantinople, capital city of the Byzantine Empire, a construction which, in its turn, had derived from earlier buildings in Anatolia, Persia and Syria.

The problem in supporting a dome, which has a circular or elliptical base, upon four or more free-standing piers set upon a square or polygonal plan, is to marry the two forms. The drawings illustrate the gradual development in solving this problem. 'A' shows the Pantheon type of structure, a circular-based dome supported on circular walling. 'B' illustrates the next stage where an octagonal base is provided to support the dome by building across the angles of the walls constructed on a square plan. 'C' indicates the structure of such angle-filling which is the *squinch* (see SQUINCH). This method was used by the Romans and appears in many Byzantine and later European buildings but was not suited to support a large dome nor one constructed upon piers or columns.

The method evolved in Byzantine construction to solve the problem of carrying the dome upon free-standing piers was the use of the *pendentive* and this system was widely employed in European Renaissance and Baroque architecture. A pendentive is a spherical triangle. In using

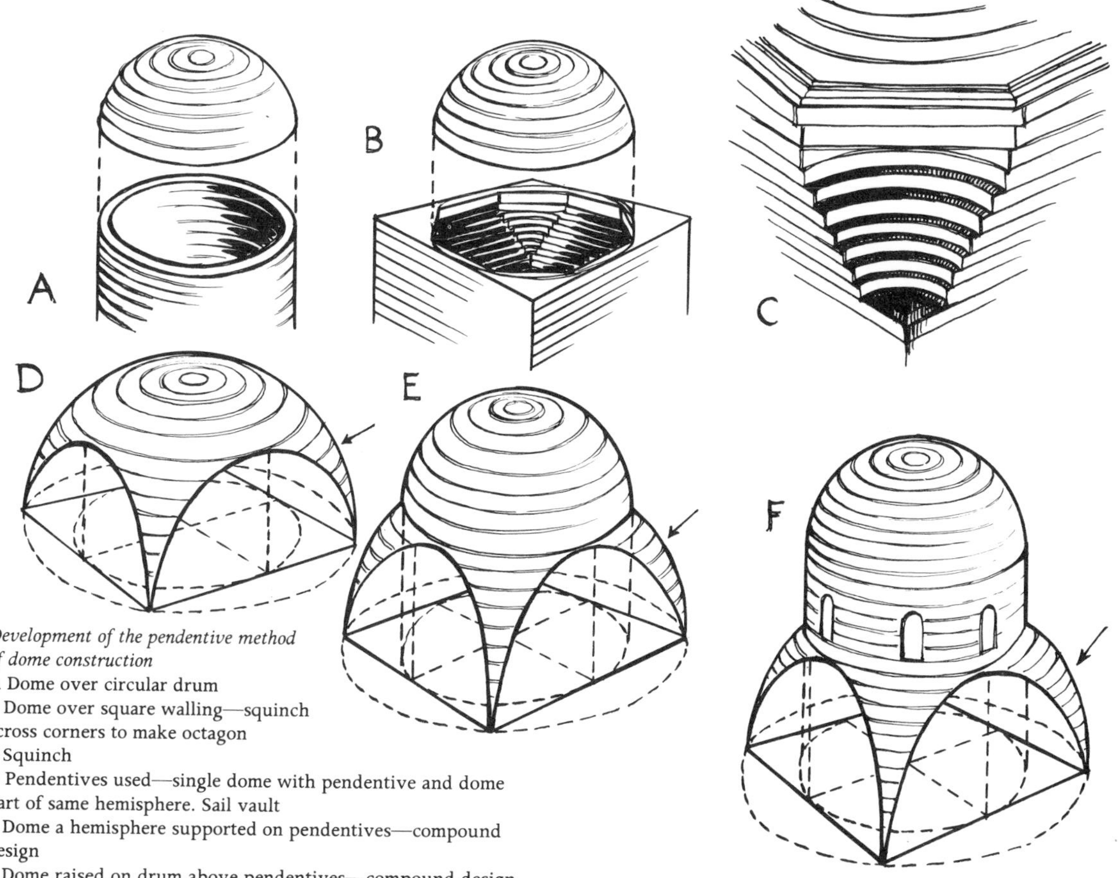

Development of the pendentive method of dome construction
A Dome over circular drum
B Dome over square walling—squinch across corners to make octagon
C Squinch
D Pendentives used—single dome with pendentive and dome part of same hemisphere. Sail vault
E Dome a hemisphere supported on pendentives—compound design
F Dome raised on drum above pendentives—compound design

Interior of dome, Church of St Stephen, Walbrook, London, 1672–9. Architect: Sir Christopher Wren

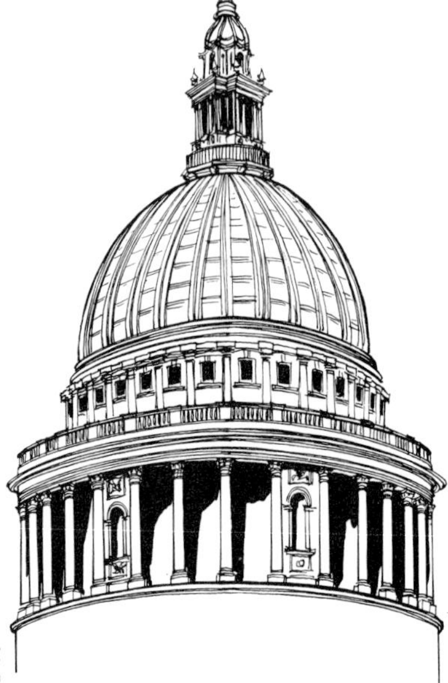

Lantern, dome and drum of St Paul's Cathedral, London, 1675–1710. Architect: Sir Christopher Wren

Cupola, Royal Hospital Chelsea, 1682–92. Architect: Sir Christopher Wren

St Peter's Basilica, Rome. Drum and dome carried on pendentives supported on piers, 1547–90. Architects: Michelangelo and della Porta

this form of construction the triangular spaces between the square section of the plan of the piers and the circular section of the base of the dome are built as if they are parts of a lower, larger dome, so that their section is like that of an arch carried across the diagonal of the square space to be covered. The lower dome possesses a horizontal section which is concentric with the plan of the intended dome. As the lower dome is too large to fill the square space, it is cut off in vertical planes formed by the four sides of the square. When the four remaining parts of the lower dome have been built high enough to form a complete circle within the square section, this circle provides the basis for supporting the actual dome. This is shown in 'D', a domical structure which, if not further developed, is known as a *sail vault* because it gives the appearance of a sail filled with wind anchored at the four corners. In 'E' the dome is set in position, supported on its lower dome, that is, the pendentives. The typical Renaissance or Baroque dome is seen in the final stage, 'F', where a dome is carried on a circular drum which is pierced by window openings, the drum standing upon pendentives. Internally the dome may be painted or coffered (see COFFER). The pendentives are often decorated with paintings or mosaics, as at St Peter's Basilica in Rome, while the drum is articulated with a classical order (see CLASSICAL ORDER). Externally most large domes carry a lantern (see LANTERN) (see also BAROQUE ARCHITECTURE; BYZANTINE ARCHITECTURE; RENAISSANCE ARCHITECTURE; SQUINCH and VAULTING).

DOOR, DOORWAY, DOOR FURNITURE The entrance, which may be opened and closed, to a building or room. The form of the doorway has evolved in consonance with architectural styles and may be arched or rectangular. Doorways, generally made of stone or wood, are usually framed with a series of mouldings and many are decoratively carved. This door-frame or door-case is termed the 'architrave'. The doors, of stone, wood, metal or glass, are operated by means of hinges, pivots or a sliding mechanism.

Saxon doorways were small and usually round- or triangular-headed; doors were of wood (see SAXON ARCHITECTURE). Romanesque doorways acted as a decorative focus for the buildings, being usually the most richly ornamented feature, notably in ecclesiastical structures (see ROMANESQUE ARCHITECTURE). The round-arched doorway was deeply recessed and multi-moulded and the wooden door was often square-headed, leaving an intermediate stone panel—the tympanum—to be carved lavishly in high relief (see TYMPANUM).

During the Middle Ages the Gothic pointed arch predominated for doorway design. In large buildings, especially cathedrals, these arches were moulded and carved with the current style of ornament (see GOTHIC ARCHITECTURE and GOTHIC ORNAMENT). The sides of such doorways (see JAMB) were shafted. These shafts or columns generally stood free and they had capitals and bases. The shape and proportion of the arch altered as time passed, becoming wider and flatter until it culminated in the later fifteenth century in the four-centred style (see ARCH). Such

Stone shafted early Gothic doorway. Wood door with ironwork fittings. Bolton Priory Church, Yorkshire, early thirteenth century

Carved wood drawing room doorway. Levens Hall, Cumbria. Late Elizabethan

Saxon doorway, Brixworth Church, Northamptonshire. Re-use of Roman bricks

Fourteenth-century carved stone doorway. Wooden door with iron scrollwork

Stone doorway, in the west front of Chester Cathedral, *c.* 1500–1520

Church of St Margaret Lothbury, City of London. Stone Corinthian columns and pediment, seventeenth century. Architect: Sir Christopher Wren

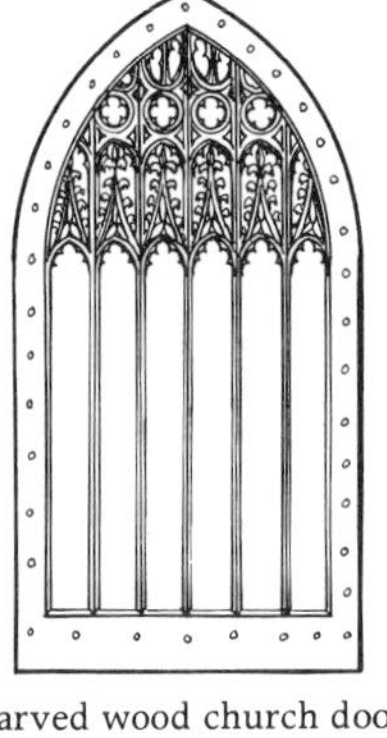

Carved wood church door, 1350

Stone doorway with glass and iron fanlight at 20 St James's Square, London, 1777–89. Architect: Robert Adam

Church of St Edmund, Lombard Street, London. Cornice supported on consoles, seventeenth century. Architect: Sir Christopher Wren

Carved stone doorway in the Church of St Andrew-by-the-Wardrobe, City of London, seventeenth century. Architect: Sir Christopher Wren

Venetian door. Carved stone doorway with wood door at The Royal Society of Arts, John Adam Street, London, 1772–4. Architect: Robert Adam

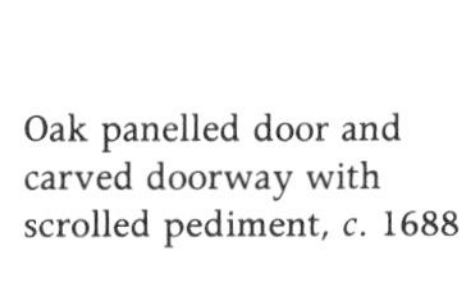

Oak panelled door and carved doorway with scrolled pediment, *c.* 1688

Perpendicular and Tudor Gothic doorways were characterized by a square hood-mould over the arch, the spandrels being filled with carved ornament (see HOOD-MOULD and SPANDREL). Medieval doors were mainly of wood, often vertically panelled and sometimes carved with Gothic tracery, foils and cusps (see CUSP; FOIL and TRACERY). Doors were usually hinged and door furniture was of wrought iron, sometimes decorative and complex in design.

The classical doorway, in use from the second half of the sixteenth century, was of rectangular shape surrounded by a moulded, often carved, door-case. Many designs were flanked by columns or pilasters which supported an entablature (see CLASSICAL ORDER) and, often, a pediment which might be triangular, curved, broken or scrolled (see PEDIMENT). Some cornices were supported by *consoles*. In the eighteenth century, notably the second half, many doorways were enclosed in a round arch, the lunette above the door being filled with glass panels enclosed by decorative iron work in fan design (see FANLIGHT and LUNETTE). The *Venetian door* of the time was composed of an arched central doorway flanked by tall, flat-topped windows (see also VENETIAN WINDOW).

The classical door, usually of wood, single or double, was panelled; at first this was in two or three square or rectangular panels, then in eight or ten, but by the eighteenth century, most often in six panels. These were sunk or raised (see MOULDINGS) and were decorated by carving or metal ornament. Most doors were hinged. Door furniture, especially in the eighteenth century when architects such as Kent or Adam designed their own architectural detail (see ADAM, ROBERT and KENT, WILLIAM), showed especially fine metal craftsmanship. Door furniture now included the door knob, finger and kicking plates, spindles and escutcheons. By this time also the earlier oak or pine doors had been replaced by polished mahogany ones.

The parts of a door are shown in the illustration of a classical example. A *door sill* is a threshold designed to

Door furniture at Saltram House, Devonshire, *c.* 1769. Architect: Robert Adam

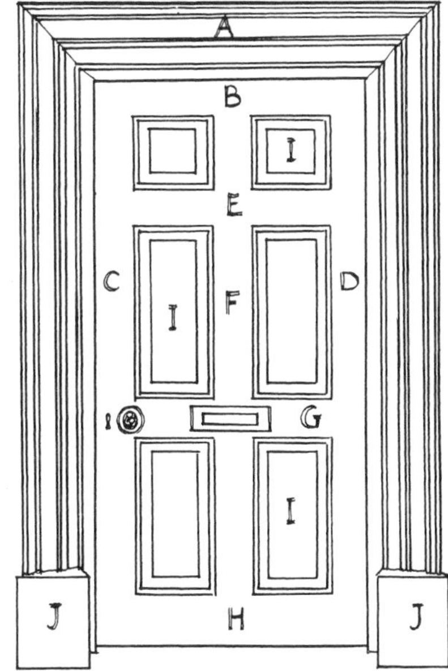

Parts of a door and doorway
A Architrave B Top rail C Shutting stile D Hanging stile E Frieze rail F Muntin G Lock rail H Bottom rail I Panel J Plinth block

keep out the rain; it is a horizontal member fitted at the bottom of a door jamb. A *door stop* is a projecting strip attached to or part of the frame, which forms a stop to the door. A *wicket door* is a small door incorporated into a larger one (see PANELLING).

DOSSERET

Dosseret in Byzantine capital. Church of S. Vitale, Ravenna, Italy, AD 526–48

A deep four-faced impost block, often with curved sides, set between the capital and the springing of an arch. Seen especially in Byzantine structures but also in some Romanesque ones to support wide arch voussoirs (see ARCH; VOUSSOIR).

DOVETAILING A method of fastening pieces of wood where the joint is composed of tenons cut in the shape of the spreading tail of a dove (see MORTISE).

DOWEL A pin of wood, metal, slate or other material for securing together by penetration two sections of wood, stone or concrete.

DRESSINGS Worked and finished stones used in architectural features such as doorways and window openings.

DRIP The projecting member of an upper moulding, for example a cornice, which is generally channelled underneath in order to throw off rainwater and so prevent it running down the wall below. The channel is called a *throat* (see also HOOD-MOULD).

DROP In architecture, any feature of a pendant character. The term may refer to the guttae, the small, conical drops depending from the mutules in a Doric entablature (see CLASSICAL ORDER) or to the carved ornament depending from a staircase newel (see STAIRCASE). It may also be applied to the pendant ribbed decoration in a plaster ceiling (see CEILING), the termination in Gothic tracery (see TRACERY) or any other ornament which hangs down. (For *drop arch*, see ARCH.)

EGYPTIAN HALL A hall with an internal peristyle of columns (see PERISTYLE) and a misnomer in that it is an interior designed in classical form and has no connection with Egyptian architecture. Such an apartment was described by Vitruvius and adopted by Palladio. It then became favoured by the English Palladians as in, for example, Lord Burlington's *Assembly Rooms* in *York* (see BURLINGTON, LORD; PALLADIAN ARCHITECTURE and VITRUVIUS).

ELEVATION, FAÇADE An external face or front of a building. 'Façade' is often used to refer especially to the principal front. An 'elevation' is also a drawing of a building made in projection on a vertical plane.

ELIZABETHAN ARCHITECTURE The building style of the reign of Queen Elizabeth I (1558–1603). Architecturally this was a time of transition between the English late Gothic traditions and the Renaissance forms then paramount in Italy and much of western Europe. English vernacular design was still to be seen in the smaller buildings, mainly houses, constructed in stone or brick or by timber-framing methods. These buildings were externally characterized by their asymmetry, their sloping, gabled roofs and modest-sized rectangular window openings; the interiors were decorated by ribbed and pendant plaster ceilings, two-stage carved chimneypieces and inlaid and carved wood-panelled walls.

Elizabethan England was a time of extensive building activity, this energy directed not, as in the Middle Ages, towards the erection of cathedrals and churches, but largely to the construction of country houses. At all levels of society, from aristocratic landowner to yeoman farmer, there was a deep desire to build a more spacious, splendid and modern home. It was mainly in the larger of these that the new Renaissance forms of building were experimented with. Wealthier landowners travelled in France, Flanders (and a very few reached Italy), bringing back with them ideas of the new classical forms to be introduced into their new houses.

Knowledge of the purer classical strain to be seen in Renaissance structures in Italy, based upon ancient Roman building, was available in England in the publications of Vitruvius, Palladio, Alberti and others (see PALLADIAN ARCHITECTURE and VITRUVIUS). Serlio's treatise was widely used (see SERLIO, SEBASTIANO) also Shute's later version (see SHUTE, JOHN). At this time though, the English were attracted particularly by the vigour and exuberance of the Flemish as well as the more sophisticated French interpretations of Italian Renaissance design. In Franch Englishmen were in sympathy with the châteaux of de l'Orme and Bullant as well as Lescot's work at the Louvre. In Flanders, even more, they felt an affinity with the work of Floris in the Antwerp Town Hall and with de Key in that of Leiden. The builders they employed in the construction of their new country houses drew exhaustively upon the books of designs and ornamental detail published in French, Flemish and German treatises. The illustrations in these books displayed a wealth of vigorous, rich ornament in the form of strapwork and cartouches, decorative orders, cresting and gabling. English builders incorporated these exciting new forms into their buildings, caring little and understanding less if their orders were incorrectly proportioned or employed according to the results of centuries of development in the antique world (see CLASSICAL ARCHITECTURE; CLASSICAL ORDER). It did not matter because Elizabethan builders were not, in general, using these orders constructionally but as a decorative finish upon a building of medieval construction.

And so the Elizabethan great houses present a mixture of old and new concepts. Of the Renaissance features symmetry was the most fundamental. The medieval house design which had grown up round a closed, four-sided court, was replaced by a more compact one built on an

Little Moreton Hall, Cheshire.
Half-timber, 1559–80

Entrance porch (frontispiece).
Cobham Hall, Kent, *c.* 1594

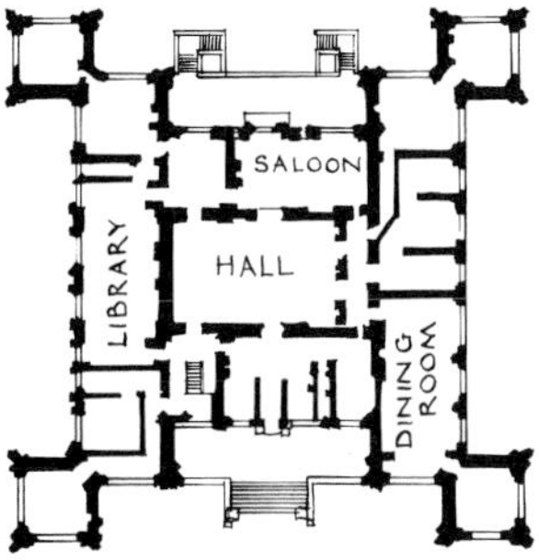

SALOON
HALL
LIBRARY
DINING ROOM

Ground plan, Wollaton Hall

Wollaton Hall, Nottinghamshire.
Stone, 1580–8

Carved oak pilaster and panelling, *c.* 1600

Gate of Honour (upper part). Gonville and Caius, Cambridge, 1573–5

Carved stone fireplace with carved oak overmantel, *c.* 1600

Main chamber, 1575–80. Ribbed and pendant plaster ceiling; carved and inlaid wall panelling; heraldic window glass

open 'E'- or 'H'-shaped ground plan; it was a rectangular block with projecting wings at each end. The characteristic two- or three-stage entrance porch (the frontispiece) (the centre bar of the 'E' or 'H') provided a focal centrepiece and, on each side of this, the apartments, the windows, the gables, the chimney-stacks and other architectural features were arranged symmetrically, one side of the building balancing the other. Another new feature was the much greater area of window glass in relation to that of the walls. Also, the skyline was broken dramatically and picturesquely by curving decorative gables and ornamented chimney-stacks and shafts. Among the older, more traditional features were the late Gothic mullioned and transomed window frames and the construction methods.

Characteristic examples of the Elizabethan great house include *Longleat House*, Wiltshire (1550–80), *Montacute House*, Somerset (1588–1601), *Hardwick Hall*, Derbyshire (1591–7), *Burghley House*, Northamptonshire (1580s). Rather smaller and more traditional timber-framed examples are magnificently represented at *Speke Hall*, Lancashire (1598) and *Little Moreton Hall*, Cheshire (1559–80). (See CEILING; COUNTRY HOUSE; CREST; GABLE; GALLERY; RENAISSANCE ARCHITECTURE; SMYTHSON, ROBERT; STAIRCASE).

ELMES, HARVEY LONSDALE (1814–47) An architect of great promise whose reputation rests, because of his early death at the age of 34 from tuberculosis, on one major work. This is *St George's Hall* in the city of *Liverpool*.

After three years of study at the Royal Academy Schools and afterwards a short time in architectural practice, in 1839 Elmes won the competition by his design to build St George's Hall; the following year he was again successful in competition for the new *Assize Courts* in the city. It was decided to amalgamate the two functions in one building and Elmes designed the scheme which comprised the crown court at one end of the structure, the civic court at the other and included a great central hall for concert performances. Work began in 1841.

Elmes's building is regarded as one of the most outstanding in Greek Revival style yet the 25-year-old designer had never had the opportunity to visit Italy or Greece. The monumental exterior dominates the large open space in which it is sited in the centre of the city, the giant Corinthian Order controlling the design and unifying the features of the differing functions of the structure. The south end is completed with a portico and pediment, the north is apsidal. The flights of approach steps adjust the design to the steepness of the site and the long horizontal lines of these, the entablature and the attic emphasize the unity of the design. Inside, the great vaulted roof of the large concert hall, based on the design of the Baths of Caracalla in Rome, was constructed of hollow bricks. After Elmes's death Sir Robert Rawlinson was the engineer in charge of building this vault, 80ft in span. Cockerell (see COCKERELL, CHARLES ROBERT) was responsible for the completion of the rest of the interior of the chamber with its monumental marble piers and classical statuary. The hall was opened in 1854 with a performance of Handel's *Messiah*.

EMBRASURE A wall opening with sides slanted or splayed from within often to be found in fortified buildings. In a battlemented parapet, 'embrasure' is the same as 'crenelle', that is, the space between merlons (see BATTLEMENT).

ENCAUSTIC A decorative process where substances were fixed by heating or burnt into the surface of the basic material. An example was the ancient method of fixing colours in a painting by the application of hot wax. Others include enamelling, and the firing of painted earthenware (see also TILES).

ELMES, HARVEY LONSDALE
St George's Hall, Liverpool, 1839–54

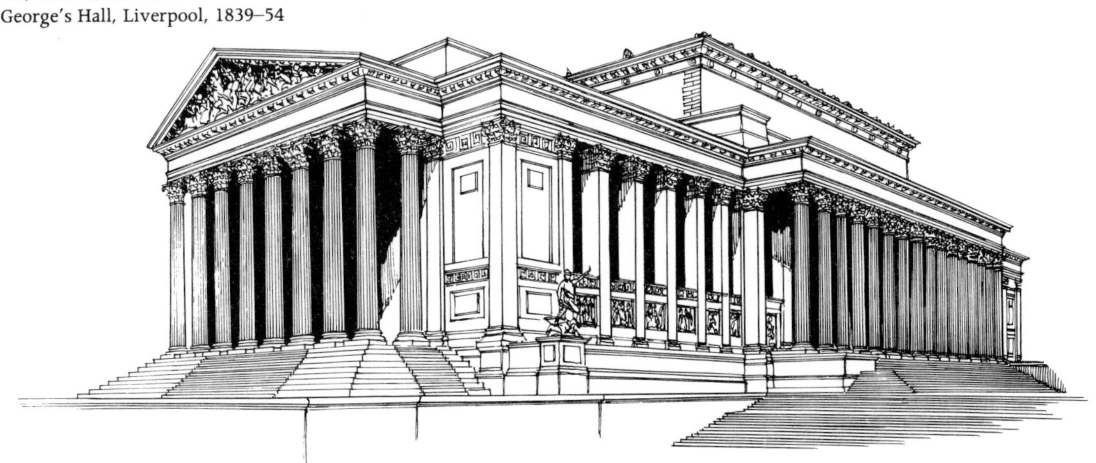

ENCEINTE In fortified building, the main curtain walling or ramparts, reinforced by towers and gates, which enclosed the castle (see CASTLE).

ENFILADE From the French *enfiler* (='to thread' or 'to string' and so to make an opening from one end to another). The word was applied in architecture to the custom of lining up the doorways in a suite of rooms so that, when the doors were all open, a long vista was obtained. This feature of interior design was introduced in the middle of the seventeenth century and was characteristic of Baroque planning. As 'in enfilade', the expression was also used in landscape gardening to describe trees planted in long rows to provide such vistas.

ENTERCLOSE, INTERCLOSE A partition dividing two parts or apartments in a building; this may be a screen or a passageway.

EXEDRA A Greek word which, in ancient times, referred to a seat out-of-doors, or to a room with seats and opening into a portico of a gymnasium or palestra where people met for conversation or where they might listen to the lectures and disputations of philosophers.

More generally, in classical architecture, the exedra may be any semicircular or polygonal recess in a wall or the colonnaded interior of an apse.

F

FACING MATERIALS Facing is the finish applied to the exterior surface of a building. When the building is referred to as *cased*, this indicates that such a facing is made of a high-quality material usually finer than that of the structure of the building. *Rendering* is the covering of a wall with a mortar or plaster mix (see also PARGETING; PLASTERWORK). External walls are generally rendered with two coats and, when left plain, the finish is just referred to as a rendering. If gravel or shingle is thrown on to this surface before it sets, partly to provide a protective coating and partly for decoration, this is known as *roughcast*. *Pebbledash* is similar but usually an extra coat of about a quarter of an inch in thickness is laid over the rendering and small pebbles or flints attached to it while it is still soft.

Mosaic as a facing is composed of small pieces of coloured glass, marble or stone pressed into a mastic or rendering to form a decorative, often pictorial, finish. The Romans referred to each tiny cube of coloured material as a *tessera* (pl. *tesserae*) (see also CLADDING; *Flushwork*, under BUILDING MATERIALS; STONE; and TILES).

FANLIGHT The name given to a window above a door which, as was usual in the eighteenth century, is semicircular and has glazing bars radiating outwards in the form of a fan. Later the word came to apply to any window above a door or even an upper part of a window which hinged to open.

FANLIGHT
No. 13 Mansfield Street, London, 1780s

FASTIGIUM A Latin word used in architecture to refer to the summit of a gable or roof-ridge of a building.

FENESTRATION The arrangement of windows in a building façade (see WINDOW).

FERREY, BENJAMIN (1810–80) A Victorian ecclesiastical architect who was responsible for a number of churches typical of their period and mainly on the accepted Gothic Revival pattern, for example, *St Stephen's, Rochester Row, London* (1845–7) and *St James's Church, Morpeth* in Northumberland (1843–6). For nearly 40 years he was diocesan architect to Bath and Wells, during which time he carried out a good deal of restoration work on *Wells Cathedral* and the nearby *Bishop's Palace*.

FINIAL A finishing or terminal ornamental feature which crowns a spire, pinnacle, gable, canopy, pediment, or staircase newel or the bench ends of pews.

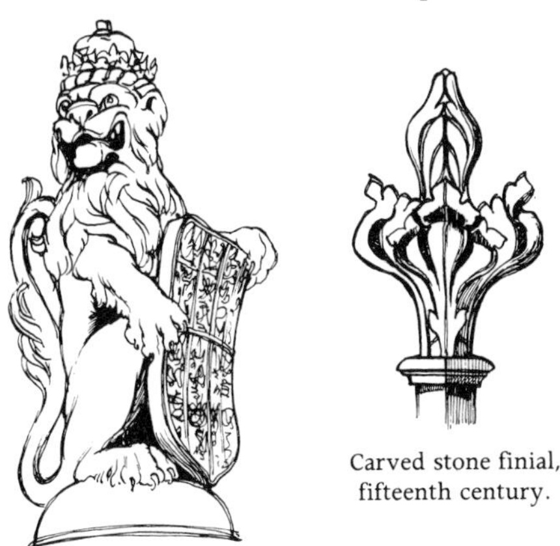

Carved stone finial, fifteenth century.

Carved stone finial: entrance way, Hampton Court Palace, Surrey. Tudor

FLÈCHE An extremely slender spire made of wood or metal rising from the ridge of a roof and often set over the crossing of a church in place of a tower; also known as a *spirelet*. '*Flèche*' is a French word meaning 'arrow' or 'shaft'. The feature was often adopted in French church architecture because it caused fewer problems of stress and thrust than a tower which would be heavier. A notable example is the *Cathedral of Notre Dame* in *Paris*. A more modern instance, in England, is that of the post-war *Coventry Cathedral* (see CHAPEL; SPIRE).

FLEUR-DE-LIS Modern French term for the lily-flower, a plant of the genus Iris. Older spellings include *fleur-de-lys* and *flower-de-luce*. In architecture as well as textile design the fleur-de-lis stems from the conventionalized motif which was borne upon the royal arms of France under the monarchy. This was the heraldic lily which, according to some sources, derived from the iris, according to others, from the head of a sceptre or battle-axe.

FLEURON A flower-shaped ornament.

FLITCROFT, HENRY (1697–1769) Under the patronage of Lord Burlington, Flitcroft worked as a draughtsman and architectural assistant then, with the earl's further assistance, he filled various posts in the Office of Works finally becoming Comptroller in 1758.

Flitcroft's work was traditional, even slavishly, Palladian as is evidenced by the vast but uninspired façade of *Wentworth Woodhouse* in Yorkshire (*c.* 1740) but his town houses, such as *No. 10 St James's Square* in *London*, were

FLÈCHE
Cathedral of Notre Dame, Paris, from the south-west, 1180–1330

FLITCROFT, HENRY
Church of St Giles-in-the-Fields, London, 1731–4

more interesting. His best-known church owes a good deal to Wren and even more to Gibbs' St Martin-in-the-Fields nearby; this is *St Giles-in-the-Fields*: a building later to be overshadowed, almost eclipsed by Centrepoint (see PALLADIAN ARCHITECTURE).

FLUSH Level with the surrounding or adjacent surface; on the same plane. So, a *flush bead moulding* is one in which the rounded moulding is sunk till its outer surface is flush with the wall or door panel. Similarly, in *flush pointing* the mortar is filled out to be level with the face of the brickwork.

FOIL In Gothic tracery, one of the small arcs separated by cusps. The number of these in the design is expressed in the name: trefoil (3), quatrefoil (4), cinquefoil (5), multifoil (many) (see CUSP; TRACERY).

Quatrefoil Trefoil

FOLIATED Enriched by carved leaf ornament; features or surfaces may be so decorated.

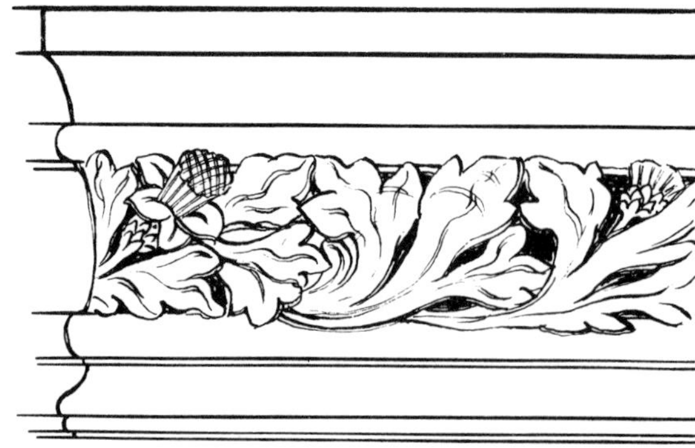

Foliated moulding: Compton Wynyates, Warwickshire, *c.* 1540

Foliated capital: Lincoln Cathedral choir, thirteenth century

FOLLY In architecture, a costly, but generally useless structure which is thought to indicate the foolishness of the builder. The term refers particularly to constructions sited in parkland; some are fantasy buildings, others express the vanity of the owner. Many are pseudo-classical or Gothic ruins, representing a fashionable eighteenth- or nineteenth-century whim. An alternative term is *eye-catcher*, as follies were often designed to terminate a vista.

FONT A vessel which contains the consecrated water for baptism. The font is usually to be found in the nave of a church, near the west end (see CHURCH DESIGN AND STRUCTURE). Fonts were generally made of stone, the basin sometimes lead-lined. A number of late medieval examples retain their elaborate carved wood canopies.

FRAMED BUILDING A structure carried on a frame

FONT
Carved stone font, Eardisley Church, Herefordshire, Norman

rather than on load-bearing walls (see STEEL-FRAME CONSTRUCTION; TIMBER FRAMING).

FRIEZE A deep band, plain or decorated with sculpture or painting, extending round the upper walls of a room below the cornice (for the classical frieze see CLASSICAL ORDER).

FRONTISPIECE The main façade or entrance of a building (see ELIZABETHAN ARCHITECTURE; JACOBEAN ARCHITECTURE).

FRY, EDWIN MAXWELL (*b.* 1899) One of the pioneers in Britain in the 1930s of the modern movement in architecture. Among his early houses is the flat-roofed, severely plain pacesetter for its time, *Sun House* in Frognal Way, *Hampstead* (1935) (see MODERN ARCHITECTURE). As executant architect working with a committee of others he again set a trend in building a low-cost block of flats named *Kensal House* in Ladbroke Grove in London (1936).

During these years Maxwell Fry helped a number of architect refugees from Nazi Germany. He was in partnership between 1934 and 1936 with one of the most famous of these, Walter Gropius, with whom he designed the *Village College* at *Impington*, built 1936–9. The scheme for the building of village colleges had originated with Henry Morris, the Secretary for Education to the Cambridgeshire County Council. These colleges were intended as centres

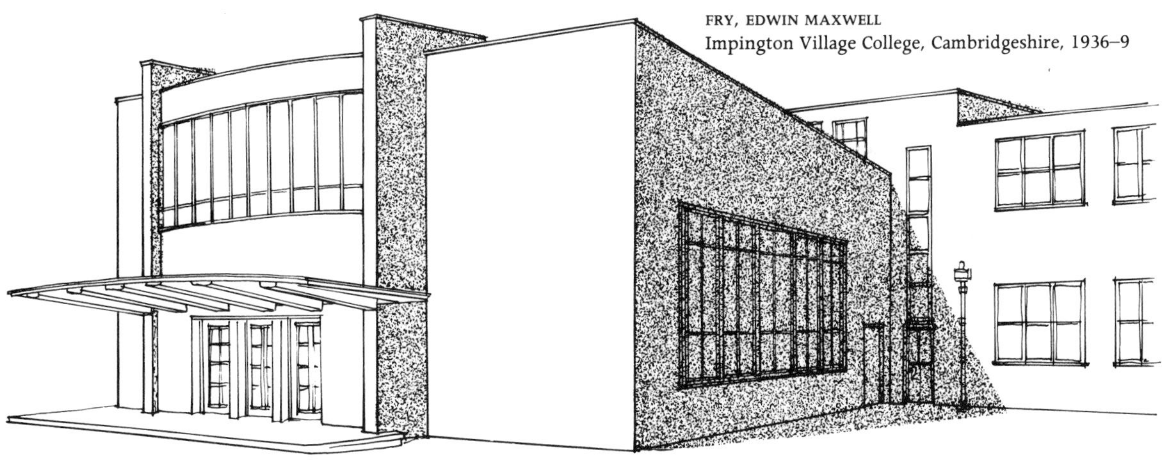

FRY, EDWIN MAXWELL
Impington Village College, Cambridgeshire, 1936–9

Kensal House, Ladbroke Grove, London, 1936

Buttress gablet: Palace of Westminster, London, 1836–65

Dutch gable: 'Swakeleys', Middlesex, 1629–38

Crow-stepped gables: Sutton Place, Surrey, 1523–30

Shaped gables: Trerice Manor House, Cornwall, *c.* 1573

of cultural and social life in rural areas and to cater for all age groups. The first, at Sawston, was opened in 1930; Impington followed. It was the first such college to be built on modern lines with simple shapes, plain façades and large windows.

After the Second World War Maxwell Fry became leader of the Fry, Drew Partnership, a firm which carried out a great deal of work abroad which included housing, university and commercial building in Nigeria, Ghana, India and Kuwait. Work in Britain included the *Colleges of Veterinary Science* and *Engineering* at *Liverpool University* (1961), the *Headquarters Building* for *Pilkington Brothers Ltd*, at St Helens, Lancashire (1961–5) and *Kingston House* in Bond Street, *Hull*, comprising offices and shops (1968). In 1964 Maxwell Fry was awarded the RIBA Gold Medal for Architecture.

FUNCTIONALISM A movement fashionable especially in the 1920s in which it was considered that the paramount duty of an architect was to design and construct buildings which functioned well. Aesthetic and artistic considerations should be regarded as subsidiary to this fitness for purpose.

GABLE The triangular upper part of the end wall of a building which rises to the slopes of a pitched roof. The entire wall is known as a *gable end*. The angle of the pitched roof varied over the centuries and in some periods of architecture the straight sides of the triangle became curved or stepped. These more decorative gables date chiefly from the sixteenth and seventeenth centuries. The stepped gables, known as *crow-stepped* or *corbie-stepped gables*, were generally of earlier date than the *shaped gable* which has multi-curved sides, convex or concave. A *Dutch gable* is crowned with a pediment and in a *hipped gable* the top part slopes back. A *gablet* is a small decorative gable set over a buttress, niche or other feature (see also BARGE BOARD; BRICKWORK).

GADROONING A form of decoration characterized by a series of convex curves, like inverted fluting, used as a border.

GALILEE A porch used as a chapel at the western entrance of a church. In the early Middle Ages such a chapel was reserved for penitents or for women and, in some instances, the word 'galilee' was applied to the western end of the nave, a part less sacred than the remainder of the church. The origin of the word is not certain; one suggestion is that it is a reference to the fact that Galilee is on the outer edge of the Holy Land. Particularly fine examples of galilee survive at Durham and Ely cathedrals (see also CHURCH DESIGN AND STRUCTURE; NARTHEX).

GALLERY

1. In a church a long, narrow chamber or passage constructed above the aisle in an upper storey and generally open to the body of the church through an arcade (see TRIBUNE). In many churches there is a gallery at the west end to contain the organ loft and to accommodate a choir or congregation. Also, a gallery may be a projecting structure supported on corbels or columns found on the exterior as well as the interior of a church.
2. In later medieval halls a minstrels' gallery was often constructed over the screens passage at the end of the hall opposite the daïs (see DAÏS; SCREENS PASSAGE).
3. In large Elizabethan and seventeenth-century houses the gallery was a narrow apartment built on the first or second floor along the full length of the longer elevation of the building; it was furnished with windows on three sides and fireplaces on the fourth (see COUNTRY HOUSE; ELIZABETHAN ARCHITECTURE; JACOBEAN ARCHITECTURE).
4. An apartment for the display of paintings and sculpture.
5. The upper tier of seats at a theatre.

GALLET, GALLETING A gallet is a pebble or a chip of stone. Galleting is where such pieces of material are pressed into mortar while still soft. The purpose is decorative or to reduce the quantity of mortar required.

GARDEROBE A chamber to house safely stores, clothes or valuables (wardrobe); also, a privy. In castles and medieval houses the garderobe was built into the thickness of the stone wall or projected outwards from it so that it could be drained into a moat or river.

GARGOYLE A decorative feature projecting from a wall to throw off rainwater. This was often in the form of a waterspout which, especially in medieval architecture, might be carved into a grotesque animal or human form.

GARGOYLE
Thaxted Church, Essex, fifteenth century

The banqueting hall at Haddon Hall, Derbyshire. The minstrels' gallery is over the screens passage, fourteenth and fifteenth centuries. The side gallery (right) dates from *c.* 1600. It was constructed to give access to the upper floors in the house

(*Below*) Baroque church gallery extending all round the interior, its passage interrupted only by the High Altar. Sør-Fron Church, Gudbrandsal, Norway. Architect: Svend Aspaas, 1786–92

GATEHOUSE An entrance gateway to a city or building which contained an apartment to house the official responsible for checking the entry and egress of visiting persons.

From Roman times onwards, and throughout the Middle Ages, towns, castles, abbeys and larger houses were protected by fortifying walls and entrance was only possible through the gatehouse. Medieval towns were encircled by such walls, pierced at intervals by well defended gatehouses. Much of this walling has now disappeared but a number of gatehouses survive such as the *Landgate* in *Rye, Sussex* (1329) and the *west gateway* in *Canterbury* (*c.* 1378).

In castle building the gatehouse of a fourteenth-century Edwardian castle had become an important centre of defence (see CASTLE); a large castle might have several of these but generally there was one principal gatehouse, larger and stronger than the others (see also BARBICAN). The usual ground plan was rectangular with flanking drum towers, often at front and rear. These would contain staircases. On the first floor would be a spacious room. In the centre of the gatehouse, at ground level, was the entrance arch defended by a portcullis (see PORTCULLIS) and, behind this, a stout double door of oak, secured by iron bars fitted into sockets in the walls on either side. At the rear of this door was generally a small, wooden-roofed room with a further portcullis behind it. At the back of this a doorway then opened at either side into the guard room and, perhaps, a small prison cell. Typical *castle gateways* survive at *Caerphilly, Harlech* and *Beaumaris* in *Wales* and at *Carisbrooke* in the *Isle of Wight*. A fine *abbey gatehouse* is that at *Battle* in Sussex (*c.* 1340).

During the fifteenth century gatehouses became more elaborate despite (or probably because of) the decline in the need for fortification. This trend continued during the first half of the sixteenth century and Tudor gatehouses were lofty, elegant and decorative architectural features, presenting an imposing entrance to all kinds of buildings from houses and palaces to university quadrangles. The military value of a gatehouse had almost disappeared but the structure was retained for the accommodation it provided as well as for its architectural impact. Among the more interesting surviving examples are the *palace gateways* at *Hampton Court* (1515–25) and *St James's* (*c.* 1530) in London, the *university gateways* at *St John's College* and *Trinity College* (1518), both in Cambridge, the *entrance*

Micklegate Bar. City gatehouse and walls of York, 1198–1230. Stone

The Nevill gatehouse, Raby Castle, Durham, fourteenth century. Stone

Landgate, Rye, Sussex, 1329

St James's Palace, London. *Temp.* Henry VIII. Brick

Battle Abbey, Sussex, *c.* 1340. Stone

Layer Marney, Essex, 1500–1525. Brick and terracotta

The Great Gate, Trinity College, Cambridge, 1518. Brick and stone

West Gateway, Canterbury, Kent, *c.* 1378. Stone

Constable's Gate, Dover Castle, Kent, 1230 and later. Stone

Coughton Court, Warwickshire, 1509. Stone

gateway to *Canterbury Cathedral* (1517), and those built for the *great houses* of *Hengrave Hall* in Suffolk (1525–38), *Coughton Court* in Warwickshire (1509) and *Layer Marney* in Essex (1500–25). Most of these are of traditional Tudor design, built in brick or stone, with tall octagonal shafts at the corners. In the second half of the century the gatehouse was gradually replaced by the Elizabethan entrance porch (see ARCH; BRICKWORK; ELIZABETHAN ARCHITECTURE; FRONTISPIECE; JACOBEAN ARCHITECTURE).

GAZEBO On occasion a turret or lantern on the roof of a house (see also BELVEDERE) but more often a pavilion or summerhouse set on an eminence in a garden or parkland so as to command a view.

GEORGE, SIR ERNEST (1839–1922) An architect with a large London and country-house practice, George was influenced by the architecture of Norman Shaw (see SHAW, NORMAN) and indeed carried out a great deal of work on Shaw's *Bedford Park* scheme in London. Also in the capital his firm (he worked with a succession of partners) was responsible for a number of building projects in, for example, *Collingham Gardens* (1881–7), *Harrington Gardens* (1881–2) and *South Audley Street*. He also designed *Claridge's Hotel* in Brook Street (1894–7) and the *Royal Academy of Music* in Marylebone Road (1910–11).

Sir Ernest's work was often in brick with terracotta decoration and characteristic were his Flemish stepped and curved gables, and decorative bay windows. He designed many large country houses which were less freely ornamented than his London work. They were well planned and designed and were laid out for comfort in tasteful elegance. His influence on his contemporaries and successors was considerable; Dawber and Lutyens both studied under him (see DAWBER, SIR GUY and LUTYENS, SIR EDWIN).

GEORGIAN ARCHITECTURE English architecture mainly classical in design built during the reigns of the four King Georges (1714–1830). For the development of the different versions of this work see ADAM, ROBERT; BASEVI, GEORGE; BURLINGTON, EARL OF; BURTON, DECIMUS; CAMPBELL, COLEN; CHAMBERS, SIR WILLIAM; CLASSICISM; COCKERELL, CHARLES ROBERT; COUNTRY HOUSE AND MANSION; CUBITT, THOMAS; DANCE, GEORGE; FLITCROFT, HENRY; GIBBS, JAMES; HAMILTON, THOMAS; HARDWICK, PHILIP; HOLLAND, HENRY; INWOOD, HENRY WILLIAM; JAMES, JOHN; KENT, WILLIAM; LEONI, GIACOMO; LEVERTON, THOMAS; MYLNE, ROBERT; NASH, JOHN; PAINE, JAMES; PALLADIAN ARCHITECTURE; PAPWORTH, JOHN BUONARROTI; PEMBROKE, EARL OF; PLAYFAIR, WILLIAM HENRY; REGENCY ARCHITECTURE; SMIRKE, SIR ROBERT; SOANE, SIR JOHN; STUART, JAMES; TAYLOR, SIR ROBERT; TERRACE ARCHITECTURE; TOWN PLANNING; WARE, ISAAC; WILKINS, WILLIAM; WOOD, JOHN and WYATT, JAMES.

GERBIER, SIR BALTHAZAR (*c.* 1592–1663) Gerbier was born in Middelburg but later, as a Protestant refugee from France, he migrated to England where he settled in 1616. A friend of Rubens, he was a man of many parts, numbering diplomacy, languages, draughtsmanship and invention among his accomplishments. He was knighted in 1628. He published a number of works, notably *Counsel and Advice to All Builders* (1664). Little of his architecture survives; one particular example which is accredited to him is the *York Water Gate* in London (*c.* 1626). This gateway was designed, when Gerbier was in the employ of the Duke of Buckingham, as an entrance to Buckingham's York House in the Strand. In the seventeenth century, when the Thames was in use as a highway, this entrance opened on to the actual riverside; now it stands detached in the Embankment Gardens. Built by the master mason Nicholas Stone, the openings are flanked by rusticated half-columns in the Tuscan Order, the central ones being surmounted by a carved pediment, below which are the arms of Villiers; on each side is a recumbent lion.

GIANT ORDER Also known as a *colossal order*, it consists of columns or pilasters extending through two or more storeys of a façade.

GIBBERD, SIR FREDERICK (1908–84) After studying at the Birmingham School of Architecture, then spending four years as an articled pupil, Gibberd became one of the comparatively few English architects to adopt the International Modern style in the 1930s (see MODERN ARCHITECTURE). Typical were his blocks of flats in London: *Pullman Court, Streatham* (1934–5); *Park Court, Crystal Palace* (1935–6); *Ellington Court, Southgate* (1937). He wrote several books, *The Architecture of England* (published 1938) and *Town Design* (1953) for instance. In 1943 he became Principal of the Architectural Association and was twice Vice-President of the Royal Institute of British Architects. He was elected ARA in 1961 and RA in 1969. He was knighted in 1967.

It was in the post-war period that Gibberd achieved a considerable reputation in such commissions as his terminal and passenger-handling buildings at *London Airport*. This was in the 1950s; in the same years at *Harlow New Town* in Essex he was appointed Architect Planner. He designed some of the buildings as well as being responsible for the Civic Water Gardens, in which he displayed his outstanding talents in landscaping and garden design. His work at Harlow continued into the 1960s (see TOWN PLANNING).

Gibberd's most notable structure is probably the *Roman Catholic Cathedral* of *Liverpool*, built to his designs in 1962–7 to replace Lutyens's abandoned building (see LUTYENS, SIR EDWIN). This Liverpool Cathedral is an unusual conception, constructed on a circular ground plan—the centrally planned church of the Renaissance ideal (see RENAISSANCE ARCHITECTURE); but it is no eclectic construction, showing as it does the imaginative use of modern structural opportunities. It resembles an immense marquee with a glass lantern and metal crown above. The cathedral is built upon the vast podium of its ill-fated classical predecessor and has an outside sacramental chapel and altar where open-air services are held. Inside, the spatial handling and use of both natural and artificial lighting lend something of the spiritual quality which can be sensed in the great medieval cathedrals. The natural lighting emanates entirely from the coloured glass of the lantern and from the narrow strips of glass in the nave walls. Reminiscent of Barcelona Cathedral in Spain, chapels are inserted into these walls all round the circle, squeezed in between the great sloping buttresses which offset the thrust of the 2000-ton lantern. Even on the dullest winter day the light is rich and glowing; in the sunshine, it becomes magical. The altar is set in the centre of the floor; above is the delicate metal baldacchino (see BALDACCHINO).

Gibberd also won the competition for the quite different *Central London Mosque* in Regent's Park (1970–7) and undertook the controversial and difficult scheme for the reconstruction of *Coutts Bank* in the Strand (1966–75).

Gibberd was noted for his specialization in large-scale planning and the construction of industrial complexes which encompass buildings set in extensive landscape sites. *Hinkley Point Nuclear Power Station*, Somerset is one such example and *Didcot Power Station*, Berkshire (1964–8) another. The *Kielder Reservoir* in Northumberland, designed as a recreation centre for the north-east, is a six-mile-long lake set in forest land. Gibberd won the Gold Medal of the Royal Town Planning Institute in 1978.

GIBBERD, SIR FREDERICK
Metropolitan Cathedral of Christ the King, Liverpool, 1962–7.
Architect: Sir Frederick Gibberd.
1. Metal framework crown 2. Stained glass lantern tower 3. Roof over nave 4. Podium, built as a roof to the crypt of Lutyens's cathedral. Now extends as a piazza for open-air services 5. Side chapels 6. Entrance to car park under podium 7. Main entrance to cathedral

GIBBS, JAMES (1682–1754) A gifted and highly individual architect of the first half of the eighteenth century, Gibbs was the inheritor of the mantle of Wren (see WREN, SIR CHRISTOPHER), a fact clearly displayed in his handling of the orders and his church steeples, but his work also evidenced his thorough knowledge of the Italian Baroque, this tinged with the influence of the English Baroque forms of Vanbrugh and Hawksmoor (see VANBRUGH, SIR JOHN; HAWSMOOR, NICHOLAS).

Gibbs was a Roman Catholic and a Scot; these factors, combined with his political affiliations which tended towards Toryism and Jacobitism, meant that he was not favoured by the Whig government in power, and so his opportunities were hindered in important architectural commissions, particularly those sponsored by the established Church.

Born in Aberdeen, Gibbs left his native Scotland while still a young man to live in Rome, where he first began to study for the priesthood but was later accepted into the Studio of Carlo Fontana, the architect, who was at the time at work on St Peter's Basilica. He remained with Fontana until 1709, gaining an understanding of the Italian Baroque style, which gave him what was at that time an unusual advantage over his British colleagues.

In his first important commission after he returned to Britain, the church of *St Mary-le-Strand*, in *London* (1714–17), Gibbs showed his debt both to the Roman Baroque and to Wren. The body of the church, particularly his treatment of the superimposed orders, was clearly influenced by the years in Rome; the east end, the west porch and, especially, the steeple are in the Wren tradition. Gibbs

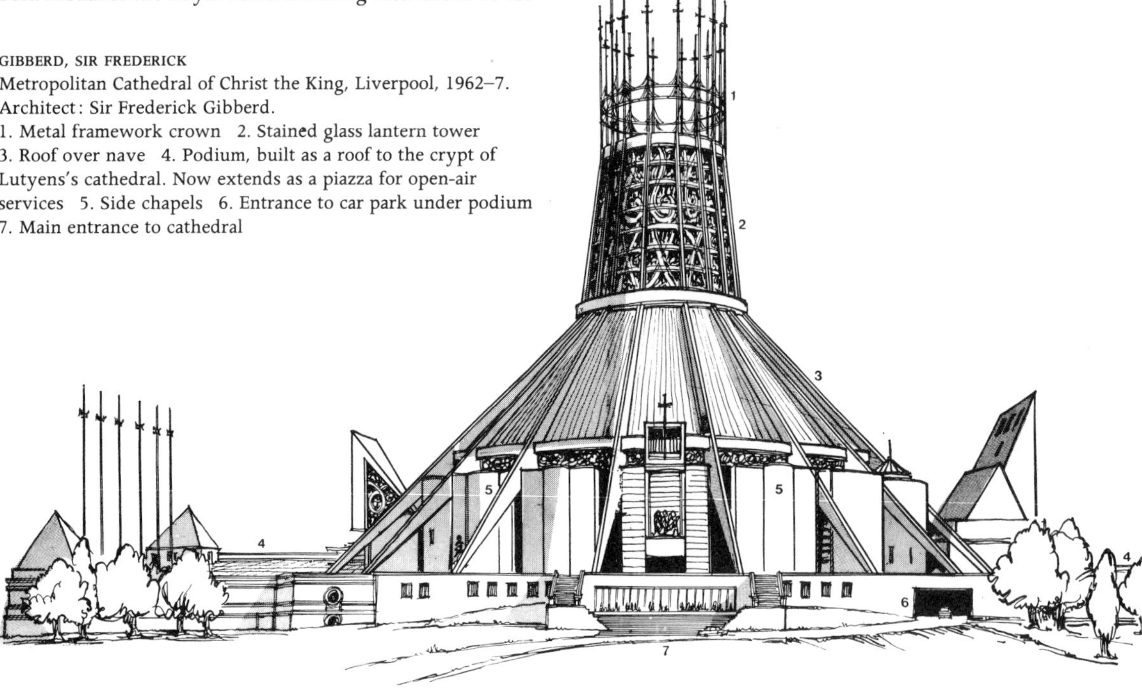

Fellows' Building, King's College, Cambridge, 1724

Church of St Martin-in-the-Fields, London, 1722–6

Church of St Mary-le-Strand, London, 1714–17

GIBBS, JAMES
The Radcliffe Library, Oxford, 1737–49

continued his ecclesiastical work by completing the neighbouring church of *St Clement Danes* (a Wren church to which Gibbs added the steeple) and by designing the smaller church of *St Peter,* in Vere Street in London.

Gibbs's masterpiece, *St Martin-in-the-Fields* in Trafalgar Square in *London,* was built 1722–6. An important building, its design influenced the pattern of Anglican church structure in Britain and even more so in America, where many versions may be seen. In the monumental temple portico in the Corinthian Order Gibbs adopted a Palladian characteristic into his individual style, though the steeple design still owed much to Wren. Gibbs broke with tradition in his contruction of this steeple. In order to save space and to provide a compact design he built the tower inside the west wall so that it emerges from the roof immediately behind the portico. This is in contradistinction to Wren and Hawksmoor who designed such towers to stand with the base visibly on the ground. The church has five bays and is aisled. It is covered by an elliptical barrel vault.

Gibbs's contribution to complete works in domestic architecture was not extensive. Notably in this field he designed the attractive *Sudbrooke Lodge* at *Petersham* in Surrey in 1726 and the larger country house at *Ditchley* in Oxfordshire in 1720. There followed his *Fellows' Building* at *King's College Cambridge* (1724) and the nearby *Senate House* (1722). The Cambridge buildings, which show his forceful Italian Baroque decorative work in the interiors, were both part of an ill-fated ambitious combination project. The former building was part of a great quadrangle which included the medieval chapel and the latter of a scheme comprising a university library and administrative centre. Both schemes foundered under the weight of endless university wrangling.

Gibbs's most original university work was the *Radcliffe Library* at *Oxford* (1737–49), in which he returned to Roman Baroque (with a Mannerist flavour), designing a boldly exuberant cylindrical building covered by a cupola. A late work was a church, that of *West St Nicholas,* in his home town of *Aberdeen* (designed 1741 but not built until 1752–5).

Both through his work, notably St Martin's and the Radcliffe Library, and his books, Gibbs exerted a strong influence upon later architects and builders, not only in Britain but in America. One book in particular became very well-known and was adopted as a useful guide by builders. This was his *A Book of Architecture,* published 1728, which included many drawings of his own work as well as others from English and Continental sources.

GIBBS SURROUND A design of window frame or doorway in which blocks of stone are set at intervals round the architrave or jamb. The head is generally finished by a triple keystone. Named after James Gibbs and popularized by him, though used also by other architects.

GLASS It is not known for certain when and where glass was first made. Fusion of sand and soda probably took place accidentally in an open fire: the process can produce glass and was described by Pliny, the first-century Roman scholar. The earliest use of glass seems to have been in the form of a green glaze poured over beads or domestic artefacts in order to give them lustre; examples have been found in the Middle East dating from about 4000 BC. Pure glass objects made in Mesopotamia and later Egypt are known from the time of about 2500 BC. The earliest glass vessels seem to have been made in about 1500 BC and moulded glass from 1200 BC; containers were also produced by winding molten glass threads round a clay or sand core.

The vital discovery, one as central to glass-making as the wheel was to pottery, was the use of the blowpipe. This is believed to have occurred in Syria in the first century BC. The blowpipes, similar to those of today, were hollow iron tubes, some 4–5ft in length; they had a knob at one end and a mouthpiece at the other.

The ingredients needed to make glass were then, as now, soda ash, lime and pure silica sand. The purity of the sand is important as the presence of even a small quantity of impurities, such as iron oxide, will colour the glass and affect its consistency and transparency. Nowadays a greater variety of ingredients is incorporated in

GIBBS SURROUND
On the south front of Stourhead, Wiltshire

order to produce glass of a range of qualities for different purposes. For instance, lead crystal glass, used for lenses and fine tableware, is made from sand, potash and lead oxide; borax is needed for heat-resistant glass. To make glass, the raw materials have to be heated to a sufficiently high temperature to fuse them together. In early times this was done in clay pots over wood fires or in stone and brick furnaces. The high temperature had to be sustained over a long period; this was not easy to achieve so melting was carried out in two or more stages.

Before the present century the main architectural use for glass was in windows. Such glass was made in countries occupied as part of the Roman Empire, chiefly in Egypt and Syria, Greece, Italy and Gaul. Windows were glazed in many Romano-British houses. After the departure of the Romans domestic window glass became a rare luxury in Britain, to be enjoyed only by kings and wealthy citizens until well into the fifteenth century, though many churches had stained glass windows from the thirteenth. All kinds of substitutes were used in the comparatively small medieval window openings (see WINDOW). These included thin sheets cut from horn or alabaster, and pieces of mica, oiled linen, paper or parchment dipped in gum arabic. Each area used the materials most easily to hand as had been the case with the marble sheets incorporated into the beautiful wheel window in Troia Cathedral in southern Italy.

By the sixteenth century in Britain domestic glass was in more general use but it was still valued so greatly that wooden lattices were fitted to protect it; and the windows were taken out of large houses while the owner was away for any length of time in order to save wear from the weather. Glass was made in Britain at this time in many parts of the country but on a small scale. Its quality was not very good and no-one expected it to be completely transparent, colourless or flat. The fuel in use was wood, which was available in quantity in most regions, so local supplies of ingredients could be used, the impurities giving a greyish or greenish-brown colour to the product.

Almost all the coloured glass used in stained glass windows and the best of the white glass was imported from the Continent, which is why it was so expensive. Up till this time the best and purest white sand was to be found in northern France, Flanders and north-western Germany. The glass made in northern France was generally called *Normandy glass*, and that which arrived via the Rhine *Rhenish*.

Cylinder glass

In Britain the usual way of making glass until the eighteenth century was the cylinder method. This *cylinder*, or *muff glass*, *broad glass*, and *green glass*, as it was also named, was hand-blown. The craftsman would gather a lump of molten glass (or *metal* as it was called) on to his blowpipe. He then blew it into a sphere and, by swinging it and twisting it in the air, he would blow it into a hollow sausage shape. A hot iron was then used to cut off the ends and slit the resulting cylinder open. It was then cooled and flattened out in an annealing oven into a panel. Annealing was a process which cooled the molten glass more gradually than if it had been permitted to cool in the normal air temperature, and so stresses and strains were avoided which would have made the glass too brittle. The size of the cylinder glass panels was limited. In the Middle Ages they were generally about 25in × 14–15in.

In the early seventeenth century two factors altered the English custom of small glass-making establishments producing indifferent-quality glass from many centres all over the country. One was the increased demand for glass (owners of small properties were now expecting window glass); the other was the depletion of the English forest timber stock. This became so serious that James I forbad the use of wood as a fuel for various industries, of which glass was one. It became necessary to heat the furnaces with coal and, as the transport of coal was so costly (by

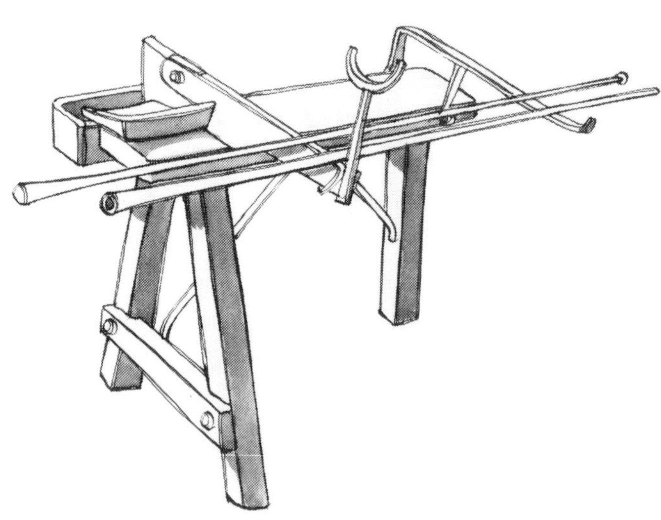

Glass bottle-maker's chair with blowing irons. Displayed in Science Museum, London

Glass furnace in operation showing blowing and swinging and flattening the parison (blob of molten glass). From Agricola, 1556. A Blowing irons, D Forceps. E Mould. Photo: Science Museum, London

Finished 'table' of crown glass. By courtesy of Pilkington

sea being the only feasible method), it was cheaper to move the glass-making concern to the coalfield and transport the sand and other ingredients. Thus the manufacture of glass was set up in fewer centres, eventually concentrated primarily in south Lancashire and Tyneside. It was fortuitous that, having moved north to be near the coalfields, the glass-makers should find in particular the superbly suitable sands of the Lancashire coast between Southport and Liverpool. Both main centres were ideally placed for the transport of their finished glass to Britain and to America by sea from the Mersey and the Tyne.

It was not easy to adapt the glass industry from wood as a fuel to coal. The English evolved a design of furnace which was most satisfactory and became world leaders in this respect. They still had to rely, though, on Continental craft-workers who were more skilled and experienced than the British counterparts, and for much of the seventeenth century used foreign workers, mainly French, to make their window glass.

Crown glass

This method of making window glass had been practised in Normandy in the Middle Ages; the product was often referred to in England as *Normandy glass*. It began to be made in England in the sixteenth century but only to a limited extent, and it was not until the later eighteenth century that it replaced cylinder glass as a better product more suitable for the larger panes of Georgian windows (see WINDOW). Glass made by this method possessed a natural and lustrous fire finish; it did not come into contact with any surface during manufacture and so was brilliant and transparent. It was more costly to produce because it was first formed into a flat circle or 'crown', and more of the material had to be wasted in cutting it up for window panes.

In the crown method the glass-worker blew a globe from the molten glass, or metal, which he had previously rolled into a pear shape. He then transferred this globe to an iron rod called a *pontil* or *punty* and broke off the blowpipe. After re-heating the glass he spun and twisted the rod round and round so that, through centrifugal force, its form opened up into a flat circular plate. Depending upon the quantity of molten glass and the speed of rotation of the punty, the plate could be spun up to a diameter of five feet. The punty was then removed and this plate, which was known as a *table of crown glass*, was placed in an annealing oven. The table was thicker in the centre and thinner towards the edges so panes of glass made in this way were not quite even in thickness. The centre knob where the punty had been attached, known as a *bullion* or *bull's eye*, was discarded to waste in good-quality glass.

Plate glass

This type of glass was made to a much greater thickness than crown glass, of materials as pure as possible; it was then ground, using sand, to remove all flaws and unevenness, then polished, using rouge, until a lustrous finish was obtained. Because of the extensive work involved in the grinding and polishing, plate glass was costly. Made by the same method as cylinder glass, plate glass was manufactured in England from the early seventeenth century but, because of its high cost of production, it was a luxury article, its use being confined mainly to coach windows and mirrors.

Sir Robert Mansell introduced the making of plate glass about 1620 and employed Italian craftsmen to manufacture mirrors. He used only the best-quality soda, lime and washed white sand because in the thicker glass any irregularity or discoloration would be more apparent. In the second half of the seventeenth century fine-quality mirrors were being made in the Duke of Buckingham's manufactory at Vauxhall. It was in 1835 that *Baron Justus von Liebig*, the German chemist, observed in experimentation a possible method of making a deposit of metallic silver on glass. It was this observation which led to the later process of silvering glass for making mirrors; this incorporated a shellac coating and red lead was used for backing. The process replaced the earlier one of coating with tin foil amalgamated with mercury.

The name 'plate glass' seems to have derived from its use for mirrors as these were originally called *looking glass plates*. However, even by the earlier eighteenth century, plate glass was still considered to be too costly to use extensively for window glazing. The French had evolved a method of casting plate glass instead of making it in cylinders which had to be cut and flattened out. In this process the molten glass was run directly on to a flat table where it was rolled out. By its contact with the surface of the table and that of the roller, both sides of the glass lost their transparency and a great deal of grinding and polishing was necessary to restore this and make an even, lustrous glass.

Making plate glass by casting was a process which the English were slow to adopt because an extremely high capital outlay was needed to establish a factory capable of it. The French had gained a near-monopoly of the process in France and Germany and exported to England. For the English to undertake such production from scratch would need extensive premises and costly equipment. It was not until the 1770s that demand for larger windows of high-quality glass rose sufficiently to attract capital to build such plant. At a new factory at Ravenhead in St Helens it was decided to manufacture cast plate glass and the huge casting-hall there produced its first glass in 1776. (It was nicknamed the 'Cathedral' because of its immense pointed brick arches; the hall survives.)

During the nineteenth century a number of factories were established in Britain to manufacture cast plate glass. It was in the last quarter of the century that demand for large-size panes grew fast, for factories, department stores and the bigger houses as well as for large mirrors. By this time also a number of improvements had been introduced into the process of manufacture: better grinding and polishing equipment and the mechanization of handling processes.

Sheet glass

This was an improved method of making cylinder glass but one which enabled much larger panes to be produced. It was developed on the Continent in the eighteenth century and was ideally suited to glazing windows, but its widespread use was held back in Britain because of the effects of the window tax which had been imposed in 1696. This tax, and the excise duties in force between 1745 and 1845, related to the number of window openings in domestic buildings and to the quantity and weight of glass used. This militated against sheet glass which was thicker than the crown glass produced by centrifugal action. It was only after successive adjustments and reductions in window taxation in the early nineteenth century that, in the 1830s, manufacture of sheet glass in Britain began to replace that of crown glass. One notable example of its use was in the 900,000 square feet of glazing incorporated into the Crystal Palace erected in Hyde Park in 1851 (see INDUSTRIALIZED BUILDING; PAXTON, SIR JOSEPH).

Window-glass manufacture in the twentieth century

In the years following the First World War methods were adopted and gradually perfected for making window glass by a continuous drawing process. Chance Brothers of Birmingham had been the first to develop a system of passing molten glass between rollers, in 1887. From this, the continuous rolling process evolved, the molten glass being drawn in a perpetual band, day and night, from immense tank furnaces. The modern method of heating these tanks is by oil, gas or electricity, to temperatures of 1300°–1500°C.

There were three main types of window glass produced in this way. The *sheet glass* was drawn in a broad ribbon vertically in a tower, then passed through rollers which changed its direction to the horizontal. *Figured glass* flowed horizontally in a band through rollers which impressed a pattern upon it. In both cases the continuous band of glass would subsequently pass through an annealing process, usually in the form of a long tunnel in which the temperature was gradually reduced.

The third type was *plate glass* which continued to be produced by the casting method until 1923. After this, plate glass was also made in a continuous manner, in a process called *rolled plate glass*, the molten glass flowing down an inclined plane between two water-cooled rollers. It emerged from this as a flat ribbon of uniform thickness. It was then cut up, inspected and passed on to a further continuous process of grinding and polishing, to be followed by annealing. Ford had developed in 1923 in conjunction with Pilkington such a continuous rolling method for narrow widths of glass for motor windscreens. In 1935 Pilkington introduced their system for grinding and polishing both sides of the plate glass simultaneously.

Float glass

This remarkable development, based upon the brain-child of *Sir Alastair Pilkington*, has completely revolutionized the making of plate glass and has rendered superfluous the costly and lengthy processes of grinding and polishing to which this type of glass had been subject during its whole history of manufacture. Even modern equipment had not done away with this.

Sir Alastair's theory, put forward in 1952, was that the molten glass should be floated along on a bath of molten tin, leaving the furnace at a temperature of 1500°C, then held at 1000°C by a chemically controlled atmosphere until the surfaces had become flat and parallel; the ribbon of glass would then have cooled sufficiently to be removed without the surface being marked. Over this temperature range the tin would remain molten and yet be sufficiently dense to support the glass. Pilkington experienced many teething troubles in the early attempts at the manufacture of float glass. They announced it in 1959 but improvements continued to be made. These included the Pulsed Electrofloat process introduced in 1975 which produces a smooth, coloured patterned glass.

The float process, which produced glass of great brilliance and clarity, made Pilkingtons at St Helens one of the world leaders in production of flat glass and manufacturing costs were significantly reduced. Pilkingtons have now licensed the float process to 31 manufacturers in 21 countries. As glass became cheaper as a building material, architects used it in greater and greater quantity, sometimes, as with glass curtain-walled structures (see WALLING), to the discomfort of the users of the buildings.

Special types of glass

Several varieties of these have been developed, mainly in the twentieth century, to supply particular needs. The best known is probably *safety glass*, which was given great impetus by the production needs of the motor industry in the 1920s for car windscreens. There are three chief ways of making glass which does not splinter: by incorporating wire mesh into it, by lamination and by a heat treatment which would make it liable to break up into harmless pieces when struck by a sharp object. *Wired glass* was first made in 1855 in England by a man called Newton but was first successfully manufactured commercially by Siemens in Dresden, Germany, in 1891 using a process devised by Tenner. The American (Schuman) method was evolved in 1892 and this was adopted by Pilkington in 1895. The wire mesh was pressed into the glass while it was still molten. Wired glass is still made. The presence of the wire does not make the glass stronger but on impact the wire holds most of the glass fragments in place.

The first patent for *laminated glass* was the Englishman John Wood's in 1905, but the first commercially successful venture was *Triplex* based on the Frenchman

Edouard Benedictus's idea of 1909. Since then many improvements have been made in laminated safety glass, all of which have involved the use of two layers of glass with a layer of plastic sandwiched between. From the 1940s the plastic has usually been a polyvinyl acetate type which was flexible at low temperatures and was self-bonding. Now the 'sandwich' is bonded together under heat and pressure.

Making sheet glass in the eighteenth century. Splitting open the cylinders. Photo: Science Museum, London

Four-inch-thick fibreglass, Supawrap 100, being laid between the joists of a domestic attic. Photograph by courtesy of Fibreglass Ltd

A relatively new form of safety glazing is *organic coated glass*. In this the coating, such as a plastics film, is applied to one or both sides of the glass. When breaking on impact, the glass adheres to the coating.

Modern processes have made available to the architect a variety of types of special glass; these include *non-reflective glass*, used widely for glazing pictures, *solar-control glass* and *one-way vision glazing*. There are two chief types of solar-control glass which is intended to reduce excessive heat from the sun and to protect furnishings from fading. One is tinted, generally grey, green or bronze, and a sun-reflecting coating is put on or in the glass during or after manufacture. The other is laminated and contains a specially tinted interlayer. Such glass cuts down glare and heat and can absorb up to 98 per cent of ultra-violet solar radiation.

One-way-vision glass has been adopted extensively in office design and supermarket stores. There are two principal glazing methods in use. In one, the one-way mirror consists of a sheet of float glass lightly silvered to give the impression of a mirror to the viewer from the outside. This glass is joined to another sheet by a special heat process and a viewer from inside can see through the mirror, but only if this room is semi-darkened. The other type of one-way-vision glazing is a single sheet of float glass made with vertical silvered strips incorporated in it. In this design the observer can use a well-lit room but can be seen if the viewer on the other side approaches very close to the glass. This type of stripview glass has a certain deterrent influence on supermarket thieves as it is visibly a security device.

Since the Second World War glass has been used increasingly in the building industry. Toughened glass can form glass walls which are either self-supporting or hung from a structural frame. Glass fibre is in extensive use for heat insulation purposes and in fibrous form such glass is now incorporated in a wide variety of materials—cement, plastics, rubber, for instance—for reinforcement purposes.

Stained glass

The origins of the making and early use of coloured glass are not precisely known but the craft is of considerable antiquity probably stemming from the Near East. Stained glass was made in ancient Egypt but the date at which it was first used for decorative window design is unknown. It was during the Middle Ages that the finest stained glass windows were produced in Europe. They were incorporated into cathedrals and churches everywhere, their primary purpose being, as was that of the sculptured porticoes, to tell the Bible story to a largely illiterate Christian population.

Two integral parts were essential to the making of a pictorial stained glass window: the pieces of coloured and white glass and the armature or supporting framework. The pieces of glass made up a translucent mosaic which was held together by lead. This was a most suitable material since it is malleable even when unheated and has a low melting point, so rendering easy the necessary casting into strips. As the craft developed the lead was not only a holding medium but became a part of the design, stressing by outline the drawing of the picture.

Because of its fragility only a small proportion of the vast quantity of stained glass windows made have survived. The earliest examples extant in Europe are the eleventh-century windows in *Augsburg Cathedral* in Germany and *Le Mans Cathedral* in France. Since these are not of primitive quality of design or craftsmanship it seems certain that there existed a quantity of earlier work which has been lost.

Glass was coloured by adding different metallic oxides to the ingredients for white glass. Considerable variety of shades was obtained, partly because the oxides were used in an impure state and partly depending upon the temperature attained in manufacture. In general, copper oxide produced a ruby red, manganese a purple, cobalt a blue, iron a green or yellow and small quantities of gold a rose red.

There were three chief methods of making coloured glass. The most usual was by fusion of the materials and in this the glass was coloured all through. In a second way the coloured pigment was burnt into the surface of the glass and the third was coloured by *flashing*. In this process the blowpipe was first dipped into molten coloured glass and a bubble was blown, then it was dipped into white molten glass and, after blowing and working, the final glass panel of white glass was coloured on one side with a layer of the desired shade. This method was at first used particularly for ruby glass as this deep colour was not sufficiently translucent for window design; but later the method was applied to other colours also in order to vary the shades. As mentioned earlier (page 187), most of the medieval coloured glass in England was imported from France and Germany.

The method used to make a stained-glass window in the Middle Ages is well-documented. A twelfth-century account tells us that the design was drawn by an artist and this was then transferred to a cartoon which was made on a whitewash-coated table. The shapes, sizes and positions of the pieces of glass were indicated on the cartoon as were the colours to be used. The glass sheets were chosen and cut up into the pieces which would be needed. Before the introduction of a diamond cutter in the late sixteenth century, this was done preliminarily by a heated dividing iron which first cracked the glass along the desired line of cut, then the iron was gently drawn along this line until the piece broke off. Any rough edges were smoothed off by a *grozing iron* which was a flat piece of metal notched at one end. The cut pieces of glass were then laid on the table over the cartoon and the artist painted on with a brush his detail design of faces, hands, hair, drapery etc. The paint was made from a metallic oxide (usually iron or copper), powdered glass and a gum to make it adhere. Finally the glass pieces were transferred to be laid out on an iron plate, first covered with ashes, and fired in a clay and dung kiln to fuse the paint on to the coloured glass. A high firing temperature was obtained by burning beechwood.

After the glass had been fired and cooled the next stage was the *leading*. The lead was cast in moulds into strips about three-sixteenths of an inch wide on an 'H' form in section, that is, with grooves at the sides to accommodate the glass. The pieces of glass were laid out on a table and piece by piece fitted into the lead strips, like a jig-saw puzzle, the strips being cut to size as required. Wooden battens held the whole window in position while the leads were first fixed by closing nails then soldered together. Cement or putty was forced into the crevices between the glass and the lead to make the whole window fit tightly and be watertight. The window was then fitted into the stonework opening by means of lead strips soldered to leads and attached to iron saddle-bars which fitted into the masonry. Larger windows were set into a complex and decorative metal armature. As tracery design developed in the fourteenth century the stone tracery held the lead-framed glass panels of the window head (see TRACERY; WINDOW).

The style and presentation of the pictorial stained glass window gradually changed over the centuries. The monumental single-figure designs of the eleventh and early twelfth centuries were replaced in the years 1150–75 by pictures contained within medallions which were bordered in geometrical motifs. Thirteenth-century glass, at least until the last quarter of the century, is noted for its rich colours and jewel-like sparkling and glowing windows as can be seen, for example, in *Canterbury* and *Lincoln Cathedrals*.

The years 1260–1325 are notable for the beautiful *grisaille glass* of many cathedrals and churches. Grisaille is treated largely in monochrome, the decoration chiefly in silvery-grey, hence the name, derived from the French *gris* ('grey'). Several reasons have been put forward for the lack of colour used in this period. It has been suggested that there was not enough money available to pay for colour, and also that, in the fourteenth century, it was because there was a Cistercian ban on colour and pictorial windows. Whatever the reason, the best glass of these years was largely monochromatic and drawn in an almost three-dimensional manner. There were large areas of clear quarries (a quarry or quarrel is a square or diamond-shaped pane of glass) surrounded by borders of monochrome foliage decoration with an occasional medallion of colour in between. One of the largest and finest examples of this work can be seen in the Five Sisters window in the north transept of *York Minster*. Each of these windows is 50ft high. The grey monochrome floral pattern is relieved by red and blue glass strips.

An early-fourteenth-century innovation was the discovery of the ability to make a yellow stain by applying a solution of silver. This formed a clear transparent film on the glass and could be varied in shade from pale yellow to deep orange. Applied to blue glass, it produced beautiful vivid greens.

Fifteenth-century glass was characterized by a greater sophistication in the handling of colour and a more stylized, formal way of designing floral motifs. In addition to the variations in shade offered by the yellow staining, the technique of abrasion was developed wherein parts of the colours could be abraded by an iron tool or a whetstone, so giving a greater palette of colour as well as more modelling. The designs became more complex and the lead-work was kept to a minimum in order not to obscure them. In floral ornament the seaweed pattern replaced the traditional leaves of oak, ivy and vine. Stylized diaper patterns and heraldic motifs were widely used.

In the sixteenth century the Gothic tradition and English craftsmanship in stained glass window design declined in favour of Renaissance forms and the import of foreign, largely German and Flemish, craftsmen. Realistic landscapes, heraldic design, classical figures or architectural scrolls replaced the religious scenes. Painting on glass gradually superseded coloured glass. Transparent coloured enamels were used; these were capably and realistically handled but were less rich, as the light shone through the glass, than the fused coloured glass had been. These windows were treated as complete pictures with one large scene per window; they resembled transparent oil paintings.

With the Gothic Revival in the nineteenth century stained glass returned to English churches. Often rich and dark and generally serious, the work was, in a number of instances, heavy and ornate. *William Morris* and *Burne-Jones*, in particular, produced some interesting work in their attempt to revive the medieval spirit as can be seen in, for example, *Birmingham Cathedral* and the *Church of the Holy Trinity* in Sloane Street in *London*.

A modern and most effective method of making stained glass windows was developed at Buckfast Abbey in Devon. In this, one-inch-thick pieces of coloured glass are cut to the size required by the design and stuck down with gum arabic to a wooden mould which is the exact size of the finished panel. When the gum is dry, fine quality concrete is poured into the mould and fills the interstices between the glass instead of using lead. The concrete is shaken into position by an electric vibrator and wire and iron bars are inserted where needed for reinforcement. This method of setting thick coloured glass into concrete gives a rich, glowing effect to the interiors of churches. The technique originated in France where there are a number of examples. An interesting one in Britain is the *Church of Our Lady of Fatima* in *Harlow New Town*, built 1958–60 to the designs of the architect *Gerald T. Goalen*. The glass was designed and made by the monks of Buckfast Abbey.

GODWIN, EDWARD WILLIAM (1833–86) A Victorian architect and decorative designer whose work was more austere and less ornate than that of most of his contemporaries. Godwin was born in Bristol and set up architectural practice there in 1854. In the succeeding decade he designed a number of houses in Gothic style and two *town halls*: that of *Northampton* (1861–4) and *Congleton* in Cheshire (1864–7). Both town halls are in Gothic style, possessing character and charm. The Northampton example is the larger and more decorative, having richly carved ornament on the façade and window openings. Congleton Town Hall is smaller and plainer and has a castellated tower reminiscent of Italian medieval civic work such as the Palazzo Pubblico in Montepulciano (1332). In 1865 Godwin moved to London where he built some of the early houses at Bedford Park (see SHAW, NORMAN) as well as a number of small London houses and he designed a range of domestic furniture.

Congleton Town Hall, Cheshire, 1864–7. Architect: E. W. Godwin

GOTHIC ARCHITECTURE The style of architecture current in Europe between the later twelfth century and the middle of the sixteenth. Clearly definable and recognizable, Gothic architecture is characterized by the pointed arch, the ribbed vault, the flying buttress, the traceried window, the slender pier, panelled stonework and the lofty steeple. Not all these features are specifically Gothic and several were known and used in different parts of the world at an earlier date but it is the fusion of these forms into a delicate, resilient structure, each part dependent upon and related to the others, which creates a Gothic building. This style of architecture, seen at its most impressive in the great medieval cathedrals (see CHURCH DESIGN AND STRUCTURE) has a vertical emphasis, the pointed arches, buttress pinnacles, spires and vaults all seeming to soar upwards in an apparent striving towards the heavens; this is in contrast to the classical structure where the emphasis of the lines of the entablature is essentially horizontal (see CLASSICAL ARCHITECTURE).

The term 'Gothic' was coined in a later age as one of disapprobation and contempt. It was the sixteenth-century artist and historian Giorgio Vasari who used the term and, in so doing, was merely expressing the thinking of his time, equating medieval architecture with barbarism. To a post-Renaissance scholar, the Middle Ages had advanced only a small way beyond the sixth-century Goths; it was the Renaissance which brought greatness back to architecture.

Gothic architecture did not suddenly come into being in the twelfth century. It evolved gradually from the Romanesque (see ROMANESQUE ARCHITECTURE) and, for some decades during the twelfth century, features of both forms were to be found, side by side, in many buildings. The earliest structures completed in the Gothic style were in the Île de France near Paris and the style soon spread to Britain. It was one which evolved and grew to maturity over four whole centuries in Britain, developing early and lasting long.

There were four distinct styles or interpretations during this long period, each growing out of the one before and pointing the way to its successor. Each change made steady progress away from the solidity of the Romanesque structure towards the seemingly ethereal fragility of the soaring spires and delicately panelled stone and glass of the late fifteenth century. Buildings became larger and higher; walls, securely buttressed, became thinner, window and doorway openings larger so that the wall area was reduced. The knowledge of structure in masonry was extended and with this advance in technique came the means to erect buildings which were shells of stone ribs and pillars. As the area of solid stone wall shrank, so the architectural design became more complex. The miracle of immense stone structures, pierced by great openings and carved tracery, was made possible by the engineering development of the stone vault and its associated abutment (see BUTTRESS; VAULTING).

It was Rickman (see RICKMAN, THOMAS) who classified the English styles of Gothic architecture in the early nineteenth century. He divided up the years from 1066 until the mid-sixteenth century into four periods which he called Norman, Early English, Decorated and Perpendicular. Since the time of Rickman, other writers have intro-

Ely Cathedral West Tower, 1150–75. Note the lancet openings and arcading

Wells Cathedral interior, 1192–1230. Note the simple ribbed vault and moulded arcades

Salisbury Cathedral from the north-west, 1234–58. Tower and spire 1334–80. Note the lancet windows and buttress design

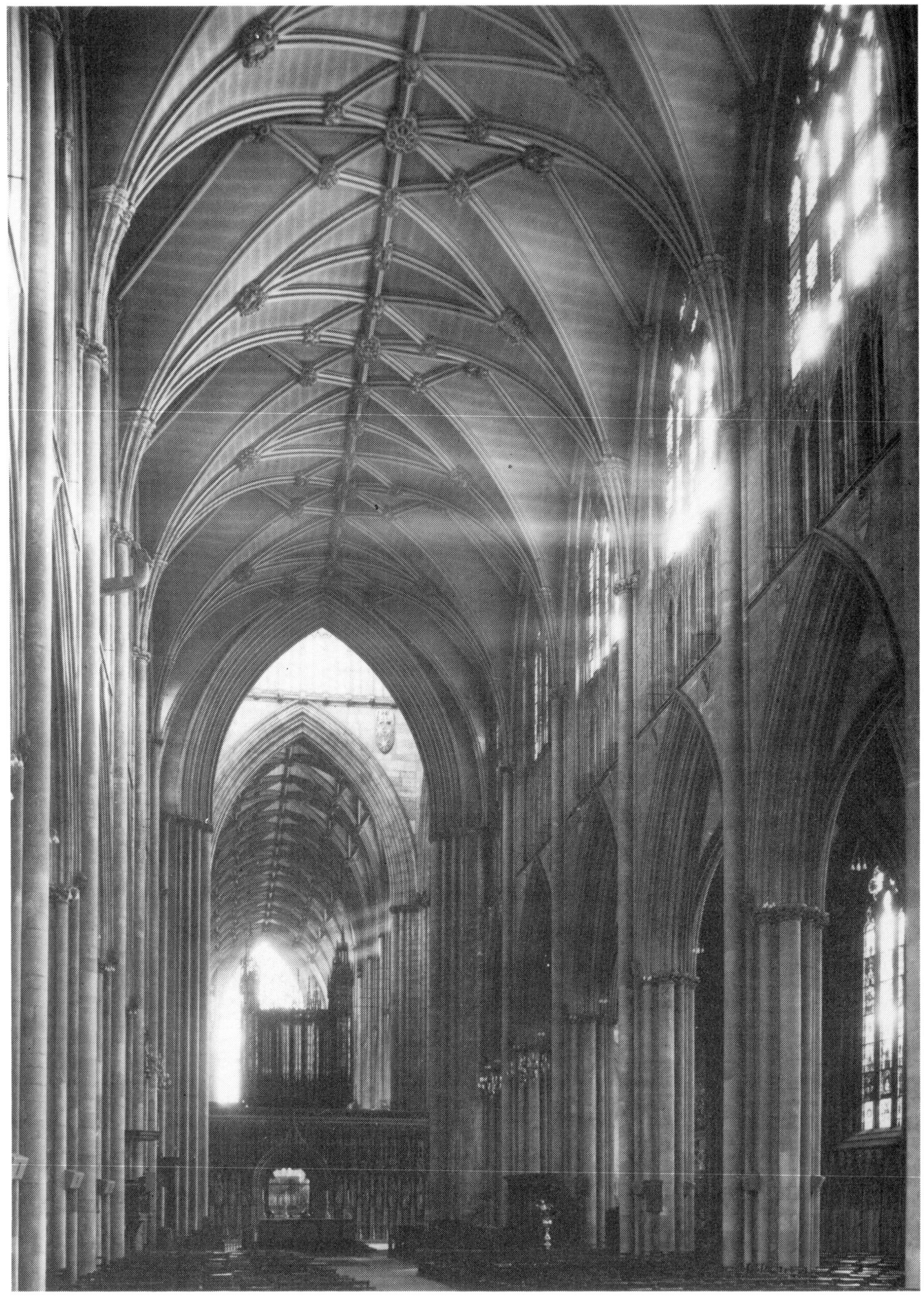

York Minster Interior 1291–1341   Note the lierne vaults and clerestory window tracery

duced different forms of classification, names and dates for Gothic architecture but Rickman's description and nomenclature survived. However, it is now recognized that one should not be too dogmatic in applying specific dates to these divisions because one style merged gradually into another, creating a transitional period between when some features of the older style were in use contemporaneously with some of the newer forms. The speed of this progress varied considerably from one part of the country to another.

The early Gothic work was called by Rickman *'Early English'*, but it is also referred to as *'Lancet'* (after the form of window design—see WINDOW) or as *'First Pointed'*. Sometimes it is described as the springtime of the style as it is characterized by a simplicity and freshness, a certain austerity of form and a beauty of proportion. The chief characteristics of Early English Gothic architecture are plain quadripartite ribbed vaults, slender spired towers, lancet (narrow untraceried) windows, single or grouped, and tall piers with clustered shafts, simple moulded or foliated capitals and tall bases. *Salisbury Cathedral* is a superb example of the period in which the style developed fully—between 1200 and 1275.

Rickman's next phase of Gothic design is what he called *'Decorated'* and this term, like the others now used—*Geometric, Curvilinear, Flamboyant*—refers to the tracery and design of the window heads (see TRACERY). The Decorated or *Middle Pointed* style lasted for about a century, from 1275 to 1375. It is characterized by larger, wider windows with decorative heads, the structure of these and the correspondingly smaller wall area made possible by the development of the flying-buttress system (see BUTTRESS), as was also the greater complexity of stone vaulting design (see VAULTING). Ornamentation became richer in the form of stone carving, painting and coloured window glass. *Exeter Cathedral* is a classic example.

The final phase of Gothic architecture, Rickman's *'Perpendicular'*, lasted a very long time in Britain, from the late fourteenth century until well into the sixteenth, when it became *Tudor Gothic*. It changed gradually during this time but not greatly. The name refers to the vertical lines which marked both the tracery of the windows and

Exeter Cathedral west front, 1328–75. Decorated style. Note the tracery of the great west window

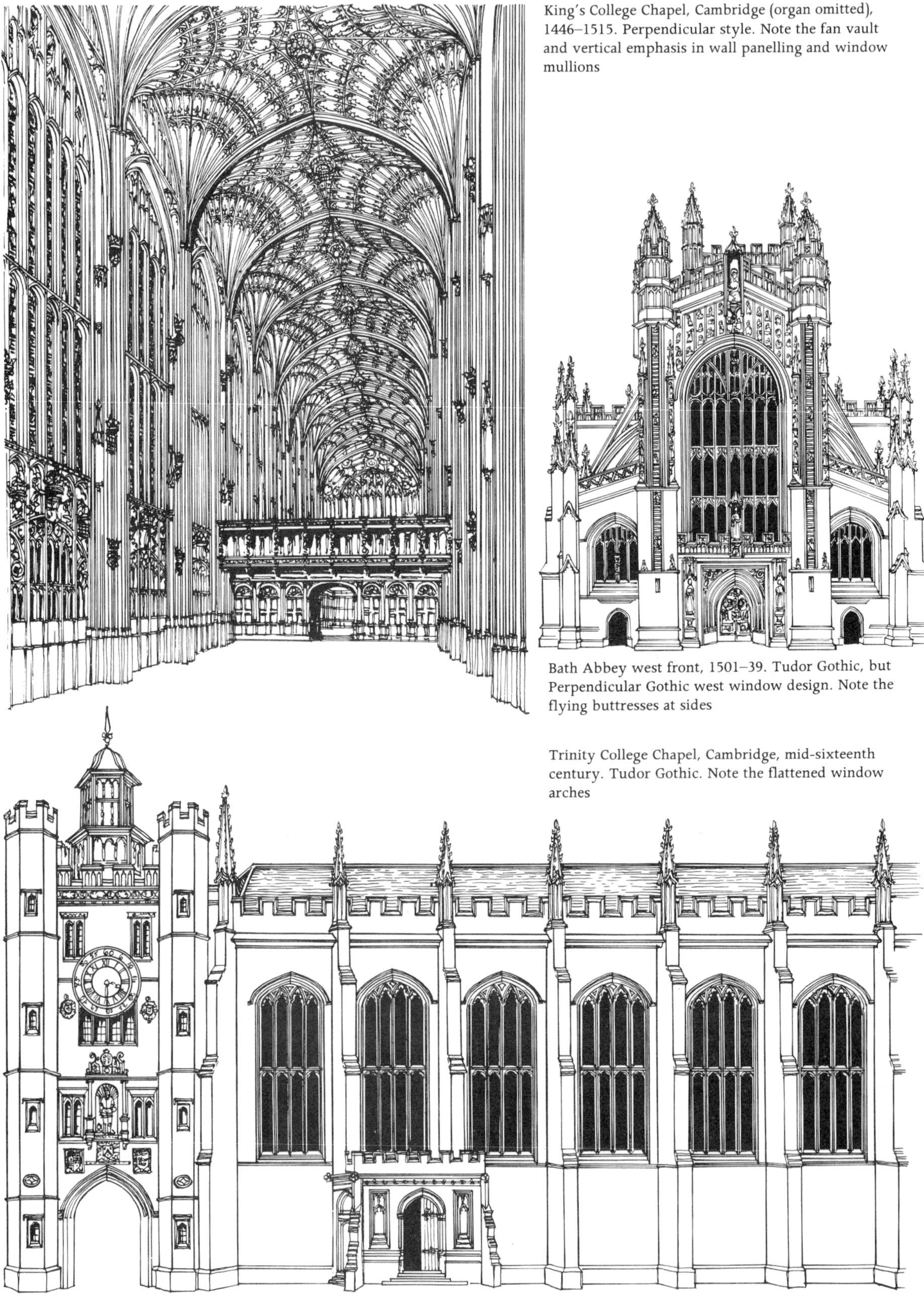

King's College Chapel, Cambridge (organ omitted), 1446–1515. Perpendicular style. Note the fan vault and vertical emphasis in wall panelling and window mullions

Bath Abbey west front, 1501–39. Tudor Gothic, but Perpendicular Gothic west window design. Note the flying buttresses at sides

Trinity College Chapel, Cambridge, mid-sixteenth century. Tudor Gothic. Note the flattened window arches

the articulation of the stone panelling of wall surfaces. In the roofing vaults these took the form of fan-shaped panelling, of which many fine examples survive, such as the *Chapel* of *King's College, Cambridge* (1446–1515). The flying buttress reached its final decorative form as did the beautifully panelled and pinnacled towers, the magnificent hammerbeam open timber roofs and the immense traceried windows. Interiors were light and delicate, lofty and spacious, with a minimum of wall area supporting a maximum of window and doorway openings. Of the impressive numbers of great buildings of this time to survive, especially notable are the *Henry VII Chapel* in *Westminster Abbey* (1503–19), *Bath Abbey,* Somerset (1501–39) and the rebuilt naves of *Canterbury* and *Winchester Cathedrals* (fifteenth century). For further information on design and features of Gothic architecture see ABBEY; ARCADE; ARCH; BUTTRESS; CAPITAL; CHURCH DESIGN AND STRUCTURE; COLUMN; CUSP; DOORS AND DOORWAYS; FINIAL; FOIL; GOTHIC ORNAMENT; IMPOST; MOULDINGS; PIER; PINNACLE; ROOF; SPIRE; SPRINGING; STEEPLE; TOWER; TRACERY; TRUMEAU; TYMPANUM; VAULTING; WINDOW.

St Botolph's Church, Boston, 1425–1520. Perpendicular style. Note the vertical lines in wall panelling and window tracery

GOTHIC ORNAMENT This style of ornament displays a richness and variety of form in both foliated and geometric carved decoration. The treatment and style changed gradually during the centuries so that the ornament of each of the Gothic periods may be recognized by certain characteristics.

The *dogtooth* ornamental form (also known as 'shark's tooth') is particularly typical of the early Gothic work of the late twelfth and earlier thirteenth centuries (Early English) and appears in different sizes in many mouldings. It is shaped like a pyramid cut into four leaves which meet at the central apex. *Diaper* decoration (see DIAPER WORK) is also typical and at this time *crockets* were introduced; the name is said to be derived from the shepherd's crook which was then adopted by the Church as a symbol of the Bishop's Office (see CROCKET).

Carved foliage decoration was widely used in Early English work. Apart from crockets, it can be seen on capitals and in window and doorway mouldings. Characteristic is the formality of the stiff-leaf foliage of the capitals which rises stiffly from the necking and falls over in clusters of leaves and flowers (see CAPITAL). The scrolled or arabesque foliated carving on panels and in mouldings is notable for its vigour and flexible curves.

Carved foliage in the Decorated period of the years 1275–1375 is characterized by its naturalness, its richness

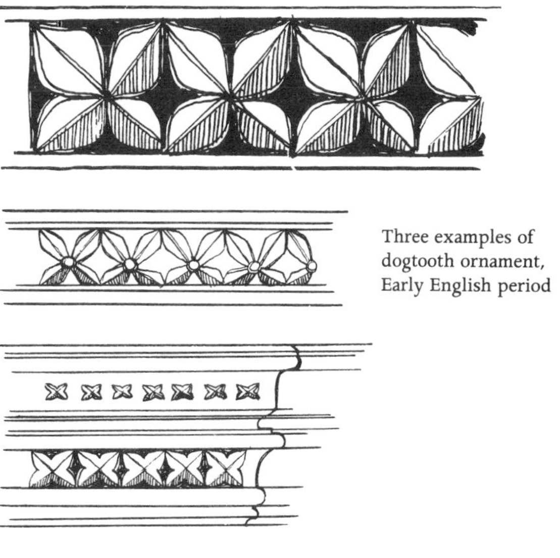
Three examples of dogtooth ornament, Early English period

Foliated carving, thirteenth century

Foliated capital,
Lincoln Cathedral,
thirteenth century

Foliated capital,
Decorated period, St
Alban's Cathedral
nave

Foliated capital, *c.*
1300, Southwell
Minster

Foliated capital,
Wells Cathedral, thir-
teenth century

Four-leaved
flower ornament
Decorated period

Diaper decoration, *c.*
1350

Carved stone corbel,
Exeter Cathedral,
fourteenth century

Thirteenth-century
foliated capital

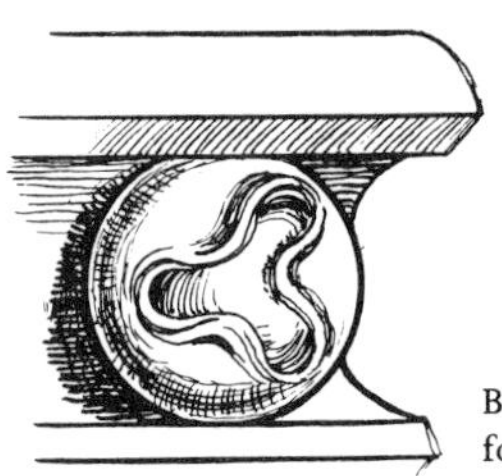

Ball-flower ornament,
fourteenth century

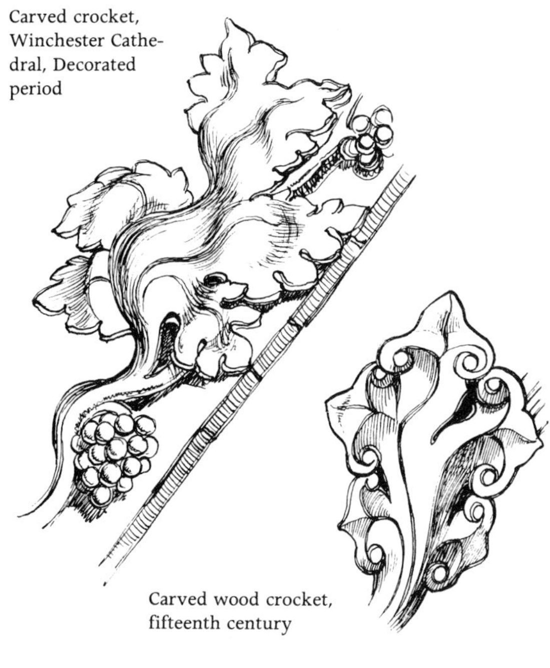

Carved crocket, Winchester Cathedral, Decorated period

Carved wood crocket, fifteenth century

Tudor flower, Perpendicular period

Carved ornament, St Osyth's Priory, Essex, Tudor Gothic, 1527

and its undulating form. A wide variety of natural leaves served as inspiration: ivy, vine, oak, rose and many more. Sculptural forms also became more naturalistic, using animals, birds and human figures.

In more formal, architectural vein, especially typical is the *ballflower* ornament which is a globular flower, partly opened to display a small sphere. It is set repetitively in hollow mouldings in many architectural features. Also typical is the *four-leaved flower*, its petals radiating symmetrically from a raised or depressed centre.

Panelling in its various forms is the chief decorative theme in Perpendicular Gothic architecture. In larger buildings especially, entire walls are so covered that doors and windows are discernible only by their pierced openings. Above, vaulting echoes the same panelled and cusped theme. More decorative ornament includes carved foliage, grotesque figures, animals and angels. The last of these frequently adorn brackets, bosses and buttress or pew finials. A specifically fifteenth- and early sixteenth-century motif is the *Tudor flower*. Used especially in brattishing for screens and cresting, it is a formalized design based on a fleur-de-lis or ivy leaf which stands upright and alternates with a small trefoil, ball or lily form (see BRATTISHING). Heraldic and geometric motifs were also widely used.

GOTHIC REVIVAL In Britain, medievalism and its expression in Gothic architecture never completely died. Classical design dominated the building scene for over 200 years from the time of Queen Elizabeth I onwards but, intermittently, the Gothic flame flickered. During the sixteenth and seventeenth centuries this was mainly because architects were asked to complete an unfinished medieval building in a form which would blend with the original work. Wren did this in a few of his city churches in London (see WREN, SIR CHRISTOPHER), *St Michael, Cornhill* (1672–1721), in Perpendicular Gothic style for instance, and *St Dunstan-in-the-East* (1698), where he added a spire in a form rather more Wren than Gothic. At *Oxford* in 1681 he completed Tom Tower at *Christ Church* with a design which merged reasonably with Wolsey's quadrangle and hall. *Kent* (see KENT, WILLIAM) performed a similar task with his gatehouse intended to fit in with the Tudor building at *Hampton Court Palace* in London (1732).

In the early eighteenth century one or two architects produced a different variant on the Gothic theme, one tinged with the power and movement of the contemporary Baroque scene evidenced, for instance, by *Vanbrugh's* own castellar house at *Greenwich* (see VANBRUGH, SIR JOHN) and *Hawksmoor's* north quadrangle at *All Souls' College, Oxford* (1715–40). When though, as Surveyor of the Fabric at *Westminster Abbey* (from 1723) Hawksmoor was responsible for the long-awaited building of the western towers, he produced a design which, if still recognizably Hawksmoor, blended satisfactorily with the medieval structure (see HAWKSMOOR, NICHOLAS).

During the second half of the eighteenth century a literary and romantic Gothic (or Gothick), encouraged by the pattern books of Batty Langley (see LANGLEY, BATTY), was introduced into domestic architecture and became a fashion. Still limited to a minor role compared to the dominant classical theme, it offered an alternative to those who were tiring of the restrictive formality of the Palladian style. *Horace Walpole* was early in the field when he introduced his controversial conception of a Gothic country house. In 1750 he created his villa at Strawberry

Hill in Twickenham by enlarging and 'medievalizing' the existing cottage. In this 'Strawberry Hill Gothic', as it came to be called, he decorated the interiors with cusped and panelled ceilings and crocketed arches. The results were two-dimensional only, charming and delicate, the product of excellent eighteenth-century craftsmanship and elegance but with little of the medieval spirit.

In the succeeding decades of the century a number of architects tried their hand at building in Gothic. It was still a romanticized and picturesque version, often dramatic in effect and personalized in detail. Characteristic were *Sanderson Miller*'s hall at *Lacock Abbey*, Wiltshire (1753–5) and *Henry Keene*'s *Arbury*, Warwickshire (1776). Even *Adam* (see ADAM, ROBERT) ventured into Romantic medievalism with castellar domestic exteriors (though the interiors were usually more recognizably Adam), as can be seen at *Culzean Castle* in Ayrshire, Scotland (1776–92).

Some of the most successful and adventurous architectural essays into romantic Gothic were the work of *Wyatt* (see WYATT, JAMES), who, over many years experimented with the style, from his early design at *Lee Priory* in Kent (1782–90) to his last house of *Ashridge Park*, Hertfordshire, begun in 1806 and completed after his death in 1813. Ashridge, the best known of the survivors, contains a central hall which takes up the entire height of the tower. Wyatt's most spectacular Gothic house was *Fonthill Abbey*, Wiltshire, which he designed for the wealthy William Beckford from 1795. This immense house was

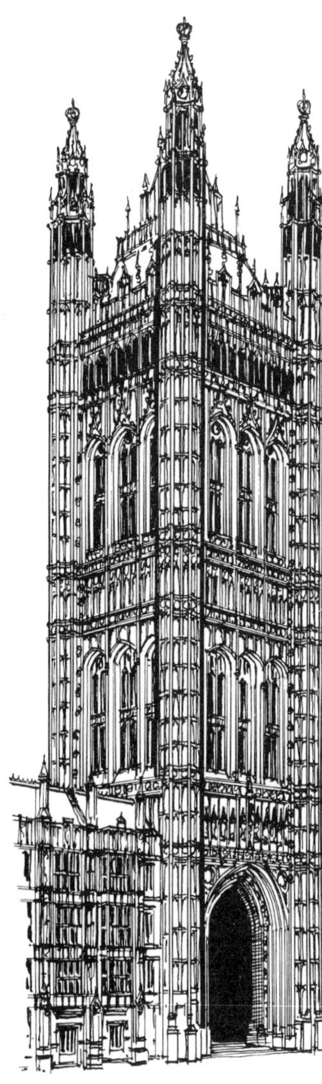

The Victoria Tower, Palace of Westminster, London, 1836–65. Architects: Sir Charles Barry and A. W. N. Pugin

All Souls' College, Oxford, 1716–35. Architect: Nicholas Hawksmoor

like a cathedral, cruciform in plan, some 300ft in length and with a 278ft tower over the crossing. The great hall inside was 80ft high. Haste in building, due to the client's impatience, the architect's indolence and consequent inadequate supervision, led to the omission of specified support arches for the tower which, in 1825, collapsed; the house was later demolished.

During the early decades of the nineteenth century the study of Gothic architecture was still not taken very seriously. Architects designed in medieval form using the decorative media and general features but taking liberties with the proportions, structure and, most of all, materials. They approached medievalism in a manner similar to that which Elizabethan builders had practised when they first utilized the Renaissance architectural forms on their traditional structures (see ELIZABETHAN ARCHITECTURE). Gothic builders in the years 1800–40 supported their vaults by means of slender columns and piers of iron and covered their vaults with plaster ribs and panelling, both instead of stone. The shapes and forms were Gothic but the proportions and treatment were not.

Most architects of the time designed in both classical and Gothic styles, varying their work according to the needs of each commission. Gothic was thought to be more suited to church and university building, classical for civic and public work. Typical of the universities was *Wilkins*'s contribution at *Cambridge*, the screen and gateway at *King's College* (1822–4) and the New Court at *Corpus Christi College* (1823) (see WILKINS, WILLIAM), also *Rickman* and *Hutchinson*'s 'bridge of sighs' at St John's College, also in Cambridge (1826) (see RICKMAN, THOMAS). Among the many churches of the time being erected, especially in the rapidly growing urban areas, are some examples which show inexperience in handling Gothic but a growing understanding of the style: *St Luke's Chelsea* by *Savage* (1820–4), *St Peter's Brighton* by *Barry* (1823–8) and *Edward Garbett*'s church at *Theale* in Berkshire (1820–30) are characteristic (see SAVAGE, JAMES and BARRY, SIR CHARLES).

From the 1840s the Gothic Revival became more serious. Archaeological study made the work more competent and the buildings more closely related to their medieval prototypes. The most outstanding structure of this time was the *Palace of Westminster* in London, rebuilt in Perpendicular Gothic style after the fire of 1834 by *Barry* and *Pugin* (see BARRY, SIR CHARLES and PUGIN, A. W. N.). It remains the greatest English neo-Gothic building, finely and dramatically designed and containing craftsmanship and ornament of the highest quality. It is probably fortunate that it was conceived before the Gothic Revival had gathered impetus, which was soon afterwards.

The Revival was seriously established in Britain by idealists and thinkers rather than architects. The movement was espoused by men who advanced it on moral and theological grounds. They were desperately sincere and had a deep belief that to design great architecture a man should be moral and good in heart. They believed that the Middle Ages was the greatest period of human endeavour and of the human spirit and that the arts and architecture of that time were the most beautiful. They aimed to re-create such architecture. They had a horror of architectural sham and thought that any material which had not been available for use in the Middle Ages should not be employed in Gothic Revival ones. They abhorred the work of the years 1780–1840 when architects had used cast iron and plaster in imitation of stone.

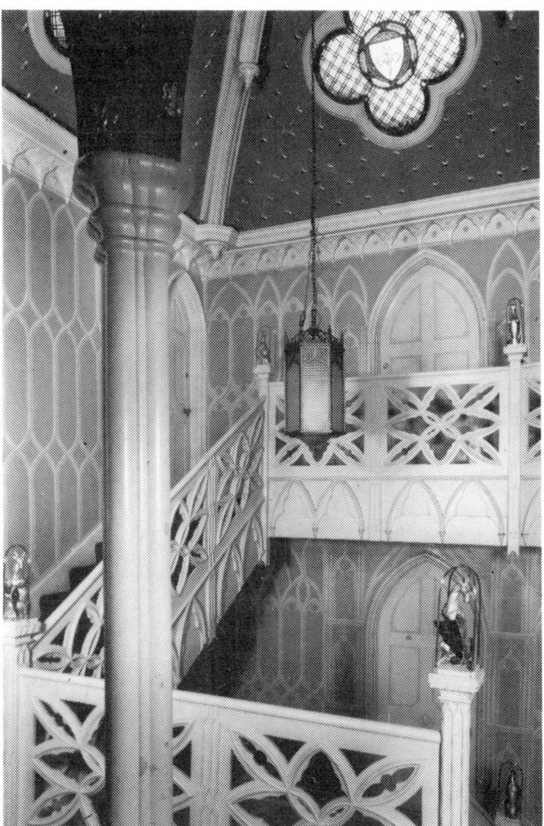

Strawberry Hill, Twickenham, the staircase

One strong influence on architectural design was the *ecclesiological movement* which stemmed from Oxford and Cambridge. Supporters of the movement believed that, not only was Gothic the true style, especially for ecclesiastical architecture, but that it should be specifically of late thirteenth- to early fourteenth-century type, or 'Middle Pointed' as they termed it (see GOTHIC ARCHITECTURE). From 1841 they published a monthly journal, *The Ecclesiologist*, which laid down rigid guidelines on Gothic design. Another forceful influence was *Ruskin* and a third was *Pugin* (see RUSKIN, JOHN and PUGIN, A. W. N.).

Despite nineteenth-century striving for a re-creation of medieval architecture, the buildings of the Gothic Revival period are recognizably different from their prototypes of

Screen and gateway, King's College, Cambridge, 1822–4. Architect: William Wilkins

Scarisbrick Hall, Lancashire, 1837. Architect: A. W. N. Pugin

Fonthill Abbey, Wiltshire, from the north-west, 1795–1807. Architect: James Wyatt

Entrance porch, Keble College Chapel, Oxford, 1868–82. Architect: William Butterfield

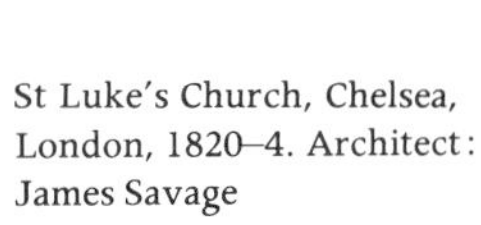

St Luke's Church, Chelsea, London, 1820–4. Architect: James Savage

St Paul's School, Hammersmith, London, 1881–5 (now demolished). Architect: Alfred Waterhouse

Bridge over the river Cam, St John's College, Cambridge, 1826, based upon the 'bridge of sighs' in Venice. Architects: Rickman and Hutchinson

St John's Church, St Leonards-on-sea 1881. Architect: Sir Arthur Blomfield. Restored after wartime damage by Goodhart-Rendel.

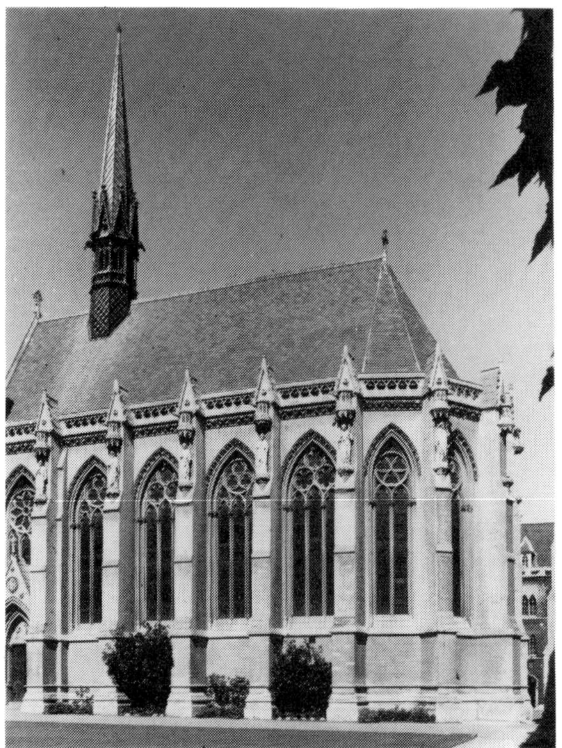

GOTHIC REVIVAL
Exeter College Chapel, Oxford, 1856–9, based upon the Sainte-Chapelle, Paris. Architect: Sir George Gilbert Scott

the Middle Ages. Partly this was a question of craftsmanship. Medieval work evolved over hundreds of years. A large body of craftsmen spent their lives carving, modelling, painting and working in plaster, glass, iron or wood and passed on their knowledge and experience to their sons and grandsons. In the nineteenth century, after several hundred years of classical design, Barry and Pugin had to train a new school of craftsmen to build the Palace of Westminster. Their work was excellent but, after 1850, the pace of building accelerated and demand far exceeded supply in all classes of craftsmen. So means of mass-production of decorative features had to be developed. It is this which gives the hard, repetitive finish to a nineteenth-century finial or capital. Medieval buildings were decades in the constructing; nineteenth-century ones were completed in a year or so. There was also a difference in creed and purpose. Medieval buildings arose from the religious feeling of the time. In the nineteenth century religious fervour was strong but it was not the sole basis for life.

The Gothic Revival in Britain was at its height between 1855 and 1885. Known as the High Victorian Gothic period its chief architectural designers were *Street, Waterhouse, Scott* and *Butterfield.* These architects, and many others, covered the country with Gothic structures: town halls, hotels, university and school buildings, railway stations and country houses. Pressure on architects from the Ecclesiological Society to follow the accepted line was great but, as the pace of building increased in order to supply the needs of a rapidly expanding population, some compromise had to be made and a greater variety of Gothic source material was tapped. By the 1870s and 1880s High Victorian Gothic design was based upon Lancet, Romanesque and Perpendicular forms as well as 'Middle Pointed' and many buildings even showed the influence of Venetian, French and Flemish medieval origins (see also BARRY, SIR CHARLES; BLOMFIELD, SIR ARTHUR; BODLEY, GEORGE FREDERICK; BURGES, WILLIAM; BUTTERFIELD, WILIAM; CARPENTER, RICHARD CROMWELL; CHAMPNEYS, BASIL; GODWIN, EDWARD WILLIAM; HAWKSMOOR, NICHOLAS; LANGLEY, BATTY; PEARSON, JOHN LOUGHBOROUGH; PUGIN, A. W. N.; RICKMAN, THOMAS; RUSKIN, JOHN; SALVIN, ANTHONY; SAVAGE, JAMES; SCOTT, SIR GEORGE GILBERT; SEDDING, JOHN DANDO; STREET, GEORGE EDMUND; WATERHOUSE, ALFRED; WILKINS, WILLIAM; WREN, SIR CHRISTOPHER; WYATT, JAMES; WYATVILLE, JEFFRY.

GRAND TOUR During the seventeenth century interest had been steadily growing in visiting and studying in Europe the remains of the ancient classical world as well as the newer works of art and architecture of the Renaissance. Members of aristocratic families, in particular, travelled for some months at a time in France, the Low Countries and Italy.

In the early eighteenth century this desire for travel and research grew rapidly in all the countries of western Europe, especially among Englishmen, Frenchmen and Germans. People travelled distances according to their means. The nobility undertook the Grand Tour of France and Italy, lasting perhaps two or three years, and stayed part of the time as guests with friends and relatives and partly in inns and rented lodgings. They collected antique and Renaissance sculpture, paintings, books, coins and ceramics as well as blocks of marble and stone and brought them back to decorate their homes. Often it became necessary to build new galleries and libraries there to house their treasures. This travel by the nobility, and also by artists and architects led to increased knowledge. Interest was aroused in travel further afield, to Greece, Dalmatia and even as far as Syria. *Robert Wood*'s journey, accompanied by *Bouverie* and *Dawkins,* to Palmyra was one such journey. The contribution of the Dilettanti Society in this field in Britain has already been mentioned (see DILETTANTI SOCIETY and STUART, JAMES), but expeditions were made from other countries and these led to important publications which extended the knowledge and understanding of the ancient world. Most notable of these were de Caylus's *Recueil d'Antiquités Eqyptiennes, Etrusques, Grecques et Romaines* (1752), Le Roy's *Ruines des plus beaux Monuments de la Grèce* (1758), Winckelmann's *History of Ancient Art* (1763) and Dumont's *Temples of Paestum* (1764).

This widening of the field for classical research made

clear to both patron and architect in western Europe that Greece, not Rome, was the originator of the classical form and that, in many instances, the Greek was purer and more beautiful. This was a new concept in the mid-eighteenth century and led in many countries to controversy in architectural and academic circles, a situation now colloquially referred to as the 'battle of the styles', as pro-Greek and pro-Roman factions took sides in their attitude to classical architectural design.

GROTESQUE Term used to describe a fantasy type of ornamentation in the form of painting, carving and stucco, incorporating human and animal representations as well as those of mythology interwoven with floral decoration. The word derives from 'grotto' because the Romans ornamented the interiors of some buildings in this way—structures which, by the time they were excavated, were below ground level.

In the seventeenth and eighteenth centuries artificial caves or grottoes were built into some large houses. The walls of these were shaped into rock and shell formation and water cascaded from them.

GROUT A thin mortar used as a filling for joints in wall and floor surfaces.

GRUMBOLD A family of masons who worked in *Cambridge*, mainly on university building, during much of the seventeenth century. *Thomas Grumbold* (*d.* 1657) carried out a considerable quantity of work at *Clare College*, on the east and south ranges and the bridge over the Cam, in the years 1638–41. *George* also worked there in the same period.

Later, *Robert Grumbold* (1639–1720) was responsible for the west range at Clare College between 1662 and 1676, after which he went to Trinity College to carry out Wren's designs for the library there (see WREN, SIR CHRISTOPHER). He returned to Clare College in 1683 to work on the north range (which included the hall and library) and, in 1705–7, the Master's Lodge. Both these commissions show the influence which working for Wren had upon Grumbold's work.

HAMILTON, THOMAS (1784–1858) A Scottish architect who was a leading exponent of the Greek Revival style in Edinburgh. His outstanding achievement in the city was the *Royal High School* (1825–9), built on the lower slopes of Calton Hill and more recently adapted to the needs of the proposed Scottish Assembly building. This is a powerful design in which the hall is presented as a projecting Doric Temple portico. Hamilton's other works in Scotland included the *Municipal Buildings* in *Ayr* (1828–30) and the *Royal College of Physicians* in *Edinburgh* (1844–6).

HANSOM, JOSEPH ALOYSIUS (1803–82) Born in York, he was first articled to an architect. In 1830 he won the competition for *Birmingham Town Hall* with a design on Roman temple lines. Three years later he achieved fame as inventor of a 'Patent Safety Cab'. He registered and sold this invention which subsequently was

East range, Clare College, Cambridge, 1638–41. Architect: Thomas Grumbold

improved when it became known as the 'hansom cab'. In 1842 he founded the journal *The Builder*.

Thereafter most of Hansom's architectural designs were ecclesiastical work for Roman Catholic clients. Notable among these buildings were the *Cathedral* at *Arundel* in Sussex, the *Cathedral* at *Plymouth* and the *Jesuit Church* in *Manchester*.

HARDWICK, PHILIP (1792–1870) The chief member of one of the architectural dynasties of the nineteenth century, Philip Hardwick was noted for his monumental, somewhat severe classical buildings, for instance, his work for the *St Katherine's Dock* Company. His name was given added prominence more recently when his best-known design, the imposing *Doric entrance arch* fronting

HAMILTON, THOMAS The Royal High School, Edinburgh, 1825–9

HANSOM, JOSEPH ALOYSIUS Birmingham Town Hall, built to Hansom's design, 1832–45

Euston Station in London (1836–9), was demolished in 1962 to make way for the 'new station improvements', despite widespread protests from learned societies and committees and members of the architectural and engineering professions (see also RAILWAY ARCHITECTURE).

Great entrance arch, Euston Station, London (1836–9, now demolished). Architect: Philip Hardwick.

Parish Church of St Marylebone, London, 1813–17. Architect: Thomas Hardwick

Philip's son, *Philip Charles Hardwick* (1822–92) took over his father's practice in 1847. He continued the work at Euston Station, building the great hall in 1849, which was 60ft in width and covered by a coffered ceiling. In 1848–51 he was responsible for *Aldermaston Court* at *Newbury*.

Earlier members of the Hardwick family included Philip's grandfather, the architect *Thomas Hardwick* (1725–98), and father, also *Thomas Hardwick* (1752–1829), several of whose buildings survive. These include the parish church of *St Marylebone* in London (1813–17), which is an imposing classical church with pedimented Corinthian portico and a square tower topped by a circular colonnade and cupola, *St John's Wood Chapel* (1814), also in London, and *Wanstead Church* in Essex, built 1787–91.

HARRISON, THOMAS (1744–1829) A Yorkshireman who returned to England to architectural practice in 1776 after spending several years studying in Rome. His work chiefly comprised castles, houses and bridges in the Midlands and the north of England and included the *bridge* at *Lancaster* over the Lune (1783–8) and that at *Chester* over the Dee, the 200ft-span, single-arched stone *Grosvenor Bridge*, built in 1827–33. Two of his larger projects were *Lancaster Castle* (begun 1788) and *Chester Castle* whose building lasted from 1793 to 1822. Both these castles incorporated a courthouse, gaol and armoury; the Lancaster example was in Gothic style, that at Chester in classical.

HAWKSMOOR, NICHOLAS (1661–1736) With Vanbrugh and Archer, one of the famous triumvirate of English Baroque architects (see ARCHER, THOMAS and VANBRUGH, SIR JOHN). Of Nottinghamshire farming stock, Hawksmoor early became interested in building and architecture. At the age of 18 he went to London to work for Wren as his domestic clerk and quickly absorbed the skill and knowledge which made him a valued assistant. From about 1684 onwards he worked with Wren in different capacities on all the great architectural projects of the day: Chelsea Hospital, the city churches, St Paul's Cathedral, Hampton Court Palace and Greenwich Hospital (see WREN, SIR CHRISTOPHER). Hawksmoor was appointed to a number of posts as, for instance, when he became in 1689 Clerk of the Works at Kensington Palace and, nine years later, Clerk of the Works at Greenwich where, in 1705, he became Deputy-Surveyor of Works.

From about 1700 Hawksmoor began to assist Vanbrugh in a similar manner (see VANBRUGH, SIR JOHN). He worked in close co-operation with Vanbrugh at Castle Howard, at Blenheim, also at Greenwich when Vanbrugh had taken over responsibility there from Wren. Hawksmoor had gained immense technical knowledge and experience from his years of working for Wren and it is certain that he was able, particularly for Vanbrugh's first commission at

The Clarendon Building, Oxford, 1712–15

St Mary Woolnoth, 1716–24

Christ Church, Spitalfields, 1714–29

West front, Westminster Abbey, London. Towers designed by Hawksmoor, 1734, built by John James, *c.* 1745

Castle Howard, to assist this gifted man who, at that time, was inexperienced in the field of architecture.

It was from the early years of the eighteenth century that Hawksmoor emerged as an architect in his own right. His personal style owed much to Wren, also to Vanbrugh but it was neither as elegantly classical as the work of the former nor as massively and exuberantly Baroque as that of the latter. Hawksmoor's surviving buildings display a specific originality which is an unusual blend of bold Roman design and medieval architecture. Unlike a number of his colleagues, for instance, Archer or Gibbs (see ARCHER, THOMAS; GIBBS, JAMES), he did not travel or study abroad and so acquire a close appreciation of Italian Baroque design. His emphasis, through books, was upon the contribution of ancient Rome.

Apart from the stone house of *Easton Neston* near Towcester, with its façade articulated by a giant order of Corinthian pilasters standing upon a rusticated base, upon which Hawksmoor completed work in 1702, his architectural reputation rests upon his contribution to university and ecclesiastical building.

He made designs and drawings for several grandiose schemes at both Oxford and Cambridge but much of this was not translated into actual building. His most important university monument is his work at *All Souls' at Oxford*. In 1710 Christopher Codrington, fellow of the college, died and left his library and money for housing it to his college. It was decided to rebuild the north quadrangle with the new Codrington Library, the Hall and Buttery. These buildings, designed by Hawksmoor, and built between 1716 and 1735, are externally in Gothic style to harmonize with the earlier chapel but are of classical form within. The pinnacled towers, in particular, provide an interesting, powerful silhouette, almost on cathedral scale (see GOTHIC REVIVAL). In contrast, in Roman classical vein, with giant Doric portico, Hawksmoor designed the *Clarendon Building* in the city, built as the University Printing House in 1712–15; different again is the more Baroque screen wall to the High Street of the Queen's College (1733–6).

In 1711 the New Churches Act was passed which provided for the building of 50 new churches to minister to London parishioners mainly in the then expanding suburbs. This was the first large-scale church building scheme in the capital since Wren's rebuilding of the City Churches after the Great Fire. In the first 30 years of the eighteenth century, however, only 12 churches were built, six of them by Hawksmoor. His architectural reputation stands, in no small measure, upon these highly original, individualistic designs. They are all different but all display vitality and power. Four are on Greek cross plan, two are more rectangular: all have boldly dramatic towers. One church, *St Mary Woolnoth* (1716–24) is in the City of London. It is built on squarish plan, much of the lower part is rusticated, above which is a rectangular tower with Corinthian columns. Another church, *St George Bloomsbury* (1716–31) is in London's West End; this is traditionally fronted by a Roman Corinthian portico. The other four churches in London's East End, constitute the most striking and unusual group. They are *St George-in-the-East* (Wapping, 1714–29), *Christ Church, Spitalfields* (1714–29), *St Anne, Limehouse* (1714–30) and *St Alphege, Greenwich* (1712–14) of which the steeple was completed later by John James (see JAMES, JOHN).

In 1723 Wren died and Hawksmoor succeeded him as Surveyor to Westminster Abbey in which capacity he designed the western towers to harmonize with the whole structure though the work was not completed until after his death.

HERRINGBONE WORK An arrangement in the construction of a wall or floor in which stones, bricks or tiles are laid diagonally to form a zig-zag design.

HIGH-RISE BUILDING The skyscraper was conceived and named in America where, by the 1880s, conditions were ripe for this type of architectural development. In the big cities, notably New York and Chicago, steeply rising land values provided the incentive to build high and the structural means to do so had become available. The story, though, did not begin in America but in England, where nearly a century earlier, textile mills for Britain's industrial revolution were being erected with cast-iron framing. This was a type of contruction, not yet an architectural style, but a functional, commercial means to an end which developed widely in Britain in the first half of the nineteenth century, being utilized in churches, civic structures and factories, culminating in the ferro-vitreous triumph of Paxton's *1851 Exhibition Building* in Hyde Park (see IRON AND GLASS; IRONWORK; PAXTON, SIR JOSEPH).

In America the desire to build high, at first for commercial and office needs, was frustrated for several decades by the requirement of transporting the occupants of the buildings from floor to floor and by the problems of load-bearing external walls. As early as 1849, *William Johnston* was erecting his seven-storey *Jayne Building* in *Philadelphia* in an architectural style which, though eclectic, displayed the vertical design format for the façade which was later to become characteristic of such high-rise structures.

Further building of this type followed but it was not until the development of the passenger lift (elevator) that it became feasible to put up structures of more than five or six storeys. The hoist for raising and lowering goods had been in use for centuries but it was not considered safe for passengers in case the rope broke. It was *Elisha Graves Otis* (1811–61) who adapted the hoist for passenger use. In 1852 he devised a safety mechanism consisting of spring-controlled pawls which, if the rope gave way, would engage ratcheted guide rails fitted into the sides of the lift shaft and so hold the cage in position. In 1854 in

HIGH-RISE BUILDING
Chilehaus, Hamburg, Germany, 1923. Architect: Fritz Höger

Senate House, London University, 1933–7. Architect: Sir Charles Holden

The Woolworth Building, New York, 1913. Architect: Cass Gilbert

The Lomonosov State University, Hill of Lenin, Moscow, USSR, 1949–53. Architects: Rudniev, Chernisev, Abrosimov, Chrjakov and Nasomov

New York Otis personally demonstrated this device and within a few years passenger lifts were being installed in office blocks and taller buildings resulted.

The next essential development to enable buildings to rise above about ten storeys was the steel-framed structure. Until the early 1880s tall buildings up to this height were being erected on traditional load-bearing lines but, to rise still higher, required impracticably thick walls at base in order to carry the load above. It was the emergence of the load-bearing metal framework, structurally independent of the external walling, which made the true skyscraper possible. An early landmark in this development was the *Home Insurance Building* in *Chicago*, built in 1883–5 by *William Le Baron Jenney*. In this he devised an iron and steel framework of columns, lintels and girders. This building was quickly followed by the fully developed steel skeleton construction of the *Tacoma Building* in the same city, where the walls were merely cladding, by *Holabird and Roche* (see STEEL-FRAMED CONSTRUCTION).

Despite these revolutionary structural ideas which made tall skyscrapers possible, architectural design continued to be largely eclectic, the wall cladding being dressed with classical columns and entablatures or, as in *Cass Gilbert's* (1859–1934) 52-storey *Woolworth Building* of 1913 in *New York*, in Gothic detail. The leader in designing an architectural style suited to take advantage of the new structural method was *Louis H. Sullivan* (1856–1924), who built his elevations to accentuate the height and with continuous pilasters to stress the steel-frame construction rather than to hide it as traditional builders had done. His *Wainwright Building* in *St Louis* (1890–1) is characteristic of this. A few years later, in 1894–5, came his masterpiece, the *Guaranty Building* in *Buffalo*, based on almost free-standing piers which anticipated the later use of *pilotis* (see MODERN ARCHITECTURE). The elevations are sheathed in terracotta and rise to a decorative, non-eclectic cornice.

From the early years of the twentieth century European architects began to build higher but until after 1945, did not attempt to follow the American example of the tall structures of the 1920s and 1930s: the *Empire State Building* of 1930–2, for example, rises through 85 storeys. Much of the early European multi-storey building was of traditional type, the form of the steel structure being concealed by the cladding as in the *Ritz Hotel* in London of 1906. Even in the 1930s, with plain, more modern design, showing repetitive fenestration, the structure is not utilized to provide architectural interest: *Shell Mex House*, London (1929–32) and *London University's Senate House* (1933–7) are typical (see HOLDEN, SIR CHARLES). Only the minority of European architects in these years followed the more original Sullivan line: *Adelaide House* in London is one example (see BURNET, SIR JOHN), while *Fritz Höger's* (1877–1949) *Chilehaus* in *Hamburg* is a particularly striking and successful building of this type.

Since the Second World War all over the western world high-rise building has become prevalent, not just for office and commercial needs but for housing also. Shortage and high cost of land have produced an incentive for this type of construction and, in the 1950s and 1960s especially, the tower block layout was adopted by architects and planners as an ideal new design for living with its economy of space and open-plan garden design. Technical advances in building materials and construction have made such structural methods more practical, for example, the substitution of welding for riveting, the increased employment of mechanical on-site plant, wide scale prefabrication and the extensive adoption of reinforced concrete (see CONCRETE; INDUSTRIALIZED BUILDING; MODERN ARCHITECTURE).

The style of such high-rise building has varied from

Kalinin Prospekt, Moscow, USSR, 1960s. Architects: Posokhin, Indoyantz and others

one country to another according to materials available and the national trend. Steel-framing is more characteristic of America, Britain and West Germany, concrete of Italy and France. Glass curtain walling was ubiquitous in the 1950s and early 1960s but was soon found to have considerable drawbacks in certain climatic conditions. Especially characteristic of the USSR is the traditionally grand scale of the projects. During the years 1945 to the early 1960s the Stalinist form of classical architecture was superimposed upon high-rise building producing innumerable skyscraper 'wedding cakes', versions of which appeared in the cities of Eastern Europe. Only after 1965 has the international modern style begun to take over there also.

Since the early 1970s the enthusiasm felt by architects, planners and town councillors for the 'vertical garden city' concept has been dampened by the gradual realization of some of the social implications inherent in this type of urban living, particularly with regard to the

Centrepoint, St Giles's Circus, London, 1962–6. Architects: R. Seifert and Partners

The Pirelli Tower, Milan, Italy, 1956–9. Architect and Engineer: Gio Ponti and Pier Luigi Nervi

elderly and parents with young families. In Britain, the decline in high-rise housing was triggered off by the dramatic collapse of one corner of the 22-storey system-built block of Ronan Point in the London borough of Newham (1968). Similar collapses occurred in several European countries. In the early 1980s the full scale of the need for rebuilding and reinforcing many system-built tower blocks is becoming apparent as investigation reveals many instances of inadequate on-site inspection techniques.

HOLDEN, SIR CHARLES (1875–1960) Senior partner in the firm of Adams, Holden and Pearson, he was the designer of *London University's Senate House*, a plain, tall structure, typical of its time (1933–7) (see HIGH-RISE BUILDING). Not dissimilar but more interesting and successful is his *Broadway House* in *London*, the office headquarters of the London Transport Executive (1927–9). On a triangular site, the building is constructed over St James's Underground Station, being on cruciform plan in order to accommodate the station. The architecture is very plain but there is a sense of power in the way in which the block towers upwards in diminishing stages. Portland stone is used for facing and for Sir Jacob Epstein's controversial (at the time) sculptural decoration, 'Night' and 'Day' (see also RAILWAY ARCHITECTURE).

HOLDEN, SIR CHARLES
Broadway House, Westminster, London, 1927–9: London Transport offices

HOLFORD, LORD WILLIAM GRAHAM (1907–75) Born in South Africa, Holford studied architecture at Liverpool University and became a Rome Scholar in 1930. He practised architecture, serving as President of the Royal Society of British Architects from 1960–2, but he is best known for his work in town planning. A leader in this field in his generation, he succeeded Abercrombie in 1937 as Professor of Civic Design at Liverpool University, and, again, in 1948, as Professor of Town Planning at University College, London, a post which he held until 1970 (see ABERCROMBIE, SIR LESLIE PATRICK).

William Holford was engaged in many town planning projects during his professional life. Best known in Britain are his ideas for the replanning of Piccadilly Circus, work on the precinct of St Paul's Cathedral, the post-war plans for the City of London in conjunction with Holden (see HOLDEN, SIR CHARLES), and work on the 1947 Town and Country Planning Act. His work was also widely known abroad, particularly in respect of the development of Canberra in Australia, Brasilia and in South Africa.

HOLLAND, HENRY (1745–1806) Son of Henry Holland of Fulham, a master builder under whom he trained. In 1771 the young Holland became assistant and partner to the landscape gardner Lancelot Brown (see BROWN, LANCELOT) who had earlier worked with Holland senior. Gradually the younger Holland took over the architectural side of Brown's practice, as in his work at *Claremont*, Surrey (1771–4). In 1773 he married Brown's daughter.

In common with other architects of his time Holland sought to supplement his income from architectural practice by undertaking speculative building work in London. In 1771 he leased an area of land in Chelsea from Lord Cadogan and developed it into an estate called *Hans Town*: this comprises Sloane Street, Hans Place and Cadogan Place. Much of the building has since been altered or demolished (see TERRACE ARCHITECTURE).

One of Holland's early commissions was to design *Brooks's Club* in London (1776). This brought him into contact with members of the Whig aristocracy which

Brooks's Club, St James's Street, London, 1776

HOLLAND, HENRY
Southill, Bedfordshire. South front, 1796–1800

yielded further important commissions and an introduction to the Prince of Wales for whom he carried out his chief work at *Carlton House* in *London* (1783–95 but dem. 1827). Here, on the north façade, he built a large-scale Corinthian portico, which led into his remodelled Ionic hall. To front the portico, Holland designed a screen of coupled Ionic columns. Also for the Prince of Wales he went on to create the *Marine Pavilion* at *Brighton*, transforming the old house into a royal residence: this Nash turned later into the Royal Pavilion (see NASH, JOHN).

Holland built or remodelled a number of country houses of which the best are *Berrington Hall*, Herefordshire (1778–81) and *Southill*, Bedfordshire (1796–1800); the latter he rebuilt for Samuel Whitbread. Much of Holland's work has been demolished or rebuilt but Southill, still the home of the Whitbread family, survives with very little alteration. Like all Holland's work it is tasteful neo-classicism (see CLASSICISM), restrained, meticulous in detail and excellently planned. Holland's style owed much to the Adam manner but his neo-classicism is in a lower key and has more of a French flavour than Adam's (see ADAM, ROBERT).

HOOD-MOULD A projecting moulding built over an arched opening to protect it from rainwater, also known as a *dripstone*. If the protecting moulding is of rectangular shape it may be termed a *label*: the carved terminal decoration is a *label stop*.

HYPAETHRAL Roofless, open to the sky.

HYPOCAUST An underfloor chamber of brick or stone constructed in ancient Roman buildings for central-heating purposes. Hot air in the basement furnace passed through wall flues to heat all the rooms (see ROMAN DOMESTIC ARCHITECTURE). The term is derived from two Greek words meaning 'the place heated from below'.

HOOD-MOULD

Carved stone label stop, fourteenth century

Hood-mould, Little Wenham Hall, *c.* 1270

HOOD-MOULD
Stone moulded label, Hengrave Hall, 1538

HYPOGEUM An underground chamber or vault.

HYPOSTYLE A large room the roof of which is supported upon many pillars.

ICONOSTASIS In the Eastern Church, the screen which separates the sanctuary from the main body of the church and upon which the icons (sacred pictures) are displayed (see BYZANTINE ARCHITECTURE; CHURCH DESIGN AND STRUCTURE).

INDUSTRIALIZED BUILDING The process of replacing craftsmanship in building by the mass-production of materials and decorative and structural features began on a small scale in the late eighteenth century. The Industrial Revolution brought steam power which was to revolutionize the machine tool and engineering industries. By the 1840s important developments were beginning to take place in the making of iron (and later steel), of glass, of bricks and concrete (see BRICKWORK; CONCRETE; GLASS; IRONWORK). Builders, following the example of Cubitt, reorganized their method of employing labour (see CUBITT, THOMAS).

By the early nineteenth century, particularly in the construction of factories, bridges and textile mills, mass-production of parts, chiefly iron and glass, was being experimented with. The *Iron Bridge* at *Coalbrookdale* was one famous example (1779), *Bunning's Coal Exchange* in *London* another (1847–9). Paxton's ferro-vitreous structure for the Great Exhibition of 1851, the *Crystal Palace*, was an early instance of a completely pre-fabricated building, a construction which, despite a large labour force, could not possibly have been erected in the short time available by traditional means (see PAXTON, SIR JOSEPH).

The growth of such industrialization in building accelerated gently from the mid-nineteenth century onwards but it has only been since 1945 that it has achieved total dominance because of a shortage and high cost of labour, skilled and unskilled. Such shortages also occurred immediately after the First World War and in the 1920s the need to make good the lack of building at the time led to the adoption of standardized and prefabricated building methods, examples being steel window frames to fit walling units, pre-cast concrete panels for walling and roofing at speed, and steel framing for building structures.

The even greater need to build quickly after 1945 because of the devastation in towns following World War II led to wide-scale prefabrication in parts of Europe, particularly of houses. The government in Britain sponsored several firms and schemes to erect temporary houses which became popularly known as 'prefabs'. One such firm was Arcon, which took its name from the firm of architects which designed the houses, the construction being handled by Taylor Woodrow Construction Ltd. The Arcon single-storey house consisted of some 2500 parts made by 145 different manufacturers. It was designed to be delivered complete to the building site from storage depots in four trucks. The first of these carried the steel structure and panels, the second the cladding and wooden floors, the third the internal partitioning and the last the kitchen and bathroom unit, finishes and trim. The construction was of light steel-framing clad externally with asbestos-cement sheeting and lined internally with plasterboard. Floors and internal doors and framing were of wood.

As the post-war emergency building programme slowed, prefabrication was less widely employed until, in the 1970s, building costs rose sharply and again a more extensive use of factory-made units took place and standardization, the essential concomitant of the prefabricated method, became more fully effective. The standardizing of separate building parts had been vital from the earliest experimentation but a system to establish an overall three-dimensional unit of measurement was now needed. Britain had been slow to adopt this system, known as *modular design*, which ensures the accurate fitting of all building parts of whatever material and wherever or by whomsoever manufactured. The Modular Society had

Ironbridge, Coalbrookdale, Shropshire, over River Severn, 1779

Arcon Mark II prefabricated house, first erected 1944. Cantilever porch contains boxes for fuel and refuse

Millbank Tower, London, 1963. Architects: Ronald Ward and partners. Glass and metal walling

been formed in Britain in 1953 to promote such a system of uniformity. Its members were drawn from all concerned with the building industry from architects to clients and craftsmen. The work of the Society is now handled by the British Standards Institution which deals with the problems of the industry. Le Corbusier had put forward a system of proportion in 1951, based upon the male human figure, to be used in building which he called Le Modulor (see MODERN ARCHITECTURE).

During the twentieth century many technical advances have taken place in the manufacture of materials which have made new building methods possible. As early as 1918 in San Francisco, *Willis Polk* introduced the 'curtain wall' of steel and glass which, hanging in front of the building's framework, separated this from the cladding. After 1945 glass curtain walling was taken up in many parts of the world where architects emulated the famous American examples in New York: the *United Nations Headquarters Building* (*Wallace K. Harrison*, 1947–50), the *Lever Building* (*Skidmore*, *Owings* and *Merrill*, 1950–2) and the *Seagram Building* (*Mies van der Rohe* and *Philip Johnson*, 1955–8).

With the development of reinforcement and prestressing, concrete has become the ubiquitous twentieth-century building material. The adoption from the 1950s, by large building firms of on-site pre-casting methods has economized greatly in transport and handling (see CONCRETE). Other technical advances of the post-1945 period have included float glass and solar glass (see GLASS), asbestos-cement panelling, plasterboard, plastics and fibreglass, aluminium and steel (see STEEL-FRAMED CONSTRUCTION) and all kinds of laminated-wood and particle-board products (see also HIGH-RISE BUILDING and MODERN ARCHITECTURE).

INWOOD, HENRY WILLIAM (1794–1843) The son of an architect, *William Inwood* (*c.* 1771–1843), Henry Inwood after training in his father's office travelled in Greece, particularly Athens, where he made a detailed study of the ancient classical architecture; in the 1820s and 1830s he published the results of his work. Father and son worked together on the majority of the family's commissions with the younger man supplying the knowledge and experience for the Greek Revival style of buildings which they preferred. One such structure was so successful that it is recognized as one of the great buildings in this style in Britain: it is *St Pancras Church* in *London*, built 1819–22. The design follows the general pattern of Gibbs's St Martin-in-the-Fields (see GIBBS, JAMES), where a steeple in diminishing stages rises behind a great portico, but the Inwood church draws on a selection of the great Athenian monuments for its inspiration: the Ionic portico from the Erechtheion and the theme of the tower from a blend of the Choragic Monument of Lysicrates and the Tower of the Winds. The body of the church is a large hall with an apse at one end and portico at the other. Inside, the hall is galleried with a flat ceiling above. The detailed decoration is rich and of meticulous quality. This was an expensive church for its day, costing £70,000.

St Pancras Church, London, 1819–22

Another attractive Inwood church is *All Saints* in *Camden Town*, also Greek Revival but this time with a circular colonnaded steeple rising behind a semicircular Ionic portico (see REGENCY ARCHITECTURE). In Gothic vein, the architects completed the rebuilding of the tower of *East Grinstead Church* in Sussex in 1813 after the death of Wyatt (see WYATT, JAMES).

IRON AND GLASS The nineteenth century was very much the age of iron, the use of which became increasingly important for both structure and decoration (see IRONWORK). By the 1820s and 1830s, as a result of the technical improvements in the making of both iron and glass (see GLASS), the idea of combining the use of these two materials for specific types of building was experimented with widely. Employed together they were regarded as more fireproof than, for example, wood and glass, though by 1850 it was being realized that an iron skeleton to a building could collapse dangerously when a

Galleria VIttorio Emmanuele II, Milan, Italy, 1865–77. Architect: Giuseppe Mengoni

Palm Stove, Royal Botanic Gardens, Kew, 1844–7. Cast-iron and glass units. Length of structure 362ft

Peter Jones's Department Store, Sloane Square, London, 1936–9. Architects: William Crabtree and others

State Department Store, GUM. Red Square, Moscow, 1889–93. Architect: A. N. Pomerantsev

fire reached a certain temperature. (Indeed, this was later proven to be only too true, on the night of 1 December 1936 when the Crystal Palace was so speedily and almost totally destroyed by fire.)

An early use of these materials was for conservatories and glasshouses. Wood framed the glass panels in many designs but gradually it was replaced by iron. *Humphrey Repton* built a ferro-vitreous structure at Brighton and this was followed by the much larger *Great Conservatory* at *Chatsworth* (see PAXTON, SIR JOSEPH), and the still extant *Palm Stove* in *Kew Gardens*. The building of this remarkable early Victorian monument, 362ft in length, was supervised by *Decimus Burton*; it was erected by *Richard Turner*, the Dublin engineer, in 1844–7 (see BURTON, DECIMUS). It was a remarkable structure for its time, comprising 45,000 square feet of greenish glass. Inside, a decorative iron spiral staircase gives access to an upper gallery from where the tall plants can be closely viewed.

It was soon discovered that iron and glass were ideal materials from which to build structures such as sheds and station concourses for the developing railway systems of Europe (see RAILWAY ARCHITECTURE) and many fine examples resulted, for instance, *Kings Cross* in *London* (*Lewis Cubitt*, 1851–2; see CUBITT, THOMAS) and *Duquesney's Gare de l'Est* in *Paris* (1847–52). Great iron and glass domed coverings were erected over important public buildings such as *London's Coal Exchange* by *J. B. Bunning* (1846–9) and *Sidney Smirke's* Reading Room which he added in 1854–5 in the court of his brother's *British Museum*. Then in 1851 came the realization of the potential of these materials for prefabrication when the *Crystal Palace* was erected in Hyde Park in less than five months (see INDUSTRIALIZED BUILDING; PAXTON, SIR JOSEPH).

Iron and glass continued to complement each other in building as the century advanced though, as both quality and quantity of steel production so dramatically improved (see IRONWORK), steel increasingly often replaced iron for structural purposes. In many European cities great under-cover shopping arcades or galleries were constructed where people could stroll, chat at café tables or window-gaze. A number of these survive: the *Galleria Vittorio Emmanuele II* in *Milan* is an impressive example. Another is the fantastic department store in Moscow's Red Square called GUM. Built 1889–93 (see IRONWORK) the interior of this great building comprises three parallel barrel-vaulted galleries, each about 1000ft in length, with balconies and walkways at different heights, all serving shops. There are iron connecting walkways from one section to another. The interior is like the nave and aisles of a church though the aisles are nearly as wide and high as the nave. There are hundreds of shops and stalls all covered above by an iron and glass domed roof.

In the twentieth century steel and glass have been used characteristically in the form of the glass curtain wall, introduced in America at the end of the First World War (see INDUSTRIALIZED BUILDING). An early and notable British example is *William Crabtree's Peter Jones'* department store in London's Sloane Square, built 1936–9. The glass-and-steel curtain wall curves round two elevations of the building on its corner site. Another use of this type of construction was in the new pharmaceutical factories designed by *Sir E. Owen Williams* for *Boots Pure Drug Company* at *Beeston* in 1932 (see MODERN ARCHITECTURE; WILLIAMS, SIR OWEN). Glass, steel and concrete are used with cantilevered façade construction. A dramatic and, in its day, controversial building was that of the *Daily Express* newspaper in London (1932) which was faced with black, toughened glass. Since the Second World War glass curtain walling has become ubiquitous, seen especially in tall buildings, again following the example of America (see HIGH-RISE BUILDING; MODERN ARCHITECTURE; STEEL-FRAMED CONSTRUCTION).

IRONWORK Iron had been regarded as a durable utilitarian material since the early Middle Ages but its use was limited by the lack of power and technical knowledge which hampered both quality and quantity of production. The iron in use at this time was *wrought*, that is, hammered, to beat out impurities and form a desired shape. It was the development of the tall blast furnace in response to the urgent needs for iron firebacks, utensils, weapons and agricultural implements which made it possible to produce a molten metal which could be poured into shaped moulds: that is *cast iron*. In the taller blast furnace the iron ore fed in continuously at the top took longer to penetrate to the bottom and in so doing absorbed more carbon from the charcoal fuel thus lowering the melting point of the iron by 350° and making it possible to liquefy it. This cast iron lacked the tensile strength of wrought iron but was strong in compression. Water wheels were used to power the furnace bellows and, where needed, the hammers; by 1600 Britain had a good supply of iron for the needs of the time.

Soon after this the diminishing timber supplies made it inevitable that coal had to be used to replace the wood fuel for smelting. This caused severe problems: the iron so made was brittle and lacked strength due to the sulphur content of the coal. Not until after 1709 when the experiments of *Abraham Darby* (1677–1717) led to an understanding that the coal must first be coked, as well as the later studies of his son *Abraham Darby II*, was iron of satisfactory quality being produced with coal. Two further innovations in the second half of the eighteenth century immensely improved production both in quality and quantity so that more ambitious uses could be found for iron in bridge and aqueduct structures and in the building of factories to house heavy machinery. One of these was due to the great ironmaster *John Wilkinson* (1728–1808) who, in 1776, installed a Boulton and Watt steam engine in his Shropshire works, so improving the power potential. The other stemmed from *Henry Cort*

Wrought-iron balustrade with stone stairs, 1700–1710

Iron balustrade and mahogany handrail, Heveningham Hall, 1778–84. James Wyatt

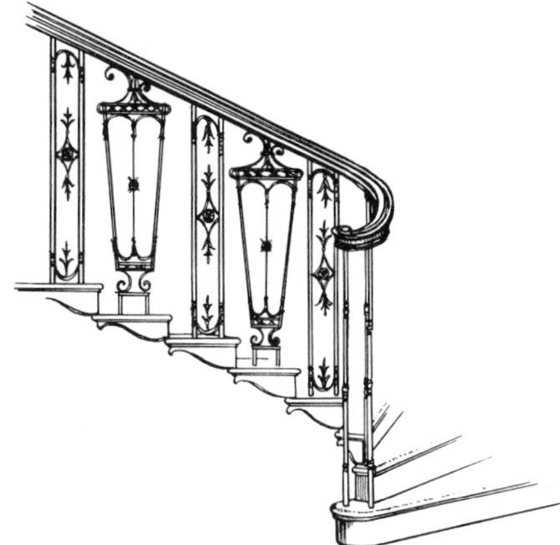

Iron balustrade and mahogany handrail, Woodhall Park, 1778–82. Thomas Leverton

Iron fanlight, Bryanston Square, London, *c.* 1800–1810

Seaside ironwork, Brighton Sea Front, Sussex, late nineteenth century

Regency bow window and iron balcony, Brighton, Sussex

Entrance gates, Royal Botanic Gardens, Kew, *c.* 1866

Station-master's Office, Paddington Station, London, 1852–4. Architect and Engineer: M. D. Wyatt and I. K. Brunel

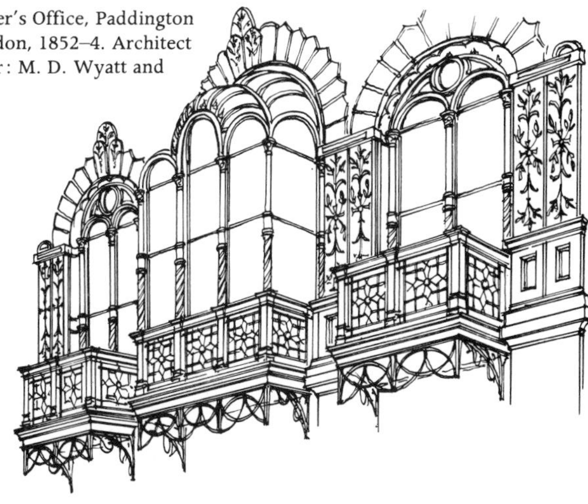

(1740–1800) who introduced in 1784 the action of puddling. This was a process of stirring the molten iron which freed it from impurities and so rendered it less brittle. The cast iron 'pigs' produced in Cort's coking furnaces could then, if required, be rolled into bars suited for making into wrought iron.

The way was now clear for an extensive use of iron, both cast and wrought for structural and decorative purposes. It would still rust and so needed painting—the age of steel was still far in the future (see STEEL-FRAME CONSTRUCTION) but, from the 1780s until about 1900, iron was utilized for almost all building needs: railings, balconies, staircase balustrades, reinforcement to wood and masonry, supporting columns and beams, window and door frames and, indeed, whole constructions of bridges and buildings.

Iron was widely used particularly for balconies, railings and staircase balustrades from the 1760s onwards. Even earlier, Inigo Jones had built his attractive round 'tulip' staircase at the *Queen's House* at *Greenwich*, 1618–35 (see JONES, INIGO), but it was in the second half of the eighteenth century that architects in general used iron for decorative balustrades in conjunction with stone or marble (often cantilevered) staircases: Chambers, Leverton, Adam, Holland and Wyatt created many beautiful examples (see ADAM, ROBERT; CHAMBERS, SIR WILLIAM; HOLLAND, HENRY; LEVERTON, THOMAS; WYATT, JAMES).

In Regency times iron balconies became an essential part of external architectural design and this custom continued during the first half of the nineteenth century. By 1820 iron was also being more widely used for structural purposes. Increasingly it was employed to strengthen timber and masonry. It was also acting as a reinforcement to concrete construction as in, for example, the Paris Panthéon (see CONCRETE). Iron supporting columns were being introduced into the building of halls and, especially, factories and mills many of which have to bear the weight of heavy machinery. Some textile mills, indeed, contained a comprehensive iron skeleton. Iron was being used for Gothic vaults and complete staircases as in Nash's 'Chinese-style' staircase in the *Royal Pavilion* at *Brighton* (*c.* 1818, see NASH, JOHN). Iron columns were increasingly being introduced for supporting parts of churches such as galleries and roofs, as for instance in two *Liverpool* churches of the time, *St George's, Everton* and *St Michael, Toxteth Road*. However, such use of iron was strongly deprecated by Pugin and the Camdenians as being 'sham' and, by the 1830s and 1840s was being strongly proscribed (see GOTHIC REVIVAL; PUGIN, A. W. N.).

In the second half of the nineteenth century wrought iron became increasingly important for heavy structural work. Beams for floors and roof trusses were manufactured which would withstand considerable loads in railway stations, civic and industrial buildings. In *New York* in 1848, *James Bogardus* (1800–74) erected his first four-storeyed factory structure of iron piers and lintels: he went on to further and more ambitious iron urban buildings and others emulated his example for factories, department stores and apartment blocks. In Britain in 1851 at *Balmoral Castle* the Prince Consort ordered a prefabricated iron ballroom. At *Saltaire* in Yorkshire much of Sir Titus Salt's magnificent new *textile mill* (1854) was of iron construction. In 1889 in *Paris* was erected the tallest of nineteenth-century structures in wrought iron: *Gustave Eiffel's* 984ft *tower* to commemorate the century of the start of the French Revolution.

ISOMETRIC PROJECTION A method of drawing objects in three dimensions similar to the axonometric system but in isometric drawing the plane of projection is equally inclined to the principal axes of the building to be drawn. Thus, an illusion of normal perspective is obtained because all dimensions parallel to the axes are correctly scaled (see AXONOMETRIC PROJECTION, drawing C, where the inclination is unequal, 60° and 30° respectively).

JACOBEAN ARCHITECTURE The building and decorative style of the reign of James I of England (1603–25) which was largely a continuation and extension of the pattern set during the years of Queen Elizabeth I (see ELIZABETHAN ARCHITECTURE).

As in the preceding 50 years, there was little ecclesiastical building and only a limited expansion of the universities. Building activity was concentrated in the domestic field where a number of great mansions were erected and many smaller but also fine quality homes (see COUNTRY HOUSE). Jacobean work is generally on a larger scale than Elizabethan, more sumptuous, stately and lavishly decorated. The house plan is still usually 'E' or 'H', the windows large and gables decorative, straight- or curved-sided in the Dutch manner. The two-storeyed entrance porch (see FRONTISPIECE) is impressive, its classical form still evidencing Jacobean dependence upon Flemish, rather than Italian, source material.

Inside, the plaster ceilings, in strapwork pattern, are richly, even extravagantly ornamented over almost the whole surface (see CEILING). The two-stage chimneypiece, extending from floor to ceiling, dominates each major interior (see CHIMNEY, CHIMNEYPIECE). Any Jacobean house of note contains its long gallery where woodwork and plasterwork are of high decorative quality (see GALLERY). Here, as in the reception rooms, the whole inte-

The staircase of Hatfield House, Hertfordshire, 1607–12

Entrance porch of Bramshill House, Hampshire, 1605–12

South (entrance) front of Blickling Hall, Norfolk. Architect: Robert Lyminge, 1619–25. The clock tower dates from the 1820s

Jacobean drawing-room, *c.* 1615–20

rior began at this time to be designed in one unit in classical form, pilasters or columns dividing the wall vertically into sections with windows, doorways and chimneypiece flanked as focal centres of interest. The room is treated as a classical order with horizontal mouldings dividing the walls into entablature support and base or pedestal (see CLASSICAL ORDER). The classical detail may still be inaccurate by Italian standards but the format was becoming accepted. The great staircase, which had begun its evolution in the Elizabethan house, had now developed into a magnificent feature. Still oak and heavily built and carved the staircase now ascended easily in short straight flights round an open well (see STAIRCASE).

Notable among the Jacobean great houses which survive are *Hatfield House*, Hertfordshire (1607–12); *Bramshill House*, Hampshire (1605–12); *Knole House*, Kent (*c.* 1605 onwards); *Aston Hall*, Birmingham (1618–35); *Charlton House*, Greenwich (1607–12); and *Chastleton House*, Oxon (1603–12) (see also RENAISSANCE ARCHITECTURE).

JAMB The vertical side members of a doorway, window or fireplace opening.

JAMES, JOHN (1672–1746) The son of a clergyman, James began his career as a carpenter, later carrying out more general building work at both Greenwich Hospital and St Paul's Cathedral. James is best known for the *Church of St George* in *Hanover Square*, London, which he designed in 1720 and in which he set a pattern for later London churches with his impressive free-standing, pedimented portico of six Corinthian columns: an example which was followed by several distinguished architects, for example, *Hawksmoor* in *St George, Bloomsbury* and *Gibbs* in *St Martin-in-the-Fields* (see GIBBS, JAMES and HAWKSMOOR, NICHOLAS). In 1713–14 James rebuilt the *Church of St Mary* at *Twickenham* on to an existing fifteenth-century western tower.

James was a competent, conscientious architect of the early eighteenth century, often following on and completing the work of more famous architects as when he built the tower to finish Hawksmoor's *St Alphege* in *Greenwich*. Also, in 1736, he succeeded Hawksmoor on the latter's death as Surveyor to the Fabric of *Westminster Abbey* after which he completed the western towers to Hawksmoor's designs.

JOIST One of a parallel set of beams upon which floor boards are laid or to which ceiling laths are fastened.

JAMES, JOHN
Church of St George, Hanover Square, London, 1720–5

JONES, INIGO (1573–1652) This self-taught (son of a Smithfield clothmaker) artist and designer of costumes and décor for Court masques brought Italian Renaissance architecture to Britain and, in so doing, created a stylistic revolution.

Architectural style in Britain had progressed slowly from the various stages of Gothic design to the classical forms of Flemish mannerism imposed upon a medieval base (see ELIZABETHAN ARCHITECTURE; JACOBEAN ARCHITECTURE; MANNERISM). In the later years of the reign of James I of England, when Inigo Jones introduced Italian Renaissance forms, this was almost a century after French architects had begun to experiment with them in their château designs. After such a long delay the English movement, initiated by Jones, emerged mature as may be seen in his BANQUETING HOUSE in London.

The architectural career of Inigo Jones also took time to become established. He seems to have visited Italy briefly in his late twenties where, in Florence, he attended stage performances of the Medici Court. This stood him in good stead when, later in England, he became a stage designer for the Stuart Court. It was in 1613 that Inigo Jones took the opportunity offered to him by the great collector, Lord Arundel, to tour Italy and France in search of works of art. He spent one-and-a-half years travelling during which time he studied both the antique Roman building remains and the later Italian and French examples based upon them, making careful drawings and measurements as he went. When he returned to England he had acquired a thorough first-hand knowledge of such buildings—most unusual for an Englishman at this date.

He had ample time to study in Rome and Naples as well as Genoa and the Veneto. He became particularly interested in the work of *Andrea Palladio* (1508–80), comparing this with the copies of Palladio's books *I Quattro Libri dell'Architettura* and *Antichità di Roma* which he had brought with him.

Back in England in 1615 Inigo Jones became Surveyor of the King's Works and from then until 1642 he worked continuously on the royal projects. Despite his long years in this office, it is a great loss to British architecture that so little of his work survives. Though Parliament severely limited what could be spent on civic and official building and there was little ecclesiastical construction, he carried out some 40 works of which only a handful are extant.

Although so few of his buildings exist, his importance in the history of English architecture cannot be too strongly stressed. He was the first English architect to work in the wider manner on the pattern set by the Italians, from Brunelleschi and Alberti onwards and later by the French, led by men such as de l'Orme, Bullant and Lescot. These Renaissance architects were rarely masters of only one profession; most were, for example, painters, sculptors, mathematicians as well as architects. They did not only design a part, or even the whole of a building, as the medieval men had done, leading from their position as master masons, but envisaged a wider, more extensive scheme and controlled the operation of all the artisans employed on the project, responsible only to the client.

Inigo Jones's reputation as the first Englishman to practise architecture in this manner is assured, even though his two chief surviving buildings in London are all that remains of two extensive royal palace schemes. Based directly upon Italian Renaissance forms and owing nothing to the mannerism of Flanders and Germany, they were a revelation to patrons and architects alike in early seventeenth-century Britain. The *Banqueting House* (1619–22), replacement of an earlier building, was intended to be part of James I's ambitious scheme for his *Whitehall Palace*; it still fronts the thoroughfare of Whitehall. It was intended for court masques and formal royal banquets and was based on the antique Roman basilican theme. Two classical orders are used, one above the other in Roman manner, Ionic below, Composite above. Inside the building, constructed on two levels, the lower being intended for less formal gatherings, the upper banqueting hall is a double cube (110 × 55 × 55ft). The exterior orders are repeated in pilaster form and above is the superb ceiling, an allegory of the government of James I, painted by Rubens in 1636 at a cost of £3000.

Though for long in use as the Imperial War Museum the Banqueting House has since been refurbished for ceremonial state occasions, its original purpose.

The Banqueting House is Jones's masterpiece but no less interesting is his first Italian Renaissance building, the

Palazzo Chiericati, Vicenza, Italy, begun 1550. Architect: Andrea Palladio

The Banqueting House, Whitehall, London, 1619–22. Architect: Inigo Jones

Queen's House at Greenwich, begun in 1616. This was designed for James I's queen, Anne of Denmark, but soon afterwards she died and work was suspended until the 1630s when the building was finished for the next queen, Henrietta Maria. This beautiful little house owes its survival to the intervention of yet a third queen, Mary II, who insisted on its retention in the Greenwich Hospital scheme of the later seventeenth century. The Queen's House is a small two-storeyed Italian palace and, like the Banqueting House, owes much to Palladio's work at Vicenza. In this instance the inspiration is the Palazzo Chiericati but, like all Inigo Jones's work, it is no mere copy but highly personal and original, restrained and characteristically national in its simplicity. The lower storey is a rusticated basement. Above, the Ionic order is confined to the central loggia and this, like the double-curved approach staircase on the terrace elevation bears the stamp of Palladio. Inside, the hall is a 40ft cube; a gallery round this gives access to the queen's apartments (see IRONWORK).

Of Jones's ecclesiastical work the *Queen's Chapel* at St James's Palace in London (1623–5) survives as Marlborough House Chapel but his ambitious and extensive reparations to *St Paul's Cathedral* were consumed in the Great Fire of London of 1666. The Queen's Chapel was Jones's first ecclesiastical work; as there was no classical tradition at the time for that type of architecture in England, he based the chapel on antique temple pattern. The interior is an aisleless rectangle covered by a coffered segmental vault and lit mainly by a large Venetian window (see VENETIAN).

Inigo Jones was involved in a number of ambitious schemes for planning in London, notably for a rebuilding of Whitehall Palace for Charles I and layouts in streets and squares, classical in theme in the manner in which Italian architects were working in Rome and Pienza. *Covent Garden* was one such project. Here, Jones was commissioned to build a residential square, known for many years as a 'piazza'. The houses had uniform façades with a giant order used in pilaster form; below were

Iron balustrade and handrail of staircase in the Queen's House, Greenwich, 1616–35

The Queen's House, Greenwich, 1616–35

arcades. This was London's first such homogeneous square; little remains of it and much of the houses and St Paul's Church there have been rebuilt more than once over the years. So little survives of the various schemes upon which Inigo Jones was engaged, and many were abortive, but the influence of his ideas upon his pupils and successors was certainly not negligible (see WEBB, JOHN). We now know that there can be little of Jones's actual work at *Wilton House*, Wiltshire and the famous Double Cube Room, restored and rebuilt after the fire of 1647, was more likely to have been the work of his pupil and nephew *John Webb* but this superb interior bears much of the stamp of Inigo Jones's quality and originality in interior decoration.

Inigo Jones's influence in his time was primarily in the field of royal patronage but his ideas and his interpretation of Palladio were revived more than once, not least in the era of Palladianism in eighteenth-century Britain (see BURLINGTON, LORD; CAMPBELL, COLEN; KENT, WILLIAM; LEONI, GIACOMO; PAINE, JAMES; PALLADIAN ARCHITECTURE; TAYLOR, SIR ROBERT).

K

KENT, WILLIAM (1685–1748) A man of varied talents, Kent was landscape gardener, furniture designer, painter and architect, not an intellectual yet the personality of the Palladian school of architecture in Britain (see PALLADIAN ARCHITECTURE). Born in Yorkshire of humble origins, Kent went to Rome, where for ten years he studied painting and made a living buying paintings for the houses of English patrons. There, in 1715, he met Lord Burlington and, later in 1719, returned with him to England where he lived for the rest of his life under the Earl's patronage at Burlington House.

On their return to England Kent worked for some time as a decorative painter; he also edited for his patron the *Designs of Inigo Jones*, published in 1727. In the early 1730s, under Lord Burlington's guidance, he turned to architecture and, through his patron's influence, acquired important commissions and became a fashionable architect in the 1730s and 1740s.

Kent's masterpiece is *Holkham Hall* in Norfolk which he designed in 1734 for Thomas Coke, Earl of Leicester, whom he had also met in Rome. (Much of the building was finally executed after Kent's death by *Matthew Brettingham*.) The exterior of Holkham is classic English Palladian, severe, correct and monumental, its design strongly influenced by Lord Burlington himself. The interior is in complete contrast. This is Roman splendour tinged with the exuberance of Baroque, the décor, furniture and furnishings rich and colourful. The entrance hall, built in Derbyshire marble in shades of cream and white marked in red, is based on Roman basilican plan though its order and decoration owe much to the Temple of Fortuna Virilis in Rome: this is one of England's finest interiors. The order is Ionic, the ceiling elaborately coffered (see ALABASTER).

William Kent was noted for his interior decorative work and also for his furniture design and ornamental detail. His style was robust and boldly Baroque with a lavish use of gilt and colour. Apart from the glowing interiors of Holkham he was also responsible for decorating the interior of *Houghton Hall* in Norfolk (see CAMPBELL, COLEN; COUNTRY HOUSE AND MANSION) and *Chiswick House* in London (see BURLINGTON, EARL OF). In 1742–4 he designed *44 Berkeley Square* in London where he successfully created a palatial home within the more restrictive confines of a terraced town house (see TOWN HOUSE).

In the civic sphere in London, Kent produced in 1732 a scheme for the new Houses of Parliament. This did not get beyond the drawing-board stage but more fortunate was his plan of 1734 for the *Treasury* in Whitehall while, nearby, his *Horse Guards* still stands. This he designed

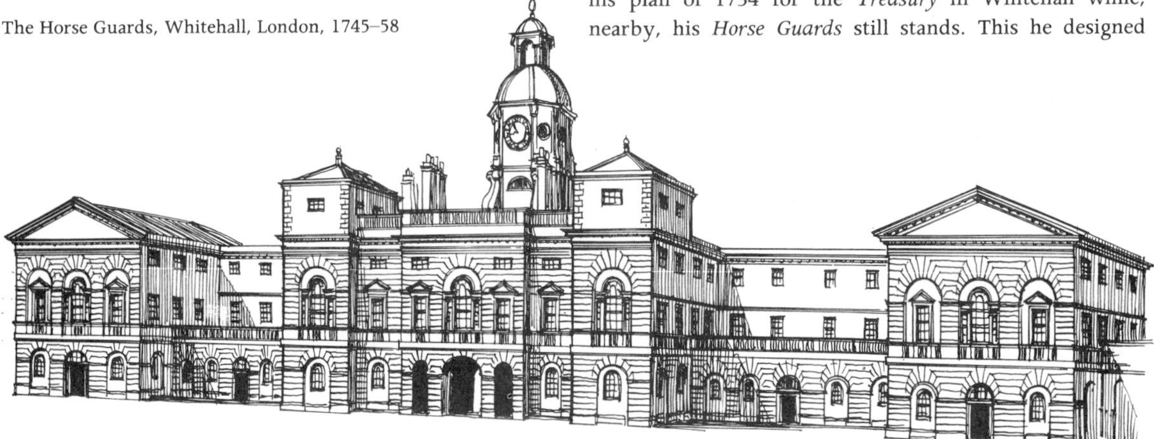

The Horse Guards, Whitehall, London, 1745–58

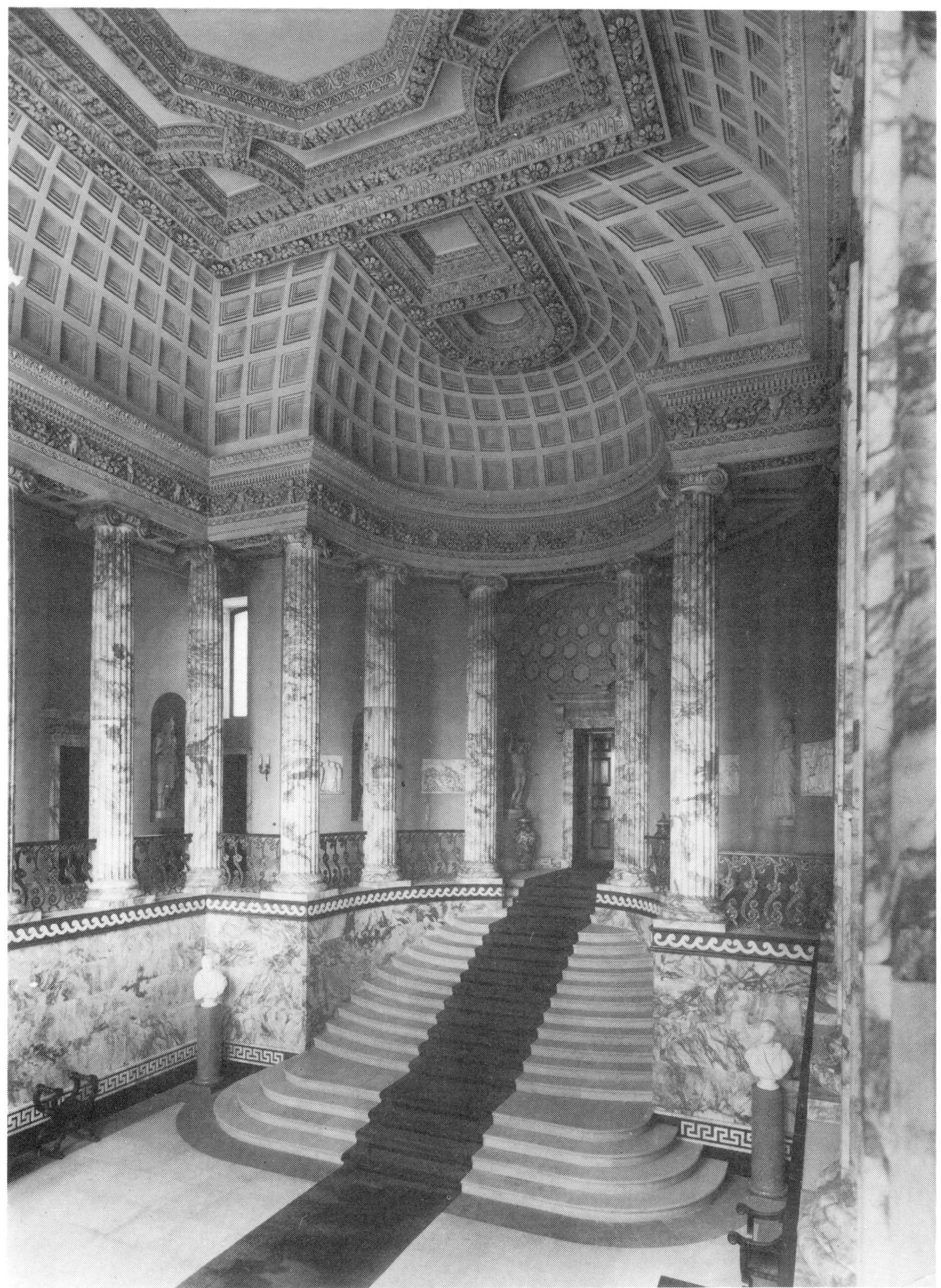

Holkham Hall, Norfolk, begun 1734: the entrance hall

much as an echo of Holkham; it was built in the 1750s to his designs after his death.

Though William Kent was a member of the Palladian School in Britain, he was not a devoted *aficionado* of the style. He was indebted to Lord Burlington as his patron and so designed as the Earl would have wished. Kent himself was equally willing to work in other styles as he did when he ventured into Gothic (albeit in classical dress) at *Esher Place* in Surrey and more notably, at *Hampton Court Palace* in the Clock Court in 1732 (see GOTHIC REVIVAL).

Kent's contribution to the essentially English version of landscape gardening in the eighteenth century was notable. He led the revolt against the Continental seventeenth-century formal garden layout and initiated a trend towards studied naturalism, pointing the way for 'Capability' Brown and others (see BROWN, LANCELOT) in providing the English parkland setting in which to display the contrasting severity of the formal Palladian house. Holkham in Norfolk and *Stowe* in Buckinghamshire are examples of this.

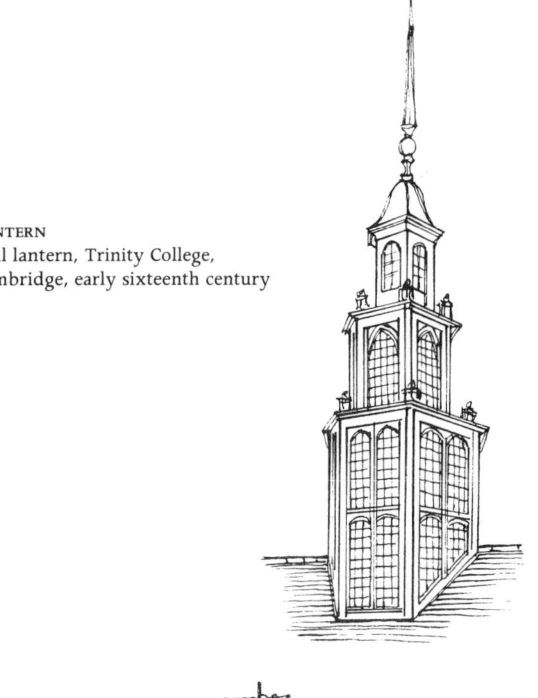

LANTERN
Hall lantern, Trinity College, Cambridge, early sixteenth century

L

LANGLEY, BATTY (1696–1751) The son of a gardener, he followed in the family tradition, then set up an academic establishment for architectural drawing. Batty Langley is known chiefly for the many books of drawings and information on the architectural mode which he was responsible for publishing for the guidance of builders and craftsmen. Among others these included *A Sure Guide to Builders or the Principles and Practice of Architecture Geometrically Demonstrated* (1729), *The Builder's Compleat Assistant* (2nd edition 1738) and *Ancient Masonry both in the Theory and the Practice* (1734). In 1741 he published his attempt to relate the new fashions in the revival of Gothic architectural design to the classical formula of five orders in his *Gothic Architecture Restored and Improved*: an attempt which was not a success.

LANTERN A small circular or polygonal structure surmounting a dome or hall roof for the purpose of admitting light and air.

LASDUN, SIR DENYS LOUIS (b. 1914) One of the outstanding architects of post-war Britain, noted for the variety and originality of his schemes, a clear, fearless approach to design and a sympathetic preference for the use of modern materials (notably concrete) in the tradition

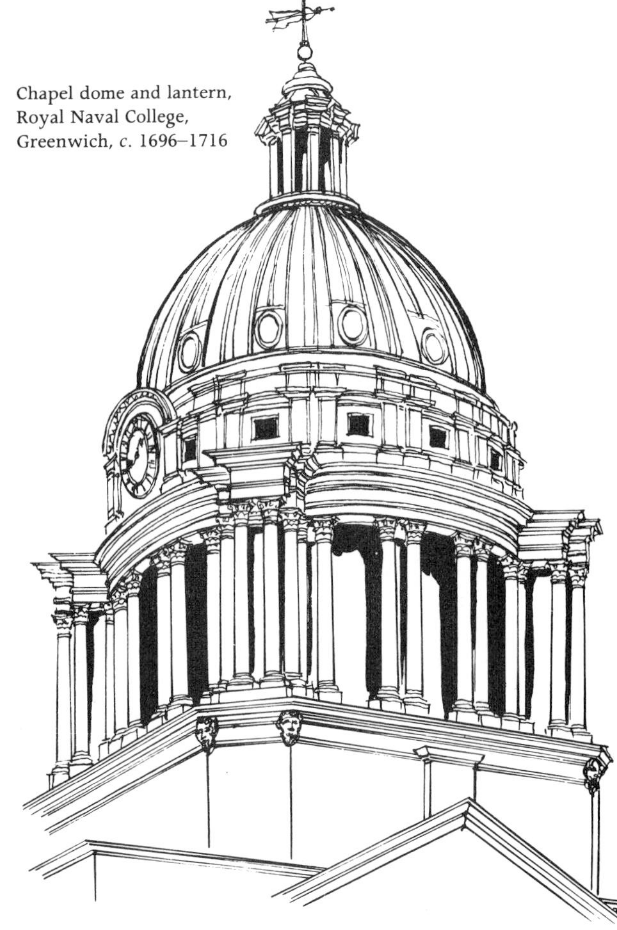

Chapel dome and lantern, Royal Naval College, Greenwich, *c.* 1696–1716

LASDUN, SIR DENYS LOUIS
Fitzwilliam House, Cambridge University: hall and library, begun 1959

'Cluster' block of flats at Claredale Street, Bethnal Green, London, 1958–9

of the early leaders of the modern movement (see MODERN ARCHITECTURE).

Before the Second World War Lasdun worked with Wells Coates (see COATES, WELLS WINTEMUTE) in the years 1935–7 then, in 1938, became a partner in the Tecton Group (see TECTON). After the war, in 1958, partnered by Drake, Lasdun devised the 'cluster' block design in *Bethnal Green* in London. This was an interesting and effective plan for housing in a densely populated area. Four rectangular concrete blocks were connected to a core by bridges. The advantage of the 'cluster' over a solid block is that light and air are admitted more freely. Other interesting projects of this period were luxury flats in *St James's Place* and the *Royal College of Physicians* in Regent's Park, both in London.

Lasdun went on to carry out a considerable quantity of work at the universities, at Liverpool, Leicester and London. At Cambridge, of particular interest is his *Fitzwilliam House,* comprising the hall and library. He was then responsible for the planning of the new *University of East Anglia,* at Norwich (1962–3).

Lasdun's most important work is the *National Theatre* on London's *South Bank* (1967–76). It comprises three auditoria (seating almost 2000 people) with their subsidiary accommodation, arranged on different levels. Concrete is used throughout for exterior and interior surfaces, the exterior being designed in terraces which, with the tower of the Olivier Theatre, are the principal features when viewed from the opposite bank of the river.

LEONI, GIACOMO (*c.* 1686–1746) A Venetian architect who moved to England in the early years of the eighteenth century where, in 1715, he superintended the publication of a lavish edition in English of Palladio's *I Quattro Libri dell'Architettura,* having spent some years in preparing new engravings to replace Palladio's woodcuts; the text was translated by Nicholas Dubois. Leoni

LEONI, GIACOMO
Lyme Park, Cheshire, south front, *c.* 1725–35

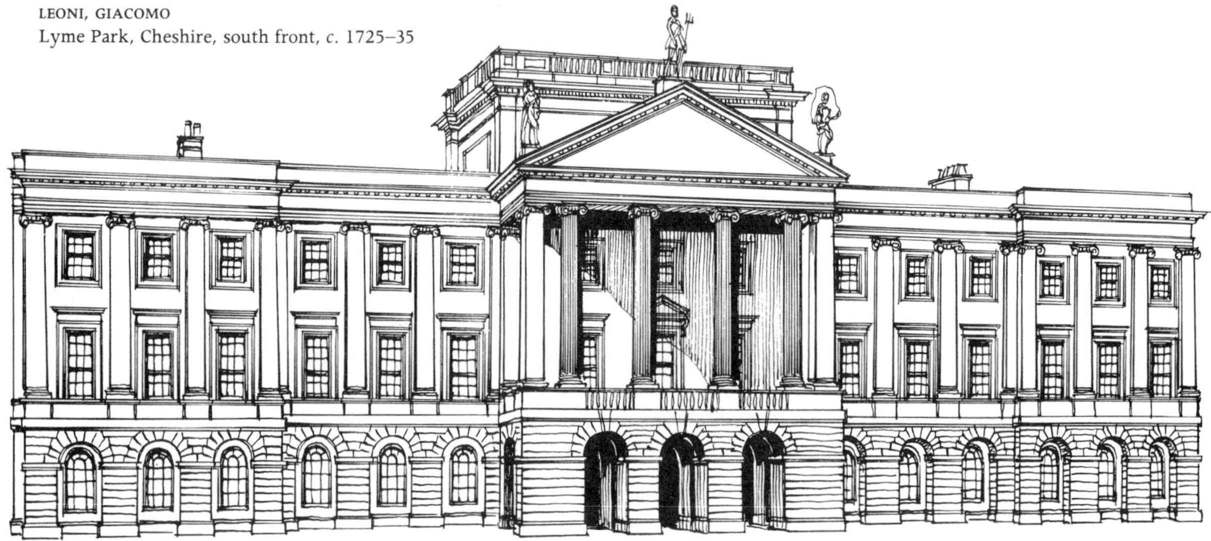

followed this in 1726 with his three-volume translation of Alberti's *Architecture*.

Leoni's own building work was in Burlingtonian Palladian style. He was a pioneer in its introduction to town house architecture at *Queensberry House*, Burlington Gardens in London (1721 but considerably remodelled in 1792). His surviving contribution to country house architecture includes *Clandon Park*, Surrey (1730–3) and *Lyme Park*, Cheshire where between 1725 and 1735 he redesigned the south front and portico (see PALLADIAN ARCHITECTURE; PORTICO).

LESENE A pilaster without capital or base, a pilaster strip as seen in Saxon stone buildings, for example, *Worth Church*, Sussex and the tower of *Earl's Barton Church*, Northamptonshire (see SAXON ARCHITECTURE).

LETHABY, WILLIAM RICHARD (1857–1931) A Devon man, Lethaby studied at the Royal Academy Schools in London then later in Europe after winning the Soane travelling scholarship of the Royal Institute of British Architects. He spent 12 years in the office of Norman Shaw (see SHAW, NORMAN) becoming his principal assistant and an admirer of his work. In 1889 he set up practice on his own, building houses and most notable in 1902, the stone church of *All Saints* at *Brockhampton* in Herefordshire: in simplified Gothic style, this original design was ahead of its time. In 1906 Lethaby was appointed Surveyor to the Fabric of Westminster Abbey.

Lethaby's influence on British architecture was much more as a scholar and a teacher than as a practising architect: indeed, his building output was small. From his early life he had greatly admired the concepts and ideals of Morris and Webb (see MORRIS, WILLIAM; WEBB, PHILIP). The architectural designs of Webb, who was a great friend, influenced some of Lethaby's own work. Of perhaps greater significance was Lethaby's achievement at the Central School of Arts and Crafts in London which he helped to promote then, after its foundation in 1894, became its first principal. Here, for the first time, were set up workshops where crafts could be taught: a monument to Morris's ideas. Lethaby remained at the 'Central' until 1911. From 1900 to 1918 he also held the Chair of Design (of which he was the first professor) at the Royal College of Art.

Notable among Lethaby's many published works were *Mediaeval Art* (1904), *Architecture* (1912), *National Architecture and Modernism* (1918–21), *Westminster Abbey Re-examined* (1925), *Philip Webb and his work* (1935) and, most original and influential, his collection of essays, published 1922, entitled *Form in Civilisation*.

LEVERTON, THOMAS (1743–1824) He is not classed among the great architects of his time but his work, though not on the grand scale nor great in quantity, has a delicate, tasteful quality, often akin to that of Adam, whose style he closely followed. He employed an ex-pupil

Woodhall Park, Hertfordshire, 1778–82

of the Adam brothers, *Joseph Bonomi*, as his assistant (see BONOMI, JOSEPH).

Leverton was the son of an Essex builder, under whom he trained. Little is known of his architectural studies and there is no record of his visiting Continental Europe.

He is best known for his interiors, particularly of town houses, as in *Bedford Square* in London (from 1775), for instance in numbers 1 and 13: the latter was his own home from 1796 until his death (see TERRACE ARCHITECTURE). *Woodhall Park* in Hertfordshire (1778–82) is one of his best-known country houses in the Adam style (see ADAM, ROBERT). Of especial interest here he designed an Etruscan-style entrance hall with fluted ceiling and walls decorated with painted medallions, also the curving staircase with its delicately formed iron balustrade and, above, a domed ceiling delicately fluted in fan decoration.

LINTEL A horizontal member spanning an opening and supporting the wall above it (see MASONRY).

LOGGIA A gallery or arcade open on at least one side and often colonnaded.

LONGHOUSE A long, low type of dwelling introduced into Britain by the Norsemen from Scandinavia. By the ninth century AD immigrant farmers were building these in stone in northern Scotland, Orkney and Shetland. The blocks were infilled with turf and the roofing was of thatch or heather on timber structure and weighted down with heather ropes and stones.

LOGGIA
Loggia d'onore at the Palazzo del Tè, Mantua, Italy. Architect: Giulio Romano, 1526–34

LONGHOUSE
Dartmoor longhouse, Lettaford, Devon. Granite walls, roofed originally with thatch

The longhouse has survived for centuries in remote areas as a sturdy building, resistant to wind and generally housing in one half the farmer and his family and in the other the farm cattle and stock. The illustration shows a surviving longhouse on Dartmoor where the walls are constructed of granite blocks. An immense lintel stone covers the low, square doorway leading into the living area.

LOUVRE An opening usually with turret or lantern covering (see LANTERN) on the roof of a medieval hall or kitchen to provide ventilation and allow smoke or steam to escape from the hearth below. Some louvres were fitted with boards to keep out the rain.

In later times the term 'louvre' (louver, luffler, lever) was applied specifically to the slanting boards or their replacement by slips of glass.

LUNETTE A semicircular opening, window or panel usually to be found above a door.

LUTYENS, SIR EDWIN LANDSEER (1869–1944) Like Soane a century earlier (see SOANE, SIR JOHN), Lutyens early dedicated himself to architecture, was absorbed by it and contributed to it all his life. During his working life he dominated the English architectural scene; he was far and away the most talented British architect of his time and it is arguable that a combination of his genius and force of personality were important factors in British reluctance to adopt modern architectural methods, materials and designs, until after the Second World War. Lutyens's designs encompassed a wide variety of themes and concepts but he was at heart an Edwardian and an individualist.

Lutyens was above all things an artist; his taste was impeccable and one of his greatest architectural qualities was his innate sense of proportion in the relationship of line, tone and mass. Like Chambers (see CHAMBERS, SIR WILLIAM) he was capable of infinite attention to detail: he was a perfectionist. His work is sometimes criticized for its traditional quality, for its use of traditional materials and for his adherence to established proportions and methods yet, although he designed much of his work in classical idiom, he transposed the styles to his own conception and a Lutyens Doric Order or Roman ornament is readily recognizable as such. In this he had Adam's and Wren's faculty for making these forms and motifs personally his own (see ADAM, ROBERT; WREN, SIR CHRISTOPHER). Whatever the influence upon his style—Arts and Crafts Movement, Classicism, Shaw, George or Webb—he interpreted it with superb authority (see GEORGE, SIR ERNEST; SHAW, NORMAN; WEBB, PHILIP).

Edwin Lutyens was born in Surrey, eleventh child of a large family. In childhood his health was delicate, causing him to spend much of his time at home where he learnt early to study for and by himself. At the age of 16 he began his studies at the College of Art in South Ken-

'Heathcote', Ilkley, Yorkshire, 1906

Britannic House, Finsbury Circus, London, 1920–6

Page Street Estate, Westminster, 1928

Headquarters of the Press Association and Reuter Building, Fleet Street, London, 1935

sington and two years later became an articled pupil in the office of Sir Ernest George.

When barely 20 he set up his own practice in London. At that time there were still enough people in Britain with money to build large houses and to employ an architect to design them. In this Lutyens was fortunate and from then until 1914 he built up a large country house practice. His houses of the early part of this period show the influence of both George and Shaw; they were generally on irregular plan, informal, often built of brick or half-timber in Elizabethan or Queen Anne manner. They were also refreshingly original, each displaying unusual, often brilliantly handled features and planning individual for each commission. Characteristic is his first house, *Munstead Wood*, Surrey, commissioned in 1896 by the gardener Gertrude Jekyll. Soon followed *'The Orchards'*, *Godalming* and *'Goddards'*, *Abinger Common*, both in Surrey and the attractive brick *Deanery* at *Sonning* in Berkshire (1899–1901), delightfully set in gardens landscaped down to the river Thames.

Towards 1900 Lutyens's houses became still more varied, in designs as well as materials, and in some cases more formal and imposing. *Tigbourne Court* in Surrey (1899) is a striking example in brick and stone (see COUNTRY HOUSE AND MANSION); another is *Marshcourt*, Hampshire (1902), a Tudor design in chalk and stone. In 1909 came the more classical, symmetrical, large brick house of *Great Maytham* in Kent and, a year later, *Nashdom Abbey* in Buckinghamshire in stone. Others include *Little Thakeham* in Sussex (1903) and *Overstrand Hall* in Norfolk. Lutyens adopted his more 'correct' and full-bodied classical approach for the first time in *Ilkley* in Yorkshire where in 1906 he built *Heathcote* of the local stone to suit the quite different landscape and colouring of the Pennine Moors in contrast to the Surrey hills. His last country house, *Middleton Park*, Oxfordshire (1935) was also in classical form.

In more romantic vein, he carried out a thorough and ingenious restoration of *Lindisfarne Castle* on Holy Island (1903–12) and, in 1910, began the 20-year-long construction of that fantastic granite pile, *Castle Drogo* in Devon.

Lutyens worked on two large housing schemes, quite different from one another in purpose, conception and construction. One was the central part of *Hampstead*

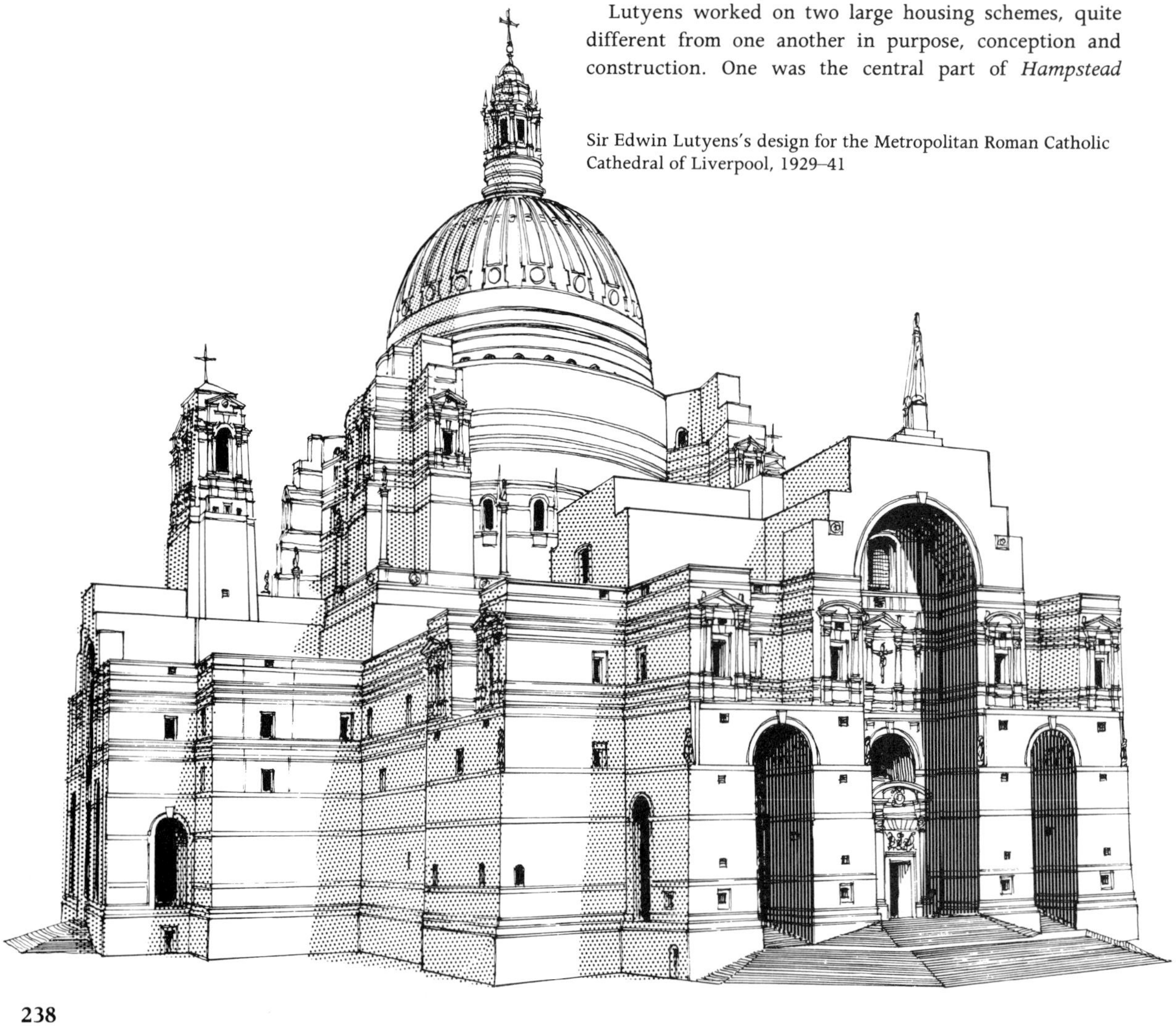

Sir Edwin Lutyens's design for the Metropolitan Roman Catholic Cathedral of Liverpool, 1929–41

Garden Suburb, begun in 1906 and planned as a project of high-quality architecture for top-class town housing (see TOWN PLANNING). The other was a low-cost re-housing scheme undertaken in 1928 at *Page Street, Westminster*. In an original, largely successful attempt to lend distinction to the block architecture forced upon him by financial stringency, Lutyens used light grey bricks, Portland stone and white Portland cement to form a chequer board pattern which would remain durable and clean, giving an austere but impressive effect. Today the area is dingy and the novelty of the design less remarkable.

After the First World War Lutyens began his career of civic architecture and developed his restrained classical style though, in each case, the design was fresh and unusual and fitted to its site and purpose. For the *Midland Bank*, apart from his branch bank buildings, he erected the immense head offices in Poultry in the City of London. This building is a vast cliff of Portland stone rising to six storeys, on a frontage 188ft in length. Much of the main elevation is rusticated with the Doric Order used only sparingly.

Of his many other imposing office blocks in London, two are particularly noteworthy: the seven-storey *Britannic House* at Finsbury Circus, its classical façade curving to the form of the circus (1920–6); and the much plainer headquarters of the *Press Association* and *Reuter Building* in Fleet Street (1935). There are two further examples in *Pall Mall*, number 120 built in 1928 and number 68 (1929).

Lutyens, like other leading architects of the 1920s, designed a number of war memorials. To him we owe one of the simplest yet the most famous: the *Cenotaph* in Whitehall. In 1919 this was erected in wood and plaster for the peace procession of that year. The design immediately impressed both the public and artistic critics. It was commissioned to be perpetuated in Portland stone. Lutyens himself called it the Cenotaph, intending to convey the semblance of an empty tomb raised up on a high pedestal. The very simplicity of the design is misleading: it is a simplicity of profound subtlety. As in the high period of Greek architecture, there are no true vertical or horizontal planes: all are subject to refinements. The verticals, if extrapolated, would meet at a point 1000 ft above ground level. The horizontals are imperceptibly curved so that their common centre is some 900ft below the level of the base of the monument.

Lutyens embarked upon two very large-scale schemes. One was the extensive civic work at *New Delhi* in India which was a great personal triumph. The other was his design for the colossal *Metropolitan Roman Catholic Cathedral* in *Liverpool*, of which only the crypt and sacristy were built when work ceased for the duration of the Second World War.

It was in 1928 that the Roman Catholic Archbishop of Liverpool decided to build a great cathedral and commissioned Lutyens to design it. In this design the architect incorporated his ideas on the adaptation of classicism to modern architecture. If it had been built it would have been a tremendous monument to modern neo-classicism in Britain. It was a domed building intended to rise higher (and the cupola to be of greater diameter) than St Peter's Basilica in Rome. The summit of the cross was to be 509ft above the ground, nearly as high as the Minster at Ulm, the highest spire in Europe. The materials were to be grey granite and warm brown brick. Four million bricks were actually laid. The crypt was completed, sunk in living rock, testimony today to a superb standard of craftsmanship in brick, but, after the war, the estimated cost of Lutyens's cathedral quickly rose from three million to 27 million pounds and to complete it became impracticable. A competition was held for a new cathedral (see GIBBERD, SIR FREDERICK).

MACHICOLATION A defensive feature in the building of castles and fortified houses where a parapet projected forward from the wall and was supported on corbels. Openings were left in the floor of the parapet so that missiles and boiling oil could be aimed at the attackers below. Examples are illustrated in BARBICAN (Lewes Castle) and CASTLE (Hurstmonceux Castle).

MACKINTOSH, CHARLES RENNIE (1868–1928) Scottish artist, architect and designer whose highly original work broke dramatically with the late Victorian traditions and deeply influenced modern architecture and design in Europe. His ideals were deeply rooted in Scottish architectural traditions; he was an admirer of both Ruskin and Lethaby (see RUSKIN, JOHN; LETHABY, WILLIAM RICHARD).

Mackintosh was a student at the Glasgow School of Art. In 1889 he entered the architectural firm of Honeyman and Keppie and, at the same time, produced a variety of designs in furniture and decorative craftwork which were Art Nouveau in theme, though Mackintosh's Art Nouveau was astringent and often more angular than flowing in form and line (see ART NOUVEAU).

In 1896 the firm, with Mackintosh's design, won the competition for the new *Glasgow School of Art*. Completed in 1909, this is Mackintosh's masterpiece, displaying an austerity in its clear, defined proportion which anticipated twentieth-century functionalism (see FUNCTIONALISM).

In 1896 Mackintosh carried out the first of a number of

commissions for Miss Cranston (in Buchanan Street), who opened a series of tea-rooms in *Glasgow*. He remodelled the interiors, designing coloured window glass, lighting effects and furniture for them very much in the Art Nouveau manner. Of particular interest were the tea-rooms in Argyle Street and Ingram Street and, perhaps the most successful design, the Willow Tea-rooms in Sauchiehall Street in 1904.

Mackintosh designed a number of houses, notably *Windyhill, Kilmacolm* in 1899 and *Hill House* in *Helensburgh* (1902–3); but after 1913, when he left his architectural firm, where he was then a partner, he devoted himself largely to painting and left the architectural scene.

MACKMURDO, ARTHUR HEYGATE (1851–1942) An English architect who is known more for his decoration and furniture designs than for his buildings. Mackmurdo was for some time a pupil of James Brooks (see BROOKS, JAMES) but also studied in Oxford in Ruskin's drawing school. In 1874 he accompanied Ruskin to Italy then, on his return to Britain, set up architectural practice on his own, designing a number of houses. He also met and became friends with Morris (see MORRIS, WILLIAM).

Imbued with some of the ideals and concepts of both Ruskin and Morris, Mackmurdo founded in 1882 the Century Guild around a group of architects, designers and artists of like mind. The Guild aimed to establish the decorative crafts as arts of distinction on a par with painting and sculpture and not merely of commercial value. This was an early instance of the several arts and crafts guilds which were being set up in the late nineteenth century under the inspiration of Morris (see ASHBEE, CHARLES ROBERT).

In his own decorative work in book illustration, furniture design and interior décor, Mackmurdo introduced motifs in swirling linear forms which ante-dated the Art Nouveau themes of the succeeding decade (see ART NOUVEAU).

MANNERISM This term is interpreted architecturally in two principal ways. In one sense it is applied to classical architecture which displays a rigid form of academic classicism. In the other, more common usage, it refers to the use of classical forms and motifs in a different manner from that traditionally accepted. For example, in sixteenth-century Italy, great architects, notably Michelangelo, Romano and Vasari, intentionally broke some of the antique and Renaissance classical rules in order to create a new, original effect. Another instance, this time in England, may be seen in the Elizabethan and Jacobean Renaissance domestic buildings where the orders, being imperfectly understood, were employed incorrectly and decoratively rather than structurally (see COUNTRY HOUSE AND MANSION; ELIZABETHAN ARCHITECTURE; JACOBEAN ARCHITECTURE).

MANOR HOUSE The mansion belonging to the lord of the manor; the chief house of a large estate or village. As an architectural term, a late medieval country house.

By the beginning of the fifteenth century the practice of fortifying rural houses had been largely abandoned: drawbridge and portcullis (see CASTLE; PORTCULLIS) had given place to a bridge over the moat and a decorative but less military gatehouse, the upper storey of which often served as a chapel. Beyond the gatehouse the house was laid out round a courtyard. The buildings were raised from one to three storeys and their rooflines at differing levels were broken by tall chimney-stacks and gabled ends. Building materials were determined by local availability: stone, brick, flint and half-timber were all in use. Window and doorway design followed the contemporary pattern (see DOOR, DOORWAY; GOTHIC ARCHITECTURE; WINDOW).

With more settled conditions and less need for defensive features, manor houses became more spacious, the extra available space being devoted to providing greater privacy in bedrooms and reception rooms. The hall still

MANOR HOUSE
Stone moated house: Great Chalfield Manor House, Wiltshire, *c.* 1480

often extended through two storeys but there were also a solar or great chamber and other private apartments (see SOLAR).

Fifteenth-century manor houses survive in many parts of Britain. Of considerable interest are *Great Chalfield Manor House,* Wiltshire (c. 1480), *Lytes Carey,* Somerset (1400–50), *Cotehele,* Cornwall (1485 onwards), *South Wraxall,* Wiltshire (fifteenth century), *Ockwells,* Berkshire (1466) and *Great Dixter,* Sussex (partly fifteenth century). A description of the development of such houses from the mid-sixteenth century onwards is given in COUNTRY HOUSE AND MANSION.

MASONRY The craft of building with stone, of cutting and carving, dressing and laying the material.

Cut blocks or rough-hewn pieces of stone were usually bound with mortar (see CONCRETE) but the craft of dry-stone walling (without mortar) has been practised since ancient times. In several early cultures, Mycenaean for example, immensely large stones were used which were so heavy that they remained in position; the interstices were then filled with smaller stones. Such masonry is referred to as *cyclopean*: the term originated with the classical Greeks who found it difficult to credit that such vast blocks had been laid by men and attributed the construction to the mythical Cyclopes.

In Britain and northern Europe most stone buildings which survive from pre-sixteenth-century date are of rubble construction: even after this, cut stone was so costly that its use was reserved for facing and for dressings of only the most important structures. Rubble walling is built up from smallish pieces of stone of varying shape. Such stones might be arranged without any particular design. This is *random rubble construction.* Some rubble walls may be coursed and in others the stones might be roughly squared. Some Roman walling consists of squared stones set diagonally in course, giving a lattice pattern: this was known as *opus reticulatum* (see WALLING).

As time passed, not only the major buildings—cathedrals and abbeys, mansions and civic structures—but those of more modest size, were finished or faced with smoothly dressed stone. This was cut into blocks then hammered or tooled to be laid in courses between fine mortar joints. The best, most sophisticated stonework was *ashlar* which was cut precisely in vertical and horizontal faces at true right angles, smoothly finished and laid in horizontal courses with vertical joints. From the early seventeenth century onwards all important stone buildings for civic use were ashlared.

Only certain stone is suited to ashlar finishing (see STONE). A good result may be obtained with, for example, granite but in general a high quality *freestone* is required; this is a term usually applied to oolitic limestones such as Portland stone or to sandstone of specific types. A freestone is one which has a fine grain, does not possess strongly marked laminations or bedding planes and may, therefore, be 'freely' worked with chisel or saw. Such freestone is also necessary for carved decorative work and for dressings of, for instance, window tracery, door surrounds, lintels, quoins, arches, pediments, classical columns, capitals and bases, gables, buttresses and para-

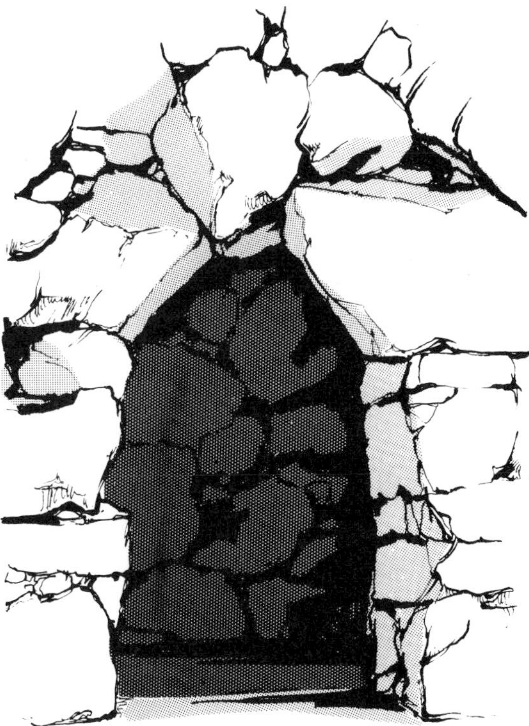

Cyclopean construction: The Gallery, Tyrins, Greece, thirteenth century BC

Etruscan dry-stone construction with massive lintel stone: the Porta Saracena, Segni, Italy, fourth century AD

Bitonto Cathedral doorway decoration, Apulia, Italy, 1175–1200. Carved stone-work

(*right*) Petworth House, Sussex, late seventeenth century. Ashlar and carved stonework.

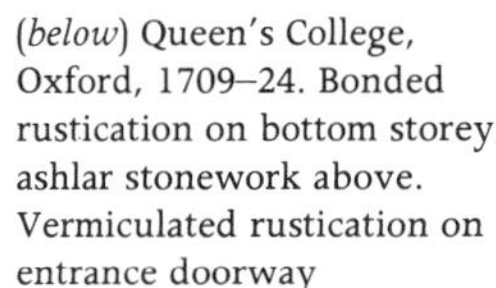

(*below*) Queen's College, Oxford, 1709–24. Bonded rustication on bottom storey, ashlar stonework above. Vermiculated rustication on entrance doorway

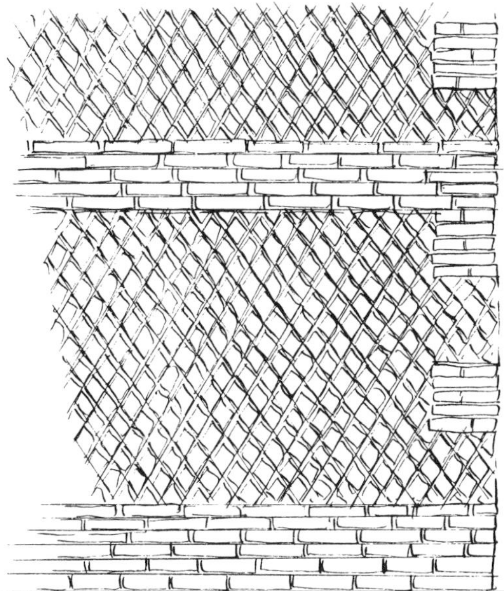

Roman walling: *opus reticulatum* with brick. Ostia, Italy, second century AD

pets (see ARCH; BUTTRESS; CLASSICAL ORDER; DOOR; GABLE; LINTEL; PARAPET; PEDIMENT; QUOIN).

One method of providing a decorative quality in stonework which was employed extensively in eighteenth- and nineteenth-century classical architecture was *rustication*. In this type of surface treatment the mortar courses were recessed and the stone blocks (which were ornamented in different ways) projected to be proud and so gave a light and shade effect. Rustication was chiefly used on basement or lower storeys and on columns, its decorative character contrasting with the smooth ashlar finish of the *piano nobile* and floors above it.

A glossary of masonry terms

Ashlar: blocks of stone worked to perfect faces and beds with square angles laid in regular courses with fine joints.

Bed (natural) of stone: the way in which the stone was laid in the ground where it was quarried. Most stones will weather better and last longer if laid on the same plane in building.

Coursed stonework: laid in horizontal courses.

Cyclopean stonework: constructed of immensely large pieces.

Dressed stone: squared stone.

Dressings: cut, smoothed and shaped stone for sills, mouldings, quoins, lintels, arches, framed openings, gables, etc.

Dry-stone walling: a method of construction where no mortar is used to bind the stones together.

Freestone: a fine-grained, easily worked stone without marked laminations or bedding planes.

Rag, ragstone: hard, coarse type of stone which is not freestone.

Rubble

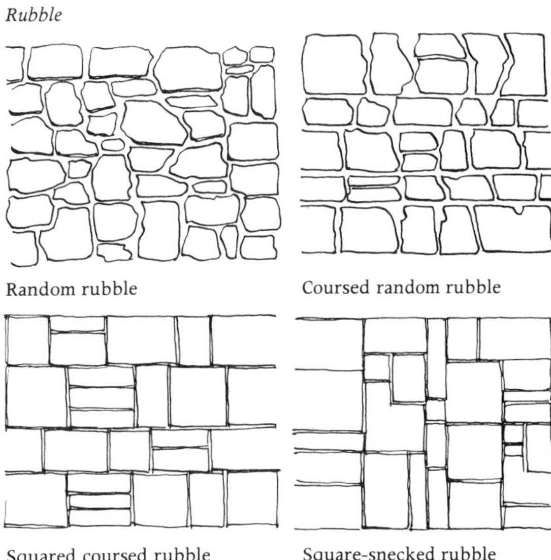

Rubble: stones of differing sizes laid in a variety of ways and bound with (often thickly applied) mortar.

Coursed random rubble: stones of varied unshaped form laid in horizontal courses.

Opus incertum: random rubble of Roman construction.

Opus reticulatum: Roman rubble walling of square-shaped stones laid on end to form a diamond pattern.

Ragwork: rubble walling composed of polygonal stones, generally used as a weathering face.

Random rubble: stones of differing size and shape laid without any discernible pattern.

Regular coursed rubble: walling of square stones laid in courses.

Square-snecked rubble: walling in which snecks (small stone blocks) are laid in order to prevent the development of long vertical joints.

Rustication: square ashlar or decorative blocks of stone laid to project forwards from the recessed mortar courses.

Banded: plain rustication with stressed horizontal joints.

Chamfered: the block edges are chamfered.

Rustication

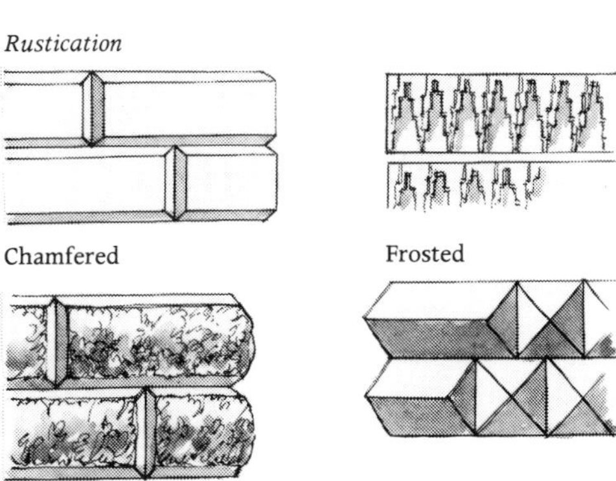

Diamond-pointed: blocks cut in planes or facets as in a diamond.
Frosted: where the surface of the blocks is carved to represent icicles.
Rock-faced: the block faces cut in a roughened manner to imitate a natural rock face.
Vermiculated: the surface of the stones is carved to represent the random path of worms.

MATTHEW, SIR ROBERT HOGG (1906–75) Scottish architect and town planner whose reputation and influence extended far overseas. This was partly due to his untiring work for the International Union of Architects (whose President he was from 1961 to 1965) as well as for the Commonwealth Association of Architects, but also because of his expertise and outstanding qualities of character and leadership. Sir Robert Matthew's influence on architectural standards as an academic, architect and town planner extended beyond the buildings which he personally designed.

Matthew was the son of a noted Edinburgh architect, John Matthew and, after studying at the Architectural School in the Edinburgh College of Art, began his professional career in his father's office. Most of his life was spent in Scotland where he began work in the public service at the Department of Health for Scotland, becoming their chief architect and planning officer in 1945.

MATTHEW, SIR ROBERT HOGG
New Zealand House, London, 1963

The following year Matthew went south on his appointment as Architect to the London County Council. From then until 1953 he revitalized this department, making it efficient, lively and world-famous, one which talented young architects were eager to join. Notable achievements of the department at this time were the *Alton Housing Estate* at *Roehampton* on the outskirts of London (1952–7) and the *Royal Festival Hall* on London's riverside, designed with *Sir Leslie Martin* in 1951.

In 1953 Matthew returned to Scotland to become (until 1968) Professor of Architecture at Edinburgh University and to work as consultant, lecturer and advisor to various bodies all of which involved extensive travelling. He also returned to private practice this time as senior partner of the firm Robert Matthew, Johnson-Marshall and Partners among whose notable achievements were the new *York University* begun in 1963 and *New Zealand House* in London. Matthew was knighted in 1962 and became President of the Royal Institute of British Architects in the years 1962–4; he received the RIBA Gold Medal in 1970.

MAUFE, SIR EDWARD BRANTWOOD (1883–1974) A Yorkshireman who, after studying at Oxford, was articled to W. A. Pite before setting up in private practice for himself. Maufe is primarily known as the architect of *Guildford Cathedral* which, begun in 1936 in modernized, even emasculated Gothic dress, is a monument characteristic of its time. It occupies a magnificent site on the outskirts of the town on the summit of Stag Hill; it is only the second Anglican cathedral to be erected on a new site since the Reformation. Unfortunately, the view of it from the town and the surrounding countryside has been partially obscured by the later building of the University of Surrey on the lower slopes of the hill.

The cathedral is constructed of brick, of the same type of clay as the soil on which it stands: indeed, it was necessary to sink 750 deep piles into this clay in order to carry the weight of the structure. The tower and interior,

MAUFE, SIR EDWARD
Church of St Thomas, Hanwell, Middlesex. Brick church, 1933

which were completed after the Second World War, make use of modern structural methods and materials. In the interior, in particular, this is so. In order to ensure a clear view of the altar for the whole congregation, ferro-concrete has been employed for the vaulting so enabling a nave to be built which possesses a wider span than that of any other English cathedral (see CHURCH DESIGN AND STRUCTURE).

Maufe designed several churches, notably *St Saviour* in *Acton* and *St Thomas* in *Hanwell*. He built a number of branch banks for *Lloyds*, the *Playhouse Theatre* at Oxford, *Morley College* in London and several country houses, for example, *Kelling Hall* in Norfolk.

MAUSOLEUM A monumental building to house a tomb or tombs. Named after the Mausoleum of Halicarnassos in Asia Minor (modern Bodrum), which was built for Artemisia in memory of her husband King Mausolus after his death in 353 BC.

MAY, HUGH (1621–84) Was, in conjunction with his contemporaries Pratt and Webb (see PRATT, SIR ROGER; WEBB, JOHN) instrumental in introducing into England the unpretentious classical style of domestic architecture now named Dutch Palladian. May had spent some years in Holland with the exiled Duke of Buckingham during the Commonwealth years in England and his only surviving house is *Eltham Lodge* in Kent built in 1664 for Sir John Shaw; it is a building which closely resembles the Mauritshuis at The Hague.

Dutch Palladian houses were so-called because this style of building, which originated in the Netherlands, was based upon the designs of Palladio (see JONES, INIGO; PALLADIAN ARCHITECTURE). For a long time they were described in England as 'Wren-style' houses, incorrectly because a number of them were built before Wren was practising as an architect; indeed, Wren designed little domestic work (see WREN, SIR CHRISTOPHER). These houses, like Eltham Lodge, were mostly built of brick with stone dressings (see MASONRY). The emphasis was classical in symmetry and the horizontal stress. In plan they were rectangular with an entrance in the centre of each long façade approached by entrance steps, flanked by pilasters and surmounted by a pediment.

On May's return to England after the Restoration, he built a number of houses, notably *Berkeley House*, Piccadilly (1665), and later became architect to *Windsor Castle* where he carried out extensive important remodelling, but these works, like most of May's architectural contribution, have been destroyed or replaced. During his lifetime, and for many years afterwards, his name was overshadowed by that of Wren.

MAY, HUGH
Eltham Lodge, Kent, 1664

MENDELSOHN, ERICH (1887–1953) An innovator and pioneer experimenter in the international modern style of architecture developing in Germany in the early 1920s. He envisaged bold, sculptural forms, dramatically expressed in light and shade, which he created with extensive use of glass, steel and ferro-concrete. Characteristic of this early Expressionism was his design for the *Einstein Tower* at *Potsdam*, a physical laboratory and observatory purpose-built in 1921 for Professor Einstein's research work. Equally dramatic were his pace-setting *Schocken department stores* at *Stuttgart* (1926) and *Chemnitz* (1928) and his *Columbus Haus* in *Berlin* (1929–31).

MENDELSOHN, ERICH
De la Warr Pavilion, Bexhill-on-Sea, Sussex. Architects: Mendelsohn and Chermayeff, 1935–6

In 1933 Mendelsohn moved to England where he went into partnership with another émigré, the Russian-born *Serge Chermayeff*. Their best-known work in England is the *De La Warr* arts and entertainment *Pavilion* at *Bexhill-on-Sea* (1934–5). This glass, steel and concrete building comprises a theatre and restaurant and, in the centre of the façade, its chief architectural feature, a curving section which provides seating from which the benefit of the sun's rays may be enjoyed the whole day long.

However, Mendelsohn did not stay long in England. In 1934 he went to visit Palestine and, in 1941, settled in America, leaving notable monuments of his work in both countries. Of particular interest were his Medical Centre of the *Hadassah University* in *Jerusalem* (1936–8) and, in the USA, his *Maimonides Hospital* in *San Francisco* and the synagogues and Jewish community centres which he designed in several American cities (see MODERN ARCHITECTURE).

MODERN ARCHITECTURE A term universally applied to a twentieth-century style which was born and slowly developed in a number of countries after the First World War and which has culminated in the current buildings of glass, concrete and steel based on module construction being erected all over the world (see INDUSTRIALIZED BUILDING).

Other names have been given to this type of architecture, for instance 'international', 'rational', 'functional', but no more comprehensive or apposite name has been suggested to describe these differing structures which appear to have no link with past styles. Not all building since 1918 can be termed modern architecture: indeed, until about 1950 only a minority of work could be so classified. The bulk of construction was of traditional, eclectic design and it was only a handful of pioneers who created modern architecture in the inter-war years.

The term 'international style' was coined in the 1930s to express the fact that this modern building type transcended frontiers and was being adopted spontaneously and simultaneously on both sides of the Atlantic, throughout Europe and beyond. But this was not just because it spread as an architectural style but because, more fundamentally, the social structure of society in so many countries had a need for the type of buildings which it produced and at a cost and speed which such methods made possible (see INDUSTRIALIZED BUILDING).

The idea, though, that internationalism in architecture meant the same type of buildings being put up everywhere was, by the 1950s, found to be unsound. National traditions were soon making themselves apparent based, as they have always been, on climate, resources, individual mode of living and economic necessity. Although modern architecture everywhere utilized similar materials and methods of construction, national differences arose. Those countries with an advanced steel industry, the USA, Germany, Britain, for example, used steel-frame construction (see STEEL-FRAME CONSTRUCTION) based on the rectangular block which was then curtain-walled or concrete-faced. In Italy and Spain, where steel was less readily available, there was greater emphasis on the use of ferro-concrete and parabolic curves and vaults. Glass curtain-walling was, especially before the comprehensive development of solar glass control, unsuited to countries with a hot, sunny climate and here the traditional desire for colour was evidenced in mosaic and external mural decoration.

Modern architecture did not, of course, just appear, fully formed, in the years after 1918. It evolved from several earlier movements. In the last two decades of the nineteenth century designers were creating buildings still partly eclectic in inspiration and still constructed from traditional materials—stone, brick, timber—but, in reaction to the overdecoration of mid-nineteenth-century work, much simpler in design with clean lines and a minimum of ornament. In England there were Webb, Shaw, Voysey, the Arts and Crafts Movement and then Lutyens (see ASHBEE, CHARLES ROBERT; LETHABY, WILLIAM RICHARD; LUTYENS, SIR EDWIN LANDSEER; SHAW, NORMAN; VOYSEY, CHARLES ANNESLEY; WEBB, PHILIP). In Holland, at the turn of the century, *Hendrik Berlage* (1856–1934) was adapting traditional Dutch brick building into the modern idiom in his *Diamond Workers' Trade Union Building* and housing estates in *Amsterdam*. *Jensen Klint* (1853–1930) was carrying out a similar exercise in Denmark in his *Gruntvig Church* in *Copenhagen* (from 1913). There was *Sigfrid Ericsson*'s (1879–1958) *Masthugg Church* of 1914 in *Göteborg* in Sweden and the most personal interpretation of all in Scandinavia can be seen in the great structures of the Finnish architect *Lars Sonck* (1870–1956), for example, *Tampere Cathedral*, built 1902–7, in rough-hewn granite blocks. There was also that decorative, romantic movement Art Nouveau which showed itself in differing guises in many European countries (see ART NOUVEAU).

These few examples among the many which were being evidenced in various countries bore testament to the deep desire of architects and designers for a change of style. But it was pressure engendered by two other vital factors which provided the catalyst for a complete stylistic break with the past. The first of these was the nineteenth-century population explosion in Europe which, together with the effects of the Industrial Revolution, made urgently necessary an increased rate of building for all purposes. The second, later, factor was the extensive destruction caused by two world wars which necessitated the rebuilding of whole towns as well as individual sites. This urgent need greatly hastened the technical development of new and improved materials, so making it possible to erect on a large scale structures more cheaply by mass-production methods. The combination of these factors has brought about a transformation in twentieth-century building which has killed for ever the architectural industry founded on individual craftsmanship.

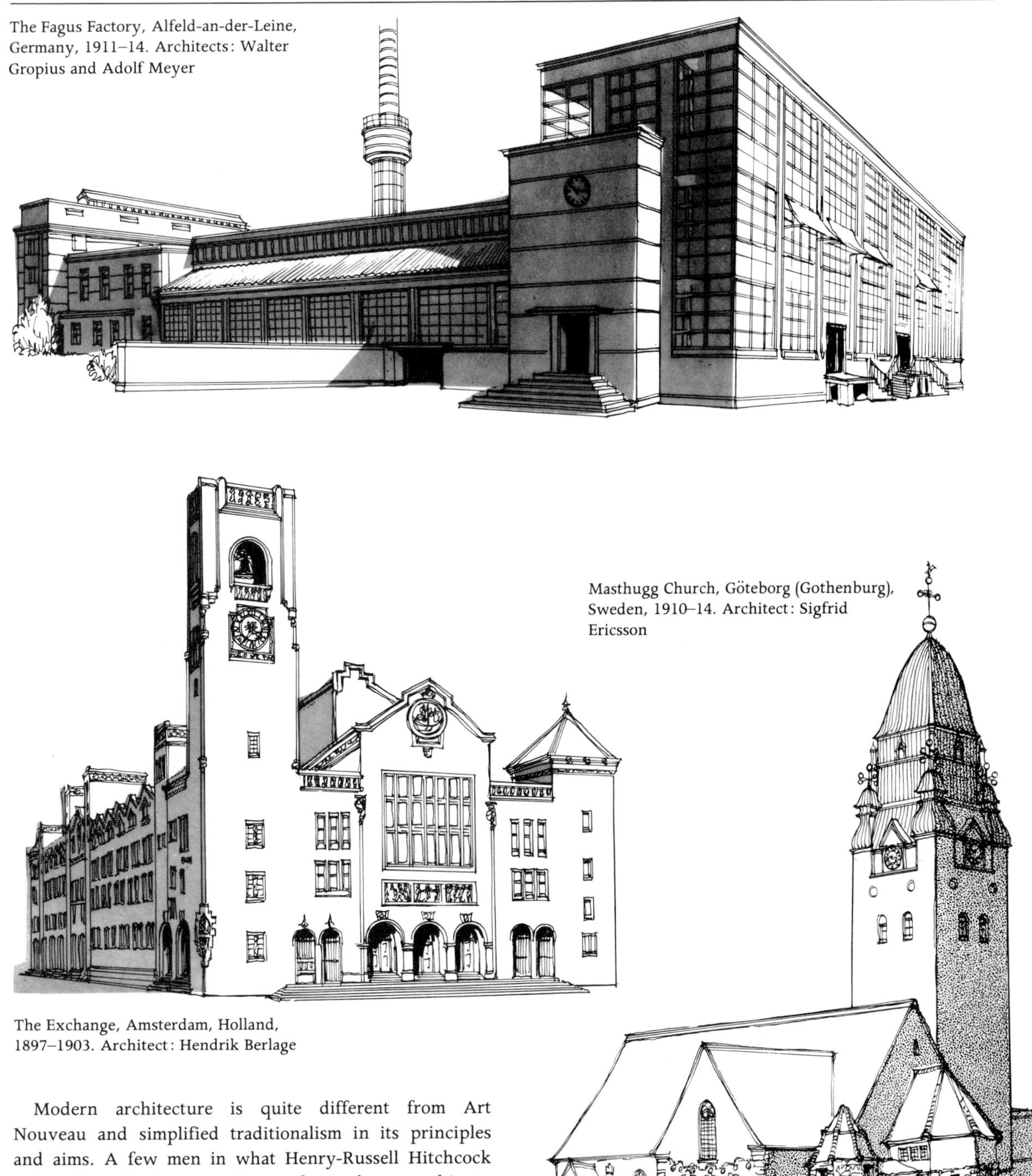

The Fagus Factory, Alfeld-an-der-Leine, Germany, 1911–14. Architects: Walter Gropius and Adolf Meyer

Masthugg Church, Göteborg (Gothenburg), Sweden, 1910–14. Architect: Sigfrid Ericsson

The Exchange, Amsterdam, Holland, 1897–1903. Architect: Hendrik Berlage

Modern architecture is quite different from Art Nouveau and simplified traditionalism in its principles and aims. A few men in what Henry-Russell Hitchcock calls the first generation of modern architects (*Architecture: Nineteenth and Twentieth Centuries* by Henry-Russell Hitchcock, Penguin Books, 1977), were experimenting with these new ideas before 1918. Two of them are better known for their futuristic ideas and projects than for work actually built. The Italian *Antonio Sant'Elia* (1880–1916) was fascinated by the romantic aspects of technology, especially in the USA, and planned cities for Italy. His *Città Nuova* projected in 1914 was exhibited in Milan. It envisaged skyscrapers, pedestrian precincts and traffic moving on overhead roadways at two or three different levels. He was expressing his ideas for an ideal socialist society. Sant'Elia was killed in action in 1916, but his drawings and designs survive and they strongly influenced the work of other architects in the 1920s.

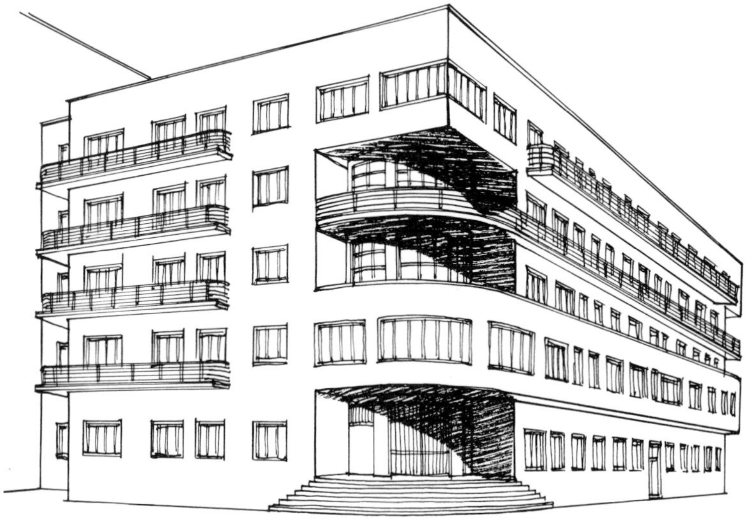

Apartment block for the Società Novocomum, Como, Italy, 1927–8. Architect: Giuseppe Terragni

Stockholm City Hall, Sweden, 1909–23. Architect: Ragnar Östberg

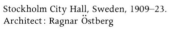

Workers' club: 'Club Rusakov', Moscow, USSR, 1925–6. Architect: Konstantin Melnikov

In France *Tony Garnier* (1867–1948) designed in the early years of the century an ideal industrial town which he called the *Cité Industrielle*. Also futuristic and, as in Sant'Elia's *Città*, traffic was separated from pedestrians and industrial areas from leisure ones. Garnier also illustrated flat-roofed buildings supported on *pilotis*, clad with glass and steel and with extensive use of concrete (see TOWN PLANNING).

Another group of architects and engineers were experimenting with reinforced and pre-stressed concrete. In France *Eugène Freyssinet* was pioneering the industrial use of the material in his great parabolic-vaulted airship hangar at Orly in 1916 (see CONCRETE), while *Auguste Perret* (1874–1954) was using it to build apartment blocks and, later, his most famous structure, the *Church of Notre Dame* at *Le Raincy* on the outskirts of Paris.

In this church was illustrated the structural possibilities of the material. The wide, light interior is covered by a segmental vaulted roof carried solely on slender reeded columns while the walls, which bear no load, are composed of pre-cast concrete units largely filled with coloured glass.

Because of the slenderness of the columns and the richness of the glass, this church possesses a spiritual atmosphere and unimpeded sight and sound of the altar for everyone. It became a prototype for churches all over Europe for decades from *Karl Moser*'s (1860–1936) *Church of St Anthony* in *Basel* in Switzerland (1926–31) and *Domenikus Böhm*'s (1880–1955) Expressionist churches in Germany to *Spence*'s post-war *Coventry Cathedral* (see CHURCH DESIGN AND STRUCTURE; SPENCE, SIR BASIL).

Elsewhere in Europe other architects were experimenting with new ideas and materials. From 1896 onwards, from his practice in Vienna, *Adolf Loos* (1870–1933) was building houses of reinforced concrete in Austria, France, Switzerland and Czechoslovakia. After his appointment in 1907 as architect to AEG, *Peter Behrens* in Germany was developing the combined use of steel, glass and concrete in original schemes of industrial architecture: his *Turbine Factory* in *Berlin* (1909) was an important example. This was followed by the large, impressive AEG plant at Riga in the USSR (1913) (see BEHRENS, PETER).

Much earlier, in the 1880s, on the other side of the Atlantic, *Louis Henry Sullivan* and *Frank Lloyd Wright* (1869–1959) had begun to create the first examples of modern architecture. Sullivan's contribution was mainly in pioneering the large commercial project in modern dress, producing functional yet decorative buildings which took all possible advantage of up-to-date structural methods (see HIGH-RISE BUILDING).

Wright began his career working with Sullivan, for whom he conceived a great admiration, carrying out most of the domestic commissions. He left in 1893 to set up practice on his own after which he became the most important figure in the modern architectural scene in America. His career, which spanned nearly 70 years, developed broadly in three different phases. In the first, up to the First World War, he was chiefly designing houses in what he described 'the house as a shelter'. These structures displayed his deeply held opinion that detached country houses should be designed as an integral part of the landscape, a view later equally strongly professed by a number of Finnish architects. Wright's designs were termed 'prairie houses' because so many of them were built in the Middle West of America, which Wright referred to as the prairie. They were low and spreading with gently sloping rooflines, very plain and clean-lined, built in traditional materials in warm, rural colours blending softly into their setting.

The most important formative years for modern architecture were those between 1918 and 1939. This next generation of architects in America and many European countries were mostly born between 1880 and 1890. The work varied from country to country but the architects were united in their rejection of eclecticism and of ornament (both in reaction to nineteenth-century building). In consequence their work tended to be starkly uncompromising. Primarily they were concerned with the proper use of material and architectural structure.

There were several, but related, movements within the main trend. One was a form of 'expressionism' derived from contemporary art in which dramatic forms and curves (as in parabolic arches) predominated, particularly as evidenced in Germany about 1920: examples include *Behrens*'s *I. G. Farben* complex at *Höchst* (1920–4) (see BEHRENS, PETER), *Hans Poelzig*'s (1869–1936) *Grosses Schauspielhaus* in *Berlin* (1919), *Fritz Höger*'s (1877–1949) *Chilehaus* in *Hamburg* (see HIGH-RISE BUILDING; also MENDELSOHN, ERICH).

Another movement was 'constructivism' which originated in Moscow soon after the Revolution of 1917. An abstract art movement, it affected architecture by putting the accent on the structure of a building, discarding ornament as trivia. Few constructivist buildings ever got off the drawing-board, largely due to the troubled and economically difficult period in which they were designed. One of the leaders of the movement was *Eliezer M. (El) Lissitsky* (1890–1941).

Allied to these two movements in the 1920s was the third, best-known, 'ism': functionalism (see FUNCTIONALISM). The need for a building to be designed suitably for its purpose had always been a tenet of good architecture but one which had to a certain extent been lost sight of in nineteenth-century eclecticism. The leaders of the modern school were impressed by the theme of structure, of making it visible and unashamed, not covered by a classical or other decorative façade. They were intrigued by the new technology and by engineering projects and the shapes evolved: spheres, cylinders, cubes, cones. They worked out the economics of building in these forms, endlessly repeated, to facilitate cheap production. Some of the results were disappointing especially when the functionalist theory was taken to extremes, postulating that if a building were efficiently designed for its purpose it must, *ipso facto*, be beautiful. It took time for architects to adapt to the freedom made possible by modern structural methods in order to make the best of the new materials and so create interesting architecture.

It was a paradox of these inter-war years in Europe that so many of the original thinkers and designers of modern architecture, these men who also possessed the courage to defy the established architectural traditions, were nationals of countries which submitted to totalitarian government; a type of government which rendered it impossible for the architects to retain integrity in their work. They emigrated, were imprisoned or submitted to dictation in their architectural commissions.

This happened in the USSR where, from 1920, younger architects in particular saw the post-revolution years as an opportunity to introduce a new architectural style fundamentally suited to socialism. The State now took responsibility and handled finance for all building and, in the years 1925–32, several architects (with little contact yet possible with the West) began empirically to design modern structures with the new methods and materials. The most successful of these was *Konstantin Melnikov* (1890–1974) who became known for his *Workers' Clubs*. These were multi-purpose buildings comprising facilities for a theatre, cinema, library, reading and discussion rooms and light entertainment. The *Club Rusakov* in *Moscow* (1925–6) survives. After 1932 the régime clamped down on all such 'bourgeois' experimentation and imposed its own emasculated classical form.

In Italy, in the early 1920s it was *Giuseppe Terragni* (1904–43) who led the modern school. In 1926 he helped to found the *gruppo sette*, seven architects who joined the *Movimento Italiano per l'Architettura Razionale*. They enunciated a new architectural theme, searching for clarity, order, honesty in use of materials and an end to eclecticism. They were all young and inspired by the Bauhaus project (see BAUHAUS) in Germany and Frank Lloyd Wright's work in America. Terragni's architecture includes some buildings in *Como*, notably the apartment block of 1927, and flats in *Milan*, the Casa Rustici in the Corso Sempione (1934–5). His colleagues included *Giuseppe Pagano, Mario Ridolfo* and *Giovanni Michelucci*. But by the mid-1930s here also the State was dictating the architectural form in a guise worthy of Mussolini's ambitions for a new Roman Empire: architects had to conform or leave.

The greatest national loss of architectural talent was in Germany. Here, by 1920, was developing an architectural school of vigour and originality which was attracting men of great ability dedicated to the new form of architectural expression. By 1933 most of them had emigrated, chiefly to Britain and the USA. Best known of this group were *Walter Gropius* who headed the Bauhaus from 1919 (see BAUHAUS) and *Mies van der Rohe* (1888–1969), both of whom finally settled in the USA where they made a significant contribution to American architecture and education until the late 1960s.

One of Gropius's early works in Germany was the *Fagus Factory* at *Alfeld-an-der-Leine*. Today it does not appear to be especially unusual but in 1911 it was a revolutionary prototype, heralding the glass curtain-walling method of cladding to become so prevalent after 1950. It is one of the few of Gropius's buildings to have survived in Germany. One of Mies van der Rohe's projects still extant there is the *Weissenhof housing estate* at *Stuttgart* begun in 1927.

Among the other talented men practising modern architecture in Germany in the 1920s were *Behrens* (see BEHRENS, PETER), *Mendelsohn* (see MENDELSOHN, ERICH), *Fritz Höger* (see HIGH-RISE BUILDING), *Hans Poelzig, Domenikus Böhm* and *Paul Bonatz* (1877–1951) who designed *Stuttgart Railway Station* (1914–27).

Of the countries in western Europe where architects remained free to develop their own style of work, the northern group of Scandinavia, Holland and Britain largely retained a traditional approach, particularly towards materials. In Holland and Scandinavia brick remained, as it had been since the days of the Hanseatic League, the basic material for all types of building. Several architects were developing a modern style which was plain, attractive and functionalist but few structures evidenced any revolutionary change. Characteristic in Holland was the work of *Michael de Klerk* (1884–1923), *Jacobus Oud* (1890–1963) and *Willem Dudok* (1884–1974). The two former men chiefly designed housing estates in *Amsterdam, Rotterdam* and the *Hook of Holland*. Dudok was City Architect at *Hilversum* when he built the *town hall* there (1928–32): a plain but finely proportioned and detailed brick building which was subsequently widely imitated in Holland. The outstanding Swedish contribution of these years was *Ragnar Östberg*'s (1866–1945) *City Hall* in *Stockholm* (begun in 1911 and opened in 1923); the elegant brick tower is a well-known Stockholm landmark. Characteristic of work of this kind in Denmark is *Aarhus University* begun in 1931.

Genuine modern architecture was uncommon in Britain before 1950: most of the building was traditional and often eclectic, though in a simplified form (see BLOMFIELD, SIR REGINALD; DAWBER, SIR GUY; LUTYENS, SIR EDWIN LANDSEER; MAUFE, SIR EDWARD; NEWTON, SIR ERNEST; SCOTT, SIR GILES GILBERT; THOMAS, SIR PERCY; WEBB, SIR ASTON). Then in the 1930s a number of Continental architects went to Britain as political refugees. Few of them stayed for long. The opportunities in Britain for modern architecture were very limited; the British profession was still dominated by the traditionalists. Soon these refugee architects continued their journey, on to America; but even their short stay in Britain had encouraged modern building.

Walter Gropius came in 1934. He designed one or two buildings, notably *Impington Village College* with *Maxwell*

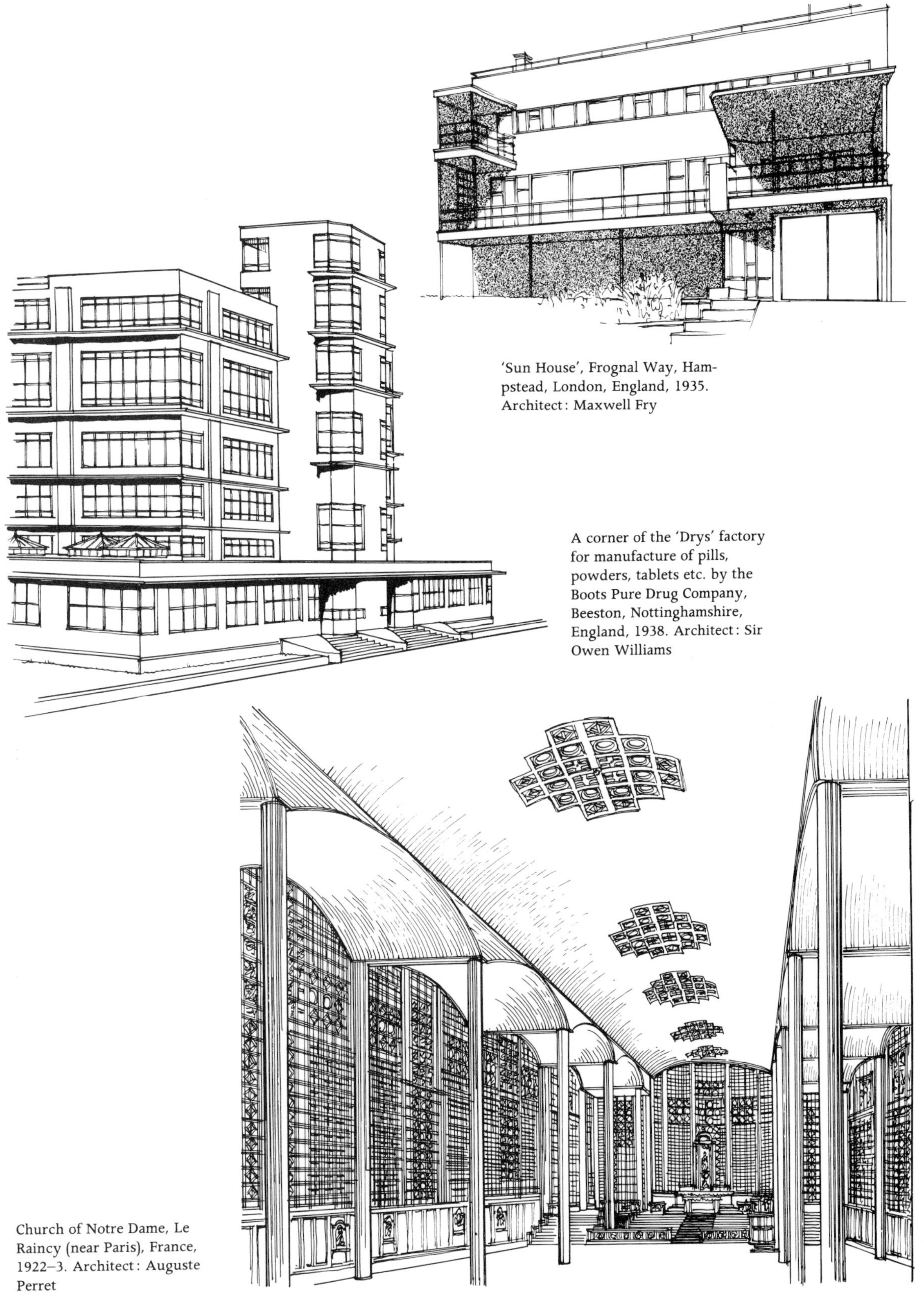

'Sun House', Frognal Way, Hampstead, London, England, 1935. Architect: Maxwell Fry

A corner of the 'Drys' factory for manufacture of pills, powders, tablets etc. by the Boots Pure Drug Company, Beeston, Nottinghamshire, England, 1938. Architect: Sir Owen Williams

Church of Notre Dame, Le Raincy (near Paris), France, 1922–3. Architect: Auguste Perret

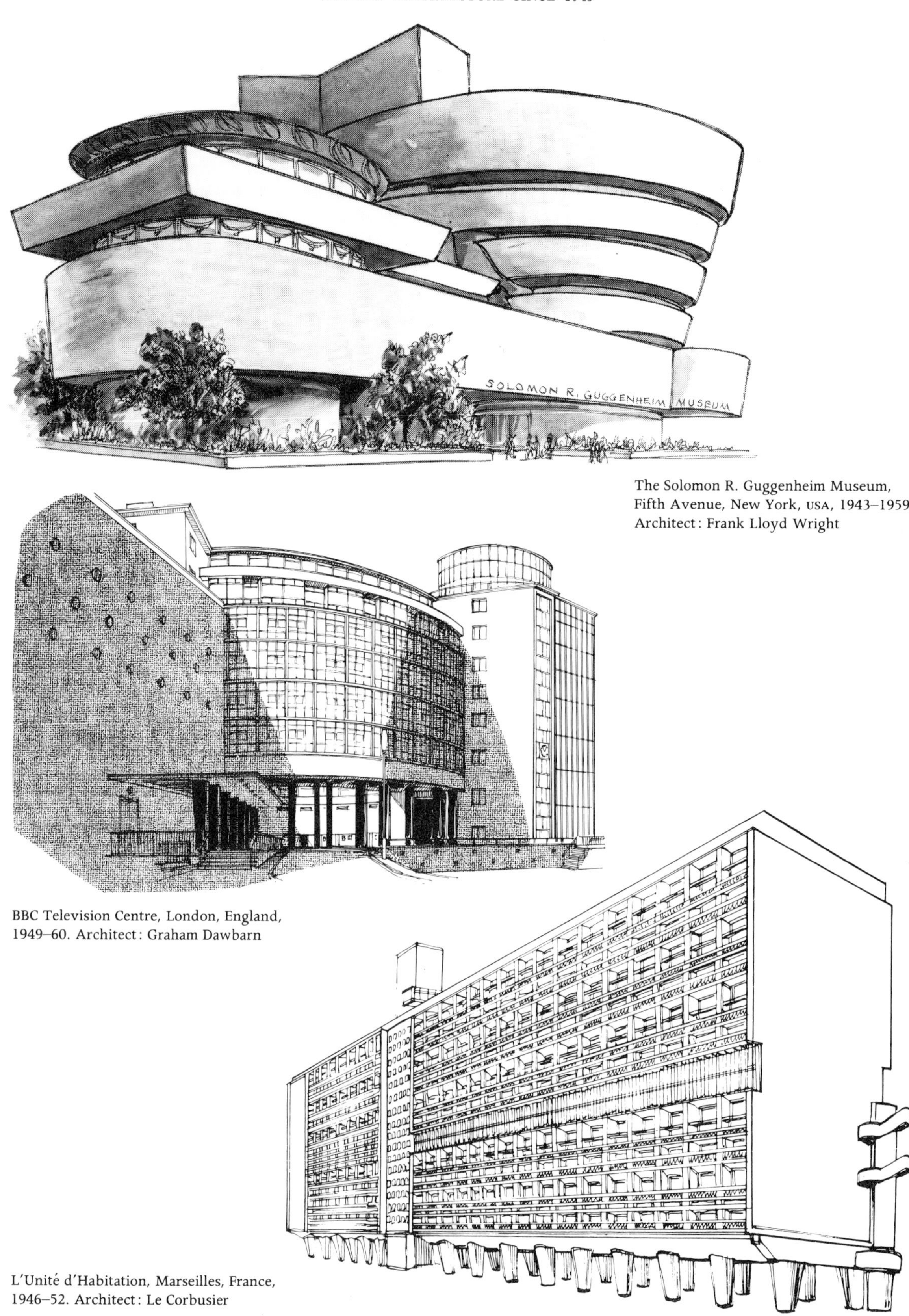

The Solomon R. Guggenheim Museum, Fifth Avenue, New York, USA, 1943–1959. Architect: Frank Lloyd Wright

BBC Television Centre, London, England, 1949–60. Architect: Graham Dawbarn

L'Unité d'Habitation, Marseilles, France, 1946–52. Architect: Le Corbusier

Fry (see FRY, MAXWELL). Mendelsohn also came (see MENDELSOHN, ERICH), so did Behrens (see BEHRENS, PETER). *Berthold Lubetkin*, like *Serge Chermayeff* (see MENDELSOHN, ERICH), was of Caucasian origin. He founded the firm of *Tecton* which built the *Highpoint flats* and *Finsbury Health Centre* in 1938 (see TECTON).

The lead given by these Continental refugees was followed by some of the younger British architects who broke away from the traditional school led by Lutyens and Scott to design functionally in steel, concrete and glass. In 1931 a number of them helped to found the MARS Group (Modern Architectural Research) in order to organize research needed for the modern building industry and to represent their country abroad (see BURNET, SIR JOHN; COATES, WELLS WINTEMUTE; FRY, MAXWELL; IRON AND GLASS; TECTON; WILLIAMS, SIR OWEN; YORKE, FRANCIS REGINALD STEVENS).

Since 1920 modern French architecture has been dominated by the Swiss architect Charles Edouard Jeanneret (1888–1965), usually known as *Le Corbusier*, who, with Frank Lloyd Wright, was a great world leader of the modern movement in architecture. He became established as an architect with advanced original ideas immediately after the First World War. Like Wright, he concentrated on house design but of a different type. Le Corbusier specialized in low-cost housing and planning in flats on estates. He envisaged the housing unit as a 'machine for living in'. Extraneous and unnecessary features were stripped off, leaving a very simple structure with flat roofs and plain walls. He evolved the *piloti* system. Pilotis were free-standing reinforced concrete columns upon which the house or apartment block stood: the rectangular box on stilts has been with us ever since. He was absorbed in the social problems of housing people in cities and developed his ideas in his book *Urbanisme*, published 1925.

In America modern architecture had become the almost universal mode of building. The skyscraper office structures of the first two decades of the century had now become the pattern for city centre architecture for all kinds of needs. Glass curtain-walled structures were being erected in quantity. Noteworthy and impressive is the

'Falling Water', Pennsylvania, USA, 1936–7. Architect: Frank Lloyd Wright

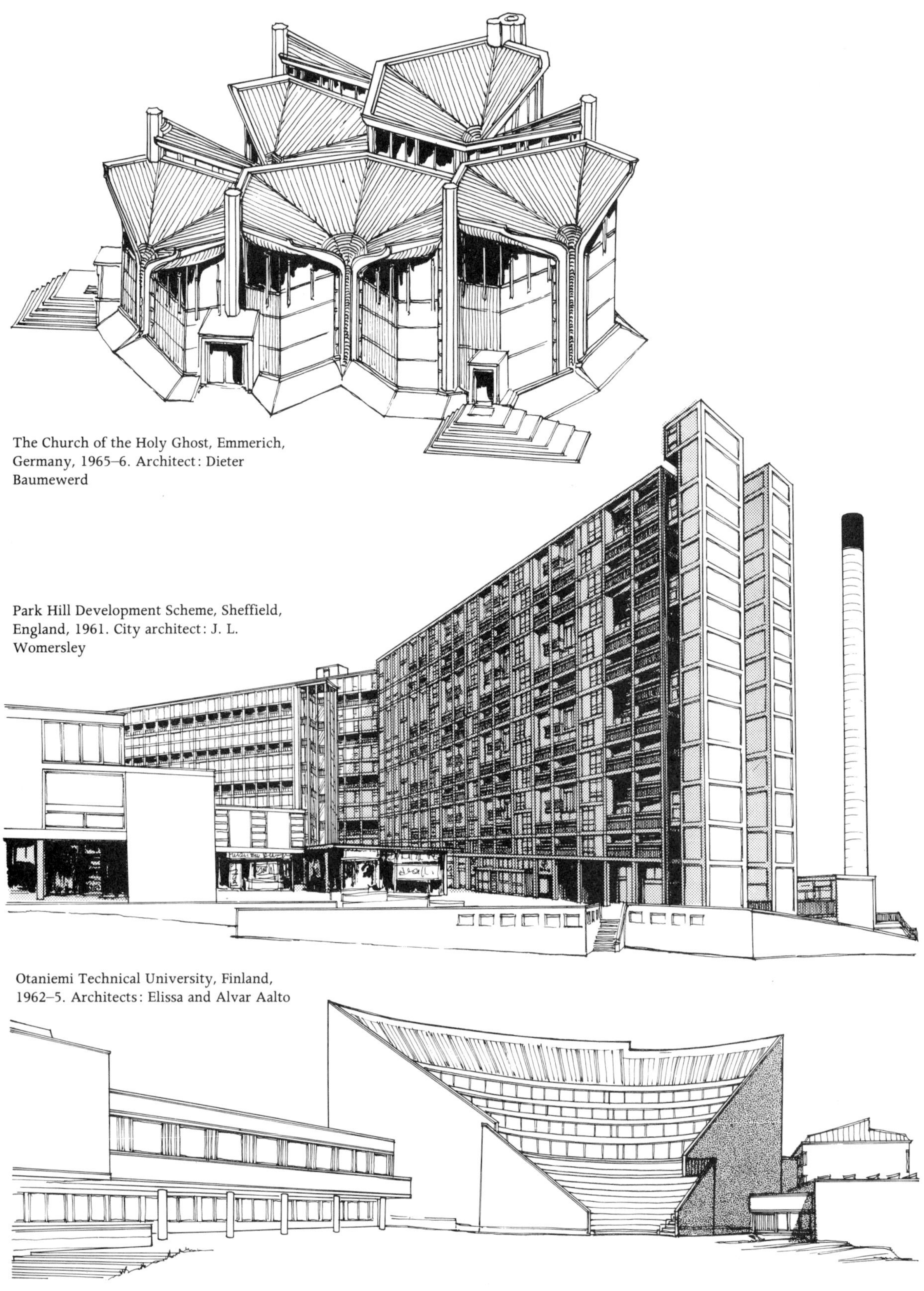

The Church of the Holy Ghost, Emmerich, Germany, 1965–6. Architect: Dieter Baumewerd

Park Hill Development Scheme, Sheffield, England, 1961. City architect: J. L. Womersley

Otaniemi Technical University, Finland, 1962–5. Architects: Elissa and Alvar Aalto

Rockefeller Center in New York (completed 1940); it comprises fourteen tall structures grouped round a piazza (see HIGH-RISE BUILDING; INDUSTRIALIZED BUILDING; IRON AND GLASS; STEEL-FRAME CONSTRUCTION).

Many American architects were becoming internationally known, *Richard Neutra* (1892–1970), for instance, the chief exponent of the California school of high-quality, lavish domestic architecture. Frank Lloyd Wright's work had now entered its second, less active phase. Apart from the remarkable Imperial Hotel in Tokyo, carefully designed and built (1916–22) to withstand earthquake tremors, much of his building was for individual houses in which he had partly abandoned his use of traditional materials in favour of pre-cast concrete blocks which were intended to provide a continuity between structure and decorative surfacing. He was also exploring the structural possibilities of concrete as a material. A dramatic instance of this is the house *'Falling Water'* built in a woodland area which is cantilevered over a waterfall.

After the Second World War modern architecture was widely adopted as the accepted building style. In Europe destruction caused by war and the cessation of building construction for five years made an extensive programme of reconstruction urgently necessary. Modern materials and means of building were brought into use to achieve the task so steel, concrete, brick and aluminium were in general use. Social changes were apparent also; in *Rotterdam*, devastated by war, it was a case of starting from scratch and one new benefit to emerge was the pedestrian precinct, later to become commonplace in the ruined cities of western Europe. The *Lijnbaan* of 1953 was an important prototype (see TOWN PLANNING).

In France *Le Corbusier* quickly won international fame with his low-cost housing scheme, the *Unité d'Habitation*, the first of which was built in *Marseilles* in 1947–52. It was his answer to accommodating large numbers of people quickly and cheaply. The 'Unité' in Marseilles comprises one immense rectangular block carried on a double row of massive central supports. It contains 350 flats in eight double storeys; there is a storey for shops half-way up and communal facilities on the roof. Other 'Unités' followed, in Nantes (1952–7), West Berlin (1957) and Briey-la-Forêt (1960).

In 1950 Le Corbusier built his highly acclaimed and personal and original *Pilgrimage Church* of *Notre Dame du Haut* at *Ronchamp* (see CONCRETE). In total contrast to the 'Unités', this is a massive, rough-cast concrete church of essentially plastic design. Superficially rurally simple it is, inside and out, a masterpiece of studied sophistication. Of equal importance and world-wide influence is his *Dominican Convent* of *La Tourette* at *Eveux-sur-l'Arbresle* near Lyons begun in 1956 which revives the brutalist theme begun in the 'Unités' (see CONCRETE). The entire layout of conventual buildings and church is starkly and uncompromisingly constructed of raw concrete. Again a superficially simple design is meticulously handled, especially

'The Crystal Cathedral', Garden Grove Community Church, California, USA, 1976–80. Architects: Philip Johnson and John Burgee

the lighting, both natural and artificial, to give to the interior of the church in particular a spiritual atmosphere. This commission inspired a number of later ones by different architects, for example, the award-winning *Dunelm House* at the *University of Durham* (1963).

A world-wide building boom got under way in the early 1960s, the speed and scale of which was fuelled by the growing range of new technical developments in the construction industry. Mechanical on-site plant was utilized ever more extensively, prefabrication was widely employed, a greatly increase use of pre-stressed concrete led to on-site pre-casting and a complex range of new materials became available: plastics, fibreglass, laminated products and chipboards. Large areas of glass curtain-walling became more acceptable in consequence of an increased deployment of air-conditioning systems and solar glare control. Standardization of parts accelerated the pace of building (see INDUSTRIALIZED BUILDING). Ideas and projects carried out by a number of engineers and engineer-architects had a marked influence on architectural design: notable in this field was the Italian *Pier Luigi Nervi* (see CONCRETE) and, in Britain, Ove Arup (see ARUP, SIR OVE).

In western Europe modern architecture assumed a more vital and imaginative form in some countries than in others. The Italians produced some interesting designs particularly in those where reinforced concrete was employed. In the 1950s the *Termini Railway Station* in *Rome*, the most outstanding of its kind at this time, was finally completed under the direction of *Eugenio Montuori* (b. 1907) and in *Milan Gio Ponti* (1891–1979) built, in conjunction with Nervi, the *Pirelli Tower* (see HIGH-RISE BUILDING). In the following decade came the curving concrete façades of the *Busto Arsizio Technical College* (Castiglione and Fontana) and *Michelucci*'s original design for the *Church of S. Giovanni* on the Autostrada del Sole near Florence; this was dedicated to those who lost their lives in the construction of this remarkable mountain highway.

By the later 1960s West Germany was recovering from the large-scale devastation of her country and the loss of a generation of architects through emigration. Here, as in several other countries, Italy, Finland, the USA, Japan, for example, reaction was setting in against the limitations of the rectangular box and hard right angles engendered by steel-frame construction (see STEEL-FRAME CONSTRUCTION). The plain surface was giving way to texture and the geometric shape to a sculptural, articulated form as in the expressionism of the 1920s, later evidenced in Le Corbusier's Ronchamp church. Characteristic of the lively new designs in concrete is *Dieter Baumewerd*'s *Church of the Holy Ghost* at *Emmerich* (1965–6). Here interest is maintained by the changing planes and angles while inside the walls, faced with abstract-patterned glass, and the unusual handling of the lighting are especially effective. Symbolic is the altar cross in blood-red metal made from burnt and devastated war materials. Different but of considerable interest is *Gottfried Böhm*'s (b. 1920) new *town hall* at *Bensberg* which is amalgamated in one scheme with the old castle and blends admirably.

It was in Finland that the promise of originality in modern architecture, which had shown itself in the 1930s, began to be realized after 1945. Led by *Alvar Aalto* (1898–1976), supported by his talented colleagues, a Finnish school of architecture evolved. The Finns have adapted their modern building to suit their difficult climate and not to obtrude upon their landscape. Finnish modern architecture, apart from its fine and original designs, interesting form and detail, has an unusually high standard of quality in material, building and finish. That this is possible in a country most of which is in extreme cold and darkness for much of the year, where the population is a bare five million and not wealthy, should shame those richer lands of the West whose performance has been markedly much lower. Aalto concerned himself with the development on the island of *Säynätsalo* and the town centre at *Seinäjoki*. His versatility and national qualities are shown particularly at the *Technical University* at *Otaniemi* near Helsinki.

Of the many notable post-war Finnish architects should be mentioned *Aarne Ervi* (1910–77), chief architect of the justly famous new town of *Tapiola* near Helsinki, begun in 1952, also *Aarno Ruusuvuori* (b. 1925), architect of the striking tent-like *Church of Hyvinkää* (1961) in white shining concrete and glass and *Reima Pietilä* (b. 1923) and *Raili Paatelainen* who built the remarkable and unusual 'baroque in modern dress' *Kaleva Church* at Tampere (1964–6).

British modern architecture in the 1950s and 1960s compared favourably with that of other countries in quality of building, planning and layout and, particularly in social needs as in new towns and universities but there was a monotony and dullness of design and an over-emphasis on the rectangular block. Of the more successful works should be mentioned the *Royal Festival Hall* in London (1951) (see MATTHEW, SIR ROBERT), *Coventry Cathedral*, consecrated 1962 (see CHURCH DESIGN AND STRUCTURE; SPENCE, SIR BASIL), the *BBC Television Centre* of 1949–60 designed by *Graham Dawbarn* (1893–1975), the steel and glass Thameside tower at *Millbank*, built in 1963 by *Ronald Ward and Partners* and, rather more unusual, the *Metropolitan Cathedral of Liverpool* (see GIBBERD, SIR FREDERICK).

These decades also saw a marked 'brutalist' movement in Britain evidenced in a forceful undisguised use of materials (mostly concrete, brick or steel) in powerful, simple designs. It was a form of architecture which aroused strong reactions, both for and against (see CONCRETE). The theme owed much to Le Corbusier but stemmed also from earlier ideas in the Europe of the 1920s and 1930s. Notable British exponents included *Alison* and *Peter Smithson* (Economist Cluster, London, 1964), *Sheppard, Robson and Partners* (Churchill College, Cambridge, 1960s), *Sir Denys Lasdun* (The National Theatre, London, 1967–76), *Stirling and Gowan* (Ham Common housing development, 1958), *Sir Basil Spence* (University of Sussex, 1961 onwards), and *Owen Luder* (the Tricorn Centre, Portsmouth, 1967). The *Park Hill* Development Scheme in *Sheffield* built from 1961 under the aegis of the City Architect *J. L. Womersley* illustrates the effect of brutalism in a large-scale project. The scheme was highly praised by the architectural profession but public comment has been less than kind.

Since 1970 architecture in Britain has, as elsewhere, shown more variety and interest. Modern architecture is still to a large extent an architect's style of building but the social and aesthetic qualities are now being more carefully evaluated and understood. Greater thought and sympathy are also being given to the blending and scale of the modern work with the older buildings in the vicinity.

For a more detailed account of modern architects and architecture in Britain see ARUP, SIR OVE; CASSON, SIR HUGH; CONCRETE; GIBBERD, SIR FREDERICK; HIGH-RISE BUILDING; HOLFORD, LORD WILLIAM GRAHAM; INDUSTRIALIZED BUILDING; LASDUN, SIR DENYS; MATTHEW, SIR ROBERT;

The Bonaventure Hotel, Los Angeles, USA, 1974–6. Architect: John Portman

POWELL, SIR PHILIP; SHEPPARD, SIR RICHARD; SMITHSON, ALISON AND PETER; SPENCE, SIR BASIL; STEEL-FRAMED BUILDING; STIRLING, JAMES; TOWN PLANNING.

The USA, after the Second World War, did not face the same problem of urgent rebuilding as many European countries but its population, swollen by immigration, was growing rapidly and there was also a marked movement westwards. In many cities older areas were rapidly demolished and replaced by new layouts. In the 1950s and 1960s several of the well-known older architects were still practising. In his seventies *Frank Lloyd Wright* was carrying out large commissions and his controversial *Solomon R. Guggenheim Museum* in *New York* was only completed shortly after his death in 1959, at the age of 91. *Ludwig Mies van der Rohe* (1886–1969), master craftsman of the soaring structure in glass and steel, who had survived the Nazi era in Germany to commence a new long and prestigious one in America, continued to build impeccable structures of severe and elegant simplicity, for example, his *Lake Shore Drive* apartments in *Chicago* (1948–51) and, with *Philip Johnson* (b. 1906), the *Seagram Building* in *New York* (1956–8).

In America, as elsewhere, there was a perceptible change appearing in the architectural scene. The tall rectangular box, totally glazed and totally plain, was still being erected, the *United Nations Secretariat* in *New York* (1947–50 by *Wallace K. Harrison*) and the *John Hancock Tower* in *Boston* (1968–77 by *Henry Cobb* and *I. M. Pei*), for instance, but alternative ideas were being sought. Buildings were being grouped; trapezoidal and cylindrical shapes replaced the rectangle; glass curtain-walling was being made more interesting by being broken in stepped surfaces. *Philip Johnson*, long master of the steel and glass tower, designed some of these, in Houston, Minneapolis, and in Los Angeles. Other architects, *Eero Saarinen* (1910–61), for example, began to experiment with a personal version of expressionism as Le Corbusier had done in his Ronchamp church, Frank Lloyd Wright in his Guggenheim Museum and Nervi in his sports structures. Saarinen's buildings at *Dulles International Airport*, Washington D.C., (1958–63) are an instance of this.

After the Second World War Europe gradually ceased to be one of the most important centres for the modern movement in architecture. Extensive important schemes were being developed in, for example, South America, Australia, South Africa and Japan. At first these were assisted or inspired by architects from Europe or the USA but gradually the world became more architecturally self-sufficient and a greater richness and variety of building resulted as in Brasilia, Mexico City, Sydney and Tokyo.

MODULE A unit of measurement by means of which the proportions and detailed parts of a building may be regulated.

In classical architecture the column shaft diameter (or half its diameter) at base was so used; this was subdivided into minutes which represented one sixtieth of a full diameter (see CLASSICAL ARCHITECTURE; CLASSICAL ORDER; COLUMN).

In more modern work Le Corbusier proposed a system of measurement based upon the proportions of the human male figure; he called the system *Le Modulor*. The module has become of vital importance in the necessary standardization of parts in present day mass-produced building (see INDUSTRIALIZED BUILDING; MODERN ARCHITECTURE).

MONOLITH A single block of material shaped into a column or monument.

MORRIS, ROGER (1695–1749) A master carpenter and builder who was responsible, in conjunction with his patron the Earl of Pembroke, for several well-known Palladian structures notably *Marble Hill House, Twickenham* (1724–9), the *White Lodge* in *Richmond Park* (begun 1727) and the *Palladian Bridge* at *Wilton House* (1736–7) (see PALLADIAN ARCHITECTURE; PEMBROKE, EARL OF). At Marble Hill House the Great Room, which was designed as a 24ft cube, was closely modelled upon the single cube room at Wilton House. As at Wilton, it was originally decorated in white and gold, the walls hung with Van Dyck portraits, though at Marble Hill these were copies.

MORRIS, WILLIAM (1834–96) Though not an architect, Morris exercised a strong and lasting influence upon architects of his own and later generations. He became interested in architecture while at Marlborough School then went up to Oxford where he met one of his life-long friends, the artist Edward Burne-Jones. In 1856 Morris entered the Oxford office of Street as a pupil (see STREET, GEORGE EDMUND) and while there formed another important friendship with Webb (see WEBB, PHILIP). Morris only

MORRIS, ROGER
Marble Hill House, Twickenham, 1724–9. South (garden) front

spent one year in Street's office then took up painting under the guidance of Dante Gabriel Rossetti.

It was in 1859, when Morris got married and commissioned Webb to design for him and his wife a new home built in traditional materials in simple vernacular style (the Red House in Bexley Heath) that the various influences of people and studies in his life came together to direct his future actions. Morris was a dedicated socialist, a medievalist and a craftsman. He abhorred the trend towards mechanization and the current over-decoration and use of spurious materials. He wanted to re-establish quality in craftsmanship and simplicity in design. Unable to find suitable textiles and furniture for his new home he began his career as a decorator. With such friends as Rossetti, Webb, Burne-Jones and Madox Brown he formed a small company which began business in 1862.

This firm, later called Morris and Co., became known for high-quality design and workmanship in the making of textiles, wallpaper, furniture, coloured glass and murals. Morris's ambition was to elevate the craftsman once more to the position which he had held in medieval society. His socialist ideals held that art should be 'by the people for the people'. He was reluctant to come to terms with the unpalatable fact that, in the 1860s, the cost of producing articles by the individual craft method could not compete with that of the mass-produced item. The well-to-do flocked to buy the firm's products but Morris had failed in his desire to bring these to the ordinary people: costwise they were out of reach of the average buyer.

Morris could not put the clock back but his reintroduction of quality design and the use of genuine materials profoundly influenced a new generation of architects and designers (see ART NOUVEAU; ASHBEE, CHARLES ROBERT; MACKINTOSH, CHARLES RENNIE; MACKMURDO, ARTHUR; VOYSEY, CHARLES ANNESLEY).

MORTISE (MORTICE)

1. In a wooden joint the mortise is the cavity cut into one member to receive the *tenon* of the intersecting member (see PANELLING).
2. The mortise type of lock is fitted into a recess in the edge of the door so cannot be removed without breaking the door.

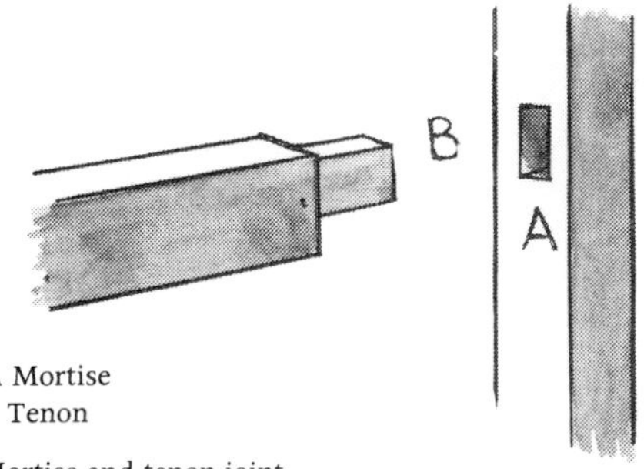

A Mortise
B Tenon

Mortise and tenon joint

MOTTE AND BAILEY CONSTRUCTION See CASTLE.

MOULDINGS Modelled surfaces given to parts of a building, for instance, an arch, a jamb, a panel, a capital, an entablature. Many mouldings are purely decorative, intended to define and accentuate the architectural character of the structure but some, as in the case of a cornice or hood-mould (see CORNICE; HOOD-MOULD), are designed to protect a vertical surface by projecting outwards so keeping rain or snow away from it.

MOULDINGS

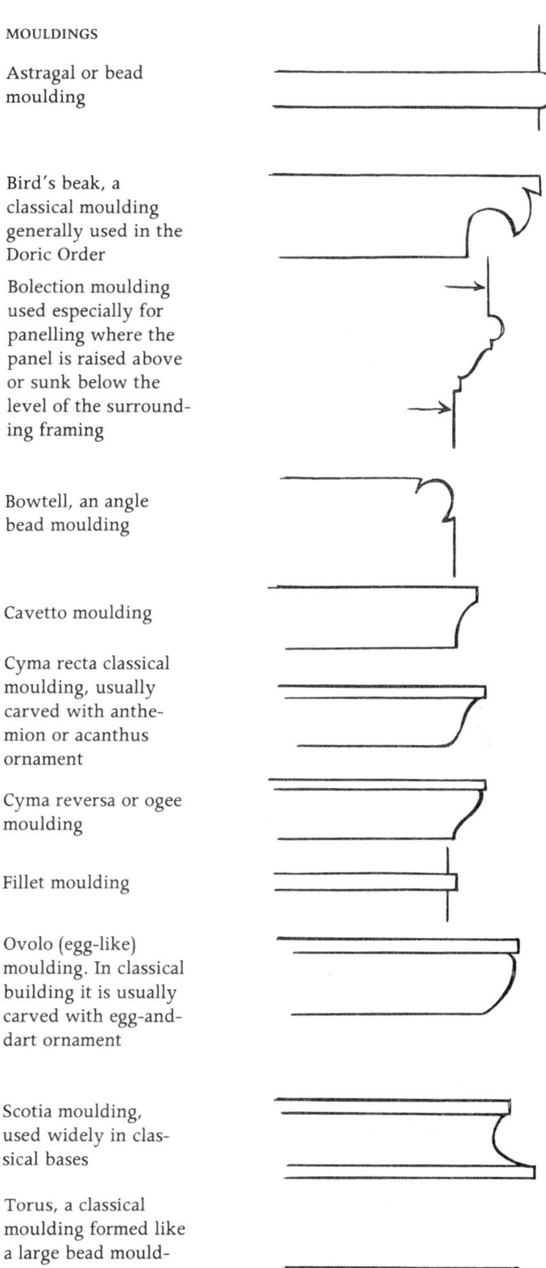

Astragal or bead moulding

Bird's beak, a classical moulding generally used in the Doric Order

Bolection moulding used especially for panelling where the panel is raised above or sunk below the level of the surrounding framing

Bowtell, an angle bead moulding

Cavetto moulding

Cyma recta classical moulding, usually carved with anthemion or acanthus ornament

Cyma reversa or ogee moulding

Fillet moulding

Ovolo (egg-like) moulding. In classical building it is usually carved with egg-and-dart ornament

Scotia moulding, used widely in classical bases

Torus, a classical moulding formed like a large bead moulding, often carved with guilloche ornament

Mouldings may be employed singly but more often are grouped in a selection which has been proved empirically over the years to be attractive. In the case of classical architecture this process has been carried further so that specific groupings of mouldings have become mandatory with certain orders. Many mouldings are decorated with carving and/or colour. Again, by experience, it has been shown that certain mouldings are suited to be carved with a specific design. Both mouldings and their ornament are characteristic of certain periods of building and are of great assistance in identifying architectural style (see CLASSICAL ARCHITECTURE; CLASSICAL ORDER; CLASSICAL ORNAMENT; GOTHIC ARCHITECTURE; GOTHIC ORNAMENT; ROMANESQUE ARCHITECTURE; ROMANESQUE ORNAMENT).

The extensive variety of mouldings are of three main types: flat or square, convex, concave. The *fillet, corona* and *dentil* (see CLASSICAL ORDER) are flat or square-faced; convex mouldings include the *astragal* or *bead, bowtell, ovolo* and *torus* while the *apophyge* (see APOPHYGE), *cavetto* and *scotia* are concave. Some mouldings comprise a combined convex and concave curve, notably the *ogee* (see OGEE) and *cyma*. Many mouldings are known by more than one name according to whether they were used in classical or Gothic architecture. Illustrated examples of the most popular mouldings are given below.

MOUNTFORD, EDWARD WILLIAM (1855–1908) Architect of a number of civic schemes in classical style. Much of his earlier work was in the *Battersea* area of south London, for instance, the *Free Library* (1888), the *Polytechnic* and the *Town Hall* (both 1890–7). All these commissions were carried out in restrained early Renaissance style, using brick and stone. In similar vein but more ambitious and stately is his *Sheffield Town Hall* (1891–6) with a slender lofty clock tower at one corner. Mountford went on to a rounder, more Baroque version of classicism in his *Liverpool College of Technology* (1896–1902) and, in 1902, the *Central Criminal Courts* in *London*.

MYLNE, ROBERT (1733–1811) The son of a Scottish master mason, he was born in Edinburgh; from 1754 he spent five years studying in France and Italy where his work showed considerable promise. Mylne's contribution was as both engineer and architect. He built many bridges, his first commission being for *Blackfriars Bridge* in *London*, for which he won the open competition and which was built 1760–9. Two features of the bridge (at the time unusual) were the elliptical arches and the

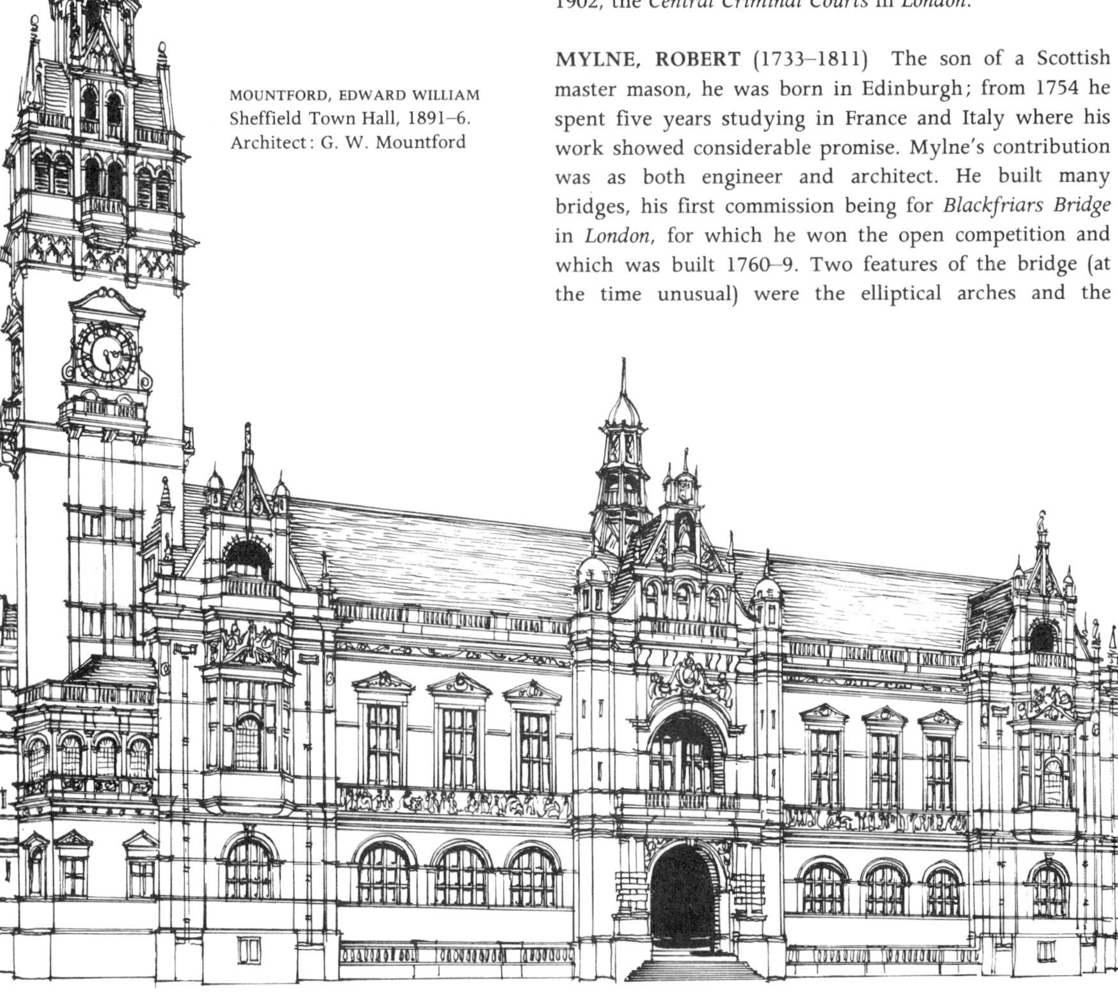

MOUNTFORD, EDWARD WILLIAM
Sheffield Town Hall, 1891–6.
Architect: G. W. Mountford

double columns mounted on each breakwater: the bridge was demolished in 1868.

Mylne's architectural work included the elegant house at the top of *Richmond Hill* in Surrey: *The Wick* (1775) which set a pattern for many similar houses. His public buildings included the *City of London Lying-in Hospital* (1770–3, demolished 1903) and the rebuilding of the east front of the *Stationer's Hall* on Ludgate Hill in London (1800) in neo-classical style.

NAOS In a Greek temple, the sanctuary chamber containing the cult statue (see TEMPLE). In a Byzantine church, the sanctuary.

NARTHEX In a Byzantine or early Christian church, a vestibule extended transversely across the western end of the building, separated from the nave by a screen or wall and set apart as an area for women and penitents. Also known as an *antenave* or *antechurch* and, later, as a *galilee* (see ANTECHURCH; BASILICA; BYZANTINE ARCHITECTURE; CHURCH DESIGN AND STRUCTURE; GALILEE).

NASH, JOHN (1752–1835) An exact contemporary of Soane (see SOANE, SIR JOHN), Nash was a contrast to him in every way. He was not austere or restrained but an ebullient extrovert. Whereas Soane's architecture was personally original and particularly adapted to effective interiors, Nash was in his element in handling the large-scale scenic exterior scheme. A man of his time, Nash worked in all styles in Gothic, Italian Renaissance, Palladian and Greek; he built rustic cottages, castellated mansions and picturesque villas.

John Nash was the son of a millwright. He began his architectural career as an apprentice to Taylor (see TAYLOR, SIR ROBERT) but, impatient as he often was, soon left and tried to work on his own. He established a new venture to build houses in London which were of brick faced with stucco and painted to look like stone (see PLASTERWORK). Financially this was not successful so he retired to the country and gradually built up a large practice in which he joined with Repton (see REPTON, HUMPHRY), Nash designing country houses and Repton laying out the grounds. The output of this practice was tremendous but, by 1802, the partnership was ended and Nash had returned to London where he spent much of the rest of his life working on extensive schemes for his patron the Prince Regent.

One such commission was the *Royal Pavilion* at *Brighton* where Nash indulged his flair for the picturesque (see HOLLAND, HENRY; PICTURESQUE ARCHITECTURE). In Brighton the royal stables had been designed and built by *William Porden* in 1803–5 in a fashionable Indian style, influenced by the recently completed *Sezincote* in Gloucestershire (see COCKERELL, SAMUEL PEPYS). (These stables became an Assembly Room in 1867, and then in 1934 were remodelled as the Dome Concert Hall.) When the Prince's favourite architect, Nash, was asked to design a palace, he began work in 1815 modifying the villa built originally by Holland, planning it to be in the Indian manner. As work progressed his enthusiasm led him towards a mixture of sources so that the finished building might be more accurately described as 'Indian Gothic with a flavour of Chinese', especially in the interiors.

Nash's contribution to architecture lies not in his eclectic experimentation nor in the originality of his classical design but in his brilliant versatility as a town planner. His extensive *Regent's Park* terraces, the old *Regent Street* and *Carlton House Terrace* represent a far-reaching achievement in town planning of modern dimensions carried out in a picturesque version of eighteenth-century classicism. Here was the logical extension of the schemes by Wood in Bath (see WOOD, JOHN).

Nash was given a unique opportunity in 1811 to design and carry out this tremendous London project. It was made possible by the coincidence of the availability of the land at a time of prosperity and an informed and enthusiastic royal patronage. With this combination of circumstances, plus energy and good health, Nash was enabled between the ages of 60 and 80 to see a considerable proportion of his scheme built. The layout comprised a large area covering the present-day Regent's Park, St James's Park, Regent Street and Trafalgar Square.

In 1811 Marylebone Park (the northern part of the proposed scheme and an area of 554 acres) reverted to the Crown. This was farmland which was intended for development. Three architects presented plans, but Nash's ideas were so much more ambitious and revolutionary than the others that the Prince Regent gave the project energetic support. The Nash scheme was nothing less than a whole 'garden city' for the wealthy in the centre of the metropolis. The concept included a park with graceful villas, a lake, a canal, crescents and terraces with intermittent focal centres. The *pièce de résistance* was to be a royal route from the Prince Regent's Park, where a summer palace was to be built, to his Carlton House in the Mall via the future Regent Street.

Nash's scheme was accepted and he began work in 1812. When he died 23 years later, much of his vast concept, in which he energetically participated until the end, had been realized. Some of his best ideas had had to be abandoned—the double circus, the summer palace and a number of villas. Today Regent's Park is only a part of the original plan and Regent Street has been totally

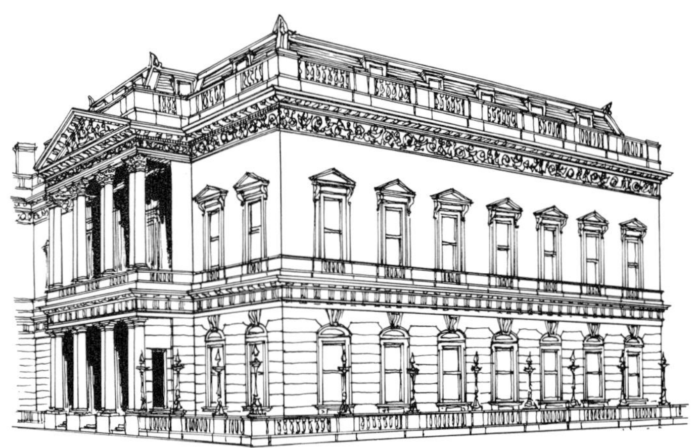

The United Services Club, London, 1828

All Souls' Church, Langham Place, London, 1822–5: the portico

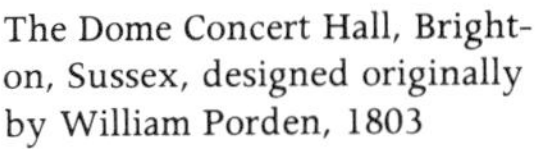

The Dome Concert Hall, Brighton, Sussex, designed originally by William Porden, 1803

The Royal Pavilion, Brighton, Sussex, 1815–20

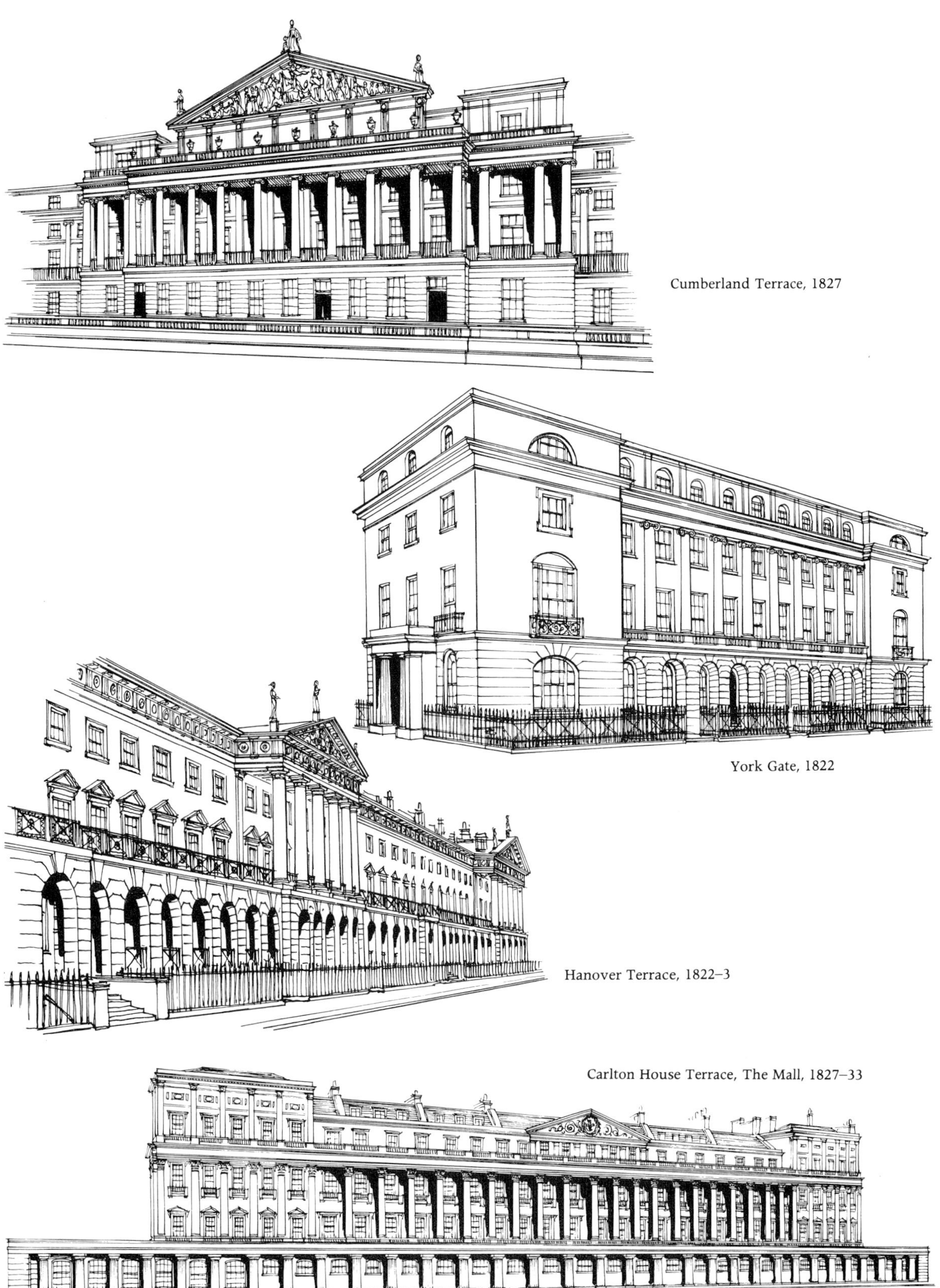

Cumberland Terrace, 1827

York Gate, 1822

Hanover Terrace, 1822–3

Carlton House Terrace, The Mall, 1827–33

rebuilt, though the line of the quadrant has been preserved. The terraces have survived, restored and adapted to modern use and in the restoration, some of the slapdash detail and proportions, which the builder had carried out to Nash's sketchy drawings and without adequate supervision, have been improved.

The crescents and terraces were built between 1812 and 1832. The earliest was *Park Crescent* at the top of Portland Place, planned as a circus of coupled Ionic columns only one half of which was built. Fronting the park are the monumental *Cumberland Terrace* and imposing *Hanover, Cornwall* and *Chester Terraces*. In 1827–32 Nash replaced Carlton House in the Mall with *Carlton House Terrace* and St James's Park was laid out.

Regent's Park lay at the northern end of Nash's royal route, Carlton House Terrace at the southern. Between the two he designed the great boulevard which, commencing at Park Crescent, swept down the Adam Portland Place to Nash's own *All Souls' Church* (1822–5), changed direction slightly to continue as Regent Street with a quarter circle (the Quadrant) at the lower end (Piccadilly Circus) to bring it into line with Lower Regent Street and Waterloo Place. There were problems with commercial interests in Regent Street as Nash insisted upon absolute architectural symmetry but these problems were solved and the scheme was architecturally and financially successful. Nash's Quadrant was built in 1818–20. It was rebuilt in 1906–23 (see BLOMFIELD, SIR REGINALD; SHAW, NORMAN).

In 1825 Nash was creating a new scheme aimed to connect Bloomsbury and Whitehall and, from 1831, a new square at the north end of Whitehall was formed: Trafalgar Square. But, except for St Martin-in-the-Fields (see GIBBS, JAMES), all the buildings here were erected later by other architects (see WILKINS, WILLIAM).

Of Nash's other London work, the *Haymarket Theatre* (1820) survives much as he designed it, as does the *United Service Club* in Pall Mall (1828). Nothing remains of his ill-fated project at Buckingham Palace except the *Marble Arch*, which he had based upon the Arch of Constantine in Rome and planned as a triumphal entrance archway to the palace forecourt. The arch was removed to its present site in 1851 after Edward Blore had completed Buckingham Palace (see BLORE, EDWARD; REGENCY ARCHITECTURE).

NEWTON, SIR ERNEST (1856–1922) A pupil of Shaw (see SHAW, NORMAN), Newton was very much influenced in his earlier work by that of the older architect. He excelled in country house design both in the vernacular style sympathetic to the Arts and Crafts ideals but also in a more symmetrical, simple yet traditional classical form. His work in a wide range of materials, notably brick, stone, tile and weatherboarding, was always well-considered and tasteful. Characteristic of his domestic commissions were *'Feathercombe'*, near *Godalming* in Surrey, *Flint House, Goring-on-Thames* and, a late example, *'Luckley'* at *Wokingham* in Berkshire (1907).

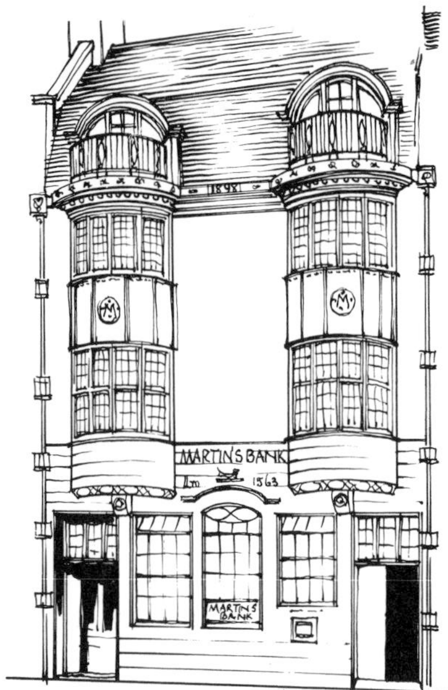

Martin's Bank, Bromley, Kent, 1898.
Architect: Sir Ernest Newton

Newton carried out a good deal of work in the *Bromley* area of Kent. In the town itself is an interesting group of three buildings in the High Street where it leads out of the Market Square. In the group, erected 1898, is the *Royal Bell Hotel* decorated with pargeted (see PARGETING) strapwork panels, the bow-window-fronted *Martin's Bank* and number 181 next door. Also in the town, in Plaistow Lane, is an earlier instance of Newton's work, the tile-hung *'Gables'*.

NICHE A recess in a wall or pier designed to contain a statue or decorative object. Many niches are semicircular in plan and are arched.

NOG, NOGGING A nog is a small block of wood. Nogging is the infilling of the walls of a timber-framed building (see TIMBER FRAMING). The most common type is *brick nogging*, where bricks are laid to form patterns between the timbers.

NOSING The rounded edge of a projecting moulding. Most commonly applied to the rounded edge of a stair tread (see STAIRCASE).

NOGGING
Brick nogging: market hall from Titchfield, Hampshire, in the Weald and Downland Museum, Sussex

OEILLET, OILLET A small hole in cloth or the eye of a needle, from the French *oeil* (= 'eye').

In architecture the term is applied to the narrow slit openings in medieval fortified walls which terminate in tiny circular openings through which arrows could be shot (see CASTLE).

OFF-SET A horizontal or sloping break in the face of a wall caused when the upper part of the wall is of lesser thickness. In medieval architecture a buttress off-set (or set-off) is sloped (see BUTTRESS; WEATHERING).

OGEE A double-curved form comprising a concave and convex section (see ARCH; MOULDING).

ORMOLU A gilded bronze or brass used in architectural decoration and furniture mounts, particularly in the eighteenth century. The word derives from the French *or moulu*, literally 'ground-up gold', though the French term for ormolu is *bronze doré*. Neo-classical architects, Robert Adam for instance, used ormolu widely as decorative material on marble, stone and wood in chimneypiece and door furniture design (see ADAM, ROBERT).

Now ormolu is an alloy of copper, zinc and tin which possesses the colouring of gold.

OVERHANG, OVERSAIL A part of a building projecting outwards over a lower part (see TIMBER FRAMING).

PAINE, JAMES (1717–89) Although he was born and lived in the south of England, much of his large country house practice was in the north and Midlands. Like Taylor, with whom he shared much of the architectural work in the years of the mid-eighteenth century (see TAYLOR, SIR ROBERT), Paine worked for much of his life in the Palladian tradition (see PALLADIAN ARCHITECTURE): not for him were the new-fangled theories on the origins of classical architecture (see GRAND TOUR). His exterior work was monumental and correct and it was only in his interior designs that Paine allowed himself to be influenced by current fashion so that a lighter, more elegant rococo and neo-classical character appeared. *Nostell Priory* in Yorkshire was one example of this (begun about 1737, it was one of Paine's earlier commissions though Adam took over the interior decoration in 1765 (see ADAM, ROBERT). The *Mansion House* in *Doncaster* (1745–8) was another.

Later Paine became more adventurous. He began to base his house planning upon Roman antique originals, as at *Kedleston* in Derbyshire, where he erected the central block of the house (1759–60) and planned in it the monumental colonnaded hall contiguous with the pantheon form of circular saloon (see Pantheon in CLASSICAL ARCHITECTURE). But, in 1761, Adam was appointed to take over and it is to him that we owe the decoration and completion of these remarkable interiors as well as the building of the south front of the house (see ADAM, ROBERT). At *Worksop Manor*, Nottinghamshire (1763–7; only the north side was completed and it was later demolished), Paine planned an immense Egyptian hall after Vitruvius (see VITRUVIUS) and, in the 1770s, designed and built at *Wardour Castle*, Wiltshire, another pantheon-like circular hall approached by a sweeping staircase.

Towards the end of his life, while High Sheriff of Surrey, Paine designed several Thames bridges: at Richmond, Chertsey, Kew and Walton: only *Richmond Bridge* survives mainly as it was built (1774–7). He published his collected works in *Plans, Elevations and Sections of Noblemen and Gentlemen's Houses*: the first volume appeared in 1767, the second in 1783.

PALLADIAN ARCHITECTURE A style based on the designs and concepts of the sixteenth-century Italian architect *Andrea Palladio*.

Palladio (1508–80, born Andrea di Pietro della Gondola) was the pre-eminent architect of his day in the Veneto area of northern Italy. His work was of high quality, known for its originality and variety, sound building structure and pleasing yet dramatic appearance. His buildings exercised a far-reaching influence on the architecture of western and nothern Europe in the seventeenth and eighteenth centuries, and the Palladian style then spread eastwards to Russia and westwards to America.

Palladio was the first important professional architect: he studied, trained and worked only in this one art. His Renaissance predecessors and contemporaries, Michelangelo for example, prided themselves on being masters of more than one discipline. Palladio followed Renaissance tradition in basing his architectural concepts upon those of ancient Rome. He re-thought these, studied the publications of Vitruvius (see VITRUVIUS), the symmetry of the buildings and town planning of Roman antiquity, and the theory of harmonic proportions (a system of proportions relating architecture to music; it was explored in antiquity and revived by early Renaissance architects such as Alberti). Palladio made hundreds of on-the-spot drawings, not only in Italy but in Dalmatia and Provence. He published his studies, designs and ideas in several books of which two, *I Quattro Libri dell'Architettura* and *L'Antichità di Roma*, were translated into many languages and so spread his theories abroad.

Palladio's own work was a mixture of these sources and the classicism of Bramante as well as the Mannerism of Italian architects such as Michelangelo and Vignola (see MANNERISM). Most of his buildings are in Vicenza and Venice. These include churches, palaces and villas as well as civic works such as the commission which brought him fame, the remodelling of the great fifteenth-century 'Basilica' in the centre of Vicenza where he imposed a pattern in his handling of the two superimposed orders (Doric and Ionic) with entablatures broken forward over each column instead of the then more usual emphasis on the uninterrupted horizontal cornice line.

In his many palaces and villas he followed what he thought to have been the ancient Roman practice but, as Roman domestic remains are fragmentary, he based his plans on temple design. He adapted what he knew of Roman building to the needs of the sixteenth century, finding often unusual and ingenious solutions to problems while careful to maintain both symmetry and effect. For example, in Vicenza, in the *Palazzo Chiericati*, he brought the loggia (a feature generally confined to palace courtyards) on to the façade; then for emphasis he stepped forward the central mass but otherwise retained the unbroken entablatures. The palace is a finely balanced instance of his art in the handling of light and shade and mass as well as detail.

In his villas Palladio introduced the idea of temple-front porticos which he mistakenly believed were characteristic of ancient Roman houses. He varied the theme from villa to villa but probably the best-known version is the *Villa Capra* (the Rotonda) near Vicenza in which the whole of the *piano nobile* is raised on a square podium and each of the four sides is fronted by an identical hexastyle portico; within is a central domed hall. This is the ultimate in domestic symmetry corresponding ecclesiastically

View of the Villa Capra (Rotunda), begun 1567, near Vicenza, Italy. Architect: Andrea Palladio

Ground plan of the Villa Capra

Palazzo della Ragione (Basilica), Vicenza, Italy. Re-clothed by Palladio from 1549

Holkham Hall, Norfolk, begun 1734, the garden front. Architect: William Kent

The Mauritshuis, The Hague, Holland, 1633 (re-modelled *c.* 1718). Architects: Pieter Post and Jacob van Campen

Queensberry House, London, 1721 (incorporates later work). Architect: Giacomo Leoni

Church of S. Giorgio Maggiore, Venice, Italy, from 1565. Architect: Andrea Palladio

to the Renaissance concept of a centrally planned church. The villa served more than once as a pattern for eighteenth-century country houses as at Chiswick and Mereworth (see BURLINGTON, EARL OF; CAMPBELL, COLEN).

In his churches Palladio also used the Roman temple pattern. He developed a type of façade design which incorporated two or more interpenetrating orders differing in scale. He employed this method to solve the old problem of relating the façade to the differing heights of nave and aisles: Palladio made his nave order larger and higher than that of the aisles. His two outstanding churches are in Venice: *S. Giorgio Maggiore* (1565) and *Il Redentore* (1577–92).

In England the first exponent of Palladian design was

Palladian Bridge at Wilton House, Wiltshire, 1736–7. Architects: Lord Pembroke and Roger Morris. The design is based upon Palladio's triumphal bridge

Roakeby Hall, Yorkshire. Entrance front (south). Architect: Sir Thomas Robinson, 1725–30

Inigo Jones who had studied ancient Roman remains in conjunction with Palladio's treatises (see JONES, INIGO). The beginning of a pure Renaissance style was also initiated in Holland in the second quarter of the seventeenth century, strongly influenced by Palladio. As in Inigo Jones's work in England, neither the Dutch nor the English examples were copies of the Italian architect's designs but were nationally individual interpretations: in Holland an important example is the *Mauritshuis* in *The Hague* (1633). This Dutch Palladian style was introduced to England in the second half of the century in the domestic building of such architects as May, Webb and Pratt (see MAY, HUGH; PRATT, SIR ROGER; WEBB, JOHN).

The chief English revival of Palladianism was in the eighteenth century in the years 1720–60 under the leadership of Lord Burlington and Colen Campbell. Many books were published giving detailed text and drawings for the guidance of architects and builders. The outstanding contribution of this Palladian school was in country house building (see COUNTRY HOUSE AND MANSION), but all over England Palladian houses were being erected in these years, from large mansions to small houses and terraces. Most of the work was by builders who based their designs on houses they had seen or on drawings in books on architecture, for example, *Vitruvius Britannicus*; Kent's editing of *Designs of Inigo Jones*; Lord Burlington's *Fabbriche Antiche*; Vardy's *Designs of Inigo Jones and William Kent*; and, of course, Dubois's translation of Palladio's *I Quattro Libri dell'Architettura* illustrated by Leoni. Apart from the architects there was an informed aristocracy who sent their sons on the Grand Tour of Europe (see GRAND TOUR) to study its classical sites and Renaissance buildings for two or three years. On their return these men became patrons of practising architects and artists.

For further information about architects who built in the Palladian style in England see BURLINGTON, EARL OF; CAMPBELL, COLEN; FLITCROFT, HENRY; KENT, WILLIAM; LEONI, GIACOMO; PAINE, JAMES; TAYLOR, SIR ROBERT; WARE, ISAAC; WOOD, JOHN.

PANELLING The practice of lining interior walls with wooden boarding became customary during the thirteenth century. This was not in the form of panelling but used boards placed vertically and overlapping one another as in a clinker-built boat (see also CLAPBOARD). This *wainscoting*, as it was called, was skilfully tongued and grooved so presenting one overlapping face and one which was flush.

The word wainscot later came to refer to any form of wood covering for wall surfaces. In the early thirteenth century the term was used to mean the material rather than the practice of covering and most often referred to a high-quality oak imported from Russia, Germany and Holland along the Baltic coast though it was occasionally used for soft woods also. The origin of the word wainscot is not certain, but it is thought to derive from an early

Carved oak panelled door, 1515–30

Oak panelled door, *c.* 1590

Carved Elizabethan panelling

Carved linenfold panelling

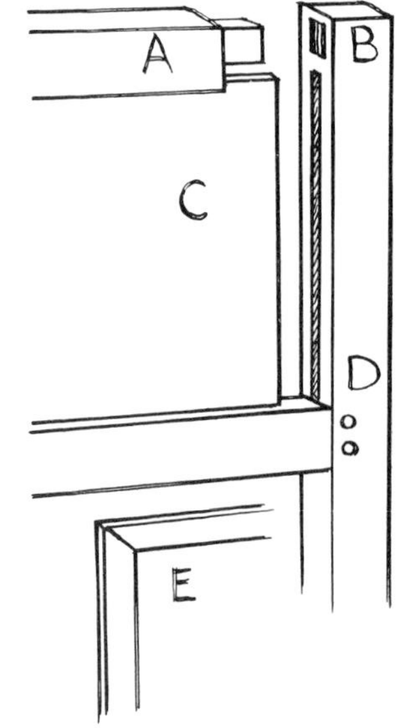

Panel and frame construction
A Rail with tenon
B Stile with mortise
C Panel
D Wood pegs
E Back of panel with tapered edges

Carved oak panelling, early sixteenth century. House near Waltham Abbey. Photo: Victoria and Albert Museum

Linenfold panelled room, *c.* 1500

Bedchamber, *c*. 1575. Carved oak panelling inlaid with different woods

Dining-room, *c*. 1640–5, wainscoted in oak in the Doric Order

Door panel detail in the library at Osterley Park House, Middlesex, from 1761. Architect: Robert Adam.

English form of wagon ('wain'); this imported timber was also used for the making of wagons.

During the fifteenth century panel-and-frame construction of 'joined' woodwork (that is, made by the joiner) was introduced into England from Flanders. This was a great advance on boarded wood covering, as it was less rigidly fixed so making it less liable to warp as it allowed 'freedom of movement in the atmosphere'. In panel-and-frame construction the panels (made of thin sheets of wood) were tapered on all four sides and fitted into narrow grooves in a framework of thicker vertical strips (stiles) and horizontal strips (rails). The stiles and rails were then united by mortise-and-tenon joints (see MORTISE) and fastened by squared and tapered oak pegs inserted into round holes. Such panelled construction was then widely employed for centuries to line walls and ceilings, for doors and furniture (see CEILING; DOOR).

Early panelled woodwork was not usually decoratively carved though it was often painted in coloured designs. From the late fifteenth century onwards different forms of carved ornamentation became characteristic of certain periods. In the years *c.* 1490–1550 this was the *linenfold panel,* where is represented in each panel a piece of material folded vertically. In later examples a refinement was introduced in which the appearance of an embroidered border was simulated by means of punches. The term 'linenfold' is a nineteenth-century one; it is believed that during the Middle Ages it was called *lignum undulatum* ('wavy woodwork'). A variation of the linenfold design is one which is now referred to as *parchemin* since it resembles a piece of parchment curling up at the corners. This is ribbed, the stopped ends being ogivally curved (see OGEE).

Solarium door, Sherborne Castle, Dorset, *c.* 1860

During the sixteenth century greater variation appeared in panelling. An early design had a central roundel decorated by a carved profile head or heraldic device then, after 1550, a profusion of English Renaissance motifs (see RENAISSANCE ARCHITECTURE) appeared and pilasters enriched the stiles. Alternatively, inlay provided the ornamentation, using holly, laburnum, bog oak and fruit woods to give colour, as well as paint and gilt. From the 1630s the whole wall was more often designed as a classical order, the panelling, window and door openings fitted into a scheme comprising entablature, pilasters and plinth (see CLASSICAL ORDER; COUNTRY HOUSE AND MANSION; PLINTH).

During the seventeenth and eighteenth centuries the panels were often left plain but could be sunk or *fielded* (that is, raised in the central area); or the whole panel was raised by the use of a bolection moulding (see MOULDINGS). By the eighteenth century deal or pine had replaced oak as wainscot material and this was painted all over in a light colour, the restrained area of border carving being picked out in gilt or ornamented with ormolu.

PAPWORTH, JOHN BUONARROTI (1775–1847) A prolific architect and a man of great versatility, being also artist, furniture- and glass-designer, landscape gardener and architectural writer. It was this versatile quality which led his friends and colleagues to dub him 'Michelangelo' so causing him later to add Buonarroti to his name. He was the son of John Papworth, the leading stuccoist of his day. When John Papworth junior showed promise of considerable artistic talent, on the advice of Chambers (see CHAMBERS, SIR WILLIAM), he was entered to be trained as an architect.

PAPWORTH, JOHN BUONAROTTI
House in Lansdown Terrace, Cheltenham, *c.* 1825. Architect: J. B. Papworth

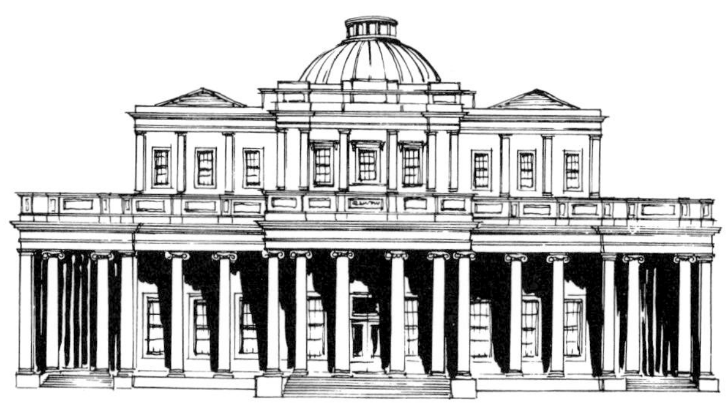

PAPWORTH, JOHN BUONAROTTI
The Pittville Pump Room, Cheltenham, 1825–30. Architect: J. B. Forbes

Papworth designed a number of country houses and was responsible for completing and altering many more. He contributed to Ackermann's *Repository of the Arts* (1809–28), to W. H. Pyne's *Royal Residences* (1818–20), Britton and Pugin's *Public Buildings of London* (1825–8) and a variety of other projects and publications.

In the 1820s Papworth designed a number of urban schemes in the manner initiated by Nash (see NASH, JOHN). In Dulwich he laid out the *Brockwell Estate* between 1825–30 for the glass manufacturer John Blades and completed the interior of *Brockwell Hall* there for him in 1824–9 (the house had been built in 1811–13 by Roper).

In the same period in Cheltenham, Papworth was laying out the *Montpellier* and *Lansdown Estates* and it is for his work in Cheltenham, much of it for Pearson Thompson, that Papworth is now best remembered; his name is so linked with the town's Regency development that buildings there were often ascribed to him without foundation. Notable on the Montpellier Estate was the *Pump Room* of 1826, a building which he designed with a circular domed hall after the Roman Pantheon set within a colonnaded rectangle.

It is interesting to compare the contemporary achievement in the town of *John Forbes* (b. 1795) on the *Pittville Estate*. Forbes's main project here, for Joseph Pitt the great landowner, was the *Pittville Pump Room* (1825–30) built like Papworth's Montpellier Pump Room, as a rotunda within a colonnade. Forbes's Ionic colonnade is more finely proportioned and his Pump Room behind is more imposing; it is a great assembly hall based on Roman Baths plan (see ROMAN BATHS). Much of the rest of the estate was laid out after both Forbes and Pitt died (see TERRACE ARCHITECTURE).

PARAPET A low wall built along the edge of a bridge, balcony or cornice for reasons of safety. Parapets may be battlemented, pierced or ornamentally carved (see BATTLEMENT).

PARCLOSE In a church, a screen dividing the main part of the interior from a chapel or shrine.

PARGETING In the early Middle Ages the term was applied to any external wall covering of coarse mortar plaster (see PLASTERWORK). 'Pargeting' now has a more specialized meaning; it describes a decorative design in plaster applied to the exterior of a building and, most commonly, one which is timber-framed (see TIMBER-FRAMING), the plaster being used as a panel of ornamental infilling. The designs may be incised or in relief.

Pargeting (pargetting, parge work, pargetry) is a peculiarly English decorative form, in favour from Elizabethan times and through the seventeenth century, after which, with the slow decline in timber construction, pargeting also was practised less and less. Surviving examples date from the second half of the sixteenth century onwards when the craft was being established, though there are a few records of earlier work. A majority of examples are to be found where there is a wealth of timber-framed buildings and especially in Essex and Suffolk and, to a lesser degree, in Hertfordshire, Cambridgeshire and Norfolk.

Earlier pargeting is generally incised, most often in what is termed 'combed-work' or 'stick-work', after the equipment used to make the design. Relief ornamentation followed, at first in simple designs often in borders and using geometrical motifs. This decoration gradually expanded into floral, animal and heraldic motifs and then complete scenes or all-over patterns. As the atmosphere dirtied the plaster it was lime-washed or colour-washed at intervals so the design gradually became blurred. Eventually, in all too many instances, the cumulative weight of the layers of lime-wash became too great and the plaster broke away and required renewal.

PARQUET, PARQUETRY *Parquet* is a floor-covering of thin pieces of polished hardwood laid in patterns, most commonly herringbone.

Parquetry is, like marquetry, a veneer comprising different-coloured woods inserted into it to form a design but, whereas marquetry may display varied types of patterns, parquetry is expressed in geometrical forms. Such a veneer may be used for flooring, panelling or furniture.

PAVILION It may take several forms:

1. A projecting part of a façade of a building, usually at the ends or the centre.
2. The terminating blocks attached by side wings to the central mass of a building.
3. A separate, small structure of ornamental type to be found in a garden or park.

PARGETING
Pargeting at Providence House, Chester, built 1652

PAXTON, SIR JOSEPH (1803–65) Son of a Bedfordshire farmer, Paxton worked in gardens from boyhood. In 1826 he was appointed by the Duke of Devonshire to superintend the gardens at *Chatsworth*. Here he gained great experience in building glasshouses, at first the traditional rectangular type with wooden framing, but later he experimented with curved glass panels, iron supporting columns and a novel roofing structure. His best known work at Chatsworth was his *Great Conservatory* begun in 1836 (now demolished). Paxton went on to landscape gardening design, fountain and waterway engineering and

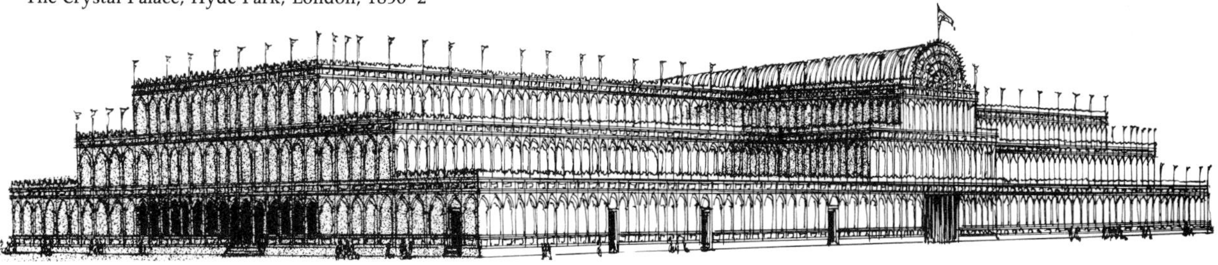

PAXTON, SIR JOSEPH
The Crystal Palace, Hyde Park, London, 1850–2

town planning, and played a limited part in railway and country house projects, for example *Mentmore Towers*.

The building with which Paxton's name is indissolubly linked is the great glass-and-iron structure erected in Hyde Park to house the Great Exhibition of 1851 and aptly dubbed (in *Punch*) the *Crystal Palace*. A competition was held in 1850 for this structure and a number of outstanding architects and engineers submitted designs. Paxton's were not at first received favourably by the Committee so he published them in the *London News*. Public response was overwhelmingly in favour of his unusual and original concept and the Committee capitulated, not least because Paxton's was the only entry to fulfil the competition proviso that the winning design should be capable of being erected quickly then subsequently dismantled and re-erected elsewhere.

Paxton's Crystal Palace was a prefabricated glasshouse of vast dimensions: it was 1848ft long, 408ft wide and over 100ft high. It contained 3300 iron columns, 2150 girders, 24 miles of guttering, 600,000 cubic feet of timber and 900,000 square feet of glass. Hailed as a ferro-vitreous triumph, nevertheless its roof framework was largely of wood. The building was a landmark in construction for its day, for its size, speed of construction and most of all as the first prefabricated structure. Parts were standardized and made in quantity. They were assembled on the site.

In 1852 the Crystal Palace was dismantled and reassembled (with a number of different features) at Sydenham in south London. Here it remained until its spectacular conflagration in 1936 (see INDUSTRIALIZED BUILDING; IRON AND GLASS).

PEARSON, JOHN LOUGHBOROUGH

St Augustine's Church, Kilburn, London, 1870–80. Architect: J. L. Pearson

PEARSON, JOHN LOUGHBOROUGH (1817–97) Primarily a church architect building in thirteenth-century Franco-Gothic style, he also designed a few country houses. Pearson trained under Salvin and Hardwick (see SALVIN, ANTHONY; HARDWICK, PHILIP) then set up in practice on his own in 1843. Many of his commissions were for London churches some of which were severely damaged during the Second World War. Excellent surviving examples of his work include *St Augustine, Kilburn* (1871–80), *St Michael, Croydon* (1880–5) and *St John, Upper Norwood* (1880–7). Characteristic of this work are his stone-ribbed vaults with brick infilling.

Pearson's last great work was *Truro Cathedral* in Cornwall, begun in 1880. Finely built in greyish granite it represents the swansong of the late but impressive Gothic Revival in thirteenth-century French medieval manner. The cathedral was consecrated in 1887 and completed in 1903 by Pearson's son after his father's death. The plan is traditional, with aisled nave, choir and transepts, and circular baptistery. The spired western and central towers rise to dominate the centre of the town.

PEDESTAL A base to support a statue, a column or a decorative feature such as an urn. In classical architecture a pedestal is divided into three parts: at the top is the cornice (see CORNICE), below this the dado (see DADO), and, at the base, the *plinth* (see CLASSICAL ARCHITECTURE; CLASSICAL ORDER).

PEDESTAL
Pedestal and urn in the dining-room at Saltram House, Devon, 1779–80. Architect: Robert Adam

Open pediment: Longleat House, Wiltshire, late seventeenth century (*left*)

Broken pediment: Pembroke College Chapel, Cambridge, seventeenth century (*right*)

Segmental pediment: Knutsford Church, Cheshire, 1744

Scrolled pediment: Uppark House, Sussex, 1688–9

PEDIMENT In classical architecture the triangular, low-pitched gable above the entablature which completes the end of the sloping roof (see CLASSICAL ARCHITECTURE; CLASSICAL ORDER; TYMPANUM).

Pediments of differing forms are also used as decorative features above doors, niches and windows. In Renaissance, Mannerist and Baroque work these may be broken, open, segmental or scrolled (see BAROQUE ARCHITECTURE; MANNERISM; RENAISSANCE ARCHITECTURE). The term *broken* is generally applied where the horizontal base moulding is incomplete in the centre. An *open* design is where the apex of the triangle is absent. The *segmental* pediment has curved top members in the form of a segmental pediment or one where the scrolls curve inwards from concavely curved mouldings.

CLASSICAL PEDIMENT
Greek temple pediment, Temple of Hera, Paestum, Italy, *c.* 460 BC

PELE (PEEL) TOWER A small, defensive structure built chiefly in the border areas between England and Scotland during the late Middle Ages. Cattle could be housed on the lower floor while the entrance for human habitation was often on the first floor with access by ladder or retractable stairway.

PEMBROKE, EARL OF (1693–1751) Like Lord Burlington (see BURLINGTON, EARL OF), an amateur architect and aristocratic patron of the English Palladian school during the first half of the eighteenth century (see MORRIS, ROGER).

PENDANT Something which is suspended. In architecture the term is applied particularly to a boss which depends, as in a late medieval stone-vaulted or timber-trussed roof. Pendant ribbed ceilings were characteristic of Elizabethan interiors (see BOSS; CEILING; ELIZABETHAN ARCHITECTURE; TIMBER-TRUSSED ROOF; VAULTING).

PENNETHORNE, SIR JAMES
Museum of Mankind, Burlington Gardens, London. Architect: Sir James Pennethorne

PENNETHORNE, SIR JAMES (1801–71) Early Victorian architect and town planner with a large practice, much of it in government work. Pennethorne began his training in Nash's office in 1820 (see NASH, JOHN) and in 1825–35 was the architect's chief assistant, building among other work two of the 'villages' in Regent's Park.

By 1850 Pennethorne had become an important government architect and was designing a number of buildings in London mainly in classical style. In 1852 he added the west wing to *Somerset House*, respectfully echoing Chambers's work (see CHAMBERS, SIR WILLIAM). He built the *Stationery Office* (Westminster) in 1847 and, in the same period, the *Public Record Office* in Chancery Lane (begun 1851), this time in chastened Gothic dress; on the interior he made extensive use of iron as a structural and decorative material. His last commission (1866) was the elaborately ornamented edifice in Burlington Gardens, built for *London University* but now housing the Museum of Mankind. Pennethorne laid out a number of London's well-known thoroughfares: New Oxford Street, New Coventry Street, Cranbourn Street, for example, as well as developing districts in Lambeth, Hackney and Kennington.

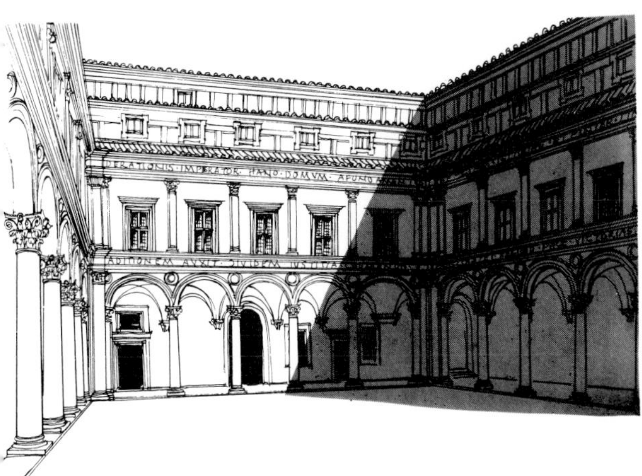

PERISTYLE A row of columns surrounding a temple, court or cloister; also the space so enclosed, to be seen in a classical temple, stoa and domestic architecture then revived in Renaissance palace design (see RENAISSANCE ARCHITECTURE; ROMAN DOMESTIC ARCHITECTURE; TEMPLE).

PEW A fixed wooden seat in a church. Medieval pews were generally finished at the aisle by *bench-ends* which were often capped by finials known as *poppy-heads*; this carved decoration might be of foliage, animals or human figures. *Box pews* were of later date. They were enclosed wooden compartments with doors hinged to open.

PIAZZA An open space, generally square or rectangular, surrounded by buildings. In seventeenth- and eighteenth-century England the term was sometimes inaccurately applied to an arcaded covered way.

PICTURESQUE ARCHITECTURE The 'picturesque' was a concept of the later eighteenth century largely involving landscaping of a romantic and dramatic nature which might include hills and crags, streams and waterfalls and dark woodlands. The term when applied to architecture was associated with small rustic or castellar, asymmetrical buildings in such romantic settings. In the early years of the nineteenth century certain architects (see NASH, JOHN) and landscape gardeners (see REPTON, HUMPHRY) for a while specialized in the picturesque.

PIER, PILLAR A pier is a solid brick or masonry support; it is not a column or pilaster (see COLUMN; PILASTER) in that it does not carry the characteristic capital and base of a classical order (see CLASSICAL ORDER). A pier

PERISTYLE
Ducal Palace, Urbino, Italy. Architect: Laurana, 1465–9

Palace of Emperor Charles V, Alhambra, Granada, Spain. Architect: Pedro Machuca, 1526–50

Nave box pews in the Church of Walpole St Peter, Norfolk, *c.* 1630

Piers in Mainz Cathedral, Germany, 1085–1239

Piers and compound piers in the nave, Lund Cathedral, Sweden, from c. 1140

Compound piers in the nave,
Abbey Church of Fontrevrault, France, 1104–1150

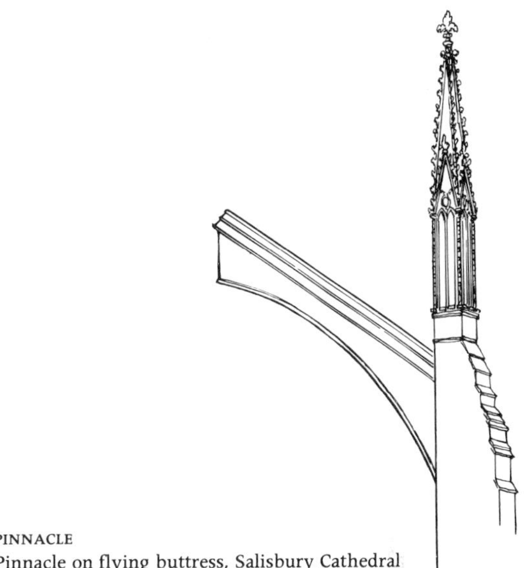

PINNACLE
Pinnacle on flying buttress, Salisbury Cathedral

is generally square in section and may support a lintel or thrust of an arch. The arch which springs from such a pier is called a *pier arch*.

The solid wall between doors and windows in a building is a pier or *pier wall*; a mirror hanging on such a wall is a *pier glass* and a table similarly placed is a *pier table*.

In Romanesque and Gothic architecture a pier (also in this context often called a *pillar*) of square or multi-sided section encircled by detached or attached shafts is referred to as a *compound* or *clustered pier* (see COLUMN). A half-pier, carrying one end of an arch and bonded into a wall, is known as a *respond*.

PILASTER A column of low projection and rectangular form projecting from a wall and evidencing the same characteristics of the relevant classical order (see CLASSICAL ORDER; COLUMN).

PINNACLE A small, slender spire, often crocketed (see CROCKET) acting as a termination to a buttress or parapet.

PIRANESI, GIOVANNI BATTISTA (1720–78) A Venetian architect and engineer who built little but exercised a tremendous influence upon European neo-classical architecture in his time through his illustrations and publications. In 1740 Piranesi visited Rome and was so impressed by the dramatic appearance of the classical ruins that he decided to embark on recording the city's great monuments in his etchings. He soon settled in Rome and, over many years, made his dramatic, imaginative reconstructions of the grandeur of ancient Rome, stressing powerfully in scenes of strongly contrasted light and shade the immense scale of the buildings. He published his *Le Antichità di Roma* in four volumes which was a record of his archaeological excavations and reconstructions and his *Vedute di Roma*, a collection of views of ancient and modern Rome. Towards the end of his life he published *Vedute di Paestum* which were his views of the Greek temples in southern Italy.

Piranesi was a dedicated and passionate 'Roman' in the contempory 'battle of the styles', refusing to accept the originality and beauty of Greek architecture in the classical world. His controversial *Della Magnificenza ed Architettura de' Romani* (1761) is a defence of his views on the total supremacy of Roman classicism.

Like Robert Adam (see ADAM, ROBERT) to whom he dedicated one of his publications, Piranesi did not believe that the Romans had abided by rigid rules in their classical design and in his *Parere sull'Architettura* (1765) recommended contemporary architects to use the Roman originals as models for a new interpretation of the classical style, not as models to copy.

PISCINA In a church or chapel a stone basin (with a drain) set into a niche or recess in a wall near and south of the altar. The purpose of the basin is for washing the vessels used in Mass or Communion. In some churches the piscina is free-standing on a pillar and is then termed a *pillar piscina*.

PLASTERWORK During the Middle Ages plaster, for both exterior and interior wall covering, was made from lime, sand and water mixed with various other ingredients which, it had been empirically discovered, would help to bind the mixture and prevent it cracking. Such ingredients included animal hair, dung and blood, feathers, straw and hay.

PLASTERWORK
Plaster frieze, Levens Hall, Cumbria. Elizabethan

The best-quality plaster available, introduced into England about 1255–60, was *plaster of Paris*. This was made by burning gypsum (calcium sulphate) and mixing with water to produce a much finer, harder plaster. In England it was called plaster of Paris because in France at that time the chief source of gypsum was in the Montmartre area of Paris. The use of this imported material was reserved for fine finishes in important buildings because of its higher cost but it became more readily available when gypsum deposits in England were discovered and worked. These were primarily in the valleys of the rivers Trent and Nidd and on the Isle of Purbeck. On some of these sites the material (also known as 'English alabaster') was mined for alabaster to be used in interior decorative work (see ALABASTER) and the smaller pieces were burnt to make plaster.

The ornate and decorative plaster ceilings and walls of the sixteenth-, seventeenth- and eighteenth-century buildings were derived from the Renaissance plasterwork initiated in fifteenth-century Italy, where Italian craftsmen experimented with a type of plaster which had been used by the Romans. This was malleable and fine, yet set slowly (giving time to work the design); it was very hard. They called it *stucco duro*. It contained lime and some gypsum but also powdered marble. Craftsmen in Elizabethan England (see ELIZABETHAN ARCHITECTURE) adopted both stucco and Renaissance forms of decoration and incorporated empirically a variety of extra ingredients, differing from area to area but including, for example, milk, eggs, ale and beeswax.

Plaster ceiling detail, Hatchlands, Surrey, 1759–62. Architect: Robert Adam.

During the eighteenth century, when decorative plasterwork became more delicate and complex, a number of patent stucco compositions were marketed which, it was claimed by their makers, were easier to work and would be finer and harder. For instance, Mr David Wark patented one in 1765 and M. Liardet, a Swiss clergyman, another in 1773. The firm of Adam Bros. purchased both of these patents and obtained an Act of Parliament in 1776 authorizing them to be sole makers and vendors of the material. They called it 'Adam's new invented patent stucco' (see ADAM, ROBERT).

Improvements were also being made to stucco to stand up to exterior use. John Nash (see NASH, JOHN), for example, developed a material made from sand, brick-dust, powdered limestone and lead oxide and used it to face buildings in imitation of stone. Later, cement was added to plaster for exterior work and, by 1840, various patent gypsum plasters were being produced, Keene's Cement for instance.

Finally, for interior needs, *plasterboard* began to replace plaster facing for walls and ceilings. This first appeared as a result of a lack of plasterers immediately after the First World War. Panels were manufactured which consisted of a layer of gypsum plaster sandwiched between sheets of strong paper. With the return of the plasterers the use of plasterboard declined but was revived with the even more urgent needs after the Second World War. By then, when its use had become widescale, the product had been greatly improved and could be applied directly to both brick and concrete surfaces. The joins could now be almost invisible, and a backing of aluminium foil was added to improve thermal insulation (see BUILDING MATERIALS; CEILING; PARGETING).

PLAYFAIR, WILLIAM HENRY (1790–1857) The son of the Scottish architect *James Playfair*, designer of the neo-classical *Cairness House* in Aberdeenshire (1791). W. H. Playfair was a leading figure in creating the 'Athens of the North', the Greek Revival later stages of *Edinburgh*'s New Town which had been envisaged and begun by Robert Adam (see ADAM, ROBERT and HAMILTON, WILLIAM). In 1817 Playfair was asked to complete Adam's unfinished University buildings. He then went on to design Edinburgh's largest Grecian structures: the *Royal Scottish*

PLAYFAIR, WILLIAM HENRY
Edinburgh viewed from the top of the Scott Monument.
A Church of Tolbooth St John B Outlook Tower C New College (W. H. Playfair) D Castle E National Gallery of Scotland (W. H. Playfair) F Royal Scottish Academy (W. H. Playfair) G St Cuthbert's Church H St George's Church I Princes Street in Charlotte Square (planned by Adam, built 1811–14 by Robert Reid to different design)

Academy (1823–36) and, behind it, the later *National Gallery for Scotland* (1850–7). Set at the foot of the Mound, below the castle and the gardens, these are two very impressive Doric monuments.

Playfair also contributed to the buildings on *Calton Hill*, the *Observatory* and some Grecian monuments one of which was based upon the Athenian Choragic Monument to Lysicrates. Though much of his work was in the Greek vein, Playfair also designed in neo-Gothic (the Edinburgh *New College*, 1846–50) and in neo-Renaissance (the Edinburgh *Donaldson's Hospital*, 1842–54).

PODIUM A continuous base or pedestal to a building. A *stylobate* acts as a continuous base to a row of columns (colonnade). In classical temple design the stylobate is the platform on top of the steps which constitute the *crepidoma* (see CLASSICAL ARCHITECTURE; TEMPLE).

POLYCHROMY The use of different colours in a variety of materials to give a decorative effect, both internally and externally, to buildings.

PORCH, PORTAL, PORTE-COCHÈRE, PORTICO A *porch* is a covered entrance to a building and may be found in all architectural styles. In many churches and houses the porch is extended upwards to provide a room over the entrance opening. Some late medieval and Elizabethan houses contain interior porches where one room leads to another. These are decorative but also functional in that the closed doorway keeps out the draughts.

A *portal* is a more elaborate imposing entrance and a *porte-cochère* is one which is wide enough to permit the passage of wheeled vehicles. If the entrance has a covering in the form of a classical colonnade (see CLASSICAL ARCHITECTURE; COLONNADE) it is termed a *portico*. Such porticos take different forms; some are based on the classical temple design with a superimposed pediment (see TEMPLE), others may be semicircular.

PORTCULLIS A defensive mechanism in fortified buildings constructed in an entrance gateway. It consists of a heavy grating of iron, or wood reinforced by iron, which is fitted into grooves in the side of an entrance to slide up and down as required (see BARBICAN; CASTLE; GATEHOUSE).

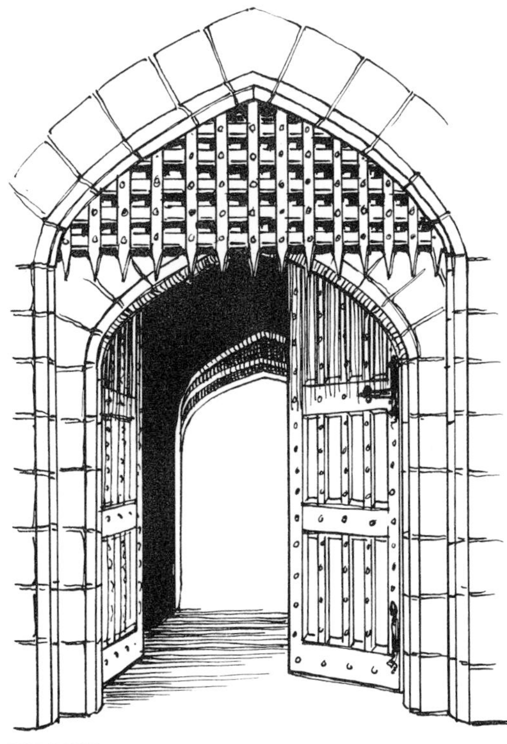

PORTCULLIS
Raised portcullis at Bodiam Castle, Sussex

Norman porch and staircase, Canterbury Cathedral, *c.* 1150–65

Porch with room above, Studley Priory, Oxfordshire, late Elizabethan

Portico, south front of Lyme Park, Cheshire, 1720–6. Architect: Giacomo Leoni

Porch, Belgrave Square, London, 1825. Architect: George Basevi

Porte-cochère at City Hall, Cardiff Civic Centre, 1897–1906. Architects: Lanchester, Stewart and Rickards

South porch, Gloucester Cathedral, *c.* 1420

Portico, St Paul's Church, Deptford, London, 1730. Architect: Thomas Archer

POSTERN A small, private side or rear entrance to a palace, monastery, castle or town. The word *sallyport* is also often used to mean a postern gate. This derives from a passageway entrance for troops to use in a fortified building when about to make a 'sally'. In architecture 'sallyport' generally refers to the entrance to an underground passageway which leads from one part of a palace, castle or town to another. The postern gate survives at the Citadal of *Mycenae* (*c.* 1350 BC); the gateway is built into the fortified wall and the passageway leads to a secret cistern outside the walls.

POWELL and MOYA (Sir Philip Powell, b. 1921; John Hidalgo Moya, b. 1926) Two young architects who formed a partnership in 1946 and became known when they won the competition for the *Pimlico* housing estate on the Thames embankment built 1948–62 and called *Churchill Gardens*. The estate, which won the Royal Institute of British Architects' London Bronze Medal, is of good-quality building and attractively laid out. The heating system which was originally installed was unusual in that the exhaust heat from Battersea Power Station opposite on the other side of the river was used to supply the estate of 1600 dwellings.

The simple directness of style and quality of building produced by this partnership has continued since the 1940s. In 1955 they designed new buildings for the *Mayfield Comprehensive School for Girls* at *Putney* in south-west London where the original grammar school was being expanded. There followed the *Festival Theatre* at *Chichester* (1962), hospitals in Slough, Swindon and High Wycombe and university extension work at *Oxford* and *Cambridge* (Brasenose College 1961, Christ Church 1967; and the new Wolfson College 1974 at Oxford and St John's College, Cambridge 1966). Of particular interest is London's first (since the 1930s) great purpose-built and highly successful museum, the *Museum of London* (1976).

PRATT, SIR ROGER (1620–85) Having received his education at Magdalen College, Oxford, Pratt then studied law at the Inner Temple. In 1643 he began several years of travel and study in the Low Countries, France and Italy, having been left a private income on his father's death in 1640. Pratt was a friend of Sir John Evelyn whom he met in Rome. He was also a close follower of the work of Inigo Jones (see JONES, INIGO). He paid careful attention to his architectural studies in Europe and made copious notes and drawings.

After his return to England in 1649 Pratt soon began work on re-designing the burnt-out house at Coleshill, Berkshire for his cousin Sir George Pratt. It appears that the elderly Inigo Jones visited Coleshill and gave advice but the house was very much Pratt's own work. He was a gentleman amateur architect but a very important contributor to English architectural history. At Coleshill and in his other houses he introduced a pure Renaissance classical style of building, simple and symmetrical and in the tradition of Palladio and Jones (see PALLADIAN ARCHITECTURE).

Coleshill House, built 1650–62, was typical of his work. It was built on rectangular plan and consisted of a half-basement, two floors and an attic storey with dormers. Tall classical chimney-stacks and a central lantern broke the roofline. The exterior was astylar (see ASTYLAR), the horizontal line emphasized by string course, cornice and

PRATT, SIR ROGER
Coleshill House, Berkshire, 1650–62. Architect: Sir Roger Pratt

Belton House, Lincolnshire, 1684–6. Mason-contractor: William Stanton

balustrade. There was no pediment and no break in the wall surfaces. The house was divided by a central corridor with principal rooms on each side. The staircase was a notable, original design for its period. It dominated the two-storey hall with its great double-flights. The deeply recessed compartmented plaster ceiling was a model for its time. Sadly, Coleshill was gutted by fire in 1952 and then demolished.

During the 1660s Pratt built several houses but none has survived unaltered. Of these *Kingston Lacy* in Dorset (1663–5) was altered by Barry in the 1830s (see BARRY, SIR CHARLES), and *Horseheath* in Cambridgeshire (1663–5) was demolished in 1777. Of considerable importance as a prototype was his *Clarendon House, Piccadilly* (1664–7) which unfortunately was demolished after only a few years in 1683. It was larger than Coleshill, having projecting wings and a central pediment; it was widely imitated until the rise of the Palladian school, in the early eighteenth century; William Stanton's *Belton House* in Lincolnshire (1684–6) is a notable instance of this.

In 1663 Pratt was appointed to be a member of the commission set up to consider the restoration of St Paul's Cathedral in London. When, in 1666, the Great Fire of London settled this problem, he was also one of the Commissioners appointed by Charles II to supervise the rebuilding of the City. In 1668 he was knighted for his work in this respect but soon afterwards retired from the architectural scene to his estate at *Ryston* in Norfolk where he took up life again as a country gentleman and rebuilt his house there in 1669–72.

PROPYLAEUM The entrance structure—gateway, porch or vestibule—to an (especially a sacred) enclosure. A famous example in ancient Greek architecture is the propylaeum on the *Acropolis* hill in Athens leading to the temple area.

PUGIN, AUGUSTUS WELBY NORTHMORE (1815–52) Son of the French artist and draughtsman *Auguste Charles Pugin* (1762–1832) who came to England in 1793, a refugee from France, and became chief draughtsman for Nash (see NASH, JOHN). The elder Pugin (helped later by his son) made a great number of superbly detailed drawings for a wide range of architectural publications, mainly on Gothic architecture and decoration: these were the first important works which provided the information on measurement and detail for designers and builders to work in pure Gothic decorative style. Most influential of these publications were *Specimens of Gothic Architecture* (2 vols. 1821–3), *Illustrations of the Public Buildings of London* (2 vols. 1825–8), *Examples of Gothic Architecture* (2 vols. 1828–31), *Gothic Ornament from Ancient Buildings in England and France* (1831).

A. W. N. Pugin gained a wide knowledge and great practice from helping his father and making drawings himself. Throughout his life he continued to produce hundreds of sketches and detailed finished drawings in ink and wash, both on-the-spot studies of actual buildings and original designs of his own buildings for architecture, furnishing, interior decoration and all kinds of detail work in the Gothic tradition. While still in his teens Pugin was employed to design furniture for Windsor Castle and for the theatre. Soon he was operating his own business, designing and making furniture and architectural details in various materials.

In 1834 Pugin was converted to Roman Catholicism which he embraced with passionate fervour. With equal fervour he became devoted to expressing his feeling in a suitable architectural and decorative mode—in Pugin's view, the style of the medieval period *c.* 1280–1340 or, as it was termed in the nineteenth century, 'Second Pointed Style'. He regarded the Middle Ages as the greatest era in human history, a time when men were inspired to live and work for the glory of God and when buildings such as the great cathedrals were erected in this spirit. He abhorred Renaissance architecture and even more vigorously the eighteenth- and early nineteenth-century Gothic work of such architects as Wyatt (see WYATT, JAMES). He complained that not only was their work not authentic in style but that they employed sham materials as in, for example, using plaster to repair stone vaults or iron as a supporting medium.

To prove his theories Pugin spent several years touring the country making beautiful drawings of medieval and Renaissance and later buildings. He then published his famous book (1836) which he called *Contrasts; or a Parallel between the Noble edifices of the Fourteenth and Fifteenth Centuries and similar Buildings of the present day. Showing the Decay of Taste*. The book was finely illustrated and compared the buildings of the great medieval past with those of later ages. It was a passionate plea for the purity of the medieval Catholic spirit but Pugin's choice of pairs of buildings to contrast was often highly prejudiced, the medieval example being of high quality and the more recent one of inferior standard.

'Contrasts' brought him fame and notoriety. He followed it with other books evidencing more balanced and cogent arguments and ones which illustrated his deep understanding of Gothic architecture, its structure, design and decoration. His work showed a comprehension greater than anyone else had achieved since the end of the Middle Ages. His books exerted a lasting and wide-ranging influence on the Gothic architecture designed and built throughout the whole Victorian period, greater than almost any other architect's contribution at this time and certainly greater than Pugin's own architectural work, commissions which often suffered from lack of adequate financing. Most influential of Pugin's publications were *The True Principles of Pointed or Christian Architecture* (1841), *The Present State of Ecclesiastical Architecture* (1843) and *Glossary of Ecclesiastical Ornament* (1844).

Pugin designed a number of churches and was

St Marie's Church, Derby, 1838–9

St Giles's Church, Cheadle, 1841–6

Oriel window and decorative detail, Palace of Westminster, London. Architect: Sir Charles Barry

St Giles's Church, Cheadle

Scarisbrick Hall, Lancashire, 1837–67

Carlton Towers, Yorkshire. Remodelled by Edward Welby Pugin, 1873–5

responsible for enlarging and altering several monastic and collegiate building groups. In all of these he put into practice his knowledge and understanding of Gothic structure and he was especially interested in the detail of furnishings and decoration in wood, metal, painting and glass. Some of his work has been later altered or damaged as at *Southwark Cathedral* but a quantity remains. The exteriors are correct and austere, the interiors richly and darkly Byzantine and often polychromatic. Notable examples include: the *Roman Catholic Cathedral* (St Chad) of *Birmingham* (1839–41) and the churches of *St Marie, Derby* (1838), *St Giles, Cheadle,* Staffordshire (1841–6), *St Augustine, Ramsgate* (1846), *St Marie, Uttoxeter* (1839) and *St Oswald, Liverpool* (1840–2).

His work survives at a number of houses where he altered or re-designed part of the building as, for example, at *Chirk Castle* in Clwyd where he worked in the interior 1845–7. The chief example is *Scarisbrick Hall,* Lancashire (1837–67), a large Gothic house with a tall, slender corner tower. The house displays some fine Gothic detail and carved ornament. It was completed after the architect's death.

The most important commission with which Pugin was involved was the building of the new *Palace of Westminster* (begun 1840) for which Barry had won the competition (see BARRY, SIR CHARLES). Pugin made the designs and supervised the work for all the interior wall decoration, the decorative art, the stained glass, the fittings, furniture, carpets and all ornament. He made superb working drawings for all the exterior ornament also including sculpture and carved mouldings. Despite damage during the Second World War, much of Pugin's work survives to show his perfectionism and the scholarly quality of his professional design and craftsmanship. The Palace of Westminster is Pugin's greatest memorial. The acrimonious dispute over the relative contribution to the building of Barry or Pugin eventually petered out but much of the work survives.

Pugin died at the early age of 40, insane in a private asylum in Ramsgate. But, even in 1851, the previous year, he was still tirelessly working at the Palace of Westminster and arranging the Medieval Court for the Great Exhibition. He undertook this work with his usual enthusiasm while making clear his scorn for the actual building, 'the greenhouse' as he called it (see INDUSTRIALIZED BUILDING; IRON AND GLASS; PAXTON, SIR JOSEPH).

After 1852 Pugin's son *Edward Welby Pugin* (1834–75) continued his father's work and practice completing outstanding commissions. One of his chief works was the great house of *Carlton Towers*, the Yorkshire home of the Dukes of Norfolk, where in 1873–5 Pugin re-cased the Jacobean house in Gothic dress and enlarged the building though much of the design—the great hall, staircase and chapel—was never built.

Much of Edward Pugin's capital and energies was spent in the costly litigation by which he sought to prove that his father's contribution to the Palace of Westminster was greater than that of Barry. The pointless struggle ruined his career and probably hastened his early death.

PULPIT A raised structure from which a preacher in church or chapel addresses the congregation and from where he delivers his sermon. Known as the *ambo* in early Christian churches, the upper part of the pulpit is usually reached by means of a flight of steps; it may be free-standing or attached to a nave wall or pier. Many pulpits are elaborately carved and/or inlaid and are covered by a decorative canopy or tester. Some pulpits are sited against an exterior church wall for open air preaching to a larger audience.

Exterior pulpit: Prato Cathedral, Italy. By Donatello and Michelozzo, 1434–8

PULPITUM Like a rood screen (see CHURCH DESIGN AND STRUCTURE), but a screen supporting a gallery (which may house the organ) and sited to divide the nave of a church from the chancel.

A pulpitum, constructed of stone and decoratively carved, is usually to be found in a cathedral or major church. It is often canopied, containing statues of saints and apostles.

PULVIN A convexly rounded cushion-like form. The term *pulvin* is used as an alternative to 'dosseret' in Byzantine architecture (see DOSSERET). A *pulvinated frieze* is one which has a convexly curved section.

QUADRANGLE A square or rectangular courtyard surrounded by buildings often designed as one architectural scheme; a layout commonly found in large medieval houses and in university colleges and schools.

QUADRIGA A sculptured group surmounting a building or monument which is in the form of a chariot drawn by four horses abreast. The quadriga on top of the Constitution Hill Arch at Hyde Park Corner in London is a noted landmark of the capital city. The arch was designed by *Decimus Burton* (1825–8) but the present-day quadriga by *Adrian Jones* was not set in place until 1912 (see BURTON, DECIMUS; TRIUMPHAL ARCH).

QUIRK A sharply 'V'-shaped moulding usually set between a convex moulding and a fillet.

QUOIN From the French *coin* (='corner' or 'angle'), the external angle of a building. *Quoins* or *quoin stones* are the dressed stones forming the angle; these are generally laid alternately one large and one small to each face and often rusticated (see MASONRY). In Saxon architecture *long-and-short work* refers to quoins laid so that long vertical slabs alternate with long horizontal ones (see SAXON ARCHITECTURE).

Quoin
A Long-and-short-work quoins at Earl's Barton Church, Northamptonshire
B Quoins at St Catharine's College Chapel, Cambridge, 1704

RAILWAY ARCHITECTURE The nineteenth century was the age of the great engineers, the railways and the development of ferro-vitreous construction (see IRON AND GLASS): all three were closely linked and interdependent. Early railway stations were unpretentious (*Crown Street, Liverpool*, 1830, for instance) and were often just open sheds. Soon, especially at the great termini, the railways needed buildings which involved them in architecture. Much of this construction was in iron: railings, footbridges, brackets, trusses, cantilevers. Classical and Gothic features were manufactured in this material only, due its strength, the columns became more attenuated. Most railway stations were built under the direction of a principal architect and a principal engineer. The architect expressed his classical or Gothic architectural ideas in iron, then built a stone or brick façade in his chosen style, a front which often had no stylistic connection with the functional parts of the station behind it. The engineer looked ahead to develop the newer material into different forms and, often, architect and engineer were not in tune with one another's ideas.

Many great stations were built in the half-century between 1835 and 1885 but a large proportion of these have been demolished or rebuilt. Even the later ones, preserved until the 1960s, are in a number of instances now under threat as their functional rôle declines or is changing. In London, the *Euston Arch*, which fronted Euston station, was lost in 1961 (see HARDWICK, PHILIP) and the 1844 structure of *London Bridge Station* by Henry Roberts and George Smith has long been replaced. Also lost or considerably altered were *Brighton* (David Mocatta, 1841), *Dover* (Lewis Cubitt, 1843–4), *Carlisle* (Sir William Tite, 1848) and *Lime Street, Liverpool* (John Franklin, 1839). The architect/engineer partnership of *Francis Thompson* and *Robert Stephenson* was responsible for several fine stations and bridges, notably the *Trijunct Station* at *Derby* (1839–41 and now demolished) but also *Chester Station* (1847–8) which fared better.

Of the great London termini built in the second half of the century three survive in a not-too-altered condition: St Pancras, Paddington and King's Cross. The first two of these retain the large hotel which it was railway tradition at this time to build in front of the engineering sheds. At *Paddington* the hotel on the south façade is an earlier building by *Philip Hardwick*. The engineer for the station (as for the Great Western Railway) was *Isambard Kingdom Brunel* (1806–59) and the architects *Matthew Digby Wyatt* and *Owen Jones* (see WYATT, JAMES). The great parallel sheds remain (a fourth one added later), the roofs of glass and wrought iron supported on cast-iron columns.

The hotel fronting *St Pancras Station* in the Euston Road has long been a controversial building but disapproval and disdain have gradually given way to admiration. Scott (see SCOTT, SIR GEORGE GILBERT) won the competition to build the hotel two years after *R. M. Ordish* and *W. H. Barlow* had begun work on the shed of the new terminus for the Midland Railway. Built at the peak of the railway construction boom of the 1860s, the station was a magnificent achievement, its shed nearly 700ft long and, for a long time at 245ft in width, the greatest span in the world. The High Victorian Gothic hotel fronting is a famous London landmark. Constructed in characteristic polychrome manner, using red brick, granite in two colours and contrasting stonework, the long façade is broken by towers and turrets, chimney-stacks and gables.

King's Cross Station is quite different. Designed and built by the *Cubitt* brothers, *Lewis* and *Joseph* (1850–1), the striking façade, with its two semicircular arches each 70ft wide, is directly related to the vast arched roofs of the halls behind. Though the original roofs, built of laminated wood, have now been replaced by steel, the appearance of this practical, no-frills construction has been comparatively little altered; only the forecourt additions detract from the massive simplicity of the design (see CUBITT, THOMAS).

The twentieth-century contribution to railway architecture in London was largely in the building of new stations for the expanding network of underground lines for the capital. This work was initiated in the 1920s by Frank

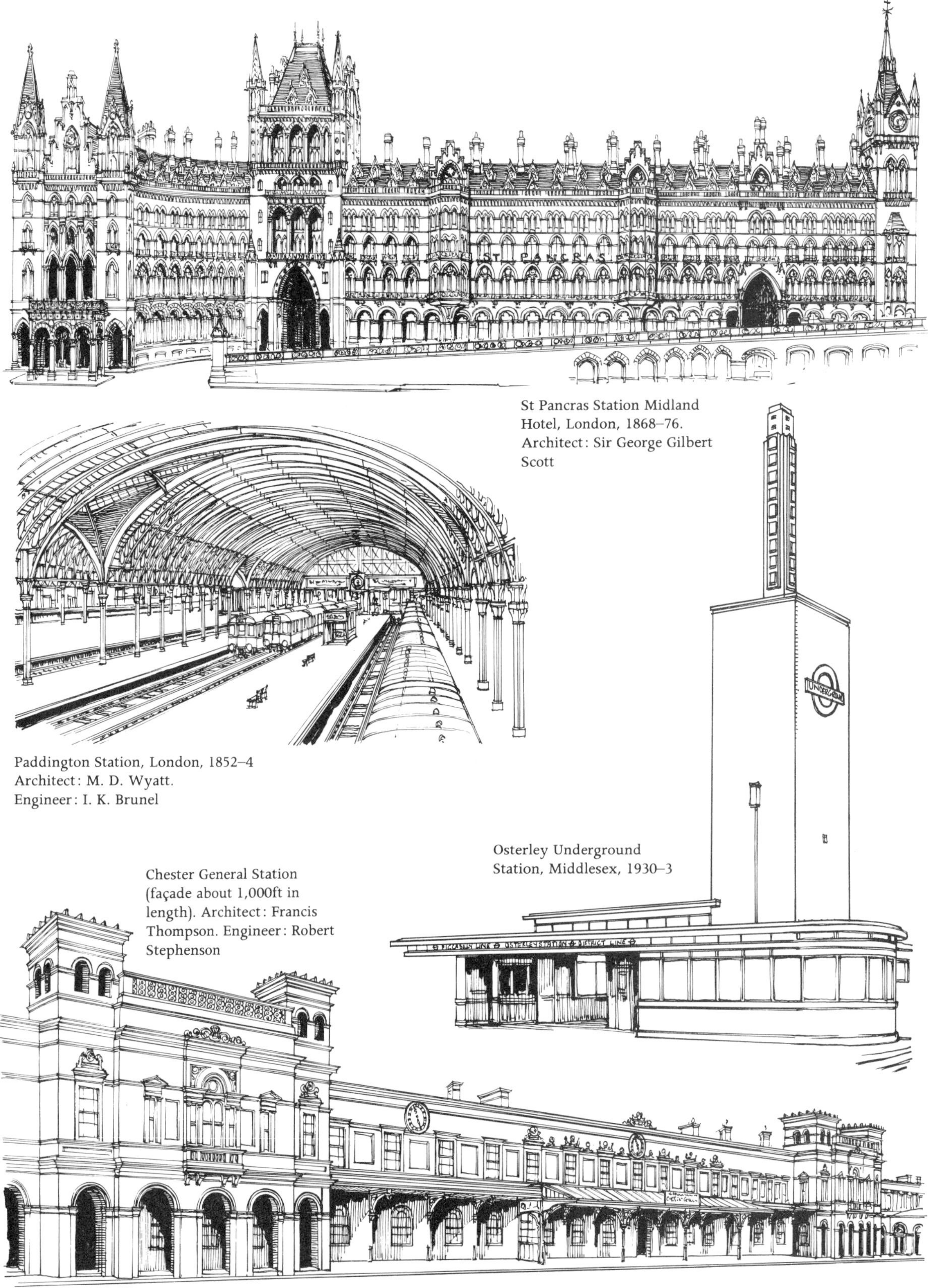

St Pancras Station Midland Hotel, London, 1868–76. Architect: Sir George Gilbert Scott

Paddington Station, London, 1852–4
Architect: M. D. Wyatt.
Engineer: I. K. Brunel

Osterley Underground Station, Middlesex, 1930–3

Chester General Station (façade about 1,000ft in length). Architect: Francis Thompson. Engineer: Robert Stephenson

RAILWAY ARCHITECTURE
King's Cross Station, London. Architects: Lewis and Joseph Cubitt, 1852

Arnos Grove Underground Station, London, 1932

Pick, head of the London Passenger Transport Board and carried out under the supervision of Charles Holden (see HOLDEN, SIR CHARLES). He designed over 30 stations, notably for the Northern and Piccadilly lines. Of these, the simple forms in brick and concrete of the Piccadilly Line Underground Stations at *Arnos Grove, Sudbury Town, Park Royal* and *Osterley* (1930–3) are characteristic yet varied.

RAINWATER HEAD A squarish container of metal, usually lead or iron, ornamentally enriched, which surmounts the upper end of a rainwater pipe in order to collect the water from roofing gutters and convey it into a down-pipe.

RAMPART A defensive wall of stone, brick or earth surrounding a town or castle (see CASTLE).

REBATE, RABBET A channelled groove cut along the edge or face of a structure or piece of furniture so that another part may be fitted into it: seen particularly in door and window construction.

REDMAN, HENRY (d. 1528) A master mason who worked at *Westminster Abbey* and other important buildings in the early sixteenth century. Redman became King's Master Mason at the Abbey in 1519 and, a little later, architect to Cardinal Wolsey at Hampton Court.

St John's College, Cambridge University. New Court, 1827–31, Gothic design. Architects: Thomas Rickman and Henry Hutchinson.

Ickworth House, Suffolk, 1796–1830, in the classical style. Architect: Francis Sandys

The Paragon, Blackheath, London, *c.* 1790, in the classical style

Lansdown Crescent, Bath. Architect: John Palmer, 1789–93. Terrace architecture in classical dress

Southgate Grove, Middlesex, 1797. Architect: John Nash

Classical porch at Grosvenor Crescent, London, 1825–6

Dining-room, *c.* 1795. Style of James Wyatt, neo-classical

Park Crescent, Regent's Park, London, begun 1812. Architect: John Nash. Classical design

St Mary's Church, Wyndham Place, London, 1823–4, in the classical style. Architect: Sir Robert Smirke

Seaside terrace house with bow windows, *c.* 1800

Moggerhanger House, Bedfordshire, 1806–11, in the classical style. Architect: Sir John Soane

All Saints' Church, Camden Town, London, 1822–4. Architects: W. and H. W. Inwood. Greek Revival design

REEDING A decorative form resembling fluting in reverse (see CLASSICAL ORDER; COLUMN) which comprises closely packed, parallel, convex mouldings.

REGENCY ARCHITECTURE Literally, architecture of the years of the Regency of George, Prince of Wales (later George IV), 1811–20. In the arts and architecture the term 'Regency' is in fact used to refer to a longer period, *c.* 1790–1830, which spanned the intermediate and transitional time between the end of Georgian Britain and the approach of Victorian.

It was in the 1790s that the pace of regurgitation of past architectural styles quickened and developed but in the years before 1830 the trend was still characterized by a light-hearted romantic approach. New sources of inspiration were experimented with and quickly abandoned in favour of something else: such sources might be neo-classicism, Greek revival, Chinese or Indian forms or literary handling of Gothic. Regency architects worked empirically, trying to create something of their own so the Regency version of a style was not a slavish copy of the original; it was an idea, a fresh conception. Because of this Regency architecture is interesting and of quality in its own right.

In all guises Regency work was usually sparingly decorated, and well proportioned and detailed. Typical are Nash's Regent's Park terraces, Wyatt's Gothic houses and Soane's Byzantine and Greek interiors of the Bank of England. For more detail on Regency design and buildings see BASEVI, GEORGE; BURTON, DECIMUS; HOLLAND, HENRY; INWOOD, HENRY WILLIAM; LEVERTON, THOMAS; NASH, JOHN; SMIRKE, SIR ROBERT; SOANE, SIR JOHN; WILKINS, WILLIAM; WYATT, JAMES.

RELIEVO Term of Italian origin meaning the projection in relief sculpture and ornament. *Basso-relievo* is low relief, *mezzo-relievo* of moderate projection, and in *alto-relievo* the work stands out in high relief.

RENAISSANCE ARCHITECTURE The French term *Renaissance*, used also in English, describes the revival (literally 'rebirth') of the classical culture of ancient Rome.

The Renaissance (*rinascimento* in Italian) began in fourteenth-century Italy where, first in the world of literature and then in the visual arts of sculpture and and painting, studies were being made of the ancient classical culture which seemed so apt to depict and express the new humanist philosophies which were beginning to replace the established theological doctrines current in the Middle Ages.

The movement came rather later in architecture where *Brunelleschi* in early-fifteenth-century Florence was the first architect of note to revive the classical style; and even this had more of Tuscan and Romanesque than of classical Rome (see ROMANESQUE ARCHITECTURE). The study from the early fifteenth century of the manuscripts of the Roman architect and engineer Vitruvius, who had lived in the first century BC (see VITRUVIUS), led to the later, purer Roman style under *Alberti*, then *Bramante*.

The High Renaissance in architecture, the great age of the Renaissance in Italy, was the sixteenth century (the *cinquecento*). There were many architects of notable stature and the quality of work produced in building and decoration was superb. It was a time when a high proportion of men of high intellect, talent and initiative became artists for it was in this field that there was opportunity for both financial reward and repute. *Donato d'Agnolo Lazzari* (1444–1514), usually called Bramante, was the leading architect of the High Renaissance in Rome. His work, though personal, was closely based on that of ancient Rome. His buildings possess great harmony of parts and proportion. His small chapel erected in the courtyard of *S. Pietro in Montorio* is a perfect example. This little building, based upon the form of a Roman circular temple (but domed in Italian Renaissance manner), has achieved a reputation quite disproportionate to its size. Called the '*tempietto*', it is built upon the supposed site of St Peter's crucifixion (see TOWN PLANNING).

Many palaces and villas were erected in sixteenth-century Italy in Renaissance style. Wealthy patrons would commission a town palace (on a limited site because of high land costs) and a more spacious suburban villa further out of town. The palace would have a High Renaissance street façade, the entrance doorway of which would lead, as it had done in ancient Roman palaces, into a classical, arcaded courtyard. *Antonio da Sangallo's Farnese Palace* in Rome is an elaborate example of this. Further north-east in the Veneto area *Michele Sanmichele, Il Sansovino* and *Andrea Palladio* were building their palaces and villas.

From Italy the Renaissance movement in art and architecture spread westwards in Europe but its character and decorative forms were gradually adulterated in its passage, each country imprinting upon the pure Italian form of Roman classicism the favoured taste of its own interpreters. In Italy itself in the second half of the sixteenth century the Renaissance movement was running out of steam and turning towards Mannerism and, later, Baroque (see BAROQUE ARCHITECTURE; MANNERISM).

In England, apart from isolated instances such as the early introduction, at the behest of Henry VIII, of Renaissance artistic forms by *Torrigiano* in his tomb for Henry VII in *Westminster Abbey* (1512–18), contacts between sixteenth-century Protestant England and Catholic Italy were limited and few of the Italian artists who came westward to France extended their travels further. When classicism was finally introduced into architecture in Britain in the time of Elizabeth I, it was based upon French and Flemish sources, the English builders taking their information from books of drawings and designs published in Flanders and France, augmented by the impressions of aristocratic travellers who returned

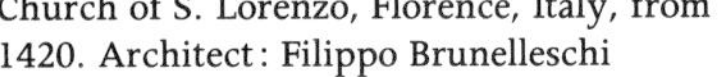
Church of S. Lorenzo, Florence, Italy, from 1420. Architect: Filippo Brunelleschi

Farnese Palace, Rome. Architects: before 1514 Antonio da Sangallo, after 1546 Michelangelo

Façade entablature of the church of S. Francesco, Rìmini, Italy, 1446. Architect: Leon Battista Alberti

Church of S. Maria Novella, Florence, Italy, 1470. Architect: Leon Battista Alberti

Palazzo Bevilacqua, Verona, Italy, *c.* 1530. Architect: Michele Sanmichele

Church of S. Pietro in Montorio, Rome. Chapel in courtyard called 'Il Tempietto', 1500–1502. Architect: Bramante

Centrally planned Church of S. Maria della Consolazione, Todi, Italy, *c.* 1520. Style of Bramante

Detail of vault of Pazzi Chapel, Florence, Italy, 1433. Architect: Filippo Brunelleschi

Detail of doorway of S. Andrea

Main doorway of Church of S. Andrea, Mantua, Italy, 1472. Architect: Leon Battista Alberti

Montacute House, Somerset, 1588–1601

Gate of Honour at Gonville and Caius, Cambridge University, 1573–5

Entrance porch of Audley End House, Essex, 1603–16

Longleat House, Wiltshire, 1550–80

The Queen's House, Greenwich. Architect: Inigo Jones, 1616–35

to commission their homes (see COUNTRY HOUSE AND MANSION; ELIZABETHAN ARCHITECTURE; JACOBEAN ARCHITECTURE). The purer Italianate Renaissance architectural form only came to England when it was introduced, early in the following century, by Inigo Jones. He based his work upon more than one Italian source, notably the remains of ancient Rome and the buildings of the High Renaissance in Rome and the Veneto (see JONES, INIGO; PALLADIAN ARCHITECTURE).

REPTON, HUMPHRY (1752–1818) Until almost the age of 40 Repton lived the life of a country gentleman but then, having lost a great deal of money in a business venture, he decided to take up landscape gardening (a term which he coined) so becoming a professional in an area where, up to then, he had taken an enthusiastic and knowledgeable interest.

Repton stepped naturally into the shoes of 'Capability' Brown (see BROWN, LANCELOT). He grasped the opportunity of the gap left by Brown's death (1783) and quickly established a reputation for layout of gardens and parks to suit a new generation of country house owners. He believed strongly in the need to stress the affinity between house and garden and to make the garden a foil to the architecture. For some years he worked in partnership with Nash (see NASH, JOHN), providing the landscape setting to the architect's buildings. After the dissolution of the partnership (1802), Repton's sons carried out the architectural role for him. Repton broke with Brown's tradition in the design of the area immediately surrounding a house where he (Repton) preferred to lay it out in more formal terraces, creating a more intimate scale for flowerbeds in the vicinity of the buildings. In all Repton

Burghley House, Stamford, 1564–89

was responsible for handling the landscape work for about 200 gardens and parks (see PICTURESQUE ARCHITECTURE).

RETAINING WALL Also known as a *revetment*, a wall built to hold back water or support an earth bank.

RETICULATED Adjective applied to a decoration or construction resembling a net (see *opus reticulatum* in MASONRY; TRACERY).

RETURN The point where a wall, moulding or pipe continues but at a direction angled to the original one; to be seen, for example, in the dripstone of a doorway or window opening (see HOOD-MOULD) or a water drain pipe which changes direction by 50° from the vertical down the side of a building to feed the drain in the ground (see also STAIRCASE).

REVEAL The side of a jamb (see JAMB) of a doorway or window which is between the outer wall and the door face or window glass. If the jamb is slanted diagonally instead of being at right angles to the window glass, it is called a *splay*.

RIB A decorative and/or structural raised band of stone or brick in a vault or ceiling (see CEILING; VAULT).

RIBBON DEVELOPMENT The custom prevalent mainly between 1918 and 1935 of building houses in a narrow band along both sides of a (usually new or modernized) main road. Such uncontrolled and unwise speculative expansion was stringently curbed by the passing in the UK of the Ribbon Development Act in 1935.

RICKMAN, THOMAS (1776–1841) An architect who trained first for medicine but after a short period practising as a doctor gave up this work and became an insurance clerk. In his thirties Rickman, having taught himself to draw, began to travel the country drawing churches: in these studies he is believed to have visited nearly 3000 buildings. He became deeply interested and knowledgeable in ecclesiastical Gothic architecture and in 1817 began architectural practice.

It was in this same year that the work for which Rickman is best known was published (see GOTHIC ARCHITECTURE). This was a book entitled *An Attempt to Discriminate the Styles of English Architecture from the Conquest to the Reformation*. In this, the first serious study of the development of the styles of medieval architecture, Rickman laid down his suggested classifications and periods, applying the names—Norman, Early English, Decorated, Perpendicular—which have since become so familiar through constant repetition by succeeding writers. The book, which was widely read and used, ran to many editions.

In 1818 *Henry Hutchinson* became Rickman's first pupil then, three years later, his partner. Together, during the succeeding decade, they designed many churches, also their best-known work, the *New Court* at *St John's College, Cambridge*. This was built in the years 1827–31 in Perpendicular Gothic style. Behind a screen wall with traceried windows and central gateway there is a square block with surmounting lantern (see REGENCY ARCHITECTURE). The stone bridge there over the river Cam, the Bridge of Sighs, so-called after the Venetian prototype, was mainly Hutchinson's contribution.

Hutchinson died in 1831 and Rickman continued building churches. He built a great many altogether, mainly in Perpendicular Gothic style; he was one of the last Victorian architects to do so before the power of the ecclesiologists was felt. Though the New Court at St John's College was a most successful essay into picturesque Gothic architecture, Rickman's churches were less so. Here he showed himself more an antiquarian scholar than a Gothic architect but his understanding and knowledge of medieval Gothic was greater than that of his contemporaries, though he did not hesitate to adopt the ideas and materials of his time such as plaster vaults and cast iron columns and tracery. Examples of his churches include *St George, Edgbaston*, Birmingham (1819–22, enlarged 1883–4, demolished 1960), *St Peter, Preston* (1822–5), *Ombersley Church* (1825–9) and *Hartlebury Church* (1836–7), both in Worcestershire and *St George, Barnsley*, Yorkshire (1821–2).

ROCOCO A decorative style, the term derived from the French *rocaille* and *coquille*, the former meaning 'rock-work' or 'stone-work', the latter the 'shells'.

In architecture and decoration, rococo represented the final phase of the Baroque. It spread from France as a reaction to the majestic, imposing yet heavy buildings and ornament characteristic of the earlier style (see BAROQUE ARCHITECTURE). After France the rococo forms quickly became popular in many of the countries where Baroque had flourished: Germany, Austria, Switzerland, Spain and Portugal in particular.

The rococo style in England is primarily a decorative one displayed mainly in interiors. Exteriors were fairly plain, the new designs being characterized by an absence of orders and symmetry and by an ornament which was lighter and more elegant than the more serious, weighty Baroque. Inside all was a gay playfulness; gone were the high relief and heavy gilding, the large painted schemes, the dark coloured marbling and the formal orders. The rococo decoration which surrounded window and door openings and enclosed ceiling and wall schemes was in dainty low relief, composed of ribbons, scrolls, arabesques, wreaths of flowers, seaweed and shells; birds and animals and a suggestion of Chinese and Gothic motifs were skilfully introduced to give variety. Colour schemes

Carved wood chimneypiece painted white, English, *c.* 1770

The Winter Palace, Leningrad, USSR, 1754–62 (Rastrelli)

Town-hall balcony, Bamberg, Germany, 1732–7

ROCOCO
Interior decoration, Hôtel Soubise, Paris, 1732–9 (Boffrand)

Palacio Mateus, Vila Real, Portugal, *c.* 1720

Palace of Sanssouci, Potsdam, Germany, 1745–7 (Von Knobelsdorff)

were also light in white and pastel tones, gilt being delicately and sparingly applied. Wall mirrors increased the illuminative effect.

Rococo design was to be seen only to a limited extent in England, its use mainly confined to stucco wall decoration, chimneypieces and doorway surrounds. Examples showing the varied adaptations of the style in different countries are shown on page 381 (see TOWN PLANNING).

ROMAN BATHS Known as *thermae* (from the Greek *thermos*, = 'hot'), these were an institution which was an integral part of life in the Roman Empire. Living conditions at home for those who were not well-to-do lacked space and comfort and the public baths provided free, or at least cheaply, the daily means for the population to relax, chat, carry out business or social affairs, bathe, receive massage and medical treatment, eat and drink and

The tepidarium, forum baths, Pompeii, Italy, AD 79

take part in athletic sports and entertainment. In Imperial Rome alone there are estimated to have been over 800 thermae of different sizes and accommodation. In the larger establishments there were restaurants, theatre, gardens and fountains, a sports stadium, rest rooms and large halls where poets and philosophers exchanged views and authors gave lectures or read their latest works.

In the bathing establishment itself the operation was long and often complicated. The bather began the process in the hot room (the *caldarium*); these were small compartments with hot water baths. He then received a scrubbing down treatment which included scraping with a strigil. Afterwards he plunged into a cold water swimming bath (in the *frigidarium*) and was then massaged and oiled. The baths provided warm rooms in winter, as in the large moderately heated room (the *tepidarium*), and cool, shady gardens in summer, where strollers could walk or sit and relax under the roofed peristyles which surrounded the open courts (see PERISTYLE).

The heating system was by hypocaust (see HYPOCAUST): hot air from furnaces under the building was passed through hollow tiles and bricks in the walls and under the floor. The temperature could be regulated for the needs of the different rooms.

There are remains of many examples of thermae, particularly in Rome. Large establishments were built by most emperors, for instance Nero (60–71), Titus (80), Trajan (110) and Constantine (320). The most important remains are those of Caracalla (206–17) and Diocletian (284–304). These two immense layouts in Rome illustrate the extensive type of baths. At *Caracalla* the main building block alone covers 270,000 square feet and contained the great central hall measuring 79ft by 183ft; this was covered by an intersecting barrel vault and was divided into three bays. The vault was supported on eight massive stone piers fronted by granite columns each 38ft high. The *Baths of Diocletian* were even larger and accommodated 3,200 bathers. Here the structures are not entirely in ruin because in 1563 Michelangelo converted the tepidarium into the nave of his church, *Santa Maria degli Angeli*, and retained the circular caldarium as an entrance vestibule with its domical roof now decorated with caissons. The three-bay nave has also retained the original vault though the marble facing has gone.

At *Pompeii* three sites of public baths have been excavated. These are smaller and less well equipped than those in Rome but are in a much better state of preservation. At the Forum Baths, for example, the tepidarium is in remarkable condition and still possesses a barrel-vaulted ceiling with rich stucco decoration, stucco-ornamented walls and, on piers surrounding the room, the figures of miniature Atlantes 2ft high (see CARYATID).

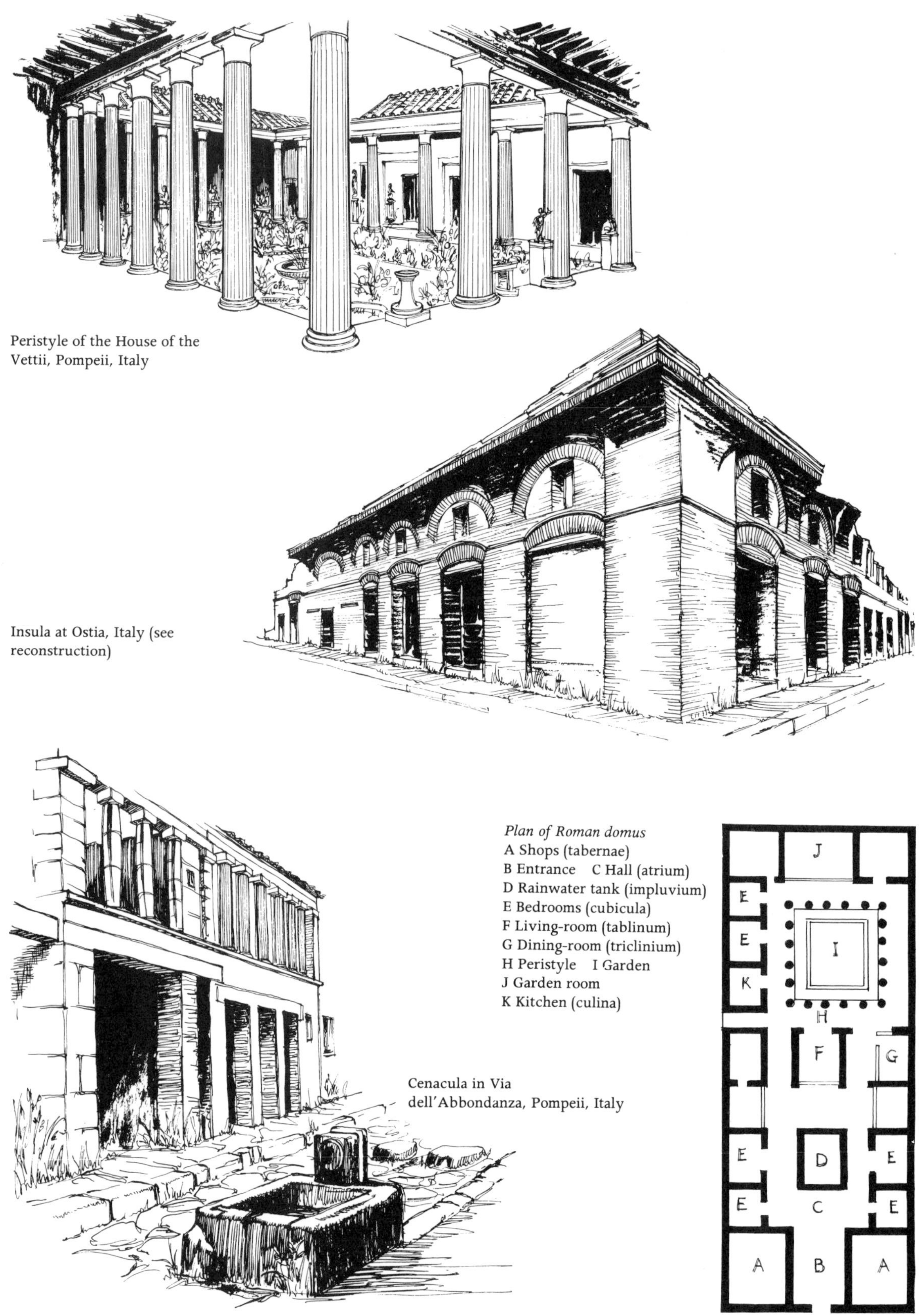

Peristyle of the House of the Vettii, Pompeii, Italy

Insula at Ostia, Italy (see reconstruction)

Plan of Roman domus
A Shops (tabernae)
B Entrance C Hall (atrium)
D Rainwater tank (impluvium)
E Bedrooms (cubicula)
F Living-room (tablinum)
G Dining-room (triclinium)
H Peristyle I Garden
J Garden room
K Kitchen (culina)

Cenacula in Via dell'Abbondanza, Pompeii, Italy

There was no hypocaust here; heating was by charcoal brazier. The frigidarium is small and circular in plan. The caldarium, also in good condition, had a hypocaust and wall flues; it is also barrel-vaulted and stucco-decorated.

At *Ostia*, the port of ancient Rome, there are extensive remains in good condition of two thermae, the Baths of Neptune which contain magnificent mosaic floors in the bathing rooms as well as an immense gymnasium (*palaestra*); and the Forum Baths which still possess their public latrine with 20 marble seats and washing facilities.

ROMAN DOMESTIC ARCHITECTURE Three kinds of home were developed: the town house (*domus*), the apartment block (*insula*) and the country house (*villa*).

The layout and form of the *domus* was based upon the Greek house of which many had survived from the Greek colonization of southern Italy. The early *domus* was almost identical with such Greek homes but, as time passed, the houses built for well-to-do Roman city dwellers became larger and more complex though the basic layout remained much the same. Most houses were one-storeyed though some had a second floor added to part of the building.

The *domus* street façade was narrow. The centrally placed entrance porch was often flanked by shops. The site was a long rectangle which extended well back from the street. There was no front garden, the open garden spaces were enclosed within the walls and rooms of the house so giving both shade and privacy. The front porch led directly into a court (the *atrium*) the centre of which was open to the sky. The rooms surrounding the atrium were roofed so that the tiled surfaces sloped inwards down on all four sides to the *compluvium* which was the open square in the centre. This admitted light and air, also rain which poured down the sloping roofs to be directed into a centrally placed tank or basin (the *impluvium*) so collecting the rainwater which was then piped to a further tank beneath the house. The atrium roofing was supported on columns or by wooden beams.

Reconstruction of insula at Ostia, Italy (see existing remains)

According to the size of the house the atrium then led into one or more garden courts, the peristyles (see PERISTYLE). Rooms were arranged round these, the sloping roofs over them supported on colonnades so giving shade round the edge of the garden and sun in the centre where there was generally set a fountain or fish pond or, perhaps, a sculptural group (see plan). A number of examples of *domus* of different sizes survive at Pompeii (all, naturally, of pre-AD 79 date) and later ones can be seen at Ostia.

While the *domus* was the home for middle-class or wealthy families, the poorer city-dweller lived in a flat (*cenaculum*) in an apartment block (*insula*). At Pompeii these *insulae* were usually only two-storeyed but in Rome and at Ostia Antica (the port of Rome where a number survive) they could rise to four or more storeys. In Imperial Rome it is believed that there were more than 40,000 such *insulae* built along streets and round squares in the city. Life in a *cenaculum* was overcrowded and lacking in most basic amenities. The construction was generally of brick and concrete with vaulted roofs. The ground floor fronting the street was usually given over to shops.

The *villa* was the suburban or country house. It was a larger, more spreading structure, laid out on a site of considerable area. It was a self-contained unit comprising farm buildings and accommodation for slaves, servants, artisans and family. It would include areas for cattle and horses, as well as for threshing; there were structures for making wine, for baking, and for textiles, a smithy and cellars for storage. Villas designed for wealthy men were extensive and architecturally magnificent. Possibly the most famous example was the Emperor Hadrian's palatial villa at Tivoli begun in AD 118. It covered several square miles of terraced hillside and included several thermae, stadia, halls, theatres, magnificent gardens, terraces and fountains as well as the imperial apartments (see CLASSICAL ARCHITECTURE; CLASSICAL ORDER; CLASSICAL ORNAMENT).

ROMANESQUE ARCHITECTURE The style current in eleventh- and twelfth-century Europe based upon the use of the round arch and characterized by massively thick walling, small windows and the clear division of the interiors (notably churches) into compartmented bays articulated by vertical shafts extending from floor to ceiling beams: a structural form derived from the restrictions imposed by earlier designs in timber building.

The appearance of Romanesque architecture varies considerably from one part of Europe to another due to the history of local building style and the particular source of the Romanesque form. In general, there are two basic types, one developed in central Europe and one to be seen in the north and west. The first of these springs, as the name Romanesque suggests, from Roman classical design.

West front doorway, Selby Abbey Church, Yorkshire, 1160–70. Note the chevron ornament on the arch mouldings

Carved ornament on south doorway, Kilpeck Church, Herefordshire, *c.* 1140

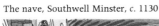

The nave, Southwell Minster, *c.* 1130

Worms Cathedral, Germany, from the south-west, *c.* 1110–1200

South doorway detail ornament at Iffley Church, Oxfordshire, *c.* 1170

Cloister base at Königslütter Abbey Church, Germany, *c.* 1135

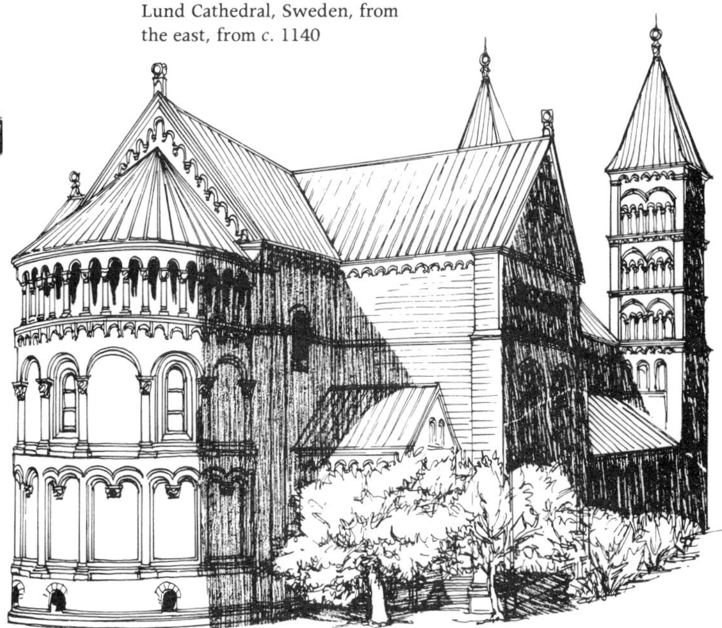

Lund Cathedral, Sweden, from the east, from *c.* 1140

Carved capital in church of S. Martín, Frómista, Spain, 1066

It is in central and southern areas of Europe, such as northern and central Italy, south-east France, southern Germany and Spain, that most examples of Roman building survive. From these, more numerous in the tenth and eleventh centuries than now, Romanesque masons developed their own designs using the round arch and (inspired by classical columns and capitals) arcading and tunnel vaults. They adopted the Roman basilican building plan for their churches with its division into nave and aisles, its timber roof covering and its apsidal termination which they set behind the high altar. These builders used foliated motifs as well as those derived from animals, birds, human figures and devil-monsters. Their decoration was rich and vigorous, their façades and porticoes sculptured all over, depicting biblical scenes (see ROMANESQUE ORNAMENT).

The Romanesque work of the north and west of Europe was less closely affiliated to that of ancient Rome. Ninth-century Carolingian architecture was influential in the formation of a Romanesque style based on that of Imperial Rome, but stronger still was that of Normandy established during the tenth century and taken to Britain where Romanesque architecture is frequently referred to as 'Norman'. The Norman influence was also felt in southern Italy and Sicily, creating in these two widely dissimilar areas (Britain and Italy) buildings of like character but adapted to indigenous needs. Indeed, the similarities between Norman architecture in the Italian south and that of Britain are notable. The great *cathedral churches* of *Trani, Troia, Bitonto* and *Molfetta* have the same massive walling, small narrow window openings and decorative western façades.

In the two great churches of William of Normandy in *Caen* may be perceived the Romanesque style characteristic of northern Europe along the whole Baltic coast from Holland to Poland and in Scandinavia, Britain and northern France. These churches, *S. Etienne* (L'Abbaye-aux-Hommes) and *La Trinité* (L'Abbaye-aux-Dames) were originally built in the years 1066–77 though some later alterations have been made. On the exterior there is a strong vertical emphasis in the western fronts with their twin tall towers. The walling is plain, broken only by round-headed doorways and window openings. The eastern ends are apsidal with accompanying ambulatory (see AMBULATORY; APSE). The interiors are clearly articulated, the tall shafts spanning nave arcade, triforium and clerestory.

Early Romanesque masonry by the Normans in England was massive, masons building the walls of great castles and cathedral churches up to 24ft thick at base for safety and to compensate for the wide jointing and poor-quality mortar. Decoration was limited and windows small, partly for defence and partly in order not to weaken the walls further. Twelfth-century work was less massive, the masonry more fine-jointed and there was a greater display of carved ornament (see ROMANESQUE ORNAMENT). While discounting the loss of the majority of buildings which were not made of stone and the subsequent Gothic alteration and enlargement of stone buildings, the quantity of Romanesque work which survives in Britain is a tribute to the strength of construction of Norman builders.

Many western façades and doorways as well as complete naves of large churches built in the eleventh and twelfth centuries are extant in Britain, for example *Tewkesbury Abbey Church, Rochester Cathedral, Southwell Minster, Gloucester* and *Ely Cathedrals* and *Malmesbury Abbey Church*; but *Durham Cathedral* is the prime instance as almost the whole structure is in this style. At Durham also may be seen the very early stone ribbed vaults (see VAULTING) which roof nave and choir. The masons building in the tenth and eleventh centuries were not sufficiently skilled to vault major spans so most buildings of this date have timber roofs and it was only slowly that, due to fire risk, these were replaced, usually in the Gothic period (see GOTHIC ARCHITECTURE), by stone.

An important feature of both northern and southern Romanesque church building is the eastern apsidal termination where it is not uncommon to see one central large apse flanked by two smaller ones. This is very characteristic of German and Scandinavian examples and of those in France, Switzerland, Italy and Spain. In the south where churches tend to be wider and lower the apses are much taller. Early instances of this derivation from the Roman basilican plan survive in a number of Italian-built churches of Lombardic style in modern Yugoslavia, for example in *Zadar* the Cathedral and *S. Grisogono*.

After 1100 the English plan began to diverge from this Continental pattern by playing down the importance of the eastern apse (apses). First the transepts were built forward with chapels to be flush with the central apse. Later the apses were altered to a square termination by building on a Lady Chapel to the east end, so doing away with the ambulatory. *Norwich* and *Canterbury Cathedrals* are two of the few English greater churches to preserve their ambulatory and apsidal termination (see also ARCADE; ARCH; BASE; CAPITAL; CHURCH DESIGN AND STRUCTURE; DOOR, DOORWAY; PORCH; TYMPANUM; UNDERCROFT; WINDOW).

ROMANESQUE ORNAMENT Particularly in early work, mouldings were cut very simply, with shallow hollows, chamfers and fillets and only sparingly decorated. Later work showed wide rolls or rounds, hollows and splays, profusely carved with ornament (see MOULDINGS).

This later Romanesque carving was, in Britain, chiefly geometric in form. Most common was the *chevron* or zig-zag decoration used especially in the deeply recessed mouldings of the round arches (*Iffley Church*, Oxfordshire, *Selby Abbey*, Yorkshire) and the *billet*, which consisted of cylinder-shaped stones set alternately with spaces in a hollow moulding. There was also *star* ornament, a four-

Carved ornament on the Schottenportal, church of S. Jakob, Regensburg, Germany, *c.* 1180

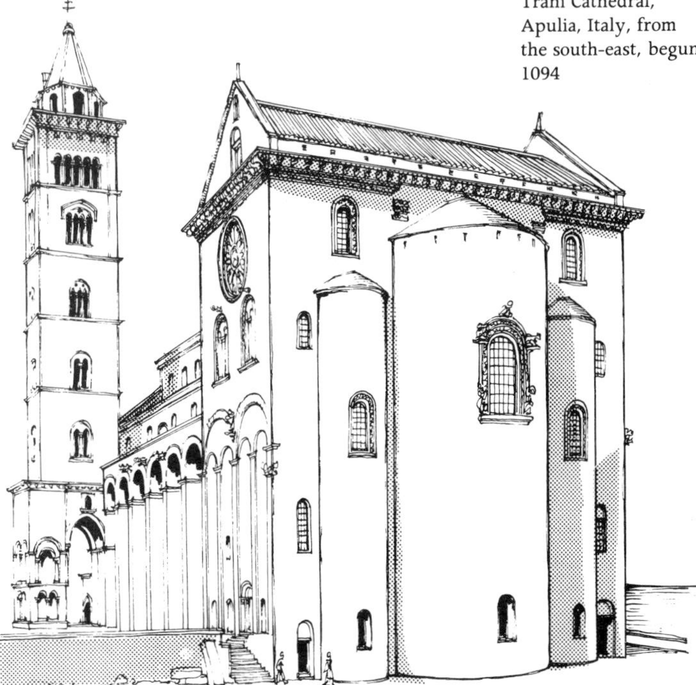

Trani Cathedral, Apulia, Italy, from the south-east, begun 1094

Capital on the west portal of the church of S. Trophîme, Arles, France, 1150–80

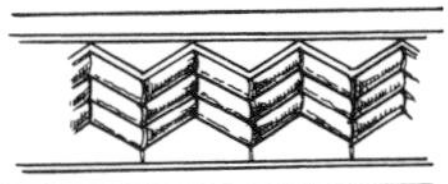

Chevron ornament

Chevron ornament

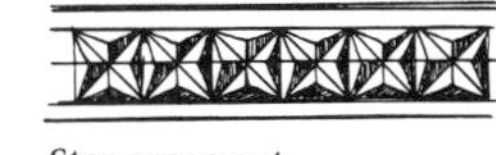

Star ornament

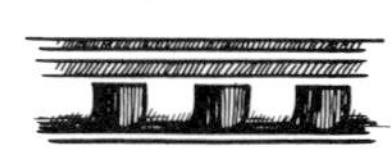

Billet ornament

Interior looking east: Abbaye-aux Dames (La Trinité), Caen, France, 1063–1125

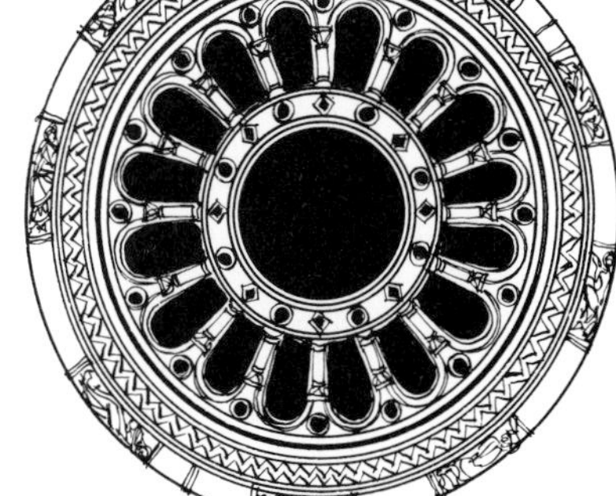

Wheel window at Basel Minster, Switzerland

Carved doorway detail at Kilpeck Church, Herefordshire, *c.* 1140. Romanesque ornament

Cloister capitals at Cefalù Cathedral, Sicily, 1131–48. Romanesque ornament

Carved doorway voussoirs at Kilpeck Church, Herefordshire, *c.* 1140. Romanesque ornament

pointed star cut into the moulding, a *lozenge*, a diamond-shaped decoration, and *cable* or *scallop*.

Deeply cut sculptural decoration became richer in the years approaching 1200. This was used to decorate doorway arches, jambs and tympana (see TYMPANUM) and capitals. All kinds of floral and animal forms were carved, as well as human figures and representations of devils and monsters; there were also figure compositions showing biblical scenes.

In general, English examples were more ornamental and less sculptural than Continental ones; the Herefordshire school of sculpture is of especial interest here as it produced on a small-scale carvings of vigour and imagination comparable in richness and variety to French Burgundian work, as for example at *Kilpeck Church*. The *beak-head* ornament was typical of English ornament; in this the heads of birds and beasts were carved in a hollow moulding so that their beaks or tongues would overlap into the adjacent round moulding (as on the façade of Lincoln Cathedral). Capitals were often foliated and sometimes depicted animals and human figures (*Canterbury Cathedral* crypt, for instance).

In Mediterranean areas, where there existed extensive remains of Roman building, both capitals and architectural detail were ornamented in a form much nearer to classical design, using acanthus leaves, anthemion, volutes and egg-and-tongue decoration (see CLASSICAL ORNAMENT).

ROOF The outside upper covering to a building. For the interior of such covering see CEILING; TIMBER TRUSSED ROOF.

Terms used to describe types and parts of roofs

Compass: a ridged roof not a curved, flat or lean-to design (see *Ridge*).

Gabled: a ridged roof terminating in a gable at each end (see GABLE).

Gambrel: a design which is finished at the ridge in a small gable.

Half-hipped: in which the ends are sloped at the top and gabled below this.

Helm: where a square tower rises to four sloping faces each descending to a gable.

Hipped: where the ends slope down to the cornice instead

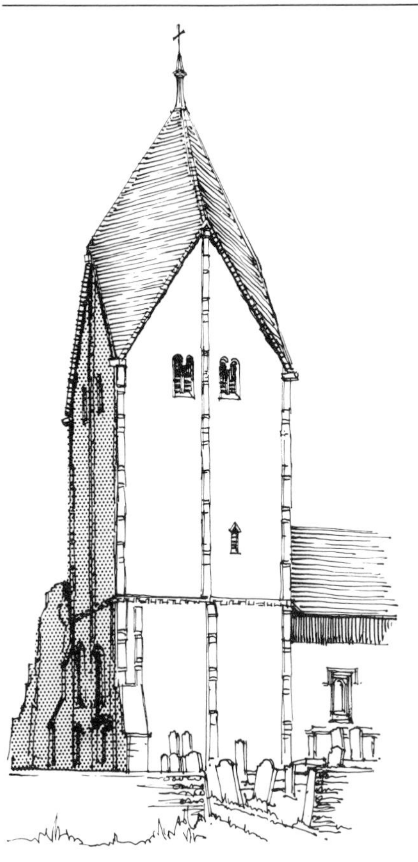

Helm roof: Sompting Church, Sussex. Saxon tower, eleventh century

Hipped roof: House on The Parkway, Welwyn Garden City, Hertfordshire, *c.* 1930

Gable (saddleback) roof: Manor House, Boothby Pagnell, Lincolnshire, *c.* 1180

Parabolic roof: central railway station ('Termini'), Rome, 1947–51. Architects: Eugenio Montuori and others

of terminating in gables.

Lean-to: a single-sloping roof built against a wall which rises above it.

Mansard: a roof with two angles of slope, one steeper than the other, named after the seventeenth-century French architect François Mansart.

Parabolic, paraboloid: forms of roof to be seen in modern architecture, particularly in reinforced concrete construc-

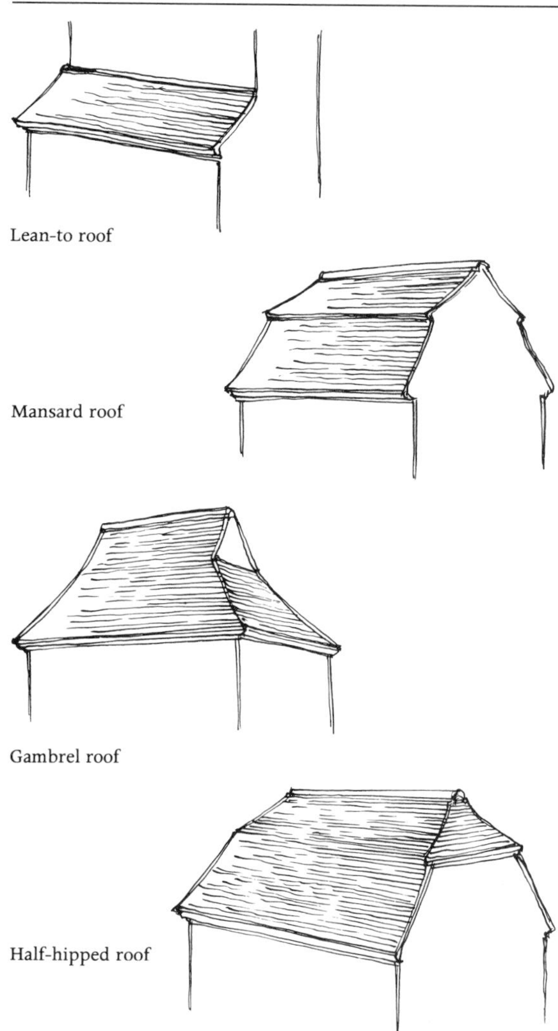

Lean-to roof

Mansard roof

Gambrel roof

Half-hipped roof

tion where they were extensively experimented with and constructed by engineers such as *Pier Luigi Nervi* in Italy. Such designs are based upon the form of the *parabola*, which may be defined as 'the path taken by an object which when expelled or thrown, travels originally at a uniform speed to fall eventually to earth under the influence of gravity'. The parabolic curve was first defined and named by Apollonius of Perga (modern Turkey) about 225 BC. A *paraboloid* roof is one some of whose plane sections are parabolas (see CONCRETE). A variation upon this is the *hyperbolic paraboloid* roof which is constructed in a double curve of hyperbolic form one of which is inverted.

Pitch: the angle of slope of a roof.

Rake: as pitch.

Ridge: the upper angle of a roof.

Saddleback: a gabled roof; the term is most commonly used for the roofing of a tower.

ROTUNDA A circular building, often colonnaded, or a room of circular plan which is generally domed: the Pantheon is a Roman example (see CLASSICAL ARCHITECTURE).

ROUNDEL A circular panel, usually decorated, in glass, stucco or carved and inlaid wood.

RUSKIN, JOHN (1819–1900) Although he was not an architect—he was a writer and art critic—Ruskin's influence upon the architecture of his age was widespread. He used his considerable literary gifts to persuade the artists and architects of nineteenth-century England to adopt his moral principles in relation to the buildings which they designed. Like Pugin (see PUGIN, A. W. N.), he preached a hatred of sham in architecture, a love of medieval Gothic forms, a disgust of classicism in Renaissance art and literature and the theory that goodness of spirit and greatness of architecture would go hand in hand. As a Protestant he

Gothic ironwork: interior, University Museum, Oxford, 1855–9

RUSKIN, JOHN
The University Museum, Oxford, 1855–9. Architects: Deane and Woodward

exerted an influence greater than Pugin's and the depth of this influence, on both architects and members of the public, was immeasurably increased by his magnificent prose and sincere enthusiasm.

Ruskin's two most famous works of artistic and moral criticism were *The Seven Lamps of Architecture*, published 1849, and *The Stones of Venice*, 1851–3. His seven lamps were Sacrifice, Truth, Power, Beauty, Life, Memory, Obedience. These qualities he related to the ideal forms of architecture. For instance, Truth represented his theme that only genuine materials should be used in building and one material should not be hidden behind or within another. Therefore vaulting should be of stone as in medieval Britain, not of plaster masquerading as stone, and likewise columns should be of stone with rubble core or, if of cast iron, visibly so, not an iron armature concealed within a stone column, so reducing its diameter and altering its proportions. Truth also meant that craftwork (carving, sawing, planing etc.) should be handwork and not carried out by machine. Beauty could only be expressed within an art form based upon nature as in medieval foliated carving.

Like Pugin, Ruskin supported certain styles of medieval Gothic work in Europe. He approved, as did Pugin, English architecture of Decorated Gothic design, that of the years 1275–1375, but, unlike Pugin, he extended his approval to Italian early Gothic work, to Pisan Romanesque and, as he extolled in his *Stones of Venice*, Venetian Gothic. In this he enthusiastically reintroduced to Britain the study of Venetian Gothic, a subject which had long been by-passed by English critics. In the influential chapter *The Nature of Gothic* he also traced a relationship between the warm satisfaction experienced by a craftsman in carrying out his work and the beauty of the finished achievement. It was this correlation which in turn inspired Morris in his attempts to turn the clock by re-establishing the craftsman in the high position which he had held in medieval society (see MORRIS, WILLIAM).

Many years later, in the 1880s, Ruskin experienced disillusion with some of the thoughts which he had expressed in his youthful enthusiasm. He had helped to establish the Gothic Revival. He had been one of its most fervent prophets and protagonists. Many well-known architects had followed his ideals and designed in styles which he had favoured. He lived to see the movement reach maturity and he was then less sure. He was horrified by some of the excesses perpetrated in its name. It was really medieval Gothic which he had loved.

Often Ruskin entered with enthusiasm with the architects into the creation of a building, following through its stages of construction with close interest but, in a number of instances, the completion of the work failed to satisfy him. A notable example of this was the building of the *University Museum* at *Oxford*, designed in 1855 by *Sir Thomas Deane* (1828–99) and *Benjamin Woodward* (1815–61). Ruskin was absorbed during the four years of construction in the medieval architectural forms, the carved sculpture and the detail of the iron and glass interior but he was regretful of the final result.

SALVIN, ANTHONY (1799–1881) A northerner, Salvin moved to London where he became a pupil of Nash (see NASH, JOHN). After this Salvin was in practice on his own account for nearly 60 years, designing chiefly in the domestic field: in total he built and altered over 75 country houses.

Much of Salvin's work was medieval in style, and he referred to a variety of periods. He acquired a wide and thorough knowledge of fortified architecture and was often called upon to advise, build and restore castles, for example the *Tower of London, Windsor Castle, Alnwick Castle* and *Caernarvon Castle* as well as castellated houses. When building a new structure, as at *Peckforton Castle* in Cheshire (1844–50), Salvin often indulged his penchant for the Picturesque. Here is a Victorian fortress, dramatic and powerful and as inconveniently planned as a medieval castle might have been, its kitchen over 50 yards distant from its dining-room.

Salvin's most attractive and interesting work is in Elizabethan and Jacobean vein and *Harlaxton Manor*, Lincolnshire his masterpiece. This was designed early in his career (he had already built two Tudor Gothic houses, one at *Mamhead*, Devon, 1826–37, the other at *Moreby*, near York, 1827–33) and at Harlaxton he was acceding to the strongly expressed wishes of his client in moving to the later, Elizabethan form. Harlaxton was begun in 1831. Most of the exterior in warm-coloured stonework was built to Salvin's designs and it displays a clear resemblance to Burghley (see ELIZABETHAN ARCHITECTURE). In the centre of the entrance façade is an enormous gatehouse with flanking towers and a central, semicircular oriel window; behind rises a square tower topped by an octagonal-based cupola. In Elizabethan tradition also is the skyline, a controlled riot of chimney-stacks, turrets, finials and gables. The decoration too is authentic, though restrained, with its strapwork and heraldic beasts. In the late 1830s *William Burn* (1789–1870) was brought in to complete the interiors which he carried out mainly in a Baroque style.

Harlaxton Manor, Lincolnshire. Architect: Anthony Salvin, 1831–40

SAVAGE, JAMES (1779–1852) Designer of a number of good churches for the Commissioners, both Gothic and classical.

By the early years of the nineteenth century the Industrial Revolution in Britain had caused such a great migration of workers from rural to urban areas that new centres of population were formed which were not served by a local church. To meet this situation in 1818, the Church Building Society was formed and, with Parliamentary support, a Church Building Act was passed which provided that one million pounds should be spent on the building of new churches. The money would be allocated under the supervision of the Church Commissioners, since which time these churches have been referred to as *Commissioners' Churches*. A few years later another half-million pounds was allocated and the eventual total of churches so built was 214. Most of the churches are in London suburbs and the industrial areas of Yorkshire, Lancashire and the Midlands. Well-known architects who built one or more of the churches included Nash, Smirke and Soane (see NASH, JOHN; SMIRKE, SIR ROBERT; SOANE, SIR JOHN).

James Savage designed several Greek Revival churches for the Commissioners, the most distinguished of which is *St James's Church, Bermondsey* (1827–9). In *St Luke's Church, Chelsea* (1820–4), Savage made (what was unusual at that date) a serious attempt to construct a Perpendicular Gothic church in medieval manner. The vaults are of stone, not plaster, and are supported by flying buttresses. It is a large, costly church with good detail and proportion (see GOTHIC REVIVAL).

St James's Church, Bermondsey, 1827–9. Architect: James Savage

SAXON ARCHITECTURE Remains of Anglo-Saxon building in England date from two different periods: the seventh and early eighth century, and the tenth and the early eleventh century. Between the two took place the devastating Viking raids which destroyed much of early Saxon culture.

Most Anglo-Saxon work was constructed in wood and wattle and daub but the more important churches and monasteries were built of stone. The work of the earlier period was centred in two main areas; the southern one in Kent followed the Roman Christian tradition stemming from St Augustine, while the northern one, in Northumbria, was centred around Hexham and Lindisfarne, and had closer affinities with Celtic monasticism.

The seventh-century Canterbury school in the south produced churches on the basilican plan as in Rome though, due to the lesser experience of British builders, these were simpler than the prototypes. Instead of, as in Rome, a row of columns supporting the arcaded wall which divided nave from aisles, there were plain walls broken only by an opening on each side which led to a series of chambers. On the Roman pattern there was also an apsidal chancel at the east and narthex at the west. Examples of this type included the *Church of St Peter and Paul* at *Canterbury* (*c.* 600), the *Church of Reculver* in Kent (*c.* 669) and *St Peter-on-the-Walls* at *Bradwell* in Essex (*c.* 660). The Reculver church is ruined and the Bradwell church the best survivor, though it has lost its apse and chapels.

The Northumbrian churches, in contrast, were built in the simpler Celtic design of tall, aisleless nave and rectangular chancel as in the small church at *Escomb*, Co. Durham (late seventh century). Even the great *monastic churches* of *Jarrow* and *Monkwearmouth*, Tyne and Wear (*c.* 675–84) were of this pattern. In 664, after the Synod of Whitby, Northumbrian monasticism followed the principles of Roman Christianity and, by the end of the century, impressive northern churches were being built on the basilican plan; those at Hexham, York and Ripon were of this type. At *Hexham Abbey Church*, Northumberland, the Saxon crypt survives. It was constructed in 674, barrel-vaulted in stone in the Roman manner.

Both geographically and architecturally half-way between these two types of seventh-century Anglo-Saxon church is *All Saints', Brixworth*, Northamptonshire which was founded about 676. For so early a building it is a large structure, nearly 100ft in length. It was built of

Interior of Deerhurst Church, Gloucestershire, tenth century

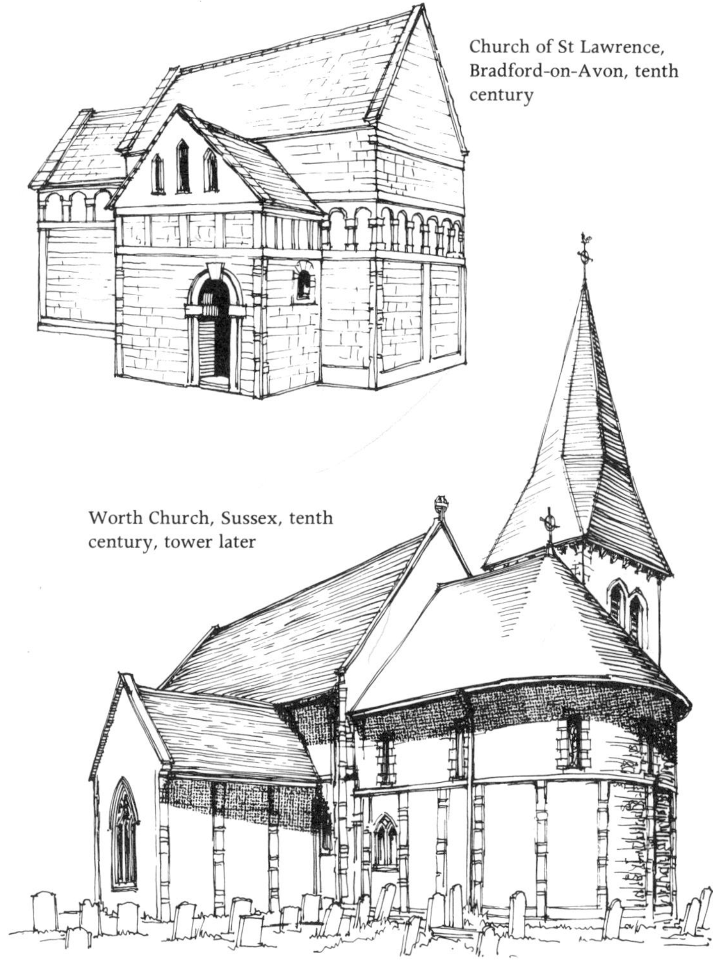

Church of St Lawrence, Bradford-on-Avon, tenth century

Worth Church, Sussex, tenth century, tower later

Tower doorway, Earl's Barton Church, Northamptonshire

Crypt of Repton Church, Derbyshire, tenth century

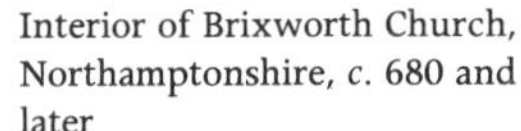

Interior of Brixworth Church, Northamptonshire, *c.* 680 and later

Baluster shafts: Saxon porch, Church of St Peter, Monkwearmouth, Tyne and Wear

Tower window at Barton-on-Humber Church, Humberside, tenth century

Pilaster strips: tower, Barton-on-Humber Church, Humberside, tenth century

Saxon tower: Church of St Peter, Monkwearmouth, Tyne and Wear

rag-stone and re-used Roman brick as an aisled basilica with eastern apse.

Most of the surviving Anglo-Saxon architecture in Britain stems from the later period; some of the work was rebuilt after the Viking raids, some was new building. The extant churches are the smaller ones; although 30 Benedictine monasteries were constructed during the tenth and early eleventh centuries, they were rebuilt by the Normans and little Saxon work remains above foundation level. Of these smaller churches the majority are simple in plan and structure. Typical is the church of *St Lawrence* at *Bradford-on-Avon* near Bath which was remodelled from an eighth-century building. Its walls are of large blocks of local stone, well cut and fitted. There is a simple high nave and rectangular-ended chancel separated by a narrow chancel arch. *Boarhunt Church* in Hampshire is a similar example. Some small churches of this time were built on apsidal plan, for instance, *Wing Church*, Buckinghamshire, *Worth Church*, Sussex and *Deerhurst Church*, Gloucestershire.

One of the most characteristic features of Anglo-Saxon architectural decoration are the *pilaster strips* (see LESENE) which are particularly to be seen on the towers. This is essentially a decorative form of the tenth and eleventh centuries. It appears to be linked to earlier structural work in timber but also to Carolingian neo-Roman wall treatment. Notable examples of pilaster strip decoration of towers or walling may be seen at *Earl's Barton Church*, Northamptonshire (*c.* 1000), *Sompting Church*, Sussex (eleventh century) (see ROOF), *Barton-on-Humber Church*, Humberside (tenth century), *Barnack Church*, Northamptonshire (tenth century), *Worth Church*, Sussex (tenth century) and *Bradford-on-Avon Church* (tenth century).

Other notable characteristics of Saxon building include the unbuttressed thin walling, the long-and-short work (see QUOIN) and the window and doorway design. Window openings were round- or triangular-headed, set singly or in pairs. They were often double-splayed: that is, they had a narrow opening which splayed inwards and outwards. In double windows the two lights were usually divided by a turned baluster shaft which supported the impost (see ARCH). This was a long, rectangular block of stone carried through the whole thickness of the wall, the baluster being set nearer to the outer face. Doorways, similarly, were round- or triangular-headed.

SCAFFOLD A temporary structure to provide secure access for exterior building work. The vertical poles are called *standards* and the horizontal ones (parallel to the wall) *ledgers*. Horizontal poles fixed into the walls and extending from them at right-angles are *putlogs*.

SCAGLIOLA A composition of gypsum, glue, isinglass and, often, marble fragments, made to imitate marble. This cheaper substance was very durable and took a high polish. It was known to the Romans and in eighteenth-century England was widely used for floors, coloured veneers and decorative inlay, and as covering for table tops and chimneypieces.

SCOTT, SIR GEORGE GILBERT (1811–78) Born of a religious but not wealthy family, he entered an architect's office when quite young, then worked in the office first of Henry Roberts and then of Sampson Kempthorne. For financial reasons Scott had difficulty in starting a practice and much of his early work was in gaols and workhouses, *Reading Gaol* (1842–4), for example. Later he went to the Continent where he studied French Gothic cathedrals and churches. All his life he preferred to design in Gothic, particularly an English version of French High Gothic of the years 1280–1340.

Sir George Gilbert Scott represents the quintessence of High Victorian Gothic architecture. He led his age in the Gothic Revival (see GOTHIC REVIVAL) and was responsible for an immense output of such work. His office was concerned with the initiation, creation, restoration and alteration of some 730 buildings. He was a highly professional, competent architect but his work lacked the individuality of his notable contemporaries: Street or Butterfield or Waterhouse (see BUTTERFIELD, WILLIAM; STREET, GEORGE EDMUND; WATERHOUSE, ALFRED). Their architecture is always immediately recognizable by this quality; Scott's is not but it typifies the mid-Victorian Gothic Revival. He popularized the movement, he believed in it, he worked industriously to further its ends because he genuinely thought it to be the most suitable architectural style for all building, secular and commercial as well as ecclesiastical and civic. In his book *Remarks on Secular and Domestic Architecture, Present and Future* (1857) he propounded these views.

Scott worked on a great number of churches and cathedrals. Of his own buildings, his first notable church, that of *St Giles, Camberwell* in London, which he designed with his then partner *W. B. Moffat* (1841–4), was one of his best. Here he showed his understanding of Gothic building (not too common at this date) and set a Middle-Pointed pattern for future work. St Giles is an impressive church, cruciform in plan, 150ft in length, with a lofty tower and spire. With St Giles, Scott began to establish a reputation as a Gothic Revival architect in England. In 1844 he confirmed this internationally when he won the competition for the *Church of St Nicholas* in *Hamburg* and built there an impressive German Gothic church. He went on to build other churches in Britain, *St George* in *Doncaster* (1854), for example, and *St Matthias* in *Richmond*, one of many constructed to serve newly expanding communities.

Scott's ecclesiastical work included a great deal of restoration, highly skilled and careful in quality. That he tended to 'over-restore' and 'improve' was characteristic of his day. By today's thinking he certainly rebuilt more than was required but without his timely intervention

Church of St Matthias, Richmond, Surrey. Architect: Sir George Gilbert Scott

much more of the structure of Britain's principal cathedrals would have been lost. Among those which he restored are *Hereford, Winchester, Ely, Salisbury, Lichfield* and *Peterborough* as well as *Westminster Abbey* for the fabric of which he was Surveyor. Also in the ecclesiastical field Scott was responsible for the new *chapels* at Exeter College, Oxford and St John's College, Cambridge. *Exeter College Chapel* (1856–9) is a successful large-scale work which, built on the site of the previous chapel, dominates the quadrangle. Scott based it upon the Sainte-Chapelle in Paris and the French influence on the Oxford building is strong (see GOTHIC REVIVAL). *St Mary's Cathedral* in *Edinburgh* was one of Scott's last and most interesting ecclesiastical works.

Kelham Hall, Nottinghamshire, 1857 onwards

When the Prince Consort died in 1861 it was decided to hold a competition for a national monument to house his shrine in Kensington Gardens. Scott won the competition and considered that the monument, built 1863–72, was one of his best works. The essence of High Victorian taste, its popularity slumped in the early twentieth century but has since returned to favour, viewed tolerantly as a classic of its age. Scott based his design on a medieval/Byzantine

The Albert Memorial, Kensington, 1863–72

shrine and encrusted the monument with the richest of ornament in marbles, enamels, precious metals and inlay.

As to large-scale secular commissions, Scott was forced by Lord Palmerston and the government to design the *Foreign* and *War Offices* in *Whitehall*, for which he won the competition in 1856, in classical style. Reluctantly he eschewed Gothic and produced a richly handled Italian Renaissance palace. He returned to Gothic with his *Midland Railway terminus hotel* at *St Pancras*, London (see RAILWAY ARCHITECTURE). Of his many houses *Kelham Hall*, Nottinghamshire is typical. Its Gothic romanticism clothed in red brick, the house is yet stolid and fails to inspire.

Sir George Gilbert Scott was the founder of an architectural dynasty which spanned more than a century. Of his sons both *George Gilbert Scott* (1839–97) and *John Oldrid Scott* (1842–1913) were Gothic architects. Though less famous than their father they designed churches of a more spiritual medieval quality. George Scott was responsible for the churches of *St Agnes* in *Kennington* (1877) and *All Hallows* in *Southwark*. His brother John built the *Norwich Catholic Church* (see also SIR GILES GILBERT SCOTT).

SCOTT, SIR GILES GILBERT (1880–1960) Grandson of the Victorian architect (see SCOTT, SIR GEORGE GILBERT), Giles inherited the family talent for architecture and, by the age of 50, had received a host of honours: he was a Royal Academician, a past president of the Royal Institute of British Architects, and holder of their gold medal; he was knighted and, in 1944, was awarded the Order of Merit.

Giles Gilbert Scott was a Roman Catholic and developed an early interest in church architecture. At the age of 18 he became an articled pupil in the office of the church architect *Temple Moore*. His name was quickly brought to professional and public notice when, as a young man of 22, he won the competition for the new *Anglican Cathedral* of *Liverpool*: a work which became his greatest achievement and to which he gave considerable time and study during the whole of his long life. Now at last almost complete, this is a building in traditional Gothic form, probably the last of its kind and size to be built, but it has an original fresh appearance, its lines clean and stressing the vertical. The cathedral is built of local sandstone,

SCOTT, SIR GILES GILBERT Anglican Cathedral of Liverpool from the south-east, 1903–78. Architect: Sir Giles Gilbert Scott

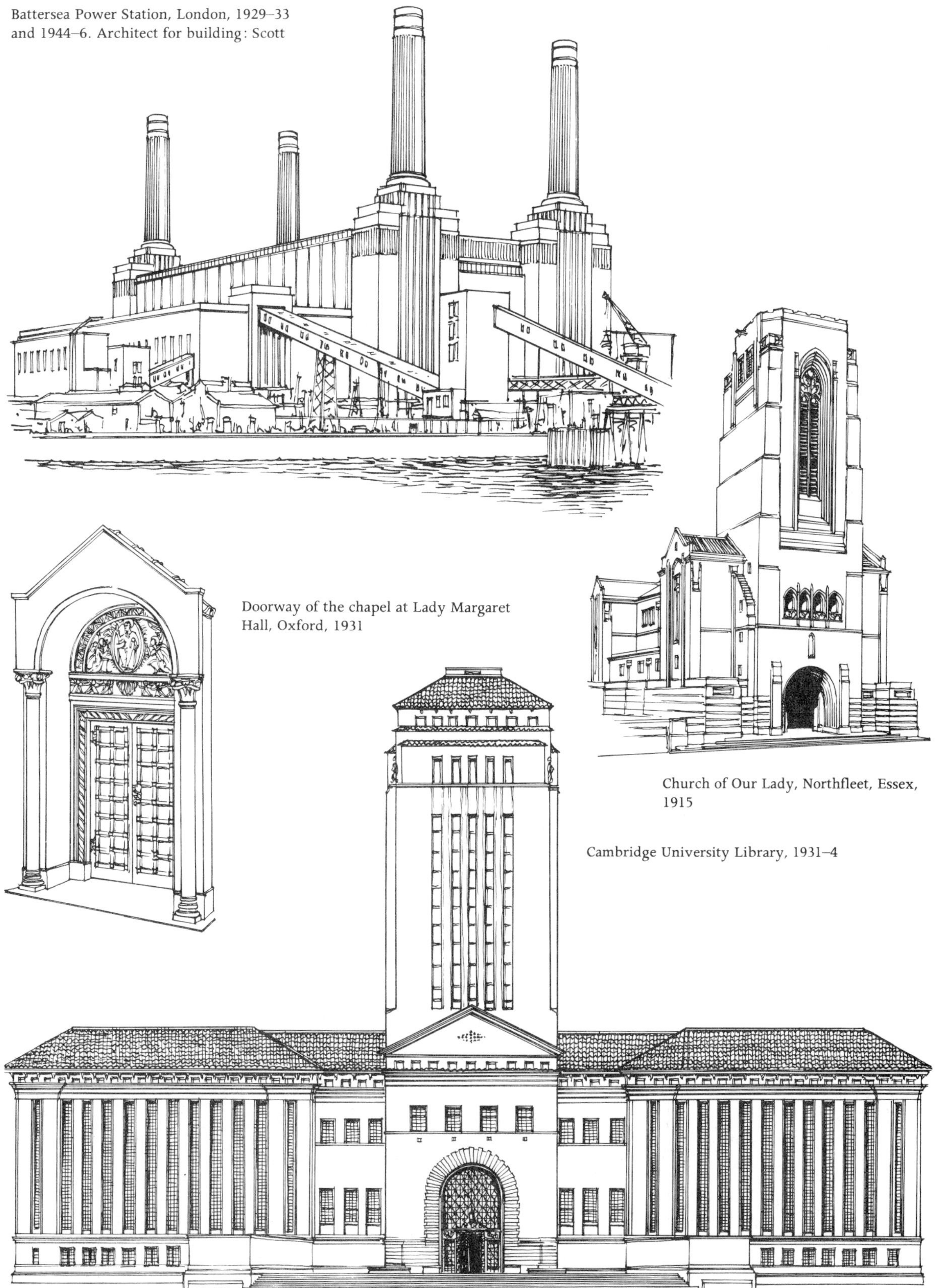

Battersea Power Station, London, 1929–33 and 1944–6. Architect for building: Scott

Doorway of the chapel at Lady Margaret Hall, Oxford, 1931

Church of Our Lady, Northfleet, Essex, 1915

Cambridge University Library, 1931–4

soft red in colour set with wide white joints. Its foundations are of brick and concrete. The exterior roofing is of reinforced concrete beams, some of which are hollow for circulation of warm air and the Roman method of underfloor heating is used. The interior is impressive, spacious and lofty. Its floor area is more extensive than that of any other British cathedral.

Scott was not entirely a traditionalist. There was great variety in his work but he rarely ventured wholeheartedly into the modern idiom. Like that of his grandfather, his practice was very large and his achievement extended over 60 years. It was diverse indeed, ranging from his Gothic cathedral to power-station and bridge design.

He built many churches and chapels, traditional and mainly Gothic but all with a personal interpretation of the style and evidencing high-quality materials and building. Typical are his *Church of Our Lady, Northfleet*, Essex (1915), *St Paul, Liverpool* (1916), *St Alban, Golders Green* in London (1932) and *St Andrew, Luton* (1932). His chapels show greater variety and interest, notably that at *Charterhouse School, Godalming*, Surrey (1922–7), as well as the *Ampleforth Abbey Chapel* in Yorkshire. In Byzantine vein is the *Lady Margaret Hall Chapel* at *Oxford* and his *Church of St Alphege* in *Bath* (see BYZANTINE ARCHITECTURE). Like his grandfather, Sir Giles carried out a considerable amount of ecclesiastical restoration work as at, for example, *St George's Chapel, Windsor* and *Chester Cathedral*.

Scott was widely employed in collegiate work. One of his most extensive commissions in this field was at *Cambridge* where, between the world wars, he designed the large *University Library* and, adjacent to it, the *Memorial Court* of *Clare College*. At *Oxford* he was responsible for the new building for the *Bodleian Library* (1936–46). Like much of his secular work these are traditional buildings in modern dress.

Among his varied commitments in London, Sir Giles designed additions to *County Hall* (1937), and the *Phoenix Theatre* (1930). Of greater interest and of much higher standard was his rebuilding of the *House of Commons* and the *Guildhall* after war damage. Here his Gothic work was impeccable; the Guildhall roof, in particular, is a fine reconstruction.

In the 1930s Scott carried out a number of commissions using a plain, monumental, and high-quality brickwork. His industrial complex for *Guinness Brewery* in north-west London was an important example (1933–6). Better known is his work at *Battersea Power Station* where he was called in as consulting architect in 1930. This project set the pattern for British power stations with his brick structure fronting the Thames. The work was not finally completed until 1955. An original concept for its day, a harmonious marriage of architecture and engineering, *Battersea Power Station* is now a listed building. Scott continued his connections with power stations and bridges until the end of his life. At the age of 79 he was advising on the design of the *nuclear power station* at *Berkeley* and, at the same time, was active consulting architect for the *Forth road bridge*. In the years 1939–45 he was architect for the new *Waterloo Bridge* in London, built of reinforced concrete faced with Portland stone slabs: a design of sophisticated simplicity making full use of modern materials and means of construction.

There were other architects of note in this third generation of Scotts. Sir Giles's brother *Adrian* was the architect of *Cairo Cathedral* and his cousin *Elizabeth Whitworth Scott* won the competition with her design for the *Royal Shakespeare Memorial Theatre* at Stratford-upon-Avon. This attractive brick theatre was built on the river's bank in 1928–32. It is a functional, unpretentious building, well constructed from quality materials which harmonize with its setting.

The Royal Shakespeare Memorial Theatre, Stratford-upon-Avon, 1932. Architects: Elizabeth Scott, Chesterton and Shepherd

SCREENS PASSAGE A passageway separated from a medieval hall by a decorative screen above which was often constructed a gallery, reached by ladder or staircase. In many houses the front entrance gave ingress to this passage and the screen (known as a *speer* or *spere*) prevented draughts from this opening, as well as from the doorways which led off the other side of the passage to the buttery, pantry, kitchen etc., from reaching the hall. It also provided a covered way through which food could be brought into the hall.

SCROLLED ORNAMENT A spiral form of decoration to be found in both classical and Gothic architecture. In classical orders the Ionic, Corinthian and Composite capitals have scrolled volutes (see CLASSICAL ORDER; VOLUTE).

SEDDING, JOHN DANDO (1838–91) A pupil of Street (see STREET, GEORGE EDMUND), Sedding was an architect and decorative designer active mainly in the ecclesiastical field. For many years he lived in the West Country where he restored and built churches, for example *All Saints', Falmouth* (1887–90). Other Sedding churches included *St Clement* near *Bournemouth* (1873–93) and *St Peter* in *Ealing* (1889–92).

His best known and most successful church is in *Chelsea* in London. This is the *Church of the Holy Trinity* in Sloane Street built 1888–91. It is constructed in red brick with stone dressings and horizontal banding; the style is, broadly, fourteenth- and fifteenth-century Gothic. The interior was freely ornamented in both Gothic and Italian Renaissance manner partly by Sedding and partly, after his death, by others. Notable was Burne-Jones's east window and the church ironwork by Henry Wilson.

SEDILIA Plural form of the Latin *sedile* (= 'seat'). In a church sedilia are canopied seats recessed into the south wall of the chancel near the altar for the use of clergy.

SERLIO, SEBASTIANO (1475–1554) Italian painter and architect, Serlio was born and studied in Bologna then spent 13 years in Rome, a pupil of Baldassare Peruzzi. He left Rome in 1527 and, after some years in Venice, worked in France where he set the pattern for the French Renaissance town house (*hôtel*) in his design for the Cardinal of Ferrara.

Serlio is chiefly remembered, not so much for his architecture, but for his publication of *L'Architettura* which became the working guide for masons and architects in western Europe, particularly France and England. The work, fully entitled *L'Architettura e Prospettiva di Sebastiano Serlio, Bolognese* was published in six volumes between 1537 and 1575. Finely and copiously illustrated, many of the drawings bequeathed to Serlio by Peruzzi, this work provided for the first time a clear, and practical guide to ancient Roman and Italian Renaissance architecture. It remained the standard work for over a century.

SGRAFFITO Derived from the Italian verb *sgraffiare* (= 'to scratch'), it is also known as *scratchwork*. A form of decorative plasterwork wherein a top coat of white plaster is incised to reveal a coloured layer beneath.

SHAW, RICHARD NORMAN (1831–1912) The most influential architect of the last three decades of the nineteenth century whose work was largely eclectic but who brought to whatever past style he was using a personal, fresh approach which lent individuality to the building. Shaw put aside the harsh colouring and over-ornamentation of the High Victorian period and returned to the simpler vernacular styles of the past, basing his designs on medieval or Tudor half-timber building, Jacobean or Queen Anne prototypes; only in his later work did he embrace a more formal classical theme.

Norman Shaw was born in Edinburgh then moved to London with his family as a boy. He studied for a number of years under *William Burn*, the Scottish domestic architect, then at the Royal Academy Schools where he won Gold and Silver Medals and the Travelling Scholarship with which he studied for three years in France, Italy and Germany. Shaw was a fine draughtsman and in 1858, on his return to England, published some of his work in Europe in *Architectural Sketches from the Continent*. He then entered Street's office (see STREET, GEORGE EDMUND) where, for four years, he was principal draughtsman and assistant, acquiring important experience.

In Burn's office Shaw had met *William Eden Nesfield* (1835–88) and the two young men found that they shared many ideas and ideals with regard to Gothic Revival design and the need for a return to a more basic and traditional architecture. They set up in practice together, an informal partnership, each designing his own commissions but each influencing the other in the development of their work.

In the 1860s Shaw began to build up a large domestic practice. He built many country houses of different sizes, but predominantly large, and a number of town houses chiefly in London. He used a variety of styles and materials, moving from one to the other with consummate skill and rarely abandoning any one style completely. He used half-timber, brick, stone and combinations of these. His earlier work, especially in country houses, is generally more medieval and informal, his later work more classical, based on Wren and Queen Anne traditions. Despite his preference for the vernacular, Shaw did not hesitate to utilize more modern means of construction, concealed iron structure for instance, and concrete. At the same time he revived fifteenth- and sixteenth-century romantic features in his interiors, characteristically the two-storeyed hall and the inglenook fireplace. His magnificent house *Cragside* near *Rothbury* in Northumberland (1869–84) is an instance of the latter. The dining-room inglenook was inspired by Fountains Abbey; the later drawing-room two-stage chimneypiece was designed by

196 Queen's Gate, South Kensington, London, 1875

Bedford Park, London, from 1876; housing estate by Shaw, Adams, May and others

First Alliance Assurance Building, Pall Mall, London, 1882

Albert Hall Mansions, Kensington, London. Brick apartment block, 1879

New Scotland Yard, London, 1886–90

Bryanston House, Dorset, 1890

Lethaby (see LETHABY, WILLIAM ROBERT), who was Shaw's assistant at the time. Made of Italian marbles, it is beautifully carved in an early Renaissance manner: the chimneypiece weighs 10 tons.

Characteristic of Shaw's fine country houses of the 1870s are *Grim's Dyke, Harrow Weald* (1872) and *'Wispers', Midhurst* in Sussex (1875) (see COUNTRY HOUSE AND MANSION). Both are 'early Tudor' half-timber designs with tall, brick chimney-stacks, barge-boarded gables and deep oriel and bay windows. They are well-built and picturesque, on a rambling and informal plan. Other examples include *Merrist Wood, Guildford* (1877), *Adcote,* Shropshire (1877) and *Pierrepoint, Farnham,* Surrey (1876).

Much later, in the 1890s, Shaw turned to the classical idiom for his country houses, designing *Bryanston House* in Dorset in 1890 and enlarging *Chesters* in Northumberland from 1891. Bryanston is a symmetrical country house on an eighteenth-century scale, comprising a central block and two projecting wings. The central mass contains a large hall 15ft × 24ft and a further hall 44ft × 36ft. The house is built of brick with stone angle and window dressings. It is a well-planned, spacious house, one of the last in England to be built on such a scale. Chesters is also magnificent in scale, built of stone with a slate roof.

For his London town houses Shaw generally preferred the Queen Anne style in brick. He built several in *Queen's Gate* in South Kensington, numbers 196 (1875) and 180 (1885) (see TOWN HOUSE) and the larger, more classical 170

(*above*) 170 Queen's Gate, South Kensington, London, 1888

Entrance front of Cragside, Northumberland, 1869–84. Architect: Norman Shaw

(1888). Characteristic also were *Lowther Lodge* in Kensington (1875), his own house in *Hampstead, 6, Ellerdale Road* (1875) and *Swan House* (1876) on the Embankment in *Chelsea* (see TOWN PLANNING).

Shaw built a number of churches but he adhered to the traditional style of the time for ecclesiastical work: Gothic. Here also he preferred the simple church, plain and built of local materials where possible. An early example, *Holy Trinity Church* in *Bingley*, Yorkshire (1866–7 and now demolished) was still clearly influenced by Street; it had a strong, solid, well-proportioned tower and spire. In the same county at *Ilkley* his *St Margaret's Church* (1878) is different. Here is a long, low unpretentious building with Perpendicular traceried windows. *Swanscombe Church* in Kent (1873) is a flint-and-stone example and *All Saints', Leek*, Staffordshire (1886) is a typical plain parish church with squat tower over the crossing.

Shaw designed several commercial city buildings in the 1870s and 1880s. These were influential designs and very decorative. *New Zealand Chambers* in Leadenhall Street in *London* (1871–3) was in red brick with Jacobean-styled ornamental plasterwork. The *First Alliance Assurance Building* on the corner of *Pall Mall* (1882–3) was a Flemish gabled design in brick and Portland stone. Much plainer and more formal was his *Second Alliance Assurance Building* designed with Newton (see NEWTON, SIR ERNEST) in 1903 in classical form in stone.

The best known of Shaw's public buildings in *London* was *New Scotland Yard*. His original building (1887–90) was a single large block on the Embankment near Westminster Bridge. Subsequently, in 1900, another similar building was added. The main block he planned in castellar form like a medieval keep with turrets. It is built of Dartmoor granite with dressings of stone and bands of brick in subtle polychromy. The roof is steeply pitched with banded chimney-stacks and gabled in Flemish manner. Though New Scotland Yard has long since moved to new premises, the old building survives.

At the turn of the century it was decided to rebuild Regent Street and much of Piccadilly Circus but retain the curve of Nash's Quadrant (see NASH, JOHN). Shaw was asked to produce designs for this. In 1905 he did so, proposing an Italian Renaissance scheme and the colonnaded portion forming the northern elevation of the *Piccadilly Hotel* was completed in 1908. After this the scheme foundered in disputes and costs. When Shaw died in 1912 most of his scheme was incomplete. It was finished to a simplified design after the First World War by Blomfield (see BLOMFIELD, SIR REGINALD).

SHEPPARD, SIR RICHARD HERBERT (1910–82) Leading architect in the firm of Richard Sheppard, Robson and Partners who became known with his winning design in the competition held for the new *Churchill College* at *Cambridge University* in 1959. This is a modern, 'brutalist' version (see CONCRETE) of the traditional Cambridge layout of residential courts. The accommodation is built in brick in low rectangular blocks surrounding small courts all grouped round the main buildings which are of concrete.

A considerable proportion of Sheppard's work has been in the educational field. This has ranged from the early *Churchfields Comprehensive School* at *West Bromwich* of 1958–60 to, in the 1960s, new science buildings and administrative centre at *Loughborough University*, residential and teaching accommodation at the *West Midlands College of Education* and student hostels for *Imperial College of Science* in *London*. In the 1970s the firm embarked on a considerable range of more interesting college buildings a number of which have been commended. This work includes the electrical engineering department, refectory, cafeteria and kitchen at *City University* in Northampton Square in *London*, new campus buildings at *Manchester Polytechnic* and extensive additions to *Durham, Leicester* and *Brunel Universities*.

Sheppard has designed a number of office development schemes in London. He has also evolved several imaginative and practical multi-purpose complexes, for instance, at *Welwyn Garden City* in Hertfordshire (1973–5), his *Leisure Centre* includes a theatre, restaurant, exhibition and banqueting halls, library and discotheque. More ambitious is his *Wood Green Shopping City* (1972–80) with its extensive layout comprising shopping, parking and housing areas.

SHINGLE A slice of wood used for roof and wall covering. In England shingles were widely employed for all kinds of roofing from Roman times until the end of the Middle Ages; after this, mainly because of the fire hazard, clay tiles replaced shingles to a great extent and the latter were retained chiefly for roofing cottages and church steeples. The traditional wood for English shingles was oak, each tile being about 5in × 10in, laid with an overlap and fashioned to be thicker at the lower edge.

SHUTE, JOHN (d. 1563) Architect and painter but known especially as the first English author of a book on classical architecture. The work was entitled *First and Chief Groundes of Architecture* and was published in 1563. Shute had travelled in Italy during 1550 but his book was based mainly on the manuscripts of Vitruvius and the works of Serlio (see SERLIO, SEBASTIANO; VITRUVIUS).

SILL, CILL The horizontal piece of timber or stone set into the base of a window or doorway opening and projecting outwards from the face of the wall in order to throw off rainwater.

SKEW In an oblique plane, slanting; the adjective is applied to a part of a structure at an angle from the rest as in, for instance, the coping of a gable or the sloping section of a buttress set-off (see BUTTRESS). In this context *skew-back* may refer to a stone block or abutment supporting the foot of an arch. Similarly *skew-corbel* refers to a stone set into the base of a gable to support the sloping coping above (see CORBEL).

SLATE A hard, fine-textured, non-porous rock formed originally by great heat and/or pressure mainly from clay, shale or volcanic ash. The chief parts of Britain where slate is to be found are Wales, the Isle of Man, the West Country and Cumbria.

Slate may be used for masonry purposes and, in modern times, has become a desirable, if expensive, cladding material for facing steel and concrete buildings. The beautiful Lake District slate is particularly suited for this and improved equipment for quarrying and sawing the material has greatly increased its use.

Traditionally slate has been utilized for many purposes due to its fissile character. It may be split easily along its natural laminae and so may be employed as thin or thick slabs for paving, walling, stairs, water tanks, shelves or even building fittings such as chimneypieces.

Its most common use has been as roof-covering since, in addition to its other properties, slate is very durable, being resistant to both frost and atmospheric pollution. The Romans roofed with slate and, though the material fell into disuse after their departure, it reappeared in the early Middle Ages. The ubiquitous use of Welsh slate for roofing stems from the later eighteenth century. The architects of the time were quick to perceive the advantages in economy of the thinner, smoother slates from Wales for the greatly increased rate of building in the enlargement of towns following the Industrial Revolution. With the nineteenth-century development of the railways, the transportation of slate was facilitated to any major town in the land.

Slate-hanging began to be a popular method of wall cladding in the later seventeenth century and this custom grew to a climax in the years 1780–1830. The material was particularly suited to the seaside building expansion of the time since it was resistant to a salt-laden atmosphere; it was widely used in the West Country. Like tile-hanging (see TILES), this was a weather-proofing building method but it also became a decorative one as variations in slate shapes were experimented with.

SLEEPERS In a building, supporting beams which carry joists. In turn, walls which support such beams are termed *sleeper walls*.

SMIRKE, SIR ROBERT (1780–1867) Leading architect of the Greek Revival in the years 1810–45 with an exceptionally large London practice much of which was concerned with public building.

Robert Smirke was the son of the artist Robert Smirke RA. He studied at the Royal Academy Schools in 1796–9, gaining both Gold and Silver Medals. In 1801–5 he travelled on the Continent, chiefly in Italy and Greece, studying and drawing. On his return to England he was commissioned to build *Lowther Castle* in Cumbria (1806–11) and this was followed by *Eastnor Castle*, Herefordshire (1812–20), both in the medieval style.

Smirke's first important commission in London was the rebuilding of *Covent Garden Theatre* (1808–9) which had been burnt down in 1808. Here he established himself as a Greek Revival architect, designing a long façade with Greek Doric portico: a novelty in London at the time. The theatre was once again destroyed by fire in 1856, this time rebuilt by E. M. Barry (see BARRY, SIR CHARLES). Smirke also completed the building of the *Royal Mint* on Tower Hill in 1807–9; this building has since been greatly altered.

Smirke's introduction to London of this monumental Greek classical design brought him recognition and in 1813 he joined Nash and Soane (see NASH, JOHN; SOANE, SIR JOHN) as one of the official architects to the Office of Works. He became a Royal Academician in 1811 and was knighted in 1832.

His best known works in London were the *General Post Office* in St Martin's-le-Grand (1824–9, demolished 1912) and the *British Museum* (1823–47) both large-scale Grecian buildings. The British Museum is Smirke's masterpiece. He was a highly professional and competent architect, his work was academic and authentic but it lacked the spark

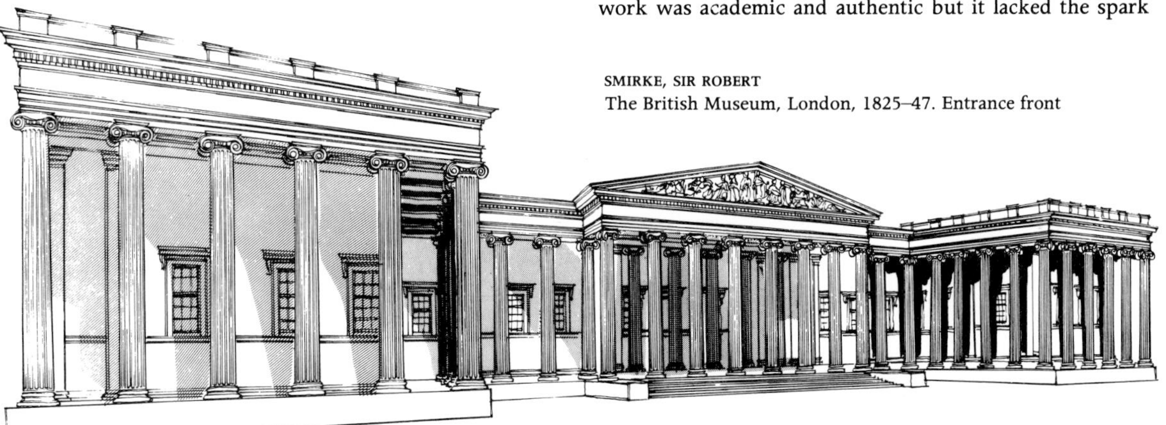

SMIRKE, SIR ROBERT
The British Museum, London, 1825–47. Entrance front

of outstanding ability. In comparison with Nash and Soane and, even more, with his contemporary in Germany, Karl Friedrich von Schinkel, architect of the not dissimilar *Altes Museum* in *Berlin*, Smirke's work was almost dull, but the British Museum possesses monumental dignity. It is one of the most imposing Greek buildings in London, its Ionic colonnade of 48 columns taken uninterruptedly round the quadrangle of the south elevation.

The work of Smirke's large practice in London included various club houses, the *Oxford and Cambridge Club House, Pall Mall* (1836–8) for example, *King's College* in the *Strand* which formed the east wing of Somerset House (1830–5) and the *Royal College of Physicians* in *Trafalgar Square* (1822–5). He was one of the architects advising the Parliamentary Commissioners on the building of new churches from 1818 onwards (see SAVAGE, JAMES) and contributed four himself. The best of these is *St Mary's Church, Wyndham Place* in London (1821–3) which was built on a terminal site on the Portman Estate and is fronted by a semicircular Greek Ionic portico. Another example is *St Anne's Church, Wandsworth* (1820–2) with similar tower and also an Ionic portico.

Smirke designed many buildings outside London, town and country houses, churches and civic structures. Much of this work was classical, mostly in Greek vein and in his favourite order—Ionic. Characteristic are his *Shire Halls* (*Gloucester*, for instance, 1814–16), the *Council Office* at *Bristol* (1824–7) and *St George's Church,* Brandon Hill, *Bristol* (1823), the last-named, unusually, in the Doric Order.

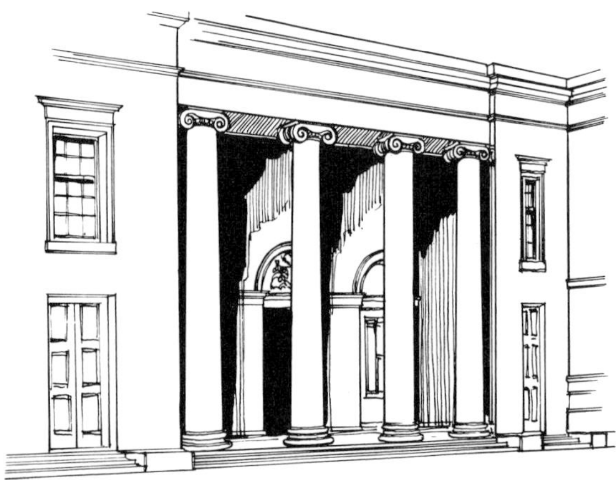

The Shire Hall, Gloucester, 1814–16

Sydney Smirke (1798–1877), Robert's younger brother, was his pupil and later joined him in a number of commissions such as the *Oxford and Cambridge Club House*. Sydney Smirke later rebuilt the *Carlton Club House* in Pall Mall in 1854–6 (demolished 1940). He is best known for his addition to the *British Museum* of its circular *reading room* by means of covering the central court with a cast-iron domed structure (1854–7).

SMITH, FRANCIS (1672–1738) A successful master builder and son of a bricklayer, Francis Smith was responsible for the construction of a number of large houses in the Midlands in the 1720s and 1730s. Some of his work was for the architect James Gibbs (see GIBBS, JAMES) such as *Ditchley House* in Oxfordshire and the rebuilding of *All Saints' Church, Derby* but, in many of his houses, Smith acted as his own architect.

Smith settled in Warwick early in the eighteenth century. Much of his work was in this vicinity and he became known as 'Mr Smith of Warwick'. He was employed as surveyor to the buildings of the county and became Mayor of Warwick in 1713 and again in 1728. His house designs tended to a sameness, one closely resembling another. In style they were a little outdated, still evidencing Baroque features in the later 1720s when Palladianism had become the architectural vogue. His best house was *Sutton Scarsdale* in Derbyshire (begun 1724 and now in ruins). Similar, especially on the exterior, is the surviving *Stoneleigh Abbey*, Warwickshire (1714–26).

SMITHSON, ALISON (b. 1928) and **PETER** (b. 1923) A husband-and-wife team of architects who became known after the Second World War as leading exponents of the *avant-garde* concepts of modern building and design then interesting younger architects. Their *school* at *Hunstanton* in Norfolk (1954), illustrating the influence of Mies van der Rohe, first aroused considerable interest; they then became associated with the 'Brutalist' movement of the 1950s and 1960s (see CONCRETE).

A more important commission was the scheme in St James's Street to provide offices for the *Economist* newspaper together with a bank and apartments. The aim was to create a building group which would not be incompatible with the scale of the eighteenth- and nineteenth-century building in the area and which would give open vistas from one part to another. The second part of the intention is more successfully realized than the first; the tower is set back but, despite this, it is too tall to blend sympathetically with the nearby Boodles Club.

The low-cost housing scheme in *Robin Hood Gardens* at *Bromley-by-Bow* in London (1968–72) is yet another expression of the urban planning theory repeatedly postulated in the 1950s, characterized by ubiquitous and dreary pre-cast concrete slabs made up into rectinilear structures.

SMYTHSON, ROBERT (*c.* 1536–1614) The best known of the master masons intimately concerned with the building of the Elizabethan great houses and the establishment of the Elizabethan form of classicism in domestic architecture. Smythson was one of the principal masons at *Longleat House* in Wiltshire where he worked in the years 1568–80 (see RENAISSANCE ARCHITECTURE) and from 1576 he was also at *Wardour Castle* in the same county.

Smythson's most important achievement was at

SMYTHSON, ROBERT
Entrance front of Burton Agnes Hall, Yorkshire, 1601–10

Wollaton Hall, Nottinghamshire (see ELIZABETHAN ARCHITECTURE). Wollaton was a new house begun in 1580 and it seems likely that Smythson was concerned with its design and building from the beginning: he spent the rest of his life at Wollaton and he was buried there. At Wollaton he held the position of Surveyor (the nearest Elizabethan equivalent to architect), not master mason as at Longleat. The house is square in plan, completely symmetrical on all four sides and with a turret at each corner. An immense hall (which is all that survived internally from the fire of the early seventeenth century) fills what would have been the courtyard in an earlier type of English house. Among Smythson's drawings are plans and elevations, as well as details of the characteristically Elizabethan hall screen. Smythson evolved the design and ornament of Wollaton from a variety of sources. The decoration of the exterior (which survives almost unaltered) and that of the hall interior are clearly derived extensively from the Flemish publications of Vredeman de Vries; there is much of Serlio (see SERLIO, SEBASTIANO) and the Loire châteaux also in the design but, overall, the house is traditionally English in spirit.

Smythson is believed also to have been concerned with the design of *Hardwick Hall*, Derbyshire (1591–7) which, like Longleat, is more classical in its horizontal emphasis and in its simplicity of ornamental treatment and so less Flemish in its Renaissance interpretation: Hardwick represents the summit of Elizabethan country-house achievement. A house certainly based upon designs by Smythson is *Burton Agnes* in Yorkshire, built in the first decade of the seventeenth century

SOANE, SIR JOHN (1753–1837) Born near Reading, son of a bricklayer, Soane determined early in life to become an architect and this dedication to and love of architecture stayed with him strongly all his 84 years. In 1768 he was articled to Dance (see DANCE, GEORGE, THE YOUNGER) and four years later became an assistant to Holland (see HOLLAND, HENRY). He won both Silver and Gold Medals at the Royal Academy Schools and, in 1778–80, studied in Rome on a Travelling Scholarship; while there he spent some time in the north in Florence and other cities and also explored the early Greek buildings in the south at Paestum and in Sicily.

Soane's career really began with his appointment as Surveyor to the *Bank of England* in 1788, a post which he held until 1833 when failing eyesight led to his retirement from the post. At the Bank he developed his highly individual architectural style. His work here (almost completely lost in the rebuilding of the 1930s) was monumental, stripped of all superfluous ornament and relying on simple, pure lines and fine proportions. Soane was in part a neo-classicist but his inspiration was multi-centred; he took, for instance, structural themes and decorative treatment from Byzantine sources. He fused these different concepts into a highly personal architectural style. In his later work especially, his designs became increasingly austere and linear, his domes and arches shallower and more segmental. His spatial handling and lighting were outstandingly original. The simplicity of his barely ornamented masses foreshadowed modern architecture but no designer then followed his lead. He was never content with less than perfection; he paid meticulous care to detail as well as to the general design.

In the 45 years during which Soane was architect to the Bank, he built the screen wall round the awkwardly shaped triangular site and rebuilt most of the interiors. Work on the Bank Stock Office was begun in 1791 and the Rotunda in 1796. From 1800 onwards several halls were redesigned and decorated. He took advantage of the

Pitzhanger Manor, Ealing, London, 1800–1803

Tyringham Hall, Buckinghamshire, 1793–9. Dome added later

Tyringham Hall: bridge in grounds

Holy Trinity Church, Marylebone, London, 1826–7

St John's Church, Bethnal Green, London, 1826–8

Dulwich College Art Gallery and Museum, 1811–14 (restored after 1944 war damage)

specific needs of the building, for instance the security problems which limited window openings to high-level positions: Soane introduced light through lunettes set high in the walls and a Roman style oculus in a centrally placed shallow dome. He gradually eliminated three-dimensional orders from his designs, replacing columns and advanced entablatures with low projection, almost linear forms of simplified classical elements.

It seems likely that it was at Paestum and Sicily that Soane began to appreciate the beauty of the monumental, archaic Greek Doric Order. These same sturdy fluted columns without base, supporting heavy abacus and entablature, which had so horrified Sir William Chambers and his colleagues, had an austere power which appealed to Soane. At *Moggerhanger House* in Bedfordshire (1809–11; see REGENCY ARCHITECTURE) Soane used this order; at *Tyringham Hall*, Buckinghamshire the portico is Ionic.

Soane's own two houses, the country residence of *Pitzhanger Manor* at Ealing (1800–3), now the public library, and his later town house at *13 Lincoln's Inn Fields* (1812–13) illustrate his more mature style. The Ealing house is fronted by Ionic columns carrying advanced entablatures but the town house is representative of his more linear, austere approach. It is this house and its contents, now the Sir John Soane Museum, which he left to the nation by Act of Parliament in 1833 as a museum for 'the study of Architecture and the Allied Arts'. One of his most original later works is the *Dulwich Art Gallery* (1811–14). Commissioned as a result of a bequest which stipulated that the tomb of the founder must be incorporated, Soane made this mausoleum (lit from above) the central feature of the principal elevation. This is an original, austere brick building characteristic of Soane and owing little to either neo-classicism or any other previous style.

Soane made three contributions in the 1820s to the Commissioners' Churches (see SAVAGE, JAMES). Of somewhat similar design, they have suffered some subsequent alteration and enlargement. They are *Holy Trinity, Marylebone, St John, Bethnal Green* and *St Peter, Walworth.*

Soane was elected an Associate of the Royal Academy in 1795 and a full member in 1802. Four years later he succeeded George Dance as Professor of Architecture at the Schools there where, for the remainder of his life, he gave to his regular lectures the same meticulous care and attention that he lavished upon his architecture.

13 Lincoln's Inn Fields (now the Sir John Soane Museum), London, 1812–13. Architect: Sir John Soane

SOFFIT The under-surface of any part of a building: arch, vault, balcony, cornice, lintel for example (see ARCH; STAIRCASE).

SOLAR In the fourteenth, fifteenth and sixteenth centuries a private withdrawing-room situated on the first or

Manor house solar, *c.* 1475–85

second floor of a house intended to permit the owner and his family to retire to away from the noise and smoke of the great hall. The solar was usually reached by means of a staircase ascending from the daïs end of the hall (see MANOR HOUSE).

SPANDREL The roughly triangular space, which may be decoratively carved or left plain, bordered by the mouldings of certain architectural features. For example, a spandrel may be the surface of a vault between two adjacent ribs, it may be the surface between the outer string of a staircase and the floor (see STAIRCASE), or it may be the surface between two arches in an arcade. Most commonly a spandrel is the area in an arched window, fireplace or doorway opening framed by the horizontal and vertical lines of the dripstone and the mouldings of the arch (see HOOD-MOULD).

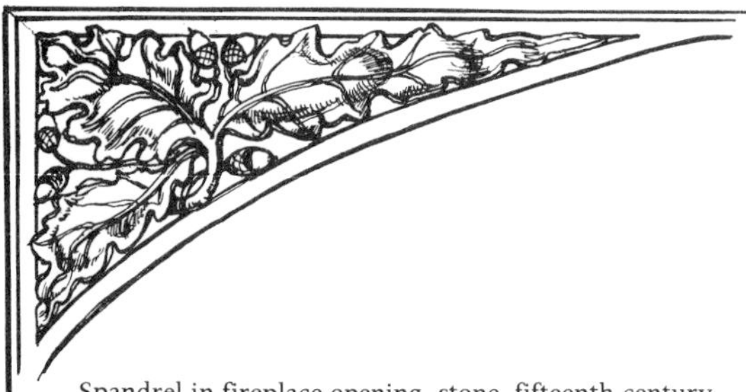
Spandrel in fireplace opening, stone, fifteenth century

Spandrel at Thaxted Church, Essex, fifteenth century

SPENCE, SIR BASIL (1907–76) Born in India of Scottish parentage, Spence went to school in Edinburgh; he then studied at the Edinburgh Architectural School and later at London University. Early in his career he spent a year in Lutyens's office (see LUTYENS, SIR EDWIN LANDSEER), where he worked on drawings for the Viceroy's House in Delhi. After war service in the army he was elected to the Royal Academy and was President of the Royal Institute of British Architects in 1958/9.

Spence's architectural commissions have been numerous and varied. They have included blocks of flats, churches, single houses and housing estates, industrial buildings, hospitals, theatres and designs for university expansion. Soon after the Second World War he became known for his exhibition work. He had begun to design in this field earlier when he was responsible for the Imperial Chemical Industries' pavilion for the Glasgow Exhibition of 1938. In the 1940s this was followed by the Britain Can Make It Exhibition of 1946 and his contribution to the *Festival of Britain* on London's South Bank in 1951; here, his *Sea and Ships building* displayed imaginative spatial handling.

Of the great quantity of building which Spence designed after 1950, two projects in particular enchanced his reputation and made his name known to the general public: the new *Coventry Cathedral* and *Sussex University*. It was in 1951 that Spence's design was chosen by the assessors from the 219 entries submitted in the competition to build a new cathedral at Coventry to replace the late Gothic cathedral of St Michael severely damaged during the war. Building began in 1954 and the cathedral was consecrated in 1962; a record time for such a construction in modern times.

Spence's design aroused criticism at first, partly because it is modern in its methods of construction, lighting, heating and decoration and does not, as at Guildford (see MAUFE, SIR EDWARD) and Liverpool (see SCOTT, SIR GILES GILBERT), follow a Gothic tradition in plan and layout, and partly because Spence set his new cathedral with its axis at right-angles to that of the old. From a different viewpoint Spence was also criticized for not being sufficiently modern in his design and Coventry Cathedral is, as the architect has himself stated, a traditional one.

As time has passed and both public and architectural critics have become familiar with Coventry Cathedral, it has been adjudged a success. Spence's foresight in incorporating not only the surviving steeple of Old St Michael's in his scheme but also its chancel walls, has been vindicated. The chancel remains, with their Perpendicular traceried windows, provide a decorative screen surrounding an atrium in front of the cathedral.

Coventry Cathedral is built of warm-coloured sandstone, a material which is pleasantly set off by the chapels of greenish slate (see CHURCH DESIGN AND STRUCTURE). Inside there is a strong impression of unity. The general design and the light from the tall nave windows in the saw-tooth walls are focused towards the altar and the Sutherland tapestry. The floor is of dark polished marble, the walls plain white. The ceiling is an immense canopy of reinforced concrete giving an impression of a medieval stellar vault in modern dress. In Coventry Cathedral Spence has created a building eminently suited to decora-

SPIRE
Broach spire, thirteenth century

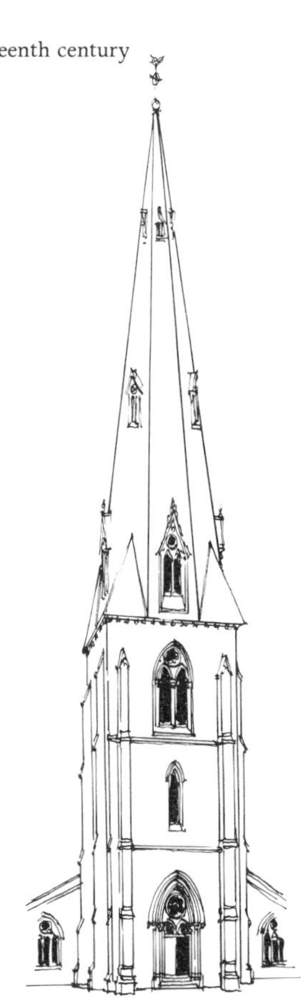

tion by his choice of artists and craftsmen. Of exceptional quality here is *John Piper*'s baptistery window of 195 lights in richly glowing glass, *John Hutton*'s engraved glass entrance screen and, on the exterior, *Sir Jacob Epstein*'s 25ft-high bronze group of St Michael and the Devil.

At *Sussex University*, the first of the seven new English universities planned after the Second World War, Spence used a brick-and-concrete format, combining the two materials skilfully in an arcaded style. Falmer House, the first building constructed, is laid out on traditional English university courtyard lines, the segmental arches being repeated all round, only varying in proportion over three storeys.

Spence returned to this theme in subsequent work for educational buildings also in his *Household Cavalry Regiment Buildings* in Knightsbridge (1970) where the façade is successful though the controversial tower is more mundane. The architect's *British Embassy* in *Rome* (1968–71) is a suitably impressive and lavish design.

SPIRE A tall, tapering structure of polygonal or conical form built on to the top of a tower, particularly characteristic of Gothic architecture. Spires were made of stone or of wood. Wooden spires were covered by shingles or lead (see SHINGLES). Most spires were octagonal and the towers upon which they were constructed had only four sides. To overcome this structural difficulty spires were of two main types, the *broach* and the *parapet*.

Most of the earlier spires were of broach design. In this form squinches (see SQUINCH) were built across the tower corners, inside at the top, to support the other four sides

Falmer House, Sussex University, 1960–2. Architect: Sir Basil Spence

of the spire. On the exterior, pyramidal buttresses, called broaches, followed up the spire sides for some distance, the apex of these finishing in the centre of the side of the spire face. In the parapet designs, characteristic especially of Perpendicular Gothic spires, the parapet acted as a support to a narrower spire and also provided a walkway for access and repairs. Such slender spires—when especially narrow they were called *needle spires*—were often reinforced by flying buttresses which extended from the spire sides to corner pinnacles on the tower (see also FLÈCHE).

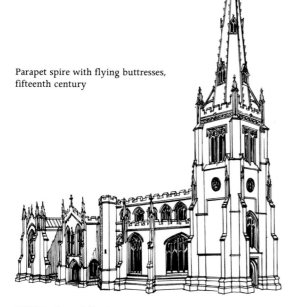

Parapet spire with flying buttresses, fifteenth century

SPUR In architecture:

1. A sloping buttress.
2. A defensive projection from a wall.
3. A supporting strut or stay.
4. A carved decorative feature between a circular base moulding and the square plinth on which it stands (see BASE).

A *spur stone* is one which is erected at the corner of a building to protect it from damage by passing traffic.

SQUINCH A series of arches each corbelled out in advance of the one below, built across the corners of a square tower or chamber to support an octagonal or circular feature such as a spire or dome (see DOME; SPIRE).

SQUINT Also known as a *hagioscope*, it is a small opening cut obliquely in a wall or pier of a church to permit a view of the altar from the aisles or transepts.

STADDLE STONES Mushroom-shaped stones placed on the ground to support timber structures containing grain or hay. Their purpose is to raise the building above the dampness of the earth and to prevent entry by rats and mice.

STADIUM In ancient Greece in early times a stadium was a foot racecourse. The word derives from *stade*, the unit of measure (about 600ft or 186m) which was the length of the standard foot race. Later the stadium was used for general athletic competition, musical performances and dramatic spectacles. Most Greek examples were set into the hillside and provided unroofed seating for spectators.

The stadium in Athens was built in 331 BC and accommodated 50,000 spectators. It was rebuilt in marble in

The stadium, Delphi, Greece, sixth century BC

Flaminio Stadium, Rome, in reinforced concrete. Engineer: Pier Luigi Nervi, 1958–9

1896 for the first Olympic Games of modern times. Several examples survive in a fair state of preservation as, for instance, that at Delphi (holding 7,000 spectators) which is built high up the mountainside above the theatre.

The modern stadium, used for sports and spectacles of all kinds, is commonly built of reinforced concrete and is often partly or wholly roofed with plastic materials.

STAIRCASE During the Middle Ages many staircases were of the *newel* type; that is, the steps were constructed in a winding or spiral manner round a central post. Such staircases could be of wood or stone and were often built into turrets or the thickness of stone walls. Alternatively there were stone stairs which led up the exterior of a building from one floor to another or wood-ladder stairs built inside for the same purpose; these often had handrail and newel but no risers (see **Glossary** below). By the fifteenth century straight, single-flight staircases were being constructed inside buildings.

In the later sixteenth century the *dog-legged* staircase was developed. The Elizabethan great house was large enough to accommodate this more massive construction (see COUNTRY HOUSE AND MANSION; ELIZABETHAN ARCHITECTURE). There was still no central well and the broad flights, which were joined by a landing, returned parallel to one another, with balustrades directed to one newel at the landing.

In the early seventeenth-century Jacobean building the *open well* staircase had evolved from the dog-legged design. In this type the flights ascended the walls of a square well leaving an open space in the centre between the outer strings and newels. Many seventeenth-century staircases were on the grand scale. They were made entirely of wood, usually oak, and were constructed with heavy decoratively carved balusters, string and newels: treads were broad, risers low. The ornamental panel balustrade, carved elaborately in scrolls and foliage, was more characteristic of the second half of the century.

Eighteenth-century and Regency staircases were less massive; many were very beautiful and showed a high standard of craftsmanship. Some were entirely of wood, generally mahogany; others had stone or marble steps. Balusters were turned in bobbin, vase or twisted manner according to date and the balusters became slenderer as the century progressed. The balustrade was now of *open-string* design, the balusters standing individually directly upon the treads in groups of two or three. After the mid-century there was greater variety in staircase design. Many examples had mahogany handrails, delicately made wrought-iron balustrades and stone or marble steps. Some designs were in straight flights, others were on a circular or elliptical plan, the steps cantilevered, one end built into the wall (see CANTILEVER).

During the nineteenth century cast iron was widely used in staircase construction, not only for balusters but also for handrail and newels. Gothic forms were widely incorporated into the balustrade construction. Some staircases were mass-produced and simple, others elaborately ornate. In contrast, the modern staircase has tended to simplicity and, in many designs, returned to the medieval no-riser ladder construction.

Glossary of terms

Those marked * are the subject of a separate article.

Baluster: see BALUSTRADE.
*Balustrade**.
Cockle stair: a winding stair.
Curtail step: the lowest step (steps) of a stair in which the outer end is carried round in a scroll.
Dog-leg stair: one in which the flights, joined by landings, return parallel to one another.
Flight: a continuous series of steps leading from one landing to another.
Geometrical stair: one generally built on a circular or elliptical plan in which each step rests upon the one below and one end of which is built into the wall.

Adam staircase, *c.* 1775, at 20 St James's Square, London

Exterior stone flight of steps in fourteenth-century castle

Wooden ladder-type staircase leading from hall floor to gallery, fifteenth century

Spiral or newel stone staircase in late thirteenth-century manor house

Winder
Oak newel staircase, *c.* 1550.

Carved oak closed-string dog-legged staircase, *c.* 1600, Elizabethan

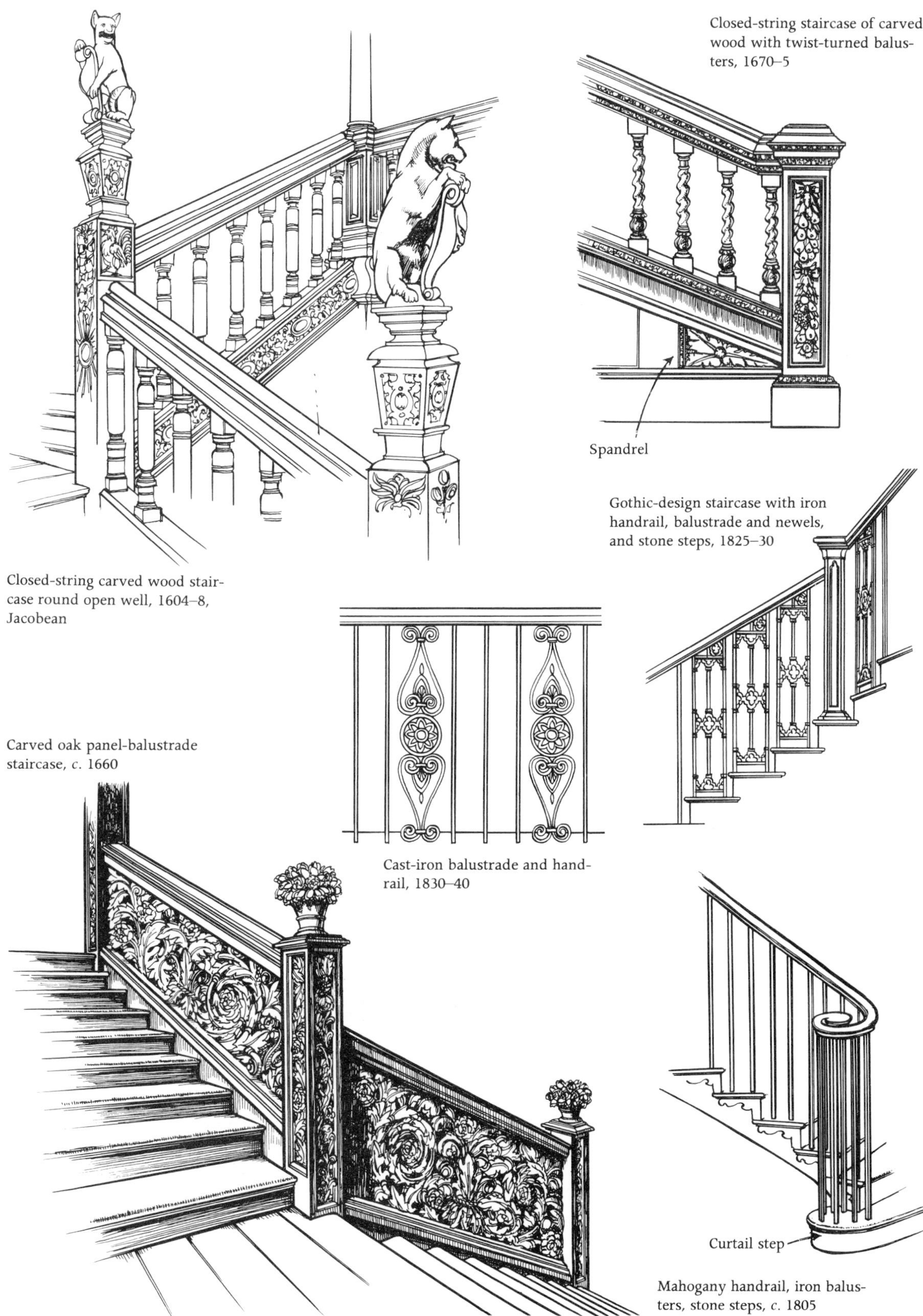

Closed-string staircase of carved wood with twist-turned balusters, 1670–5

Closed-string carved wood staircase round open well, 1604–8, Jacobean

Gothic-design staircase with iron handrail, balustrade and newels, and stone steps, 1825–30

Carved oak panel-balustrade staircase, *c.* 1660

Cast-iron balustrade and handrail, 1830–40

Mahogany handrail, iron balusters, stone steps, *c.* 1805

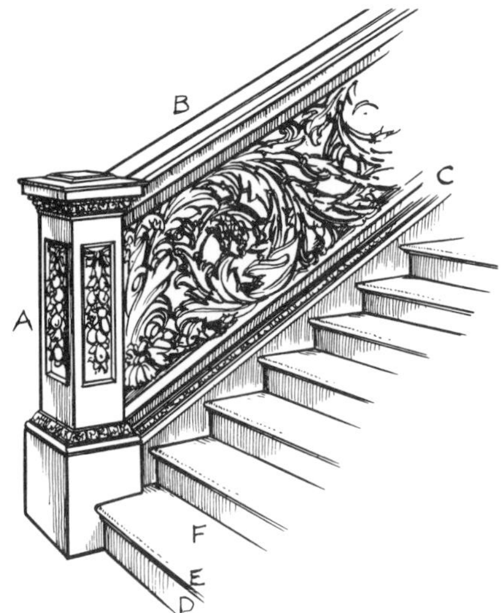

Closed-string carved wood staircase with pierced panel balustrade, *c.* 1680
A Newel B Handrail
C String D Riser E Nosing
F Tread

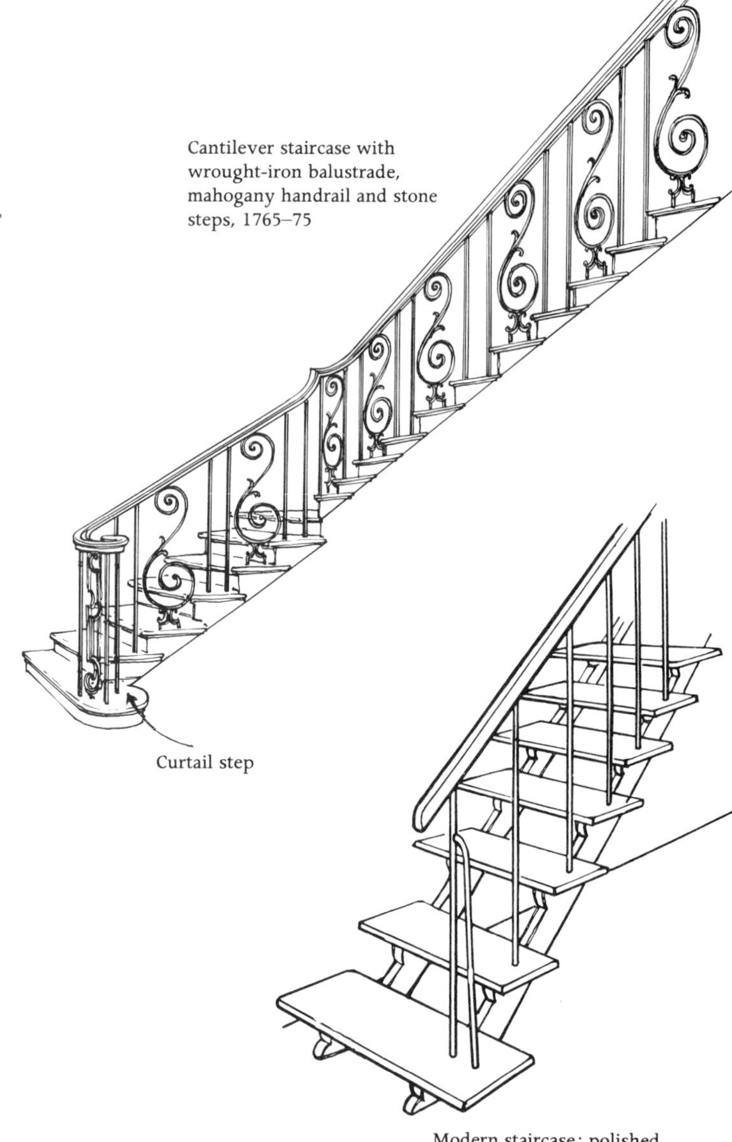

Cantilever staircase with wrought-iron balustrade, mahogany handrail and stone steps, 1765–75

Modern staircase: polished wood treads, no risers, metal balusters

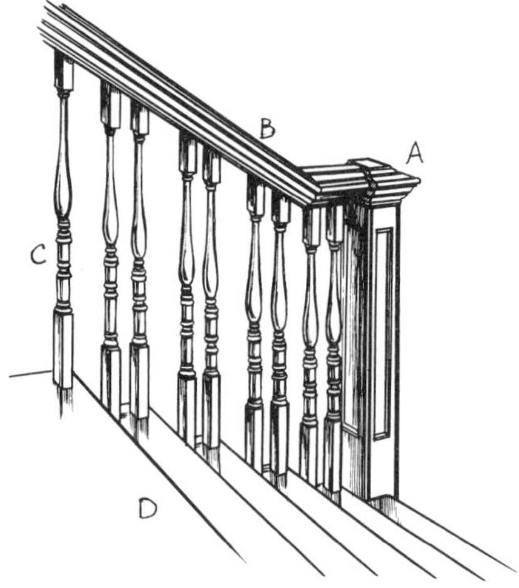

Open-string wood staircase, *c.* 1700
A Newel B Handrail
C Vase-turned balusters
D Tread

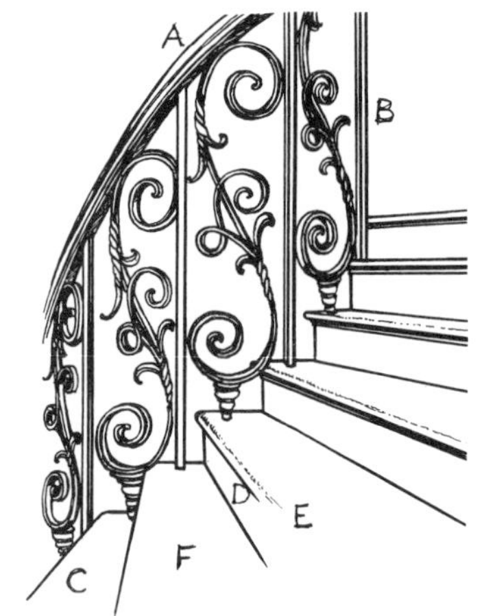

Open-string geometrical staircase, *c.* 1790
A Handrail
B Wrought-iron balustrade
C Tread D Riser E Nosing
F Winder

Newel: the main post at the angle of a staircase to which the string and handrail are fitted. In a *newel staircase* the post is a central pillar round which the steps of this type of spiral stair wind.
*Nosing**.
Rise: in a *step*, the vertical distance between the upper surface of two consecutive treads; in a *flight*, the height from top to bottom.
Riser: the vertical front part of each step.
Scotia: a concave moulding under the nosing of a step.
*Soffit**: under-surface of a stair.
*Spandrel**.
String: the inclined baulk of timber supporting the steps of a staircase. A *closed-string* stair is one where the balusters, of equal length, stand upon the sloping string. An *open-string* (or *cut-string*) stair is one where the balusters stand directly upon the treads, two or three per tread, so that their height varies according to their position along the handrail.
Tread: the horizontal upper surface of a step.
Turnpike stair: a spiral staircase.
Vice, Vyce stair: a newel staircase.
Well: the open space in the centre of an open-well staircase, that is, between the outer strings of the stair flights.
Winder: a tread which is wider at one end than the other, to be found in a spiral or geometrical staircase or one which turns a right-angle corner.

STEEL-FRAME CONSTRUCTION
Bessemer converter steel plant, Ebbw Vale, 1860. Photo: Science Museum, London

STALLS Compartments or divisions of an area. The word referred in early times to the division of a stable into compartments, one for each animal. Similarly, the term came to mean the divisions into allocated spaces for the seating of clergy in the choir of a church. In medieval churches choir stalls are often the recipients of magnificent decorative wood carving and, in cathedrals and major churches, these are usually canopied.

Choir stalls also often possess carved undersides to the seats which are hinged to lift back. These rich and varied carvings are brackets which, when lifted up, gave some support and relief from standing to the occupant during lengthy services. Such a bracket is called a *misericord*, a term derived from the Latin *misericordia*, meaning 'pity' or 'mercy'.

STAY Structurally a brace or strut (see TIMBER TRUSSED ROOF).

STEEL FRAME CONSTRUCTION Steel had been made in small quantities until the early eighteenth century in Europe by the cementation process and from 1740 by the wootz method ('wootz' is a corruption of a Canarese word for a crucible steel made in southern India). This was introduced commercially into England by *Benjamin Huntsman* (1704–76) who re-melted the blister steel in closed crucibles to produce a steel with better, more uniform carbon content. Steel contains more carbon than wrought iron but less than cast iron (see IRONWORK). In order to make it more cheaply a way had to be found to remove the excess carbon and impurities from the molten pig iron and with a smaller quantity of fuel.

It was *Henry Bessemer* (1813–98) in England (also *William Kelly* in America) who revolutionized steel-making with the discovery that this could be done, by blowing a stream of air through it to create a higher temperature. Bessemer designed his 'converter', a vessel in which this process was carried out and which could then be tilted in order to pour out the molten metal into ingots.

Meanwhile *Frederick Siemens* (1826–1904) was developing with his brother *William* in Germany his idea of heat regeneration in which hot waste gases could be utilized to pre-heat the fuel and air entering the furnace. At first solid fuel was used but William Siemens invented the gas-producer in 1861; this converted the solid fuel into gas which made it possible to obtain a high working temperature of 1650°C from the use of low-grade coal as well as utilizing scrap iron. These advantages led by 1870 to the growth of the *open-hearth* method of steel-making as an alternative to the Bessemer process and by 1900 this had become the principal way of making steel.

Most of the steel required in the early decades of the twentieth century continued to be made by the open-hearth method until after 1945, but this has now been superseded by the *oxygen-lance* process where pure oxygen is injected into molten steel through a water-cooled lance inserted into the mouth of the converter vessel. Another method (first developed commercially in 1900 in France) using an arc furnace, where an electric arc is struck between electrodes to melt the metal, produces about 20 per cent of British steel.

Today a wide variety of alloy steels is available for specific functions and needs, for example to be especially hard, heat-resistant or stainless. For building and engineering structures alloy steels have been developed to possess great tensile strength. Alloy steels are made by adding specific amounts of other elements during manufacture. At first such alloys were produced accidentally—Michael Faraday prepared alloy steels in laboratory experiments as early as 1819—but commercial development came only with the burgeoning production of steel in the late nineteenth century.

It can be seen, therefore, that by the 1860s it was becoming possible to use steel as a structural material to replace iron but it was not until the 1890s that the full possibilities of the material for architectural construction were completely realized. It was the coinciding of the availability of cheaper, better steel from the open-hearth process with the needs of metal framing for commercial skyscraper building which established the vital importance of the material (see HIGH-RISE BUILDING; INDUSTRIALIZED BUILDING; IRON AND GLASS).

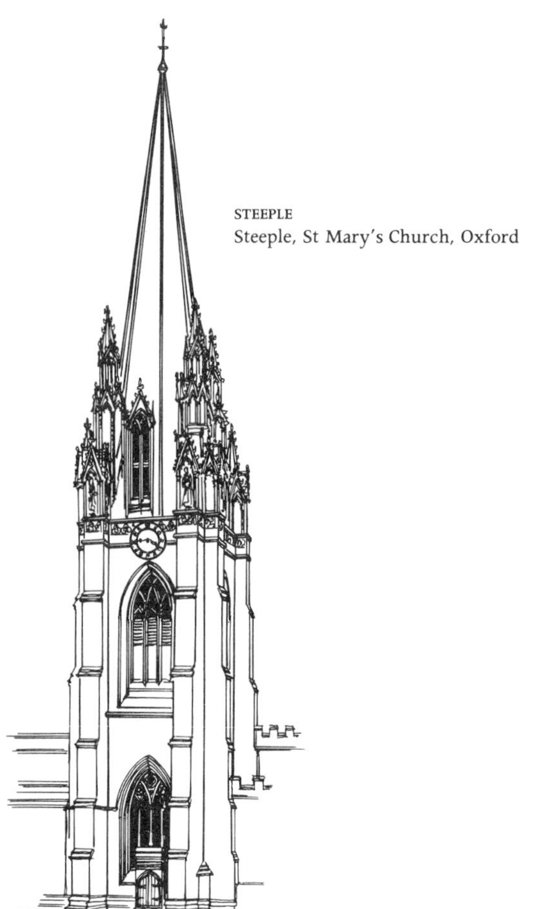

STEEPLE
Steeple, St Mary's Church, Oxford

STEEPLE The combined tower and spire of a church.

STEUART, GEORGE (*c.* 1730–1806) Designer and builder of a number of country houses of which *Attingham Park* in Shropshire (1783–5) is the best known; this is a graceful neo-classical house on the traditional pattern.

Steuart's most important achievement is *St Chad's Church, Shrewsbury* (1790–2) which stands on a fine site above the town. It is an imposing design of unusual conception having a circular nave and free-standing tower; it can accommodate a large congregation.

STIRLING, JAMES (b. 1926) Individualist and architect of original ideas, the controversial personality of contemporary British architecture. Each succeeding commission completed by Stirling arouses dissent among professional colleagues, architectural critics and users of his buildings. He has been variously described as the 'best architect of his generation' and 'a designer of fascist architecture', and his work as 'anti-architecture'.

James Stirling was born in Glasgow but grew up and was trained in Liverpool. He worked for some time in the office of Lyons, Israel and Ellis where he met *James Gowan* (b. 1924) and the two architects set up practice together. Among their early works was the *housing estate*

STEUART, GEORGE
St Chad's Church, Shrewsbury, 1790–2. Architect: George Steuart

at *Ham Common* near London (1955–8), a flirtation with the current wave of New Brutalism (see CONCRETE). They went on to build the *Engineering Faculty Building* at *Leicester University* (1959–63) which established their reputation. This was a more spectacular design comprising offices and lecture theatres in a tower and single-storey workshops where they extensively employed patent industrial glazing complemented by vivid red tiling.

The two architects then parted company and Stirling went on to become much better known and exhibit a range of different interpretations of modern techniques and materials to suit varied commissions. In the 1960s, as with so many British architects, he was responsible for a quantity of work at the universities which were then expanding quickly. He built the *History Faculty Building* at *Cambridge* (1964–7) and the *Florey Building* for Queen's College at *Oxford* (1966–71). Both these complexes are bold and powerful. Large areas of glass are used with strongly coloured brick and glazed tiling. The buildings are statements of solid geometry, uncompromising but not without interest. According to some of the academic users they are uncomfortable and suffer from building faults, leaking glass, noise disturbance etc. The architect feels that they have not been well maintained.

Stirling went on to design geometrical concrete blocks for housing at *Runcorn* (1967–76) reminiscent to a degree of Le Corbusier (see MODERN ARCHITECTURE) and residential accommodation at *St Andrew's University* (1964–8). These long, low blocks in reinforced concrete have been described, among other things, as a concrete IBM card. This is hardly to do them justice for, although there is verity in the simile, there is also a repetitive rhythm. In the *Training Centre* at *Haslemere* in Surrey designed for *Olivetti* (1969–72) there was another change of approach. A complex built in glass, aluminium and plastic, this is the 'wet look', with the sharp angles rounded off, and curving, flowing surfaces. The buildings are eminently functional, particularly the impressive multi-purpose glazed gallery.

In the 1970s (in practice since 1971 with Michael Wilford) Stirling concentrated on work abroad where he has achieved an international reputation especially in Germany and the USA. He has held professorships of architecture at Yale and Düsseldorf, was recipient of the Alvar Aalto prize for architecture in Finland (see MODERN ARCHITECTURE) and has won a number of competitions for important commissions. These include the *Rice University School of Architecture* extension at *Houston*, Texas (1979–81), the *Staatsgalerie* complex, including the new *Staatstheater* in *Stuttgart*, Germany (1977–83) and the *Wissenschaftcentrum* in Berlin (1980, for completion in 1984). In England, Stirling's latest important commission is the long-awaited *Clore Gallery* now being built to house the Turner Collection at the *Tate Gallery* in London (the foundation stone was unveiled in April 1983).

It is said, by some writers, that in these later works Stirling has turned towards eclecticism, chiefly of neo-classical derivation, to harmonize with existing buildings. In Stuttgart, for instance, the original Staatsgalerie was built in 1825, a neo-classical structure. The Tate Gallery also is in classical form. But Stirling's stripped neo-classicism bears little relationship to Soane's or Schinkel's; it is, like all Stirling's work, individualistic and personal and essentially of the present day. His work of the 1980s is more sophisticated and less strident than that of the 1960s; it has more sympathy but it is still striking and never repetitious. Although he has received most acclaim from Europe and America since 1970, his own country has not forgotten Stirling. The Royal Institute of British Architects awarded him their Gold Medal in 1980.

STOA In ancient Greek architecture a roofed promenade, colonnaded in front and walled at the rear, where doorways lead into the various buildings. In Byzantine architecture a covered hall the roof of which is supported by rows of columns.

Long stoas were characteristic architectural features of the market place (*agora*) of ancient Greek cities. These single- or double-storey structures contained shops, offices, temples, so enabling people to shop and carry out their business protected from the sun and rain.

STOA
The Stoa of Attalos, *c.* 150 BC in the agora of Athens. Restored 1953–6 by the American School of Classical Studies in Athens

STONE The best of all traditional building materials for durability and architectural and artistic quality. In Britain, for many centuries, due to difficulties of transportation, building in stone was confined to the considerable areas of the country where it was easily available. Also, because of the cost of quarrying and of working the material, its use was limited to the ability of the client to pay.

There is great variety in type and quality of building stone in Britain. Over 90 per cent of such stones are limestone and sandstone and, according to district, there are a great number of different limestones and sandstones. Limestone consists mainly of carbonate of lime, sandstone of particles of quartz usually with other minerals incorporated such as mica and felspar.

The remaining building stones are largely granite and marble, both of which are employed chiefly because they will take a high polish. Most forms of granite are igneous rock; that is, they were formed when molten material cooled. Granite is extremely hard and is crystalline. It is

STIRLING, JAMES
New Staatstheater, Stuttgart, Germany (part of Staatsgalerie complex). Architect: James Stirling

highly durable, being impervious to water and resistant to atmospheric pollution in towns. Its hardness, however, makes if difficult to decorate. Marble is a crystalline form of limestone of which there are comparatively few examples in Britain. These include the Irish Connemara marble and that quarried on the Island of Iona. See also related articles on ALABASTER; BUILDING MATERIALS; BRICKWORK; COADE STONE; MASONRY; SLATE; TERRACOTTA; TILES.

Selected list of widely used building stones

Ancaster: a granular limestone from central Lincolnshire.

Bargate: a calcareous sandstone from the Guildford district of Surrey.

Barnack: a limestone from the area around Peterborough used extensively during the Middle Ages.

Bath: an oolite limestone widely employed for building since before the Norman Conquest.

Caen: a limestone from Normandy imported in quantity by sea to the south-east of England in the early Middle Ages.

Carboniferous limestone: a hard stone from many hilly areas such as the northern Pennines, the Derbyshire Peak District and the Mendips.

Carstone: a hard sandstone impregnated with iron oxide, and so brownish in shade, to be found chiefly in Cambridgeshire and Norfolk.

Chalk: a form of limestone used for building especially along southern coastal areas of England (see also BUILDING MATERIALS).

Clipsham: a hard limestone of cream to buff colour from southern Lincolnshire.

Collyweston: a Northamptonshire limestone used chiefly for stone slates.

Connemara marble: a dolomitic limestone, greenish in shade marked with white, from County Galway in Ireland.

Cotswold: a limestone of varying quality from a wide area in south-west England, used extensively from the early Middle Ages onwards for building and roofing.

Craigleith: a carboniferous sandstone, no longer quarried, but known particularly for its extensive use for the buildings of Edinburgh.

Granite: a hard, durable, crystalline, igneous rock containing a number of minerals, notably quartz, felspar and mica. Granite will take a high polish but is extremely hard to cut so decorative mouldings were rarely possible before the advent of power tools. Because of its durability and resistance to atmospheric pollution and water, granite is often used as a cladding material. Aberdeen is probably the city where it has been most extensively utilized. Granite has been chiefly quarried in Scotland, Ireland, Wales, Cumbria and Devon. Its colour, determined mainly by its felspar content, ranges from red and pink to grey, greenish tones to white, often in a mottled pattern.

Hopton Wood: a beautiful limestone in cream and grey or brownish tone which may be polished and so suitable for sculptural use. Quarried in Derbyshire, Cumbria, Yorkshire and County Durham.

Iona: a green and white marble quarried on the island.

Ironstone: a stone which has been impregnated with iron.

Ketton: a Northamptonshire limestone quarried chiefly between the fifteenth and nineteenth centuries.

Magnesian limestone: one which contains carbonate of magnesium and is found mainly in eastern Yorkshire.

Malmstone: a soft, friable sandstone containing lime mostly quarried in south-east England.

Marlstone: a limestone containing iron which gives it a reddish colour used especially during the Middle Ages and found in several Midland sites.

Millstone grit: a strong, durable carboniferous sandstone of dark colour, quarried from Roman times in the Pennine regions of Yorkshire and Lancashire also southwards to Derbyshire and northwards to Northumberland.

New red sandstone: the chief building stone of the west Midlands. *Old red sandstone* (older geologically) can be more varied in colour from red to purple, pink or brown. It is found in Devon and Cornwall, also Scotland, Wales and Ireland.

Portland: a limestone of fine and even texture, probably the best building stone of England. Stone from the Isle of Portland in Dorset was quarried by the Romans and continued to be worked on a small scale during the Middle Ages but, because it was hard and difficult to work, did not come into extensive use until, in the seventeenth century, water power and frame saws made the cutting of large blocks a possibility. It was Wren in his rebuilding of the City of London who first popularized its use because of the ability to cut large blocks at the quarry (see WREN, SIR CHRISTOPHER).

Purbeck: a limestone from the Isle of Purbeck in Dorset. Purbeck 'marble', the crystalline limestone from the Corfe Castle area of Dorset, which could be highly polished, was immensely popular during the Middle Ages for interior ecclesiastical work, especially for column shafts, as can be seen in many cathedrals and churches, most notably those built in the Early English and Decorated Gothic periods: the prime example is Salisbury Cathedral. Early access to the sea at Poole made it possible to transport Purbeck marble via river systems to many other parts of England especially in the south.

Serpentine marble: a Cornish marble from the Lizard peninsula which is usually dark green and marked like a snake's skin. Will take a high polish and is ideal for sculptural decoration.

Sussex marble: a greyish-blue crystalline limestone widely used during the Middle Ages and later.

Tufa: a lightweight sponge-like limestone formed by water precipitating a lime deposit from older adjacent limestone. A material widely used in ancient Rome especially for vaulting because of its lightness and extensively utilized in England from the time of the Roman occupation until about 1400.

Wealden: a Sussex sandstone.

Weldon: a fawn-coloured limestone.
York: a hard, fine, even-grain, pale brown sandstone from Yorkshire, some of which is strongly laminated, in which case it is widely used for paving.

STOREY, STORY The stages, set one above the other, of which a building is composed or the space between two floors of a building. In Britain the lowest storey, which may be wholly or partly below ground, is the basement. At ground level is the ground floor (in America this is known as the first floor) and above this one the first, second, third floor etc. In many periods of design, and especially in classical architecture, the first floor is the principal one, for which the Italian term *piano nobile* is often used. The top floor rooms, which might be lit by dormers and have sloping ceilings, are attics (see also ATTIC). An intermediate storey between the ground and first floor is called a *mezzanine* or *entresol*.

STRAPWORK A Renaissance surface decoration of Flemish origin composed of ornamented interlacing broad bands or straps to be seen especially in late Elizabethan and in Jacobean building in England on ceilings, friezes and wood panelling (see JACOBEAN ARCHITECTURE).

STRAPWORK
Strapwork ceiling design: Athelhampton, Dorset

STREET, GEORGE EDMUND (1824–81) Born in Essex, Street studied when young in Winchester under Owen Carter. At the age of twenty he entered Scott's office (see SCOTT, SIR GEORGE GILBERT), where he worked for five years then, in 1849, set up in practice for himself. Street travelled extensively in Europe; in France and Germany in 1850–1, then Italy in 1853. His Italian work led to the publication in 1855 of his *The Brick and Marble Architecture of Northern Italy*, a work which, like Ruskin's publications (see RUSKIN, JOHN), had a strong influence on the architecture of his time. During the years 1861–3 Street visited Spain three times and in 1865 his *The Gothic Architecture of Spain* appeared; this was an important book finely illustrated with his own drawings.

Meanwhile, in 1852, Street, who had become a protégé of Bishop Wilberforce of Oxford and thus Diocesan Architect, was commissioned to build the new training college for clergy in the area, the *Oxford Diocesan Theological College* at *Cuddesdon*. He set up practice in Oxford, building among other projects *St Mary's Church* at *Wheatley* (1855–68) which is a stone church in Early English (First Pointed) style. It is a simple, rather severe, church with lancet and plate-traceried windows and a solid square tower capped by a traditional spire.

Soon after the Wheatley church was begun, Street moved his practice to London. He designed many churches in various interpretations of High Victorian Gothic, mainly 'Middle (Second) Pointed' English Gothic but some churches also showing French or Italian influence. Many of his designs were uncompromisingly severe but all were of high-quality workmanship in design, detail and building finish. Street was a perfectionist; he was intellectually honest and an untiring worker. He was a deeply religious man, of High Church persuasion and a member of the Ecclesiologist Society. His most important churches are *St James the Less* in *London* (1860–1) and *St Philip and St James* in *Oxford* (1852–65). The London church (in Westminster) is built of polychrome brickwork, mainly in deep red with black banding. On the exterior at one corner stands a tall steeple; the large interior is richly decorated in brick, ceramic, marble and stone. SS. Philip and James is a characteristically individual Street design with a French Gothic flavour. Other Street churches include *All Saints, Clifton*, Bristol (1863–8), *St Paul, Herne Hill* (1858), *St John, Kennington* (1870–4), *St Peter, Bournemouth* (1853), *St John, Torquay* (1861–71) and, a pleasant country church, *St Mary* at *Fawley*, Berkshire (1864–6).

Street held several diocesan appointments and, in this capacity, carried out a great deal of ecclesiastical restoration work. For instance, at *Bristol Cathedral*, he rebuilt the nave and west front (1868–88). In 1871 he became an RA and was also Professor of Architecture at the Royal Academy Schools. He served a term as President of the Royal Society of British Architects. He received a number of recognitions for his studies of European (particularly French) Gothic architecture.

Church of St James the Less, Westminster, London, 1860–1

The Law Courts, Strand, London, 1868–80

St Mary's Church, Fawley, Berkshire, 1864–6

Oxford Diocesan Theological College, Cuddesdon, 1852–78

Street is best known for his chief secular work, on which he spent much of the last 15 years of his life: the *Law Courts* in the *Strand* in London. He won the competition for this complex in 1866 but it was a commission which dragged on for many years (the site being changed more than once) and he died before the building was finally complete. The Strand front was a difficult one, very long and narrow and Street's irregular stone façade is successful in breaking up what might have been, in the hands of a less able architect, a monotonous elevation. The work is severely Gothic in his favourite thirteenth-century castellated style. Inside, the architect's treatment of the Great Hall is very fine.

STRESSED SKIN CONSTRUCTION A constructional method which utilizes the load-carrying capacity of a skin material fastened to a framework so that the complete unit acts integrally thus increasing its flexural strength. Made-up panels of such units are manufactured for use for floors, walls and roofs. Timber is most frequently employed for this purpose, plywood being glued or mechanically fastened to a timber framing, but any material with tensile strength may be suitable, for example metal and some plastics.

STUART, JAMES (1713–88) A draughtsman and painter whose reputation in architecture was made by the publication from 1762 onwards, in conjunction with *Nicholas Revett*, of their books of drawings of ancient Greece (see DILETTANTI SOCIETY; GRAND TOUR).

Stuart set out on his European travels in 1742, paying his own way from his earnings derived from painting fans. He stayed in Rome for some years then, in 1748, accompanied by colleagues, visited Naples. Both Revett and Stuart were interested in studying Greek architecture at first hand and received financial support for a proposed expedition to Athens from the Dilettanti Society. They set out in 1751, returning in 1755. The first volume showing the results of their studies was published in 1762. Entitled *The Antiquities of Athens measured and delineated by James Stuart FRS and FSA and Nicholas Revett, Painters and Architects*, the measured drawings were by Revett while Stuart's contribution was more modest being confined to views engraved from his gouache drawings.

It was Stuart who became well-known from this publication of which the second and third volumes appeared after his death in 1789 and 1816 respectively. Commissions in painting and architecture were offered to him but, due to indolence and disinterest, he actually built very little. He is known only for his surviving work of the Doric Temple at *Hagley Park*, Worcestershire (1758), his interior decoration at *Spencer House* in London (*c.* 1760), *15 St James's Square*, London (1763–6 but interiors altered *c.* 1791 by Wyatt) and the park buildings at *Shug-*

STUART, JAMES
15 St James's Square, London, 1763–6

SWAG

Swag

Festoon

borough, Staffordshire (1764–70); these comprise a triumphal arch (based on Hadrian's Arch in Athens) and copies of the Athenian Tower of the Winds and Monument of Lysicrates.

The influence on British architecture of the *Antiquities of Athens*, like Robert Adam's later publications, was primarily an interior decorative one: the Greek Revival was far in the future. The neo-classical interiors of architects such as Adam, Wyatt and Holland as well as the ceramic products of Wedgwood were affected by these studies of ancient Greece but the excavations at Herculaneum and Pompeii were arguably the stronger influence.

SUMMER Also *sommer*, the principal beam in a building supporting the floor joists. *Bressumer* is similar but often refers to a main beam spanning an opening or the façade of a structure (see BRESSUMER).

SURBASED, SURMOUNTED A dome or arch whose rise is less than half its span (see ARCH) is 'surbased'. A dome or arch whose rise is greater than half its span is 'surmounted'.

SWAG An ornamental motif composed of draped fabric suspended from two points and hanging in a curve between: similar to a *festoon*, which is in the form of a floral decoration.

T

TABERNACLE The ornamental niche or receptacle placed above or behind the altar in a church to contain the Holy Sacrament.

Tabernacle work is the decoratively carved woodwork of canopies over choir stalls, niches and pulpits.

TALMAN, WILLIAM (1650–1719) A contemporary of Wren (see WREN, SIR CHRISTOPHER) and an important country house architect; few documented examples of his work survive. In the years 1689–1702 he was Comptroller of the King's Works, after which he was replaced by Vanbrugh (see VANBRUGH, SIR JOHN). His work shows both Italian and French influences. Most of his designs, which were for large houses, utilize a giant order in pilaster form.

An early Talman house was *Stanstead Park* in Sussex (1686) but this was later remodelled then finally burnt down in 1900. At *Chatsworth House*, Derbyshire he rebuilt the south and east fronts (1687–96) and was in charge at *Dyrham Park*, Gloucestershire from 1698, where he designed the east (entrance) front and the Orangery. He then rebuilt the south front of *Drayton House*, Northamptonshire in 1702. At *Uppark* in Sussex he designed the house (*c.* 1690) to which wings were added later. At *Hampton Court Palace* Talman, serving as Comptroller

TALMAN, WILLIAM
South front, Chatsworth House, Derbyshire. Rebuilt 1687–96 by William Talman

under Wren, carried out a good deal of work especially in the interiors and in laying out the grounds.

TAMBOUR The general meaning of the word is 'drum'. In architecture, therefore, it may refer to:

1. The core or bell of a Corinthian or Composite capital (see CLASSICAL ORDER).
2. The walls of a circular building surrounded by columns.
3. The circular walls of a building supporting a dome as in the Roman Pantheon (see CLASSICAL ARCHITECTURE).
4. The circular walls of a lantern above a dome.

TAYLOR, SIR ROBERT (1714–88) Son of a mason, Sir Robert Taylor was apprenticed at the age of 18 to the sculptor Henry Cheere. At the end of his term of apprenticeship his father sent him to study in Rome but in 1743 lack of finance resulting from his father's death compelled

Uppark, Sussex, *c.* 1690. Architect William Talman

TAYLOR, SIR ROBERT
Sharpham House, Devon. Remodelled from *c.* 1770 by Sir Robert Taylor

him to cut short his studies and return to Britain.

Taylor practised as a sculptor for some time but then decided to take up architecture where, by patient study and hard work allied to an acute business sense, he built up a large architectural practice mainly patronized by city merchants. Taylor was in mid-century a Palladian architect, sharing most of the work available with Paine (see PAINE, JAMES). He was appointed to a number of important and useful positions among them in 1764 Surveyor to the Bank of England, in 1769 Architect of the King's Works, in 1788 Surveyor of Greenwich Hospital. He was knighted in 1782.

Sir Robert Taylor was a highly professional and competent architect but not an inspired or original one. His work reflected the architectural styles of his day so that until 1765–70 he was designing in the Palladian tradition, one of a second generation of such architects and carrying on the work of Campbell and Kent (see PALLADIAN ARCHITECTURE). After this his work became lighter, the decoration more delicate as he gradually adopted a neoclassical approach. This was to be seen most notably in his interiors of the 1770s for the Bank of England but his work here, like that of Soane who followed him (see SOANE, SIR JOHN), was lost in subsequent rebuilding.

A large proportion of Taylor's architecture has been destroyed or rebuilt. Of his surviving work *Heveningham Hall*, Suffolk (1778–*c.* 1780) was the largest house. The north façade is traditional in pattern with central block

Heveningham Hall, Suffolk. North front 1778–86. Architect: Sir Robert Taylor

flanked by pedimented side pavilions, all rusticated on the lower storey with first and second storeys spanned by a giant Corinthian Order. It is an extensive, impressive elevation. The interior of Heveningham was completed, after Taylor was dismissed, by Wyatt (see WYATT, JAMES). In Devon Taylor transformed the earlier stone house of *Sharpham* from c. 1770 into a Palladian one.

Of his smaller villa-type houses *Danson Hill*, Kent (*c*. 1760–5) and *Asgill House*, Richmond, Surrey (*c*. 1760–5) survive as do also his London buildings *Ely House*, Dover Street (*c*. 1772) and *3–6 Grafton Street* (1771–3). Taylor was also responsible for the graceful stone bridge over the River Thames at *Maidenhead*, Surrey (1772–7).

TECTON The name of a group practice of architects formed in 1932 by *Berthold Lubetkin* (b. 1901). Lubetkin was born in Georgia (now USSR). He studied in Moscow and practised for a short while in the USSR before continuing work in Paris. He moved to England in 1930.

In the 1930s the name of Tecton quickly became synonymous with modern methods of design and building particularly in the use of reinforced concrete: such work was uncommon in Britain at that time (see MODERN ARCHITECTURE). The group first built the luxury block of flats (*Highpoint*) at Highgate in north London (1935) to which a second block was added three years later. They became particularly known for their work at the *Zoological Gardens* in London, for example for the moulded concrete *Penguin Pool* there. In 1938–9 they were responsible for another pace-setting design, the *Finsbury Health Centre*. It was the consulting engineer of the group, *Ove Arup*, who was responsible for much of the enterprising methods of handling concrete for the Tecton buildings (see ARUP, SIR OVE).

Tecton was disbanded during the Second World War and, though reconstituted in the late 1940s, did not recover its initiative in leading the field of modern work. Over 30 years later, in 1982, Lubetkin was finally awarded the Gold Medal for Architecture by the Royal Institute of British Architects.

Highpoint flats, Highgate, London, built by Tecton, 1938

TEMPLATE, TEMPLET

1. A pattern or mould used for marking out shapes on materials.
2. A block of stone bedded on to a brick pier or wall to spread the load of the joist or beam above.

TEMPLE A sacred edifice devoted to divine worship and containing the symbol of the deity.

The classical temple of Greece and Rome was built not to accommodate worshippers as in a Christian church but to house the likeness of the deity. Earliest Greek Temples were based upon the design of the Mycenaean megaron in the Bronze Age palaces. They consisted of rectangular halls with frontal porches supported on columns. The Greek desire for symmetry led to the development of a portico at each end (see PORTICO) and enclosed a chamber to house the cult statue (see NAOS) and, later, another smaller room behind to serve as a treasury.

According to the size of temple the number of columns in the portico varied. Smaller temples had only four columns in their porticoes (tetrastyle form), larger examples had six (hexastyle), eight (octastyle), ten (decastyle) or twelve (dodecastyle). In each instance, there were generally twice as many columns in the lateral colonnade as in the portico. All temples were raised on a continuous basement, usually of three steps. This stepped base is called the *crepidoma*, the platform of which is the *stylobate*. The entrance doorway was normally in the east wall behind the portico columns and designed so that sunlight would fall upon the cult statue in the naos. Windows were rare. Light was admitted through doorways and roof skylights. Roofs were low-pitched with a ridge pole. The triangular space at each end of the temple was closed by a wall (see TYMPANUM) and protected by a raking cornice. The pedimental tympanum was generally enriched with sculpture. The rafters were covered by tiles and these were finished at the sides in a gutter with waterspouts (*antefixae*) at intervals. *Acroteria* decorated the three angles of the pediment (see CLASSICAL ORDER).

Greek temples were designed for external effect, the worshippers remaining outside round the altar. The naos was plain and solidly walled, the sculptured and painted decoration being mainly on the exterior surfaces and confined to the frieze, pediments and acroteria. In large temples the width of the naos was too great to be spanned by wooden beams so interior colonnades were built to divide the space longitudinally. These colonnades were two-tiered in order to support the roof. Such interior colonnades have been lost from most Greek temple remains but may be seen at, for example, the *Temple of Hera* at

Peripteral hexastyle Greek Temple of Aphaia, Aegina. Early fifth century BC. This partial restoration is cut away to show two tiers of interior columns
A and B Acroteria
C Antefixae

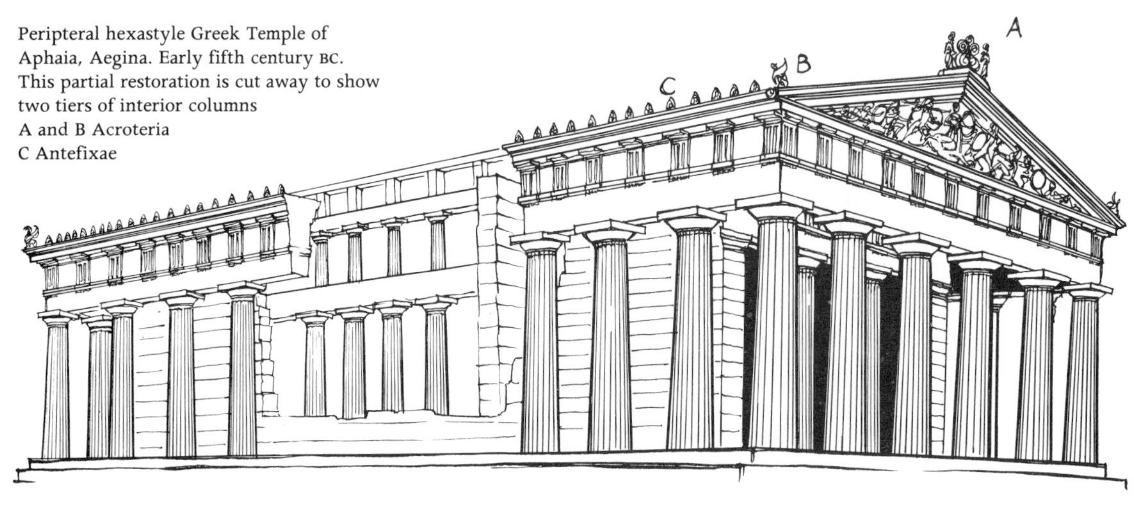

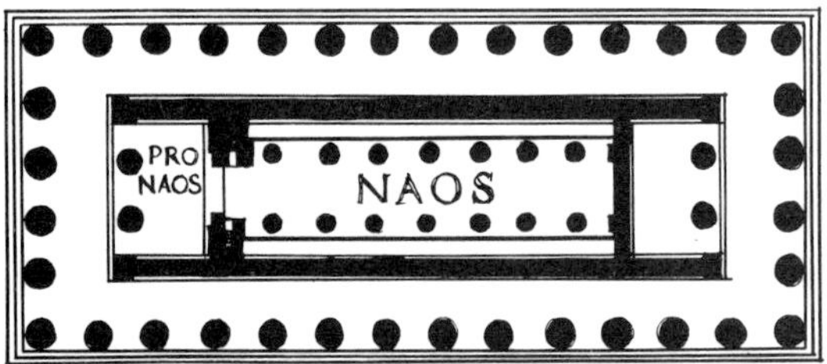

Plan of Temple of Hera, Paestum, Italy, *c.* 460 BC. Peripteral hexastyle Greek temple

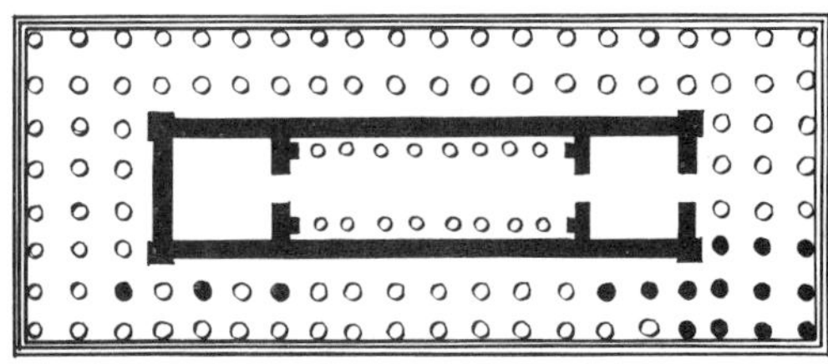

Plan of Olympeion (temple dedicated to Olympian Zeus), Athens, begun 174 BC. Dipteral octastyle Greek temple

Etruscan temple from Alatri (restored)
A Acroteria

Interior of Temple of Hera at Paestum showing second tier of columns inside naos

Roman Temple of Vesta in Forum Boarium, Rome, 30–10 BC. Peripteral circular temple (entablature replaced by a modern roof)

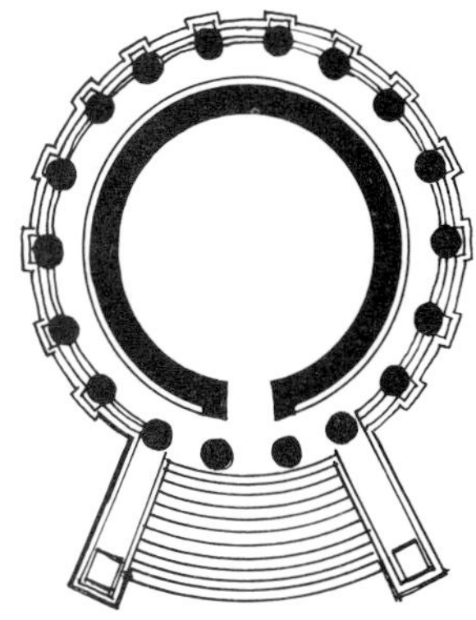

Plan of peripteral Roman temple like the Temple of Vesta

Etruscan antefixa. In form of Gorgon's head from Capua. Terracotta, sixth century BC

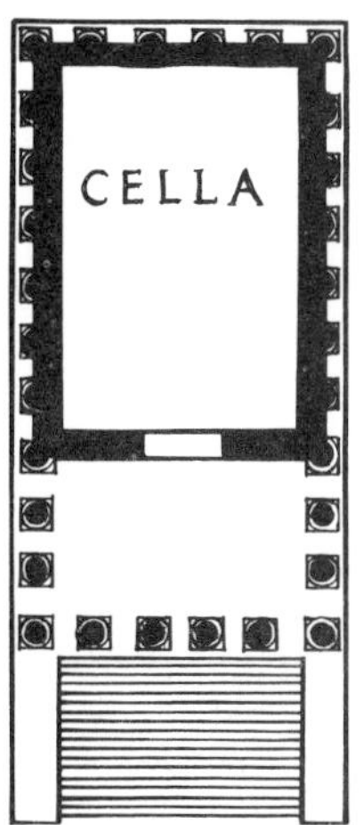

Plan of pseudo-peripteral hexastyle Roman temple: Maison Carrée, Nîmes, France, *c.* 16 BC

Plan of (pseudo-peripteral tetrastyle) Roman Temple of Fortuna Virilis, Rome, second century BC

Roman temple: the Maison Carrée, Nîmes, France, *c.* 16 BC. Pseudo-peripteral hexastyle temple

Paestum in Italy and the *Temple of Aphaia* at *Aegina* near Athens (see CLASSICAL ARCHITECTURE).

There exist extensive remains of *Etruscan temple* foundations but knowledge about the superstructure is more speculative. Vitruvius (see VITRUVIUS) provides a clear description of a late example which has a three-chamber interior, the cells placed side by side and dedicated to different deities. Much of the structure was of wood with decoration in terracotta and painting. A temple from *Alatri* has been re-erected and restored and stands in the court of the Villa Giulia in Rome.

Roman temple design is based upon the Greek prototype but the Roman cult chamber, the *cella*, was longer than the Greek naos in order to accommodate the sculpture and treasures brought from Greece. The cella was often widened at the expense of the peristyle so that the lateral ambulatories disappeared and half-columns were engaged with the walls to line up with the columns of the front portico: such a design is called *pseudo-peripteral*, a *peripteral* building being one which is surrounded by columns. Roman temples were usually raised on a podium rather than three steps and were approached via a staircase flight on the entrance front. Some Roman temples were circular, like a Greek tholos (see THOLOS) and comprised a circular cella with encircling colonnade.

Glossary of terms used in classical temple building

Adytum: an inner sanctuary.

Anta: a pilaster built against the wall on either side of a temple portico. When the portico has columns between such antae so that they range with the front wall, the portico is described as being *in antis*. Thus, a *distyle in antis* temple has two columns between the antae.

Cella: the main chamber in a temple which houses the cult image.

Crepidoma: the stepped base of a Greek temple.

Dipteral: describes a peristyle composed of a double row of columns.

Epinaos: the open space under the portico roof at the rear of a temple behind the naos.

Monopteral: describes a temple supported by a colonnade but without walls.

Naos: see NAOS.

Opisthodomus: an enclosed area at the rear of the naos in a Greek temple, often utilized as a treasury.

Peripteral: describes a temple enclosed by columns (see also PERISTYLE).

Pronaos: the area enclosed by side walls in front of the naos behind the portico.

Prostyle: where the portico columns stand in front of the pronaos.

Pseudo-dipteral: describes a temple where the peristyle is a double row of columns except for the part immediately surrounding the naos walls where there is only a single row.

Pseudo-peripteral: describes a temple where the lateral columns are engaged with the cella wall; characteristic of Roman temples.

Pteroma: the passageway or ambulatory between the naos walls and the peristyle.

Temenos: the sacred precinct surrounding or adjacent to a temple.

TERRACE ARCHITECTURE A terrace is a row of houses built adjoining one another and designed in a uniform manner.

The idea of planning town houses (see TOWN HOUSE) by the street, or even bounding all sides of a square, had been experimented with in the seventeenth century by *Inigo Jones* in *Covent Garden* in London (see JONES, INIGO). This concept of giving a uniform Palladian treatment to a street of houses tended to lapse in Britain after Inigo Jones's time and owners had their town houses built individually on similar, though not identical, patterns. From about 1750 town expansion began to accelerate quickly which made it economically and architecturally profitable to treat houses as one terraced façade. Ground landlords started to let their sites in larger blocks instead of, as previously, in areas large enough to accommodate only one or two houses. A few streets and squares in London were built within repetitive Palladian façades but the city where the idea was first fully developed was *Bath*.

It was between 1720 and 1730 that the value of the mineral waters in Bath was re-discovered and they were popularized for their alleged medicinal qualities. With royal patronage Bath quickly emerged from being a small town to a summer resort for health and entertainment. The leading figure in the consequent replanning and enlargement of the town was *Wood* (see WOOD, JOHN). By his work he helped to revive the popularity of Bath stone from the local quarries (see STONE). He had a masterly conception of town planning in terraces, streets and squares (see TOWN PLANNING). He did not visualize town houses simply as individual units but as part of a complete architectural layout for the city. In 1728–35 he built *Queen Square*, then went on to *South Parade* and, his masterpiece, the *Circus* which was completed in the 1760s by his son.

After John Wood died in 1754 a new generation of architects carried on his work, expanding and developing the idea into large-scale civic planning. The contours of the land posed problems. The city centre was sited on the low-lying land flanking the River Avon and the hills rose, sometimes steeply, around. The architects not only dealt with that problem, they took advantage of it. They built curving crescents and terraces on the edges of these hill crowns, giving fine vistas of both city and countryside. They built in stone in a Palladian manner on the grand scale.

John Wood, the younger, was one of these architects. He built the most impressive of these hill terraces, the *Royal*

Terrace-building in Bath: Pulteney Street with Holburne of Menstrie Museum in centre distance. Architect: Thomas Baldwin, 1785

Terrace-building in Bath: Camden Crescent. Architect John Jelly

Victorian terrace-building in stone: Blenheim Terrace, Manningham Lane, Bradford, Yorkshire, *c.* 1855

Terrace-building in London: Bedford Square. Partly by Thomas Leverton, 1780

Terrace-building in London. Pelham Crescent, South Kensington. Architect: George Basevi, 1820–30

Terrace-building in Brighton. Lewes Crescent, Kemp Town. Architect: H. E. Kendall

Terrace-building in Cheltenham. The Promenade, 1825–30

Terrace-building in London. Fitzroy Square. Architect: Robert Adam, 1790

Early Victorian terrace-building in London. Milner Square, Islington. Architects: Gough and Roumieu, 1841–3

Regency terrace-building in Hove: Brunswick Square. Architects: Wilds and Busby, *c.* 1826

Regency terrace-building in Brighton: Royal Crescent. Brick faced with black glazed mathematical tiles, *c.* 1800

Regency terrace-building in Hove: Brunswick Terrace. Architects: Wilds and Busby, *c.* 1825

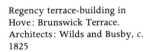

Crescent (1767–75). Here 114 Ionic columns front 30 houses in a uniform stone façade constructed on a major axis of 538ft: it remains one of the finest instances of terrace building in Britain (see WOOD, JOHN). Among the many other terraces in Bath of especial interest are *Lansdown Crescent* (1789–93) by *John Palmer* (see REGENCY ARCHITECTURE), *Camden Crescent* (1788) by *John Jelly* and *Pulteney Street* (1785) by *Baldwin* (see BALDWIN, THOMAS).

The influence of the terrace architecture in Bath was far-reaching. It encouraged architects in London and other towns in the later eighteenth and early nineteenth centuries to develop the theme in an endeavour to house their growing urban populations in housing of pleasing aesthetic quality at a reasonable price. In the later decades of the eighteenth century *London* began to follow Bath's example. Most of the leading neo-classical architects contributed. Arguably the most impressive of these schemes was the *Adelphi* achieved, despite financial, engineering and legal problems, by the *Adam brothers* (1768–74). The scheme provided palace façades to front the River Thames, high up to give a magnificent view. Houses of great beauty and good amenity were built there with offices, including stabling, water supply, heating etc. The theme was a late Roman palace; it bore a close resemblance (despite different architectural treatment) to the Palace of Diocletian in Split, Yugoslavia which had been so carefully studied *in situ* years before in 1757 by Robert Adam (see ADAM, ROBERT).

The Adam brothers undertook two other major speculative building enterprises in London streets. In *Portland Place* Robert Adam planned a *Grande Place* on the Continental pattern, surrounded by individual palaces, each different and especially designed for a wealthy patron. He interested a number of aristocrats but the advent of the American War of Independence (begun 1775) curtailed the desire for financial speculation and the scheme was shelved. It was a decade later when the houses in Portland Place were finally built by James Adam. The thoroughfare is a stately one and some of the houses survive but, in comparison with the usual Adam standard, they are stereotyped and repetitive; also, due to James's inadequate supervision during building, the standards were below par. *Fitzroy Square* was designed by Robert Adam in 1790 but built after his death. The south and east sides were constructed largely to his designs though the interiors have been altered.

Holland also undertook this type of speculative building in *Hans Town* (see HOLLAND, HENRY) as did *Leverton* in, for example, *Bedford Square* (see LEVERTON, THOMAS) while in the early decades of the nineteenth century Nash was establishing a vogue for stucco-faced brick terraces at Regent's Park (see NASH, JOHN). It was from 1800 that the steady but accelerating growth of the capital began to transform London from a normal city surrounded by pleasant villages—Hampstead, Chelsea, Blackheath for example—to a sprawling metropolis (see TOWN PLANNING). *Burton* and *Cubitt* were carrying out large-scale speculative development and, though not architects, were building to a high standard (see BURTON, JAMES; CUBITT, THOMAS) as were also the architects *Decimus Burton* and *Basevi* (see BURTON, DECIMUS; BASEVI, GEORGE).

Aside from the need for housing the increasing population of London and manufacturing towns, other, small centres of population were expanding rapidly due to leisure interests: these were the spas and sea-side resorts. Bath had been the eighteenth-century spa example. During the Regency the population grew at other spa towns such as Cheltenham, Tunbridge Wells and Buxton. In *Cheltenham, Papworth* and *Forbes* were the chief architects (see PAPWORTH, JOHN BUONARROTI). *Carr* contributed at *Buxton* (see CARR, JOHN) and at *Tunbridge Wells Decimus Burton* acted as architect for his father's building (see BURTON, JAMES).

Chief among the expanding sea-side resorts were *Brighton* and *Hove*, popularized by the Prince Regent and developed from the village of Brighthelmstone. Between 1800 and 1850 some two-and-a-half miles of sea-front terraces were laid out from Hove in the west to Kemp Town in the east. Today there are gaps where later development has intervened but a great deal survives. Here is the culmination of Nash's Regent's Park terrace ideal. There is no particularly local presentation, the work is mainly faced with painted stucco, as in London.

Many architects contributed to the building of the Brighton and Hove sea-front terraces. Of particular quality and distinction is the great length of *Brunswick Terrace* (*c.* 1825) built by *Charles Busby* and *Amon Wilds*; it is divided into two sections by the intervening *Brunswick Square* (*c.* 1826) by the same architects. Nearby is *Decimus Burton*'s *Adelaide Crescent* while, at the other end of the sea-front, are the magnificent terraces and squares of Kemp Town. On a more intimate scale is the *Royal Crescent* (see TILES). The Burtons, father and son, also contributed to the expansion at *Hastings* and *St Leonards*.

By 1830 terrace architecture was well established. It had been found to be the most economical way to build houses saving materials, land and time. The quality of such terraces as well as the architectural style varied enormously during the nineteenth century from style-less back-to-back houses, through middle-class brick terraces often in polychrome Gothic-style brickwork, to elegant classical schemes for the well-to-do. Despite the spread of high-rise building in modern times (see HIGH-RISE BUILDING; MODERN ARCHITECTURE), terrace architecture is still with us.

TERRACOTTA A fired earthenware material introduced to Britain from Italy in the sixteenth century for moulded decoration on buildings. The Italian word means 'baked earth'. Terracotta is harder and less porous than brick; its mix includes grog, that is, previously fired earthenware ground to a power (see BRICKWORK; COADE STONE).

TERRAZZO A hard finish suitable for floors and walls made from marble chips set in cement, then ground and polished.

TESSERAE A tessera is the small cube of material—glass, stone, marble—used in mosaic work. A *tessellated* finish for floors and walls is one in which the tesserae are embedded.

TESTER A canopy suspended or supported over a bed, throne, pulpit, tomb etc. (see BALDACHIN).

THOLOS
Tholos at Delphi, Greece, *c.* 390 BC.

THOLOS A Greek word for a circular building with a domed or conical roof. Remains of *tholoi* survive at Olympia, Epidauros, Delphi and Athens. The Delphi tholos, which has been partly reconstructed, stands upon a circular crepidoma and had a ring (48ft diameter) of 20 Doric columns inside which was the naos wall then an inner ring of ten Corinthian columns. The roof over the naos was conical and there was a lower sloping one over the peristyle.

THOMAS, SIR PERCY (1883–1969) One of the principal builders of modern South Wales between 1920 and 1950. Sir Percy Thomas was born in South Shields but spent his childhood in Cardiff. In 1911 he set up architectural practice there with Ivor Jones. He built the *Technical College* at *Cardiff* (now the University of Wales Institute of Science and Technology), *University College Swansea* (University of Wales) and carried out further collegiate work at *Aberystwyth* and *Bangor*.

Sir Percy's most important work is the *Civic Centre* at *Swansea* (1930–4). This scheme, comprising an assembly hall, administrative offices and law courts, was built on a spacious site in a park outside the centre of the town. The buildings are grouped round a courtyard, the exterior outward-looking walls faced with Portland stone, the inner courtyard ones with brick finish. The city hall is characteristic of the best of architecture of these years. It

Main doorway of City Hall, Swansea

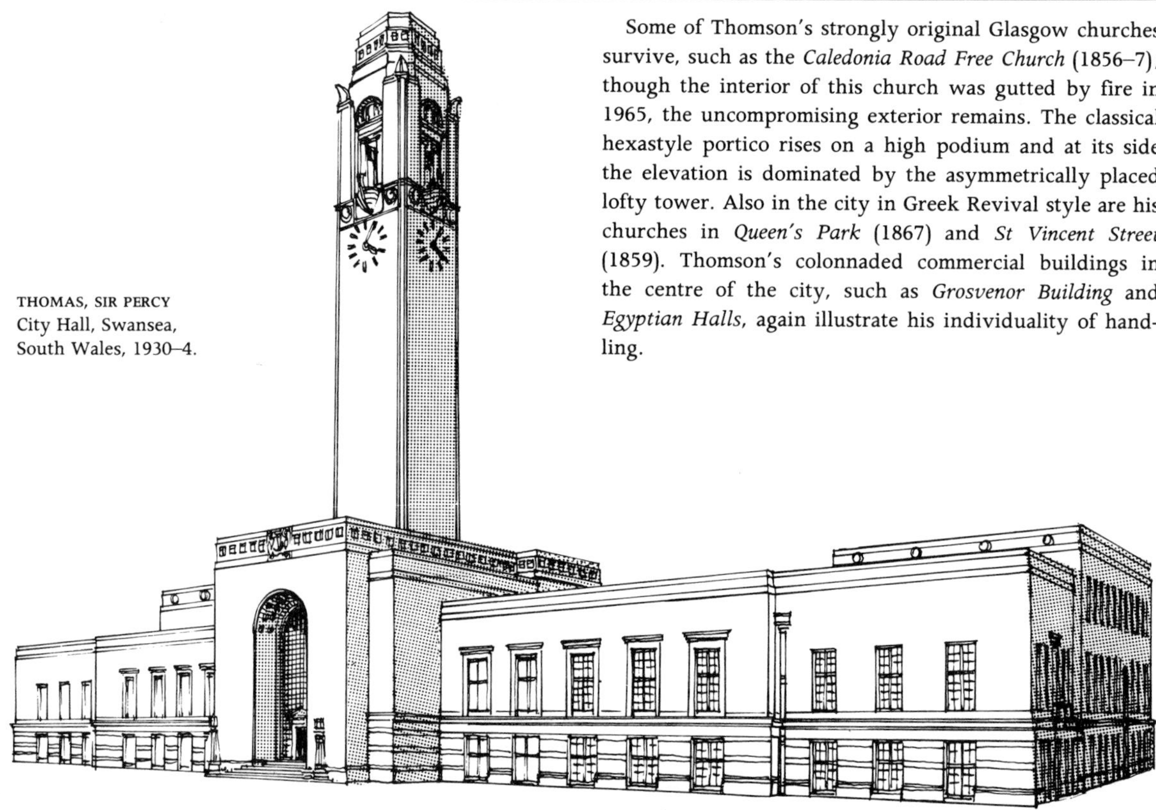

THOMAS, SIR PERCY
City Hall, Swansea, South Wales, 1930–4.

is very plain and unornamented, its long, low front elevation broken by a central block rising to a slender clock tower 160ft high. The fenestration is classical as is the tall, round-headed doorway with caissons under its arch.

Sir Percy had an extensive industrial practice. He acted as consulting architect for the *Steel Company of Wales* in their Works at Abbey and Margam, the *Carmarthen Bay Power Station* and the *British Nylon Spinners' Factory* at Pontypool. He was awarded the Royal Institute of British Architects' Gold Medal for Architecture in 1939 and was, unusually, twice its President in 1935 and 1943. He retired from his firm of Sir Percy Thomas and Son in 1961.

THOMSON, ALEXANDER (1817–75) A talented and unusual architect for his time, Thomson lived and worked most of his life in *Glasgow* where he built mainly in the Greek Revival style to which he brought his own individual approach. Because he was designing in this style in the 1850s and 1860s when, even in Scotland where the architectural fashion for the Greek mode lingered later than it had in England, the Gothic Revival was getting into its stride, he was known as 'Greek' Thomson. The greatest formative influence upon his work was that of the great German architect of the first half of the century, *Karl Friedrich von Schinkel*. Thomson's bold and forceful terrace building (1859–74), *Moray Place, Great Western Terrace*, for example, shows this particularly.

Some of Thomson's strongly original Glasgow churches survive, such as the *Caledonia Road Free Church* (1856–7); though the interior of this church was gutted by fire in 1965, the uncompromising exterior remains. The classical hexastyle portico rises on a high podium and at its side the elevation is dominated by the asymmetrically placed lofty tower. Also in the city in Greek Revival style are his churches in *Queen's Park* (1867) and *St Vincent Street* (1859). Thomson's colonnaded commercial buildings in the centre of the city, such as *Grosvenor Building* and *Egyptian Halls*, again illustrate his individuality of handling.

TILES Like bricks, tiles need to be fired in a kiln and, over the centuries, were often made at brick kilns. Tiles are fired to be harder and smoother than bricks and, as with terracotta, more care needs to be paid to the mix (see BRICKWORK; TERRACOTTA).

Tiles are used for covering roofs, walls and floors. The Romans used baked roof tiles but, as with brick-making, the manufacture in England of tiles died out after their departure until (it is not known exactly when) production began again in the early Middle Ages. The most usual medieval roof covering was thatch or wood shingles (see BUILDING MATERIALS; SHINGLES) but the fire hazard in towns led to the re-adoption of stone or baked tiles.

Floor tiles, often very decorative, were widely in use in the later Middle Ages but the custom of *tile-hanging* of walls began in the late seventeenth century. Also known as *weather-tiling* because its purpose was chiefly to afford protection from rain and snow, tile-hanging can also be ornamental and designs of hanging vary. The tiles were hung on wood battens plugged to the walls or were pegged or nailed into the mortar courses. This method of wall covering has always been more traditional in the south of England while slate-hanging was more practised in the north (see SLATE).

Varieties of tile

Brick tile (also known as a *mathematical tile* or a *weather-tile*): a design of tile introduced in the eighteenth century

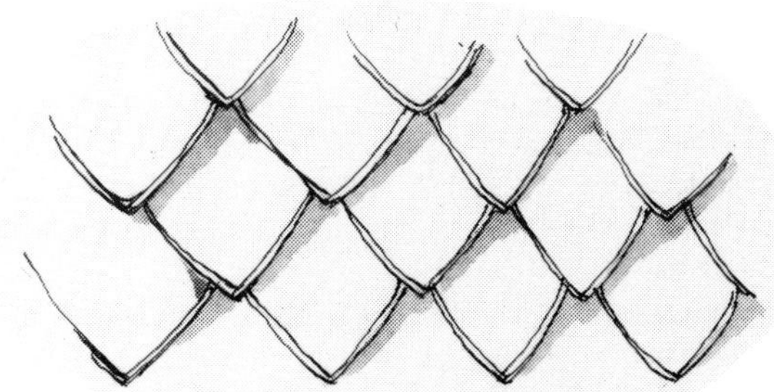

Roman stone-tile roofing

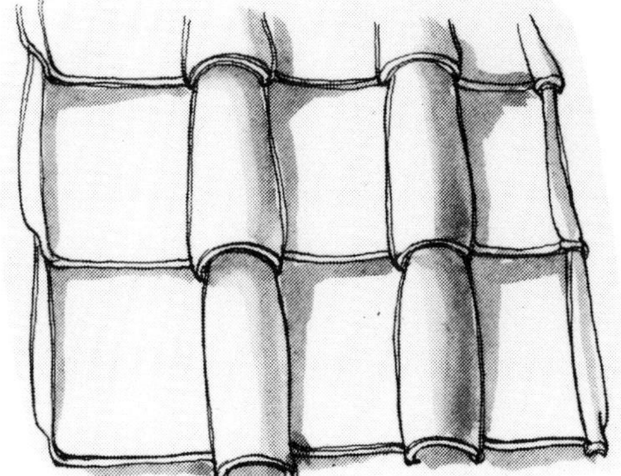

Roman roof tiling with alternate imbrices and tegulae

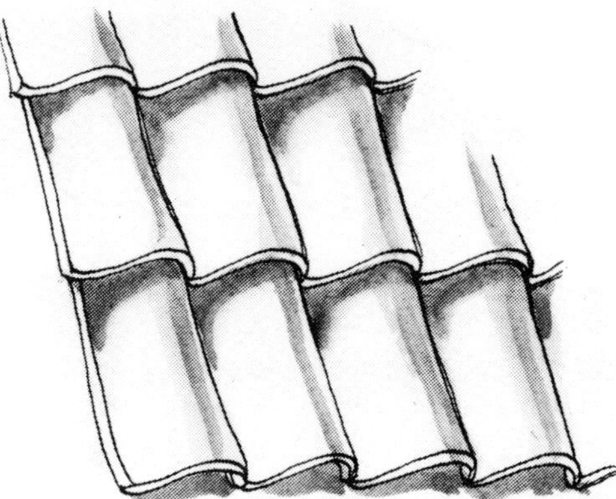

Pantiles

and in use mainly in the period 1760–1830. The tiles were mostly the same size as bricks and were applied to walls to provide a tile skin to the surface. The tiles could be nailed to wooden boards or battens, as in tile-hanging, or could be used to cover other materials such as timber or brick. Their main purpose was to bring the walling surface up to date in current fashion, so, for example, replacing red bricks with white, black or cream colouring, or giving half-timber the appearance of brick.

These tiles were excellent for weather-proofing and were used by many of the leading architects of the time, for instance *Henry Holland, Samuel Wyatt* and *Sir John Soane*. Mathematical tiles were employed most extensively in Sussex and Kent. *Patcham Place* near Brighton (*c.* 1760)

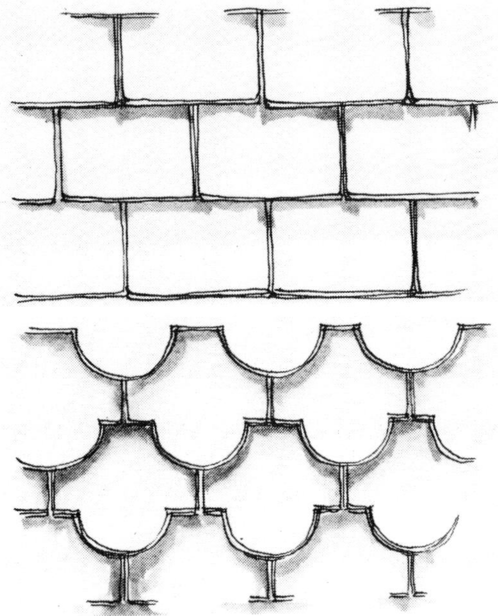

Different designs of tile-hanging

Black glazed mathematical tiles at Royal Crescent, Brighton, *c.* 1800

Oak timber-framed house, late fifteenth century. Wattle-and daub infilling (daub of mud, manure and chopped straw). Re-erected 1967 in Avoncroft Museum of Buildings, Worcestershire

Timber-framed hall-house, built *c.* 1400 and enlarged *c.* 1515 and later reconstructed at Weald and Downland Open Air Museum, West Sussex

is one example where two elevations are faced with black tiles; the *Royal Crescent* in *Brighton* is another (*c.* 1800), where the red brick façade is covered with black glazed tiles.

Encaustic tiles: decorative coloured and glazed tiles used on both walls and floors. Particularly to be seen in mediaeval buildings and in the nineteenth century.

Harmus tile: one covering a joint between tiles.

Imbrex tile (plural *imbrices*): a Roman rounded tile used in roofing to cover the joints between flat tiles which were called *tegulae* (singular *tegula*).

Pantile: large S-shaped curved tiles used for roofing, first imported from Flanders in the 1630s and manufactured in England from the early eighteenth century.

Plane, plain tile: flat tile.

TIMBER-FRAMING Wood has probably been used as a structural material more than any other over the centuries in Britain. The country was fortunate in possessing, at least until the seventeenth century, vast areas covered with forest mainly of hardwood trees. Much of this was oak and this hard and durable wood was used for the majority of timber construction.

A timber-framed building is one where the walls are made up as a framework of timbers with the panel spaces filled in with other materials such as wattle and daub or laths and plaster (see BUILDING MATERIALS: PARGETING), brickwork (see BRICKWORK; NOGGING) or wood boarding (see CLAPBOARD, WEATHERBOARD). This type of construction is also known as *half-timbering* because the timbers are halved or cleft, not complete logs. This is different from the whole-log type of construction used more widely in Europe in areas such as Scandinavia and the Carpathian mountain parts of Rumania and Hungary where softwoods of pine or fir represent the chief available material.

There are several designs of timber-framing, most of them of a box-frame type with horizontal and vertical timbers and added struts and braces. Usually the frame is constructed upon a base or footing of a material which will be more impervious to damp, such as a low wall of stone or brick. Upon this a baulk of timber is laid horizontally; this is a *sill* or *plate*. Strong upright posts called *studs* are mortised into the sill and their upper ends are tenoned into another horizontal timber plate. In a single-storey building this is called a *wall plate* as it supports the lower ends of the roof rafters. In a two- or three-storey building, it is a *summer* or *bressumer* as it is carrying the floor joists of the floor above (see BRESSUMER; SUMMER).

In many instances the upper storeys will project over the ones below on some or all sides of the building; such an overhang is known as a *jetty*. When the upper storeys

Timber-framed manor house and gatehouse, Lower Brockhampton, Herefordshire, *c.* 1400

are jettied on two or more sides, additional support is given by an internal cross beam stretching diagonally to the corner post; this is a *dragon beam*. Several possible reasons are advanced for the practice of jettying, the main ones that it gave more floor space to the upper storeys, which was important in confined town sites, and that it protected lower storeys from rain and snow at a time when there were no down-pipes and gutters.

Timber-framed houses of the later periods, the fifteenth and sixteenth centuries in particular, were often very decorative. Barge boards were ornately carved (see BARGE BOARD) and the box-framing was infilled with quatrefoil, trefoil and star decoration in wood carving.

Timber-framed buildings were, to a certain extent, prefabricated. The larger timbers would be cut and prepared near the site but the smaller ones could be made in a carpenter's workshop and brought to the place where the building was to be erected. The infilling was put in as the framework was constructed so each floor was completed in turn. Half-timber structures are not difficult to dismantle and re-erect and many have survived because of this. Two open-air museums in particular have rescued many such structures which might have been lost otherwise. These are the Weald and Downland Open Air Museum near Singleton in West Sussex (from 1970) and the Avoncroft Museum of Buildings near Bromsgrove in Worcestershire (from 1963).

The softwood timber structures of Europe needed painting for weather protection. The oak half-timbering of Britain was less in need of such sealing and sixteenth- and seventeenth-century painting was usually by water paint and so not noticeably strong in tone or colour. The more permanent black painting of the timbers was mainly carried out in the nineteenth century with a tar derivative from coal production.

Elizabethan timber-framed inn: The Feathers Hotel, Ludlow, Shropshire

TIMBER-TRUSSED ROOF An open interior roof system composed of a rigid construction of timbers (the *truss*) which were tenoned and pinned together to provide a stable combination to resist all thrusts (see ROOF).

Until the late sixteenth century such open timber roofs covered the large interiors of the majority of buildings: the trussed roof was the equivalent in wood to the vault of stone (see VAULTING). The earliest type of construction was by the use of *crucks* (see CRUCK BUILDING) but such interiors lacked headroom and gradually a more advanced structure evolved to cover the main interiors. There was considerable variety of design and, as the centuries passed, they became more elaborate.

In general, the medieval roof was gabled at each end with a fairly steep pitch. A long beam, the *ridge-piece*, extended horizontally along the length of the apex and further beams (*purlins*) were set at intervals parallel to the ridge down the pitch from apex to wall top where a timber called a *wall plate* was laid along it. This was secured by stone *corbels* (see CORBEL). At right angles to these timbers were laid the *rafters*; these were affixed to

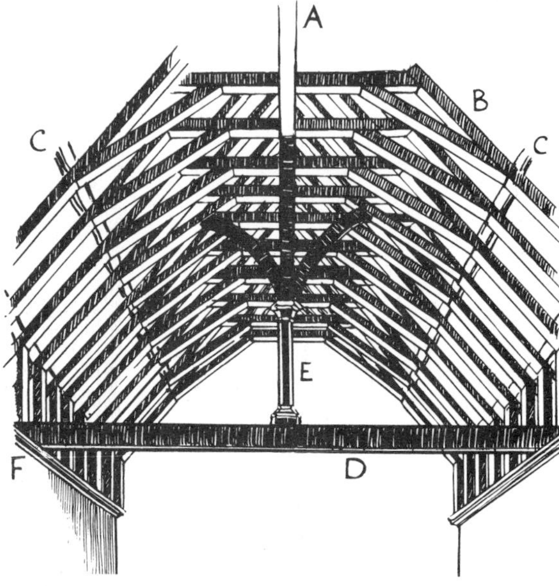

Tie-beam and king-post timber-trussed roof
A Collar purlin B Rafter C Purlin D Tie beam E King post F Wall plate

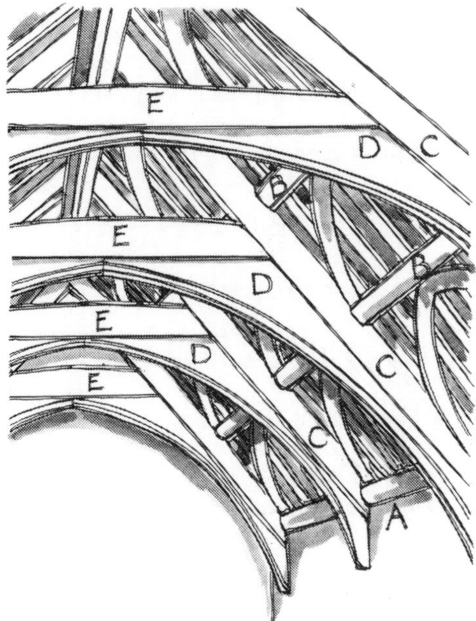

Arched-braced collar-beam roof
A Wall plate B Purlin
C Principal rafter
D Arch brace E Collar beam

Tie-beam and crown-post roof: Great hall, Oakham Castle, Leicestershire, *c.* 1190

Braced collar-beam roof: The hall, Rufford Old Hall, Lancashire, 1463–1505

Double false hammerbeam hall roof: Gifford's Hall, Stoke-by-Nayland, Suffolk, *c.* 1500
A Hammer beam
B Hammer post C Corbel
D Brace E Wall plate
F Purlin G Principal rafter
H Collar beam

Hammerbeam roof: St Mary's Church, Woolpit, Suffolk, 1439–51

the wall plate at the lower end and the ridge-piece at the upper. At intervals, marking the bays (see BAY; CRUCK BUILDING), were heavier timbers called *principal rafters*; between were slenderer *common rafters*.

One of the simplest structures utilized a *tie beam*. This was a massive beam thrown across the interior at wall plate level to counteract the outward thrust of the roof on the walls. It was pinned or tenoned into the wall plates and often curved slightly upwards in the centre. On this tie beam was usually set a vertical post or posts to strengthen the structure. *Collar beams* were like tie beams but set higher up in the roof above wall plate level. Straight *struts* and curved *arch braces* were introduced for reinforcement. *Coupled roofs* were constructed without tie or collar beams. They gave better interior visibility and enhanced the lofty appearance of the roof.

The later, more complex phase was represented by the *hammerbeam roof* which evolved at the end of the fourteenth century. The *hammer beams* were like abbreviated tie beams. Extended at wall-plate level, they were supported from corbels by means of arch-braced wall posts and both corbels and beam ends were often decoratively carved into figures or animals. The shorter hammer beams gave better visibility than the tie beams and reduced lateral pressure. The vertical *hammer posts* rose from the inner end of the hammer beams to a collar beam above which joined the purlins. The whole roof was gilded and painted and often decoratively carved.

Glossary of terms

Arched brace: a curved supporting, reinforcing timber.
Collar beam: a timber which ties the principal rafters together at a high level in the roof.
Collar purlin: a purlin running the length of the centre of the roof under the collar beams.
Coupled roof: a design which has no tie or collar beams.
Crown post: a vertical post standing in the centre of a tie beam and supporting a collar purlin or collar beam. Usually braces or struts connect the crown post to the collar purlin and collar beam.
Double hammerbeam roof: a system in which there are two sets of hammer beams and posts, one above the other.
False hammerbeam roof: here the hammer posts are tenoned into the inner end of the hammer beams instead of being supported upon them, so making a less strong structure.
Hammerbeam roof: horizontal hammer beams, supported from corbels on arch-braced wall posts, extend at wall plate level towards the centre of the roofing space. Braced hammer posts rise vertically from the inner end of the hammer beams to a collar beam above.
King post: a central vertical post rising from tie beam to ridge-piece.
Principal rafters: chief timbers rising from wall plate to ridge and carrying the purlins.
Purlins: timbers, running parallel to the ridge, which carry the common rafters.
Queen posts: a similar design to a king post but here there are two vertical posts instead of one.
Ridge-piece: the main timber running along the apex of the roof.
Strut: a straight brace.
Tie beam: the main tie timber extending horizontally from one side of the roof to the other at wall-plate level.
Wagon roof: a continuous wooden roof in half-cylindrical form: the wooden equivalent to a stone barrel vault (see VAULTING).
Wall plate: the main timber running along the top of the wall from one end of the roof to the other.

TITE, SIR WILLIAM (1798–1873) A Victorian architect with a large practice, chiefly in railway and civic building, who also held a number of public appointments. His best known civic commission is the *Royal Exchange* in

TITE, SIR WILLIAM
Windsor and Eton Riverside Railway Station, Berkshire, 1850.
Architect: Sir William Tite

Saxon tower of church of Earl's Barton, Northamptonshire, eleventh century

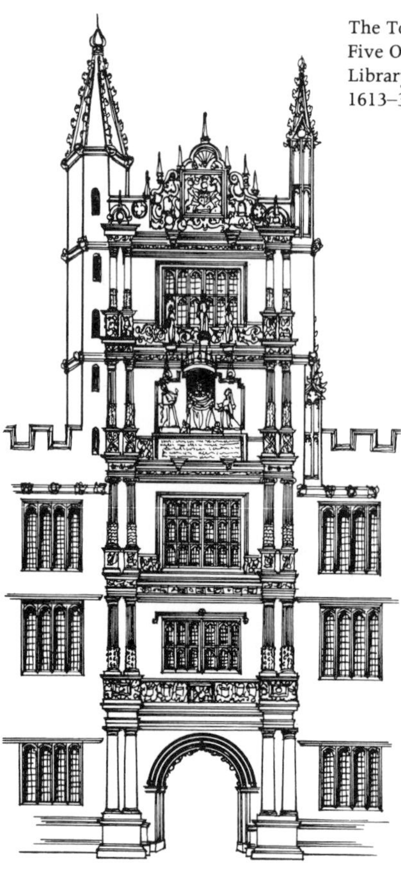

The Tower of the Five Orders, Bodleian Library, Oxford, 1613–36

Magdalen College, Oxford, *c.* 1490–1509

The Clock Tower (housing Big Ben), Palace of Westminster. Begun 1843

South-west tower of York Minster, 1432–74

The Town House, Aberdeen, *c.* 1865

TITE, SIR WILLIAM
The Royal Exchange, London, 1842-4. Architect: Sir William Tite

London; this he built in 1842–4 after winning the competition for a new structure to replace the previous Exchange which had been destroyed by fire in 1838. Tite's Royal Exchange is dominated by its forceful eight-column Corinthian portico with sculptured pediment which, despite its early date, is characteristic of a mature Victorian work, weighty in comparison with Dance's Mansion House nearby (see DANCE, GEORGE, the elder).

Tite was responsible for a number of railway structures (see RAILWAY ARCHITECTURE). Among his best designs was *Carlisle Railway Station* (1847) and also that at *Perth* (1848). His smaller stations included that at *Nine Elms, Vauxhall*, London (1838–40) and the rural, Gothic Revival station, complete with royal porch, of *Windsor and Eton Riverside*.

TOWER A tall structure, part of a building or separate, square, circular or polygonal in plan and following the architectural style of its time. Towers were built for defence as in castles, as landmarks or to carry bells as in churches, as clock towers in civic or domestic structures or purely for architectural and aesthetic interest (see CASTLE; CHURCH DESIGN AND STRUCTURE; CIVIC ARCHITECTURE; GOTHIC ARCHITECTURE; GOTHIC REVIVAL; ROMANESQUE ARCHITECTURE; SAXON ARCHITECTURE).

TOWN HOUSE Apart from the large mansion designed for the wealthy patron which stood detached within its own extensive grounds and was therefore not unlike the country house built for the same owner, town houses throughout the ages, because of high land values, have been restricted in frontage measurement. Until the outbreak of the First World War palatial houses were still being designed for well-to-do clients by all the leading architects: Barry's *Bridgewater House* in London was characteristic of its time (see BARRY, SIR CHARLES) as was Adam's earlier work at *Northumberland House* in the Strand (see ADAM, ROBERT).

The typical town house, though often spacious within, has been built on more modest lines. It has always reflected the current architectural style. In Britain the progenitor was the Roman *domus* (see ROMAN DOMESTIC ARCHITECTURE) which had a narrow frontage, often with shops on the ground floor, but extended a considerable distance back from the street to accommodate suites of rooms built round open garden courts. From the Middle Ages onwards the layout of the garden courts, the idea of which had evolved in the warmer climate of Mediterranean lands, was abandoned in favour of a rear garden and orchard. Larger town houses contained many rooms and extended upward for one or two storeys (see TIMBER-FRAMING).

By the later seventeenth and the eighteenth centuries the classical style of town house (see CLASSICAL ARCHITECTURE; CLASSICAL ORDER) was generally of three storeys with further accommodation for servants in roof dormers. Such larger houses were planned to give accommodation for lavish entertainment and maximum privacy for the owner behind the narrow façade. A carefully planned suite of rooms of different shapes and sizes was integrated with access by staircases and landings.

With the population explosion in towns of the nineteenth century and the accelerated growth of the comfortably-off middle classes, large numbers of solidly constructed houses were erected in the new suburban areas. Such houses were mass-produced rather than architect-designed. They were built of brick or stone in decoratively polychrome Gothic manner in styles which owed their inspiration to a variety of origins (see GOTHIC REVIVAL). These houses usually extended upwards rather than rearwards, reflecting the increasing cost of land. They had basements and the front door at just above ground level was approached by a flight of steps. They had three, four or five storeys and attic dormers in the roof above.

Much of the mass housing in towns of the twentieth century has been in flats or terraces (see HIGH-RISE BUILDING; TERRACE ARCHITECTURE). Where town houses have been erected separately or semi-detached the design has reflected the reduction in the size of the family since Victorian times and two storeys has been the normal pattern.

TOWN PLANNING The idea of designing the layout of a town for aesthetic and practical considerations, of providing order and convenience for the social and defensive needs of its citizens, is an old one. In *Ancient Greece* many cities were built on natural hills and were surrounded by walls with fortified gates and towers. In the 'city upon the hill', literally the *acropolis*, plan the principal buildings were within the walls on top of the hill and most of the houses were outside.

The grid scheme of city layout with streets crossing one another at right angles and with a uniformity of street width and building design, which became the pattern for the classical world of Greece and Rome and was later adopted in Europe and in modern America, was devel-

Octagonal towers of Alnwick Castle, Northumberland, *c.* 1350

The Norman Tower, Bury St Edmunds, Suffolk

York Minster from the south-east. Central tower, fifteenth century

Pier-head building, Cardiff. Architect: William Frame, 1896

44 Berkeley Square, London. Architect: William Kent, 1744–5

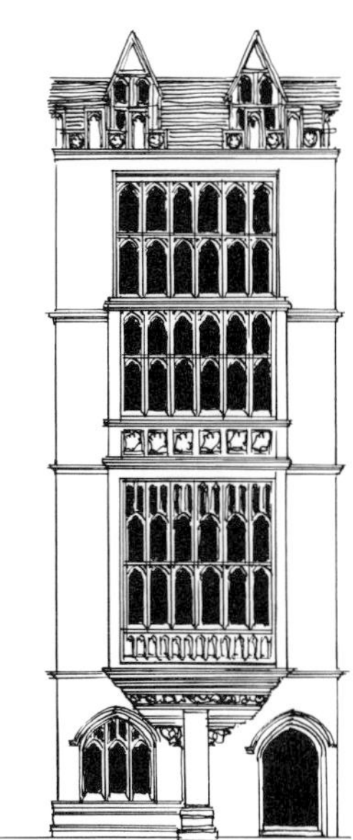

Charles Russell House, 23 Park Lane, London, 1846–8, now demolished. Architect: W. B. Moffatt

The Terrace, Richmond Hill, Surrey, *c.* 1769

20 St James's Square, London. Architect: Robert Adam, *c.* 1775

Fairfax House, York. Architect: John Carr, 1770

oped in Ionian Greece in the seventh century BC: this street pattern is known as *Milesian* because it is named after the city of Miletus on the coast of Asia Minor.

The grid street plan is believed to have originated earlier and further east, possibly in Mesopotamia, but the concept is most familiarly associated with the name of *Hippodamos*, a Greek philosopher and town planner who lived in the early fifth century BC. This is due to Aristotle who ascribed its invention to Hippodamos who was born in Miletus. In the reconstruction of the city about 475 BC, after its sack by the Persians, Hippodamos was able to put forward his ideas on urban planning. These included the concept of dividing up a city into three areas, one for public buildings, one for sacred use and the third for

TOWN HOUSE
Gothic suburban house. Polychrome brick and stone, 1860–70

180 Queen's Gate, London. Architect: Norman Shaw, 1885

63–4 Sloane Street, London. Architect: Fairfax Wade, 1897

Speculative housing: mock Tudor, brick and pebble-dash, 1925–35

Half-timber town houses and shops as from the Middle Ages onwards. This example in Bridge Street, Chester, is much restored

private homes. In Miletus, for instance, the central area was reserved for the *agora*, which was an open-air meeting place for the transaction of business comprising a market place, stoas (see STOA) and commercial halls. Residential areas surrounded the agora and excavation has revealed parts of the gridiron pattern here, containing some hundreds of uniform rectangular blocks.

It is not certain whether Hippodamos was ever in charge of laying out a town but his plans and ideas were influential in the planning of some cities, for example, Piraeus, the port of Athens, in about 470–460 BC. Other Greek cities built on similar lines include Priene, Ephesos, Corinth and Pergamon.

Roman cities were also planned as far as possible symmetrically on a grid system though, in the case of existing towns which they took over or of hill sites, geographical problems made this difficult. The city would be encircled by its own defensive walls pierced by fortified gates at points where the principal roads made their exit. Where a new city was planned the ideal layout was thought to be eight-sided.

The Roman *forum* corresponded to the Greek agora and under republican Rome had the same function. Under empire, as time passed, larger towns possessed more than one forum and the main one became the site for imposing buildings devoted to the administration of justice, commerce, bureaucracy and worship: the ordinary shops were gradually cleared away. The forum was planned symmetrically and was surrounded by colonnades (see STOA). The temples were set at various angles and not oriented as Greek ones had been (see TEMPLE).

The typical medieval city in Europe was not planned symmetrically or, in most cases, planned at all: it just grew. Schemes were made but seldom carried out. Defence was of paramount importance and within the fortified walls the church, abbey, castle and market place were dominant.

With the coming of the Renaissance in Italy came the rediscovery of the Vitruvius manuscripts, prime source of information for Roman architecture of the first century BC

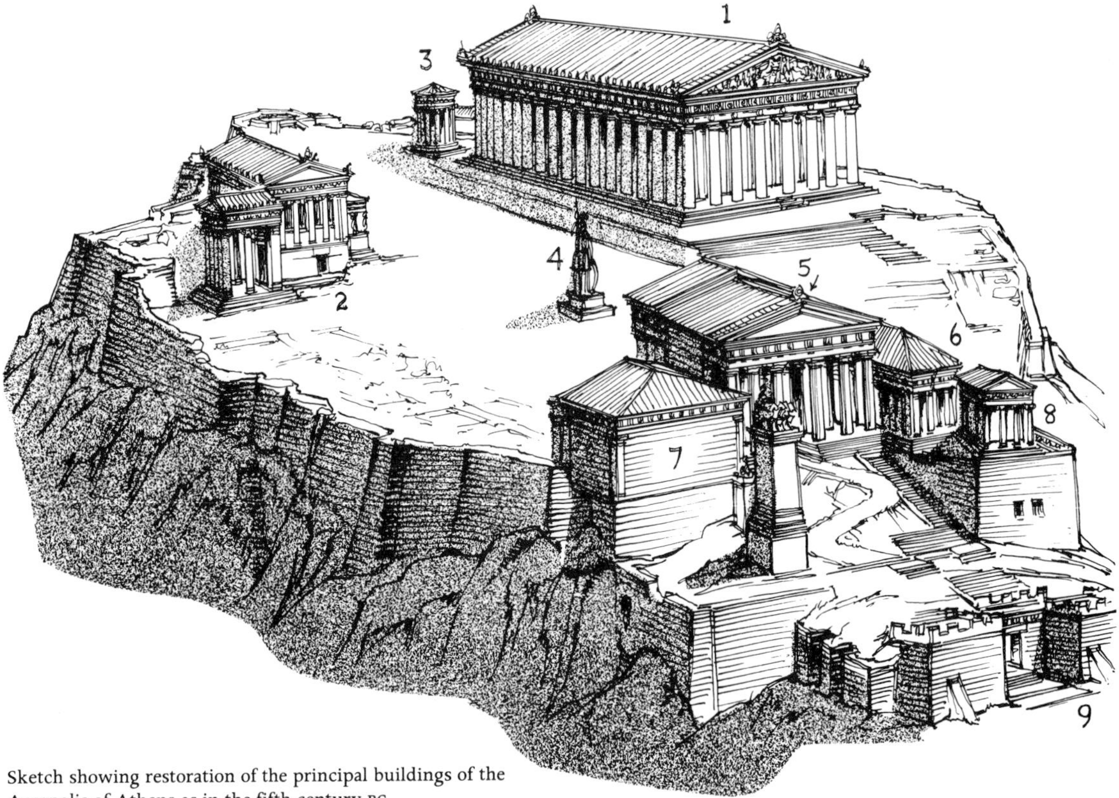

Sketch showing restoration of the principal buildings of the Acropolis of Athens as in the fifth century BC
1. The Parthenon 2. The Erechtheion 3. Ionic tholos 4. Statue of Athena Promachos by Pheidias 5. The Propylaea 6. Its southern wing 7. Its northern wing (the picture gallery) 8. Temple of Athena Niké 9. Main entrance to the Acropolis

Reconstruction of the Forum Romanum in Rome looking towards Capitol Hill
1. Tabularium 2. Temple of Concord 3. Temple of Vespasian 4. Curia 5. Arch of Septimius Severus 6. Temple of Saturn 7. Imperial rostra 8. Arch of Tiberius 9. Column of Phocas 10. Honorary columns 11. Basilica Julia 12. Temple of Jupiter 13. Temple of Juno

(see VITRUVIUS). The first volume of his *De Architectura* contains his plans for an ideal Roman city. Architects once more turned towards classical symmetry and many ideas were put forward for an ideal city plan. During the fifteenth century Antonio Avelino, known as *Il Filarete* (1400–69), wrote a lengthy treatise *Trattato d'Architettura Civile e Militare* (1460–4), in which he designed his ideal city, called *Sforzinda* in deference to Francesco Sforza, the powerful Duke of Milan. This was a radially planned star-shaped city enclosed in a circle. Several other architects produced radial plans but only one was carried out, that of *Vincenzo Scamozzi*'s (1552–1616) nonagonal fortress town of *Palmanova* near Venice (1593). Scamozzi's ideal city was dodecagonal in shape and contained a grid pattern layout not a radial one. This was more practical and was later more generally adopted. The small town of Hamina in Finland on the Soviet border was destroyed during the Russian occupation of 1713–21. It was rebuilt in the late eighteenth century by Carl Blaesingh on a plan based on Scamozzi's Palmanova. The town is still built on radial plan with the 1798 town hall in the centre.

Though few complete new cities were built for many years on symmetrical grid lines, parts and especially centres of older cities were rebuilt in a classical pattern of symmetry. *Pienza* town centre (begun 1459) was one example; others included the *Piazza dei Signori* in *Verona*, the *Piazza San Marco* in *Venice* and *Michelangelo*'s *Piazza del Campidoglio* in *Rome* (1540).

As always, it was *Leonardo da Vinci* (1452–1519) who was producing drawings of ideas far in advance of his time. He was not only concerned with planning a city in an orderly, practical way but also with segregating its traffic, transport and people. Ante-dating *Sant'Elia*'s *Città Nuova* and *Garnier*'s *Cité Industrielle* by over 400 years, he illustrated a city on different levels where the civic centre, pedestrian ways and housing were above and separated from the roads, canals and drainage beneath.

With the early seventeenth century the rest of western Europe began to develop and adapt to its own needs Renaissance ideas on town plannning. In France in the later sixteenth century Henry IV had begun to reconstruct the city of *Paris* after years of warfare. He completed the partly built *Pont Neuf*, building a new wide thoroughfare spanning the western tip of the Ile de la Cité and so linking north and south banks of the River Seine. He then developed the *Place Dauphine* on the island as a high-class residential neighbourhood. He planned two other squares, the *Place Royale* (later Place des Vosges and begun 1605) and *Place de France* (begun 1620 but completed later), both as fashionable accommodation for the wealthy. Henry's town planning was in advance of the rest of Europe. A similar scheme, derived from the French prototype, was Inigo Jones's *Covent Garden* in London (see JONES, INIGO).

In the 1630s, *Jacques Lemercier* (*c.* 1585–1654) built the small town of *Richelieu* and its attendant château for the French king's chief minister, Cardinal Richelieu. The town remains much as it was built, unpretentious, homogeneous on grid pattern with two main streets crossing each other at right angles and with two squares at intersections.

Meanwhile the city of *Amsterdam* was being rapidly enlarged. From 1612 it was carefully planned and constructed. Concentric rings of canals—the Heerengracht, the Keizersgracht, the Prinsengracht—were each lined with tall terrace houses in a style characteristic of Amsterdam. The architect who chiefly contributed to this expansion was *Hendrik de Keyser* (1565–1621).

In Italy town planning on a larger scale was attempted during the seventeenth century. The *Piazza del Popolo* in *Rome* was an early Baroque scheme (see BAROQUE ARCHITECTURE); by *Carlo Rainaldi* (1611–91), it was a prototype of the French *rond-point* theme where roads radiate from a focal centre, in this case two churches standing on island sites divided by three thoroughfares leading from the centre of the piazza to different parts of the city. The churches are *S. Maria di Montesanto* and *S. Maria dei Miracoli* built 1662–72. Another Baroque scheme in the city was the '*Spanish Steps*' which sweep in triple ascent, dividing as they go, up the steep hillside from the Piazza di Spagna to *Alessandro Specchi*'s (1668–1729) church of *S. Trinità dei Monti*.

In the north of the country the idea of designing palaces in streets instead of individually was developed in *Turin* where Carlo Emmanuele I employed his architect *Carlo di Castellamonte* to lay out the *Piazza San Carlo* and the beginnings of the *Via Roma* (1638). Work continued during the seventeenth and eighteenth centuries under Guarini and Juvara. In *Sicily*, *Giovanni Battista Vaccarini* (1702–68) replanned the city of *Catania* after its devastation in the earthquake of 1693, making it a Baroque city containing the imposing buildings of the Cathedral, the Palazzo Municipale and the three churches of S. Agata, S. Placido and S. Chiara.

In the second half of the century *Wren* in England presented his plan for the rebuilding of the *City of London* after the Great Fire of 1666 (see WREN, SIR CHRISTOPHER). It was a radical scheme to replace the maze of medieval streets which had made up the pre-Fire City and, though approved by King and Parliament, predictably foundered upon the need for practicality and the non-co-operation of the City freeholders. Wren's plan was a classical one on a geometrical grid pattern but he incorporated focal centres for important buildings such as St Paul's Cathedral, the Royal Exchange and the Custom House. These were linked by main thoroughfares which gave vistas to and from them. The City churches were given special positions and in front of St Paul's was to be a long wedge-shaped space.

A key part of the plan was a wide embankment quay along the River Thames from Blackfriars to the Tower based upon that bounding the River Seine in Paris. From the recently laid out *Piazza del Popolo* in Rome and from

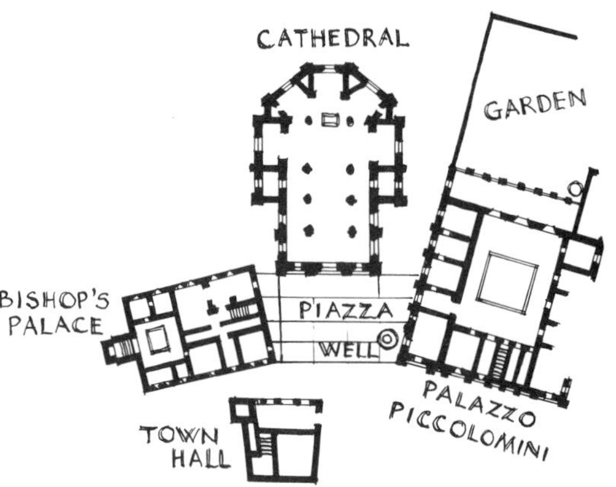

Plan of Pienza town centre, Italy. Begun 1459

Pienza, town hall and Bishop's palace

The Capitol (Campidoglio), Rome, Italy. Including the Palazzo Capitolino, Palazzo del Senatore and the Palazzo dei Conservatori, 1540–1644. Architect: Michelangelo

Piazzo San Carlo, Turin, Italy, 1638. Architect: Carlo di Castellamonte

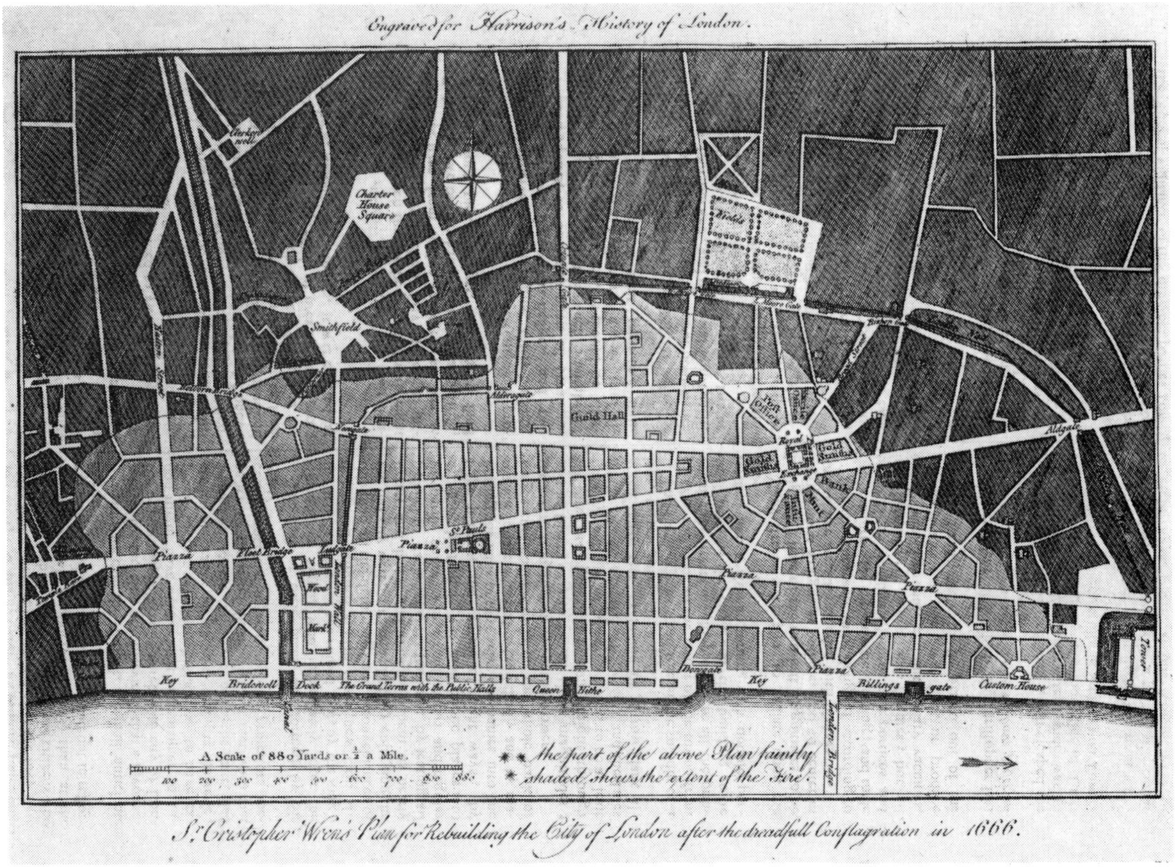

Sir Christopher Wren's plan for the rebuilding of London, 1666

Piazza del Popolo, Rome, Italy, 1662–79. Architects: Rainaldi, Fontana, Bernini
A Church of S. Maria di Montesanto
B Church of S. Maria dei Miracoli

Louis XIV's Paris Wren had taken his *rond-point* theme.

During the eighteenth century the pace of redevelopment of towns increased and planned schemes grew larger; this was particularly so in Britain and France. In Britain the city of *Bath* was being extended in terraces and crescents (see TERRACE ARCHITECTURE; WOOD, JOHN). In *Edinburgh, Robert Adam* was planning the long-awaited New Town (see ADAM, ROBERT) but most of this was laid out after his death and it was a new generation of architects who finally created the 'Athens of the North' in the early nineteenth century (see HAMILTON, THOMAS; PLAYFAIR, WILLIAM HENRY). Also in the Regency period (see REGENCY ARCHITECTURE) came *Nash's Regent's Park* and *Regent Street* (see NASH, JOHN), the development, also in *London*, of Bloomsbury, Belgravia and South Kensington (see BASEVI, GEORGE; BURTON, JAMES AND DECIMUS; CUBITT, THOMAS) and the layout of streets and squares in the spa towns and sea-side resorts (see TERRACE ARCHITECTURE).

A number of the extensive town planning schemes of the eighteenth century in France survive in a remarkably unspoilt and homogeneous condition. Most notable is the town centre of *Nancy* where, from 1750, *Emmanuel Héré de Corny* was responsible for one of the finest rococo compositions in Europe (see ROCOCO), which comprises the octagonal *Place Stanislas* (originally Place Royale) with its Hôtel de Ville and sculptured corner fountains. Through a triumphal arch one enters the tree-lined avenue of the *Place Carrière* which leads to the *Place du Gouvernement*.

In *Lyon* the *Place Bellecour* (originally Louis le Grand) was laid out by *Robert de Cotte* in 1713–38. *Jacques-Jules Gabriel* was responsible for the town-centre squares at *Rennes* (1734–43) and the now faded grandeur of the quay-side area of *Bordeaux* (1730–60); and *Guillaume Camnas* built the *Place Capitole* in *Toulouse* (1750–3). Best known is *Ange-Jacques Gabriel*'s contribution in *Paris* of the *Place de la Concorde* (originally Place Louis XV) laid out from 1757.

During the nineteenth century, as city populations expanded and European countries became wealthier, town centres were being redeveloped all over Europe. The architecture in each country reflected the national preference which selected from the wealth of current eclecticism. Thus, in *Munich* there was Greek Revivalism and Rundbogenstil; in Franz Josef's *Vienna* Ringstrasse and in *Budapest* a varied range of Gothic, Greek and

The Spanish Steps, Rome, Italy, 1723–5. Leading up to the Church of SS. Trinitá dei Monti from the Piazza di Spagna, Architect: Francesco de Sanctis. Fountain, the 'Barcaccia', by Pietro Bernini, 1628

Place de la Bourse (Place Royale), Bordeaux, France. Custom House left, Stock Exchange right. Architect: Jacques-Jules Gabriel, 1740–6

Place du Gouvernement, Nancy, France. Architect: Héré de Corny, 1750–7

Neue Hofburg, The Ring (Ringstrasse), Vienna, Austria, 1881–94. Architect: Karl von Hasenauer

Place de l'Opéra, Paris, France, 1858–64. Architects: De Fleury and Blondel. The Opera House (centre, Académie Nationale de Musique), 1861–74. Architect: J. L. C. Garnier

Stone terrace houses, Saltaire, Yorkshire, 1854–70

House, Bedford Park, London, late nineteenth century

London Country Council Becontree Housing Estate, Essex. Dormitory suburb, built mainly 1920–30

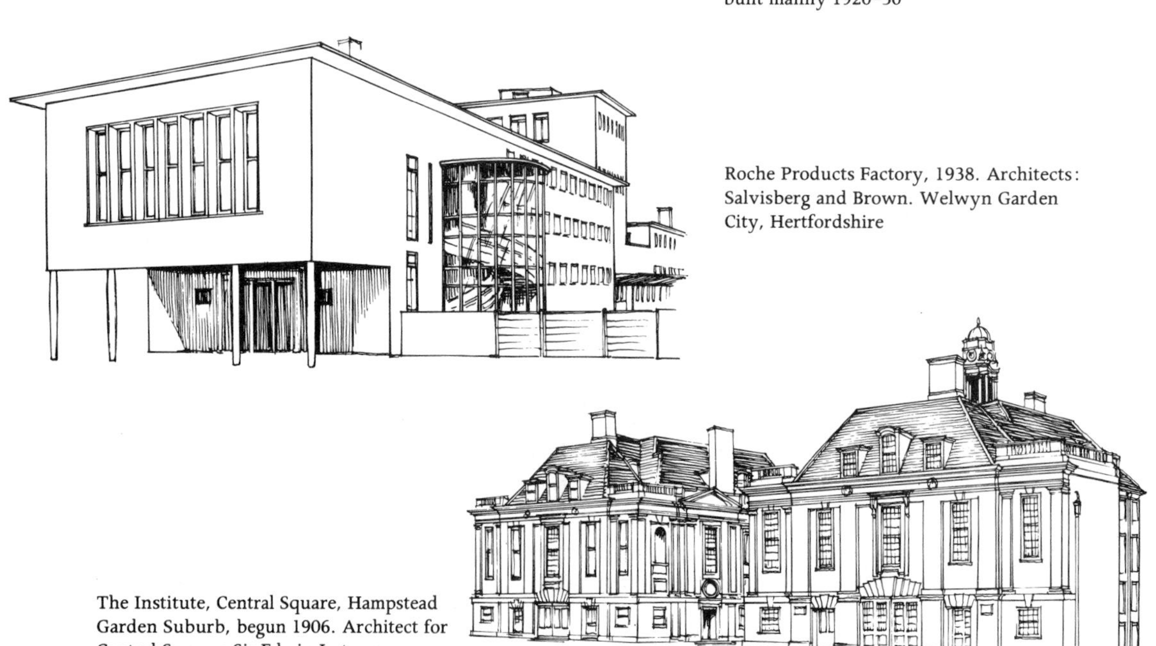

Roche Products Factory, 1938. Architects: Salvisberg and Brown. Welwyn Garden City, Hertfordshire

The Institute, Central Square, Hampstead Garden Suburb, begun 1906. Architect for Central Square: Sir Edwin Lutyens

Baroque; and in Napoleon III's Paris an urban masterpiece by *Haussman* and his colleagues who created the Grands Boulevards with their *rond-points* and richly flamboyant buildings.

In the second half of the nineteenth century other forms of town planning were also being initiated, not of imposing buildings lining wide thoroughfares, but of more humble new buildings intended to provide better housing, convenience and working conditions for the vastly increased urban population. In several countries of Europe there were appearing philanthropists, visionaries and architects with a sense of social purpose, ahead of their time and current thinking. In Germany there was Krupp at Essen, in England Sir Titus Salt in Yorkshire. Such men built 'ideal townships' for their workers, with housing, shops and amenities near the factories. These were the forerunners of the Garden City and New Town concepts of the twentieth century.

Saltaire was the first example of a 'New Town' in Britain. Sir Titus Salt, the Bradford mill-owner, built a new Italianate mill on the banks of the River Aire a few miles from the city and, around it, houses, a hospital, library, church, institute and almshouses for his workers. Each house had a parlour, kitchen, pantry, cellar, three bedrooms and an outside toilet. Built of stone in terrace form, the streets were named after Sir Titus's large family of children. The houses were well built and pleasantly situated; they were veritable palaces compared to the slums from which the Bradford workers had come.

A similar scheme on a smaller scale was initiated at *Copley*, a village near Halifax, where a Grecian-style mill and about 100 houses were built in the 1860s to a design by *W. H. Crossland*. These are stone houses, late Gothic in type.

In *Bedford Park* in *London* a different type of housing experiment was planned. This was not an industrial centre but a dormitory suburb. Initiated by Mr *J. T. Carr*, the estate was built centred round a church, a general stores and a club. Several architects worked on the project over many years: Norman Shaw, Maurice Adams, E. J. May and Sir Ernest George (see GEORGE, SIR ERNEST; SHAW, NORMAN). The houses are of brick, semi-detached or terraced, suitable for families of moderate income.

In the early twentieth century several different approaches were being tried out for providing better living and working conditions for a still-expanding urban population. Municipal schemes organized by the big city councils involved the building of housing estates. These were high-density schemes and were *dormitory suburbs* so that the occupants had to travel, in cities like London, often a considerable distance to work. The absence of a 'green belt' between one estate and another created large areas of uniform housing. There was also extensive unplanned speculative housing (see RIBBON DEVELOPMENT).

Port Sunlight Village, Wirral. Working Men's Club and gardens

Expanding upon Sir Titus Salt's ideas, several industrialists were establishing their own model housing estates adjacent to, but not an integral part of, the factory area. *Bournville* (Birmingham) stems from Cadbury and Rowntree built theirs at *York*. The most extensive and impressive was Lord Leverhulme's *Port Sunlight* in the Wirral of Cheshire. The Lever factory was built in 1888 and the housing estate has developed since then for the firm's employees. Architecturally the estate is successful. There is great variety of materials, styles and scale of buildings but all is indigenous and traditional and there is no overall architectural monotony. Several well-known domestic architects, for example Sir Ernest George (see GEORGE, SIR ERNEST) contributed. Most of the houses are of brick, stone or half-timber with pargeting. There is also a church, an art gallery, schools, a cottage hospital, library, bank, fire station, post office, shops, and an inn.

In 1906 the Garden Suburb Trust was founded to build a high-quality architectural layout for a housing area in north London: this was the *Hampstead Garden Suburb*. The chief planning experts were Sir Reginald Unwin and Barry Parker and the architect for the central part of the community Lutyens (see LUTYENS, SIR EDWIN LANDSEER). Lutyens's Central Square is a formal symmetrical plan in the Renaissance tradition. On opposite sides of the square are two churches, the Anglican St Jude and the Free Church, balancing one another in the design. Around the square are large terraced houses and the Institute buildings. The estate covered 317 acres. The architectural standard is high, as is the workmanship. The whole scheme is in red brick and tiles with white-painted woodwork.

The ideal *Garden City* was propounded in a book in 1898 by *Ebenezer Howard*. His aim was to create a new centre of population in a planned housing area which would also contain amenities such as churches, shops, schools and clubs and would produce a self-supporting community in the cleaner rural air with a higher proportion of open space per house than had been the case in nineteenth-century industrial towns. He intended that the land upon which the town was to be built should be owned by or held in trust for its community and he wanted adequate land space for a rural belt between the town and other urban areas. It was an attempt to call a halt to the increasing urban sprawl of the big cities.

The Garden City Association was formed and a company established. Two garden cities were built, both in Hertfordshire, at *Welwyn* and at *Letchworth*. Both have green belt areas and the industrial part of the town, though readily accessible, is kept apart from it. The buildings are traditional and varied comprising terraced cottages and detached houses. Roads are tree-lined, houses have gardens. There are shops, council offices, and a theatre.

After 1945 European town planners faced a tremendous task in rebuilding shattered city centres in a host of countries; they also had to come to terms, as the Americans had tried to do at an earlier date, with the explosion in numbers of the private motor car. The idea of segregating wheeled from pedestrian traffic was not a new one. *Leonardo* had postulated it in the fifteenth century (page 377), and it had been fundamental to the themes of *Sant'Elia* and *Garnier* (see MODERN ARCHITECTURE); but these were drawing-board projects. In the USA just after the First World War it had been tried out in *Radburn* in New Jersey but it was not until the 1950s and 1960s that traffic pressures forced a serious consideration of this as a satisfactory solution to everyday urban movement problems.

The method of segregation varied according to whether the subject was an existing city or a new centre of population. Many of the old cities of Europe had been so totally devastated that objections to pedestrianization of the town centre were much more muted than in, for instance, Britain or France where commercial interests were in general bitterly opposed to limiting vehicular access to their premises. The famous prototype of the city pedestrian precinct was the *Lijnbaan* of 1953–4 designed by *Bakema* and *Van den Broek* in the largely destroyed centre of *Rotterdam* in Holland. West Germany widely adopted the plan in rebuilding her northern cities shattered by aerial bombardment, for example, in *Essen, Düsseldorf, Hanover, Hamburg*. Then later in the 1970s, when commercial interests had realized the advantages of pedestrianization and the public had shown their approval, other less damaged cities followed suit as in *Munich* and *Verona*.

In the City of London, immediately after the war, Abercrombie's plans had met similar resistance to those of Wren 300 years earlier (page 377 and see ABERCROMBIE, SIR LESLIE PATRICK) and the limited *Barbican* and London Wall schemes which were finally built attracted considerable criticism. These covered a large area damaged by bombing and were built in 1959–82 to designs by Chamberlin, Powell and Bon and the City of London Planning Department. The intention was to provide a residential neighbourhood for city workers to include accommodation, a school, shops, restaurants, museum, a library, offices and an arts and conference centre. Motor traffic was to be segregated from pedestrian ways by different levels of construction connected to podia at the base of high-rise buildings. In the event the British climate proved unsuited to such a concept and traffic was only partially segregated. The most successful part of the enterprise seems to have been the cultural centre created here.

The alternative method of establishing new centres of population was on the whole more successful. These were often *satellite towns* not too far from a larger centre of population and dependent upon it for costly facilities such as universities and hospitals. Scandinavia acquired a reputation for building such quality New Towns in the immediate post-war era. Sweden in particular, having been neutral during the war, was able to develop such schemes much earlier than the war-ravaged countries

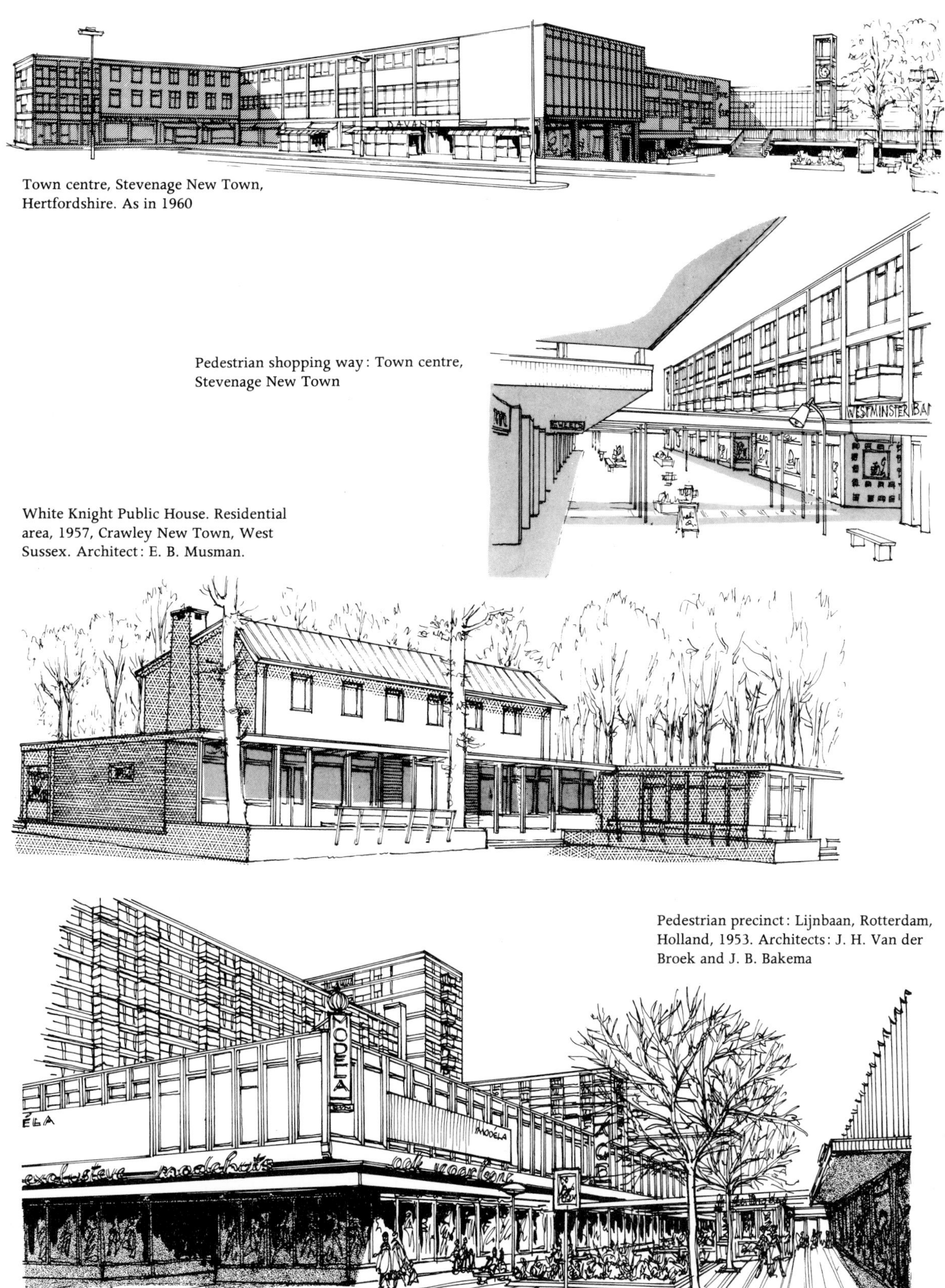

Town centre, Stevenage New Town, Hertfordshire. As in 1960

Pedestrian shopping way: Town centre, Stevenage New Town

White Knight Public House. Residential area, 1957, Crawley New Town, West Sussex. Architect: E. B. Musman.

Pedestrian precinct: Lijnbaan, Rotterdam, Holland, 1953. Architects: J. H. Van der Broek and J. B. Bakema

could do. The new towns of *Vällingby* and *Farsta* on the periphery of *Stockholm* were two examples, both well built and laid out, wheeled traffic and pedestrians largely separated, but both of limited architectural interest.

Of much higher architectural standard and more imaginative in its concept is the satellite town of *Tapiola* eight kilometres from *Helsinki* in Finland. It was begun in 1952 by its chief architect *Aarne Ervi* (see MODERN ARCHITECTURE) who designed the central area. The layout here comprises a large lake with swimming pools and fountains and behind it a pedestrian precinct shopping area and other facilities. The housing is of mixed development, pleasingly planned and naturally sited to take advantage of the wooded landscape.

Not dissimilar is the new satellite town of *Reston*, Virginia in the USA, built 18 miles from Washington. Like Tapiola it has a large artificial lake, trees and wooded areas and its houses are planned informally to blend into the natural landscape. An important feature of Reston is its stress upon segregation of pedestrian from motor traffic, a safety factor achieved by laying out roads and paths at different levels; a concept inherited from the Radburn scheme of 60 years earlier.

In Britain the *New Town* scheme was the successor to the pre-war Garden City concept. With Lord Reith as its Chairman, the New Town Committee was set up in 1945 to suggest guiding principles upon which the theme might be developed. The New Towns Act of 1946 provided for 20 such towns to take the overspill from large cities, especially London, and that they should not adjoin the city in question (see ABERCROMBIE, SIR LESLIE PATRICK).

Planning was quickly implemented on the first sites: *Hatfield, Stevenage* and *Hemel Hempstead* in Hertfordshire, *Crawley* in Sussex, *Harlow* in Essex (see GIBBERD, SIR FREDERICK). In 1955 *Cumbernauld* was begun to relieve the housing pressures on Glasgow. In the early 1960s a new generation of New Towns was planned to provide housing urgently needed in a number of key areas; notable were *Telford* (originally called Dawley) in the Midlands, *Runcorn* in the north-west, *Washington* in the north-east and two in Scotland, *Livingstone* and *Irvine*. The first of three possible new 'Cities' was started in 1967 in the Bletchley area (Buckinghamshire); it was called *Milton Keynes*. This was a much larger, more complex project envisaging a population of 250,000 by the end of the century.

The New Towns have been a success despite problems of resettling urban populations and providing interests and entertainment for the young. Each town was built with civic and cultural buildings, schools, hospital and colleges as well as a town centre well provided with large shops and adequate car parking. In the peripheral areas are churches, public houses, community centres and sports facilities. The industrial area is normally separate from the residential part of the town, pedestrianization is extensive and wheeled traffic safely controlled and segregated. The architecture is modern but each area utilizes indigenous materials. As time has passed, though, several of the earlier towns have grown larger and more densely populated than was at first envisaged. In consequence pressure upon car parking facilities and town centre, education and hospital services has mounted. There is criticism that some towns have become too large and that it would have been better to have built a greater number of smaller centres.

In older city centres important features of many schemes for urban renewal have been the maintenance of comfortable ambient air temperatures and convenience of access; this has been achieved by taking advantage of modern technology. In design, undercover shopping, car parking and entertainment facilities as well as museums and churches may be linked by moving walkways, escalators and pedestrianized streets; a mini-city being created to give comfort and ease in patronizing a variety of services. Such schemes are particularly welcome in cities which experience extremes of winter and summer temperatures: for example the re-designed *Place Ville-Marie* in *Montreal* in Canada (*Pei* and *Cobb*, 1967). Other North American examples include *New York's Lincoln Center* (*Johnson, Harrison* and *Abramovitz*, 1966) and *Chicago's John Hancock* (1967–9). *London's Barbican Centre* has already been mentioned (p. 384); in *Paris* the *Pompidou Centre* (1976) has been both vigorously praised and condemned for its architecture but is acknowledged to be successful for convenient use of its facilities.

TOWNSEND, CHARLES HARRISON (1851–1928) An architect practising chiefly in the last years of the nineteenth century and first decade of the twentieth. Townsend was born in Birkenhead and trained in an architect's office in Liverpool; he set up in practice on his own in London in the 1880s. In the 1890s Townsend, who was a talented member of the Arts and Crafts Movement, designed three particularly original and decorative buildings. Two of these were built on awkward, restricted sites in congested parts of *London*: the *Bishopsgate Institute* (1892–4) and the *Whitechapel Art Gallery* (1896 but altered 1900). He had more space available for his *Horniman Museum* in Dulwich, which is a local landmark on top of a hill. In Essex the interior of *Great Warley Church* is decorated in his characteristic style (see also ASHBEE, CHARLES ROBERT; LETHABY, WILLIAM RICHARD; MACKMURDO, ARTHUR HEYGATE).

TRABEATED Based on the post-and-lintel type of construction (see CLASSICAL ARCHITECTURE).

TRACERY The ornamental intersection of the stone mouldings in a Gothic window head; also such decorative designs in panels, vaults and screens.

Tracery appeared early in the development of Gothic architecture. The need arose from the idea of grouping

TOWNSEND, CHARLES HARRISON
Bishopsgate Institute, London, 1892–4.
Architect: Charles Harrison Townsend

two or more lights under one arch head. This created a space above, the *spandrel*, which presented an awkward feature of design. To resolve this problem the space was carved into foiled circular shapes. These were pierced, so creating the earliest form of tracery, *plate tracery*, in which stone infilling occupied a larger area than the window glass.

After the mid-thirteenth century *bar tracery* began to develop from the plate form. In this type of work the stonework was much narrower, in 'bars', and the area of glass much greater. An early design of bar tracery was *Y-tracery* were the single mullion dividing the window into two lights branched at the window head in the shape of the letter Y. After this the window area steadily grew larger, with greater width in comparison to height, and the head was encompassed by an equilateral rather than a lancet arch. The window was then divided by several mullions, giving three, five, seven and even nine lights and the tracery design became more complex.

At first the pattern was *geometrical* based on circles, trefoils and quatrefoils; then, in the fourteenth century, there were introduced flowing, flame-like shapes based on the ogee form: this was called *flowing* or *curvilinear tracery*. A variation on this was *reticulated tracery* in which the design was made up solely of circles which formed ogee shapes at top and bottom, so creating a net design. There was also *intersecting tracery* in which the mullions extended in curves to the head of the arch, crossing one another as they passed.

Further variations in the fourteenth and fifteenth centuries included *drop tracery* which was a traceried edging

TRACERY
Plate tracery: Lausanne Cathedral, Switzerland, south transept, twelfth century

Drop tracery, Antwerp Cathedral, Belgium, west front doorway, fifteenth century

Y-tracery, *c.* 1290

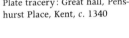

Intersecting tracery, thirteenth century

Plate tracery: Great hall, Penshurst Place, Kent, *c.* 1340

Reticulated tracery, fourteenth century

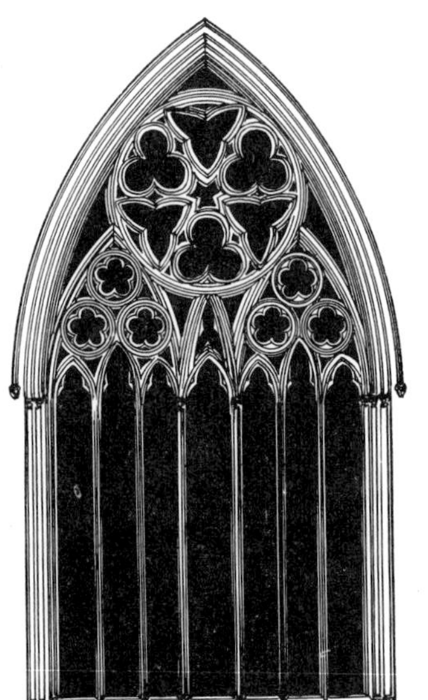

Geometrical tracery: East window of choir, *c.* 1300, Ripon Cathedral

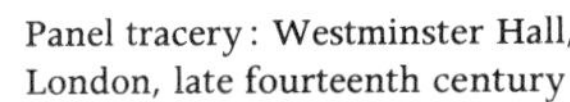

Panel tracery: Westminster Hall, London, late fourteenth century

Panel tracery: St George's Chapel, Windsor, west window, *c.* 1485–1509

Geometrical towards curvilinear tracery, Exeter Cathedral, west front, 1328–75

to an entrance arch, *Kentish tracery* which has a complex foil design to be seen chiefly in the county of Kent, and *flamboyant tracery* (which is a later French form of curvilinear tracery, sometimes to be seen in England—it flows upwards in flame-like shapes).

The last phase of tracery design came in the Perpendicular Gothic work particularly characteristic of Britain in which the window design followed the pattern of panelling seen in the fifteenth- and early sixteenth-century treatment of walls and vaults. Windows were divided vertically by mullions and horizontally by transoms to create *rectilinear* or *panel tracery*. In later examples the window was also wider than before, its head enclosed by the flatter, four-centred arch (see ARCH; FOIL; GOTHIC ARCHITECTURE; OGEE; SPANDREL; VAULTING; WINDOW).

TRIBUNE

1. In a basilica, or church on basilican plan, the apse (see BASILICA).
2. An elevated platform or rostrum.
3. In a church, a gallery (see GALLERY).

TRIUMPHAL ARCH A monumental arch erected to commemorate an important military or domestic happening or in memory or respect of an individual.

Such arches were characteristic of ancient Roman building custom and were erected especially in honour of emperors and victorious generals. They were constructed often astride a road and were pierced by one or three arched entrances; in the latter instance the central opening was for vehicular traffic and the smaller lateral ones were for pedestrians. An order was used flanking the openings in column and pilaster form; the Corinthian or Composite Order was preferred for this purpose by the Romans. The plinth, arch spandrels, frieze and entablature were enriched with carved ornament and sculpture. Above the cornice was an attic for the appropriate dedicatory inscription. A large sculptural group surmounted the arch, usually in the form of a triumphal car drawn by four or six horses (see QUADRIGA). Many Roman triumphal arches survive in Rome and other cities (see CLASSICAL ARCHITECTURE; CLASSICAL ORDER).

TRIUMPHAL ARCH
Arch of Septimius Severus, Forum Romanum, Rome, with Composite Order, AD 204

TROPHY In the antique classical world a memorial of a military victory composed of arms and spoils taken from the enemy. In art and architecture a carved decorative representation of such a composition.

TRUMEAU A French term applied to the pier between two openings or more commonly, in Gothic architecture, the central pier supporting the tympanum which divides a large portal into two parts and which is often sculptured.

TURRET A small tower.

TYMPANUM The face of a classical pediment between its sloping and horizontal cornice mouldings; similarly the area between the lintel of a doorway and the arch above it. In many instances the tympanum is sculptured (see CLASSICAL ARCHITECTURE; GOTHIC ARCHITECTURE; ROMANESQUE ARCHITECTURE; TEMPLE).

TRUMEAU
Sculptured Virgin on trumeau. Centre façade portal of Reims Cathedral, France, thirteenth century

TRUMEAU AND TYMPANUM
Madonna portal, south transept of Amiens Cathedral, France, *c.* 1280: sculptured trumeau and tympanum

TYMPANUM
Carved tympanum on Romanesque doorway of Barfreston Church, Kent

U,V

UNDERCROFT In a house, castle or church, a vaulted chamber partially or wholly underground and used primarily for storage (see also *crypt* in CHURCH DESIGN AND STRUCTURE).

VANBRUGH, SIR JOHN (1664–1726) Of Flemish descent, being the grandson of the Haarlem merchant Giles van Brugg, Vanbrugh was born in London and brought up in Chester where his father, Giles Vanbrugh, worked in the sugar business.

John Vanbrugh, like Wren, did not come to the profession of architecture until he was in his thirties; also like Wren, he was engaged in other, different careers before this (see WREN, SIR CHRISTOPHER). Vanbrugh was commissioned in the army in 1686 and spent some years in France, part of the time in prison (including a period in the notorious Bastille) on suspicion of spying. He continued his military career on his return to England in 1692 but a few years later had taken up a new profession as a successful playwright. In 1704 he became a herald and in 1714 he was knighted.

Vanbrugh's entry into the architectural profession was momentous; it came when he was asked in 1699 by the Earl of Carlisle to design *Castle Howard* for him in Yorkshire. This stupendous mansion was the new architect's first attempt at design and he owed much to Hawksmoor's experience in acting as draughtsman, advisor and administrator (see HAWKSMOOR, NICHOLAS). Nevertheless the concept was Vanbrugh's and, like all his work, was in the grand manner; it established him as the leader of the Baroque school in England. Castle Howard set the pattern for his designs which were not rigidly defined blocks, as in much seventeenth-century work, but grouped buildings of strongly articulated masses. Some of the work is coarse, particularly in detail, but Vanbrugh was a master of three-dimensional form in stone, adept at creating monumental, grandiose shapes in light and shade. His Flemish ancestry showed in his Baroque treatment of classicism, in the robustness of his porticoes, and wall articulation.

At Castle Howard the central block is surmounted by a large drum and cupola (rebuilt after the fire of 1940) which dominate the structure. Inside, the great hall is square, its giant Corinthian pilasters supporting the arches upon which the drum rises. The hall itself is spacious and imposing but the interior dome above is lofty and narrow (only 27ft in diameter and 77ft above floor level)—the

UNDERCROFT
Romanesque undercroft from original manor house: Burton Agnes Hall, Yorkshire

Garden front of Castle Howard, Yorkshire, begun 1700

Vanbrugh Castle, Greenwich, 1717–18

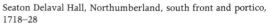

Seaton Delaval Hall, Northumberland, south front and portico, 1718–28

price that has been paid for the impressive exterior silhouette. This is a familiar problem with dome construction and one solved by many architects by building two domes, a flatter, lower one within a taller exterior one (see WREN, SIR CHRISTOPHER). On the north elevation of the house curving arcades advance to bound a great open court on each side of which are extensive groups of buildings which accommodated kitchens, stables, laundry etc. Much of this building was carried out after Vanbrugh's death.

The creation of *Blenheim Palace*, Oxfordshire (1705–25) was Vanbrugh's supreme triumph. A present from a grateful nation to the Duke of Marlborough, this immense structure seemed to be designed especially for display rather than comfort and convenience. Blenheim, Castle Howard, and the later *Seaton Delaval* were the last of a type of gigantic residence which became obsolete because of sheer size and cost; they represent domestic architecture in the grand manner.

This commission also presented Vanbrugh with his greatest difficulties. The Duchess of Marlborough made no secret of her disapproval of the choice of architect, his design and 'extravagances'. When Queen Anne's royal favour was withdrawn from the Duchess, Treasury payments for Blenheim finally ceased and so did building work. With favour restored under George I work restarted in 1716 but by this time relations between Vanbrugh and the Duchess had deteriorated so greatly that the architect was finally excluded from his own work and, after the Duke's death in 1722, Hawksmoor returned to complete building supervision.

Blenheim Palace as it stands today, in the superb setting of its park at Woodstock, is a remarkable house, both for its colossal scale and conflicting masses. The great centre block with its Corinthian portico is theatrical, even ostentatious, but its scale is absorbed in the greater compass of the complete frontage, extending to 856ft. The centrepiece is connected to the massively castellar side pavilions by curved colonnades of Doric columns. Beyond these, forming the side wings of the *cour d'honneur*, are the stable and kitchen courts surrounded by their own groups of buildings. Though quite different from the Italian Baroque of Borromini or Bernini—for there are few curves or undulations—the conception of Blenheim could be described by no other term than Baroque (see BAROQUE ARCHITECTURE). Surprisingly, in contrast to the usual

Belvedere Temple (1725–8) at Castle Howard, Yorkshire. Architect: Sir John Vanbrugh

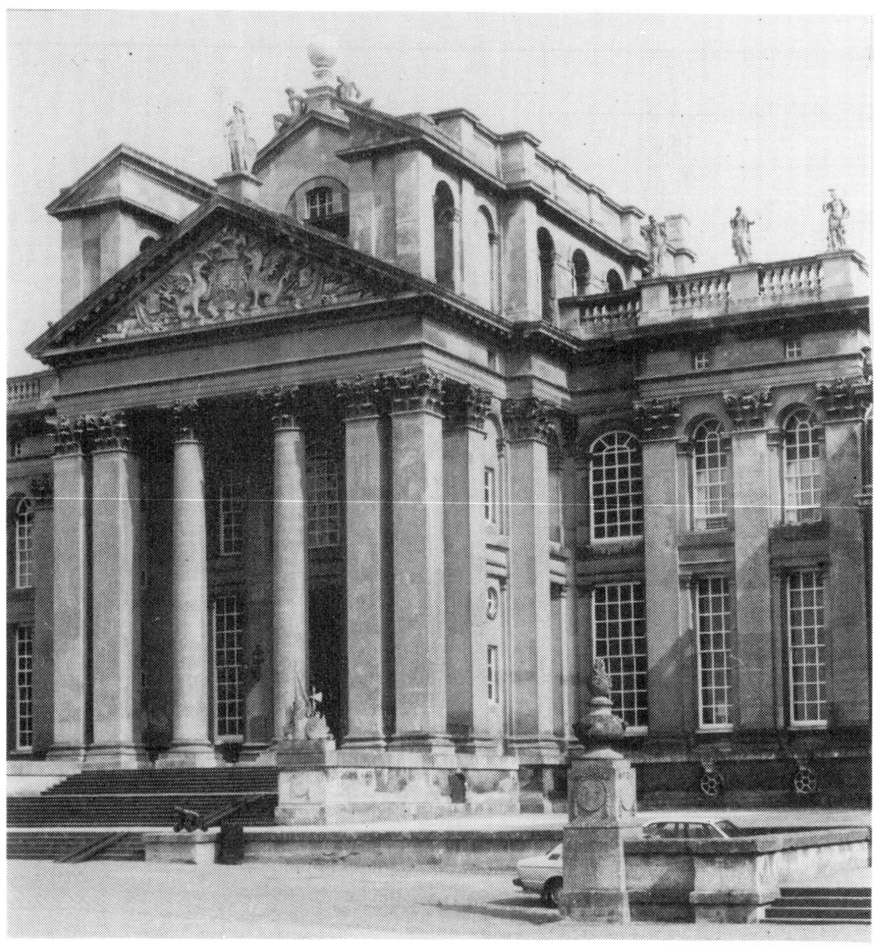

Entrance portico of Blenheim Palace

South front of Blenheim Palace

West front and gardens, Blenheim Palace

Bridge, lake and palace, Blenheim Park

Baroque treatment of rustication, pediments, portico and colonnades, the detail is often simple as, for example, in the plain window openings. Inside are the superbly decorated great hall and reception rooms including especially the magnificent ceiling and wall paintings by *Sir James Thornhill* and *Louis Laguerre*.

Vanbrugh's architectural career was less than 30 years. In this time he developed a highly personal style, always masculine, strong, forceful and displaying what Adam, who admired his work greatly, characterized as Baroque 'movement' (see ADAM, ROBERT). In 1702 Vanbrugh was appointed Comptroller of the King's Works and the following year became a member of the Board of Directors of *Greenwich Hospital* where he took a part in supervising building operations. Finally, in 1716, he took Wren's place as Surveyor in charge there and directed the completion of the Great Hall and the building of the William III block.

Much of Vanbrugh's work was in the domestic field. Surviving are *Kimbolton Castle*, Huntingdonshire (remodelled 1707–10), *King's Weston*, Gloucestershire (1712–14) and the remarkable and powerful *Seaton Delaval Hall* in Northumberland. This was built 1720–8 but was twice badly damaged by fire and left roofless for 50 years. It has now been partly restored and the great Ionic portico on the south front once more evidences Vanbrugh at his most monumental.

Of the smaller houses which he built at *Greenwich*, his own house *Vanbrugh Castle* survives. Built 1718–19, this is a personally Vanbrugh Baroque version of an early medieval castle with towers and machicolations. One of Vanbrugh's last works was the *Belvedere Temple* (Tower of the Winds) in the grounds of Castle Howard (1725–8) in which he designed his own version of Palladio's Villa Capra near Vicenza (see PALLADIAN ARCHITECTURE and see also COUNTRY HOUSE AND MANSION).

VARDY, JOHN (d. 1765) Vardy worked for many years, mainly as Clerk of the Works, in the service of the King's Works at Greenwich, Hampton Court, Whitehall, Kensington, St James's and Chelsea Hospital.

Vardy was closely associated with William Kent (see KENT, WILLIAM), publishing some of his works and erecting after Kent's death (with William Robinson) the *Horse Guards* in Whitehall. Vardy himself designed *Spencer House* in London in the Palladian style (1756–65) (see PALLADIAN ARCHITECTURE).

VAULTING An arched interior roofing made of stone or brick; in the eighteenth and nineteenth centuries such vaults were sometimes built in plaster or wood.

Vaulted ceilings were especially characteristic of Gothic architecture in the Middle Ages, and in the nineteenth-century revivals of the style (see GOTHIC ARCHITECTURE; GOTHIC REVIVAL). The Romans and, later, Romanesque builders had used the simplest style of vault, the *barrel* or cylindrical form (see CLASSICAL ARCHITECTURE; CONCRETE; ROMANESQUE ARCHITECTURE). This is like a tunnel, generally semicircular in section and supported on side walls. It is dangerously unsuited to wide spans due to the immense thrust which it exerts upon the walls.

With the development of pointed arch construction in the early Middle Ages the *ribbed vault* evolved (see ARCH). The classical arch and the Romanesque arch were both round forms. The pointed arch was not a new invention when it was adopted for the Early English style of Gothic architecture; it had long been used in the Middle East and, by the twelfth century, was also being constructed in Christian building in areas subject to North African influence such as Spain and Sicily.

The impetus towards the adoption of the pointed arch in western European ecclesiastical building stemmed from the urgent need to provide interior roofing which would be less liable to destruction by fire: a hazard to which timber roofs were particularly vulnerable. The pointed arch became the key to building such vaults of stone or brick because of its greater flexibility in construction. The difficulty of roofing the interiors of churches and monastic structures with stone, using only round arches, stemmed from the fact that nave, choir, transepts and their aisles often had different heights and widths. Also vaulting is constructed in bays (see BAY) on columns or piers and the semicircular arch lends itself to a square bay. In a ribbed vault the diagonals crossing the square were longer than the ribs connecting the sides of the bay. It was, therefore, impossible for all the ribs to be of semicircular form. Either the vault had to be domical or the diagonal ribs segmental; alternatively, the side arches had to be squeezed to become stilted (see ARCH).

Because of these problems comparatively few Romanesque buildings were stone vaulted and such vaults were of *barrel*, *groined* or *domical* type. Empirically it was discovered that the pointed arch, which could be tall and narrow (*lancet*), medium (*equilateral*) or wide (*obtuse*), was ideally suited to vaulting at various heights and spans (see ARCH). The French term for this arch, *arch brisé* (= 'broken arch'), clearly illustrates its convenience.

Over the 400 years in which Gothic architecture was the current style the increased knowledge gained by experience enabled builders to construct even wider, higher and more complex vaults. The ribbed vault construction consisted of a framework of stone ribs supported on wood centering (see CENTERING). When the spaces between had been infilled with stone pieces or bricks the whole became self-supporting. Such a structure was much lighter and more flexible than a barrel vault.

Initially ribbed vaults were of *quadripartite* design, that is, the bay area was bisected by diagonal ribs making four compartments (see BOSS). During the early fourteenth century more complex patterns were constructed, introducing intermediate *tierceron* ribs, which extended from the vault springing to the ridge rib (see ARCH) and, soon

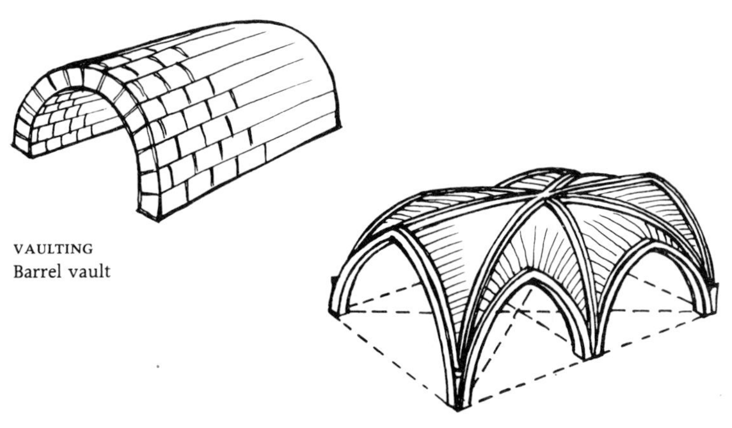

VAULTING
Barrel vault

Gothic vault over oblong compartment

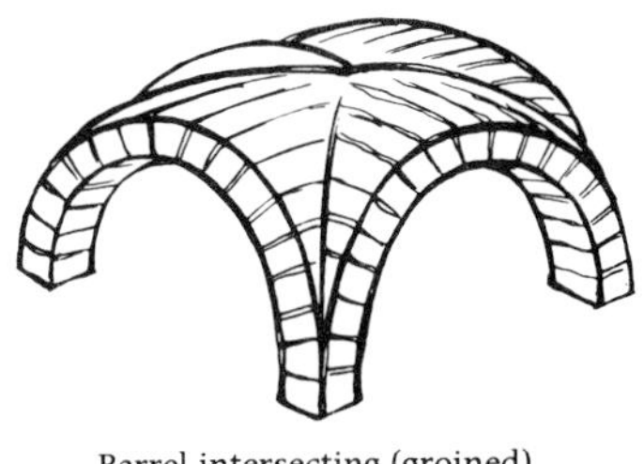

Barrel intersecting (groined) vault

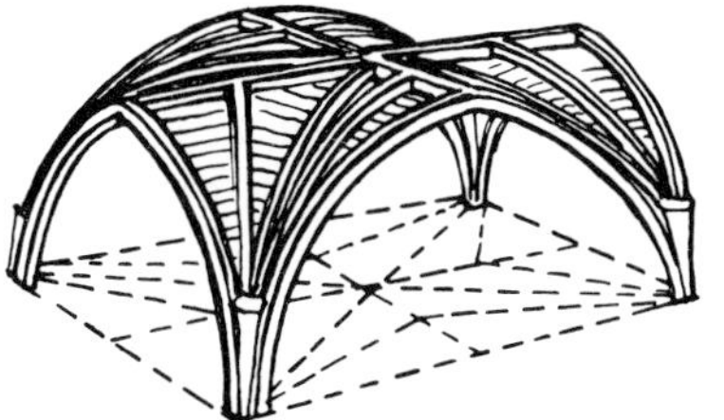

Sexpartite vault

Brick and stone groined vaults: undercroft of Palace of Diocletian, Split, Yugoslavia

Barrel vaulting: choir of Basilica of S. Benoît-sur-Loire, France

Groined vaulting: crypt of Lastingham Church, Yorkshire, 1078–88

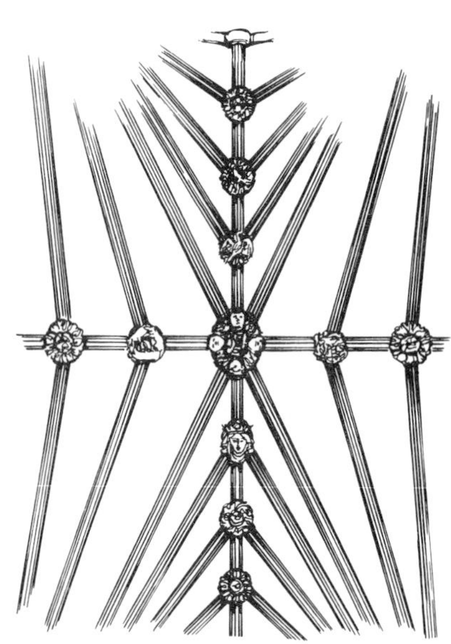

Ribbed tierceron vault, plan view: nave of Exeter Cathedral, 1353–69

Pointed barrel vaulting: Meira Abbey Church, Spain, twelfth century to 1258

Plaited, swirling vaulting: Vladislav Hall, Prague Castle, Czechoslovakia, 1487–1500

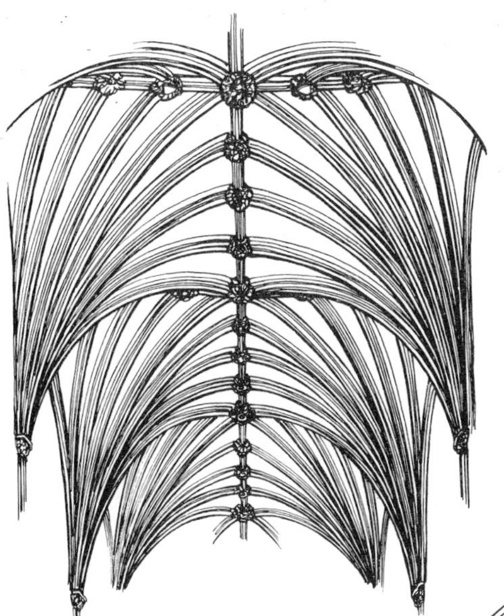

Ribbed tierceron vault: nave high vault, Exeter Cathedral, 1353–69

Lierne vault: plan view of presbytery, Gloucester Cathedral, *c.* 1350

Lierne vault: choir of Wells Cathedral, *c.* 1329

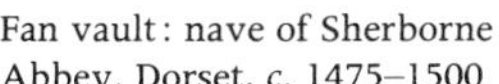

Fan vault: nave of Sherborne Abbey, Dorset, *c.* 1475–1500

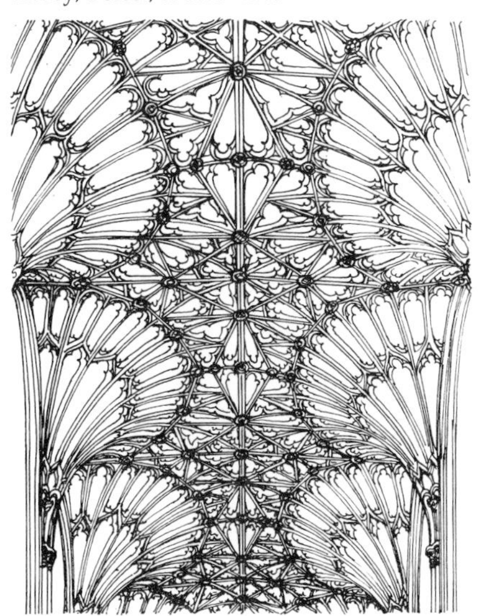

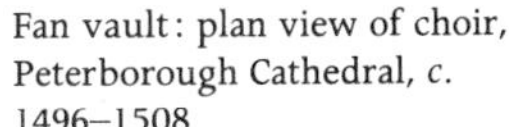

Fan vault: plan view of choir, Peterborough Cathedral, *c.* 1496–1508

Fan vaulting: King's College Chapel, Cambridge, 1446–1515

afterwards, the *lierne vault* was developed in which extra ribs (liernes) were introduced, crossing from rib to rib and making elaborate patterns.

In the final, Perpendicular, phase of Gothic architecture the *fan vault* appeared. It had evolved from the wish to build a vault which could accommodate ribs of different curvature as they sprang from the capital or vaulting shaft. The radiating ribs of a fan vault are of equal length and are bounded by a rib in the shape of a semicircle. The whole group of ribs is in the form of an inverted concave cone. Lierne ribs cross the radiating ribs so producing, as in wall and window design of the time, a panelled surface (see ARCH; GOTHIC ARCHITECTURE; TRACERY; WINDOW).

Glossary of vaulting terms

Barrel vault: also known as a *tunnel* or *wagon vault*, a continuous tunnel-like vault, most often semicircular in section but occasionally, in Romanesque building, of wide, pointed form.

Crown: the upper central surface of a vault where the ribs intersect and along which a ridge rib (if present) runs. The intersections are generally covered by a boss (see BOSS).

Domical vault: a groined or ribbed vault where the diagonal groins or ribs are semicircular in form so causing the centre of the vaulted bay to rise higher than the side arches in the centre as in a low dome (see DOME).

Fan vault: a panelled vault resembling a fan constructed in inverted concave cones, the ribs of which are of equal length as they radiate from the central springer.

Formeret: also known as a *wall rib*, a non-structural half-rib built across the side wall of a vaulted bay to balance the rest of the design.

Groined vault: also known as a *cross vault*, one where two barrel vaults intersect at right angles. The groins are the sharp edges formed where the vaulting surfaces meet; there are no covering ribs.

Lierne: a ribbed vault where lierne ribs are incorporated into the design to make a more complex pattern. Derived from the French word *lier* (='to tie'), these ribs are secondary, decorative ones which do not spring from the wall supports but extend in any direction from the structural ribs and might join any other rib.

Ploughshare vault: also known as a *stilted vault*. One in which the wall ribs spring from a higher level than the diagonal ones, so producing a web of twisted shape resembling a ploughshare. This is in order to permit better ingress of light from the clerestory windows.

Quadripartite vault: a vault of four compartments made by the crossing of two diagonal ribs.

Sail vault: see DOME.

Sexpartite vault: in which a bay of quadripartite vaulting is divided transversely into two parts to give six compartments.

Severy: a vaulting bay.

Stellar vault: one in which the lierne ribs create a star-shaped pattern.

Tierceron: a rib which extends from the vault springing to the ridge rib.

Transverse arch: one separating one vaulting bay from another. A transverse rib marks the line of separation.

Vaulting shaft: the vertical shaft from which the ribs spring.

Web: also called a *cell*, the stone or brick infilling between ribs of a vault (see BRICKWORK).

VENETIAN DOOR, WINDOW A Venetian window is a tripartite design with the central section arched and taller than the two flat-topped flanking lights. Also known as a *Palladian window* or *Serliana* because it was first illus-

Venetian window at the Horse Guards, London. 1751–8.
Architect: William Kent

trated in Serlio's *Architettura* published in 1537 (later to be translated into English) this, deriving from Palladio, was a characteristic of English Palladian architecture (see PALLADIAN ARCHITECTURE; SERLIO, SEBASTIANO).

A Venetian door is similar, the central doorway being arched and flanked by lower flat-topped windows (see DOOR, DOORWAY).

VERANDA, VERANDAH An open, roofed balcony or gallery generally supported and fronted by metal framing which may be partially or wholly glazed.

VERTUE, ROBERT (d. 1506) and **WILLIAM** (d. 1527) Two brothers who were King's Master Masons in the late fifteenth and early sixteenth centuries. They worked at *Bath Abbey*, also on other great projects of the time, notably *St George's Chapel*, Windsor and the *Henry VII Chapel* in Westminster Abbey.

VICTORIAN ARCHITECTURE Architecture of the years 1837–1901 (see BARRY, SIR CHARLES; BENTLEY, JOHN FRANCIS; BLOMFIELD, SIR ARTHUR; BLORE, EDWARD; BODLEY, GEORGE FREDERICK; BRODRICK, CUTHBERT; BURGES, WILLIAM; BUTTERFIELD, WILLIAM; CARPENTER, RICHARD CROMWELL; CHAMPNEYS, BASIL; CIVIC ARCHITECTURE; COLLCUTT, THOMAS EDWARD; COUNTRY HOUSE AND MANSION; ELMES, HARVEY LONSDALE; FERREY, BENJAMIN; GEORGE, SIR ERNEST; GODWIN, EDWARD WILLIAM; GOTHIC REVIVAL; HARDWICK, PHILIP; INDUSTRIALIZED ARCHITECTURE; IRON AND GLASS; IRONWORK; LETHABY, WILLIAM RICHARD; MACKMURDO, ARTHUR HEYGATE; MORRIS, WILLIAM; MOUNTFORD, EDWARD WILLIAM; NEWTON, SIR ERNEST; PAXTON, SIR JOSEPH; PEARSON, JOHN LOUGHBOROUGH; PENNETHORNE, SIR JAMES; PLAYFAIR, WILLIAM HENRY; PUGIN, AUGUSTUS WELBY NORTHMORE; RAILWAY ARCHITECTURE; RUSKIN, JOHN; SALVIN, ANTHONY; SCOTT, SIR GEORGE GILBERT; SEDDING, JOHN DANDO; SHAW, RICHARD NORMAN; STREET, GEORGE EDMUND; TITE, SIR WILLIAM; TOWN PLANNING; VOYSEY, CHARLES FRANCIS ANNESLEY; WATERHOUSE, ALFRED).

VILLA In both Latin and modern Italian the term refers to a country house or the country seat of a landowner or farmer. This was its meaning in Roman times; Hadrian's villa at Tivoli was a majestic example (see ROMAN DOMESTIC ARCHITECTURE). It continued to be so in the classical age of the Renaissance and later as, for example, in Palladio's, Vignola's and della Porta's villas in Italy (see PALLADIAN ARCHITECTURE; RENAISSANCE ARCHITECTURE).

By the nineteenth century in Britain a villa was designed for a well-to-do owner as a detached house in the pleasantly semi-rural suburbs of the then quickly developing towns. In more modern times the word is likely to refer to a smaller version of such a house probably occupied by a family of the professional and middle class.

VITRUVIUS *Marcus Vitruvius Pollio* (usually referred to as Vitruvius) was a Roman architect and engineer of the first century BC. Comparatively little is known of his life apart from the likelihood that he served as a military engineer under Julius Caesar; in Imperial Rome he then worked under the Emperor Augustus and was engineer of Rome's water supply. He built a basilica at Fano (now destroyed).

Vitruvius is known for his ten-volume work *De Architectura*, written and dedicated to Augustus about 25 BC and comprising a comprehensive account, based upon his own experience and a study of the Greek architects, of the aesthetic principles and design, proportion and detail of Greek and early Roman classical architecture. In the first volume he discussed the training of architects, architectural principle and town planning, in the second building materials, the third and fourth temple architecture and Greek orders. Volume five dealt with public building, six with domestic work and seven with interior decorative design. The final three volumes considered the broad aspect of the engineering side of architecture, including mechanical engineering and water supply.

De Architectura is the only complete treatise on architecture to survive from classical antiquity. Several manuscript copies were known in the Middle Ages but only when, in the early fifteenth century, it first came to be studied by the architects of the Italian Renaissance, notably *Leon Battista Alberti* (1404–72), did it come to be accepted as a basic tenet of study for the revised classical architectural form. It was first printed in Rome about 1486 and an Italian translation was prepared about 1520 under the direction of *Raphael*. Before long illustrated editions were being produced, later in most European languages (see CAMPBELL, COLEN; CLASSICISM; PALLADIAN ARCHITECTURE; RENAISSANCE ARCHITECTURE; TEMPLE; TOWN PLANNING).

VOLUTE The helix or spiral form of scroll characteristic of the classical capital of the Ionic Order and, on a smaller scale, also of the Corinthian and Composite capitals (see CLASSICAL ORDER).

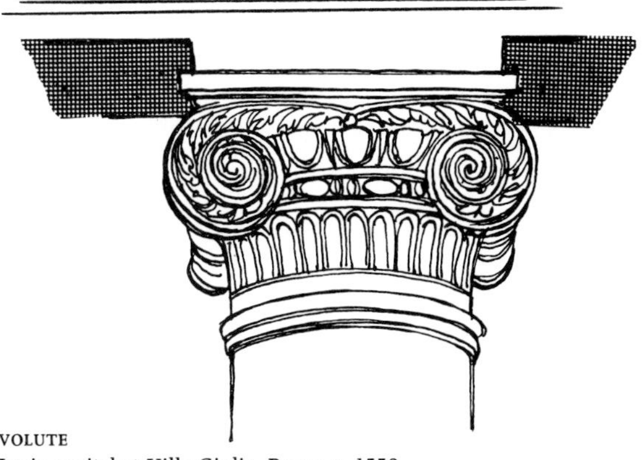

VOLUTE
Ionic capital at Villa Giulia, Rome, *c.* 1550

VOLUTE
Composite capital in church of S. Miniato al Monte, Florence, twelfth century

VOYSEY, CHARLES FRANCIS ANNESLEY (1857–1941) Born in Yorkshire, the son of a parson but grandson of Annesley Voysey the engineer and architect, Charles Voysey began his career in the office of the architect Seddon (see SEDDON, JOHN DANDO); he then went on to George Devey before setting up practice on his own in 1882. Influenced by Mackmurdo (see MACKMURDO, ARTHUR HEYGATE), he began by designing extensively in the field of interior decoration, particularly wallpaper, furniture and textiles, and soon made a considerable reputation.

Voysey then turned more attentively to architecture where his contribution was mainly in the domestic field. His first house, in 1888, was *The Cottage* at *Bishop's Itchington,* Warwickshire, where he initiated a form which he then went on to develop: an informal plan, with asymmetrical long, low elevations, gently sloping roofs, lean-to buttresses and rough-cast wall finish.

Voysey's style was personal. In breaking away from late Victorianism he followed Shaw (see SHAW, RICHARD NORMAN) in appreciating the vernacular tradition but his work was plainer, simple yet subtle, and less eclectic. Art Nouveau and the influence of Mackintosh had their effect upon his work (see ART NOUVEAU; MACKINTOSH, CHARLES RENNIE). This was on an intimate rather than grand scale and he continued to design all decorative features, inside as well as on the exterior.

In town housing Voysey designed a London house in *Bedford Park* and a pair of terrace houses near Sloane Square, *14–16 Hans Road,* both in 1891. In the terrace houses he abandoned his rough-cast finish for red brick with stone-mullioned windows. Like all Voysey's work, these façades are unpretentious but possess charm and simple, elegant detailing. His country houses include his own home *The Orchard* at *Chorley Wood,* Hertfordshire (1900), *The Pastures, North Luffenham,* Leicestershire (1901) (see COUNTRY HOUSE AND MANSION), *Perrycroft, Colwall,* Hereford and Worcester (1893) and, probably his best work, *Broadleys, Lake Windermere,* Cumbria (1898–9).

In the 1890s Voysey's work became known in Europe and the USA. Both there and at home his influence spread, his high-quality yet simple building well received by a number of architects in reaction from High Victorianism: *Mackay Hugh Baillie-Scott* (1865–1945) was one of these.

The Orchard, Chorley Wood, Hertfordshire, 1900. Architect: C. F. A. Voysey

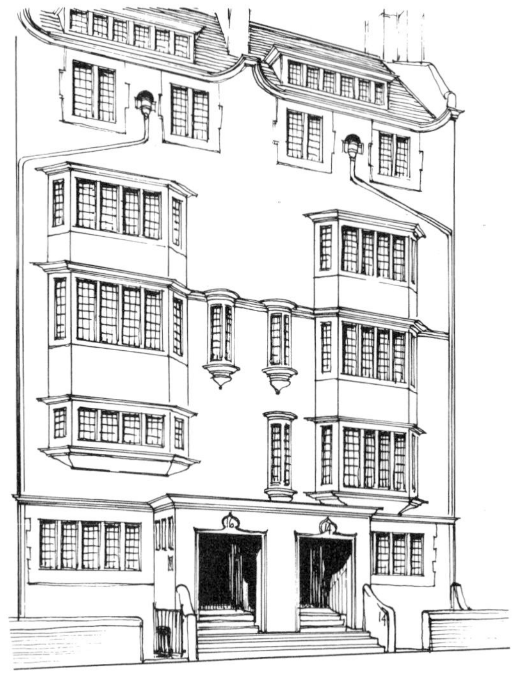

14–16 Hans Road, London, 1891. Architect: C. F. A. Voysey

VOYSEY, CHARLES FRANCIS ANNESLEY
White Lodge, Wantage, Oxfordshire, 1898–9. Architect: Mackay Hugh Baillie-Scott

WARE, ISAAC (d. 1766) For seven years from 1721 Ware was apprenticed to the architect *Thomas Ripley* (c. 1683—1758). After this he held various posts for over 30 years in connection with the Royal Works where he was particularly concerned with building work at Windsor Castle and Greenwich. He was primarily a Palladian architect and was closely associated with Lord Burlington (see BURLINGTON, LORD; PALLADIAN ARCHITECTURE). His best known work is *Wrotham Park*, Middlesex (1754), a typically Palladian house which survives almost unaltered. He also designed *Chesterfield House* in London (1749, demolished 1937), some London town houses and *Oxford Town Hall* (1751–2, demolished 1893).

In 1738 Ware published his translation of Palladio's *Four Books of Architecture* and dedicated the publication to Lord Burlington. The work is illustrated by Ware's own engravings and is still notable as an excellent translation of Palladio. In 1756 his comprehensive account of Georgian architecture was published; entitled *A Complete Body of Architecture*, it covered more than 700 pages.

WASTELL, JOHN (d. c. 1515) A notable master mason of the later Middle Ages who worked particularly at *King's College Chapel*, Cambridge where, from 1508, as King's Mason he was responsible for the fan vault (see VAULTING); and at *Canterbury Cathedral*, where he built the central tower (1490–7).

WATERHOUSE, ALFRED (1830–1905) A leading architect of the High Victorian period, designing large-scale civic, commercial and educational buildings in the Gothic style. He is noted for his innate and extensive skill in planning and controlling the design of very large and complex structures and creating interesting and dramatic masses and skylines. Waterhouse thought of architecture three-dimensionally. His work is fiercely individual and easily recognizable for its weight, dignity and power. Like many of his contemporaries, he liked to employ polychrome materials, particularly terracotta and coloured brick; some of this brickwork must have presented a strident appearance before weathering softened the hues.

Alfred Waterhouse was born in Liverpool. He was articled to the architect Richard Lane in Manchester, then travelled in Germany, Italy and France. He returned to *Manchester* where he began practice in 1856. Three years

The Prudential Assurance Building, London, 1878–9

Terracotta decoration of oriel window, Prudential Assurance Building

Terracotta capitals of main doorway, National History Museum

The Natural History Museum, London, 1873–9

Main doorway, Natural History Museum

Base detail on main doorway, Natural History Museum

Balliol College, Oxford. Façade to Broad Street, 1867–8

later he won the competition for building the *Assize Courts* in the city (bombed 1940), a design which was in a Venetian form of Gothic. His most important building in Manchester is the *Town Hall* (1869–77), standing impressively in a large square in the centre of the city. A characteristically Gothic Revival structure of considerable quality, it is a well-planned and well-handled, powerful design with a complex roofline of gables, chimney-stacks and a soaring clock tower in the centre of the main elevation (see CIVIC ARCHITECTURE).

Waterhouse moved his practice to London in 1865. In 1870 he was appointed as architect to the new *Natural History Museum* which was to be built on the site of the International Exhibition of 1862. This great museum, its impressive principal façade fronting Cromwell Road in South Kensington, is Waterhouse's most popular work. Much of the structure of the building is of brick but the façade is of two shades of terracotta, in buff and grey/blue, made by Gibbs and Canning of Tamworth. The wealth of finely detailed decoration, also of terracotta, was modelled by Dujardin of Farmer and Brindley to Waterhouse's own drawings. The main doorway, in Romanesque style, is particularly richly ornamented (see COLUMN). On the rest of the façade the sculptural enrichment depicts an astonishing variety of animals and plants; the display enchants each new generation of the public, children and adults alike. The interior construction is of iron with terracotta casing and plaster vaulting.

Among Waterhouse's large-scale buildings in less happy, red-brick Gothic construction with terracotta decoration are the surviving *Prudential Assurance Building* in *Holborn* in London (1878–9) and the *Metropole Hotel* on the Brighton sea-front (1888–9). Of similar materials but of more pleasing aspect was *St Paul's School*, Hammersmith (1881–5, now demolished, see GOTHIC REVIVAL). He also built *University College Hospital* in London (1897) and a number of churches and country houses. His most flamboyant and elaborate creation in the domestic field was his extensions at *Eaton Hall*, Cheshire (1867). Waterhouse was responsible for considerable rebuilding at Oxford and Cambridge, notably the street façade and hall at *Balliol College, Oxford* (1867–74) and, in *Cambridge*, work at *Jesus* and *Caius Colleges*.

WEATHERING

1. The wearing away of an exterior surface due to the action of the weather.
2. The inclination of exterior surfaces of sills, buttresses, parapets etc. in order to throw off rainwater (see OFFSET). A *weather moulding* is one which projects and has a weathered top surface; it is constructed to protect a window or other opening (see HOOD-MOULD).

WEBB, SIR ASTON (1849–1930) A highly successful architect of the years 1885–1914, Aston Webb designed and completed a considerable number of extensive secular schemes mostly in a varied and eclectic range of classical styles. His work was rarely original but he satisfied his eminent clients with suitable, well-proportioned and detailed compositions.

Some of Aston Webb's earlier commissions were in *Birmingham* where he designed (with *Ingress Bell*) the *Law Courts* (1886–91) and, from 1900, the *University* at *Edgbaston*: the quintessence of the 'red brick university' of the time.

In *London*, in *South Kensington*, in the early years of the new century, he was responsible for the *Royal College of Science* and the *Royal College of Mines*; and, between 1899 and 1909, he completed the *Victoria and Albert Museum*. This red-brick building with stone dressings and sculptured decoration possesses an imposing entrance fronting Cromwell Road and, above, rises a colonnaded and arched tower. Also in London, in these years, Aston Webb gave a new façade to *Buckingham Palace* (1913), laid out the architectural settings in front of the Palace for the *Victoria Memorial* and the *Mall* and built the *Admiralty Arch* at the head of the thoroughfare as a terminal feature into Trafalgar Square. Outside London he built *Christ's Hospi-*

The Victoria and Albert Museum, Cromwell Road, London, 1899–1909

WEBB, SIR ASTON
The Admiralty Arch, London, 1910

tal in *Horsham*, Sussex (1893–1904) and the *Royal Naval College, Dartmouth*, Devon (1899–1905).

Sir Aston Webb was President of the Royal Institute of British Architects 1902–4 and won their Gold Medal for Architecture in 1905. He was knighted in 1904 and became President of the Royal Academy in 1919.

WEBB, JOHN (1611–72) Little is known of Webb's life before he became pupil and assistant to Inigo Jones in 1628. For 24 years he worked with and for Jones. He revered his master (who was also his uncle by marriage) and kept in the background during those years of service so that it is not easy to distinguish his contribution from that of Jones. From him Webb received a thorough training in draughtsmanship and grounding in the understanding of Italian Renaissance architecture. He carried out many drawings for Jones's commissions, notably for designs for *Whitehall Palace*, repairs to *St Paul's Cathedral*, for *Somerset House* and, over several years, for *Wilton House*, Wiltshire (see JONES, INIGO). After the fire there in 1647 it seems likely that much of the work of

WEBB, JOHN
The King Charles II block, Royal Naval College, Greenwich, 1665–9. Architect: John Webb

restoring and rebuilding, particularly in the Double Cube Room, was Webb's contribution rather than that of his, by that time, elderly master.

After Inigo Jones's death in 1652, Webb carried out a number of his own commissions but much of this building has been altered or demolished. It included *Lamport Hall*, Northamptonshire (1655–7, since partially altered), *Belvoir Castle*, Leicestershire (1655–8, remodelled early nineteenth century) and *The Vyne*, Hampshire (1654) where he altered the interior and designed the portico.

Webb's most important surviving work is the *King Charles II's block* at the Royal Naval College, Greenwich. The *Greenwich Palace* of Tudor times had been allowed to fall into decay and Webb was commissioned to design new buildings. He planned an ambitious scheme which incorporated Inigo Jones's Queen's House (see JONES, INIGO) but only succeeded in completing this one building in 1669 before the enterprise was allowed to lapse. It was not until much later, after the accession of William and Mary, that it was decided to build at Greenwich a naval counterpart to Chelsea Hospital and, when the sovereigns gave the site of Greenwich Palace, Wren was put in charge of the project (see WREN, SIR CHRISTOPHER). Webb's King Charles block does illustrate, though, an understanding of the newer current Baroque concept in its use of the giant Corinthian Order and the rusticated façade. In this it presaged the great work of Greenwich Hospital yet to be created by Wren, Hawksmoor and Vanbrugh (see BAROQUE ARCHITECTURE; HAWKSMOOR, NICHOLAS; VANBRUGH, SIR JOHN).

WEBB, PHILIP (1831–1915) With Shaw and Voysey, Webb was influential in the revival of quality English domestic architecture in the last 30 years of the nineteenth century (see SHAW, NORMAN; VOYSEY, CHARLES FRANCIS ANNESLEY). Webb was more serious, more intellectual in his architectural approach than Shaw but he also introduced elements of past styles—Gothic, neoclassical, Queen Anne—and, like both Shaw and Voysey, returned time and time again to the English vernacular. His work was stripped of all needless decoration and was sometimes even astringent. He designed all the details of a house down to door furniture, light fittings and fire-irons: he was a perfectionist and could be uncompromising in his manner to clients who would not accept his high aesthetic standards.

Philip Webb was born in Oxford, the son of a doctor. After early architectural training he entered Street's office in Oxford (see STREET, GEORGE EDMUND) where he met Morris (see MORRIS, WILLIAM). In 1856 he set up practice in London and an early commission was to design a house for Morris on the latter's marriage. This was the *Red House* at *Bexelyheath* in Kent (1859–60). Neither large nor pretentious, this house represents a milestone in English domestic architecture of the nineteenth century. It is built of plain red brick with no polychromy. The steeply

WEBB, PHILIP
Standen, East Grinstead, West Sussex, 1891–4

pitched roofs are red-tiled. The house plan is irregular and informal, reflecting the disposition of the rooms within. Here is a revival of the English vernacular, blending characteristics from earlier ages—Georgian sash windows, seventeenth-century tall chimney-stacks and brick bonding.

Webb and Morris remained life-long friends and associates. Over many years Webb designed furniture, metalwork and glass for Morris and Co. He built a number of houses in town and country but did not develop a large practice. In *London* he built *1 Palace Green* (1868) and *19 Lincoln's Inn Fields* (1868–9). His earlier country houses included *Benfleet Hall* at *Cobham*, Surrey (1861) and *Arisaig*, Inverness-shire (begun 1863). In the 1870s came *Joldwyns* in Surrey (1873), *Rounton Grange* (1872–6) and *Smeaton Manor* (1878) in Yorkshire and, in 1880, *Clouds* at *East Knoyle*, Wiltshire.

Webb's last complete house was *Standen, East Grinstead* in West Sussex (1891–4) and the only one of his major houses to survive intact, having been owned and occupied by the same family since it was built, remaining virtually unaltered until, in 1972, it was bequeathed by the daughter of the original owner to the National Trust. Standen also retains much of its contents, the original fireplaces and fittings as well as a quantity of Morris and Co. wallpapers, carpet and furniture.

WILKINS, WILLIAM (1778–1839) Son of an architect, Wilkins was born and grew up in Norwich and then entered Caius College, Cambridge in 1796. After graduating in 1800, he travelled for four years in Italy, Asia Minor and Greece. In 1807, after his return to England, he published his *Antiquities of Magna Graecia* which contained drawings of Greek temples at Paestum in southern Italy and those in Sicily at Segesta, Agrigento and Syracuse.

Wilkins began to practise architecture in Cambridge, settling down to a career as an enthusiastic Greek Revivalist. He was by this time a fellow of Caius College and, being a classical scholar and knowledgeable about Greek architecture, was given encouragement from those, such as Thomas Hope, who wished to support the use of the Grecian style in current architecture. In *Cambridge* he won the competition to design buildings for the new *Downing College*; a large site was made available and work began in 1807. He used the Ionic Order derived from the Erechtheion on the Athenian Acropolis and had built the hall by 1821. He continued in Grecian vein at *Haileybury College*, Hertfordshire (1806–9) and at *Grange Park*, Hampshire (1809). His serious and archaeologically correct Greek styling was not unsuited to civic and collegiate work but in country house building, as at Grange Park, its monumentality appeared unsympathetic and prospective clients were not attracted to it.

Wilkins's reputation as a leading architect of the Greek Revival brought him important commissions and academic posts. He was given opportunities to develop his style in three large-scale projects. He built *St George's Hospital* at Hyde Park Corner in London (1828–9), which was later considerably enlarged. Much more impressive was his best classical work, *University College* in London (1827–8). He built the main block with its monumental Corinthian portico raised on a great podium with approach steps; the dome rose above and to the rear. The side wings were added later. The London University (as it was then) was a new collegiate concept not built on the traditional Oxford and Cambridge court system, and it was erected in the centre of a capital city.

Wilkins's most important commission was the *National Gallery* (1834–8), where he was given a tremendous opportunity to show his architectural expertise. The gallery stands on one of the finest sites in London, its long frontage overlooking Trafalgar Square and the length of Whitehall. Unfortunately he showed what had been perceptible to a lesser degree at University College: that, although his detail and handling of parts of the building were good, he seemed unable to relate these to a unified concept. The long façade, surmounted by a trivial dome, is split up into numerous fussy sections and pavilions giving a result which is an anti-climax to the site; it lacks coherence and any dramatic quality.

Wilkins's other, domestic and collegiate, work is more successful. Here he has capitulated to the current preference for Tudor and late Gothic design. He built country houses at *Dalmeny*, Linlithgowshire (1814–17) and *Tregothnan* in Cornwall (1816–18). He carried out a quantity of collegiate work at *Cambridge*, notably the *New Court* at *Trinity College* (1821–3), the hall, screen and entrance gateway at *King's College* (1824–8) where, earlier in 1819, he had designed the graceful bridge over the Cam, and at *Corpus Christi College*, where he built the *New Court*, laid out in a single unified scheme comprising library, hall and chapel (1823–7).

WILLIAM DE RAMSAY (d. 1349) Most notable of a family of masons who contributed in no small way to the development of the decorative and structural architecture of the first half of the fourteenth century (see GOTHIC ARCHITECTURE). William was a King's Mason, advising on the condition of the *Tower of London* and on the building of the presbytery of *Lichfield Cathedral*. He worked at the *Palace of Westminster*, including *St Stephen's Chapel* and most importantly at *St Paul's Cathedral* in the chapter house and cloister.

WILLIAM OF SENS (d. *c.* 1179 or 1180) French master mason, he was so-called because of his association with Sens Cathedral in France; he was invited to come to *Canterbury Cathedral* to re-build the chancel there after its destruction by fire in 1174. William worked at Canterbury until his fall from the scaffolding in 1178, incorporating in his design some features of the early Gothic style

The London University (now University College), Gower Street, London, 1827–8

King's College, Cambridge. Stone bridge over the River Cam (1819–20)

New Court, Corpus Christi College, Cambridge, 1823–7

The National Gallery, Trafalgar Square, London, 1834–8

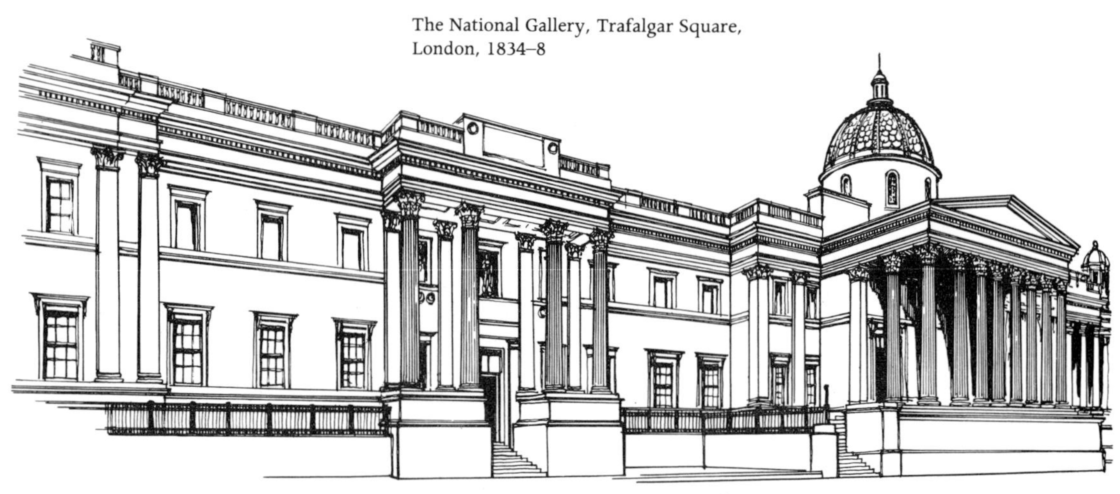

then current in the Île de France (see GOTHIC ARCHITECTURE). William was badly injured in this fall and soon afterwards returned to France. His work was continued by a mason also called William and known as the 'Englishman' to differentiate.

WILLIAM OF WYNFORD (d. *c.* 1405) Influential master mason of the later fourteenth century and a protégé of Bishop William of Wykeham for whom he worked at *Windsor Castle*; later, he was put in charge of the building of the new nave at *Winchester Cathedral*, also *Winchester College*, and the construction at *New College, Oxford*. William of Wynford is particularly noted for his contribution as master mason at *Wells Cathedral* where he completed the west front with Perpendicular Gothic towers, blending the two styles successfully and with sympathy.

WILLIAMS, SIR OWEN (1890–1969) Welsh engineer and architect, noted for his espousal of new techniques in large-scale construction particularly in that of reinforced concrete. Before the Second World War he was concerned in the design and building of the *Empire Stadium* at *Wembley* and the *Health Centre* at *Peckham*.

His outstanding contribution at this time was his pharmaceutical factory for *Boots Pure Drug Company* at Beeston, near Nottingham. On a new site here (1930–2), he built the two sections of the factory, the 'wets' for liquids, creams and pastes and the 'drys' for powders, tablets and lozenges (see MODERN ARCHITECTURE). In these buildings Williams used, on a large scale, the 'mushroom' form of construction, where the reinforced concrete supporting piers spread outwards like a mushroom cap at the top to support a slab floor above. He also utilized glass curtain-walling on a large scale (see IRON AND GLASS).

After 1945 Sir Owen was responsible for the BOAC headquarters and workshops buildings at Heathrow Airport (1954–5). He worked for many years advising on motorway construction in Britain, particularly bridge building as in the Midland Link Motorways.

WINDOW An opening in a wall of a building to admit light and air and to give a view of the surroundings.

Windows in early medieval buildings were narrow and, generally, small. This was partly for defensive reasons, partly because with the current understanding of building techniques it was deemed inadvisable to weaken the wall with larger openings, and partly because of the very

WILLIAMS, SIR OWEN
Pharmaceutical production: 'Wets' Factory, Boots Pure Drug Co., Beeston, Nottinghamshire, 1932

Asturian church window: S. Miguel de Liño, Spain, ninth century

Wheel window: Assisi Cathedral, Italy, twelfth century

Romanesque window: Salamanca Old Cathedral, Spain, 1120–78

Rose window: Lincoln Cathedral, *c.* 1325

Romanesque window: Angoulême Cathedral, France, 1100–28

Romanesque window: Trani Cathedral, Italy, twelfth century

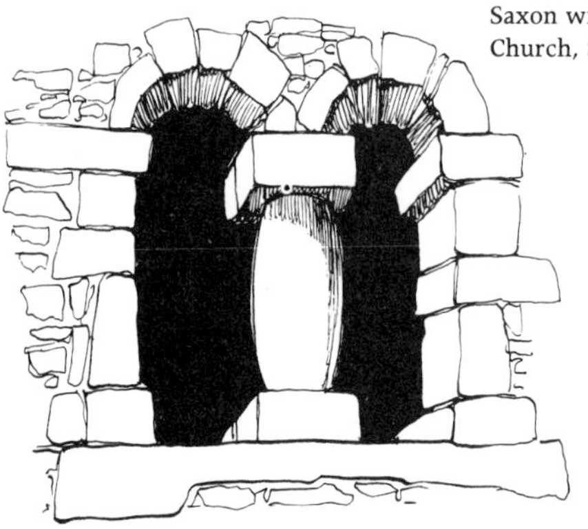

Saxon window opening: Worth Church, Sussex, tenth century

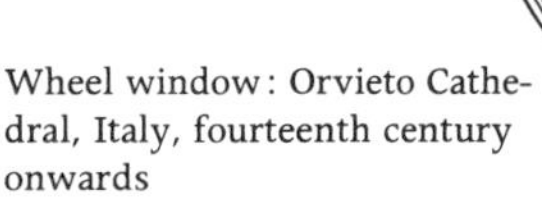

Wheel window: Orvieto Cathedral, Italy, fourteenth century onwards

limited supplies of glass available. Such windows were fitted with wooden shutters which could be barred across at night. In the day-time the stark choice was between closing the shutters to keep out the cold air, but also exclude the light, or leaving them open for illumination and so suffer the draughts. To ease the problem varied substitute materials were used instead of glass though these were less transparent (see GLASS).

Saxon window openings were round- or triangular-headed, *Romanesque* ones round-headed (see ROMANESQUE ARCHITECTURE; SAXON ARCHITECTURE). The narrow lancet window, set singly or in groups, was characteristic of early Gothic design. As time passed, the need for defence declined and building experience grew; windows then became larger and wider, the heads decorated by tracery and enclosed by arches of more obtuse or four-centred form (see ARCH; GOTHIC ARCHITECTURE; TRACERY). By the fifteenth century some windows were square-headed. *Bay* and *oriel* designs were characteristic of larger buildings.

As window design developed after the twelfth century the opening was divided by stone or wood partitions. The vertical ones are *mullions*, the horizontal ones *transoms*. Each part of the window so divided is known as a *light*.

During the sixteenth century, in larger buildings, the window area increased markedly in proportion to the wall. The glass was in small panes, often diamond-shaped, the grooved lead bars into which it was fitted (the *cames*) being of a lattice design. The smallness of the panes was due to the pliability of the lead which was unsuited, with larger panes, to withstand the force of a strong wind.

During the earlier Middle Ages few windows were made to open. The leaded lights were affixed by wire to iron bars set in the stone or wood frame. Gradually it became possible to open part of the window in casement fashion. By the later sixteenth century these casement windows had increased in size and a larger proportion of the whole window could be opened.

The seventeenth-century window in classical style (see RENAISSANCE ARCHITECTURE) was larger, square- or round-headed and had rectangular panes. By the end of the century the sliding *sash window* had largely replaced the casement design and, as the eighteenth century advanced, window openings and panes became larger and taller, the window opening extending almost the full height of the room, while glazing bars became slenderer. *Bow-fronted* windows were characteristic of the Regency period (see REGENCY ARCHITECTURE). Advances in glass-making in the second half of the nineteenth century led to the abandonment in many cases of the glazing bars of a sash window, leaving just two large panes, one upper and one lower.

The casement window was reintroduced in the early twentieth century and sash and casement have been available since. Metal-framed windows were introduced: first steel (which required painting), then in the 1930s aluminium. Since 1945 the 'picture window' and double-glazed window units have been increasingly adopted.

Glossary of terms

Bay window: one projecting outwards, set on the ground and extending upwards through one or more storeys. It may be square or polygonal in shape.

Bow window: similar to a bay window but curved. Fashionable in Regency architecture.

Bull's eye window: also known as *oeil-de-boeuf*, a circular

Cross window: The Ashmolean Museum, Oxford, 1840–5

Venetian window incorporating French window: Peper Harow, Surrey, 1765–75

Diocletian window, *c.* 1730

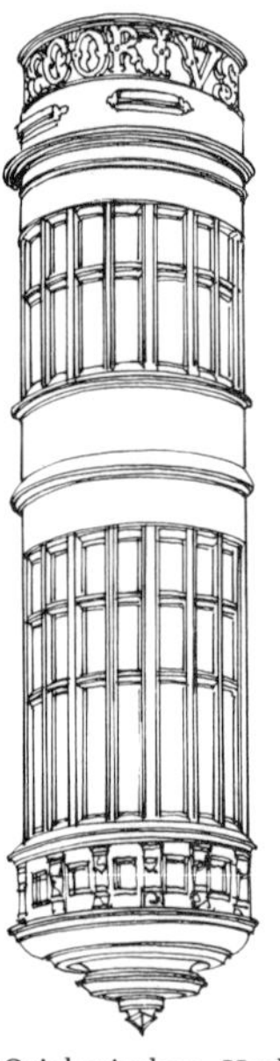

Oriel window, Harlaxton Manor, Lincolnshire, 1831–55

Stone bay window: Horham Hall, Essex, 1502–20

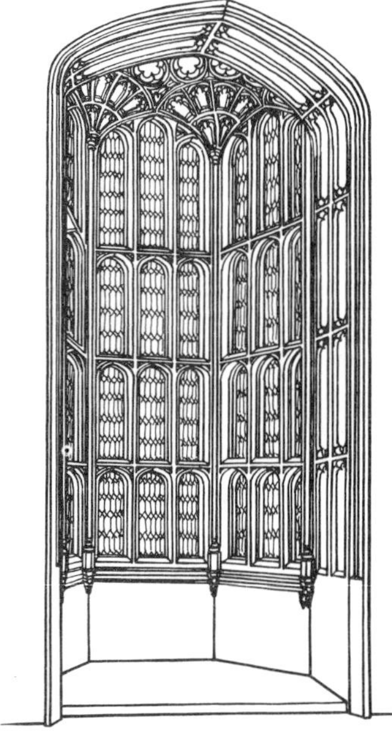

Stone oriel window; 1530–40

Bay window: Wiston Park, Sussex, 1558–78

Oriel window: St Osyth's Priory, Essex, 1527

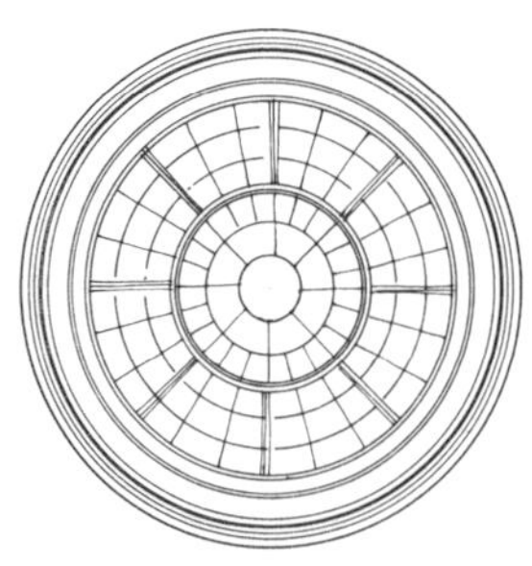

Bull's eye window: Church of St Lawrence Jewry, London, 1670–80

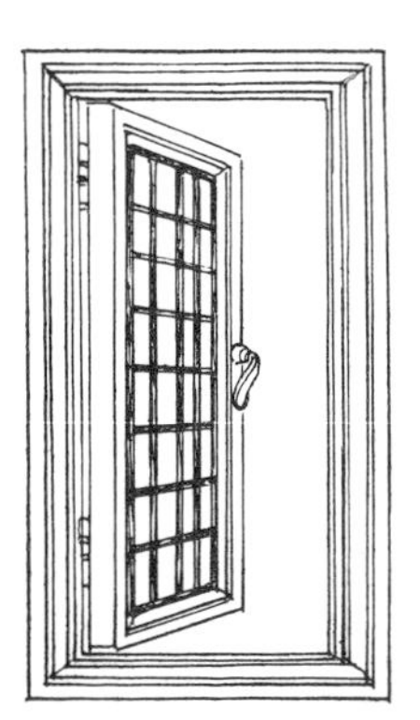

Casement window

Dormer window: Hôtel de Sens, Paris, 1475–1507

or oval window with glazing bars which radiate from a central 'eye'.

Came: a grooved bar of lead which holds small panes of window glass (see GLASS).

Casement window: a metal, stone or wooden window frame hinged along one vertical side to enable it to be opened outwards or inwards.

Compass window: a bay window.

Cross window: one with only one mullion and one transom which form a cross.

Diocletian window: a design used especially in Palladian architecture, revived from the Roman Palace of Diocletian in Split (Yugoslavia). It is of semicircular form and is divided by two mullions, the central section being larger than the side ones (see PALLADIAN ARCHITECTURE).

Dormer window: one with a vertical face set upon the inclined plane of a gable roof. The dormer will possess its own individual roofing.

Sash window: Normanby Hall, Humberside, *c.* 1820

Lancet windows: Beverley Minster, 1220–60

French window: a ground floor tall window extending down to floor level and opening outwards as a pair of doors.

Glazing bars: the wooden bars which held the larger glass panes of the windows from the seventeenth century onwards and replaced the medieval lead cames.

Laced windows: a particularly eighteenth-century style in which window openings were set vertically above one another in line and were bordered by strips of brick.

Lancet window: a tall, one-light, narrow window with a sharply pointed arch (see ARCH), characteristic of thirteenth-century Gothic architecture (see GOTHIC ARCHITECTURE). Lancets might be designed singly or in groups, usually three, five or seven.

Lattice window: where the small panes are diamond-shaped and set in lead cames arranged in a lattice fashion.

Leaded lights: where the lead cames divide the lights of a window.

Lights: the openings between the mullions and transoms of a window.

Mullion: a vertical bar of masonry, wood or iron dividing the lights of a window.

Oculus: a round window.

Oeil-de-boeuf: see *Bull's eye window*.

Oriel window: a projecting window, curved or polysided,

Queen Square, Bath, 1729–36. Architect: John Wood the Elder

The Circus, Bath, begun 1754.
Architects: John Wood father and son

Detail section of the Royal Crescent

The Royal Crescent, Bath, 1767–75.
Architect: John Wood the Younger

which, unlike a bay window, is situated on an upper floor and does not reach the ground but is cantilevered out or supported on a corbel or bracket.

Rose window: a circular window with traceried design (see GOTHIC ARCHITECTURE; TRACERY).

Saddle bar: a supporting iron bar fixed across a mullioned window to which the cames are fastened.

Sash window: the term originally applied to a window frame, generally of wood, which enclosed one or more panes of glass: the word 'sash' being a corruption of 'chassis'. A sash window then came to mean a sliding window, a style which had been in use from the fifteenth century and which had to be wedged open.

The sash window in the present sense of the term is a double-hung sash which comprises a wooden framework in two parts each holding the window glazing; these frames slide up and down in vertical grooves. The sashes (the frames) are controlled by cords and are counter-balanced by weights. This type of window made its appearance in England about 1675–80 and gradually replaced the casement design.

Transom: a horizontal bar dividing the lights of a window.

Venetian window: see VENETIAN DOOR, WINDOW.

Wheel window: a circular window with a design of spokes radiating from a central hub as in a wheel.

WOOD, JOHN (1704–54) The architect who, with his son, also *John Wood* (1728–81) initiated the creation and development of Georgian Bath (see TERRACE ARCHITECTURE).

John Wood the Elder was born in Bath, son of a local builder. By 1727, when he finally settled in the city to practise, he had already gained a wide experience, for so young a man, in building, in the current style of architecture and in the concept of designing similar town houses in a long palatial elevation. He had worked in Yorkshire, at *Bramham Park* and for some time in *London* where he was a leading builder in the development of the Cavendish Estate. He participated, among other schemes, in design and construction in Oxford Street and Cavendish Square.

As early as 1725 John Wood was working out ambitious ideas to transform his home town, basing these upon its former Roman glory. He envisaged 'a grand Place of Assembly, to be called the Royal Forum of Bath', and also a Roman sports arena—the Grand Circus—accompanied by an 'Imperial Gymnasium'. Only a fraction of his grandiose schemes were actually built for he had difficulty in attracting sufficient financial support, but by 1736 he had completed *Queen Square* in stone in a Palladian palace style, with a central pedimented feature, the giant Corinthian Order repeated in pilasters and columns along the façade and standing upon a rusticated basement. This was an echo of the work which he had seen and been involved in, in London.

Wood then turned to his more original ideas for the Forum and the Circus. Only North and South Parade were built of the Forum scheme but the *Circus* was achieved. The concept was different from Wood's original one but it was certainly based upon a Roman amphitheatre and the design represents a landmark in English urban architecture. Here is a circle of 33 houses divided into three parts by incoming streets. The design is repeated in identical manner all round the circle and comprises three stages using coupled columns in different orders—Doric on the ground floor and, above, Ionic then Corinthian: the Circus is a 'Colosseum' with the orders on the interior rather than the exterior of the structure. John Wood died very soon after the commencement of building and his son completed the work.

As a young man *John Wood the Younger* had assisted his father for a number of years working, for example, in *Liverpool* on the *Exchange* (1749–54, later the Town Hall). After his father's death he succeeded him as leading architect of Bath. In this capacity his finest achievement, which continued and expanded his father's ideas, was the *Royal Crescent* (1765–75): one of the grandest and largest of all such curving architectural sweeps (see TERRACE ARCHITECTURE). He then built the *New Assembly Rooms* (1769–71, badly damaged in the interior in 1942) and the *Hot Baths* (1773–7), both in Palladian style. Among his other buildings is *Hardenhuish Church*, Wiltshire (1779).

WREN, SIR CHRISTOPHER (1632–1723) Best known of all English architects, Wren was born at East Knoyle, Wiltshire, son of the Rev. Christopher Wren then rector of Knoyle and later Dean of Windsor. The young Christopher was brought up in a High Church tradition (his uncle was successively Bishop of Hereford, Norwich and Ely). He was educated at Westminster School which he left in 1646. He then showed early intellectual ability at the age of 15 by translating into Latin the part of William Oughtred's *Clavis Mathematica* dealing with geometrical dialling. Three years after leaving Westminster School Wren went up to Wadham College, Oxford where he graduated in 1651 and obtained his Master's degree in 1653.

It was soon apparent that the young man was outstandingly brilliant. 'That miracle of a youth', as the diarist John Evelyn described him in 1654, was then chiefly interested in science. It was here that he found full scope for his inventive mind, developing theories and experiments while still at college on some 50 problems in the fields of astronomy, physics and engineering. He carried out anatomical experimental work with Dr Charles Scarburgh, the anatomist and mathematician and a disciple of Harvey (discoverer of the circulation of the blood). Wren worked on the subjects of submarine navigation, instruments for recording weather and telescope designs, and he produced a hard paving material. His chief interest was astronomy but he also concerned himself with physics and meteorology. Isaac Newton considered the young Wren to be an outstanding student.

At the age of 25 Wren was appointed to the Chair of Astronomy at Gresham College, London and two years later returned to Oxford as Savilian Professor of Astronomy. In 1660, in conjunction with Dr Wilkins (Warden of Wadham College), Robert Boyle (the scientist) and others Wren became one of the founder members of the Society of Experimental Philosophy which, two years later, was granted its royal charter by Charles II to become the Royal Society and to include in its membership such famous names as Isaac Newton, Robert Hooke and the diarist John Evelyn.

This background was an unusual one, even in the seventeenth century, as training for an architect. Wren's formative years up to the age of 30 had been spent in practical scientific study; but architecture was not yet a profession and Wren was not the only architect of this time to have taken up the work in maturity. His scientific training had a profound effect upon his approach to architecture and all his life he retained the faculty of envisaging an extensive scheme as a whole before work was begun. He brought his mathematical ability and technical knowledge to an understanding of the structural problems of roofing large spans, providing sound support and buttressing and working out difficult site planning.

It is not known precisely when Wren became interested in architecture. In 1661 Charles II invited him to supervise the fortification of Tangier but this he declined on grounds of ill-health. His first essay into architecture was in 1663 to build a traditional classical chapel for *Pembroke College, Cambridge* at the request of his uncle, Bishop of Ely; a competent, if not notable, building. His second attempt was the *Sheldonian Theatre, Oxford* (1664–9) where he based his design upon the Roman Theatre of Marcellus which he had studied in Serlio's book of architecture (see SERLIO, SEBASTIANO). Wren's reputation as an architect was greatly enhanced by his solution to the roofing problem. The Roman original had been open to the sky and Wren wished to cover the English counterpart without using supporting columns which would obscure the view. He solved this, typically, with the aid of his colleague, the Professor of Geometry, Dr Wallis, by means of a timber-trussed roof carrying the ceiling.

In 1663 a commission had been appointed to undertake the restoration of *St Paul's Cathedral* which was, once again, in a deplorable state of disrepair (see JONES, INIGO). The commission approached Sir John Denham (the Surveyor-General), John Webb, Roger Pratt and Wren regarding reconstruction plans. This approach was a tribute to Wren's reputation as a draughtsman and model-maker for, at that time, his architectural experience was negligible.

In 1665 Wren set out on his one trip abroad. Unlike Inigo Jones (see JONES, INIGO) his first-hand knowledge of European architecture was limited and, although he studied Italian and French designs, his aim was always to produce classical buildings suited especially to his own country. There is an essential Englishness in Wren's work. His great fertility of imagination enabled him to design endless variations upon the classical theme to meet this need. He went to France as a holiday traveller and spent some months visiting châteaux and staying in *Paris*. In the city he met *Bernini* who was there to present his designs for the Louvre. He also had the opportunity to meet *Le Brun, Le Vau* and *Poussin*. Wren also went to *Versailles* to see the palace and was most impressed with Le Vau's *Collège des Quatre Nations* in Paris. He did not reach Italy but brought back a quantity of books and engravings. He had extended his architectural horizons and enriched his appreciation.

On his return to England the problem of *St Paul's Cathedral* had reached a vital stage. Pratt had advocated leaving the structure alone until it became necessary to demolish and rebuild completely. Wren put forward a reconstruction plan which was extensive. This included the replacement of the tower by a classical dome or steeple and re-casing the nave in classical form to blend with Inigo Jones's west front. In August 1666 his plan was accepted. Six days later the Great Fire settled the problem permanently.

The destruction of so much of the City of London gave Wren his great opportunity. He was fortunate that such great commissions became available to him just at the moment when he was beginning to practise. His work dominated the architecture of Britain during the 50 years from the 1660s. He was the vital force in most of the important architectural schemes of the period, directing, influencing, controlling both design and execution of such projects as the rebuilding of the city churches, St Paul's, Hampton Court Palace, Greenwich and Chelsea Hospitals and a quantity of work at the universities. Stemming from this pre-eminence there has been a tendency to attribute to him all buildings in a style similar to his own without any firm evidence; but due to the patient work of scholars, in particular those of the Wren Society, many such generalizations have now been refuted.

Within a few days of the fire in London being brought under control, plans were being submitted for the rebuilding. Among those plans was Wren's scheme for a new classical city layout with a drastic realignment of thoroughfares. The plan represented an ideal but one which was so different from the existing medieval arrangement of the city that, even without the opposition of city interests, it would have been impractical to impose it in one operation on the commercial capital of the country (see TOWN PLANNING). By October the King had appointed Wren, *Pratt* and *May* (see PRATT, SIR ROGER; MAY, HUGH) as architectural commissioners, together with three city delegates—*Robert Hooke, Peter Mills* and *Edward Jerman*—to survey the area and plan the rebuild-

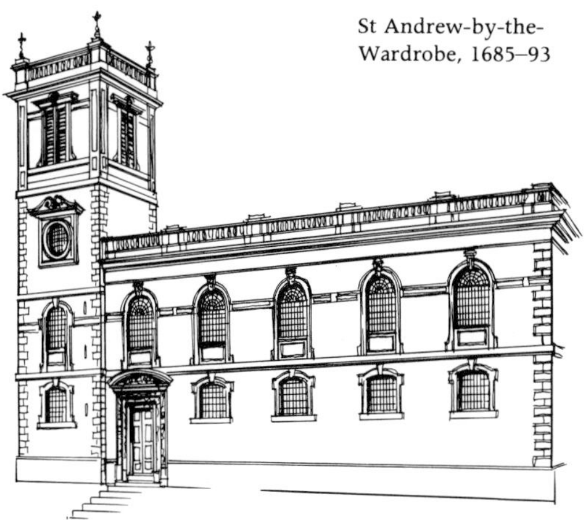

St Andrew-by-the-Wardrobe, 1685–93

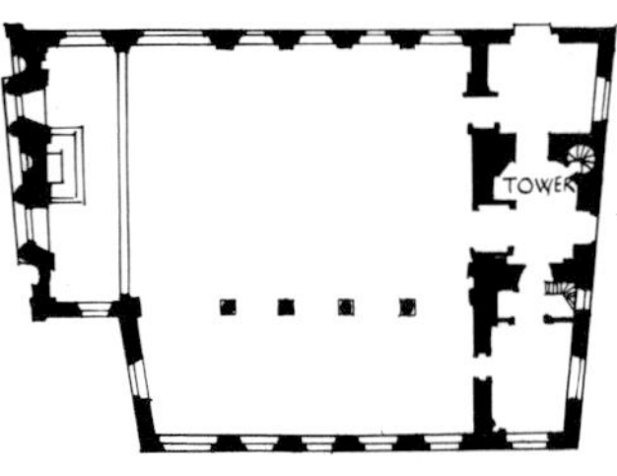

Ground plan of St Lawrence Jewry, 1671–7

Ground plan of St Mary-le-Bow, 1670–3

St Bride, Fleet Street, 1671–8. Interior restored after war-time destruction

St Bride, Fleet Street, 1671–1703

St Stephen Walbrook, 1672–9

St Benet, Paul's Wharf, 1677–83

St Edmund the King, Lombard Street, 1670–1708

St Stephen Walbrook, 1672–9

Steeple of St Mary-le-Bow, completed 1680

Steeple of Christ Church, Newgate Street, complete

ing. The city was to rise again on much the same street plan as before but the buildings should be of more permanent materials and where possible flanking wider streets. New structural standards were set up and brick replaced much of the previous timber buildings.

In 1670 a tax was ordained by Parliament to be levied on sea coal arriving at the Port of London. The income derived from this tax was designed to pay for the rebuilding of the *city churches* and St Paul's Cathedral. In the years 1675–1705 the money raised paid for the fabric of the churches while the parishes assumed the responsibility for the interior decoration and fittings.

Unlike other buildings in the reconstruction of London, Wren's authorship of these 51 churches within the city limits has not been disputed. The standard of design varies. This is due partly to site limitations, the availability of parish funds for interior work and the fact that Wren was more closely associated in detailed drawings and supervision of some churches than others. The churches were built over most of the years of Wren's long career. They illustrate, perhaps more clearly than any other examples of his work, his fertility of imagination and his ability to solve the most intractable problems of site, limitation on space and variation in style. None of the churches is quite like any other. They are nearly all classical in conception though a few were designed in Gothic to harmonize with surviving remains. The sites are most varied, few are level or possess parallel sides of equal length. *St Benet Fink* (demolished 1842), for instance, was decagonal in plan. Few churches possessed a right-angled corner. At *St Benet's, Paul's Wharf* the site was so steeply inclined that even in this small area there was a variation of 10ft in height.

Wren's qualities of versatility and inventiveness are nowhere shown more clearly than in his designs for the church steeples. He had no English classical precedent to work upon (though he did draw upon Dutch examples) and many of them are Gothic steeples in classical dress. Of particular beauty and dramatic impact are the delicate Baroque *St Mary-le-Bow*, the 'wedding cake' of *St Bride* and the *Christ Church* diminuendo on temple forms. Of equal interest and variety are the tall bell towers surmounted by lanterns ranging from the lofty *St Magnus the Martyr* and the delicate *St Martin Ludgate* to *St Margaret Lothbury* and *St Edmund the King*. Many churches have simple square towers only, such as *St Clement, Eastcheap*.

Wren varied his building materials to give colour and interest to the churches. He used Portland stone and brick, together and separately, and most churches had lead belfries and gilded vanes and crosses. In general, he designed the churches on the Roman basilican form drawing on Serlio and many other Italian sources (see CHURCH DESIGN AND STRUCTURE). The first of the city churches to be restored and re-opened was *St Mary-at-Hill* in 1676; the last was *St Michael Cornhill* in 1722. Wren was then 89 years old.

Wren made more than one design for a new classical cathedral to replace the medieval *St Paul's Cathedral* which, it was finally admitted in 1668, was irreparable. His favourite was the Great Model design of 1673, a centrally planned church surmounted by a large dome 120ft in diameter. It was rejected by the commissioners who, despite its impressive grandeur, thought it too much a break with English cathedral-building tradition. Architecturally they wanted a spire; ecclesiastically they wanted a Protestant cathedral, not one which savoured so much of Rome.

Wren's last plan of 1675 was a compromise, a Gothic cathedral in classical dress. The ground plan was cruciform with a long nave but over the crossing he had placed a dome which he then broke with a tall drum and continued with a smaller dome topped by a six-stage steeple. Charles II, who had also preferred the Great Model design, then issued the royal warrant authorizing the new design but the warrant permitted 'variations, rather ornamental than essential'. The King had shrewdly foreseen that the architect would not be slow to take advantage of this loophole. Over the years of building Wren shortened the nave, altered the transepts, substituted a quite different dome and quietly abolished the steeple. In final form the whole cathedral acquired some Baroque characteristics particularly in the later work of the west front (see BAROQUE ARCHITECTURE). In his dome construction Wren followed the double dome principle, an inner shallow form suitable for interior appearance and an outer, taller, more impressive one giving a fine silhouette. The inner dome is of brick, and surmounting this is a brick cone which supports the lantern and cross. The outer dome is of lead-sheathed timber (see DOME).

In 1669 Wren was appointed to the coveted post of Surveyor-General on the death of Sir John Denham. Both May and Webb (see MAY, HUGH; WEBB, JOHN) ought to have expected to be considered for this position in advance of the younger and architecturally inexperienced Wren but with the favour of Charles II the appointment was made. Soon the heavier administrative burden made it impossible for Wren to continue his scientific work. He chose to continue his architectural career and resigned his professorship at Oxford in 1673; in the same year he was knighted. He continued, however, actively to support the Royal Society and became its President, 1681–3. Wren remained Surveyor-General for nearly 50 years. In addition to the administrative and architectural work of the position he became Comptroller at Windsor in 1684, Surveyor at Greenwich Hospital in 1696 and at Westminster Abbey in 1699, and served as a Member of Parliament on two occasions, 1685–7 and 1701–2.

Wren was responsible in the 1670s and 1680s for a quantity of university work. At *Oxford* he completed *Tom Tower* at *Christ Church*, the lower stages of which late Gothic work had been built in 1529. At *Cambridge* he continued his early work at *Emmanuel College*, building

Aerial view of cathedral from south-west

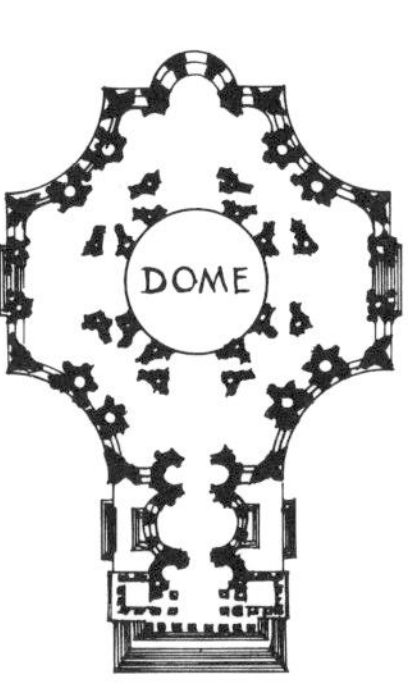

Plan, Great Model Design

The Great Model Design, 1673

The Warrant Design, 1675

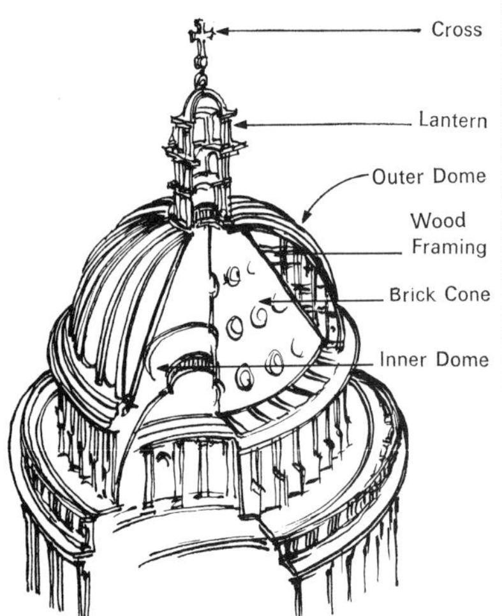

Simplified sketch of construction of dome

Nave and crossing

WREN, SIR CHRISTOPHER
The Library, Trinity College, Cambridge, 1676–84

Pembroke College Chapel, Cambridge, 1663–5

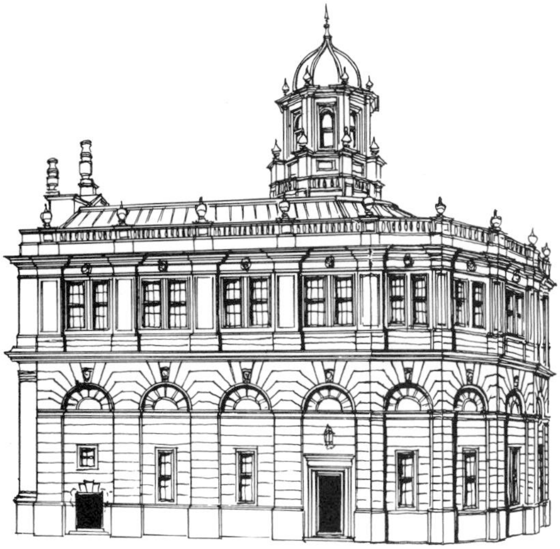

The Sheldonian Theatre, Oxford, 1664–9

Hampton Court Palace, Middlesex, east front, 1689–94

The Royal Hospital, Chelsea, river front, 1682–92

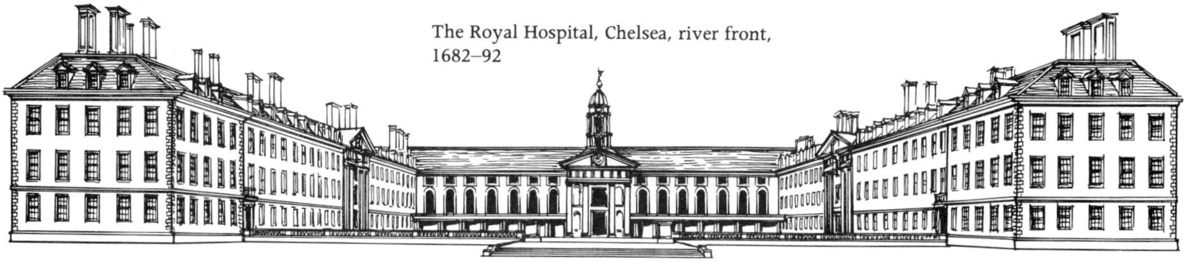

the *Chapel*, 1668–73. Like the Pembroke Chapel, this still shows his architectural immaturity, the proportions of the parts being less well balanced than in his later work. Quite different is his *Library* at *Trinity College* (1676–84); here is a masterpiece of simple perfection using superimposed orders; the lower one, Doric, is arcaded and above it the Ionic stage is fenestrated. Wren's library sealed off the fourth side of the existing Nevile's Court.

The scheme to build the *Royal Hospital, Chelsea* (1682–92) was inspired by *Les Invalides* in Paris which had been founded in 1670. The enterprise was paid for partly by the Privy Purse and partly by the Army. The site, chosen by Wren, had no space restrictions and stretched uninterruptedly to the River Thames. The layout forms three sides of a quadrangle open to the river. In the centre block are the hall and chapel fronted by a Doric portico and surmounted by a lantern. The simple, almost austere, wings in red brick and stone have pilastered pedimented pavilions and are three-storeyed with dormers above. The hospital design set a building pattern for many years.

During the 1680s Wren built a number of churches apart from those in the city of London. Several of these have been demolished or rebuilt but two in particular survive, though partly altered and later damaged during the Second World War. *St Clement Danes* in the *Strand* in London was built 1680–2, its tower completed by Gibbs in 1720 (see GIBBS, JAMES). *St James's, Piccadilly* (1676–4) has now been restored after war-time damage.

The years of the reign of William and Mary (1689–1702) were those of Wren's mature style and a particularly active time in the building of royal works and palaces. Though a quantity of his designs were not realized, a great deal was built and survives. He was asked to enlarge Nottingham House as an alternative royal residence to Whitehall Palace. The result was *Kensington Palace* (1689–96) part of which was altered in the eighteenth century. Of his work at *Winchester Palace*, *Whitehall Palace* and *Westminster Palace* nothing survives. At *Hampton Court Palace* two magnificent wings, the south and east, were built (1689–94). These palace buildings in rose-red brick with contrasting stone dressings are a solid indication of what one of his finest designs would have looked like if it had been completed.

It is at Greenwich that Wren's mature, intensely personal style of Baroque is displayed at its best. The Greenwich layout also evidences Wren's qualities as an overall planner and designer. On the accession of William and Mary it was decided to have at Greenwich a naval counterpart to Chelsea Hospital. In designing the layout for this impressive seamen's hospital Wren had to incorporate both Inigo Jones's Queen's House and Webb's King Charles II's block (see JONES, INIGO; WEBB, JOHN). This he did, designing a block balancing Webb's, laying out the design for the whole hospital and being responsible for the twin domes of hall and chapel. Hawksmoor assisted him until 1702 (see HAWKSMOOR, NICHOLAS) when Vanbrugh took over as principal architect (see VANBRUGH, SIR JOHN). The painted hall, one of Wren's finest achievements, was completed in 1704, the chapel later, in 1716 (see frontispiece). There is a grandeur and spaciousness about Greenwich (later the Royal Naval College) and a homogeneity despite the long period of building under several talented but very different architects. This last quality is in no small part due to the great talent of Wren for handling the grand scheme and the respect paid to him by the other architects who carried on his work there.

Wren dominated the architectural scene until the death of Queen Anne in 1714. He had created a style which moved over the years from a Renaissance to Mannerist to Baroque form but was still essentially personal. He had set very high standards of materials and construction and welded together a superb team of building and decorative craftsmen. But, perhaps, the lone genius had lived too long. Palladianism was knocking on the door (see PALLADIAN ARCHITECTURE) and younger men who had worked for and with him were breaking new ground. In 1718 at the age of 86, he was relieved of his Surveyorship. His dignified acceptance of the situation was made in his own words: 'having worn out by God's Mercy a long life in the Royal Service and made some Figure in the World, I hope it will be allowed me to die in peace'. This he did at the age of 91.

WYATT, JAMES (1746–1813) A member of a very large family of builders and architects (15 of whom practised architecture), James was the most gifted and best known. A man of unusual talents, he experimented with many architectural styles and excelled at most. Because of this eclecticism James Wyatt and his work are assessed by differing standards; some historians and critics regard him as a facile copyist, others as a brilliant executant.

He was the son of Benjamin Wyatt, a builder and timber merchant who also practised architecture. In 1762 James set off for Italy where he spent six years, first in Venice then in Rome learning to become an accomplished painter and architectural draughtsman. After his return to England he was brought dramatically to public notice by his selection to build the *Pantheon* in *London's Oxford Street*. Designed for concerts and masquerades, it was, internally, an impressive assembly hall on apsidal-ended basilican plan with galleried aisles and roofed by an immense cupola (see *S. Sophia* in BYZANTINE ARCHITECTURE). When it was opened in 1772 the Pantheon created a sensation. It was a tremendous success both architecturally and functionally and made Wyatt's reputation. Aristocratic patronage came his way and commissions poured in. (The Pantheon was burnt down in 1792. It was roughly on the site of Marks and Spencer's store, east of Oxford Circus.)

At this time Robert Adam (see ADAM, ROBERT) was at the height of his fame and Wyatt began to design in the

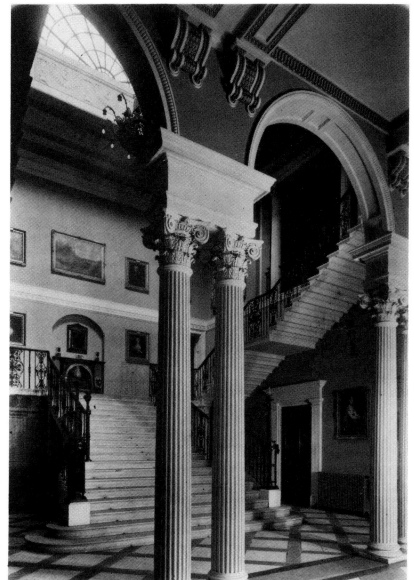

The Hall, Dodington Park, Gloucestershire, 1798–1808

Wall decoration, Heveningham Hall, Suffolk

The Orangery, Heveningham Hall, Suffolk, 1790–5

Adam manner. His success was so great that Adam complained in his *Works in Architecture* (published 1773) of plagiarism. One notable example was *Heveningham Hall*, Suffolk (*c.* 1780–4) where Wyatt was responsible for the interior of the house (see REGENCY ARCHITECTURE) which had been built by Taylor (see TAYLOR, SIR ROBERT); another was *Heaton Hall*, Manchester (*c.* 1772). Wyatt also adopted other forms of classicism as in his more Palladian manner at *Ripon Town Hall* (1799).

In 1796 he succeeded Chambers (see CHAMBERS, SIR WILLIAM) as Surveyor-General and by this time he had become the principal architect of the day. His commissions became too numerous and he began to offend clients by not giving them sufficient attention and courtesy. Despite this he continued to be very busy and, between 1800 and his death in 1813, accomplished some fine work in a more refined and severe Greek classical style. Characteristic of this work was his completion of Henry Keene's *Radcliffe Observatory* in *Oxford* (1776–94), which is based upon the Tower of the Winds in Athens, the building of *Dodington Park*, Gloucestershire (both house and church, 1793–1813) and the completion of the house at *Stoke Poges Park*, Buckinghamshire (1793–1804).

Also in these years Wyatt was designing more and more in Gothic, at first in a picturesque and romantic form, but later evidencing a more mature understanding of medieval Gothic construction and decorative detail. Examples of his work in this manner range from his university building, for example, the library and hall at *Balliol College, Oxford* (1792–4), his interiors as at *Bishop Auckland Castle*, Co. Durham (*c.* 1795), his rebuilding of the *Parish Church* of *East Grinstead*, Sussex in Perpendicular Gothic style (1789–1813) to the commission to build *Pennsylvania Castle* on the Isle of Portland, Dorset (1800). Much of his remodelling of *Belvoir Castle*, Leicestershire (1800–13) and work at *Lee Priory*, Kent (1783–90), which were in his more mature Gothic style, have been lost, though one room from Lee Priory survives in the Victoria and Albert Museum. Best known of Wyatt's surviving ambitious houses in the style is *Ashridge Park*, Hertfordshire, begun 1808 and completed by his nephew *Jeffry Wyatville* in 1817 and and also his spectacular essay into Gothic at *Fonthill Abbey*, Wiltshire (see GOTHIC REVIVAL).

James Wyatt carried out a great deal of necessary work at a number of *medieval cathedrals*, notably at Salisbury, Hereford, Lichfield and Durham. As was to a certain extent the then current attitude towards medieval Gothic workmanship, he was often over-enthusiastic in both demolition and 'restorative improvements', so earning himself the later title of 'Wyatt the Destroyer'.

Two members of the next generation of the Wyatt family became well known, James's eldest son *Benjamin Dean Wyatt* (1775–*c.* 1855) and his nephew Jeffry Wyatt. Benjamin was a competent architect but lacked his father's brilliance. He is best known for his building of

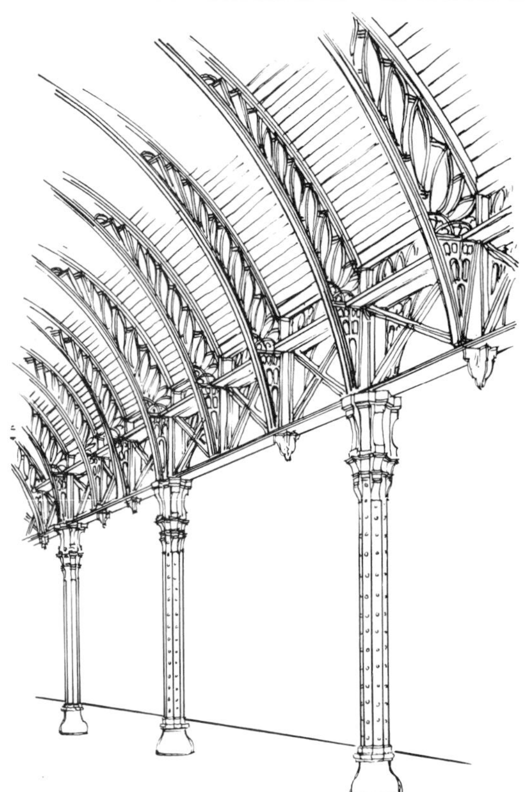

Ironwork, Paddington Station, London, 1852–4. Architect: Sir Matthew Digby Wyatt

The Theatre Royal, Drury Lane, in London (1811–12), after the previous theatre had been destroyed by fire in 1809 and his re-casing of *Apsley House* at Hyde Park Corner with the addition of a new Corinthian portico, for the Duke of Wellington (1828). Benjamin Dean Wyatt also designed for the Duke in 1815 an enormous palace to be built at his country home of *Stratfield Saye* but the plan had to be abandoned on grounds of expense.

Jeffry Wyatt (1766–1840) became well known as a country house architect; like his uncle James, he built up a large practice and designed in a wide variety of styles though, in deference to the first four decades of the nineteenth century, these were mainly different forms of Gothic and Tudor. He built new houses and carried out alterations and new work for a number of clients who owned some of the most famous houses in the land, for example, Chatsworth, Longleat, Wollaton and Woburn.

The commission for which he is best known is his extensive rebuilding of *Windsor Castle* for George IV. The King had realized on his accession in 1820 that if he was to use Windsor as a royal palace the buildings would have to be transformed in order to make good the neglect of many years. The castle had become an unsightly incongruous mass of accumulated building resulting from spasmodic and ineffectual 'patching up' and much of it was in a useless, even dangerous, condition. In 1824 Wyatt's

Heveningham Hall, Suffolk, 1788–99.
Architect for interior work James Wyatt

designs for a radical rebuilding were accepted and the King laid the foundation stone on 12 August. On the same day he acceded to the architect's request that his name be altered to *Wyatville* in order to distinguish himself from his uncle James who had earlier worked at Windsor. In 1828 Wyatville was knighted and was granted for life a residence in the Winchester Tower from where he had been supervising the work. He had been appointed to transform the castle and make it into a worthy royal residence. This he did, almost completing the work by Queen Victoria's accession in 1837 at a cost of over half-a-

Apsley House, London, 1828. Alterations by Benjamin Dean Wyatt and Philip Wyatt

Church of SS. Mary and Nicholas, Wilton, Wiltshire, 1840–6.
Architect: Thomas Henry Wyatt

Ashridge Park, Hertfordshire, 1808–13. Architect: James Wyatt

million pounds. He created a scheme of considerable grandeur, romantic in silhouette, his new Gothic building blending with the medieval to form a picturesque, castellated palace, congruous in its unified conception.

Two other members of the Wyatt family who were practising architecture in the mid-nineteenth century were brothers, sons of Matthew Wyatt (a cousin of James). They were *Thomas Henry Wyatt* (1807–80) and *Sir Matthew Digby Wyatt* (1820–77). T. H. Wyatt built up a large practice in country house design, also churches and hospitals. His most interesting project is the *Church of SS. Mary and Nicholas* in *Wilton*, Wiltshire (1840–6), built in partnership with *David Brandon*. This is an unusual bold design in Italian Romanesque style with characteristic detached campanile.

Sir Matthew Digby Wyatt was more widely known chiefly for his work in conjunction with some of the great engineers of the time. He was architect for Isambard Kingdom Brunel's *Paddington Station* (see IRONWORK; RAILWAY ARCHITECTURE) and he designed a range of the internal courts for Paxton's *Crystal Palace* (see PAXTON, SIR JOSEPH). He was also surveyor to the East India Company and worked with Scott on the *India Office*, part of the Whitehall government offices (see SCOTT, SIR GEORGE GILBERT).

YEVELE, HENRY (*c.* 1320–1400) Master mason to the King, who worked in London from 1355 until his death on royal palaces and castles, notably Westminster and the Tower. Most outstanding of his contributions were *Westminster Hall*, the nave of *Westminster Abbey* and, finest of all, the nave of *Canterbury Cathedral*.

YORKE, FRANCIS REGINALD STEVENS (1906–62) One of the pioneers in England in the inter-war years of the international modern style of architecture and founder member of the MARS Group (see MODERN ARCHITECTURE). Yorke was in partnership from 1935–7 with *Marcel Breuer*, a Hungarian pupil of Gropius from Bauhaus days (see BAUHAUS). In 1944 Yorke entered partnership with *Eugene Rosenberg* and *Cyril Mardall*. The firm had a large practice building houses and flats, hospitals, schools and colleges. Best known of their projects is *Gatwick Airport* (1957 onwards).

ZOOPHORUS A frieze ornamented by sculptural reliefs representing animals (see CLASSICAL ORDER; FRIEZE).

ZOOPHORUS
North frieze, the Parthenon, Athens, 447–430 BC.

Bibliography

Classified select list of books recommended for further reading

Dictionaries and encyclopaedias

Colvin, H. M., *A Biographical Dictionary of British Architects, 1600–1840*, John Murray, 1978

Curl, J. S., *English Architecture: an Illustrated Glossary*, David and Charles, 1977

Encyclopaedia Americana

Encyclopaedia Britannica

Fleming, J., and Honour, H., *The Penguin Dictionary of Decorative Arts*, Allen Lane, 1977

Fleming, J., Honour, H., and Pevsner, N., *The Penguin Dictionary of Architecture*, Penguin, 1977

Harris, J., and Lever, J., *Illustrated Glossary of Architecture, 850–1830*, Faber and Faber, 1966

Kay, N. W., Ed., *The Modern Building Encyclopaedia*, Odhams Press, 1957

Placzek, A. K., Ed., *Macmillan Encyclopaedia of Architects* (4 Vols.), The Free Press, 1982

Richards, J. M., *Who's Who in Architecture from 1400 to the Present Day*, Weidenfeld and Nicolson, 1977

Stierlin, H., *Encyclopaedia of World Architecture*, Macmillan, 1983

General

Airs, M., *The Making of the English Country House*, Architectural Press, 1976

Allsopp, B., *A History of Classical Architecture*, Pitman, 1965; *A General History of Architecture*, Pitman, 1960

Allsopp, B., Booton, H. W., and Clark, U., *The Great Tradition of Western Architecture*, Black, 1966

Amery, C., *Period Houses and their Details*, Architectural Press, 1974

Baker, J., *English Stained Glass*, Thames and Hudson, 1960

Barker, T. C., *Pilkington Brothers and the Glass Industry*, Allen and Unwin, 1960; *The Glassmakers: Pilkington, 1826–1976*, Weidenfeld and Nicolson, 1977

Batsford, H., and Fry, C., *The English Cottage*, Batsford, 1950; *The Cathedrals of England*, Batsford, 1960

Binney, M., and Pearce, D., Ed., *Railway Architecture*, Orbis, 1979

Braun, H., *The Story of the English House*, Batsford, 1940; *Elements of English Architecture*, David and Charles, 1973; *English Abbeys*, Faber and Faber, 1971

Brunskill, R. W., *Traditional Buildings of Britain*, Gollancz, 1982

Brunskill, R., and Clifton-Taylor, A., *English Brickwork*, Ward Lock, 1977

Camesasca, E., *History of the House*, Collins, 1971

Clarke, B. F. L., *Parish Churches of London*, Batsford, 1966

Clarke, B., and Betjeman, J., *English Churches*, Vista Books, 1964

Clifton-Taylor, A., *The Pattern of English Building*, Faber and Faber, 1972; *The Cathedrals of England*, Thames and Hudson, 1967; *English Parish Churches as Works of Art*, Batsford, 1974

Clifton-Taylor, A., and Ireson, A. S., *English Stone Building*, Gollancz, 1983

Colvin, H. M., Gen. Ed., *The History of the King's Works* (6 Vols.), HMSO, 1983

Condit, C. W., *American Building: Materials and Techniques from the beginning of the Colonial Settlements to the Present*, University of Chicago Press, 1968

Cook, G. H., *The English Cathedral*, Phoenix House, 1957; *Portrait of St Alban's Cathedral*, Phoenix House, 1951; *Old St Paul's Cathedral*, Phoenix House, 1955; *Portrait of Canterbury Cathedral*, Phoenix House, 1949; *Portrait of Durham Cathedral*, Phoenix House, 1948

Cook, O., *The English House through Seven Centuries*, Whittet Books, 1983; *The English Country House*, Thames and Hudson, 1980

Cook, O., and Smith, E., *English Abbeys and Priories*, Thames and Hudson, 1960

Copplestone, T., Ed., *World Architecture*, Hamlyn, 1963

Craig, M., *The Architecture of Ireland*, Batsford, 1982

Crossley, F. H., *Timber Building in England from Early Times to the end of the Seventeenth Century*, Batsford, 1951

Cruden, S., *Scottish Abbeys*, HMSO, 1960

Dunbar, J. G., *The Architecture of Scotland*, Batsford, 1978

Dynes, W., *Palaces of Europe*, Hamlyn, 1968

Fintel, M., Ed., *Handbook of Concrete Engineering*, Van Nostrand Reinhold, 1974

Fletcher, B., *A History of Architecture*, The Athlone Press, 1975

Gibberd, F., *The Architecture of England*, The Architectural Press, 1965; *Town Design*, The Architectural Press, 1970

Girouard, M., *Life in the English Country House*, Yale University Press, 1978

Gloag, J., and Bridgewater, D., *History of Cast Iron in Architecture*, Allen and Unwin, 1948

Godfrey, W. H., *A History of Architecture in and around London*, Phoenix House, 1962

Gombrich, E., *The Story of Art*, Phaidon, 1972

Harvey, J., *Cathedrals of England and Wales*, Batsford, 1978

Hilling, J. B., *The Historic Architecture of Wales*, University of Wales Press, 1976

Honour, H., and Fleming, J., *A World History of Art*, Macmillan, 1982

Ison, I., and W., *English Church Architecture Through the Ages*, Arthur Barker, 1972

Johnson, P., *British Castles*, Weidenfeld and Nicolson, 1979; *British Cathedrals*, Weidenfeld and Nicolson, 1980

Jones, E., and Woodward, C., *The Architecture of London*, Weidenfeld and Nicholson, 1983

Kidson, P., and Murray, P., *A History of English Architecture*, Harrap, 1962

Lloyd, N., *History of the English House*, The Architectural Press, 1975; *A History of English Brickwork*, Antique Collectors' Club, 1983

Mansbridge, J., *Graphic History of Architecture*, Batsford, 1967

Maré, E. de, *The Bridges of Britain*, Batsford, 1954

Menear, L., *London's Underground Stations*, Midas Books, 1983

Morshead, O., *Windsor Castle*, Phaidon, 1971

Mumford, L., *The City in History*, Secker and Warburg, 1961
Muthesius, S., *The English Terraced House*, Yale University Press, 1982
Nicholson, N., *Great Houses of Britain*, Weidenfeld and Nicolson, 1979
Nuttgens, P., *The Story of Architecture*, Phaidon, 1983
Petzch, H., *Architecture in Scotland*, Longman, 1971
Pevsner, N., Founding Ed., *The Buildings of England, Ireland, Scotland and Wales* (Many Vols.), Penguin Books
Pothorn, H., *Styles of Architecture*, Batsford, 1971; *A Guide to Architectural Styles*, Phaidon, 1983
Pugin, A. W. N., *The True Principles of Pointed Architecture* (Reprint of first edition of 1841), Academy Editions, 1973
Robertson, E. G., and J., *Cast Iron Decoration*, Thames and Hudson, 1977
Rosenau, H., *The Ideal City*, Methuen, 1983
Ruskin, J. *The Stones of Venice*, Collins, 1960; *The Seven Lamps of Architecture*, Noonday Press, USA, 1961
Saunders, A., *The Art and Architecture of London*, Phaidon, 1984
Savage, G., *Concise History of Interior Decoration*, Thames and Hudson, 1977
Simpson, F. M., *A History of Architectural Development*, new edition in 5 volumes, Longmans, from 1962
Simpson, W. D., *Castles in England and Wales*, Batsford, 1969
Sitwell, S., *Great Houses of Europe*, Weidenfeld and Nicolson, 1961; *Great Palaces*, Weidenfeld and Nicolson, 1964
Stanley, C. C., *Highlights in the History of Concrete*, Cement and Concrete Association, 1979
Whone, H., *Church, Monastery and Cathedral*, Compton Russell Element, 1977
Woodman, F., *The Architectural History of Canterbury Cathedral*, Routledge and Kegan Paul, 1983
Yarwood, D., *The Architecture of Britain*, Batsford, 1980; *The English Home*, Batsford, 1979; *English Houses*, Batsford, 1966; *English Interiors*, Lutterworth Press, 1984; *The Architecture of Europe*, Chancellor Press, 1983; *Outline of English Architecture*, Batsford, 1977; *The Architecture of Italy*, Chatto and Windus, 1970

The ancient classical world

Ayrton, E., *The Doric Temple*, Thames and Hudson, 1961
Boëthius, A., *Etruscan and Early Roman Architecture*, Pelican History of Art Series, Penguin, 1978
Brion, M., and Smith, E., *Pompeii and Herculaneum*, Elek, 1960
Dinsmoor, W. B., *The Architecture of Ancient Greece*, Batsford, 1950
Grant, M., *Cities of Vesuvius*, Weidenfeld and Nicolson, 1971
Lawrence, A. W., *Greek Architecture*, Pelican History of Art Series, Penguin, 1983
Macdonald, W. L., *The Architecture of the Roman Empire*, Yale University Press, 1965
Richter, G. M. A., *Greek Art*, Phaidon, 1959
Robertson, D. S., *Greek and Roman Architecture*, Cambridge University Press, 1969
Taylor, W., *Greek Architecture*, Arthur Barker, 1971
Vitruvius, *The Ten Books on Architecture*, Harvard University Press, 1914
Ward-Perkins, J. B., *Roman Imperial Architecture*, Pelican History of Art Series, Penguin, 1981; *Roman Architecture*, Abrams Publishers, New York, 1977
Wheeler, M., *Roman Art and Architecture*, Thames and Hudson, 1964

Early Christian and Byzantine

Bovini, G., *Ravenna: its Monuments and Works of Art*, Fratelli Lega, Italy
Krautheimer, R., *Early Christian and Byzantine Architecture*, Pelican History of Art Series, Penguin, 1981
Macdonald, W. L., *Early Christian and Byzantine Architecture*, Prentice-Hall International, 1962
Stewart, C., *Byzantine Legacy*, Allen and Unwin, 1959
Talbot Rice, D., *Art of the Byzantine Era*, Thames and Hudson, 1963

Saxon and Romanesque

Allsopp, B., *Romanesque Architecture*, Arthur Barker, 1971
Conant, K. J., *Carolingian and Romanesque Architecture*, Pelican History of Art Series, Penguin, 1979
Fisher, E. A., *The Greater Anglo-Saxon Churches*, Faber and Faber, 1962
Stoll, R., *Architecture and Sculpture in Early Britain*, Thames and Hudson, 1967
Verzone, P., *From Theodoric to Charlemagne. A History of the Dark Ages in the West*, Methuen, 1967

Medieval and Gothic

Butler, L., and Given-Wilson, C., *Medieval Monasteries of Great Britain*, Michael Joseph, 1979
Cook, G. H., *English Monasteries in the Middle Ages*, Phoenix House, 1961
Frankl, P., *Gothic Architecture*, Pelican History of Art Series, Penguin, 1962
Harvey, J., *The Gothic World*, Batsford, 1950; *Henry Yevele*, Batsford, 1944; *Gothic England*, Batsford, 1948; *The Mediaeval Architect*, Wayland Publishers, 1972
Rickman, T., *An attempt to Discriminate the Styles of Architecture in England from the Conquest to the Reformation*, John Henry and James Parker, 1862
Schuerl, W. F., *Medieval Castles and Cities*, 1978
Sitwell, S., *Gothic Europe*, Weidenfeld and Nicolson, 1969
Webb, G., *Architecture in Britain in the Middle Ages*, Pelican History of Art Series, Penguin, 1956
Wood, M., *The English Mediaeval House*, Bracken Books, 1983
Wright, J., *Brick Building in England, Middle Ages to 1550*, John Baker, 1972

1550–1720

Beard, G., *The Work of Sir Christopher Wren*, Bartholomew, 1982
Briggs, M., *Wren the Incomparable*, Allen and Unwin, 1953
Downes, K., *Vanbrugh*, Zwemmer, 1977; *Hawksmoor*, Zwemmer, 1979; *Christopher Wren*, Allen Lane, 1971; *The Architecture of Wren*, Granada, 1982
Dutton, R., *The Age of Wren*, Batsford, 1951
Girouard, M., *Robert Smythson and the Elizabethan House*, Yale University Press, 1983
Harris, J., *William Talman: Maverick Architect*, Allen and Unwin, 1983
Hind, A. M., *Wenceslaus Hollar and his Views of London and Windsor in the Seventeenth Century*, Bodley Head, 1922
Hook, J., *The Baroque Age in England*, Thames and Hudson, 1976
Lees-Milne, J., *The Age of Inigo Jones*, Batsford, 1953
Little, B., *Sir Christopher Wren*, Robert Hale, 1975; *The Life and Work of James Gibbs*, Batsford, 1955
Palladio, A., *The Four Books of Architecture*, Dover Publications, New York, 1965
Sekler, E. F., *Wren and his place in European Architecture*, Faber and Faber, 1956
Serlio, S., *The Five Books of Architecture*, Dover Publications, New York, 1982
Sitwell, S., *British Architects and Craftsmen 1600–1830*, Batsford, 1948
Summerson, J., *The Classical Language of Architecture*, Thames and Hudson, 1983; *Architecture in Britain 1530–1830*, Pelican History of Art Series, Penguin, 1969
Whinney, M., *Wren*, Thames and Hudson, 1971
Wittkower, R., *Architectural Principles in the Age of Humanism*, Academy Editions, 1977

The eighteenth century

Beard, G., *The Work of Robert Adam*, Bartholomew, 1978

Binney, M., *Sir Robert Taylor*, Allen and Unwin, 1983
Davis, T., *The Architecture of John Nash*, Studio, 1960
Fleming, J., *Robert Adam and his Circle*, Murray, 1962
Harris, J., *The Palladians*, Trefoil Books, 1981; *Sir William Chambers*, Zwemmer, 1970
Hussey, C., *English Country Houses 1715–1840* (3 Vols.), Country Life, 1955–8
Jourdain, M., *The Work of William Kent*, Country Life, 1948
Kearns, K. C., *Georgian Dublin*, David and Charles, 1983
Lees-Milne, J., *Earls of Creation*, Hamish Hamilton, 1962; *The Age of Adam*, Batsford, 1947
Richardson, A. E., *Robert Mylne: Architect and Engineer*, Batsford, 1955
Robinson, J. M., *The Wyatts: an Architectural Dynasty*, Oxford University Press, 1979
Stroud, D., *The Architecture of Sir John Soane*, Studio, 1961; *Henry Holland: his Life and Architecture*, Country Life, 1966; *George Dance, Architect, 1741–1825*, Faber and Faber, 1971
Summerson, J., *Georgian London*, Barrie and Jenkins, 1962; *The Life and Work of John Nash, Architect*, Allen and Unwin, 1980
Sutchbury, H. E., *The Architecture of Colen Campbell*, Manchester University Press, 1967
Watkin, D., *Athenian Stuart*, Allen and Unwin, 1983
Wittkower, R., *Palladio and English Palladianism*, Thames and Hudson, 1974
Yarwood, D., *Robert Adam*, Dent, 1970

The nineteenth century

Beaver, P., *The Crystal Palace*, Hugh Evelyn, 1977
Blomfield, R., *Richard Norman Shaw*, Batsford, 1940
Bradley, I., *William Morris and his World*, Thames and Hudson, 1978
Briggs, A., *Victorian Cities*, Odhams Press, 1963
Clark, K., *The Gothic Revival*, John Murray, 1962
Crook, J. M., *Victorian Architecture*, Johnson Reprint, 1971; *The Greek Revival*, John Murray, 1972; *William Burges and the High Victorian Dream*, John Murray, 1981
Cunningham, C., *Victorian and Edwardian Town Halls*, Routledge and Kegan Paul, 1981
Curl, J. S., *The Egyptian Revival*, Allen and Unwin, 1983
Davey, P., *Arts and Crafts Architecture*, The Architectural Press, 1980
Dixon, R., and Multhesius, S., *Victorian Architecture*, Thames and Hudson, 1978
Dyos, H. S., and Wolff, M., *The Victorian City* (2 Vols.), Routledge and Kegan Paul, 1973
Evans, J., *John Ruskin*, Jonathan Cape, 1954
Girouard, M., *The Victorian Country House*, Yale University Press, 1979
Hitchcock, H. Russell, *Early Victorian Architecture in Britain* (2 Vols.), The Architectural Press, 1954; *Architecture, Nineteenth and Twentieth Centuries*, Pelican History of Art Series, Penguin, 1982
Hobhouse, H., *Thomas Cubitt, the Master Builder*, Macmillan, 1971
Macleod, R., *Charles Rennie Mackintosh*, Collins, 1983
Margetson, S., *Regency London*, Cassell, 1971
Naylor, G., *The Arts and Crafts Movement*, Studio Vista, 1971
Olsen, D. J., *Town Planning in London*, Yale University Press, 1982
Pugin, A. W. N., *Contrasts* (Repub.), Leicester University Press, 1969
Quiney, A., *John Loughborough Pearson*, Yale University Press, 1979
Richards, J. M., and Maré, E. de, *The Functional Tradition in Early Industrial Buildings*, The Architectural Press, 1958
Richardson, M., *Architects of the Arts and Crafts Movement*, Trefoil Books, 1983
Saint, A., *Richard Norman Shaw*, Yale University Press, 1983
Shepherd, T., *London in the Nineteenth Century* (First published 1829, Repub.), Frank Graham, 1970
Stanton, P., *Pugin*, Thames and Hudson, 1971
Thompson, P., *William Butterfield*, Routledge and Kegan Paul, 1971

The twentieth century

Banham, R., *Guide to Modern Architecture*, The Architectural Press, 1962; *The New Brutalism*, The Architectural Press, 1966
Benevolo, L., *History of Modern Architecture*, Routledge and Kegan Paul, 1971
Birks, T., and Holford, M., *Building the New Universities*, David and Charles, 1972
Booth, P., and Taylor, N., *Cambridge New Architecture*, Leonard Hill, 1970
Butler, A. S. G., *The Architecture of Sir Edwin Lutyens* (3 Vols.), Country Life, 1950
Dean, D., *The Thirties: Recalling the English Architectural Scene*, Trefoil Books, 1983
Department of the Environment, *New Towns*, HMSO, 1973
Francis, A. J., *The Cement Industry: 1796–1914*, David and Charles, 1977
Gradidge, R., *Edwin Lutyens*, Allen and Unwin, 1984
Gropius, W., *Scope of Total Architecture*, Allen and Unwin, 1956
Hayward Gallery (Exhibition 1982), *Lutyens*, Arts Council of Great Britain, 1981
Jencks, C., *Late-Modern Architecture*, Academy Editions, 1980
Jones, E., and Vanzandt, E., *The City: Yesterday, Today, and Tomorrow*, Aldus Books, 1974
Kiddersmith, G. E., *The New Architecture of Europe*, Penguin, 1962
Kultermann, U., *New Architecture of the World*, Thames and Hudson, 1966
Lambert, S., *New Architecture of London*, The Architectural Association, 1963
Le Corbusier, *Towards a New Architecture*, The Architectural Press, 1970; *The City of Tomorrow*, The Architectural Press, 1971; *The Modulor*, Faber and Faber, 1977
Lutyens, M., *Edwin Lutyens*, John Murray, 1980
Macfadyan, D, *Sir Ebenezer Howard and the Town Planning Movement*, Manchester University Press, 1970
Newton, H., Ed., *A Selection of Historic American Papers on Concrete 1876–1926*, American Concrete Institute, Detroit, 1976
Osborn, F. J., and Whittick, A., *New Towns*, Routledge and Kegan Paul, 1977
Pehnt, W., *Encyclopaedia of Modern Architecture*, Thames and Hudson, 1963
Pevsner, N., *The Sources of Modern Architecture and Design*, Thames and Hudson, 1981; *The Pioneers of Modern Design*, Penguin, 1982
Richards, J. M., *An Introduction to Modern Architecture*, Penguin, 1956
Service, A., *Edwardian Architecture*, Thames and Hudson, 1977
Sharp, D., *The Picture Palace*, Hugh Evelyn, 1969
Stamp, G., *The Great Perspectivists*, Trefoil Books, 1982
Stamp, G., and Amery, C., *Victorian Buildings of London 1837–1887*, The Architectural Press, 1980
Sutcliffe, A., Ed., *Multi-Storey Living: The British Working Class Experience*, Croom Helm, 1974
Waddell, R., Ed., *The Art Nouveau Style*, Dover Publications, New York, 1977
Weaver, L., *Houses and Gardens by E. L. Lutyens*, The Antique Collectors' Club, 1981
Webb, M., *Architecture in Britain Today*, Country Life, 1969
White, R. B., *Prefabrication: a History of its Development in Britain*, HMSO, 1965
Whittick, A., *European Architecture in the Twentieth Century*, Leonard Hill Books, 1974; *Erich Mendelsohn*, Leonard Hill Books, 1956
Wingler, H. M., *Bauhaus*, MIT Press, 1980

Index

Persons and buildings are all listed individually but, for reasons of space, the following major entries should be consulted for specific details, parts and types of the subject where, in most cases, a glossary of terms is given:

ARCH, BRICKWORK, BUILDING MATERIALS, CHURCH DESIGN AND STRUCTURE, GLASS, MASONRY, MOULDINGS, PANELLING, PEDIMENT, ROOF, STAIRCASE, STEEL-FRAME CONSTRUCTION, STONE, TEMPLE, TILES, TIMBER-FRAMING, TRACERY, VAULTING, WINDOW.

Apart from country house names, buildings are generally listed under the names of towns or villages and persons under the surname.